THE POLITICS OF HONOR:
A Biography of Adlai E. Stevenson

THE POLITICS OF HONOR:

A Biography of Adlai E. Stevenson

BY KENNETH S. DAVIS

G. P. Putnam's Sons New York

To Flo

WITH ALL MY LOVE

CONTENTS

Illustrations follow page 96

PREFACE

I

A FAMILIAR metaphor haunts the minds of most serious historians and biographers as they write their books, namely that of the world as stage, history as drama, and historic personages as role-playing actors.

The metaphor has its dangers. Taken too literally it becomes essentially anti-historical in that it suggests a Cosmic Playwright in whose mind everything happened at the dawn of time, which is to say that nothing has *really* happened since. In that case all seeming change would be the mere (or false) appearance of an unchanging reality, every event would be but the manifestation of a basic timeless pattern, and the anguish of choice and the risk of action whereby the course of events seems to us to be affected would be illusions. Human freedom would then be only a cloak, a disguise for human bondage. But of course the suggestion is, in my opinion, false. I see no reason why we should deny the truth of our immediate experience in order to validate a remote and abstract theory.

The metaphor has also, however, its advantages—and especially for an American writer. We Americans are, generally speaking, deficient in historical consciousness. We live in the moment. We improvise, we invent, we solve problems in terms of the present, paying small heed to antecedents or consequences. Our typical philosophy is pragmatism, which concentrates on immediate practical efficacy, eschewing (and not wholly without contempt) general ideas, basic principles, and underlying trends or tendencies. We consequently regard history, for the most part, not as a continuing process in which all of us are involved and which imposes on each of us a burden of responsibility, but as a mere record of the past, a sequence of discrete dated events and characters whose relations, insofar as these exist, are all external. A great advantage of our metaphor is that it repudiates this view. To say that history is a drama is to emphasize precisely what the pragmatic conception ignores. It is to insist that history has meaning, that it has in some sense a plot or story or purpose, and that this may be discerned in the great continuities and regularities, the massive general tendencies or trends, which are operative at any given period. Of these, individual events and people are active elements; by these they are rendered historically significant.

There is another advantage. Our metaphor indicates and clarifies the nature of the task of a writer who has history and an historic person as his subject. For if history is conceived as drama, then the task of the biographical historian becomes akin to that of a theater reporter or play reviewer. He, the writer, is engaged to some degree in dramatic criticism. He must study out the meaning, the major theme or story line, of the play, keeping always in mind that this play is an arbitrary segment of a continuing drama and that the person who (to the extent that Necessity rules) is only an actor in it is also (to the extent that Freedom prevails) among the authors of it. Once discovered, this major theme—the dominant trend or tendency of historic events—provides a standard of criticism. In terms of it the writer may judge how well the historical person has performed, both as player of his assigned role and as a creator, an innovator who recognizes and realizes in action the possibilities of his situation.

How profoundly does this person understand the drama in which he is involved? How clearly and convincingly does he communicate his understanding? Where and when and (if possible to determine) *why* does he muff lines or miss cues or blur his character with incongruities? These are questions the writer must try to answer.

II

What is the major theme, the basic plot, the overall tendency of history in our time? It seems to me a theme simple yet grand, suspenseful between the highest hope and deepest dread, and the fact that my statement of it may seem trite (it has, indeed, often been made) detracts nothing from its truth.

The historic drama of our time, in my opinion, is the struggle of a humane and rational world order, efficiently organized and lawfully governed, to be born out of a chaos of war-making national sovereignties that have been rendered socially and economically obsolete by scientific technology and now, in consequence, threaten to destroy all earthly life, and even the earth itself as a habitable planet, armed as they are with the total weapons that scientific technology has produced. The assumption that the ultimately emergent world order must be humane and rational may seem unwarranted, the result of merely wishful thinking. But I think it is implied by all we know of human nature and evolution. A ruthlessly totalitarian world order, a universal tyranny in which individual human beings were as ants in an anthill, might function with the necessary efficiency and so maintain itself indefinitely, once it was firmly established. But how could it become firmly established? The process must almost certainly be one of violent conquest, human nature being as it is, and this, in the present state of technology and world power distribution, is self-defeating; it can lead only to that world destruction that seems increasingly to be a rational order's one alternative.

Surely this is the great lesson to be learned from the two global wars of our blood-soaked century and from the convulsive, often violently contradictory world movements that have been occurring ever since.

Here, then, is the great drama in which the subject of the present book, Adlai E. Stevenson, played his creative role, as I see it. Here, too, is the critical standard by which he, as an historic figure, must be measured. And it is a conclusion of my book (though I state it in the preface) that he measures, by this standard, very large—larger, I think, than any other major American political figure of the last two decades. I further think that he will loom even larger as the years pass, assuming that we survive our present folly and wickedness—so much so that future historians (if there is for us a future) may regard him as the dominant political figure of the 1950's and early 60's, causing these to be dubbed the Age of Stevenson as Arthur Schlesinger, Jr., has dubbed the 1830's the Age of Jackson and the 1930's the Age of Roosevelt. Of course his impact was far less than either Jackson's or Roosevelt's. He never became President. But his actual influence upon the course of events while he was alive, effecting differences between what occurred and what *would* have occurred had he not been actively present, was greater, I think, than that of either of the two men who won the office to which he aspired.

In this conclusion I may of course be mistaken. It is a summary answer to many questions of "if," and such questions are impossible precisely to answer, though they are precisely the questions most useful to the interpretative biographer and historian. But it is because I feel as I do that this portrait of Adlai Stevenson is a detailed full-length one, designed to present him, not as he seemed to be to those who saw him in only one or two of his many aspects, but as he was as a whole and in the round and, insofar as I was able to discover from a personal experience of him, in his essential being. I would be the last to claim that I have solved completely the mystery of him. I doubt that anyone will. He was a complex man who operated on many levels; he quite sharply compartmentalized his relations with other people; and there were times when he seemed not to understand himself, his own deepest motives and highest ambitions, with the certainty he needed for truly responsible decision and action. (He did insist always upon moral responsibility, and this was the root of his difficulties when he had to make personal career decisions; as no other leading politician of his time, he was a conscience-driven, conscience-burdened man.) Mystery therefore remains.

But I have tried to tell his life story interestingly, accurately, and in such a way as to give the reader the materials he needs to reach his own conclusions as to how so ordinary and even mediocre a young American as Stevenson seemed to be in the 1910's and 20's could grow—slowly, steadily, with a seeming inevitability—into greatness.

—KENNETH S. DAVIS

Princeton, Massachusetts
January, 1967

BOOK ONE

Out of the American Earth

CHAPTER ONE

IN March of 1909, his fortieth year, Lewis Green Stevenson was a slender man, of medium height, rather intense looking, almost perfectly bald (his only hair was a close-cropped fringe across his temples and around the back of his skull), with large clear wide-spaced eyes, a straight rather fleshy nose, and finely modeled lips. A cleft in his chin was matched by an even deeper cleft in his forehead, just above his nose, as though his eyebrows had been often drawn together in a frown of physical pain. And, indeed, they had been. In recent months he had begun to suffer periodically from migraine headaches so intense they totally incapacitated him for days at a time; this disability was added to a severe injury to his right shoulder, which occurred when he was fourteen and from which he would never fully recover. Its pain, though he'd never confess it, had for years been a virtually constant dull ache. It accounted for the fact that he was sometimes irritable, occasionally too sharp and quick in his responses to challenges that were only mildly hostile if hostile at all. But he was also, basically, a jolly man, and it was this basic self he showed most of the time to the world.[1]

The injury and his response to it were significant both of the quality of the man and of the family attitudes in which he'd been raised. With other boys he'd gone hunting on a Sunday, though his Presbyterian father, whose family tree was studded with Presbyterian divines, frowned upon such desecrations of the Lord's Day. Lifting his gun for a quick shot, he'd failed to pull the stock tightly against his shoulder. The recoil had sent him staggering backward, blind with pain, and by the time he reached home his shoulder, blackly bruised, was hot and swollen. But he said nothing to his parents about it—not that day, nor the next, nor the next. Not until weeks of pain had passed was the injury revealed. He was taken at once to the doctors: an operation was performed, the bone was scraped: but too much time had passed and a chronic infection had developed which the doctors could not truly cure, nor even accurately diagnose in that year of 1882. One result was a permanent slight crippling of his right arm, seldom noticed by others save when he shook hands. Shaking hands, he shoved his right shoulder forward and braced his elbow slightly against his side—and smiled.

Much of his life had been a quest for health. It had sent him West in his manhood. He'd been educated at Phillips Exeter Academy in Exeter, New Hampshire, and then at Illinois State Normal University. The latter was in the town of Normal, a community so close to Bloomington as to be virtually one with it. A distinguished former member of State Normal's faculty (from 1866 to 1872) was Major John Wesley Powell, principal architect and present chief of the U. S. Geological Survey, who had also taught at Illinois Wesleyan in Bloomington itself. Major Powell had for forty years been a friend of Lewis Stevenson's father and the friendship extended to the Stevenson son. What then was more natural than that the son should ask Powell for a place on a Geological Survey party into the Southwest, or that Powell should grant the request? Young Stevenson had had grand adventure along the Colorado; he loved the desert and believed that its climate had improved his health.

He'd adventured, too, for several months in Japan and China during the 1890's and had written some newspaper reports from the theater of war when the Sino-Japanese conflict broke out. This was enough to cause him to be labeled a "former war correspondent" in news stories about him. If the label was inaccurate, in that he'd never actually been a member of the working press, it did point to one important fact about him: one way or another his life had been, and remained, intimately concerned with newspapers. He was a lifelong Democrat whose father had entered politics with Greenback party support in the 70's, had been a champion of the "free silverites" in the 80's and 90's, had been elected Vice-President of the United States in 1892, and had in 1900 been a running mate of William Jennings Bryan when he suffered his third and last Presidential defeat.

On March 4, 1893, when Lewis was a young man of twenty-four, he had been in Washington to see his father, Adlai Ewing Stevenson, ceremoniously installed as Vice-President. The city had then been blanketed by two inches of snow; a dull gray light had fallen upon the great platform on the Capitol steps as Grover Cleveland, after an interval of four years, became again the nation's President. But the day had been bright and warm when, in the preceding June, Lewis's father had been nominated as Cleveland's running mate. Lewis had been that day in Chicago, attending the Democratic Convention, along with two of his sisters, the dark-haired eighteen-year-old Julia and the light-haired nineteen-year-old Mary. (Just three years later, in 1895, Mary, who had been so gentle, so quietly lovely, died of tuberculosis—a loss deeply felt by Lewis, as it was by all who had known her well.) His youngest sister, reddish-haired sixteen-year-old Letitia, had remained in Bloomington with their mother, in the big family home on McLean Street, facing Franklin Park. And Lewis's Grandmother Stevenson was also in Bloomington that day, staying in the house of Lewis's uncle William, a younger brother of Adlai. A reporter for the Bloomington *Pantagraph* told how the eyes of the "venerable mother" (she then approached her seventy-third birthday) glowed with a quiet pride when she was told of the great honor that had come to her son. "He has always been a good son," she'd said, "and a good man."

She was proud of all her children, worthy descendants, she felt, of ancestors of whom she was also very proud. She'd been born Eliza Ann Ewing in Iredell County, North Carolina. The man she married in 1832, Major John Turner Stevenson of sturdy Scotch Presbyterian stock, had been born there, too, just a year before she was and, like her, had moved as a child to Christian County, Kentucky, and had been raised there in the Bluewater country. Here her seven children, a girl and six boys, were born. Then, on July 7, 1852, the John Turner Stevensons had arrived in Bloomington. In the spring of 1857, at the age of forty-nine, the husband died, and ever since that tragic day Eliza Ewing Stevenson had felt herself to be living in and through her children.

Of them, none had been more loving and dutiful than Adlai. He was her second-born, the eldest son, whose lot it was to take his father's place as head of the family. He'd become a vibrant, jovial, dominant personality, immensely liked and respected even by those (and they were the majority in Republican Illinois) who strongly opposed his political views. A sparkling conversationalist with a generous outgoing personality, he'd become one of the great raconteurs of the day. The latter talent, combined as it was with a mastery of public speaking, had served him well in politics. His had been an intensely active life, but no matter how busy he was he'd sent his mother, every single day, some token of his affection and esteem for her: a letter, a few scrawled lines on a postal card, or some little gift.

This was typical of his thoughtfulness of others; it was consistent with his essential attitude toward the world. He was a man who focused so much of his attention outside himself, a man so intensely interested in other people, that he had little left of interest or attention to spend upon himself. There was no malice in him. His observations and judgments of those about him, uncomplicated by self-consciousness, were on the whole remarkably kindly; when they were not he seldom expressed them.

In September, 1854, when he was yet a student at Bloomington's Wesleyan University, he was among a group who called upon the visiting Stephen A. Douglas in the latter's room in Bloomington's National Hotel. Barely four months before, the Little Giant had pushed his Kansas-Nebraska Bill through the most turbulent session of Congress ever seen up till then—and the storm provoked by the act's repeal of the Missouri Compromise was yet rising across the land. Chief among the callers that day was the Honorable Jesse W. Fell, who was also by general consent the chief citizen of Bloomington and Normal, and the youthful Adlai had listened with rapt attention as Fell, a close friend of Lincoln, proposed to Douglas that the senator engage with Lincoln in a "joint discussion" of the issues raised by Kansas-Nebraska. Young Adlai would never forget the emphatic way in which Douglas had declined the suggestion. But when Lincoln himself entered the hotel room a few minutes later, he and Douglas greeted one another with great affection. . . .[2]

Four years later, Fell's suggestion had borne historic fruit—the series of seven great debates between Douglas and Lincoln which, though he lost the senatorial election, made Lincoln a national figure—and young Adlai Stevenson had personally witnessed the launching of the series on a crude platform at Ottawa. No man now held Abraham Lincoln in greater esteem. But Lewis Green Stevenson knew that his father had not been among Lincoln's political supporters during the Civil War. In the year of the Lincoln-Douglas debates, Adlai Stevenson, having read law in Bloomington after returning from Centre College in Danville, Kentucky, was admitted to the Illinois bar. He actively supported Stephen Douglas for the Senate that year. In April of the following year he'd met and become a good friend of Robert G. Ingersoll, in Metamora—the Ingersoll who'd later become so famous an orator and so notorious a religious agnostic. In 1860 he'd joined Ingersoll, who was himself a Democratic candidate for Congress, in strong support of Douglas for the Presidency—and four years later he'd been elected elector-at-large on the Democratic ticket and had canvassed Illinois for McClellan.

Thereafter he'd been continually active in Democratic politics. When in 1869 he moved from Metamora to Bloomington, forming a law partnership with his double first cousin, James S. Ewing, his desk was at once a focal point of the Illinois Democracy and his will a potent force in the party counsels. Twice, in 1874 and '76, he'd won election to the Congress in one of the most solidly Republican districts in the state, having become a leading spokesman for bimetallism, "fiscal reform," and drastic tariff reductions in order to help farmers and others of the debtor class in the West and South.

His fiscal views had been opposed by Grover Cleveland. So had been his views as to the proper exercise of patronage in the building up of political party organization. Appointed first assistant postmaster general by Cleveland in 1885 (Cleveland's first term), Stevenson, like most Democratic politicians, had disagreed with the President's efforts wholly to abolish the "spoils system." When Pulitzer's New York World editorially chided the President for forgetting "the obligations which an administration elected by a great historical party owes to that party," Adlai Stevenson had boldly issued a statement of agreement: "Although it is daily asserted that hundreds of postmasters are being appointed, yet the six months which have elapsed since Cleveland's accession finds only between ten and twelve percent of the offices occupied by Democrats." In the end, of course, Cleveland had been forced to yield. Adlai Stevenson himself had gained fame in his party, and notoriety among his opponents, by removing some forty thousand Republican postmasters and replacing them with deserving Democrats. He'd been dubbed "The Headsman," and for this exercise in practical politics his party had been glad to reward him with the Vice-Presidential nomination in 1892—particularly so since there was need to mollify the "silverites," Cleveland being so strong a gold-standard man.

This last, the nomination of Stevenson as a "sop to the silverites," was a piece of "politicking" that very nearly backfired on the gold-standard men. The country at large still did not know it,[3] but in the summer of 1893 Adlai Stevenson came very close to becoming President of the United States. In June of that year a malignant growth as large as a quarter dollar had been found in the roof of Cleveland's mouth, necessitating an immediate operation in which the entire upper left jaw was removed. The President made a strong recovery, and every hint of his illness, published months later in the press, was flatly denied by men close to him. But the doctors knew, and Adlai Stevenson and his son also knew, that Cleveland's life had been gravely threatened. . . .

Adlai's wife, Letitia, Lewis's mother, was as remarkable a woman as her husband was a man, and her presence beside him had been a major factor in his success. As Second Lady, she had presided with grace and charm, and with immense pleasure, over the society of Washington, yet had had an abundance of energy left over for other concerns. She had, for instance, taken an active part in the activities of the New York Avenue Presbyterian Church. (John Watson Foster, Secretary of State in 1890–93, was a leading elder of this church; Foster's grandson, named John Foster Dulles, would be not unknown to future history.) One of her fellow members was Mrs. Phoebe Apperson Hearst of California, wealthy widow of Senator George R. Hearst of California, who'd made his millions out of copper and gold mines in the West. Mrs. Hearst's power-hungry son, William Randolph, having made a great commercial success of the San Francisco *Examiner,* launched the New York *Journal* in the third year of Cleveland's administration, and with it a "yellow journalism" of which the elder Stevensons could not but disapprove —but Mrs. Hearst herself was a "great and pious lady," as the Stevensons always said, whose energy and fortune were devoted to good works. As one of Mrs. Stevenson's closest friends, she joined with Mrs. Stevenson in the founding of the Mothers' Congress, forerunner of the Parent-Teachers' Association. Mrs. Stevenson had also taken the lead in founding the Daughters of the American Revolution and had been a pioneer member of the Colonial Dames and of the Women's Clubs of America. . . .

Those had been crowded years for Lewis Stevenson, too. In November of 1893 he married his childhood sweetheart, Helen Davis, daughter of W. O. Davis, the proprietor of the Bloomington *Pantagraph*. Helen's mother had been born Eliza Fell, daughter of Jesse Fell, and the *Pantagraph* had been one of the many enterprises that Fell had launched. In the 1830's and 40's, when it was called, first, the *Observer* and, later, the *Intelligencer*, the newspaper had been a Whig organ; in the 1850's, soon after being named the *Pantagraph*, it had become an organ of the new Republican party and the earliest editorial supporter of Abraham Lincoln for the Presidency. Staunchly Republican the *Pantagraph* remained, reflecting the conservative views of Davis, under whose management it had grown into one of the most influential and prosperous papers in Illinois. Thus Davis had never been a political friend of Adlai Stevenson. Quite the contrary. But he was a kindly, pacific Quaker gentleman who would not permit political differences to blind him to another's human qualities, and he'd made no overt objection to the romance between his daughter and Stevenson's son, though it must be confessed he had no great personal liking for the latter. . . . The wedding had been the most brilliant social event of its year in central Illinois.

Lewis had taken his bride to Washington, where he served as private secretary to his father. Two years later he'd made his journey alone to the warring Far East where he'd been introduced to the Empress of China. And in Washington, of course, the newly married couple became good friends of Mrs. Phoebe Hearst. The friendship had proved rewarding when, after the Vice-Presidential term ended, Lewis again went West in quest of health. Mrs. Hearst employed him to help with the management of her mining properties in Arizona and New Mexico, particularly of the Santa Rita copper mine in the latter state. In 1899 he'd moved from Fort Bayard, New Mexico, to Los Angeles, continuing to help with management of Hearst estates. Nor had all the profit from this arrangement accrued to him. He had been a successful steward: enterprising, an effective organizer, an astute manager both of finances and of men. Mrs. Hearst had not hesitated to recommend him highly to her son when William Randolph, in 1904, having added the Los Angeles *Examiner* to his swiftly growing newspaper empire, was in search of an assistant general manager of that property. The post had been offered Lewis, and he'd accepted it.

He had become, by that time, widely known in southern California, particularly in Democratic political circles. Just a few months after his arrival in Los Angeles in 1900 he'd been the subject of an extended feature story in the city's leading paper. The occasion was his father's nomination as Vice-President on the ticket headed by William Jennings Bryan. Mounted in a family scrapbook at home, the article recorded that the Democratic national convention at which his father was nominated that year was the first Lewis Stevenson had missed "since he was a boy of six or eight." He was, the writer added, "exceptionally bright, a thorough specimen of a twentieth-century unassuming American." Other, later publicity, telling of his effective role at some party meeting or other, recorded with apparent surprise that he looked "not the type of political henchman." He looked, instead, "scholarly," but had proved himself a hardheaded politician just the same.

All this had done him no harm in the eyes of William Randolph Hearst, himself a Democratic member of Congress from New York with high political ambitions, when the Los Angeles *Examiner* became a Hearst property. The Hearst newspaper connection had, of course, made young Stevenson yet better known to the southern California public. He'd received a great deal of personal publicity, for instance, as a result of the great earthquake of April 18, 1906, which devastated San Francisco. By that time he'd moved from Los Angeles to Berkeley, into a house near the famous "Hacienda," the home of Mrs. Phoebe Hearst, and then, after a brief time, had moved back to the southern city. When news of the San Francisco disaster came, the Los Angeles *Examiner* recruited doctors and nurses, gathered together quantities of medical and other supplies, and dispatched these northward on a much-publicized special train. Of that train—the first relief train to reach the stricken city—Lewis Stevenson was in charge, and he'd done yeoman service in helping to organize relief work in the flame-swept city where hundreds had died, thousands had been injured, and scores of thousands made homeless. A number of babies, born in relief tents, were named after him by grateful parents.

It appeared to many that he might look forward to a successful public career on the West Coast.

Yet in that very year of the earthquake he had abandoned all his Western projects and returned to Bloomington, Illinois. There were several reasons. For one thing, neither Lewis nor Helen had ever felt really at home in the West; their roots ran deep into the Illinois earth and their vital interests had continued to center in Bloomington, where they visited for extended periods every year. For another thing, their parents wanted and perhaps even needed their return. Helen's father was by then a widower; he approached his seventieth year. Lewis's father was now seventy-one, and he'd more than hinted that, in his declining years, he wished that his son were beside him. But the final determinant had been the expanding enterprises of Mrs. Matthew Scott, Lewis's Aunt Julia, who had been left a widow in 1901. Adding more and more land to the extensive holdings left to her, she had soon some forty-nine farms comprising more than twelve thousand acres. She asked Lewis to become her farm manager. She offered a good salary. Without much hesitation, he accepted.

II

Bloomington and her sister community, Normal, contained in 1909 approximately thirty thousand people—something over twenty thousand in the former place, something less than ten thousand in the latter. In general plan, Bloomington was a fairly typical Midwestern county-seat town. Its center, from which all else spread out, was the courthouse square, around which were built the leading stores, banks, and hotels, plus a "Grand Opera House" in which operas were very seldom if ever performed, and a theater, the Castle, in which a five-thousand-dollar organ was installed. As the business center of the second richest agricultural county in the United States (only Lancaster County, Pennsylvania, surpassed McLean County, Illinois, in this respect), the town's economic life very largely depended on farming, but there was a healthy admixture of other economic elements: a candy factory, an insurance company destined to grow into a very large enterprise, the Alton Railroad shops, several small manufacturing concerns, and two colleges—Illinois Wesleyan in Bloomington itself, and the State Normal College in the town next door.

Many retired farmers lived along the quiet streets, and everywhere in the town the farmer's attitudes and way of life were evident. Nvertheless, Bloomington was not at all a backward community, viewed from an urban standpoint. It had a degree of sophistication far from typical of towns of its size and general composition, for it had drawn to itself a remarkable number of exceptional people. Among these, of course, were the grandparents and parents of Lewis Stevenson and his wife. Others were famous figures of the Lincoln era: Ward H. Lamon, David Davis, Leonard Swett, William F. Arny. Two "inspirational" writers, Frank Crane and Elbert Hubbard, had been Bloomingtonians; Rachel Crothers, soon to become a famous playwright, was a Bloomingtonian. So were James G. Harbord, the soldier; Margaret Illington, the actress; Clark Griffith, the baseball pitcher; and several others of equal note.

Any town so productive of celebrities must feel itself to be in the main stream of national life, and Bloomington's sophistication was increased by the presence of many wealthy, widely traveled, and well-educated people— a "Society" more brilliant than that of most towns two or three times its size. Of it, Lewis Stevenson himself, of course, was a leading member and his house among its focal points.

This house, at 1316 East Washington Street, was a two-story ten-room structure set far back from the street on the north side, with high-pitched gables bounding an attic almost large enough to be considered another story. The long lot on which the house was set had, when the Stevensons bought the place in 1906, a small grove of box elders at the back, a great sycamore tree rising above the northwest corner of the house, an ash tree, and no landscaping or shrubbery at all. Thanks to Helen Stevenson, there were soon a good many young trees and shrubs. Clingstone peach trees replaced the box elders and ginkgo trees were planted. The house was originally walled with gray clapboard, but in 1912 it was "pebble-dashed"—that is, stuccoed.

The front door of the house opened into an entrance hall from which a stairway climbed to the second floor.[4] Its walls held many mementos of Lewis Stevenson's travels to the Orient, including Japanese and Korean ceremonial swords, a carved elephant tusk, and Egyptian embroideries. From it opened three doors into downstairs rooms: the drawing room across the whole south front of the house, the dining room on the east side behind the hall, and the library.

The drawing room, with its floor-to-ceiling windows, had an astonishingly varied décor. Its walls were covered with gray grass cloth; its highly polished oak floors were almost covered with dark red oriental rugs and runners. A tiger-skin rug, brought from China, sprawled before the white-tiled fireplace and hearth, and a fire screen with a cut-velvet peacock design upon it stood at the tiger's head. On the fireplace mantel stood a Sèvres clock and a leopard modeled in white marble. There were tall wing-backed chairs in this room and tall-backed pull-up chairs, and at one end a Baldwin piano, over which was draped a brightly colored ancient Chinese mandarin coat. There was a tall richly carved cabinet, seventeenth-century Italian, on which stood a Chinese goddess, while nearby stood a plain walnut table made by some Quaker forebear in Pennsylvania, probably during the Colonial period.

But the drawing room was strictly a special occasion room, rarely entered by the children of the house save when they were brought in by their parents to bow or curtsy before guests. The library was the true "living room" of the house. A west room, it was approximately ten feet wide by fifteen feet long, though it seemed longer because at its west end were three large bay windows. A fireplace was in the southeast corner of the room. On the wall at its left hung a cross-stitched sampler containing the alphabet in various colors and a stitched-in name and date: Eliza Brown, 1825. On the wall to the right hung a framed facsimile of the three-page autobiography of Abraham Lincoln, in Lincoln's handwriting, with below it a printed statement that this had been made available to the public by Jesse W. Fell of Normal, Illinois, on March 20, 1872. It was published by James R. Osgood and Company, Boston.

It was in this room that the great-granddaughter of Eliza Brown, the granddaughter of Jesse W. Fell, the wife of Lewis Stevenson, and the mother of his two children—Mrs. Helen Davis Stevenson—spent most of her time with these children, reading to them by the hour from the books that lined the walls. In 1909, her fortieth year, she was a tall, slender woman with a long, narrow face, pale of complexion, and a mass of dark hair brushed back from her high forehead to a soft bun. Her eyes were gray and heavy-lidded, her nose straight and cleanly chiseled. She did not appear physically strong; three years before, in Berkeley, she'd almost died of pneumonia and her former strength (she'd never been really robust) had not returned to her. But there was in her appearance another kind of strength—the strength of a forceful personality—and this appearance did not belie reality.

As a girl, Helen Stevenson had studied singing in Germany and in Paris, and she often sat at the Baldwin and played accompaniments to the songs she sang: German *lieder*, French art songs, Civil War ballads, folk songs, sentimental songs of the day. The children loved to hear her. "You can't holler down my rain barrel," "Can she bake a cherry pie, Billy boy, Billy boy?," "The Bicycle Built for Two"—these they loved, and also the sad songs from the great American war about boats coming down the river, and the prisoner who dreamed of Mother dear as he sat within the stockade.

And the children loved even more to hear her read, with dramatic inflections, in her richly resonant contralto voice. Often she read from *The Family Album of Poetry and Song*, containing selections from Byron, Scott, Holmes, Tennyson, Whittier—and when she read Whittier she sometimes paused to remind her children that Whittier was a Quaker poet and that he might be said to speak more directly to them than to most people because Quaker blood flowed in their veins, too. She herself came from Quaker stock.[5] Her grandfather Fell had been raised a Quaker and so had her grandmother Hester Brown Fell. (It was Hester's mother who had cross-stitched that sampler by the fireplace.) Quaker, too, in heritage, was her father, W. O. Davis, whose forebears had settled in William Penn's colony as early as 1670. Of course all these Quakers had become Unitarians in Bloomington, but if they'd broken the confines of a rigid Quaker piety, accepting a more "liberal" faith, they'd retained many of the Quaker ways and much of the Quaker spirit—a love of peace, an inward serenity which increased rather than reduced effective activity in the world. Often, then, the mother would be led by her children's questions to tell stories about her ancestors, who were, by that same token, *their* ancestors as well—and when she did this they sensed and perhaps even pondered the mystery by which "blood" was said to flow out of the distant past through their own veins toward the future. The past was alive in them.

The past was certainly present in the library. It was a room of relics and heirlooms. Upon shelves that lined all but the fireplace wall were books that ancestors had bought and bequeathed to them: Hume's *History of England* in six volumes; the works of Tennyson in eight volumes; Prescott's *Conquest of Mexico* in three volumes; Boswell's *Life of Samuel Johnson* in four volumes; a set of Shakespeare in tall slender volumes, beautifully bound in white calf. Many of these books, the children knew, came from their grandfather Davis, who was an omnivorous reader and whose library was full to overflowing. The sewing rocker, with its cane back and seat, was an heirloom. The antique clock upon the fireplace mantel was an heirloom. So were the needle-point and crochet-covered cushions in the chairs. The dark oak writing table beside the bay window was not, but it looked as though it were and it had been built, obviously, for the ages. Equally solid was the heavy carved oak straight-back chair beside the table where, in later years, the children would study their school lessons and write their letters, using the silver inkstand and penholder on which, in the evenings, firelight dully glittered.

III

The children, in 1909, were a nine-year-old boy, Adlai—a very chubby little boy—and an eleven-year-old girl, Elizabeth, who was slender and regal, almost a perfect childish replica of her mother. The father called his son "Brute" because he was such a gentle, conscientious, well-behaved little boy; and he called his daughter "Sheep" because she was the very opposite of sheepish.

Almost every night as the boy lay in his bed he heard, before he slept, the haunting cry of a train whistle, far across the prairie beyond the town. It was a cry that always evoked in him strange and powerful emotions of which, decades later, he sometimes spoke. The sound seemed to carry into his consciousness a lyric sense of distances in space and time so vast that this warm and cozy world of his was lost in them. He sensed that his world was an island, after all—a tiny island compared to the cold emptiness by which it was surrounded. Tragedy was therefore possible. But far from frightening him or in any way dismaying him, this sense of tragic possibilities seemed to enhance his present joy. He loved the sad wail of a distant train whistle in the night. He would always love it. In the 1950's, as a mature man, one of his regrets about "Progress" would be that it banished steam locomotives from the nation's railways, and with them the long aching evocative calls of steam whistles across lonely miles of prairie.

CHAPTER TWO

T O the little boy, Adlai, American history was largely a family matter; to the man, it was of his essence. . . .

During the period from 1906 through 1911, family custom decreed that the Lewis Green Stevensons take Sunday dinner with the elderly Adlai Stevensons, where the little boy listened, fascinated, to stories of the early Stevensons and of all the collateral lines which had fused to make *him*, through his own father. The Ewings, for instance. And the Osbornes. It was after the little boy's great-great-great-grandfather, Adlai Osborne, that Grandfather Stevenson had been named, the word originally coming from the twenty-ninth verse of the twenty-seventh chapter of the Book of Chronicles, where it is recorded that one "Shapat, the son of Adlai" was placed "over the herds in the valleys" in the time of David. The founder of the American Stevensons was William, a Scotch-Irishman who'd come to Pennsylvania in 1748 and moved in 1763 to what was later Iredell County, North Carolina, where he, a farmer and notably pious Presbyterian convert, became a ruling elder of the Fourth Creek Church in what is now Statesville.[1]

This pious William Stevenson had been dubbed "Little Gabriel" because, though small in size, he was great in voice and could pray with a fervor, a fluency, and a volume amazing to all who heard him. Famous was the occasion on which, as the family put it, he "prayed the devil out of Doctor Hall." The latter, pastor of the Fourth Creek Church, was subject to fits of melancholia during which he was so convinced of his own sinfulness that he could not preach. One such spell lasted for a year and a half and might never have ended had not Little Gabriel mounted the pulpit to intercede with the Almighty on his pastor's behalf. At the close of this prayer, as long as it was fervent, delivered with stentorian volume, the Reverend Dr. Hall went slowly to the pulpit and preached again; it is reported that "he was not troubled by these melancholy spells for many years after Little Gabriel's prayer and never so seriously as before."[2]

Little Gabriel, the boy learned, was his great-great-great-grandfather and was as prolific of children as he was fervent in prayer. Of his twelve children, the eldest was killed as a soldier in the Revolutionary War. From the fifth child, James, the little boy could trace his own descent. James Stevenson had married Nancy Brevard, a daughter of Colonel Hugh Brevard, who was a leader at the Battle of Ramseur's Mills during the Revolution and was a brother of the Ephraim Brevard who authored the Mecklenburg Declaration of Independence, wherein Mecklenburg County, North Carolina, had declared her independence from England and established a government of her own by May 20, 1775, nearly fourteen months before the great Declaration that Thomas Jefferson penned in Philadelphia.

James Stevenson, with his wife Nancy, his brother-in-law, his younger brother Moses, and a large party of emigrants, crossed the mountains and settled in Christian County, Kentucky, where they established a Presbyterian church almost before they'd established their homes. James, too, was prolific of children: he had nine of them, the sixth of whom was little Adlai's great-grandfather John Turner Stevenson. He it was who married Eliza Ewing, daughter of Adlai Osborne Ewing, and fathered Adlai Ewing Stevenson I, Vice-President of the United States. They were sturdy yeoman stock, these people, farmers and Presbyterian preachers, strong of physique and equally strong in their Protestant faith. The boy was rightly taught to take pride in them.

In the late 1850's Adlai I had gone with Cousin James Ewing from Bloomington, where they'd attended Illinois Normal in the sister town of Normal, to Danville, Kentucky, where they enrolled as students in Centre College, a Presbyterian institution. The president of Centre College at that time was the Reverend Lewis Warner Green, D.D., whose daughter Adlai I was destined to marry; she became, by that marriage, the grandmother of the little boy.

This Reverend Dr. Green came from a distinguished family.[3] He had been born in 1806 on a large and lovely estate near Danville called "Waveland," established by his father, Willis Green, in 1795. Willis Green was the son of Duff Green of the Shenandoah Valley in Virginia—scion of one of the greatest Colonial families—and of Anne Willis Green, whose father, Harry Willis, was also among the greatest of Virginians. And for his second wife (his first had died at Waveland of "galloping consumption" shortly after her wedding), the Reverend Dr. Green had taken one Mary Peachy Fry, whose ancestry was quite as distinguished as his own.

She was directly descended from Colonel Joshua Fry, a graduate of Oxford who, in 1732, became professor of mathematics in Virginia's William and Mary College. Professor Fry had collaborated with Thomas Jefferson's father, Peter, in preparing a map by order of the King, the first accurate one of the "Inhabited Parts of Virginia," and had been commissioned a colonel by King George III, commanding Virginia militia during the French and Indian War. On the march to Fort Duquesne he was thrown from his horse, died of his injuries, and was buried on May 31, 1754, under an oak tree near Mills Creek, Maryland. (His command devolved upon his twenty-two-year-old lieutenant colonel, George Washington, who cut into the oak: "Under this tree lies the body of the good, the just and noble Fry.") He left a son, John, who had a son, Joshua Fry II, and this second Joshua, after returning from Oxford where he'd been sent for his education, served as a soldier in the Revolution. He then emigrated to Mercer County, Kentucky, where, having inherited a large landed estate, he was enabled to devote his energies to a school that he opened for the education of his own children and his neighbors'. Many who later became prominent Kentuckians owed their education to him.

Joshua Fry II took as wife Peachy Walker, daughter of Dr. Thomas Walker, physician, surveyor, explorer (he named the Cumberland Gap), and scientific engineer, who had become the commissar-general of Braddock's army. (His house, Castle Hill, still stood outside Charlottesville, Virginia, in the 1950's and would be visited then by the boy become a man.) One of his sons, also named Thomas, was the father of the Mary Peachy Fry, who, as a young widow (she'd married a Colonel Lawrence and had a son by him), married Lewis Warner Green.

Mary Peachy Fry Green, the little boy's great-grandmother, was a legendary figure in the family. She was a formidable aristocrat in the Southern tradition, who in all her life—at least until she came to live with her daughters in Bloomington—had never so much as buttoned her own shoes or made a cup of coffee. She was an arrogant, haughty, black-haired beauty at the time of her second marriage, and she remained arrogant and haughty— and black-haired, too—until, in her eighties, she died. But she had charm and vital force; an aura of excitement surrounded her; and if she was excessively patrician and proud and too much devoted to worldly matters, she perhaps provided a needed counterbalance to the Reverend Dr. Green's tendency toward excessive otherworldliness.

For the Reverend Lewis Green had been raised in the strict Calvinist faith, convinced of the doctrine of original sin and of the necessity of God's grace to absolve each man of his innate wickedness. Good works were needed, too. Dr. Green saw man's wickedness institutionalized in Negro slavery—not an easy view to take in his time and place and circumstances. He himself inherited some twenty-two slaves. But he joined his fiery kinsman, editor James Birney of Danville's leading newspaper, in sponsorship of the "Liberia Project," and as soon as he obtained his inheritance he not only freed his slaves but also financed the emigration of several of them to West Africa's new Negro Republic. Thus did he keep the faith.

And at the time of his second marriage this faith had been, or seemed, as solid as a rock, as bright as a beacon. Alas, he took his bride to Germany. There he studied in universities swept by that tide of skepticism which was later called the "Higher Criticism." Before long his faith was dissolved, the shining light went out. He walked in utter darkness through the streets of

Allegheny City, where he was president of the Presbyterian Theological Seminary; he yet walked in gloom when, after a period as president at Hampden-Sydney college in Virginia and of Transylvania (now the state university) in Kentucky, he returned to Danville as president of Centre College. And who knows but what his very life might have failed for lack of purpose had he not had beside him a proud, aristocratic girl whose zest for life was wholly undisturbed by metaphysical doubts?

Long years afterward his granddaughter Julia Stevenson—the little boy's aunt Julia Hardin—met an elderly lady who had been one of the Reverend Green's parishioners in the Danville Presbyterian church. This lady told Julia how, one evening, she met her minister as he walked slowly up the path to the president's house. His head was bowed, his face drawn with weariness, and she stopped him to ask, rather anxiously, how he was.

"Faint, yet pursuing," he'd replied, lifting his hat and bowing in his usual courtly way. "Faint, yet pursuing." [4]

And indeed, as Aunt Julia told her young nephew, Dr. Green, though faint with doubt and confusion, did pursue the truth until at last he found it in a more serene mature faith than any he had known before.

But there was nothing faint about the impression he made upon young Adlai I and his cousin James Ewing when they first met him at Centre College. That impression was strong and glowing—nor did it ever weaken or fade. The little boy never heard Grandfather Stevenson speak of Dr. Green save with reverence and gratitude; the same was true of Cousin James, who became Minister to Belgium and whom the boy knew as a most distinguished old gentleman with walrus mustaches, a soft pleated shirt front, and a long black frock coat.

There was always a twinkle in Grandfather Stevenson's eye, however, when in the presence of Grandmother he spoke of his first meeting with the great teacher, for it was at that meeting that he also first saw Letitia Green, the reverend doctor's daughter. It was on a Sunday. The two shy cousins, just arrived in Danville, were invited to dinner at the president's house. They were years older than most entering students, and to Letitia, then in her early teens and not uninfluenced by her mother's aristocratic ways, the two looked old indeed. And very dull. That evening her mother told her that she must include the two cousins among her guests at a party she was planning. Bitterly, she rebelled. She'd rather give up the party altogether, she said, than have it spoiled by "old" Stevenson and "old" Ewing. Her father, however, prevailed, as in such matters he always did. The party was held. The two cousins came.

"And so I met your grandmother," Grandfather Stevenson would say to his grandson and namesake. "And so we were married."

The latter event did not occur, however, until some nine years later, after the Civil War had been fought and Dr. Green had died. It was said that "his tired heart was broken by fratricidal strife," and well it might have been, for though he himself was an ardent Union man he had beloved kinsmen and close friends in both the Union and Confederate armies. All that he stood for, all that he had worked for—all kindness and love—seemed to be consumed in the conflagration. Grandmother Stevenson spoke movingly of his spiritual agony and of her own adventures as a young girl in those violent bloody years. After the battle of Perryville, fought some miles from Danville, the Confederates retreated through the latter town; the girl Letitia Green watched them stream past the president's house, worn and bedraggled. That night, as she lay abed in her room on the house's first floor, she was awakened by the sound of snipers shooting in the streets. She started up. She rushed for the door. And just as she reached it a bullet struck the pillow where her head had lain.

"Now where would *you* be," she would ask little Adlai, gently smiling, "if I had not reached that door? But never mind. I did reach it—and here you are!"

She'd been at Miss Haynes's Fashionable Finishing School for Young Ladies, at Ten Gramercy Park in New York, when news of her father's last illness reached her. To get home she'd traveled by train to Lexington and thence through the battle lines to Danville in a stagecoach repeatedly halted by soldiers who demanded her passport. When she reached home at last she was barely in time to see her father die.

Then it was, or shortly thereafter, that young Letitia, with her widowed mother, had come to live with the elder daughter, Julia, who had married Mr. Matthew Scott, formerly of Lexington, Kentucky, and now a resident of central Illinois. Flat and, in those days, relatively treeless, central Illinois seemed a dreary landscape after the lush rolling beauty of Kentucky, but Matthew Scott was a wealthy, canny man who had the means to re-create, in the raw prairie state, much of the grace and ease of the old plantation South and, so far as Dr. Green's widow was concerned, to maintain the aristocratic attitudes, too. It was inevitable, therefore, that the Widow Green (how she'd have bridled at the name!) should regard with small favor the suit for her daughter's hand which was at once pressed by Adlai Stevenson I. He was then thirty-one years old, was prosecuting attorney at Metamora and well known in political circles, but he seemed far "beneath" the Scotts and Greens. Letitia, however, knew her own mind and heart, and her mother at last gave a reluctant consent to that which she was powerless to prevent.

The wedding took place on December 20, 1866, in the Matthew Scott home. Chicago was deemed too crude a town to supply the wedding feast, or the waiters for it; everything—ices, salads, cakes, and waiters—came from that much older and more sophisticated city, St. Louis. And it came frozen by a sudden bitter cold wave. Everything had to be thawed out before the feast could proceed. Afterward, Adlai Stevenson I drove his bride to Metamora, and there she entered upon what was almost a frontier life (ten muddy miles separated Metamora from the nearest railroad) for which she seemed at first wholly unfitted. With her waspish waist and her wardrobe of silks and satins and fine muslins, she appeared too fine and frail. She wasn't, however. She quickly adjusted—and from the first the marriage was singularly happy. The tiny Letitia Green Stevenson looked up at her six-foot-tall husband with loving pride and respect. He looked down upon her in adoration and with an equivalent respect. And in their relationship with one another, in the household they established, they maintained from first to last a formality which, somehow, gave a richer meaning to all their words and all their gestures. Always he addressed her as "Mrs. Stevenson," and she addressed him as "Mr."

She appeared far from strong—and indeed, in terms of muscular power, she was far from strong. Yet she had borne many burdens without flagging. Two of her children—Lewis, and Mary, who'd died so young—had been frail and required frequent nursing, though the other two, little Adlai's Aunt Julia and Aunt Letitia, had been robust enough, and boisterous. They grew up to be beautiful girls, belles of Washington society, where Letitia of the reddish-golden hair was called "The Lily," while dark-haired Julia became "The Rose."

II

Of all his maternal ancestors, the greatest according to popular belief—certainly the greatest in influence upon the little boy Adlai—was Great-grandfather Jesse Weldon Fell.[5]

At the edge of Bloomington, with a park of several landscaped acres around it, was the first house Jesse Fell lived in after his marriage, way back in 1838, to Hester Vernon Brown. Jesse was thirty, then—and as lawyer, newspaperman, road builder, town builder, political leader, he was already a major power in central Illinois. His bride was nineteen. . . . Best man at that wedding was David Davis, Jesse's friend and law associate to whom these acres were later sold. Davis, like Fell, was later a close friend of Abraham Lincoln; he was Lincoln's floor manager during the 1860 Republican convention and became an associate justice of the Supreme Court of the United States and executor of Lincoln's will. It was Judge Davis who built the mansion that occupied the site of Jesse Fell's relatively modest cottage during the years of little Adlai's growing up; and the boy was often told by his mother that Davis had been "a *big* man, weighing about three hundred pounds."

He, the boy, had once been taken to visit Hester Brown Fell, his great-grandmother, an old, old lady whose hair was drawn tightly back against her skull in the old Quaker style, whose smile was tired and a little sad, but whose gray eyes had a rare serenity as, looking back into a full and happy life, she awaited death. Just a few months later (this was in 1907) she was dead at the age of eighty-eight, having survived her husband by twenty years. Her father, William Brown, had been the great man of Delavan, Illinois, where she was raised. A *good* man, too. All through central Illinois he was known as "Joseph" because in a year of general crop-failure he had sold his own good corn crop to his distressed neighbors for the normal price of one dollar a bushel instead of at the inflated prices others were charging. He was a man of means. From the Quaker community of Chester County, Pennsylvania—the same county that Fell came from—he'd come West with his family in a carriage, and his very first cabin had had glass panes in its windows. He could afford tutors for his children, and it was as tutor to the Brown children that Jesse Fell in 1832, having just come to Illinois, first saw his future bride.

The church where the boy Adlai's family worshiped on Sundays—a plain brick structure on the corner of East and Jefferson streets—had been founded in 1859 by Jesse Fell with his brother Kersey (who first proposed Lincoln as Republican candidate for President) and some twenty other "religious liberals." Of course Fell by then had fallen entirely away from the Quaker piety in which he had been raised (his house, incidentally, was one of the few in that community in which dancing was permitted), but this piety, as the mother explained, had never been rigidly orthodox. His father, a hatter, had forsaken the Friends for Methodism in middle years, while his mother had been a preacher of the Hicksites, who constituted the "liberal branch" of the Society of Friends and were opposed to set creeds and doctrinal statements. Thus when the slim blue-eyed young Fell started west in the fall of 1828, his mind, unhampered by religious dogma, could swiftly learn from books and practical experience. He became salesman for a book firm in Pittsburgh; he set type in a Wheeling newspaper office; he "paused for two years" (this phrase of his mother's delighted the grown-up Adlai, who always quoted it with relish) in Steubenville to study law; he passed his bar examinations in Steubenville in October, 1832; and he arrived in eastern Illinois a month later, ready to begin one of the most useful careers in Midwestern history.

At first the religious group he helped to organize in Bloomington was called the Free Congregational Society. It met in historic Phoenix Hall upon the square. A decade later, when the present church was built (with a spire, now, alas, destroyed), it became Unitarian. But from its very beginning its faith was a rational one. Human reason is man's only sure guide to truth, the members believed, and that to use one's mind honestly and well in quest of truth is therefore an act of devotion to the Supreme Intelligence. This implied a commitment to free inquiry and free speech.

The faith, the commitment, had not gone untested during the Civil War, but its greatest test came in April, 1865, after Abraham Lincoln's assassination. The news of that tragedy had been especially dismaying to Bloomington, where so many of the President's personal friends resided, and of these friends none had been more grief-stricken than Jesse Fell. He presided over a great mass meeting of sorrowing citizens, in the square, on the day after Lincoln's death and spoke there "with singular eloquence of his old friend." [6] Strong emotions were therefore aroused among members of the Free Congregational Church when its pastor, the Reverend Charles Ellis, a New Englander of fervent abolitionist views, chose in his sermon for April 23, 1865, to hold Abraham Lincoln morally responsible for his own assassination.

Before God, the minister argued, John Wilkes Booth was less to blame for Lincoln's murder than were the Founding Fathers, for these had permitted slavery to be woven as a fatal flaw into the fabric of the Republic at the time of the Constitutional Convention. As for Abraham Lincoln, he had supported this slave constitution until forced by events to issue the Emancipation Proclamation. "He had not the moral courage to step forth like a strong man in his might and do what his better nature told him was his highest duty," cried Mr. Ellis.

The effect of this, and of much more in similar vein, was an angry disturbance in the church. Mr. Ellis was barely permitted to complete his sermon. And a few days later a full meeting of church members was held for the avowed purpose of demanding the pastor's resignation.

Jesse Fell could hardly fail to deplore, personally, the assessment Mr. Ellis had made of Lincoln's character. He might well have questioned the judgment and sensitivity of a man who could so deliberately salt an open wound. Yet Jesse Fell stood firmly against the proposed action. As substitute for the proposed action he submitted resolutions which (a) refused to censure the sermon, asserting the right of any man to express his ideas untrammeled in this church; and (b) reproved the mob which had caused the disturbance last Sunday. It is evidence of Fell's persuasive power that these resolutions were almost unanimously adopted, for this meant that several members of the reproved mob must have voted for them. And the effect of all this on Mr. Ellis was instructive for a boy destined to a career in politics. For though he had been publicly vindicated, the minister voluntarily resigned his pulpit a few days later, convinced that his usefulness in Bloomington was at an end.

Fell, himself, though if anyone could be called the founder of the Republican party in Illinois, it was he, and though he was always active in politics, never permitted himself to be a candidate for elective office. He preferred that others, notably Abraham Lincoln, give official expression of his political views. Famous in history was the story of how Jesse Fell, having toured the Old Northwest and the New England states while Lincoln and Douglas engaged in those great debates Fell had suggested, returned to join his brother Kersey in urging Lincoln to become Republican candidate for President in 1860. Lincoln had become a national figure; Fell urged his friend to write out an autobiographical sketch which might be used for campaign purposes. Lincoln at first refused, saying the idea was a "foolish" one, but Fell continued to press him until finally, on December 20, 1859, Lincoln handed Fell the brief sketch whose facsimile was now framed on the wall of the library at 1316 East Washington. At once Fell sent it to his friend Joseph L. Lewis, in Westchester, Pennsylvania, and Lewis's use of it played no small part in swinging the Pennsylvania Republicans, a key delegation, behind Lincoln's candidacy.[7]

The boy Adlai learned that railroad lines ran through Bloomington largely because Jesse Fell had fought so hard in the 1830's and 40's to put them there; and the dirt road which crossed those tracks to run northward for three miles to Normal was named Fell Avenue, as well it might be, since Normal was even more completely Fell's town than Bloomington was. He was a great founder of towns, was Jesse Fell: Pontiac, Lexington, Towanda, Clinton, Leroy, El Paso—all had been largely initiated by him. And one of the towns he had started was Normal, laid out in 1854. It was called North Bloomington at first; the name was changed when the State Normal School, the first teachers' college west of the Alleghenies, was established there. For this, too, Fell was largely responsible. It was he who donated the land for the campus and who led the subscription drive that raised one hundred and forty-one thousand dollars, thus outbidding Peoria for the college; it was he who directed the inspection trip that presented the proposed site to officials in the best possible light, despite heavy rains, which had transformed the bare prairie into a sea of mud; it was he who led eighty prominent Bloomingtonians in the underwriting of the pledged funds, after lawyer Abraham Lincoln had drawn up the bond.

Among the things that made the inspectors favor this site for the college were the young elms and maples that lined the streets of Normal. Jesse Fell had planted them: he always planted trees on land he owned, and he had planted some ten thousand in Normal. After Pennsylvania, the treeless prairie country had looked so bleak to him that tree planting became a compulsion; he had become the greatest tree planter in the Middle West, supplying scores of thousands of seedlings with his own money.

In Normal was Fell Park, the site of Jesse's home, where the little boy's Grandfather Davis had been married to Eliza Brown Fell, and where Helen Stevenson, the boy's mother, had often played as a little girl. The house itself still stood, though removed from its original site—a large square structure, not beautiful at all but very comfortable-looking, with a cupola at the peak of its roof and verandas around three sides.[8]

The Davis traditions were not really very different from the Fells'. This family, too, was Quaker, and came from Chester County, Pennsylvania, where the first of the line, John, died in 1719. William Osborne Davis was of the sixth generation. He was born in a house the family had lived in, father and son, for well over one hundred years, his own father, Hibbard, having been one of the wealthiest and most respected farmers in this community. But William Osborne Davis had early evinced a dislike for farming, coupled with a yearning toward intellectual pursuits. While yet in his teens he accumulated a considerable library of serious literature—Shakespeare, Burns, Byron, Plutarch—and at the boarding school he attended, the Greenwood Dell School on the historic Brandywine, he impressed the master, a venerable Quaker named Jonathan Gauss, with his "warm heart and sensitive temperament" as well as with his scholarship. Later he himself taught in that school.

Then, at the behest of one of the Fell family, he came west, arriving in Bloomington shortly after his twentieth birthday, in the fall of 1859. He taught school that winter in Normal, became a friend of Jesse Fell's, and in 1860 went into the wilderness of the Nebraska Territory in vain search for gold. Returning to Illinois, he did guard duty in Springfield in the first year of the Civil War. In 1862, when Jesse Fell was appointed army paymaster with the rank of major by Abraham Lincoln, W. O. Davis became Fell's clerk. And in 1868 he became Fell's son-in-law, later taking over active management of the *Pantagraph,* of which he became sole editor and proprietor in 1871. . . .

He could talk wittily on many subjects, including (with some vehemence) politics, but of himself as a person, and of purely personal experience, he seldom spoke. He listened. He had a knack for drawing out other people, thus gaining an acute sense of the public temper in his community, which served him and the *Pantagraph* well.

His effect on the boy Adlai was great, and would be manifest in the man. It might be said that through Grandfather Davis the influence of Jesse Fell upon the boy was deepened and widened. For though Grandfather Davis refused to talk of himself, he talked a great deal about his father-in-law, whom he strove in many ways to emulate. There were similarities between the two. Both were shrewd, unassuming, conscientious, devoted to the public weal, peace-loving, tidy in their personal habits, and in general immensely capable.

But there were differences, too, and the differences, as personified in Grandfather Davis, were perhaps as influential. Prudence and acquisitiveness were more important in Davis's character than they were in Jesse Fell's.

There was in Fell a largeness of vision, a creative imagination, a generosity of spirit which Grandfather Davis had in far smaller degree, perhaps because he was far less robust physically. Consistent with this was the fact that neatness and orderliness, notable in Fell, were almost a passion in his son-in-law. It was as if his vital energies were so meager that he was compelled carefully to ration them.

It can hardly be said that the boy resembled his grandfather in this respect: his room was almost too cluttered to get into, being jammed with collections of coins, baggage checks, luggage tags, wood for carving, tadpoles in Mason jars, and the tiny pictures of boxers and baseball players and actresses that came in the cigarette packages of those days. He was untidy, too, with his clothes; often they lay strewn around the room.

But in another respect he and Grandfather Davis were very similar, the old man's example encouraging what seems to have been a natural tendency in the boy. The grandfather kept close track of his money. (It is recorded that his standard advice to young men was "never spend more than half your income and keep accounts" but that the wage scale on the *Pantagraph* was not high enough to make his advice practical for most of the young men he employed there. His hostility toward organized labor, particularly when it threatened his paper, was implacable and moralistic.) He carried a pocket notebook in which he jotted down all expenditures, and he deplored every form of waste and extravagance, though he and his family lived very well indeed in a material way. Even in his purchases of books—and his love and need for books was immense—his expenditures were modest.

It was Jesse Fell, however—and not his maternal or paternal grandfather— who became Adlai's favorite ancestor and even, as he'd say, his "favorite historical character." Fell was the kind of man he himself would most like to be, the "best sort of citizen," a rare combination of visionary and shrewd practical man, eminently "useful."

"He looked ahead," the man would say. "He saw possibilities where others did not. In land. In towns. In Abraham Lincoln. And he always did something about them, something effective."

Then, with a wry smile, he'd mildly regret that Great-grandfather Fell had not been just a bit more concerned to profit in a material way from his enterprise and foresight.

"Life would be simpler for me now if he had. He once owned a lot of land here in Chicago, you know—just outside the Loop. If only he'd held onto it—but he let it go for the mortgage. Oh, he did well enough financially, I suppose, but he seemed to lose interest in an enterprise at about the point at which it was about to yield really big money. He went on to something else. Judge David Davis, for instance, who started as a clerk in his office, I think, died a very wealthy man." [9]

For Jesse Fell's character and personality the man's admiration was unbounded. Though moderate and pacific, he'd say, Jesse Fell was a great natural leader of men, who'd persist patiently and stubbornly when principle was at stake. Fell was utterly fearless. He had, too, a kind of instinctive grasp of the proper balance between force and persuasion in the achievement of human goals. One of the great-grandson's favorite stories about him was of the occasion when Fell, as schoolteacher, was forced to whip a bully larger than himself. He did a thorough job of it. But afterward the youthful teacher gave the bully a lecture that mingled kindness and flattery so effectively that the bully reformed himself and became a Methodist Episcopal minister "of fine character and widespread influence."

Another favorite story revealed that Fell, for all his Quaker background, reacted in the way his great-grandson would also, as boy and as man, when pushed too far. Fell and another lawyer, in a courtroom where Abraham Lincoln was present, became engaged in an argument so heated that Fell was flatly accused of lying.

"I told him that would have to be settled outside the courtroom," Fell himself wrote years later, "so when court adjourned, we promptly went out to settle it in the time-honored way. Neither of us gained much advantage over the other, as while he was the stronger, I was quicker, and we were parted before we could finish. We had fought hard enough, however, to be willing to shake hands. In the morning we were indicted for fighting 'to the disturbance and alarm of the people'. My defense was that nobody was at all alarmed, much to Lincoln's amusement, and the indictment was quashed." [10]

III

Of all the boy's ancestral influences, then, Jesse Fell's was most important.

There was in him, however, quite a mingling of opposite traditions! He could trace out, as components of himself, the American aristocrat and the petty bourgeois, the poor artisan and the wealthy businessman, the small farmer and the powerful planter, the soldier and the pacifist, the abolitionist and the slave owner, the free thinker and the rigid Calvinist, the settled Easterner and the westering pioneer, the Unionist and the Confederate, the rabid Republican and the equally rabid Democrat. No one, in terms of heritage, could come closer to being an all-American boy. And no man, molded by such a heritage, and conscious of it, could easily yield to partial views, or become a dogmatist. The man would have a sense of alternative values, an awareness of historic relevancies and implications. He'd ponder long before deciding. But once his mind was made up, it might be better made than most men's are, with a larger view of objective truth than most men obtain. One of his own favorite quotations came from Bacon's essays, which was a favorite book of his mother's and from which she read often to her children. "If a man will begin with certainties, he shall end in doubts; but if he will be content to begin with doubts, he shall end in certainties."

Certainly his consciousness of history as a family matter made history for him a vividly human drama written by the daily thought and passion and action of individual men and women, yet written, too, in terms of a design more vast and meaningful than any individual could comprehend. There was a pattern. Hence there must be purpose. And the purpose seemed to be moral. He developed a sense of historical process, and of the need for tradition, which was rare in his America. Tradition was that strand of continuity on which historic events are strung like beads; only in terms of a living tradition could current events be understood in such a way as to make intelligent action possible; and this tradition was clearly within as well as beyond himself. Being alive, it was not fixed and rigid. Rather was it that permanence which is the very essence of change, and he himself would re-create it at the same time as he was judged by it when, through present action, he helped to shape the future.

CHAPTER THREE

IN the spring of 1899 Eliza Brown Fell Davis came to Fort Bayard, New Mexico, for an extended visit with her daughter, Helen Louise Stevenson. With her she brought the two small children of her only son, Hibbard, whose wife had died tragically some five years before. She had enjoyed the visit for only a few happy weeks when a strangely persistent physical pain, deep and gnawing, drove her back with her two grandsons to her home in Bloomington. An operation in Chicago confirmed her suspicions: she was dying of cancer. In November her husband took her to San Antonio, Texas, there to await what both knew to be a swiftly approaching end.

There was, however, a balance, a continuity: as Eliza Brown Fell Davis was dying out of the family, another new life was growing into it. The tall, slender, bearded William Osborne Davis had gray, heavy-lidded eyes that appeared always to be gazing across great distances and had always in them, even in his frequent moments of laughter, a quality of quiet sadness. His was a sensitive, brooding intelligence, quickened rather than dulled by long bouts with ill health, and he must have felt acutely that a race between death and life was being run through that bitter autumn and early winter.

Soon he would be a widower—but soon also he would be again a grand-father: Helen Stevenson was again with child. The first news had come from Fort Bayard; later news came from Los Angeles, whence the Stevensons removed that summer. Eliza Brown Fell Davis died at one o'clock in the morning of January 21, 1900. By that time Helen Stevenson was very big with child. It was a hard pregnancy. Her husband grew increasingly worried about her as January gave way to February and the time for her taking seemed overdue. He communicated his anxiety to his parents, and to the widowed father-in-law, now returned to Bloomington. The anxiety seemed more than justified on the morning of February 5; the birth, too, was hard. ... But when the Stevenson nurse, Cora Galbraith, returned from a nearby park to which she'd taken the two-and-a-half-year-old Elizabeth, she was informed that Elizabeth now had a baby brother. A perfectly *enormous* baby brother: he weighed eleven pounds and eight ounces!

It had been long decided what name Lewis Stevenson's son should bear. The telegrams that went out that day to Bloomington announced the birth of a second Adlai Ewing Stevenson. And on the next morning, in wintry Bloomington, Lewis's mother wrote to her daughter-in-law:

February 6, 1900

My dear Helen:

This proud day's sun must not set until I have sent you a line of most heart-felt congratulations to both you and the triumphant father, and a glad welcome to the dear grandson, Adlai.

That he may fill all your most ardent expectations is my earnest prayer. If the new Adlai only comes up to the splendid standard established by his two grandfathers, you will have nothing to regret in the pain and suffering of yesterday. With all good wishes and prayer for your speedy recovery, I remain

Always yours,
Letitia Green Stevenson

A week later she wrote to her son:

February 13, 1900

My dear Lewis:

You know now what it is and all it means to say "my dear boy." May he grow dearer to you each hour of his life and may he be to you and to his mother all you have been to us all these years.

Father is as happy as a king over his first grandson and real namesake. He often says if Adlai Jr. only turns out such a boy as Elizabeth is a girl his highest ambition will have been attained. How I wish it were possible to peep in upon your little household—not so very little either—this splendid, cold, clear morning!

I am so glad Elizabeth loves the boy. A child is apt to carry through life the feelings it had when its first rival arrives in the world.

*Heaven bless you and yours and make the boy in all things to be like
you, his proud father and mother.*

Devotedly,
Mother

But it was Helen's father who wrote the letter that, in later years, would
be most quoted. On the first Sunday following his new grandson's birth,
W. O. Davis wrote to his daughter from Bloomington:

Dear Helen:
*Tell Lewis that I rec'd his second letter, written since the advent of
little Adlai, this morning and I want to thank him for writing so promptly,
and while I should reply to him now I want to wait until I have written
to you.*

*We are all highly gratified to hear of the successful launching of this
little Presidential craft and to know that you are safely through it. We
have been anxious, and were filled with dread until relieved by your
telegram—but now that you are believed to be out of danger, the joy
the little cherub is to all of us, will compensate a good deal for your
tribulations. Little Elizabeth will enjoy a little brother. She will be so
wise in protecting him, and utterly spoil him, as I was spoiled by my
older sisters. Then I suppose Lewis's ecstatic condition is such that it
is hardly safe to permit him to be left alone. Bert and Lewis B. both
insist that he had his thumbs on the scales, determined that the little
fellow should outweigh little Jessie Davis Merwin. I know Lewis's delight is unbounded, and I scarcely know anyone who enjoys their children
better than he. And it is such a fine thing to have children in the household, and enjoy them. I do not know what I would do now without these
little boys of ours—they are developing so well—*

Yours lovingly,
W. O. Davis

II

It is an historic truth that Adlai Ewing Stevenson II—a placid baby,
sweet-tempered, and very fat—was in the national political news within
six months after his birth. In the summer of 1900 he and his sister were
taken by their mother, with Cora to help her, to the Davis summer cottage
at Charlevoix, Michigan. On the way they stopped in Bloomington where
Grandfather Stevenson was photographed holding his namesake in his arms.
The resulting picture showed Adlai E. Stevenson I, Democratic candidate
for the Vice-Presidency, looking with stern directness at the world, his lips
clamped tightly shut beneath a thick white mustache, his brow puckered in
a slight frown, his bald pate fringed by a fuzz of white hair. Adlai E.
Stevenson II, who was certainly very large for his age, leaned passively
against his grandfather's left side and looked away to his left, neither smiling

nor frowning, his fat little hands resting loosely on the hand that held him. The picture was published on July 20 as a four-column cut in Hearst's brand-new Chicago *American,* with the caption: "The next Vice-President and his Grandson." Below was the legend:

Governor (Theodore) Roosevelt says that this citizen of Illinois . . . in common with all other Democrats, "stands for dishonesty and dishonor, for license and disaster at home and cowardly shrinking from duty abroad." There are some citizens of Illinois who probably do not agree with Mr. Roosevelt's view, and who will probably tell him so next November.

When this infant Adlai had grown into a man he would never be sure that he actually remembered the Montrose Avenue house where he had been born. His earliest extended memories were of the life in Berkeley. And by the time the family moved there he had conferred upon his sister the nickname she would bear for the rest of her life. When he first began to talk, "Elizabeth" was more than his tongue could manage; he called her "Buff," which soon became "Buffie," and it was as Buffie that she was there-after chiefly known to her family and intimate acquaintances. She called him "Brod" (his mother called him "Laddie"), and she was indeed a very "man-aging" little girl where he was concerned.

She seems never to have regarded him as a rival for her parents' affection. She delighted in her responsibility for him, assuming toward him, from the outset, a maternal attitude—and sometimes he rebelled against her domi-nance: when they quarreled, which was seldom, it was generally because of this. But for the most part he was a quite passive recipient of her manage-ment and her adoration. She did adore him. She always would. When she compared herself with him, she saw his dominant traits as "virtues" and hers as "vices," and she'd say to herself and to others that he was so "good," so "sweet," so "gentle." Others who knew him well agreed with her in this latter judgment. He was, as a little boy, not at all aggressive. He seemed not to care at all for that limelight which to her spirit was as food and drink.[1]

But Charlevoix, Michigan, was more his home than the California cities ever were. Every summer he and Buffie were taken there by their mother, with Cora (the children called her "Codie"), for three or four months, to live in a colony of well-to-do people, many of them from Bloomington, centered in and about the Belevedere Hotel.

In January, 1907, just a few months after the family had moved from California to Bloomington, Grandfather Davis, whose health was far from good in his declining years, went to Florida, taking with him his daughter Helen and the two Stevenson grandchildren. Lewis was then in Europe. Their destination was Winter Park, Florida, where they lived for many weeks in a rented house beside a golf course. There little Adlai made friends with colored boys who caddied for the golfers, tried to play golf with them, and often brought them home, asking the servant to "give my brother some dinner." It was from Winter Park that he wrote, on March 1, 1907, his earliest extant composition—a letter to his father in Europe:

Dear father

I hope you will come home soon?

I will make you a pictire of a cow.

It was also in Winter Park that he had his first taste of formal schooling. Grandfather Davis told of it in a letter, dated January 15, 1907, to Lewis.

Adlai began attendance at the public school a week ago [he wrote]. Elizabeth conducted him the first morning and ushered him into the presence of the teacher, who assigned him a seat, and some work. He was a pretty raw scholar, had no ideas of the rules, talked out loud, and moved about with a good deal of freedom. He was dressed in the fringed suit Miss Woodbury gave him, so the scholars nicknamed him Indian. On his return home at noon, he felt quite a little chesty and told of his experience chiefly in the rough-house at the recess at 10 o'clock. He said, "There is one boy I must get rid of so I swatted him some good ones on the slats and soaked him a warm one in the face, and was oftener on top than I was under." Meanwhile some of the boys hollered, "Give it to him, Indian." It was all intended to be playful but [was] altogether different from anything in his previous career.

The incident was so amusing to Grandfather Davis and the others precisely because it was so incongruous with the little boy's temperament and usual demeanor. Once in Bloomington, a year or so later, he was "jumped" by some older, larger boys and had his nose broken in the resulting melee (later, at Charlevoix, he tripped over a garden wire in the dark and broke his nose again, permanently bending it to the left). He himself would remember that he had "many fights at school." But others remarked in him a most peaceable disposition and a distaste for fighting, if no apparent fear of being hurt himself.

From the very first he was a sensitive and almost excessively conscientious little boy. Virtually every piece of wrongdoing, in his case, was an inadvertence for which he suffered great remorse. Apparently this stern conscience was an innate part of him: certainly it was not the product of punishment, for he was not sternly raised and never suffered a corporal correction more severe than a mild slap on his hands.

His play world at Bloomington contained many of those who populated it in Charlevoix. Joe Bohrer, for instance, was a companion in both places; so was his cousin, Davis Merwin (Helen Stevenson's sister Jessie had married L. B. Merwin), who lived just two doors up the street from him and was almost exactly his age. And one of the centers of his play world was the shop Walter Williams had set up in the back yard of his father's home— the C. U. Williams home across the street from the Lewis Stevensons. Walter, who was nine years older than Adlai, was a precocious mechanical genius. He had become a master of all the mysteries of internal-combustion engines and electric motors. He was also an inventor. As a young man he would invent the Oil-O-Matic, among other things, and make himself a fortune.

Another center of his play world was the yard of the Coolidges, who lived two doors to the west of the Stevensons. Mrs. Coolidge was a sister of Sidney Smith, a Bloomington boy who had become famous as the creator of "Andy Gump" in the funny papers. Her two children, Hesketh and Betty, were among Adlai's favorite companions. Still other play places were his Grandfather Stevenson's yard, Grandfather Davis's where he and Dave Merwin played mumbledypeg with their jackknives for hours at a time, Joe Bohrer's yard, and Franklin Park, where he and his companions played ball and rode bicycles. (Tennis, in Charlevoix in the summer, early became his favorite game, and one at which, by his mid-teens, he was expert.) In Davis's pasture just beyond the fence bounding his back yard, where cows wandered, he hunted crayfish along the meandering stream and played "cowboys and Indians" and "Civil War" upon a grassy sward that would become the golf course of the country club a few years later.[2]

He was a "normal" boy. He did the things that most boys of his time and place and social class were doing. None of his playmates of those years (when he was eight, and ten, and eleven) would later remember that there was anything remarkable about him. They would recall no particular anecdotes concerning him that might reveal any marked capacity or forecast a distinguished future. He did not star in sports; he had no outstanding mechanical ability; he manifested no artistic or literary genius; he was no brilliant scholar. Far from being intellectually precocious, he seemed to lag behind most of his contemporaries at school in his mental development, though not so greatly as to make even this a distinguishing characteristic. Most people found him very likable. Older people especially were impressed by his good manners, sensing that these proceeded not merely from training but from a genuine concern for other people and for the principles of right conduct.

III

Of all the influences that played upon him, the most potent by far was family. This included not only his immediate family but also his grandparents and aunts and cousins and all those ancestors whose stories went back two centuries and more into the national history. Some outside observers claimed it was fortunate for little Adlai that he had this larger family to sustain his vital growth, since the immediate family situation at 1316 East Washington was, in their view, a not wholly happy one.

Lewis and Helen Stevenson were brilliant, witty, willful people who were scintillating company on social occasions. But they were irritable in the literal meaning of that word—sensitive, high-strung—perhaps because their general physical health was none too good. Their nerve ends seemed to be more nakedly exposed to the world than most people's are. They were therefore aware of environmental pressures too slight to enter the average consciousness; they were chafed to the point of pain by things most people can ignore. Often they chafed one another, and because each of them could use words like knives, stabbing and slashing with precision, they wounded one another deeply.[3]

One of the exacerbating differences between them had to do with their attitudes toward money. Helen was thrifty, Lewis extravagant, in money matters. To count costs was, for Helen, almost an expression of piety; not to count them was, for Lewis, an expression of human warmth. She had been horrified when she learned that before their marriage he had bought a diamond ring to be buried with his sister Mary, just because "Mary always wanted a diamond." She was more resentful than grateful when he showered upon her such gifts as an elaborate silver toilet set (her old one was "perfectly good") and a gold bracelet shaped as a coiled snake with diamonds for eyes (her taste would never have chosen it). Perhaps she sensed in his extravagant giving an element of aggression. Sometimes it was as if he felt a need to buy back affections forfeited during spells of pain-provoked irritability, an effort which might seem insulting to the person he strove thus to manipulate. At other times it was as if he enjoyed flouting Helen's cautious thrift, defying her and so getting even.

Lewis had other characteristics that, while often amusing, were certainly not conducive to peace and quiet in the home. He was often dramatic, even theatrical, in his reactions to stimuli. He kept a loaded revolver in his bedroom as a protection against burglars, and he heard far more burglars in the night than could possibly have entered 1316 East Washington.

Some outsiders believed that the relationship between Lewis and Helen Stevenson was such as to encourage the latter to become very much a mother, lavishing upon her children a loving care that even some insiders (cousins, aunts) felt to be excessive. It was a common thing in that prosperous neighborhood for children to be over-mothered, according to the lights of less privileged people. But Helen Stevenson was believed to go beyond the neighborhood average in this respect.

Her concern for her children's health amounted to an almost constant anxiety. (Lewis, too, was a health-worrier. "You'll never know what happiness is unless you are healthy," he said.) This was explainable by her own and her husband's frequent ill health; nevertheless it somewhat limited the range of her children's activity and might have encouraged in them a species of hypochondria. Both parents adopted dietary fads at various times and foisted them upon their offspring: Battle Creek foods ("Hay!" snorted Grandmother Stevenson; she'd not have such hay at her table), "fletcherizing" (chewing each mouthful of food an incredible number of times), the consumption of gallons of milk and orange juice, the use of onion soup as a specific against headaches. When exercise with dumbbells and Indian clubs was decreed, Lewis Stevenson was among the first to obey. When regulated deep breathing before open windows was the fad, no family breathed more deeply than the Stevensons. When sleeping porches were recommended, Helen Stevenson promptly built one over the back porch (this was in the fall of 1912), and Buffie and Adlai were forced to sleep there even on bitterly cold nights. Similarly with cold baths. Once when Lewis Stevenson was on a farm inspection trip in Indiana he wrote his son asking if the latter were taking his daily cold baths. "I hope so," he said. "In a lecture the other day I heard a doctor say a man would gain thirty percent resistance power (to prevent catching disease) if he had taken daily cold baths from childhood." No family was more conscious of germs.

And the mother's concern was by no means limited to matters of physical

health. She was equally concerned to form in her children habits of work
and play that would be conducive to moral probity and worldly success. The
letters she wrote to Adlai when she was separated from him were full of the
most detailed advice about his general attitudes, his social conduct, his
schoolwork. When they were together she watched over him with embarrassing closeness. If she were in the vicinity of the school at closing time, for
example, she often picked him up in her electric car, a procedure he did
nothing to encourage. Once he hid from her under a bearskin robe on the
floor of another student's car, so that he might ride home with his companions. . . .

Quarrelsomeness and love are not necessarily antithetical, however, in
such temperaments as Lewis's and Helen's. The former may manifest the
latter—and that it did so in this case is the testimony of the most intimate
observers. The Democratic Vice-President's son and the Republican publisher's daughter had known one another well from earliest childhood. They
could scarcely remember a time when they had not loved one another and
taken it for granted that they'd marry. Thus there had never been between
them that quality of courtship whereby each strives to impress the other
with his or her most lovable qualities while avoiding all that might anger or
annoy. They were utterly frank with one another; it was hardly possible for
them to be anything else. What to outsiders appeared bitter, wounding
quarrels seem therefore to have had, as essential reality, a very different
quality: a release of tensions that might otherwise have strangled love. And
this seems to have been recognized by their children.

CHAPTER FOUR

I N the summer of 1912, Lewis Stevenson proposed that the family go to a
hotel in Spring Lake, New Jersey, for a few weeks.[1] Spring Lake was near
Sea Girt; at Sea Girt, the governor of New Jersey had his summer mansion;
and the governor of New Jersey, as everybody knew, was Woodrow Wilson,
former president of Princeton and now the Democratic candidate for President of the United States. Wilson had received the nomination at the Baltimore convention despite the bitter opposition of Lewis's former employer,
William Randolph Hearst, and despite the publication of a private letter
of some years before in which the then president of Princeton expressed the
hope that William Jennings Bryan, whose fiscal policies Wilson opposed,

might be "knocked into a cocked hat." The latter fact might have given some slight pause to the elderly Adlai Ewing Stevenson back in Bloomington, but apparently it did not do so. As for the former Vice-President's son, his admiration for Wilson was unbounded.

A day or so after their arrival in Spring Lake, Lewis took his son with him to Sea Girt, to the white two-story green-shuttered colonial house where Wilson was ensconced. There, on a wide Grecian-columned porch facing the sea, the boy Adlai Stevenson was introduced to a man destined to become one of his heroes and a potent influence upon his own political thought. That autumn the boy Adlai lived a more consciously political life than he'd ever done before, having for the first time some awareness of issues as well as of personalities in a campaign. When his own grandfather Stevenson had run for governor four years before, he'd been excited because the grownups were, and he could see that politics was, for them, a matter of vital import. The parades and shouting crowds, the suspense as election day drew near—these had impressed him. But far more interesting to him personally was the fact that an extra telephone was installed in his grandfather's house to receive the returns on election night, and that this extra phone, instead of being mounted on the wall, sat on a table and had no crank. In the fall of 1912, however, hearing politics talked day in and day out, with Roosevelt damned and Taft deplored and Wilson extolled at every meal, he learned that there was something called the "Payne-Aldrich Tariff," and it was very bad because it aided "special privilege"; that Taft was a poor President because he was a "tool of the interests"; that there was something called "conservation," and it meant that you must keep selfish men from stealing the trees and minerals that belonged to all the people; that Governor Wilson had not only a "great mind" but also a "deep concern for humanity"; and that Republicans in general believed that businessmen should run the government as they did their own businesses, to make money for themselves, whereas Democrats believed that *all* people should be represented by government and *all* should be served by it, with equal justice. Of course Republicans often talked like Democrats in election years, but that was just to fool the voters.

However, Grandfather Davis—a good kind man—had been a very rigid Republican. The Merwins were Republicans. Most of their Bloomington friends, fine people all, were Republicans. To be a Republican, then, was not to be wicked, but only sadly mistaken. . . .

Shortly before ten o'clock on November 5, the *Pantagraph* office phoned the Stevenson home to tell the former Vice-President of Wilson's triumph. Take it all in all, it was an impressive victory. When the complete returns were in, it would be found that Wilson polled 6,286,214 votes, Roosevelt 4,126,020, and Taft 3,483,922. Thus Wilson lacked a popular majority, but he'd carried forty-one of the forty-eight states and obtained 435 of the 531 votes in the electoral college, and his party, for the first time in many years, controlled both houses of Congress. The Stevensons were elated; within an hour after Taft and Roosevelt had conceded, Grandfather Stevenson wired the President-elect. Next day Wilson telegraphed his thanks.

Nor was the national victory the only cause for celebration. Edward Fitzsimons Dunne, former mayor of Chicago and a long-time political friend of both Lewis and the former Vice-President, had won the governorship of Illinois, the first Democrat to do so since John Peter Altgeld's victory in 1892. This meant that Lewis would be offered an appointive office of some kind, and that his personal political prospects—for he was developing political ambitions at that time—would be greatly enhanced.

A few weeks later this expectation was fulfilled. The governor-elect asked Lewis to serve as chairman of the Illinois State Board of Pardons, and Lewis accepted. It would be the first public office he had ever held, and he prepared for it with thoroughness and enthusiasm.

They were a particularly happy, busy family that fall and early winter, with the lives of the parents as well as of the children opening out into new and rich experiences. Never had the world seemed more amiable to them; never had the political climate of Illinois and of the nation seemed more favorable to such ambitions as this highly political family might hold. Buffie, in University High School in Normal, was happily taking part in school dramatics and falling in and out of love every week. Adlai was happily exploring, and mastering, the mysteries of the family Locomobile (Lewis always called it, with a certain reverence, "The Machine"), bought in 1911, paying at least as much attention to these as he paid to his schoolwork.

Christmas came and passed with a round of parties and family feasts.

For Buffie the following days were enlivened by the presence of Margery McClelland, one of her old Charlevoix playmates, who had come for a holiday visit. She asked and received permission to entertain a group of her contemporaries, with Margery as guest of honor, including among her guests a girl named Ruth Merwin, a cousin of the Merwin children who, in turn, were Buffie's cousins. With Ruth, Buffie had formed a special friendship at University High.

The party evening came.

With it—swiftly, starkly, incredibly—came tragedy. . . .

Since it was to be a supper party and Adlai was deemed too young for it, he had his supper early that evening of December 20, 1912, going up afterward to his room. Lewis and Helen Stevenson went out to pay a neighborhood call while Buffie took her guests into the drawing room. One of the boys, Bob Whitmer, proudly offered to demonstrate the manual of arms, which he had learned at military school—if only he had a gun. Whereupon Buffie went out into the hallway and called up to Adlai, asking him to go into the attic and fetch down the old .22 rifle that was kept there. Eagerly Adlai did so.

First Bob Whitmer carefully examined the gun to make sure there were no bullets in the barrel or magazine, explaining professionally that this was always required at school. Then, with professional smartness, he executed the manual and was warmly applauded. The gun was given back to Adlai to be returned to the attic. As he left with it he excitedly imitated Whitmer's movements. The gun went off. Ruth Merwin dropped limply to the floor.

She was dead.

Later examination revealed that the ejecting mechanism had a rusty spring that had probably prevented the emergence of the single bullet. But no one was concerned with this at the moment. Everyone stared helplessly, unbelievingly, at the girl who an instant before had been gaily laughing and talking and who now lay so still upon the hallway carpet.

The dead girl's mother, Mrs. Clarence Merwin, proved herself to be "a very great woman," as the family gratefully acknowledged ever after. On that very night, in the midst of her own terrible grief, she comforted Adlai's mother, and talked to Adlai, too, telling the boy that he must not blame himself. He *must* not! She realized that this tragedy could be devastating upon anyone as sensitive and imaginative and excessively conscientious as this boy was.

The day of the funeral Helen Stevenson took Adlai, Dave Merwin, Margery McClelland, and Claire, her French maid, to Chicago on an early train. There they stayed at Aunt Julia Hardin's home; Uncle Martin Hardin had by then become pastor of the city's Third Presbyterian Church. Lewis and Buffie went to Ruth Merwin's funeral. "Adlai Stevenson, prostrated by grief, was unable to be present," the *Pantagraph* reported. When Helen and the others returned to Bloomington the tragic event was not referred to, nor was it ever mentioned again in the family, or by Adlai himself, until a reporter questioned Adlai about it forty years later.

What effect did the tragedy have upon the development of Adlai Stevenson the man?

To answer this question precisely is of course impossible. The man himself probably could not have done so if he would—and certainly he would not. When William Glasgow of *Time* magazine, with some hesitation, brought the subject up in 1952 Stevenson "looked away for a moment" and then "told me the whole story, in a quiet matter-of-fact way." [2] Later interviewers would find him similarly matter-of-fact on this subject as on all others that, though they concerned his intimate life, were necessarily exposed to the public gaze as he became an increasingly important public figure. To the facts as he recounted them, no evident emotion would adhere. Yet one need not be particularly perceptive to see that this apparent frankness was, in reality, the agency of a profound reticence. He seemed to tell all; he revealed nothing that was of the essence.

There is no doubt, however, that the tragedy did have an effect, a deep and lasting one, giving rise to some of the subtler complexities of an exceedingly complex man. It might partially account for certain distinctive traits of the mature man: a diffidence of manner, a tendency toward self-deprecation. Recurrent in his public speech, forty years later, would be the phrase: "If you please . . ." Even his far-famed wit might be shaped in part by his awareness—born of this tragic experience—that blind chance can frustrate the strongest will, that it may assume at any moment the shape of a black malevolence, that death in any case awaits us all. He who holds his head too high while striding pridefully into a country of bogs is likely to end up in the muck; better to look down humbly, accepting the absurdity of trembling knees and slippery footing. In this spirit Adlai Stevenson would make himself the butt of his own best jokes, using as a shield that which his political opponents feared as a sword.

II

During the following years Adlai and his father grew closer together. They began to share common interests. They went hunting together and occasionally played golf together. Lewis drove his Locomobile on his farm inspection trips and often he took his son with him. In the hot Illinois summers father and son would load the back of the Locomobile with a huge tin box of provisions, a tent, folding beds, and a spirit stove. Father and son would tramp together through the fields, with the tenant farmers showing them the results of new farming practices Lewis was always introducing: new rotations, new fertilizer treatments, new methods of cultivation, and at night they'd camp in a farmyard or pasture, which Lewis Stevenson always preferred to the farmhouse. They'd bathe in the morning, sometimes, in creek or river, as proud as they were happy to be roughing it. Often they were stuck in mud, for there were no surfaced roads.

Yet there remained between father and son a certain tension. They were so very different in mind and temperament: Adlai even-tempered, quiet, notably cool in judgment; Lewis volatile, gay, and quick-tempered, and inclined toward swift judgments made sometimes in the heat of anger—judgments often as quickly changed. Letters from this period seem to show that the mother and two children regarded themselves, now and then, to be in a secret alliance against the father's frequent storms. Father had to be humored. He had to be handled. One must not take his flat orders too seriously, for he was likely to reverse himself remorsefully without notice. But these same letters also reveal Lewis Stevenson's great capacity for love: one had again the sense of a warm, generous, extroverted personality battling gallantly against recurrent severe bodily pain, and losing the battle, sometimes, in an angry constrictive exasperation.

That Lewis Stevenson would have gone far in politics had his health permitted was one of the convictions of Adlai Stevenson the man—and there is considerable evidence in support of this conviction. However erratic he might sometimes be in his role of *paterfamilias,* he was in his professional life notably practical, ingenious, and imaginative. By the time his son reached high school Lewis had earned a national reputation as a leader of scientific agriculture, and a few years later he would be among the first men to be listed in *Who's Who in America* under the classification of "farmer." (He pioneered, for instance, in the use of soybeans as a major crop, making the planting of soybeans both as a cash crop and for soil building purposes a condition of the lease among his tenants.) As chairman of the Board of Pardons, he introduced many improvements in the administration of the parole laws; the governor was proud of him and could be counted on to support whatever ambitions he might have for further public service.

Politics, certainly, was in his blood, and he wanted to carry on the family's political tradition. He may even have felt an obligation to do so, after his mother and father, their lives declining through the first months of Woodrow Wilson's administration, finally died.

On Sunday, December 28, 1913, the Lewis Stevenson family, in solemn black, attended the funeral of Letitia Green Stevenson, wife of the former Vice-President of the United States. Services were held in Bloomington's Presbyterian church, which was filled to overflowing. Prominent among the mourners were members of the Bloomington chapter—the Letitia Green Stevenson chapter—of the Daughters of the American Revolution.

Her husband survived her by only five months. On June 13, 1914, Adlai Ewing Stevenson I was dead. His funeral, three days later, was the largest and most widely publicized in Bloomington's history. Dignitaries from all over the country were there, reporters scribbled notes in pads during the services as if reporting a political rally, and Pathé newsreel men had their cameras set up on tripods by the church entrance, cranking away industriously. Next day, newspapers all over the country carried a picture of the Vice-President's namesake, clad in knickerbockers, holding with his sister a crepe-draped American flag at the church door.

It was the end of an era in the Stevenson family history, and it coincided with the end of an era in world history—for barely ten days after Grandfather Stevenson's funeral, in a far country of which few Bloomingtonians had heard and of which Grandfather Stevenson's namesake had heard only because he had Serbian stamps in his stamp collection, the Archduke Franz Ferdinand, heir to the Austro-Hungarian throne, was shot to death in the streets of Sarajevo, capital of Bosnia. Six weeks later war flamed on the Russian border, and in the tiny Belgian village of Visé dazed civilians were being led before German firing squads for having dared to fire upon invading German troops. Soon all western Europe was ablaze in a conflagration that would not end until the last effective vestiges of the nineteenth century were consumed, not only in Europe but in America.

Among the casualties of the war would be the fame of Adlai Ewing Stevenson I. His career would seem to have no vital connection with the America that emerged from the war; his speeches and writings would be largely forgotten because they said little that seemed relevant to the generations of men among whom his namesake must make a life. There would remain of him, in the minds of his family and friends, the memory of an extraordinarily rich and lovable personality.

III

In August of 1914, Carl Vrooman of Bloomington was appointed Assistant Secretary of Agriculture in the Wilson administration, under Secretary David Houston. The event heightened the interest at 1316 East Washington in Wilson's farm policies, for Vrooman had married Julia Green Scott, daughter of Mrs. Matthew T. Scott, in 1896, and had thus become "Cousin Carl" to the Lewis Stevensons. He was, in some respects, a strange husband for an aristocratic heiress. Raised in Kansas through years of farm depression, he had become a Populist, the author of a book called *Taming the Trusts* and of another, *American Railway Problems,* which argued from European examples that U.S. railroads should be nationalized. In Washington he and his wife became the center of a brilliant social life in which the Lewis Stevensons, from time to time, would share.[3]

A few weeks after the Vrooman appointment there was a new beginning for Lewis Stevenson himself. The Democratic landslide two years before had swept into the office of secretary of state for Illinois a plump-faced, bespectacled young man named Harry Woods, who soon proved to be mentally unbalanced. He feuded with everyone, flew into frequent shouting rages, wrapped the most commonplace subjects in mystery. He aspired to be United States senator, filing for that office in 1914 with every confidence that he would be nominated, and spending a great deal of money on his campaign. He ran a poor third in the primary—fourth in his home Chicago ward. The blow crushed him. On the morning of October 11 his wife found him dead in his garage at the rear of his Springfield home, a bullet wound in his forehead, a revolver in his hand. Two days later, on October 13, the governor announced that Lewis G. Stevenson of Bloomington had been appointed to fill out Woods's term, which would expire in January, 1917. The appointment, a complete surprise to politicians and reporters, was made because of "my personal observation of Mr. Stevenson's conduct of the Board of Pardons," the governor said.

Lewis Stevenson moved at once to Springfield, leaving Adlai in Blooming-ton with his mother to complete the school term. The 1915 session of Illinois' General Assembly was made memorable by a bitter battle over the speaker-ship of the House. For five stormy weeks, during which angry passions flamed high and no less than sixty-seven ballots were cast without decisive result, Lewis Stevenson was the House's presiding officer. His mastery of parliamentary procedure, his adroitness in handling men, his sense of justice, his self-control under fire—all were severely tested. His greatest personal fear during this ordeal was that he might be struck down by one of those terrible migraines and become incapacitated for a day or two, but, miraculously, this did not happen. When at last the speaker was chosen, the House gave the secretary of state a unanimous vote of thanks for the impartiality and effi-ciency with which he discharged his duties.

By that time Adlai and his mother had moved to Springfield, where he was enrolled in the Springfield high school. Buffie had been enrolled, the preceding autumn, in the University School for Girls, on Lake Shore Drive in Chicago, but had so rebelled against the enforced separation from her family that she was permitted to return to the family circle in Springfield that spring. They lived in a house rented from former Governor Richard Yates. Next door lived the Medill McCormicks while the General Assembly was in session, for McCormick, publisher of the Chicago *Tribune,* was a state senator—Republican, of course—and, strange as it might seem in a later year, the two families were close friends.

In Springfield, Adlai began to be interested in girls. His favorite date was pretty, vivacious Mary Douglas Hay, daughter of Mr. and Mrs. Logan Hay, good social friends of the Lewis Stevensons.[4] Logan Hay was one of Illinois' most prominent attorneys; he was also one of the nation's foremost Lincoln scholars. He was a cousin of John Hay, Lincoln's secretary and biographer, and a son of Milton Hay, who had been one of Lincoln's close friends. Milton Hay had had a law office on the same floor with Lincoln and Herndon. Logan Hay's mother, born Mary Logan, was the daughter of Judge Stephen T. Logan, who had been senior partner of the law firm of Logan and Lincoln in the early 1840's.

Family ties were loosened in the autumn of 1915. Lewis Stevenson re-mained in Springfield as his wife and children returned to 1316 East Wash-ington in Bloomington. Adlai was enrolled in University High. Buffie, a tall slender vivid girl with an actress's temperament, had become eighteen in July, and was entered in Miss Wright's School for Young Ladies, in Bryn Mawr. She was reluctant to go, if not actually rebellious. "How ghastly to break up the home," she wrote in her diary before she left. "I suppose we will never all live together again." [5] Helen Stevenson went East with her daughter, planning to stay there for some weeks.

Before the mother left she hired as housekeeper a nineteen-year-old colored girl named Alverta Duff whose life, from that point on, would be intimately involved with Stevenson lives. She was the daughter of one Peter Duff, the son of a Mississippi slave who had come as a boy of fourteen to the house of Jesse Fell in Normal, where he was taken in and given odd jobs to do on condition that he go to school. He went to school, and by the 1900's the Duff family was highly respected in the community. Fannie Duff, Alverta's mother, feared that the big house at 1316 East Washington might be too much for her daughter, who had never worked before for anyone save her mother, and was not particularly strong, but Helen Stevenson was insistent: Adlai was being left alone for the first time and they must have a housekeeper whom she could absolutely trust to look after him.

As it turned out, Alverta's mother need not have worried. The girl was more than a superb housekeeper; she was also, from the first, a close friend of Adlai's. And decades later, one of the things she would remember about the "kind and considerate, sweet-tempered boy" was his studying at the library table at night, with the green-shaded lamp shining down over his bent, absorbed head. She believed that he studied abnormally long and hard.[6]

And perhaps he did. Having entered school so late—and having attended so erratically, with frequent long interruptions ever since—he had handicaps to overcome. But his teachers believed he limited his formal studies to a barely acceptable minimum. They repeatedly told him and his parents that he had the mental ability to make excellent marks if only he would concentrate more. He was too actively interested in too many things, they said. As it was, his grades in the fall of 1914 had averaged 77 (out of a possible 100) in algebra, 77 in English, and 76 in zoology. He was absent from Normal during the spring term, at Springfield, where his grades were if anything a little lower than his University High ones. Next year, when Alverta first knew him, his record was somewhat improved. In the fall of the 1915–16 year he averaged 86 in English, 77 in geometry, and 83 in history; in the winter he scored 91 in geometry, 93 in history, and 81 in Latin. In the spring he averaged 86 in English, 83 in geometry, and 83 in Latin.[7]

He seems to have thought he was "working extremely hard in school," in the fall of 1915. He said so in an October letter to his sister (who wrote him rather acid reports of her life at "Miss Wright's Fashionable Finishing School"), drawing at the bottom of the page a sketch of an emaciated, bespectacled professor, all head and no body, labeled "Me, 20 years hence, Professor of Latin and Greek."

IV

Lewis and Helen Stevenson had decided that Adlai should go East to college, preferably to Princeton. There were family reasons for favoring Princeton: Adlai Osborne had graduated from that institution in 1764 and Great-grandfather Lewis Warner Green had also gone there, to the Theological Seminary. Moreover Woodrow Wilson, the family's great political hero, had not only graduated from Princeton but had made his academic career there, gaining national fame as its president during the first decade of the century.

Alas, University High School had failed to prepare Adlai for the Eastern college entrance board examinations required by Princeton. Adlai took three of these early that summer. He failed all three.

One can imagine the effect this produced on short-tempered Lewis Stevenson. Lewis himself was no scholar and had no particular desire that his son become one, but he *did* want Adlai to be a "well-rounded man"—and how could the boy become that if he couldn't even get into a first-rate college? He immediately set about securing his son's entrance into Choate School in Connecticut where Davis Merwin had already gone, only to discover that, even for this, Adlai was inadequately prepared. The boy was deficient in French! Lewis arranged for a tutor and ordered his son to study, and study hard.

But, characteristically, Lewis was almost equally insistent that his son take an active interest in the political developments of that intensely political summer. It was high time, he said, that Adlai learn about such things first hand. So in early June he wired both Adlai and Buffie, ordering them to meet him in Chicago to observe the Republican National Convention. . . .

What Adlai learned during those hot and hectic days in Chicago could hardly have furthered his preparation for Choate, but it was useful to his later career. He gained a clear insight into the basic issues and essential strategy of the huge, noisy gathering. Harold Ickes helped him to understand. Ickes took Adlai and Buffie over to the Bull Moose convention, which was meeting in Chicago simultaneously with the Republican regulars. As Buffie reported, the Bull Moose was "much more fun than the Republicans!" It was also more sad for those who really cared (as Ickes did) about Progressivism, for Teddy Roosevelt virtually destroyed his handiwork by indicating that he would not accept the Progressive nomination. At the same time he urged Progressives to return to the Republican fold. Ickes, in pungent bitter phrase, explained what this meant. Once the breach the Progressives had made was closed, the Republican party would be more monolithically conservative than it had been at any time since McKinley's death, for the Old Guard was now vindicated, the party's liberal wing was discredited, and one could be sure that the former would punish the latter by denying it any real power.

For Ickes, as for most insurgents and most Democrats, too, the basic issues of the coming campaign did not lie in the realm of foreign policy, where Woodrow Wilson seemed inclined to place them. True, the lengthening shadows of war lay heavier upon the land, day by day; the threats looming across the Atlantic would make the slogan "He Kept Us Out of War" an appealing one, so long as it was balanced by the words and deeds of "Preparedness." But how could there be much difference between the foreign policy of Republicans and Democrats in a situation where there were virtually no free choices? No, the real issues lay between an extension of the New Freedom and a resurgence of McKinley Republicanism—and the Republican strategy, particularly the choice of Charles Evans Hughes as standard-bearer, was deliberately designed to blur this issue as much as possible in the general public's mind while sharpening it as much as possible in the mind of the business community.

Adlai was not permitted to go with his father to the Democratic convention, which opened in St. Louis two days after the Republican convention ended; he had to prepare for his Choate examinations, Lewis now insisted. But he followed what happened in St. Louis with close attention, and what happened afterward, too. It was right in terms of pattern that Hughes, despite his allegedly progressive tendencies, should in July begin to sound like a restrained Mark Hanna; Adlai was quite possibly less surprised by it than were Hughes's long-time personal friends. It was equally right, in terms of pattern, that the Wilson administration should advance the New Freedom, through governmental action, even while the campaign was going on: the Federal Farm Loan Act on July 17; the Jones Act, guaranteeing ultimate Philippine independence, on August 29; the Adamson Act, establishing an eight-hour day (instead of the prevailing ten) for interstate railroads, on September 3.

The latter, which caused the four railroad brotherhoods to call off a nationwide strike scheduled to begin at midnight September 4, was at once a major campaign issue, being bitterly denounced by candidate Hughes. Hughes termed it a "force bill" whose passage, in the face of threats, rendered contemptible the government of the United States. The charge, to which Wilson eloquently replied in terms of the "general welfare," disturbed Lewis Stevenson not at all. This was a good issue for Democrats, he explained. It made the labor vote secure, and it must drive into Democratic ranks those former Bull Moosers who might still be wavering between the parties.

With this, Carl Vrooman agreed. The Assistant Secretary of Agriculture came to Chicago in mid-September to confer with U.S. District Attorney Cline on what action, if any, the federal government should take to avert a threatened milk strike in that city; he came down to Bloomington afterward for a brief visit.

And Josephus Daniels agreed, also. Wilson's Secretary of the Navy came to Bloomington in September as keynote speaker at a giant Wilson rally in the Coliseum; he stayed as houseguest at 1316 East Washington, where his presence raised to its highest pitch the Stevenson family's personal involvement in the national campaign. Lewis was unable to come over from Springfield on the great day, so Buffie—at a large dinner given in Daniels' honor—sat proudly in her father's place.

Nor was Adlai's personal involvement in politics during those weeks merely a passive one of listening and reading. Lewis Stevenson was running for his first elective office, that of secretary of state, to which Governor Dunne had appointed him. He had exercised the powers of that office with such even-handed efficiency that many a Republican voter and newspaper, including the Chicago *Tribune,* now supported his candidacy, but for some reason Roger Sullivan, the powerful Democratic Chicago boss, opposed him. In consequence the primary campaign became a hard and dirty one. Several unknown men, whose names just happened to be closely similar to Lewis', filed for the nomination in competition with him; he had to hire private detectives, at considerable personal expense, to ferret out the skulduggery and protect his name on the ballot. But on September 13 he won the primary. He won by a big majority. He even carried Cook County, to everyone's surprise and Roger Sullivan's acute discomfiture. . . . Adlai made several trips with his father, to political rallies and such. He helped his father pass out cards on the streets; he also drove the family Hudson through the country roads around Bloomington, pausing every few hundred yards to tack a Lewis Stevenson placard on a telephone pole.

But despite these distractions, plus a camping holiday in northern Michigan with some Bloomington boys, Adlai managed to make up his French deficiency. In September he was notified, through his parents, of his acceptance by Choate.

CHAPTER FIVE

THE town of Wallingford, Connecticut, lying a dozen miles northeast of New Haven, contained in 1916 some ten or twelve thousand people. It was, by American standards, an ancient town, dating from 1670, a center of silver manufacturing surrounded by a rolling countryside over which great orchards and vineyards had spread for generations. The Choate School, with a campus of several hundred acres dotted with handsome buildings, lay at the town's eastern edge.

Though founded by Judge William Gardner Choate in 1896, the school was, for the most part, a creature of Dr. George St. John, headmaster since 1907. The two hundred-odd boys of whom Adlai Stevenson became one were recognized as distinct individuals, and to each, in terms of his individual needs and nature, was given the kind of liberal education through which English public schools had developed the British governing class. "Habits of efficiency and industry" and "an understanding of the enduring values and of the spirit of public service," were instilled. Grade standards were high. So were the standards by which general conduct was measured. Morality at Choate was considered to be firmly rooted in Protestant religion, and church attendance on Sunday mornings was a rigid requirement.

In this environment Adlai flourished, by the standards of formal schooling, as he had never done before, but made no outstanding scholastic record. When he again took college board examinations in May of 1917 he did approximately twice as well as he'd done the year before, passing a few of the ten to fifteen different tests which were required. In the autumn his examination record helped determine his course for his second Choate year. "I find that I can get into Princeton without taking Physics, Solid Geom., and Trigonometry by substituting 2 years of Spanish or German," he wrote his mother. "I expect to do this as it makes it much easier and Spanish is a coming language." In another letter he wrote that "Solid and Trig are worthless subjects anyway." Science courses were almost meaningless to him, then and later. He had had no grounding in the mathematical language; both University High and Choate placed their emphasis on literary subjects. Nevertheless, in early June of 1918 he reported to his mother that on his final examination he received the second highest mark in his "Trig" class; it was "88 percent and Mr. McOrmond wrote *splendid* on my book." "I got 82 in Spanish," he went on. ". . . My other marks were 78 in French, 74 in Algebra and 69 in Latin."

That same spring, Dr. St. John wrote a letter to Helen Stevenson saying that Adlai was to have a month's drill in the taking of examinations. The headmaster had observed that examinations "never do him justice," the boy having far more knowledge and a far greater intelligence than the results of formal tests would indicate.

At Choate, as at University High, Adlai's vital interests centered on extra-curricular activities, and he might well be proud of the successes he made of these, for he began under some serious handicaps.

As a latecomer in the fall of '16 he was assigned a single room and he lived alone through all that school year. He was one of the few students who did. To his physical isolation was added, at the outset, a rather acute spiritual loneliness: he discovered that he was one of only three Democrats in all the student body and that neither of the other two had a personal stake in the outcome of the elections. Alone, then, he must defend his political position against great numerical odds. Most Choate boys had inherited from their fathers a faith in the sanctity of private property and in the divine right of businessmen to rule the country, which had been rendered all the more vehement by the attacks of Populists, Muckrakers, and Bull Moosers. Some of them looked upon Adlai's Democratic loyalties as actually subversive. They were not loath to say so.

His wounds could have been only partially assuaged by the results of the balloting on November 7. By late evening of that day, Adlai knew that his father had lost his race for secretary of state. Governor Dunne had lost, too, to Frank Lowden. The boy might take some comfort from the fact that his father had run thirty thousand votes ahead of anyone else on the state Democratic ticket, had received more votes in Cook County than Frank Lowden, and had run thousands of votes ahead of Woodrow Wilson in Illinois as a whole. Nevertheless, it was a defeat. To the news of it, that night, was added the news that Woodrow Wilson had also lost. Adlai went to bed convinced that Hughes was the next President of the United States. Not until next day, when the close California vote was at last tabulated, did he learn that Wilson, after all, had won, with 277 electoral votes to Hughes's 254, and with 9,129,606 popular votes to Hughes's 8,538,221. Moreover, the Democrats retained control of both houses of Congress.

On election day Buffie and Helen Stevenson were in Lakewood, New Jersey, where they had been encouraged to remain by Lewis Stevenson, for he did not want his family to suffer the last nerve-racking days of his campaign. Next day they received from him a bright, cheerful letter that buoyed their spirits. A little later Charles Evans Hughes and Mrs. Hughes came to Laurel in the Pines, where Buffie and Helen were staying, and if he were at all embittered by the manner in which his hopes had towered to the skies, only to crash to the ground, they saw no sign of it. They reported to Adlai that Hughes was quietly dignified, a bit aloof, perhaps, but wholly admirable.[1]

The historic events that followed hard upon Wilson's reelection were educative of Adlai as future politician. Wilson's chief campaign slogan had been, "He Kept Us Out of War." The clearly implied promise was, "He Will Keep Us Out of War"—and it proved acutely embarrassing to the administration as history, no longer a flowing process, advanced with martial tread from 1916 into 1917, carrying the United States inexorably toward armed intervention.

Mid-January, 1917, saw the collapse of Wilson's attempt to negotiate a "peace without victory" in Europe. On January 31 Germany announced that all ships, including those of neutral nations, would be sunk without warning by her submarines if they entered a broadly designated "war zone." On April 2, after six unarmed American vessels had been sunk within a few weeks, Wilson asked the Congress for a declaration of war, using those eloquent phrases which would ring so hollow a few years later: "The world must be made safe for democracy. Its peace must be planted upon the tested foundations of political liberty." On April 6, the war declaration, having passed the Congress overwhelmingly, was signed by the President. . . .

The lesson was clear. Adlai Stevenson would express it again and again in the 1950's. "We cannot afford to forget," he would say, "that *how* you win in politics is as important as *what* you win." The "what," after all, is largely determined by the "how."

But of course this lesson was not one which the boy could have stated in 1917 and '18. His letters made no reference to the stupendous historical events of that spring, save that older boys were enlisting and that next fall's football team was being "ruined." For him as for others, however, the war was an intense present excitement: flags, parades, martial music, much talk of honor and glory and sacrifice, an outburst of passionate idealism that would seem, in retrospect, incredibly naïve.

In the summer of 1917 he and Buffie spent a long vacation on the H F Bar ranch, a famous dude ranch near Buffalo, Wyoming, to which they had first gone in 1915.[2] They arrived in Buffalo on July 4, witnessed there a gala celebration featuring bronco busting and auto racing, then rode eighteen miles by auto to the ranch whose setting, amidst the mountains, stirred Adlai to ecstatic comments in a letter to his mother. During that summer he was supposed to combine pleasure with further tutoring in French: his parents had hired as chaperone one Nora Caroe, who had been Buffie's French teacher at Miss Wright's school: but the arrangement did not work out as planned. For the one hundred guests at the ranch, a crowded schedule of activities was arranged, and Adlai missed so few of them that he had little time for scholarly pursuits. He bought himself a pair of bearskin chaps and spent hours every day in the saddle; he took part in the cattle roundup, riding as one of the back guards; on "Frontier Day" he won a prize in the gymkhana contest, spearing potatoes while riding pell-mell; he went on a ten-day pack trip into the Big Horn mountains with Frank Horton, owner of the ranch; he did a great deal of fly casting for trout in icy, rushing mountain streams; he climbed mountains.

When he returned to Choate his interest in journalism became intensely active. Within a day or so after the fall term opened he was heeling for the *Choate News* board. At first he seems to have felt inadequate to solicit advertising and indicated as much to his mother, but by the end of two or three weeks he had sold several hundred dollars' worth and was trying to enlist the support of his father for a final push. "I am writing you on a matter of great import, i.e., import to me," he said. "You see the *News* competition ends this Saturday and I am now fourth man in the competition. Further-more I think (and have been told so) that the board is only going to take on three men. Now an 'ad' will help me greatly and I might possibly get taken on . . . if I get a good one . . . as I am so near to third place anyway. The *News* is considered the second biggest thing in school after football and Mr. St. J. thinks it the first. . . . Do you know of any firm, co., etc. that might advertise? If you do know of one please let me know immediately." A week later Adlai won his place on the board. Soon he sent his mother "the best first issue the *News* has ever had—all the masters say so," and in the spring he became the paper's editor in chief. No triumph of his later years gave him greater pleasure than this. Proudly he wrote home on *Choate News* letterhead stationery: "pretty hard last week getting out my first *News*," but that "my efforts were well rewarded because the general opinion is that it is about the best issue of the season. When you receive it look at the picture on the right side of the front page and see if it resembles any one you ever saw before. Also read the article about the 1918 board as I wrote most of it. Also read the editorial, which is another product of my pen. Furthermore notice my name in the headlines on the Loomis Tennis match."

The latter story reported that Choate had defeated Loomis the preceding Wednesday, 4–2, and that A. E. Stevenson had beaten his man in straight sets, 6–1, 6–3.

He shared a room, that second year, on the top floor of Hill House with Harry Stearns and Jim Milholland, "the best room in the School," he wrote his mother, with a huge dormer window looking far out across the rolling Connecticut countryside. His letters spoke of "select feeds" in various rooms, of dances ("we are going to have a dance after the Taft [football] game, and Harry is going to have a girl up from Hartford for me"), and of visits in New Haven—happier letters than those of the preceding year. "I am never going to room alone again," he vowed.

His social life became quite brilliant during the Christmas holidays, which he spent in Washington with his family. On December 22, 1917, Lewis Stevenson was appointed Chief Special Investigator of the U.S. Navy by Secretary Daniels, his job being to prevent frauds in Navy food contracts. Immediately Lewis, Helen, and Buffie moved into an apartment in the Hotel La Fayette, and when Adlai joined them for the holidays he found them plunged into society. Ellen Bruce, daughter of a friend of his parents, under-took to float him, getting him all manner of invitations to dances and recep-tions. It was all so exciting that upon his return to Choate he found it hard to concentrate on his studies; he ordered Buffie to write him "all the dope" on the capital's society.

The following spring, 1918, when he became editor of the school paper, was for him a season of honors. He was elected captain of next year's tennis team. He was elected vice-president of the senior class. "By some strange freak that I can't understand," he was elected secretary of the Athletic Association, which was the student athletic governing body; "[this] strikes me as very amusing when the other two officers are the two biggest athletes in School," he wrote his mother. And, as a crowning honor, in his view, he was elected president of St. Andrews, the school's religious society for all denominations. "You didn't know your son was a young evangelist, did you?" he chortled. "If I come back [to Choate] next year, it looks as tho' I'd be a pretty big dude." Reporting these triumphs to his mother gave him great pleasure, because *she* obviously derived such pleasure from them. "How you keep your equilibrium with so much glory being thrust upon you, I do not see," she wrote him. "Certainly you have made good with both faculty and students and our pride knows no bounds!"

His mother's letters to him were full of advice that mingled Christian piety with a kind of Chesterfieldian worldliness.

> We are so pleased that you are so happy in your new room and in being an "old boy" [she wrote him in October of '17]. Of course your connections with "News" . . . make you a big factor and I think it is splendid experience for you. You will learn how to handle men, etc. etc. . . . I hope it will show you how necessary it is to gauge your strength, to allot your time, and not give of both too ceaselessly. This is just as important in becoming successful as talent. And another thing, never be annoyed or anxious. *Worried* is the common way of expressing it. It *never* helps and slowly and insidiously it ruins your mind and body. "Sufficient unto the day is the work thereof" the Bible says and you must learn never to go to bed with a business thought in your mind! Just think, you have already $500 worth of ads and while you were in C. you were a little anxious about them. Now you see it was unnecessary to be the least troubled. Please keep these things in mind and see if you can't get steadier by the discipline this work affords. To keep placid and cheerful, know all things come to those who love the Lord and doeth His works. . . . May God be with you always.

II

In late June, 1918, he joined his family, who had returned from Washington to Bloomington. He had learned that if he passed the Navy physical examination and the college entrance examinations, he might be enlisted in the U.S. Navy as an apprentice seaman, stationed at Princeton as a student trainee. He spent the summer cramming for the college board, concentrating on Virgil, while for relaxation he rode horseback with Buffie along the side roads around the town. Avidly, in the *Pantagraph* and Chicago papers, he read of American forces fighting in France, of Lenin's Bolsheviks in Russia, of the German occupation of the Ukraine. In the last week of August he returned to Wallingford, Connecticut, there to complete his cramming.

"I am each day gaining in erudition and sincerely believe that you will not recognize me in my present intellectual disguise when next we meet," he wrote his mother. "I think, if the Gods are with me, that I may pass my exams. The Virgil is, I find, an enormous task for so short a time but, as I said before, if the Gods are with me, *very close by,* I may pass." Meanwhile he had registered for the draft, as all men between the ages of eighteen and forty-five were required to do, and spent what little time he had free trying to collect *Choate News* advertising money. Before he left Wallingford for Princeton he'd collected some $550, of which his personal share was $130. "Not so bad, eh?" he asked.

On Sunday, August 31, with a Choate friend, a "corking fellow" named Eldridge Snyder, he moved into a room in the Nassau Inn in Princeton, directly across from the university campus.

Next morning Adlai entered the examination room to begin three grueling days of tests from which he emerged tired, dispirited, convinced of his failure. . . .

Three weeks later, having learned that he had been accepted, he formally enrolled in the university. Then he went to the gymnasium, below McCosh Walk, where he filled out a Naval Reserve Force enlistment blank and cheerfully submitted to the orders and medical examination. Stripped, he weighed 137 pounds—just a little less than normal for his age and height of five feet, nine inches. His chest expansion was four inches. His vision was normal (he was astounded by the number who were rejected because of color blindness), and so were his heart, his blood pressure, his lungs, his muscular coordination. By midafternoon he was officially deemed acceptable by the Navy. ("Thanks to your unceasing care I passed . . . pretty high," he wrote his mother.)

He was assigned to No. 64 Stafford Little Hall, a suite consisting of a study and two small bedrooms; he was given a bureau, desk, bed, and chair and was told he could not mount a Choate banner nor any other "decorations" on his bedroom wall. He had three roommates: Hendrik Terry of New York City ("a very nice fellow"), William E. Hale, and Ralph Goodwin, with whom he had formed a close friendship at the H F Bar ranch the previous summer.

For the first few weeks thereafter, his half-comic role as apprentice seaman was dominant over his role as a Princeton man. He was ordered out of bed at 5:55 each morning, must be properly dressed in his company's ranks outside Little Hall a few minutes later, and then must march to commons, where breakfast was served promptly at 6:15. He marched to lunch at 12:15, to supper at 6:15, to chapel on Sunday, and in between he marched and drilled for hours. When classes opened the following week, he was assigned courses in naval instruction, Spanish, law, history, and chemistry, and to these, too, he was marched in formation. He bought, for thirty-five dollars, "a good uniform to wear on liberty . . . as the Gov. stuff is not very good" and became "believe me . . . one hot looking little 'jack.' You will just about split when you see me," he predicted to Buffie and his mother. He helped organize a brass band for his naval unit, despite the fact he himself played no instrument but a mandolin. Occasionally he put to sea with his fellow seamen on Lake Carnegie, an artificial lake eight hundred feet wide and three and one half miles long, given the university by Andrew Carnegie for rowing activities. Whaleboats were used, but there were so few of these and so many seamen that most of the latter spent most of their time on the lakeshore, watching, and tying sailor's knots.

Meanwhile, in France, the Allied offensive roared on, with Americans attacking through the Argonne forest, until by November 10 the Germans were retreating so rapidly it was difficult for Allied troops to maintain contact with them. Next morning at eleven o'clock the end came. After four years, three months, and seven days of a war in which ten million men had been killed in action, every gun on the western front fell silent—and Adlai Stevenson joined his fellows in a delirious celebration of the Armistice, consuming with them a somewhat excessive quantity of beer.

In the days that followed, the relative emphasis between his two roles was reversed. No longer did the apprentice seaman dominate over the college man: he was, thenceforward, a Princetonian for whom the Navy was but a minor campus activity, until he received his formal discharge in January 1919.

BOOK TWO

An Individual Emerges

CHAPTER SIX

PERHAPS as good a way as any to assess the overall effect of Princeton on Adlai Stevenson is to contrast it with the effect of the university upon another eager youth from the Middle West, one who had been admitted precisely five years before Adlai was and whose experience of life was to have some effect, incalculable but real, upon Adlai's own. It was on September 23, 1918, that Adlai informed "Dearest Mum" of his admission to the university. ("This has been a most successful day," he wrote.) It was on September 24, 1913, which happened also to be his seventeenth birthday, that one F. Scott Fitzgerald wired *his* mother (whom, in a complicated way, he hated): ADMITTED SEND FOOTBALL PADS AND SHOES IMMEDIATELY PLEASE WAIT TRUNK. Fitzgerald then settled into a room in a stuccoed house at 15 University Place and prepared to conquer glory.[1]

The Princeton world that Fitzgerald entered was slightly smaller than the one Adlai was to know. It contained approximately fifteen hundred students, as compared with around two thousand in 1919 (Adlai's freshman class contained a little over five hundred) and it was yet, in physical appearance, not greatly changed from the Princeton of the 1890's. Nassau 1913; hundreds had them in 1918). Palmer Stadium was under construction. Street was yet unpaved (only six Princeton students had automobiles in The Gothic undergraduate commons in the northeast corner of the campus had not yet been built (it would be opened in 1915), and several of the buildings had not yet been begun that were to shift the center of the university's physical plant to a point some one hundred yards south of McCosh Walk by the time Adlai entered.

But in most essential respects this Princeton world of Fitzgerald's was identical with that which Adlai knew. Actually, as force or influence, it was a double world, with one powerful portion of it a contradiction of the other portion, equally powerful. It therefore produced in each entering student a tension which, if sometimes creative, was always dangerous. Facing Princeton's two worlds, the undergraduate was challenged either to make a flat choice between them, rejecting one while accepting the other, or to resolve their contradictions in some "higher synthesis." The student who could do neither was certain to be badly hurt and might be wholly lost.

One of the two worlds was in many ways a creature of Woodrow Wilson, whose ideal for the college was much the same as that toward which Choate, as educational process, was aimed. Education should be a living thing instead of a cut and dried system of lectures, textbook assignments, and recitations by rote. It should inspire in men a passion for public service. (He wrote: "Who is 'noble' amongst us? He who spends his energy outside the circle of self-interest.") To this end he had led his faculty into a radical revision of the curriculum, introducing the four-course honors system. He had led his trustees to approve, and had himself raised much of the money to finance, a preceptorial system modeled somewhat on Oxford's. He drew to Princeton fifty outstanding young men to serve as tutors. With them he sought to transform the undergraduate college from "a place where . . . youngsters [are] doing tasks to a place where . . . men [are] doing thinking . . . conversing about the things of thought . . . eager and interested in the things of thought."

But as Wilson led Princeton along the path of his purpose, he inevitably came into conflict with the second of the Princeton worlds, one which was essentially anti-intellectual and hostile to his concept of a college community. This second world was divisive in its effect on the student body. It sought to perpetuate attitudes and ways of life that made unyielding distinctions between men, not primarily on a basis of individual worth as measured by intellect and moral character, but on a various categorical basis of birth, wealth, social grace, and extracurricular achievement. Wilson came to regard this second world as intolerable by the university he was making. Boldly he set out to eliminate it. Instead, he was himself eliminated, having raised such a storm of opposition (involved in it was a question about the location of the Graduate College) that he was glad to escape from his college presidency into New Jersey's gubernatorial race in 1910.

The capital of this second world, so to speak, was Prospect Avenue, lined on both sides by the beautiful and luxurious homes of upperclassmen's clubs: Ivy, Cap and Gown, Cottage, Colonial, Tiger Inn, Quadrangle—some seventeen of them by the time Adlai Stevenson came to Princeton. These were the end products of a process that had begun in the late 1870's, in the social vacuum resulting from President McCosh's firm suppression of Greek-letter fraternities. Small eating clubs were formed at that time, perfectly innocent and innocuous. They did not even have names at first: each was simply a group of students having like interests and congenial tastes who took their meals together in one of the boardinghouses scattered around the town. Then, in the early 80's, one of these groups rented a small building to be used as a clubhouse. Ivy Hall, it was, on Mercer Street, built originally for the Princeton Law School. Thus the Ivy Club was born. Soon its example was followed by other groups, and the custom was established of choosing second-semester sophomores each February to replace seniors lost by graduation. Within a decade the Princeton club system was deeply rooted in the college life; and as their alumni prospered the clubs became more exclusive, their houses more elaborate, their arrangement more precise in a hierarchy of snobbism. They generated loyalties and values and codes so pervasive that no student could be entirely unaffected by them. For their members they also provided places of relaxation and social activity so luxurious as to justify, in part, a widespread designation of Princeton as "the finest country club in the East."

The whole of this process was strongly influenced by the fact that Princeton had always been the most "Southern" of Northern colleges. Before the Civil War, it often happened that half the student body came from below Mason and Dixon's line. They made integral to the developing Princeton tradition—the tradition in which the club system grew—many of the manners and prejudices, and even some of the social philosophy, of the Southern planter aristocracy.

One result was the production of a "Princeton man" who could be quite sharply distinguished from, say, a "Harvard man" or a "Yale man." (Of course such sweeping categorical generalizations are always inaccurate in detail: they ignore the real differences between the real men who are categorized: but as summings up of dominant characteristics they serve a useful descriptive purpose.) It was of the essence of the "Harvard man" that he be not a type at all but a strong individualist; Harvard seems always to have encouraged intellectualism and individualism, the latter sometimes to the point of eccentricity. Contrariwise, it was of the essence of the "Yale man" that he be a type: athletic, hearty, extroverted, ambitious, and intensely competitive. The Yale fraternity and senior-society system generally encouraged a frank and open pursuit of success, and everyone knew that he who was tapped by Skull and Bones had his financial security virtually assured. But the "Princeton man" was different from these. It was of his essence that he be neither a strong individualist (to be at all eccentric was to risk being tabbed a "bird") nor a conformist whose conformity was molded by an openly confessed ambition. He was, above all, smooth—that is, socially adroit and graceful. ("I think of Princeton," Scott Fitzgerald would have one of his fictional characters say, "as being lazy and good-looking and aristocratic.") He dressed well, talked well, danced well; he had a casual, insouciant charm, he looked upon bourgeois manners and values with amused contempt, as an aristocrat should, rather than with angry hatred, as proletarians are supposed to do.

The "Princeton man," as a matter of fact, avoided all extremes like the plague: to express strong commitments or aversions on any subject save an admittedly trivial one, like sports, was to be accused of "running it out," and to "run it out" was the deadliest of social sins. Thus, while Princeton's competitions in Adlai Stevenson's day were as fierce as any in the Yale system, it was necessary that the competitor *seem* not to be seriously competing at all. He must, above everything, maintain good form. To make one of the best clubs, for instance, was the major ambition of a great majority of freshmen and sophomores; but for that very reason one seldom saw a freshman or sophomore sauntering down Prospect Avenue. A club membership, like virtually every other ultimate reward of Princeton success, must be approached indirectly, with a careful concern for the aesthetic quality of the acts through which the approach was made.

Upon this glittering world the seventeen-year-old Scott Fitzgerald bent a gaze that was at once far more sophisticated and far more naïve than that which the eighteen-year-old Adlai Stevenson looked upon it five years later. Though abnormally conscious of class distinctions, he was unable to determine to which class he himself belonged—and his upbringing (his mother had spoiled him badly) had encouraged his belief in the injustice of a world that so often refused to defer to *his* feelings, *his* wishes. Hence his view of Princeton was colored by such personal insecurities as Adlai Stevenson had never known.

But it was also sharpened by these. The outsider who longs to get in is always aware of things which the insider, taking them for granted, doesn't really notice at all, and Fitzgerald was a sensitive observer. His vision, if badly distorted in some ways, saw at once in the Princeton landscape many subtle variations of which Adlai Stevenson (as freshman and sophomore, anyway) remained blandly, cheerfully unaware. Fitzgerald's was a calculating look. Princeton was a world he meant to conquer: he *had* to conquer it if he were to feel secure in it; and as he closely studied the terrain over which he must advance, he shrewdly assessed the various routes by which he might achieve those heights occupied by the elite of the campus. He also assessed the relative value of the weapons others had used that he might employ for conquest.

Football was of course the surest way to distinction, but a single afternoon on the freshman squad was enough to convince him, and the coach, that this way was closed to him. (He weighed just 138 pounds, as compared with Adlai's 137, and his height of five feet, seven inches, was two inches less than Adlai's.) Next in the hierarchy of prestigious activities was the

Triangle Club, annually producing a student-written musical comedy, which toured major cities during the Christmas holidays. Only slightly below Triangle, and perhaps even equivalent with it, was the *Daily Princetonian;* certainly a board member had a considerable persuasive power, and if he did not use it to command an equivalent social prestige, the fault was his alone. (One editorialist was to arouse Fitzgerald's awe by boldly attacking the club system itself!) After the student newspaper came the student humor magazine, the *Tiger,* and on approximately the same level with this was the Philadelphian Society, Princeton's equivalent of the Y.M.C.A., whose officers were invariably men of weight and influence. Considerably below all these, but still possible if one were brilliant enough, was the *Nassau Literary Magazine.*

Alas for Woodrow Wilson's dream, high scholarship never presented itself to Fitzgerald, nor to Adlai Stevenson five years later, as a possible avenue to glory; it did not even appear particularly valuable in itself. But success in any of the other above-named endeavors would assure a bid to a good club in the middle of the sophomore year. Major success would assure a bid from one of the best clubs. Accordingly, Fitzgerald concentrated on Triangle, spending much of his freshmen year writing the libretto for a show that Triangle accepted the following September and produced at the end of his first sophomore semester. He also contributed to the *Tiger* and the *Nassau Lit,* and wrote a farce produced by the Elizabethan Dramatic Club in September of 1914. The following February he was elected secretary of the Triangle Club; a little later, having rejected bids from Cannon, Quadrangle, and Cap and Gown, he went into Cottage, a very prestigious club indeed. "Though," he confessed later, "I might have been more *comfortable* in Quadrangle . . . where there were lots of literary minded boys." He was elected to the editorial board of the *Tiger* in May. He could look forward with confidence to the presidency of Triangle and, in his last year, to election to the Senior Council, the latter being the ultimate of Princeton glory.

(His confidence was curiously sustained by the fact that his strikingly handsome person was topped by blond hair. He went through the Princeton yearbooks for the ten years preceding his entrance and found, from a study of pictures of the Senior Council, that two thirds of its members were light-haired men despite the fact that "only about thirty-five percent of every class here are blonde." [2] This meant "that out of every *fifteen* light-haired men in the senior class *one* is on the senior council and of the dark-haired men it's only one in *fifty.*")

It was a brilliant career. It contained, however, a fatal flaw. If scholarship was no path to glory, a minimum of it was required by the college authorities. Fitzgerald, completely absorbed into extracurricular activities, failed to achieve the minimum. In November of his junior year, having been declared ineligible for further extracurricular enterprises and fallen ill of malaria, he dropped out of college to avoid being flunked out (as he would certainly have been) at the term's end. He came back the following year and completed his work as a junior, but he had forever lost his chance to become a power. In October of his senior year he went into the Army as the "world's worst second lieutenant," spending all his free time in the Officers' Club, first at Fort Leavenworth and then at Camp Taylor in Kentucky, writing a novel whose subject was himself, and Princeton. . . .

The whole experience hurt Fitzgerald badly as a human being. As Arthur Mizener has said,[3] it fixed permanently in him his sense of social security, and it caused him all his life long to overvalue the "badges and medals" of a "success" he had almost, but not quite, achieved.

II

The contrasts between this career and Adlai Stevenson's, amidst the same scenes and under the same external pressures, can of course be partially accounted for by differences in background, social status, and past experiences. Adlai began his race for those honors Fitzgerald prized so highly with advantages that Fitzgerald wholly lacked. He had family. He had economic security. He came from a prep school which, though small, was recognized as in all respects first rate. From the day of his enrollment he was a member of that in-group to which Fitzgerald, for all his striving, could never quite penetrate. John Harlan, the high duke of the campus, president of the class of '20, and full of other honors, was Adlai's personal friend. So were many of the other most influential undergraduates. When the Choate Club of Princeton was organized in early February, he was elected secretary. ("The rub regarding the officers is that the president and vice-president must be from the upper classes and the Sec. from the freshman class," he explained to his father. "In other words, I got elected, by some miracle, over the other freshman.") There was never any doubt that he would receive bids from the best clubs, and of these it might have been predicted that he would choose (as he did) the Quadrangle.

But such external differences in initial advantage are by no means the sole explanation of the fact that Adlai Stevenson made a success of Princeton by the standards Scott Fitzgerald employed, whereas Fitzgerald himself failed by almost any standards one might apply. Far more important, as explanation, were internal differences—those of mind and character. Fitzgerald's was a divided nature, Stevenson's an integrated one.

Stevenson's approach to Princeton's double world was far more innocent, far less complex than Fitzgerald's—and far more wise. Stevenson engaged in no such shrewd appraisal of terrain as Fitzgerald made; he merely accepted the double world as it was, uncritically, and sought to do his duty within it (fulfilling felt family obligations) to the best of his ability.

If he chose as his major activity precisely the one which, given his special aptitudes, was most likely to lead him into prominence, it was only because those same aptitudes caused him to regard journalism as an interesting career possibility. The nature of his hero worship was significantly different from Fitzgerald's. What Fitzgerald most passionately admired was glamor, popularity, power. What Adlai Stevenson most admired was the sheer ability to get things done and done well. John Harlan, his greatest hero of those years, made things function superlatively, and it was this capacity, in Adlai's view, that caused Harlan to be twice elected president of his class, to be made chairman of the board of the *Princetonian* ("he is an excellent chairman, and works awfully hard at it himself"), and to be elected not only to the Senior Council but to the chairmanship of that august body in the fall of 1919. This overall ability of course involved a measure of popularity; one could not lead men to work well together toward common goals if one were not personally liked; but the solid core of this liking must be a respect earned by objective accomplishments. To pursue popularity as an end in itself seemed to Adlai Stevenson, even as an eighteen-year-old, a senseless enterprise. (He was realistic, however, in his appraisal of the advantages he gained from Harlan's friendship—and since he had a shrewd notion that this friendship was at least partially motivated by Harlan's interest in Buffie, he was not averse to encouraging his sister, now and then, to accept Harlan's invitation to club dances and the like. In one of his letters he mentioned, as a passing remark buried in a closing paragraph, that Harlan had asked him "if Buff was going to be up here at the time of the Junior Prom" on March 15. "I think he is going to ask her," he went on, "and I think it advisable that she be here as he will probably head the Prom, if he is reelected Pres. of the class"—which Harlan was. . . .)

His career attitudes at Princeton, essentially the same as those with which he had become a power at Choate, are clearly revealed in his letters. "Thus far I have written 2 stories for the 'Prince' and both were printed," he reported home on January 29, 1919, just a week after he'd begun to heel for the *Princetonian*. "It is awfully hard work but quite worthwhile and interesting. I was talking to Jim Douglas the other day and he urged me to stay out for it. I have to write a story a day from now on." Yet when he feared that his *Princetonian* activity might dangerously impair his scholastic standing, he was perfectly prepared to sacrifice the former to the latter. "The freshman uniform tests begin tomorrow and if I fail any of them I think I will drop the 'Prince' as it takes a great deal of time and I haven't much chance of making it this competition anyway," he reported on February 8, just three days after his nineteenth birthday. By that time he was one of only thirteen men who had been retained in the competition out of the thirty-seven who had started it, but, as he pointed out, only two men were to be taken on the board. Since "several fellows are way ahead of me," he felt that his own chances were slim. But he failed no subjects in the examinations, and John Harlan joined Jim Douglas in urging him to stay out. He decided to do so "for awhile longer, as I hate to be a quitter."

In the end, having produced an exceptional quantity and quality of copy, he won the competition. By the close of his freshman year he was a member of the newspaper's board and well on his way toward a top editorial position.

The whole of this experience he made an integral part of himself—he grew into it and absorbed it into his total being—in a way Fitzgerald was unable to do either with his college experience or with his later ones. As a result, the Princeton that corrupted Fitzgerald, fixing in him his sense of insecurity, would have an opposite effect on Stevenson. The latter's college career speeded the process of continuous balanced growth (mind-body-spirit progressing as organic unit) which, from the outset, had been characteristic of him. Fitzgerald lost poise, Stevenson gained it, and that which drove sharp wedges into Fitzgerald's psyche, further splitting it, merely gave to Stevenson a wider range of possible attitudes (he would learn to employ them quite consciously, like an actor), plus a higher social polish. Princeton encouraged in Fitzgerald that fiscal irresponsibility for which he became notorious ("All big men have spent money freely," he told his mother petulantly when she remonstrated with him [4]) and which kept him continuously in debt during the years of his highest income. Upon Stevenson's attitude toward personal finances Princeton's club world had no effect whatever. He continued to be frugal.

And of all the influences that played upon Adlai Stevenson at Princeton, not the least was that of Scott Fitzgerald himself. During the early months of 1919, while Stevenson was heeling so industriously for the *Princetonian*, Fitzgerald in New York was writing short stories and garnering with them 122 rejection slips which he "pinned in a frieze around my room." In the summer of 1919, while Stevenson was again at the H F Bar ranch in Wyoming, Fitzgerald was rewriting the novel he'd first drafted while in the Army. In the fall of 1919, when Stevenson's greatest anxiety was over the fact that his mother insisted on renting a house for Buffie and herself in Princeton ("I thought it was the cruelist thing a parent could do—coming to live at a son's school," Adlai told Buffie later), Fitzgerald's novel was accepted by Scribner's. In March of 1920 Fitzgerald and Stevenson must actually have brushed elbows, though the latter had no remembrance of it in the 1950's, for Fitzgerald was living at Cottage that month, awaiting the publication day of his novel. He attended the prom. And on March 26 the *Princetonian*, which was continuing to absorb most of Adlai's extracurricular energies, carried a small advertisement that aroused some excitement in him as it did in nearly every other undergraduate. It announced the publication that day of *This Side of Paradise*, "the First Novel of F. SCOTT FITZ-GERALD, '17. . . . A Story About a Princeton Man."

According to Mizener, Fitzgerald was distressed by the small size of the *Princetonian* ad, but he could hardly have been distressed by the effect it produced: there was a gratifying rush of buyers of his book at the Princeton University store. Among them was Adlai Stevenson, who read it avidly through two or three soft April evenings. Though he refused to remember, in his later years, that it "really influenced me very much," the evidence that it did influence him is in his letters, which almost immediately began to have a somewhat different tone. His habitual self-deprecation—an attitude so different from Fitzgerald's outward pose, yet so consistent with Fitzgerald's inward feeling—began to wear a gloss of wry wit, and there were turns of phrase which echoed, if faintly, the Fitzgerald style. Always he had been remarkably sensitive to landscape beauty, and the lyric evocations of the Princeton landscape, which were among the best things in *This Side of Paradise*, touched a deep answering chord in his nature.

"I also remember saying, to girls on dates, about the book, 'It's a great human document,'" he told a friend, laughing, early in 1956. "'A remarkable human document,' I'd say, and look very wise and sophisticated of course. It was the thing to say that spring about that book."

In the same year, in the midst of a particularly grueling primary campaign he wrote to another friend who had been visiting with him about his Princeton years. "I haven't the remotest idea where I stood in my class scholastically," he wrote. "My greatest pre-occupation was with extra-curricular activities and I think I was content with what we generally called 'a gentleman's third group.' * Certainly I was never threatened with Phi Beta Kappa, nor, I fear, even tempted. It was a different time [with] different mores and there are those of us who still shed a salty tear for F. Scott Fitzgerald and the departed glories of the Princeton Country Club."

"But, oh," he added, "what a *Daily Princetonian* was produced under my mothering eye!"

III

Though he had dreaded his mother's coming to Princeton and had done all he could to dissuade her from doing so (he kept insisting that he'd be much too busy to see her often), he was forced to admit, as the sophomore year advanced, that the arrangement was "not so bad." In October of 1919 Buffie and Helen Stevenson moved into a beam-and-brick Tudor mansion

---

* In Princeton's peculiar grading system, the usual A, B, C, D, F (for failure) was replaced by seven groups, with group one being the highest grade. Groups one to five were passing, groups six and seven were failures. The third group, above which no gentleman need aspire, was equivalent to a C.

in Library Place, owned by Dean Fine. It had mullioned windows looking out over a sweep of lawn in which grew ancient gnarled apple trees and huge pines. It had a large living room with a great fireplace in which a log fire blazed cheerfully on every winter evening. And it had a garage housing the Hudson Super-six which Adlai had chosen and which he found to be very useful to him.

Soon the house became as much a center of his social life as the Quadrangle Club would be in his junior and senior years. Mrs. Stevenson engaged an efficient local Negro couple as servants, and maintained a kind of open house for Adlai's and Buffie's friends, all of whom remembered her as a very gracious hostess.

But though Adlai spent far more time in Library Place than he had said he would do, this did not belie the fact that he was, as he'd said, "very busy." He was always on the go—to classes, to Choate Club and other organization meetings, to the *Daily Princetonian* office—and when he came to his mother's house he usually carried with him a brief case loaded with books and papers.

When the Christmas holidays arrived Adlai spent them in Library Place, where the family was joined by Lewis Stevenson, who had returned to his farm management duties in Bloomington early in 1919. Most of his energies were focused, however, upon a very different enterprise. In Washington he had become interested in German Zeppelins, which, he thought, might become almost as important to the travel of the future as railroads were to the travel of 1918. Accordingly, when released from his Navy duties, he had organized a syndicate to acquire the American rights to basic patents for German lighter-than-air craft, and had managed to interest Dr. Johann Schuette, a German inventor and engineer who had built twenty-two dirigibles, in the leasing of such rights. He had lined up as investors a most distinguished list of men, including Owen D. Young, David Goodrich, William Wrigley, Jr., Marshall Field, R. B. Mellon, and Franklin D. Roosevelt. The plan was to establish a Zeppelin line between Chicago and New York, and of this plan he was full of sparkling talk that Christmas season. Adlai listened with avid interest.

They talked, too, of politics, of the tragic illness of Woodrow Wilson and of the failure of Congress to ratify the Treaty of Versailles. After the long, creative excitement of Populism and Progressivism and the New Freedom, after the enormous effort of war, the people seemed to want a rest. They seemed to be tired of reform, tired of idealism, tired of heroics, tired even of the responsibilities of self-government—and with this gathering mood of irresponsibility, an irresponsible government was perfectly consistent. When the people want a rest, said Lewis Stevenson—when they want a do-nothing government—they vote Republican. In terms of their want, they were right to do so—for though mediocrity was no Republican monopoly, God knew, there being plenty of it in Democratic ranks, it was only the Republican party which made of mediocrity a political principle. Not once since the Civil War had the Republicans put into the White House a man who approached the first-rate—with the possible exception of Teddy Roosevelt, who got in by accident—and they certainly would not do so in 1920.

Lewis Stevenson was definitely going to attend the Democratic National Convention in June. He was also planning a business-and-pleasure trip to Europe during the summer, but the trip would have to wait until the convention was over. And why didn't Adlai plan to come to the convention too?

But Adlai had other plans. He and a group of his friends were planning a European trip and they'd want to spend as much time overseas as possible before the fall term opened.

CHAPTER SEVEN

IN Princeton that autumn of 1920 Adlai Stevenson's major interest for some weeks was national politics. He was one of the organizers of Princeton's Cox-Roosevelt Club; he wrote several articles for the pro-Cox *Princetonian;* he was a member of the committee that brought Governor Cox to Princeton, where the Democratic candidate spoke at Alexander Hall; he was an usher at the great student Cox rally. The central issue of the campaign, as he saw it, was presented by the League of Nations. World peace, he argued, required a strong League, and a strong League was impossible if the United States refused to join it. Since the Democratic platform and candidates were unequivocally pledged to United States membership in the League, while a hard core of the Republican party was flatly opposed to membership, surely a majority of the American people in their wisdom would cast their ballots for James M. Cox and Franklin D. Roosevelt.

His hopes may have been buoyed by the fact that Cox's speeches were well organized, forthright appeals to the intelligence of the electorate. To Adlai, Cox's arguments in favor of the League seemed unanswerable. Nor did the handsome Senator Harding attempt to answer them. Harking back to the days of William McKinley, Harding conducted a front porch campaign, reading to visiting delegations speeches deliberately designed to obscure his position on the League, and demonstrating in general a veritable genius for platitudinous mediocrity.

But something sick and tired in the American people responded to

Harding's declaration that what the country needed was "not heroism but healing, not nostrums but normalcy, not revolution but restoration, not agitation but adjustment, not surgery but serenity, not the dramatic but the dispassionate, not experiment but equipoise, not submergence in internationality but sustainment in triumphant nationality." Few political statements in all our history can have been more hilariously absurd than this, considered merely as rhetoric (surely the Harding-coined "normalcy" was no more original that his balancing of "surgery" with "serenity"!). Yet few statements have proven more persuasive of the electorate.

Harding's victory was of landslide proportions. Only after the votes were counted did Harding discover that the central issue of the campaign had been, after all, membership in the League, and that in voting for him the people were voting against the League. The League issue, said he, was now dead.

Said Woodrow Wilson: "The people of America have repudiated a fruitful leadership for a barren independence. . . ." In doing so they had turned away from their historical and moral obligation. Soon, he predicted grimly, "we will see the tragedy of it all."

II

The mood of irresponsibility that now swept the country, however costly in the long run, was remarkably enjoyable in the short run for those who did not too much resist it with moral qualms, and if Adlai's unabated conscientiousness kept him from such experiments in sex and alcohol as many of his classmates made (he would be remembered as "rather conservative" in his fun), it did not prevent his active enjoyment of the new freedom that, in the opening 1920's, was so different, so very different, from Woodrow Wilson's.

He managed to maintain his standing scholastically in the gentlemanly third group, but his interest in his studies was peripheral. Practically never did he mention his classwork in letters to his parents or to Buffie. His sister, who was studying psychology under Carl Jung in Switzerland, protested that he was wasting too much time with "the debs of Philadelphia, etc." She said, "You seem to be quite outdoing us all in the social line" and "how frothy and futile it seems." She congratulated him upon his election to the secretary-treasurership of the Quadrangle Club, but only because "you can have a great and good influence through your position of power." She now looked upon Princeton's club system with a critical eye, being encouraged to do so by young Fowler McCormick, who was also studying at Zurich. "How about your lessons?" she asked Adlai. "Remember, this is a good time to learn!" [1]

In February he was advanced to the second highest editorial position on the *Daily Princetonian,* a triumph his father promptly reported to the *Pantagraph* but, alas, inaccurately. Soon, an irate Adlai wrote his father that he was "assailed from all sides with clippings from the Chicago *Tribune* to the effect that I am head of the *Princetonian* [when] as a matter of fact [I] am only second." Particularly galling to him was the gloating tone of the story: "The position . . . is the highest on the paper and the most sought after honor in Princeton literary life. Young Stevenson is a junior and is not yet 21 years old." Actually the story was printed on his twenty-first birthday, and "Young Stevenson" was furious. "Once more may I protest (as usual in vain I suppose) against your assumption of the duties of my publicity manager," he wrote his father. "As in the past, when I have strenuously objected, you have . . . gone ahead and, with the apparent intent of pleasing a mere child, put things in papers which were altogether wrong in point of fact and most embarrassing to me. . . . Please desist and do me a real favor."[2]

His anger may have been soothed by the birthday letter he received from his mother, though this too became a source of some embarrassment to him when, thirty-five years later, it was published in books and magazine articles about him. It was a typical example of the kind of influence his mother sought to exert over his growth. She wrote:

> *21 years old, 21 years young, 21 years wise, 21 years beloved!*
> *Your babyhood, boyhood, and young-manhood have been a natural sweet unfolding and gradual development! Round upon round. There are no dark muddy spots thus far in your career. Since you have become a reasoning being, you have made always an earnest, honest effort towards high living. This effort is character-building. The rewards are secondary in importance. . . .*
> *You have never wanted something for nothing, nor anything that was not rightfully yours. And so whatever in rewards come to you, you can rejoice over Right for the sake of Right! These, my dear, are the only principles that make for permanent success or happiness, and better never be rewarded or successful than to allow these to be forgotten for one moment. Character is better than all success and it will bring success more certainly than friends, fortune or talents.*[3]

A few weeks after writing this, Helen Stevenson was again in Europe, with Buffie, and as they traveled through France and Italy, letters from Adlai informed them that he was experiencing, in that spring of 1921, a season of triumphs. He was elected secretary of the board of trustees of Quad. He became managing editor of the *Princetonian*—the office his father had prematurely announced. He was nominated by the Senior Council as a candidate for the Council next year. This was that spring's greatest triumph. Each spring, the twelve "most prominent" men in the junior class were nominated ("that I should be considered in that category was most unexpected"), and, of these, five were elected by vote of the entire junior class. The remaining members of the fifteen-man Council would be elected in the fall. "Of course I will not be elected among the five taken on this spring but now I at least have hopes of making it next year," he wrote his mother and sister.

His prediction came true. He was not elected that spring, but he received a very respectable number of votes.

Meanwhile he again toured Europe.

Back in Princeton, in September of 1921, he plunged into the last and busiest of his college years. His classwork was heavier than it had been in earlier years, and every issue of the *Princetonian* was a challenge, a problem he spent hours helping to solve. Thirty-five years later he'd remember with acute nostalgia the long nights at the printers'.

From time to time the *Princetonian's* editor was himself in the news. In early autumn his hope of being elected to the Senior Council was realized. As a matter of fact, he received the largest vote of any among twenty-three candidates. In the spring he was appointed to two commencement committees. In the voting for "biggest politician," he received eight votes from his classmates and placed third, the winner receiving 124 votes and the runner-up nine. He was second in the voting for the man "who *thinks* he is the biggest politician," receiving 28 votes as compared with 41 for the winner. He received two votes as "the man most likely to succeed," placing eighteenth on that list, and he was ninth on a nine-man list of those receiving votes for "best all-around man outside athletics."

During the second semester of that year his mother and sister again lived in Princeton, despite Adlai's effort to discourage their coming. In late autumn he received a letter from his mother asking him to look for a house they might rent furnished; some days later he received a special-delivery letter from his father angrily demanding that he take care of this business at once. Adlai replied:

> I don't believe you would have been so peremptory in your demands . . . if you fully appreciated the exacting demands for time on an active student in the two big game weeks of his senior year. . . . Personally I can see no reason for coming to Princeton—if you want to come at all—until after Christmas—about the first of February. There is nothing doing here now and I thought perhaps the family would like to go south somewhere for Christmas—Pinehurst, Southern Pines, Camden, or some other place where mother could enjoy the weather.

He hoped that she would enjoy the weather so much she'd want to stay in the South, but he hoped in vain. Helen and Buffie Stevenson were residents of Princeton in February.

June came, as it seemed, with a rush, hard on the heels of February, so busy was he. Commencement Week came: President Hibben's reception in the lovely gardens of Prospect, the last club parties, the commencement exercises themselves: and, all at once, he was a Princeton alumnus. . . .

He would be a very loyal one, returning whenever possible to class reunions and keeping close track of university affairs. Thirty-two years later—on March 22, 1954—he returned to address the Senior Class Banquet. Bits of that speech would be often quoted, and he concluded it with some extemporaneous remarks about what Princeton had meant to him personally. He said:

> Let me add a final word, gentlemen. I came here last night in darkness, after an absence of four or five years. I came with an old friend, an old classmate. We drove a little through the campus, after dusk. It was soft, the air fresh with the beginning of spring. I thought of some words that I read here long ago, written by the English poet, Alfred Noyes, who stayed for a time on the Princeton campus. They were something like this if I am not mistaken:
>
> > Now lamp-lit gardens in the blue dusk shine
> >   Through dog-wood red and white,
> > And round the gray quadrangles, line by line,
> >   The windows fill with light,
> > Where Princeton calls to Magdalen, tower to tower,
> >   Twin lanthorns of the law,
> > And those cream-white magnolia boughs embower
> >   The halls of old Nassau.
>
> Sentimental? Yes. Nostalgic? Perhaps. Yet beautiful, true. Your days are short here; this is the last of your springs. And now in the serenity and quiet of this lovely place, touch the depths of truth, feel the hem of Heaven. You will go away then with old, good friends. And don't forget when you leave why you came.[4]

Two months later he would return to Princeton to receive her highest recognition, the honorary degree of Doctor of Laws.

III

During this same address to the seniors, Adlai Stevenson remembered that the world into which he and his classmates graduated was "happier and more hopeful" than the one into which Princeton seniors would graduate in 1954. "A terrible war to make the world safe for democracy had just ended victoriously," he said. "A noble concept, the League of Nations, had emerged from the chaotic aftermath of that elemental struggle. It was the twilight of kings, the dawn of world-wide democracy. Optimism was boundless and people proclaimed that we were on the threshold of the new era of universal and perpetual peace and prosperity."

This memory of the prevailing mood was, no doubt, an accurate one. A "golden glow" (the phrase was Charles Beard's) emanated from a press increasingly dominated, not by professional journalists, but by business interests who imposed upon the communication of news and opinion a subtle but highly effective censorship. Nevertheless, there were dark and ugly spots in the generally bright scene, and those who saw them and assessed their significance for the future were by no means as confidently happy as Adlai remembered America to have been in that summer of 1922.

Nor was he himself carefree that year. He could not decide what he wanted to do with his life.

His major interest was journalism. It was in his blood. In the years before he went off to school he spent much time during his vacations at the *Pantagraph,* doing odd jobs for the love of it. "I have many happy recollections of trips in the neighborhood with reporters to county fairs, preparing lists of ribbon winners, etc.," he wrote in a reminiscent letter in the 1950's. "In fact, I think I knew every nook and cranny of the old *Pantagraph* building and sat at linotype machines before I had long pants." If that paper had been wholly Stevenson property he would have returned without a qualm to his home town and made his career there, perhaps emulating William Allen White whose town of Emporia, Kansas, was remarkably like Bloomington in several respects. His experiences with the *Choate News* and the *Princetonian* had convinced him that he was not without ability as a newspaperman. Like White, he might be led through journalism into creative writing, for sometimes he was quite sure that what he really wanted to be was a writer. But the *Pantagraph,* as his father pointed out, was *not* Stevenson property. Uncle Bert (Hibbard O.) Davis was the paper's publisher and active manager, and there were cousins. The political editorial policy, which was so conventionally Republican, might prove distasteful. The town was not very large. The situation *could* become unhappy.

It would be wise, Lewis Stevenson insisted, for Adlai to attend law school and have a profession. How he wished that he himself had done so! His own father, and Adlai's great-grandfather Jesse Fell, had started their careers as lawyers. Such training would be useful "no matter what you do later." Adlai himself could see that this was so: the whole of human experience—economic, political, moral, even aesthetic—was reflected in the law, and from the law careers in a score of fields seemed to radiate like spokes from the hub of a wheel. Accordingly, Adlai had agreed to enter the Harvard Law School and by the time he received his undergraduate degree he was not only entered at Harvard but had also arranged to room in Cambridge with two classmates, Charles Denby and William B. McIlvaine, Jr., and a

Choate School and Harvard friend, Norman Davis, Jr., whom everyone called "B."

He had agreed, however, reluctantly. If he were not to be a newspaperman, he preferred to be a rancher in the West. Ever since the summer when he and Ralph Goodwin had first met at the H F Bar, the desire to become a rancher had competed with his desire to go into journalism, and in that summer of '22 the lure of the West was so strongly renewed that it led him into a conflict of wills with his father. Ralph Goodwin, driving his Jordan roadster from Cleveland to Wyoming, picked up Adlai in Bloomington, not long after graduation.

They went together to the T A T ranch in Wyoming, not a dude but a working ranch owned by Goodwin's sister and brother-in-law, and as the two shocked barley, stacked hay, rode the range, mended fence, and camped and fished in the mountains, they decided to try ranching together. They went so far as to look for a suitable property and notified their parents of their plans. The effect on Lewis Stevenson was explosive. Not only did he flatly refuse to give financial backing to any such venture, he also proclaimed that if Adlai were not home in time for law school he, Lewis, would come to Wyoming and bring him back.

Thus Adlai entered upon his career as a law student in a rebellious mood. The law school, he reported to his mother on September 22, "is the hardest graduate school of any kind in America" and "the most feverish place I've ever seen—everyone works *all* the time and still about 25–35 percent get dropped every year." All he'd heard since he arrived were "gruesome tales of . . . astonishing hours of work when the big reviews begin in March." Until then, he added sarcastically, it was a "comparative loaf" requiring only eight full hours of work every day. "We have so many enormous books and notebooks that we have to carry them back and forth to class in satchels," he concluded. "More bad news later." The only happy news he could report in those first weeks was that his room in Claverly Hall was "very comfortable, large, sunny, etc." and that he and his roommates had been the first new students to be taken into Lincoln's Inn, "the best of the Law School eating clubs" where there was a "splendid bunch of men" and where the food was excellent.

Cambridge seemed to him a "most unattractive place"; he doubted if he could ever "reconcile" himself to it. "Haven't seen a blade of grass, except a few square ft. on the campus [the word betrayed his assertive Princetonionism; at Harvard it's the Yard] . . . but I'm still searching," he reported in mid-October. As for Harvard University itself, "the thing that impresses me particularly is that nobody seems to know or care to know *anyone* else." The atmosphere was "entirely different . . . from Princeton—a city club rather than a country club. . . . Everything," he added in bitter resignation, "is concentrated, work, play and exercise."

By November he felt that he was gradually becoming adjusted to the hard, monotonous routine, though "we all continue to go to bed with a tacit cheer for Princeton and wake up with a groan for Harvard." (He and his roommates were overjoyed when Princeton beat Harvard in that year's football game. So was Buffie, who came up to Cambridge for the event and was taken to a tea dance at the Hasty Pudding Club by Dale Warren and her brother.) He was even discovering that "parts of the law are quite interesting" and was encouraged, very tentatively, to believe that "I may learn to enjoy it." The belief was strengthened when, on November 7, he won his first club law case.

His second semester at Harvard was somewhat happier than his first had been. Cambridge under a blanket of fresh snow became, he found, almost beautiful (soon, of course, the city snow became gray with soot, and as dully ugly as the New England winter sky). And there was a miraculous quality to the coming of spring after the long rigors of a New England winter. He found himself looking upon the greening grass (there *was* some after all, under the great elms of Brattle Street) and upon the budding trees and flowers with "an air of complacency." Through much of that spring he was working a fifty-hour week, forcing his way through heavy books "and their appalling contents of undigested knowledge": he called his experience the case of "Blackstone vs. Stevenson." "We [have] a regular schedule now— from 9 to 1 each morning, from 2 to 5 in the afternoon, and from 7:30 to 10:30 at night." But he managed to survive the spring examinations—and this, like the New England spring itself, seemed to him miraculous.

In the fall of 1924, just seven weeks after Harding had died under mysterious circumstances in San Francisco and Calvin Coolidge had become President of the United States, Adlai with five companions moved into a dilapidated old wooden house just down Mount Auburn Street from Claverly Hall, where they rented eight rooms, two baths, and a sleeping porch. He was happier in Cambridge his second year than he had been in his first. Outside the hard grind of his studies, his life was a pleasant one: football weekends at Princeton as well as Harvard; visits to New York where he saw Pavlova dance, saw a World Series game, and had an exciting talk "about democracy etc." until after midnight one night with B.'s father, the famous Norman H. Davis who had played so important a role in international affairs during Wilson's administration; weekends on Lewis Farm, Walpole, Massachusetts, the country place of Francis Plimpton's father, who was president of Ginn and Company, publishers, and chairman of the trustees of Amherst; squash in the afternoon; a good many parties in Cambridge and Boston, though he continued to regard Boston society satirically; long walks through the Cambridge residential sections which, draped in vivid autumn foliage and bathed in sparkling frostbit autumn air, no longer seemed to him wholly ugly and depressing.

But he continued to find the law "a jealous mistress and not a particularly attractive one," requiring at examination times ten or twelve hours of concentrated work every day for a week at a time. Examinations continued to terrify him; it always seemed miraculous to him that he could pass any of them; he continued to feel that his life, as yet, had no clear purpose, no defined goal. Assuming that he received his law degree and were admitted to the bar, what then? Did he really *want* to be a lawyer, devoting himself exclusively to abstracting property titles and drawing up prospectuses and helping to organize and reorganize corporations? He didn't think so. He still much preferred journalism. He was watching with close attention the exciting new venture in journalism, *Time* magazine, launched in 1923 by two Yale men of the class of '20, Briton Hadden and Henry Luce; he was impressed not only by the commercial possibilities but also by the social idealism that the youthful founders of *Time,* as yet uncorrupted by power, espoused. Last year he'd even toyed with the idea of investing some of his money in the project and going himself to work upon it, and later he sometimes wished that he had done so. . . . No, the only justification that the law had for him personally was that, as his father had said, it could lead him into something else, something more active, with a stronger appeal to his whole nature. The fact that he did not know what this would be made him more than a little restive, and even anxious, under all his day-by-day busyness.

Then, suddenly, there occurred an event which put an end to his Harvard career and, for a time, took his career decisions, or indecisions, out of his hands.

CHAPTER EIGHT

U NCLE Bert Davis, son of W. O. and successor to him as *Pantagraph* head, had been in failing health for a year or more. In the spring of 1924, in California, he died. Adlai returned to Bloomington for the funeral. He found that grief over the passing of his uncle was not the only grief that descended upon the Stevenson and Merwin families while he was yet in Bloomington.

Grandfather Davis's will, under which Uncle Bert managed the paper, had been drawn up by Davis's great and good friend "Private Joe" Fifer, former governor of Illinois. Because of an unlikely series of deaths and a lack of legal precision, the terms of this will now became ambiguous. The will had provided that the shares in the *Pantagraph* be held in life estate by W. O. Davis's children, then passed to their children. Uncle Bert had had two sons, William and Louis. William had died of illness while at a military school; Louis had been killed while training as an Army Air Force pilot at Ellington Field, in Texas, in May of 1918. Surviving, then, were five grandchildren, three Merwins and two Stevensons. The question now arose as to how the estate was to be divided between the two families. By the reading that the Stevensons favored, the will stated that the eight hundred shares of *Pantagraph* stock less ten shares that had been bequeathed to a long-time employee of the paper, would be equally divided between W. O. Davis's two surviving children, Helen Stevenson and Jessie Merwin. By the reading that the Merwins favored, the will stated that the stock was to be divided between the two families in proportion to the number of grandchildren in each—that is, in such a way as to give each grandchild the same number of shares. The former reading meant that the Stevensons and Merwins would each receive 50 percent of the property, or 395 shares. The latter reading meant that the Merwins would receive 60 percent and the Stevensons 40, or 474 and 316 shares respectively. (Lewis Stevenson fumed that he'd have had six children if he had known the will could possibly be interpreted in the latter way.) [1]

As might be expected, the situation was not clarified by long and heated family conclaves. The stakes were large, for the *Pantagraph* was a major power in central Illinois, and in all cases of this kind the human mind becomes remarkably fertile of plausible rationalizations. Certainly there was room here, too, for honest disagreement.

Finally the two families decided to institute a "friendly suit" so that the courts could decide the matter in terms of law. But of course the suit was not wholly friendly. Inevitably a good deal of acrimonious feeling was involved, and Adlai, having missed more classes than he could adequately make up, returned to Harvard in a disturbed emotional state. His mother, even more disturbed, fell ill and went to Battle Creek Sanitarium for a rest cure. "I hope and feel sure it will do you a lot of good, but nothing but *mental* peace will ever make your physical condition what it should be," Adlai wrote her out of his own travail. "Of this I feel sure, and it's all in accord with your theories anyway. So I hope you are trying to look at things as dispassionately as possible." As for himself, he was going through "the hardest weeks on record," weeks during which he put in between fifty and sixty hours of concentrated mental work, trying to catch up in time to pass the term finals. ("I do hope *I can* keep my mind functioning. . . . If I can [only] keep my spirits and my physical well-being intact. . . .") Desperately, all too aware that he was inadequately prepared, he plunged into examination week—and failed two courses.

But it had been decided that he and his cousin and boyhood companion,

Davis Merwin, should both go to work on the *Pantagraph*, while the lawsuit ground its ponderous way through the court. Accordingly, Dave Merwin became a business manager and when Adlai returned to Bloomington he became an editor of the paper, an arrangement which was maintained for almost two years. . . . There is no evidence that Adlai was dismayed by this interruption of his legal education in favor of working journalism.

II

He entered upon this new phase of his life after a brief, hectic interlude during which he was totally immersed in national politics. On Monday, June 24, 1924, the Democratic National Convention opened in New York City, and Adlai attended it in an official (if minor) capacity as an assistant sergeant at arms. The assignment had been secured for him by his father.

Lewis Stevenson was a figure of some importance in that interminable and disastrous convention. Long before the convention opened it was quite obvious to the knowledgeable that the two leading candidates of the party, William G. McAdoo and Alfred E. Smith, would eliminate one another in the balloting, neither being able to achieve even a majority of the votes, much less the two thirds then required. It was, therefore, a forgone conclusion that a dark horse would be named, and Lewis Stevenson's dark horse was David F. Houston, the Secretary of Agriculture in Wilson's administration with whom Carl Vrooman had served. Lewis Stevenson, as a matter of fact, was the guiding spirit of the Houston campaign, whose headquarters were at the Hotel Saville.

But Houston, alas for Stevenson hopes, was so dark a horse as to be almost invisible against the background of gloom in which the Democratic convention was held. Houston was a most able mind but he lacked fire; he lacked the capacity to inspire others; he could administer, but he could not lead. And Adlai Stevenson himself, writing his mother on the day before the convention opened, said that "frankly" he didn't think Houston "has much chance of getting the nomination." It looked to him "more and more as if John W. Davis was the man."

Davis had immense personal superiority, by every sane criterion of value, over Silent Cal Coolidge. The great trouble with him as a candidate was that he seemed to represent the same big business interests as Silent Cal represented: he was a corporation lawyer with Wall Street connections, being affiliated with the United States Rubber Company, the New York Telephone Company, and (worst of all) the House of Morgan. Thus his nomination would blunt the only issue, that of business domination of government, on which the Democrats might conceivably win.

Certainly this last was an issue on which the Republicans in that year were more than usually vulnerable. Only a little over two months after Harding's death, Senator Thomas J. Walsh of Montana had demanded a full Senate investigation of the mysterious circumstances surrounding the leasing of two naval oil reserves, Teapot Dome in Wyoming and Elk Hills in California, to Edward L. Doheny and Harry F. Sinclair, respectively. Soon the public was hearing a sordid tale of graft and corruption, the like of which had not been abroad in the land since the administration of U.S. Grant.

One thousand and ninety-eight delegates assembled on June 24 in Madison Square Garden. This was the old Garden (soon it would be replaced by a skyscraper) on whose roof Harry Thaw shot Stanford White. On its floor Democrats now seemed inclined to shoot one another, for it is literally true that, one terrifying night, a riot would certainly have occurred if the aisles had not been patrolled by extra scores of special-detail policemen.

The issue lay between two planks of the party platform dealing with the Ku Klux Klan. One plank, drafted by a cautious majority of the platform committee, deplored racial and religious intolerance in general terms. The other, drafted by a bold and morally outraged minority, flatly condemned the Klan by name. McAdoo forces favored the former plank, Smith forces favored the latter, and for dangerous hours the result of the battle was uncertain. (It should be noted that no such dispute had disrupted Republican deliberations; in Cleveland, where Calvin Coolidge had been nominated by acclamation, with Charles G. Dawes as his running mate, the Klan was not mentioned aloud.) The final vote was very close. Fractional votes being allowed some of the delegates, 546.15 voted for the cautiously worded plank while 542.85 voted to condemn the Klan boldly, unequivocally. Then the weary delegates, some of them more embittered than ever, others of them relieved, went back to their sweltering hotel rooms for a few hours of sleep.

Adlai Stevenson—scurrying between convention floor and hotel suites with messages to and from delegates and wire-pulling managers—saw and heard and felt it all. He sat in on strategy conferences during which every facet of the Houston candidacy was argued out. He learned thus how much shrewd planning, how much complicated thought, goes into a political campaign. But he learned, too, how crucial a role sheer chance often plays in political success or failure and that nervous control and a quick wit in moments of crisis may be more decisive than a long-range thoughtfulness.

For instance, on the night his father was to make the speech nominating David Houston, the taxi in which his father rode from the Hotel Saville to the Garden was immobilized in a crosstown traffic snarl. Precious minutes passed during which Lewis Stevenson grew desperate, for if Houston were not presented that night he might never be. Finally he leaned his head out the window and called to a traffic patrolman. "Officer!" he cried. "I've got to be at Madison Square Garden in five minutes to make the nominating speech for *Al Smith!*" The effect was magical. Immediately the cop's whistle shrilled; he leaped on the running board and, blowing his whistle and waving his arm, cleared the taxi's way through the jam and all the way to the convention hall. He even escorted Lewis Stevenson through the crowd into the hall itself, a way opening for them miraculously whenever Smith's name was pronounced.[2]

Actually the speech nominating Smith was given by Franklin D. Roosevelt, who hobbled gallantly to the platform on crutches and, following the long demonstration set off by the first syllable of "Alfred" to fall from his smiling lips, spoke very well indeed. But Adlai believed, and many others shared his belief, that Lewis Stevenson's speech for Houston was better written and at least as well delivered. Adlai was proud of his father, proud of the fact his father was being mentioned here and there among the delegates as a possible Vice-Presidential candidate, and while his father spoke it was even possible to believe that Houston, after all, might have a real chance. . . .

The belief remained alive for several days—though as those hot angry days wore on it appeared likely that the party itself was on the point of total dissolution. On the first ballot, McAdoo had 431½ votes and Smith had 241, whereas 732 were necessary for nomination. Both men gained votes on succeeding ballots. These followed one another in swift, endless succession— the tenth, the twenty-fifth, the fortieth—with Governor Brandon of Alabama standing on his chair at the beginning of each of them, screaming: "Alabama casts twenty-four votes for Oscar-r-r W. Under-r-wood!" As the number of ballots soared above fifty, with no decision in sight, fearful men recalled that the largest number of ballots ever taken in a Democratic convention had been at Charleston, South Carolina, in 1860, where after fifty-seven ballots the party had split in two, with the southern faction nominating John C. Breckenridge and the northern one Stephen A. Douglas. Yet when the fifty-eighth ballot was taken in the 1924 convention, Smith had only 221½ and McAdoo only 495; a decision was as far away as ever. McAdoo forces angrily demanded that Smith withdraw in order that the front-runner might achieve nomination, a demand they could support on every ground of practical politics. But this was not the determining factor in this situation; the ultimate determinant was a moral feeling. Those delegates who had fervently supported the anti-Klan platform plank and were outraged by McAdoo's refusal to disavow Klan support flatly refused to agree to Smith's withdrawal unless McAdoo also withdrew. So the balloting went on hopelessly, until at last, on July 9, McAdoo gave up. He and Smith released their delegates. Four hours later, on the hundred and third ballot, John W. Davis was nominated. . . .

There would follow a campaign in which Cal Coolidge pitched hay, carried maple syrup buckets, and held up long-dead fish for the benefit of cameramen, while saying very little; and in which Davis attempted to capitalize on the issues presented to the country by the Republican record. When the votes were counted in November, it was found that Coolidge had won 382 electoral votes as compared to Davis's 136 and La Follette's 13, and had received nearly fifty-eight percent of the popular vote.

III

On the whole, Adlai Stevenson enjoyed his years on the *Pantagraph*, despite the fact that the circumstances in which he worked were by no means of the happiest. He bore the title of managing editor. He supervised reporters and helped make up the paper. In the summer of 1925 he wrote a series of editorials concerning the trial of John T. Scopes in Dayton, Tennessee, for teaching evolution in the Dayton high school in violation of Tennessee law. This was the famous Monkey Trial during which William Jennings Bryan was special prosecutor and Clarence Darrow the lawyer for the defense. It became, of course, the trial of Bryan the Fundamentalist before the bar of public opinion on charges of fanaticism, ignorance, and a bigoted censorship of education. On these charges, with Darrow as his prosecutor, Bryan was convicted. Soon he would die. To Adlai, whose grandfather had been Bryan's running mate in 1900, the spectacle, for all its hilarious trappings, was sad, and his editorials were sober defenses of the principles that Bryan and the Fundamentalist party attacked: free inquiry, free speech, the separation of church and state.

The lawsuit at last came to trial in the circuit court and was lost there by the Stevensons. Naturally the Merwins were satisfied with the lower court's decision, but Adlai's family insisted on appealing the case. When the Illinois Supreme Court finally ruled, it sustained the appellate court in the Stevensons' favor: the *Pantagraph* stock was to be divided equally between the two families.

But while the case was pending on appeal the Merwins quietly acquired the ten shares of stock that W. O. Davis had given to the valued employee many years before. With them went voting control of the company, despite the court's later decision in favor of equal treatment, and with them also went Adlai's vision of a career as a newspaper editor.

Lewis Stevenson and Adlai had discussed Adlai's future while the case was still in the courts. Lewis pointed out how much time and effort and money had already been invested by and for Adlai in the law. Surely it was the part of wisdom to finish law school, since his future at the *Pantagraph* was uncertain. Adlai agreed, and he stuck to this conclusion despite the offer of an instructorship in English or history that came to him from the Lawrenceville School, near Princeton—a most attractive offer, declined with regret. Accordingly, in the autumn of 1925 he was again a law student, spending his weekdays at the Northwestern University Law School in Chicago and coming home weekends to look after *Pantagraph* matters.

At Northwestern his interest in the law quickly grew under the influence of the dean, the famous John Henry Wigmore, who became Adlai's fast friend. He caught an expanding vision of the advantages of life in a mighty city and felt challenged by the stern competition at the bar. Certainly he was strongly influenced by a trip he made to Washington during this period to serve as an usher at Charley Denby's wedding to Senator David Reed's daughter. Charley was finishing a year as secretary to famed Supreme Court Justice Oliver Wendell Holmes, who had been a good friend of Adlai Ewing Stevenson I, and who gave to his old friend's grandson one of the unforgettable afternoons of the latter's life. Before the fireplace in Holmes's Washington home the old man talked to the young one about the law, legal education, the Civil War, and all manner of things—and as he talked, Adlai gained a larger, more exciting view of the law as a career than he had ever had before. . . . In June of 1926 Adlai took his J.D. at Northwestern and immediately thereafter passed his examination for entrance to the Illinois Bar.

Then, before he settled down to a law practice for which he still had no real enthusiasm, he decided to take what he called "one last fling" at journalism. . . .[3]

IV

The idea was born at a convivial bachelor dinner following the wedding of one of Adlai's friends in June. The young men talked of Russia, and three of them—Adlai, George Norton, and Bob Page—expressed their eagerness to visit that enigmatic land and to observe, at first hand, the workings of the Communist experiment. But foreigners were barred from Russia by the Soviet government, and even if they had not been, the American State Department would have denied to private citizens permission to travel there under American passport protection. How, then, could the young men gain entrance? By becoming foreign correspondents of American newspapers, replied Adlai promptly. Immediately he became excited about an idea which grew large as he talked of it.

One of the most newsworthy figures in the world that year was Grigori Vasilievich Chicherin, Soviet Foreign Minister. It was with him that American diplomats had endeavored to negotiate over the Czarist debts repudiated by the Bolsheviks and over the compensation of Americans for their confiscated Russian property. Those negotiations had now broken down completely. Chicherin was as silent and invisible as he was newsworthy—he refused to see any of the handful of American correspondents then stationed, or marooned, in Moscow—which meant that anyone who obtained a private interview with him would have a great scoop.

Why not make this the object of a Russian expedition? asked Adlai.[4] With it, one might not only gain the newspaper accreditation necessary to the securing of a Russian visa but might also help pave the way for a settlement of some of the outstanding issues between the U.S. and U.S.S.R. Admittedly this last was a far-fetched possibility.

George Norton and Bob Page agreed that it was worth a try. Lewis Stevenson, too, was intrigued by the audacity of the idea when Adlai explained it to him: he helped Adlai obtain the necessary credentials as a foreign correspondent for the Chicago *Herald-American* and Hearst's International News Service. George Norton, meanwhile, obtained credentials as a representative of his hometown newspaper, the Louisville *Courier-Journal* and Bob Page, unaccredited, decided to come along anyway on the off chance that he could accompany his friends across the forbidden border.

Nor was this the only plot in which Adlai was involved that summer. He was also active in an attempt by Lewis and Helen Stevenson to save Buffie from the theatrical career on which she was now embarked, a risky career that was looked upon, by Adlai and Helen especially, with disapproval. She was with Gilbert Miller's stock company in Rochester, drawing fifty dollars a week and working under the direction of George Cukor, with Rosamund Pinchot, Glenn Hunter, Ilka Chase, and Louis Calhern. There seemed every chance that she would be caught halfway between success and failure in the theater, wasting her youth in that gray land of in-between, and waking up some gloomy morning to find herself a middle-aged spinster with a scattered, meaningless past and with no future at all.

Accordingly, it was decided that Adlai, on his way to New York, should stop off in Rochester and attempt to persuade Buffie to go to Italy with him and their mother. He did so. He saw Buffie act. Her role, that hot night, was a brief scene in which she entered, sat upon a bench, and spoke one line. When he took her to supper afterward he managed gently and tactfully to let her know that her work, if that night was a fair sample of it, didn't seem to him especially exciting, or glamorous either. The Italian trip would be much more exciting, much more glamorous. . . .

And so it proved.

On July 24, Adlai and Buffie sailed with Helen Stevenson on the *Conte Biancamano*.[5] A huge crowd was at the pier as the ship cast off, for on board was Generale Umberto Nobile, the hero of the hour, who had just flown over the North Pole in a dirigible. Buffie became a good shipboard friend of the heroic general, and when the ship steamed into the Naples harbor, where a great triumph awaited him, he asked her to stand beside him on the bridge.

Adlai viewed Fascist Italy through a journalist's eye, storing away facts and impressions for use in future writing. He used this material not for Hearst but for two long articles that were published in the Bloomington *Pantagraph* after he returned. Those who became interested in the development of his mind, in the 1950's, would study these articles with a considerable interest. He himself would remember them as "very critical" of Mussolini and of fascism; those who viewed them across the years of bloody chaos that Mussolini helped to produce would not see them so. He was obviously influenced by Fascist propaganda, a thing wholly new to a young American of 1926.

He said good-by to his mother and sister in the Tirol and hastened to Vienna to meet Bob Page and George Norton. All three had applied for Russian visas before leaving New York and hoped to find these waiting for them in the Soviet consulate in Vienna. Their hopes were not fulfilled. For days they haunted the consulate, being continuously put off by officials who claimed to have communicated with Moscow on the matter. After a precious week had passed, Bob Page gave up and departed, while Adlai and George Norton went down the Danube to Budapest, having arranged for the visa (if permission arrived) to be issued there. Adlai visited a friend in the American legation at Budapest; he and Norton had a good time there, but the friend's efforts to facilitate the visa were unavailing.

One evening George Norton said that he knew of a delegation of Southern Baptists who were going into Russia via Poland and suggested that they join the group. Adlai shook his head. He was going into Russia as an accredited foreign correspondent if it could possibly be done. So George Norton left him (incidentally, the Southern Baptists, with Norton among them, were halted at the Polish-Russian border), and Adlai pushed on alone to Belgrade. No visa. He pushed on to Bucharest. Here again, no visa, though his stay in Bucharest seemed to him profitable as education: he became the guest of an officer of the Rumanian Standard Oil Company, a fact that, as he reported to the *Pantagraph* upon his return, "materially facilitated his investigation into economic and political conditions in the Balkan states." He paused in Sofia. No visa. He went on to Constantinople. Still no visa. But in Constantinople he stubbornly spent two solid days in the outer office of the Soviet consulate, ostentatiously waiting, before at last he virtually gave up hope and went out to explore the fascinating city. Two days later he went back to the Soviet consulate, where officials rebuked him for his absence. His visa was ready and waiting.

If he thought this the end of his difficulties, however, he was promptly disillusioned. There remained much more severe tests, not only of tenacity but of ingenuity and physical stamina as well. The visa granted, Soviet consular officials considered their duty wholly done; no suggestions were forthcoming as to how one might travel from Turkey to Moscow. So Adlai went down to the waterfront, where he learned that a small Italian freighter, the *Diana*, was about to sail up the Asiatic coast of the Black Sea to the Russian port of Batum, at the western end of the Caucasus. He hired a man to row him out to the *Diana*, where he managed to talk the captain (in very broken Italian) into taking him as a passenger. The voyage required five days, for the little ship seemed to put in at every port along the way, and though Adlai shared his cabin with an Italian diplomat, an interesting old man on his way to Persia, and joined the ship officers shooting sea gulls with a rifle, he really did not enjoy the trip. At Batum trouble was compounded for him. All his papers, all his books, including his French-Russian dictionary and Bernard Pares' *History of Russia*, were taken away from him. Without knowing any Russian at all, he must now make his way. . . .

Afterward it would seem to him almost miraculous that he had done so. No one spoke English; almost everyone regarded him as a suspicious character. Never had he felt more utterly isolated, nor more physically miserable. He was almost always dirty and tired and hungry; it was borne in upon him that he might easily fall ill in this strange wild land, and if he did he might die untended among half-hostile strangers, for the individual life, he quickly realized, was not deemed sacred here. Yet it did not occur to him to turn back. Somehow he managed to travel along the mountains to Tiflis, capital of that Georgian republic of which Stalin was native, and from Tiflis to the oil city of Baku on the Caspian. There he obtained a train ticket for a journey northward. For five days he was locked in a train compartment with an extremely dirty and extremely bearded Russian who spoke not a word, going through Rostov and Kharkov and across an endless flat plain on which the works of man were far less various and interesting than those of the plain of Illinois. He arrived at last in Moscow, depressed by his weariness and hunger and the dreary monotony of his journey. The miserable poverty of the people (he witnessed the aftermath of the great famine along the Volga) was everywhere apparent, and it was, as he immediately saw, intensified in Moscow. His first sight, when he stepped out of the railroad station, was of a group of "wild children," "wolf children"—the homeless, hopeless orphans of war—crouched upon the cobblestones where someone had dropped and broken a jar of jam: the children scraped the stones with their fingers and licked their fingers ravenously, fighting among themselves like mangy animals.

In Moscow he stayed in a house run for stranded foreigners by the Friends Service Committee, directed by two kindly and efficient ladies to whom he was always afterward grateful—a Miss Graves of Baltimore and a Miss Higgens from England. Most of the American newspapermen ate there every day, and Adlai was thus daily associated with such famous journalists as Walter Duranty of the New York *Times*, William Henry Chamberlin of the *Christian Science Monitor*, and H. R. Knickerbocker of the I.N.S. These men were inclined to regard Adlai's project with amused skepticism, but they admired the young man's audacity and did what they could to help him. He learned from them most of what it was possible to know about the workings of the Kremlin and about the great crisis through which the Soviet Union was then passing. Lenin had died two years before and the bitter struggle for his succession between Stalin and Trotsky had been won by the former. Lenin's new economic policy (the N.E.P.), which had seemed to point toward a liberal socialism that mixed state ownership with private enterprise, was now abandoned by Stalin, who was taking steps to liquidate the kulaks (richer peasants, encouraged under the N.E.P.) and every other vestige of capitalism. He was doing so with utter ruthlessness.

"The atmosphere of fear was palpable," said Adlai Stevenson long afterward, "as palpable as the abject poverty of the masses. I never knew whether or not I was being followed, but I did know that people were afraid to be seen talking to me. One of the Russians I talked to," he added, "was Karl Radek, the old Bolshevik theoretician, who was later killed in the purge. He was head of Intourist when I was there."

His chief Moscow guide, however, was the Countess Sophia Tolstoy, who as daughter of the great writer and curator of the Tolstoy Museum was tolerated by the Communists. Several Russian refugees in America—Prince Ratislav, Colonel Voevodsky, and Ilya Tolstoy, among others—had asked him to communicate, if possible, with relatives, and Countess Tolstoy helped him to do so.

Every afternoon he called at the Foreign Office; he went there, as a matter of fact, before he'd unpacked his bag on his first weary day in Moscow. He talked with Chicherin's press secretary, who sat with his back to folding doors behind which, Adlai suspected, sat Chicherin himself, closely listening to every word that was said. Adlai, therefore, said many words. He was eloquent in his presentation of ideas concerning the Czarist debts and the expropriations, he was sympathetic and open-minded concerning Soviet problems, he admired Chicherin's proven abilities, he was convinced that a full-dress interview with the minister would be of immense value to "both our countries." The press secretary listened politely, then smilingly advised him to return next day. This continued for a month. At the end of that time the persistent young American, his money running low, was forced to give up what he finally confessed to be, in any case, a hopeless enterprise. He left Moscow without his story.

"But I've always been very thankful for that trip," he said in the 1950's. "After what I saw there, I could never believe, as so many did in the early 1930's, that Soviet Russia's way was a good way for any state to go. Some men, from the highest humanitarian motives, became Communists or fellow travelers during the Depression, but I felt that I had seen at first hand what Communism really meant, in terms of terror and brutality. All that terror and brutality breed are more terror and more brutality, and so it was in the Russia I saw."

He went to Leningrad, where he spent a week. Then he went to Stockholm by way of Helsingfors, Åbo, and the Baltic Sea, sailing for the United States from Gothenburg, Sweden. He returned to Bloomington on October 12, 1926.

There he discovered, through letters from Switzerland, that the failure of his plot concerning Chicherin had been more than offset by the success of the plot against Buffie's stage career. The latter success, in fact, was almost *too* complete, in Helen Stevenson's view.

In a hotel in Valmont, above Lake Geneva, Buffie had met a handsome young Virginian named Ernest Ives, first secretary at the American Embassy in Constantinople, who had come to Switzerland on leave. Within three days after they'd met they were planning to honeymoon in Egypt. (He'd formerly been consul in Alexandria.) Their idea was that they marry at once, while he was still on leave, but this precipitance was successfully opposed by Mrs. Stevenson, who argued that a two- or three-month separation was required by wisdom. It was finally agreed that Buffie and Mrs. Stevenson would return to Bloomington until early in 1927, when Buffie would return to Europe for a wedding in Naples.[6]

Minor complications arose when all this was explained to Lewis Stevenson. He exploded in characteristic fashion, flatly refusing to permit his daughter to marry a man he'd not even met. He would go to Naples with Buffie; he'd look this strange young man over carefully; and *then*, if he liked what he saw, he would permit the wedding to go forward. As usual in family crises, he faced a united front formed by his wife, his daughter, his son. As usual it was Adlai who smoothed things over. On the eve of the fateful voyage he sent his father a long letter for which Buffie, though she never saw it, was especially grateful. "You can't imagine what an effect your splendid letter had on Father," she wrote from mid-ocean. "He has done everything possible to help me and not fret me, and I do appreciate your tact and understanding.... You should hear OLD PAPA tell me he thinks you have a 'master mind, and altho' a boy, one of the great men he has ever known.' He has utter awe of you, as I have love and confidence."

On February 4, 1927, Elizabeth Stevenson and Ernest Ives were married in Naples. In accordance with Italian law, there were two ceremonies, a civil one at twelve noon and one in the Presbyterian church at three in the afternoon. Bride and groom departed at once for Egypt, to honeymoon until March 1.

v

By that time Adlai Stevenson was drawing $125 a month as law clerk in the old and highly respected law firm of Cutting, Moore and Sidley, with offices on La Salle Street in the heart of Chicago's financial district. He had obtained the job through his Princeton friend, M. Ogden West, with whom he had traveled in Europe in the summer of 1921. Ogden West had a brother-in-law in this firm and would himself become, in later years, a partner.

But if Adlai had obtained this highly prestigious start through a personal connection rather than through abilities demonstrated in law school, he certainly did not regard it as a sinecure. He was working as hard as law clerk as he had ever done while a Harvard law student, averaging fifty hours a week. He was stubbornly, conscientiously determined that, like it or not, he would become a first-rate lawyer, always an asset and ultimately a partner in the firm.

CHAPTER NINE

CHICAGO'S celebrated Gold Coast extends southward for a mile or so along Lake Michigan from Lincoln Park to approximately Delaware Street, itself a mile north of the Loop, and inland perhaps a quarter of a mile. In geographic terms, therefore, it is a tiny segment of the great city. In terms of power and prestige, however, its dimensions are vast, and they were even greater forty years ago when Adlai Stevenson became a member of the community they bounded: here dwelt the rich, here were the city homes of society. The Coast's glittering façade was rapidly changing. Skyscraper apartments for the wealthy were rapidly rising along the Drive itself, replacing the grandiose mansions of former years, and along the side streets— Maple and Cedar and Elm—many of the substantial dwellings were being made over into apartments and let out piecemeal to young single people who were just beginning their careers. It was into one of the latter, a brownstone house at 70 East Elm, that Adlai Stevenson moved early in 1927.

Elm Street was remarkable in that it did actually have, in its narrow parkings, some puny specimens of the tree after which it was named. (Maple, alas, had no maples, nor did Cedar have cedars.) If they were slender plants scarcely taller than a tall man's head, if their crowns were but scraps of foliage during the warm seasons, they nevertheless brought green information of the world of nature into this man-made world of pavements and walls. Stevenson was grateful for them. He was grateful, too, for a view of the lake from the front windows of his room. They faced southward and from them, at an angle, his view caught between towering walls, he could look far out across the inland sea to a watery horizon, often shrouded in mists, out of which the full moon rose on clear nights with a magical radiant beauty. On Sundays he often walked along the lake from Oak Street beach to the breakwater at North Avenue. He needed thus to renew himself after a week in the gray smoky canyon of La Salle Street.

The workday fare on which a beginning law clerk feeds is no more fattening to his ego than his salary is to his pocketbook, nor is it of such a nature as to engage, very often, the clerk's fascinated attention. Most of it is drudgery; much of it is menial. This is especially true in such financial law firms as Cutting, Moore and Sidley. A relatively small portion of the work there involved anything so dramatic as a court trial. Most of it, as a matter of fact, was designed to keep court trials from happening. Young Stevenson, therefore, had little opportunity in his law work to display his skill in oral argument, that ability to project his personality over a group of people, which he had begun to develop at Princeton.

He was, in effect, a servant of the partners, a kind of glorified office boy, to whom were assigned those tasks that were too time-consuming and routine for a partner's close and expensive attention. Yet a great deal depended upon the efficiency, the precision, with which these tasks were performed. He looked up the law as it pertained to a case a partner was handling. He wrote memoranda on questions of law. He kept a docket for a partner or for partners. He drafted simple wills and contracts. He ran all kinds of errands. And all the time he was acutely aware that he was in competition with other young men, and that there were more of these than there were eventual partnerships to reward them. The yardstick by which the competitions were graded was, in his firm, a tradition of legal work of the highest quality, extending unbroken to the year following the Civil War —the longest such tradition in Chicago.

He was immediately well-liked personally in the firm, both by his superiors and by his fellow clerks. He was uniformly cheerful, even-tempered in times of pressure, conscientious in the performance of his duties, generally sound in his judgments. His presence was no obvious threat to anyone. If he had success anxiety (and he did have some), he hid it well under casual, pleasant, unassertive good manners. If he had any brilliant potential either as lawyer or as man, it was not recognized by his superiors. They noted, however, that he steadily improved as a lawyer and that he was better at any given moment than he seemed to think he was. He claimed far less than his due: he seemed to feel that, given his heritage and initial advantages, he should do far better than he was doing.[1]

Conscience thus deprived him of self-satisfactions that others in his circumstances would have enjoyed. But it also ensured his future growth. And growth was ensured, too, by the fact that he was involved, as he had been at Choate and Princeton, in a great deal of extracurricular activity. He followed the pattern established in his school and college days. A fifty-hour week devoted to the law by no means used up all his energies. Most of these, it sometimes seemed, were held in abeyance while he performed his hired duties, to be released after hours in a great number and variety of social engagements and civic enterprises.

II

The social engagements, joined with recreational activities of many kinds, were at first predominant. He at once became a member of the Harvard-Yale-Princeton club * and played squash there two or three times a week; he was also active in the management of the club, constantly enlarging through it his circle of friendly social acquaintances. He was, of course, no stranger to Chicago's society when he first came to the city: many of the fashionable and wealthy citizens were long-time friends of his family. Their sons and daughters were, often, his own personal friends, some of whom he had known since his boyhood summers at Charlevoix and others of whom he had known in the West, or on his travels, or at Princeton or Harvard.

One long-time acquaintance, for instance, was Hermon Dunlap Smith, whom everyone called "Dutch." The Smiths had had a place across the lake from the Davis cottage at Charlevoix, and the two boys (they were almost precisely the same age, Dutch having been born on May 1, 1900) had sometimes, though seldom, played together during those idyllic summers. During their college days the two had also sometimes met. Dutch had gone to Harvard, graduating with the class of '21, and at Harvard he had been president of the *Crimson*; as a result, he and Adlai had met sometimes at conferences of Eastern college student paper executives. The acquaintanceship had been slight and casual, however, until Adlai moved to Chicago. Thereafter it quickly grew into a very warm, close friendship and would remain so.

By the spring of 1927 Dutch Smith was already very solidly established as a business executive and a member of Chicago's social elite. He had joined the Northern Trust Company's executive staff in 1922. In 1926 he had become a second vice-president of the company. In 1928 he would join Marsh and McLennan, insurance brokers, advancing ultimately to the position of president of the board in that large and prosperous enterprise. In 1923 he had married Ellen Catherine Thorne, daughter of the president of Montgomery Ward & Company, with whom Adlai had had a slight acquaintance ever since the summer of 1919, when she and Adlai had met at the H F Bar ranch.

Ellen Smith seldom gave a party to which he was not invited. He never dominated the group, nor displayed an intimidating brilliance, nor did he have (people felt this) any desire to do so. With his steady good cheer, his

* The club ceased to exist in the 1930's.

genuinely interested questioning, his close listening to answers, he helped others to put their best selves forward. Their attitude toward him was warmly affectionate, if often a little patronizing. He claimed so little for himself that they would like to have claimed a great deal for him, but there were not many who felt they could honestly do so.

There were a great many parties in those years, both formal and informal; it was the height of the Jazz Age, when the pursuit of pleasure absorbed a greater proportion of youthful energies, perhaps, than it had ever done before in America or has ever done since. Stevenson became one of a loosely organized set composed of young married couples, as yet childless, and young bachelors and unmarried women of approximately the same age, social class, and future prospects. They were constantly encountering one another at clubs and theaters and private homes—mostly the latter—and came to know one another well. Many of them had a background of money; few were wealthy in their own right, most of the men earned meager salaries, but none was really economically insecure. Many had family prestige; all would inherit a substantial property. The young men had gone to Ivy League colleges, almost invariably one of the Big Three though, now and then, one encountered a man from Williams, or Amherst, or Dartmouth. The girls had gone to Miss Finch's, or Dobbs Ferry, or some other fashionable finishing school; rarely had one of them attended a university. Doing so was not considered a necessity for girls in the upper income brackets at that time.

Among the closest of these women friends, destined to play a role of some importance in his future life, was Jane Warner. (She would marry Edison Dick in 1930; and in the 1950's he would be chairman of the executive committee of the board of directors of the A. B. Dick Company.) Her father was Ezra J. Warner (Yale, '99) president and treasurer of the great wholesale grocery firm of Sprague, Warner, and Company. It was Warner, a Republican, who urged Stevenson to become a Democratic candidate for the legislature in 1928—the first time anyone suggested that Stevenson become a candidate for public office. The young man toyed with the idea for some weeks, then gave it up as unfeasible in his circumstances. Distracted by active politics, he would never make the grade at Cutting, Moore and Sidley. . . .[2]

Another of his women friends who would be important in his future life was Alicia Patterson, the brilliant and vivacious daughter of Captain Joseph Patterson. Captain Patterson and his cousin, Colonel Robert Rutherford McCormick, had become the dominant powers over the Chicago *Tribune* by 1919 when, in part because the two strong-willed men did not get on well together, Patterson launched the hugely successful tabloid New York *Daily News*. To the captain's daughter, Alicia, Adlai was more strongly attracted in a romantic way than he was to most (if any other) of his

Vice-President Stevenson lived in this substantial house in Bloomington, one of the centers of his namesake grandson's world as a boy. The former Vice-President is seated in the front yard, his family around him. (*Courtesy, Mrs. Ernest Ives*)

Mrs. Lewis Stevenson, mother of Adlai Stevenson. (*Wide World Photos*)

Something of the psychological relation between Adlai Stevenson and his sister, Elizabeth (Buffie)—she motherly, possessive, protective—is indicated in this picture of them when they were, respectively, three and six years old. (*Courtesy, Mrs. Ernest Ives*)

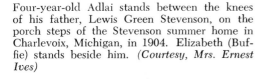

Four-year-old Adlai stands between the knees of his father, Lewis Green Stevenson, on the porch steps of the Stevenson summer home in Charlevoix, Michigan, in 1904. Elizabeth (Buffie) stands beside him. (*Courtesy, Mrs. Ernest Ives*)

Six-month-old Adlai E. Stevenson in the arms of his grandfather, the first Adlai E. Stevenson, Vice-President of the United States in Cleveland's second administration. When this picture was taken in Bloomington, Illinois, in the summer of 1900, Grandfather Stevenson was again Democratic Vice-Presidential candidate, running with William Jennings Bryan against McKinley and Theodore Roosevelt. *(Courtesy of Mrs. Ernest Ives)*

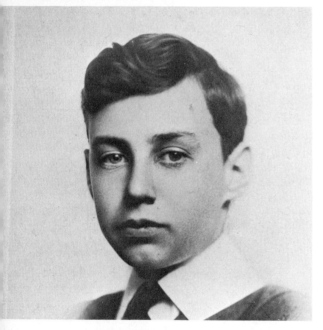

Thirteen-year-old Adlai wears an Eton collar. *(Courtesy, Mrs. Ernest Ives)*

Adlai E. Stevenson, Princeton, Class of 1922. *(Courtesy, Mrs. Ernest Ives)*

Adlai E. Stevenson, candidate for governor of Illinois in 1948, poses with (left to right) his son Adlai III; Vice-President Alben Barkley (a distant relative); and his nephew Timothy Ives at 1316 East Washington Street, Bloomington, Illinois. The old Stevenson family home has now become the home of Buffie and her diplomat husband, Ernest Ives. *(Courtesy, Mrs. Ernest Ives)*

Amid public gaiety was private sorrow at the inaugural ball of Governor Adlai E. Stevenson of Illinois in January, 1949. Seven months later the new governor was forced to announce that his wife, Ellen Borden Stevenson, who here sits glumly beside him, would sue him for divorce. Seated behind Governor and Mrs. Stevenson are Mr. and Mrs. Ernest Ives, Stevenson's brother-in-law and sister, Buffie. *(Courtesy, Mrs. Ernest Ives)*

The governor's three sons were hosts at a holiday dance for young people from all over Illinois in late December, 1951. Left to right: John Fell, the Governor, Borden, and Adlai III. *(Courtesy, Mrs. Ernest Ives)*

Governor Stevenson with his famous dog Artie in his office in the mansion, Springfield, Illinois, 1951. (*Courtesy, Mrs. Ernest Ives*)

The most famous of all Adlai Stevenson campaign photographs, the "hole in the shoe" photo taken at Flint, Michigan, during the 1952 contest. Typically, Stevenson, who is to speak in a few minutes, is still working on his speech. (*Wide World Photos*)

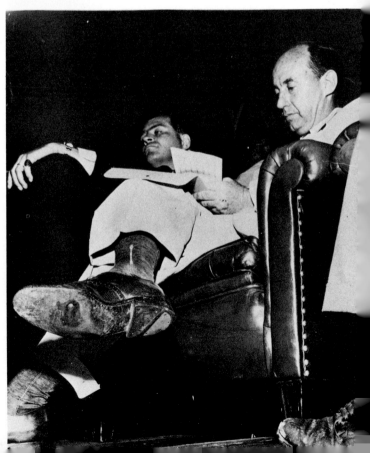

Adlai Stevenson in June, 1928, looks down at his infant nephew, Timothy Ives, son of Elizabeth Stevenson Ives and Ernest Ives, who is held by Adlai's mother while Adlai's father looks on. (*Courtesy, Mrs. Ernest Ives*)

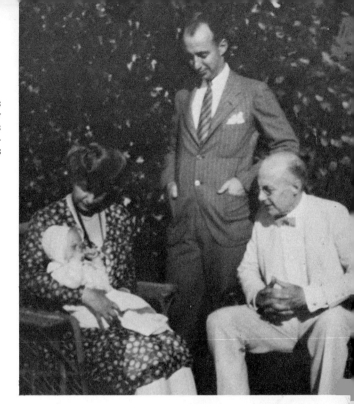

The clan gathers at the old Stevenson home in Bloomington in the fall of 1957 to celebrate the first birthday of two grandchildren. Left to right, top row: Timothy R. Ives, Ernest L. Ives, Mrs. Ernest Ives, Mrs. Adlai E. Stevenson III, Adlai Stevenson III, Governor Stevenson. Left to right, bottom row: Mrs. Timothy R. Ives, her daughter, Alison Armour Ives, Mrs. Martin D. (Julia Stevenson) Hardin (Adlai's aunt), Adlai Stevenson IV. (*Wide World Photos*)

Senator John Sparkman of Alabama, Democratic candidate for Vice-President; Stephen A. Mitchell, newly selected Democratic National Chairman; and the Democratic candidate for President, Adlai Stevenson, smile happily in the national headquarters of their party, Washington, D.C., August, 1952. (*Wide World Photos*)

Stevenson, having won the 1956 Presidential nomination despite the opposition of ex-President Truman, waves to the cheering Chicago convention. Grouped around him (left to right) are Mrs. Adlai E. (Nancy) Stevenson III, Adlai III (partially obscured), John Fell Stevenson, and Mrs. Ernest Ives. Truman, standing behind the nominee, hides his discomfiture with a smile. (*Wide World Photos*)

No one is happy in the Stevenson family party as they watch on television, in a Los Angeles hotel suite, the nomination of John F. Kennedy as the 1960 Democratic Presidential candidate. Stevenson received 79½ votes before the delegates made Kennedy's selection unanimous. Seated immediately back of Stevenson is his sister, Mrs. Ives. Seated on the floor are (left to right) Adlai III, Borden, Nancy (Adlai III's wife), and John Fell. (*Wide World Photos*)

At the Kennedy summer home at Hyannis Port, on Cape Cod, President Kennedy and Stevenson, now U.S. Ambassador to the United Nations, confer at length on U.S. strategy for the forthcoming UN General Assembly, August 5, 1961. *(Wide World Photos)*

Mrs. Eleanor Roosevelt and her great good friend Adlai Stevenson, on the platform at Madison Square Garden, where Stevenson had just completed a major campaign speech attacking the Eisenhower administration's foreign policy, October 23, 1956. *(Wide World Photos)*

Three days after the assassination of President Kennedy, Stevenson confers at the White House with Kennedy's successor, Lyndon Johnson, who urgently requests the Ambassador to the UN to remain at his post. *(Courtesy, Mrs. Ernest Ives)*

Dag Hammarskjöld, Secretary General of the United Nations, confers with Stevenson during an intermission of a meeting of the Security Council, October 16, 1961. *(Inge Morath–Magnum)*

Stevenson's flag-draped coffin lies in the Bethlehem Chapel of Washington's National Cathedral on the night of July 15, 1965, twenty-four hours after he dropped dead on a London street. *(Wide World Photos)*

At the graveside in Bloomington, Illinois, Borden Stevenson holds the folded flag, which has been removed from his father's casket and given ceremoniously to his aunt, Mrs. Ernest Ives, who sits beside him. Behind them are President and Mrs. Johnson. *(Wide World Photos)*

friends during his early Chicago years, and the attraction would remain strong all the years until her tragic death in 1963.

In the summers of 1927 and '28 Stevenson was one of a group of young men who rented a house in Lake Forest, that most famous and fashionable (at least at that time) of all the string of north shore suburbs. They dubbed their house "The Château," commuting from it to their city offices (many of them rode bicycles to the station) all through the summer. Most if not all of them became members of Lake Forest's fashionable Onwentsia Club, where dances were held every weekend and where Stevenson played a great deal of tennis during his hours off, and a good deal of golf. He rode, too. He was naturally good at games. When he was playing regularly he golfed in the lower eighties. He still played a very tough tennis game and was a good shot and a fine horseman.

Concurrent with all this informal social life was an intermittently glittering formal one, particularly during the Christmas holiday season and the weeks following it. The Jazz Age, like the Gilded Age, was one of particularly conspicuous consumption among the wealthy. During it, Chicago's debutantes were launched, not en masse as they later were, but one by one at balls costing their parents anywhere from three to five thousand dollars apiece, and sometimes more. On occasion two orchestras were employed at these affairs to ensure continuous dancing into the wee hours, and always a long stag line was required to assure each girl of a number of dancing partners in gratifying swift succession. No hostess could be personally acquainted with all the people required to fill huge hotel ballrooms; particularly was it impossible for her to know all the young men whose presence, in droves, was demanded. Hence "Miss Campbell's List," from which Miss Eliza Campbell, the social secretary employed by Chicago's society mothers, made up guest lists for her clients. Stevenson and his "Château" friends were on the list, as a matter of course.[3]

But Adlai Stevenson was not deeply susceptible to the prevailing mood of the Jazz Age, then approaching its climactic moments. He seemed to have been born knowing that, in the total scheme of things, there are no privileges: everything truly possessed must be paid for sooner or later, either through a conscious fulfillment of the obligations that privilege imposes or through a loss of personal quality, a cheapening and coarsening of personality. Even conscience—a felt knowledge of obligations, an acute sensitivity to moral values—may be a privilege in this sense. Certainly no one can live well without it, and certainly it must be paid for; it carries with it vital dangers of which Stevenson's remarkable mother was well aware.

Excessive conscience, she realized, could breed life-negating fears; it might become a kind of cowardice which kept a man from realizing that greatness which Helen Stevenson believed to be potential in her son. "Free yourself of all fear," she earnestly advised him in a letter written in April,

1927. "Fear of *anything* is devastating. . . ." It would be a "good sign" if he wanted to be "very elegant in appearance, and if you blow a little money, it will kill off scare-cat fear." Buffie, she pointed out, had "bought more finery" in her "enthusiasm in feeling well and free." Buffie might "go too far that way, but better that than an attack of fear." She urged him to "get a true knowledge" of himself and of what he really wanted out of life, and she begged him not to "be hurried" and harassed. "What is best for you to do about life will have opened up to you as time goes on." (She was also concerned, in that letter, lest her husband sap Adlai's self-confidence by "passing on his worries and fears." Poor Lewis Stevenson, certainly, was having his troubles that year, what with the continuing farm depression, Coolidge's veto of the McNary-Haugen bill on which Lewis had worked with George N. Peek and Hugh S. Johnson of the Moline Plow Company, and the collapse of the Zeppelin project for which Lewis had had such high hopes. That spring, for the first time, he sometimes impressed his son as a tired, harried old man.)

It is perhaps an unanswerable question whether art is more an imitation of life than life is of art; the two interact and modify one another profoundly. To what extent did *This Side of Paradise* reflect a certain kind of glamorous girl who emerged during the war? To what extent was the girl created by *Paradise?* No one can say. But it is a fact of literary history that the living model for the Isabelle Borge of Fitzgerald's first novel was the beautiful Ginevra King of Chicago and Lake Forest.[4] Among her neighbors and contemporaries in Lake Forest were Peggy Carry, Edith Cummings, and Courtney Letts. These three had been the "great belles," as Buffie put it, of that social life in Washington in which she was so much involved in early 1918; it was at Courtney's coming-out party in Washington that John Harlan, with Allister McCormick and several Princeton men, had given Buffie "such a rush."

Ginevra King would become the wife of John Pirie (it was the second marriage for both of them), who would be president of Carson, Pirie, Scott and Company, the large department store on State Street, by the 1940's. Courtney Letts, having at her first wedding become Courtney Letts Stillman of Washington, would at her second become the wife of John Borden of Chicago, in March, 1925. By his first wife John Borden had two daughters. The younger would marry Robert Pirie, brother-in-law of the former Ginevra King. The elder was destined to marry Adlai E. Stevenson, who thereby, for a brief period, became a son-in-law of the former Courtney Letts.

The event was being prepared in the spring and summer of 1928. . . .

III

Her name was Ellen, and to a superficial view it seemed that she too might have stepped from the pages of a Fitzgerald novel. At eighteen, she was a slender vivid dark-blond-haired girl, with plump cheeks, a firm and even stubborn jaw, heart-shaped lips, and hazel eyes through which she habitually looked out upon the world with a bright, smiling, wide-lidded stare.

She was very pretty and very rich, but these attractive qualities by no means accounted for the whole of the fascination she seemed to have for the young men who thronged around her at parties. Her attitudes mingled a childish innocence with worldly sophistication in ways that were confusing but delightful to most people. She was, some thought, rather birdlike. One tended to describe her with the adjectives one applies to the actions of birds —perky, flighty, fluttery—for though her movements were graceful and seemed, when one was with her, to flow smoothly together, one was likely to remember them as jerky, disconnected, hopping from here to there like a brilliant bird who pauses now and then to preen and to stare. The same was true of her conversation. It was very quick and gay and witty: it was, most people agreed, wholly charming: but it did have a tendency to break into pieces when one handled it with the fingers of memory. It became a clutter of impressions, a scattering of moments vivid and even brilliant, but without evident relation to one another. One sensed obscurely that she was dangerous—dangerous to others but above all to herself—and one longed to *protect* her. She was so eager for life! So anxious to grasp and shape the world into forms that expressed, beautifully, herself! She might be terribly hurt by it!

She lived, as a princess should, in a palace—a turreted sixteenth-century French château built of smooth gray stone in the latter part of the nine-teenth century by her grandfather, William Borden, who had made a fortune out of Chicago real estate. It stood at 1020 Lake Shore Drive, on the corner of the Drive and Bellevue Place. Directly across Bellevue from it stood Edith Rockefeller McCormick's great limestone mansion, for whose architectural ugliness the Borden château helped somewhat to compensate. When Ellen was a little girl she used to write verses as she lay in her bed at night, scribbling them on smuggled sheets of paper by the light of a street lamp that shone into her room. She also early evinced a taste and talent for interior decoration. She was sensitive to colors and their relations to one another, and to the balancing of a room's furnishing.

She could feel that she came naturally by her interest in writing and in the arts in general. Her mother, the former Ellen Waller of an old and distinguished Chicago family, from whom she inherited her beauty (mother and daughter looked much alike), was among the city's patronesses of the arts, with a particular interest in music. Her father's sister, Mary Borden, was a famous novelist. Aunt Mary was now Lady Spears, for in 1918, a year before she published her first novel, she had married the famous soldier and diplomat and author, Brigadier General Edward Louis Spears, who was to become a knight of the British Empire.

As for Ellen's father, John Borden, from whom she inherited many of her salient characteristics, he, too, possessed qualities that might have led him to success in the creative arts had he chosen to channel his energies in that direction. He had not so chosen: he was not, as a matter of fact, much interested in the arts at all. After receiving his B.A. from Yale in 1906, he had entered the Northwestern Law School (it was while he was a law student that he had married Ellen Waller in 1907), receiving his LL.B. and being admitted to the Illinois Bar in 1908. In the years since, he had demonstrated a restless imagination, remarkable courage, and great physical vigor. He had also revealed a penchant for daring speculations. These qualities had led him to dramatic business successes. They would later lead him to equally dramatic failures, for in him they were joined (they often are so joined) with an impatience of procedural rules, a boredom with routine, and a notable carelessness of details. In 1928, however, he was at the very peak of his success. Having inherited a fortune, he had added another to it as an associate of John Hertz in the Yellow Cab Company; then he had gone into Southwest oil and added yet another. Simultaneously he had so distinguished himself as an Arctic explorer that he was listed as one in *Who's Who*.

And not only was he explorer, sportsman, clubman, financier. On his Glenwild Plantation near Granada, Mississippi—an estate of baronial proportions—he raised purebred Shorthorn and Hereford beef cattle, and Duroc-Jersey hogs, entering outstanding animals in the great livestock expositions in Kansas City and Chicago and winning with them an occasional ribbon. At the age of forty, after seventeen years of a marriage most observers had thought to be a very happy one, he had divorced Ellen Waller Borden in order to marry, barely three months later, the glamorous Courtney Letts Stillman. To Ellen and her younger sister Betty, in the divorce settlement, went the mansion at 1020 Lake Shore Drive, and other riches, the house to be used by Mrs. Waller Borden so long as she wished to do so. But with these came a great deal of pain and bitterness, a breaking of vital strands from which the eldest daughter suffered only slightly less than her mother did.

Ellen was educated at St. Timothy's, Catonsville, Maryland—a school famous for its exclusiveness and its devotion (under Louisa McE. Fowler and Jane R. Heath) to conservative educational values. The daughters of the rich went there. Yet even among these, the teen-aged Ellen had the largest expense account (indeed it was an unlimited account) in the school, thanks to her father, who may thus have attempted to make it up to her for her broken home. After leaving St. Timothy's, she had gone for a year to Miss Sheldon's and Miss Nixon's in Florence, Italy. Then, in December of 1926, she was presented to Chicago society and became one of the most popular debutantes of her year. She was presented at the Court of St. James during one of the levees of the spring of 1928.

By the time the latter event occurred she had virtually decided that, from her many suitors, she would choose Adlai Stevenson. She had met him again and again at parties. He had become the most frequent of her escorts. He was obviously devoted to her as a *person* and not just as the leading deb, or as a great heiress. She enjoyed his sparkling conversation, his good dancing, his charming manners; and life with him, she decided, would never be boring. These things she would say to interviewers in later years. She would deny, in these later years, that she had ever really loved him. . . .

But if she did not, appearances deceived the most intimate of their friends at the time. They seemed so very much in love, so wholly delighted with one another. Her mother was delighted with Adlai, too, and encouraged the match; and when Lady Spears met him she became wholly committed to him. As for Adlai, by the spring of '28 he was writing glowing letters to his mother about this completely captivating girl who, for all her wealth and beauty, was very far from having had a happy life. He was profoundly moved by her yearning toward beauty, and very proud of her manifestations of literary talent. When the Chicago *Tribune* printed one of her verses on its editorial page, he bought extra copies of that issue and sent a clipping of it to Bloomington for mounting in the family album.*

One of the points he referred to, as he spoke of her to his family, was her *spontaneity*. She seemed to him so fully and freely and charmingly self-expressive, and she did things on the spur of the moment, in defiance of schedules and plans.

"You know," he said to his mother, "I've always planned things, and considered consequences. But she just does things as she *feels* like doing them." [5] Together they might balance one another, he felt, making up for each other's deficiencies.

Moreover, by marrying him Ellen would become a member of a family and would partake of a family life such as she had never known before. In

---

* The verse, entitled *It Must Be Mad*, was as follows:

I watch my shadow slide about *I watch it raise its fists and know*
And O, I know without a doubt   *There's no one there to take the blow*
It must be mad!   *I see it going out the door*
I watch it pick up things with care, *And wonder what it's going for:*
When I can see there's nothing there, *It must be mad!*

later years she would make a much-quoted remark to the effect that the Stevensons "must have Chinese blood in them, they all worship their ancestors so." The remark would be considered a gibe at her husband's people. But at the outset she was intrigued by the intense family feeling that all of them had, and was herself sustained by the sense of belonging to a living tradition, deeply rooted in history and growing through her husband and herself toward the future. If this ancestor worship seemed to her ridiculous in some respects, she could not but realize that it gave to every present Stevenson life a richer, deeper significance.

And this sense of vital continuity was particularly strong through the spring and early summer of 1928, for in March of that year Mr. and Mrs. Ernest Ives returned to the United States for the birth of their son, Timothy Read. He was born in Chicago on April 9. Ellen and her mother were impressed by the intense family feeling that focused on this event. So much warmth and joy surrounded it! Joy glowed in the proud father and mother scarcely more than it did in the baby's grandparents and uncle! Obviously, then, the family feeling was far more than ancestor worship; it was concerned more intensely with the future than it was with the past.

That year, as a matter of fact, it looked for a time as though new luster might be added to the Stevenson family name in the very immediate future. Almost simultaneously with the birth of Timothy Read Ives came the birth of a Vice-Presidential boom for the baby's grandfather Stevenson. The Democratic National Convention was to be held in Houston, Texas, in July, and as July approached, Lewis Green Stevenson was deemed an increasingly strong contender for nomination as Al Smith's running mate. Several leading Illinois newspapers editorialized on the subject, pointing out that Lewis Stevenson's nomination would greatly strengthen the Democratic appeal to the farm vote, a vote which should certainly have been lost to the Republicans when they, at their convention in Kansas City, rejected the principles of the McNary-Haugen Bill and proposed as a solution to the farm problem a farm board which would encourage cooperative marketing.

Buffie remained in America until July, while Ernest Ives returned to his post in Ankara. She attended the Houston convention with her parents. And there she saw her gallant father's boom die swiftly to a sputter, and then into nothing at all, as Al Smith, nominated on the first ballot, threw his support to the liberal Senator Joseph T. Robinson of Arkansas. Robinson was of course nominated: the campaign became one of Smith-Robinson versus Herbert Hoover and Kansas Senator Charles Curtis. Lewis Stevenson was not uninfluential at Houston, however. He had a hand in shaping the farm plank of the Democratic platform.

For Adlai, Lake Geneva, Illinois, held a greater vital interest than Houston, Texas, did that month. Mrs. Waller Borden and her daughters Ellen and Betty were living there, at Ceylon Court, the luxurious estate of the late Mr. and Mrs. John J. Mitchell. Adlai was a frequent weekend visitor. By the latter part of the month, he and Ellen were engaged to be married, though the formal announcement would not be made until late September. One particularly "beautiful weekend" with "the 'wife' and in-laws" began on Saturday, July 28, and when he wrote his mother about it the following Monday he said that "Mrs. Borden expects you & father whenever you can come & wants you to understand that you won't be visiting, just 'staying.'"

Three days later, on Thursday morning, he called upon Ellen's father at the latter's office, 6 North Michigan Avenue, for an interview he had dreaded but which "turned out most pleasantly." He found the elder Borden to be really "a most pleasant" man, if perhaps a bit arrogant and willful, and received from him a great deal of advice as to how and where they should live, the size and nature of Ellen's inheritance, and so on. That afternoon, Mr. McPherson, a senior partner of Cutting, Moore and Sidley, summoned Adlai to his office. "[With] quaking knees I responded, but, wonder of wonders, instead of firing me he raised my salary beginning August 1 to $200 per mo!" Adlai wrote his mother that evening. Thus emboldened, he told McPherson that he was engaged to be married and would like to have a month or six-week vacation. "To the month he acquiesced eagerly—to the 6 weeks he hesitated on the ground of example to the other young men but said he would take it up with his partners. Hereafter, August 2 will always be my lucky day."

Autumn came and passed for him in a delirium of happy, hectic activity. Everything seemed to be breaking his way, including his stock market speculations—though they, of course, were apparently breaking in favor of *everybody* who was in the market that year, else the prudent Stevenson would not have bought stocks at all. (By October 8, Zenith was up to $135, which meant that Adlai Stevenson's profits on this stock alone—if only he had sold it then—would have amounted to $8000.) On a typical weekend in early October he and Ellen motored up to Lake Forest on a Saturday afternoon, played some tennis there, then motored over to Lake Geneva for a Saturday night and Sunday at the country home of the Kellogg Fairbanks'. Mrs. Fairbanks was almost equally famous as hostess and as Janet Ayer Fairbanks, the novelist, and Ellen and Adlai had a marvelous time with her. She and Adlai got along particularly well because she was that rare creature in her stratum of Chicago society, an ardent supporter of Al Smith.

The only cloud on the bright skies of his happiness was the defeat, in early November, of Al Smith and of most of the Democratic candidates for House and Senate. Once again the Republican victory was of landslide proportions—due in part to a smear campaign against Al Smith's Catholicism and his alleged determination to bring back the open saloon, but due mainly to continuing prosperity. (Said Herbert Hoover, as he accepted the nomination: "We in America are nearer to the final triumph over poverty than ever before in the history of any land. . . . We shall soon . . . be in sight of the day when poverty will be banished from this nation.")

IV

At four-thirty on Saturday afternoon, December 1, 1928, in the small chapel of the fashionable Fourth Presbyterian Church on Upper Michigan Avenue, with the pastor, Dr. John Timothy Stone, officiating, Ellen Borden became the bride of Adlai Ewing Stevenson II. The bride wore a white velvet gown, with collar and full-length panels of a rose-point lace that had been worn at their weddings by her mother and her grandmother and her great-grandmother. Her only ornament was an antique necklace of uncut emeralds. She was given away by her father. Her younger sister, Betty, was her only attendant. William B. McIlvaine, Jr., was the bridegroom's best man. Only the immediate families and a few intimate friends, some twenty-five in all, attended the ceremony. Among these were Mrs. Louis B. Merwin, Mr. and Mrs. Davis Merwin, Mr. and Mrs. Ralph C. DeMange, and Mrs. Davis Ewing, all of Bloomington. From Chicago were Mr. and Mrs. Chauncey McCormick, Mr. and Mrs. Chauncey Blair, Mrs. Edith Rockefeller McCormick, Mr. and Mrs. John Paul Welling, and Colonel and Mrs. George Langhorne.

After the wedding Mrs. Waller Borden was hostess at a large reception for the bridal couple at 1020 Lake Shore Drive, and on the following Tuesday, December 5, Mr. and Mrs. Adlai E. Stevenson sailed from New York for North Africa, where they honeymooned for six weeks (Mr. McPherson and the partners had decided to grant the extra two weeks), motoring through Tunisia, Algeria, and Morocco.

When they returned to Chicago in mid-January, 1929, they moved into an apartment in a remodeled brownstone house at 76 East Walton Place. Here, on February 5, Adlai Stevenson celebrated his twenty-ninth birthday. His bride was not yet nineteen.

BOOK THREE

The Growing Years

CHAPTER TEN

EARLY in 1929, Lewis and Helen Stevenson were in Europe, where they visited Buffie and little Timmie and Ernest Ives in Constantinople. Helen Stevenson remained in Constantinople for several weeks, then went to the Riviera with Buffie, while Lewis traveled extensively through central and western Europe. Everywhere he encountered a bitter resentment of America's failure to join the League of Nations, or even the World Court. He spoke of this in a newspaper interview when he returned in March to Bloomington. He spoke also, to friends, of the wave of social unrest that seemed to be sweeping Europe. There could be no doubt that in Austria and Germany the failure of the United States to ratify the Versailles Treaty gave a persuasive political power into the hands of weird figures—a "crazy demagogue named Hitler," for instance—who denounced that treaty and termed it a piece of treachery by the Jews.

On the evening of March 26 Lewis Stevenson sat at a desk in the Bloomington Club, writing a letter to Buffie—all the more poignant to her because it was destined to remain forever unfinished. In the midst of it he became aware that he was unwell. Then, abruptly, his body was racked by an overwhelming pain of a kind he had never known before: he called for help and collapsed. He was rushed to Brokow Hospital. His young cousin, Dr. E. M. (Ed) Stevenson, was summoned. The doctor's diagnosis was instantaneous: Lewis Stevenson had suffered a severe heart attack and was in imminent danger of death.

Examining him with a greater care than he'd been able to do before, Dr.

Ed was astonished to discover that the Lewis Stevenson he had known, a witty active man who seemed younger than his sixty-one years, actually lived in a very old man's body. Heart, arteries, muscular tone—all were such as a doctor would expect to find in a man in his late seventies. And as Dr. Ed reviewed his patient's life in the light of present evidence, he was struck by the gallantry with which Lewis Stevenson had lived through what must have been long periods of intense pain. Only extreme tensions long continued (of these the migraine headaches had probably been a symptom) could have so ravaged a body.[1] Yet courage, buoyant courage, had certainly been one of Lewis Stevenson's salient characteristics in politics and business, where he had taken many a bitter blow without whining and without giving up.

Messages radiated from the sickbed—north to Chicago, east to Ithaca, New York, far eastward to Buffie and Helen Stevenson in the South of France. . . . The family gathered.

Adlai, with Ellen, came down from Chicago. When it became apparent that Lewis Stevenson, after all, might survive for a time, the two returned to Chicago. Thereafter Adlai virtually commuted between Chicago and Bloomington.

Once, when he was alone in the hospital room with his father, it was borne in upon him with special force that his father lay upon his deathbed, for on that day his father himself obviously believed that the end was near. Lewis Stevenson, in great pain, could hardly talk above a whisper, but he looked at Adlai in a peculiarly penetrating way as he gasped that "politics is a hazardous life, full of ingratitudes"—and it seemed to Adlai, at that instant, that his father was trying to warn him against a political career. But why? Apart from his brief and not very serious consideration of Mr. Warner's suggestion that he run for the legislature, Adlai had never considered becoming himself a politician. Nor had his father ever suggested such a career to him. Mystery was compounded when, immediately afterward, Lewis added some very earnest words about "service." Afterward Adlai could not remember precisely what these words were.

"Memory plays tricks on you when you recall moments like that," he said, many years later. "You're emotionally wrought up and later, out of all your later experience, you're likely to ascribe a greater significance to words and gestures than they actually had at the time."[2]

But he did remember, beyond power of doubt, that his father spoke with profound earnestness of the "duty to serve" and the "need to serve." There was, his father gasped, an "obligation." It all seemed very strange to Adlai at the time. Later it was one of the memories which convinced Adlai that his father had always had undisclosed ambitions for him, had always known that Adlai, with his heritage and background and personal character, was destined (or "doomed," as Adlai would sometimes say in later years) to follow a political career.

Shortly after one o'clock on Friday, April 5, Adlai and Ellen in Chicago boarded a train for Bloomington to spend the weekend at his father's bedside. At approximately the same time Lewis Stevenson, after a light lunch, dropped off to sleep. Lewis's sister Julia, Mrs. Martin D. Hardin, sat watching him. He slept quietly. But at five minutes before two o'clock he awoke and fixed upon his sister a puzzled gaze.

"Is everything all right?" he asked.

Mrs. Hardin, surprised, nodded and smiled reassuringly.

"Yes," she said. "Everything's fine."

He closed his eyes. He heaved a great sigh. He was utterly still. His sister stared at him, touched him. She called frantically to the nurse. . . .

The funeral sermon, in Bloomington's Presbyterian church, was preached by Lewis Stevenson's brother-in-law, the Reverend Martin D. Hardin, who at that time was a minister in Ithaca, New York.

Immediately after the funeral Adlai Stevenson went to New York to meet his mother, who had sailed from Europe on the S.S. *Homeric* and was on the high seas when her husband died.

II

An ending . . . Six months later it might have seemed to Adlai Stevenson that his father's death acquired, through its timing, a symbolic historical significance. In the gloomy canyon of La Salle Street, it seemed to many that the world itself was ending as, day after day, banner headlines in newspapers proclaimed the death of the great bull market. Lights burned all night in brokerage offices as calls for more margin went out, and through the panic-stricken days wild rumors swept the crowded sidewalks and offices, agitating even such islands of relative calm as the offices of Cutting, Moore and Sidley.

Adlai Stevenson suffered no real personal hardship from the deepening Depression. His wife's fortune, and his mother-in-law's, shrank in proportion to the prevailing decline in values. His father-in-law would lose millions and with them his formerly high position in Chicago's financial world. But Stevenson retained his inherited interest in the *Pantagraph*, of which he was a director and vice-president, and other substantial properties would come to him upon his mother's death. He seemed to be making satisfactory if not precisely brilliant progress toward a lucrative partnership in his law firm. He knew well that he was among the very fortunate ones.

The realization of this was heightened in him whenever he walked to and from his work, as he sometimes did; he liked to walk. Invariably, even on fashionable North Michigan Avenue, he encountered ragged, hungry, humiliated men begging in one form or another for nickels and dimes. Both pity and terror arose from the sight of long bread lines, of men sleeping under bridges and on the benches of Grant and Lincoln parks, of jungles of shacks ("Hoovervilles," they were dubbed) on the outskirts of the city, and of war veterans selling apples on street corners. The contrast between these miserable people and those with whom he associated professionally and socially was great enough to stab any fortunate one, and especially one so conscientious as he, with guilt feelings.

He could hardly feel *personally* guilty, however, and despite such anxieties as he may have felt concerning the public welfare, his own life entered smoothly upon what, in retrospect, might seem its happiest decade. As always before, it was a full, active life, containing a great variety of interests.

His work in the law office naturally continued to absorb the bulk of his time and energy. The overall effect of the Depression upon Cutting, Moore and Sidley was to expand its practice almost in proportion to the contraction of Chicago business in general, and to change its character. Probate work grew relatively less important as the firm became involved in the enormous job of picking up and trying to put back together the shattered pieces of financial structures which it, if to a lesser extent than some other firms, had helped to build in the 20's. Hence fifty-hour work weeks continued to be Stevenson's common lot, and he had difficulty breaking away for weekends or vacations.

He had energy left over, however, for an extremely active social life. He and Ellen had multitudes of friends. Regarded as one of the most attractive couples in the city, they were invited everywhere: and when in 1930 they moved from East Walton to a larger, more luxurious apartment on Lake Shore Drive, they increased the amount of entertaining they did. At every party Ellen sparkled, with her beauty and gaiety and quick intelligence, in a way that made her husband immensely proud—and some of their friends would remember in later years that he had been perfectly content to let her be the focus of attention, remaining himself in the background, enjoying her with the others.

He began to take part in civic activities. Conscience led him to work with the Lower North Side Community Council. Through this activity, and through work with Hull House, of whose board of trustees he later became a member, he saw the darker side of that economic crisis which he viewed topside through his work as a financial lawyer.

But by far the most important of his civic activities, in its effects upon the city's future and upon his own, was his work with the Chicago Council on Foreign Relations. Organized in 1922, the council was an educational enterprise designed to infuse the capital of Midwest isolationism with some knowledge of, and active interest in, American foreign policy. Most of its members were League of Nations advocates whose local aim was to counteract in part the influence of Colonel Robert McCormick's reactionary nationalism as expressed through the Chicago *Tribune*. The membership was a highly prestigious one. Stevenson's mother was on the council's executive committee in the early 30's; so were William Pratt Sidley, the head of Stevenson's law firm, and Mrs. Harriet (John P.) Welling, Stevenson's good friend. Stevenson himself was on the committee by 1930 when the council hired, as its executive director, a brilliant, dynamic young man named Clifton Utley, whose leadership would help to make the council a major influence upon Chicago's intellectual life.

Utley's introduction to Adlai Stevenson took place at four o'clock on a winter afternoon in 1930, in the office of George Richardson, manager of the Marshall Field estate and then president of the council. It was a meeting of the executive committee. Utley would not remember that Stevenson made any particular impression upon him, however—then or for many months thereafter. Stevenson was considerably younger than the other committee members, who were all very distinguished people, and he said little at these early meetings. Utley was perhaps more impressed by Ellen Stevenson, who, with her mother and younger sister, Betty (Mrs. Pirie), became a member of one of the three classes in foreign affairs that Utley taught at Lake Forest during those early Depression years.[3]

A natural correlative of council work was an active interest in International House when this was established, with Rockefeller money, at the University of Chicago in 1932. Stevenson became a member of International House's board of governors.

III

On October 10, 1930, the Stevenson's first child, a son, was born. They named him Adlai Ewing Stevenson III. Three days later the proud father informed his mother that "family matters are progressing satisfactorily—the young man is losing some of his enchanting birthday appearance—in short, he's beginning to look more human tho he still has some distance to go." Ellen was still "terribly weak." The baby was promptly dubbed "Big Boy" and soon became, in his father's opinion, the "funniest one-man show in the world," so much loved and enjoyed by his parents that they had difficulty making up their minds to follow through on long-laid plans for a vacation abroad in the late spring of 1931. Stevenson badly needed a vacation, however; he felt that he was going "stale," and his eyes were beginning to bother him.

He and Ellen sailed for Europe, leaving Big Boy in the hands of Alverta Duff in Bloomington. They visited Buffie and Ernest Ives in Copenhagen. Ives, having been transferred northward from Constantinople, was approaching the end of his tour of duty in the capital of Denmark. He'd soon be transferred to Pretoria. He and Buffie had insisted that Adlai and Ellen, and Mrs. Helen Stevenson, must visit them in Denmark before the Pretoria transfer was made, for Copenhagen, they said, was "wonderful." It was, too, as they presented it to their guests. Adlai called it an "epic experience." He also said, in a letter written to Buffie, Ernest, and his mother from Stockholm, that "Cutting, Moore and Sidley seems charmingly remote now and I haven't worn glasses for two weeks."

In Stockholm they were lavishly entertained by American legation friends of Ives's. Even the "horrible news" he heard there about the "current condition of the stock market" failed to dampen their spirits, though it sharpened Adlai's awareness that Sweden, with its mixed economy of cooperatives and of government and private enterprise, seemed remarkably immune to the world-wide economic collapse....

In late June the Stevensons were back in Chicago, refreshed and renewed. Adlai plunged again into a busy, various life, and if he had any personal anxiety, it may have been over the question of whether or not he was, in actual fact, to gain a partnership in Cutting, Moore and Sidley. Five years had passed since he joined the firm, as 1932 came on, and he was well aware that six years was about the average elapsed time for this firm between the hiring of a clerk and his acceptance, if successful, into partnership. He had no hint from the senior partners concerning his own acceptability.... But if he had such anxiety, it was more than balanced by a new strand of happiness which wove into his life in the autumn of 1931. He was again to become a father....

The second Stevenson son was born on July 7, 1932. He was formally named Borden, after Ellen's family. Informally he was dubbed "Squeak." Both children gave their parents immeasurable delight. "If laughter is an intoxicant," said the father, "I am perpetually tight." He'd remember particularly that when Big Boy was a year and a half old he suddenly took to making imaginary snowballs under the table, then rising up and throwing them hurriedly at his mother, who dodged them laughingly, or pretended to be hit by them and dismayed. Big Boy had also developed a strategy for dealing with admonishment or threatened correction. "If you ask him to do *anything* he finds uncongenial ... he takes on an injured expression and says, 'Addie got a cold!'" wrote Adlai to his mother. By that time, Squeak had become "very large and handsome" and said "ga, ga," and laughed out loud at his elder brother all the time.

They were gloriously happy.... But their bright, cheerful private lives— and the lives of the fortunate social class—stood out in stark contrast to the gloom that spread and darkened throughout the country as America sank deeper and deeper into the slough of Depression. Even if Stevenson were not (as he would insist he was not) a "very thoughtful person" at that time, the contrast could not but impress him. Later, coupled with his view of

Republican Depression policies, it would become one of the major determinants of his political feeling and thinking.

As the months passed he was forced to recognize that organized class conflict of a kind theretofore regarded as a unique European phenomenon was by no means impossible in America. Others seemed to welcome this fact; it horrified him and would have horrified him even if his class status had been less privileged, for he remained by temperament and philosophy a peacemaker, committed to reasonableness. Reasonableness itself, however, was outraged as the spring of 1932 came on. By that time forty percent of the possibly gainfully employed were unemployed in Chicago. Hunger stalked the food capital of the world, while surpluses pressed livestock and crop prices down to, and below, the cost of producing them on Stevenson farms and those other farms his father had managed.

Surely the only power great enough to challenge successfully the Great Depression was the power of the federal government. Yet government presented, to a politically minded young man, a spectacle of confusion and impotence as educative as it was unedifying through those dismal years.

Hoover's tragedy was not that he was coldhearted or indifferent to human suffering. Rather was it that he and his colleagues remained helpless prisoners of rigid, inhuman preconceptions. The President had apparently invested most of the moral energy of his highly moralistic nature in the belief that prosperity depends upon the activities of businessmen, that jobs are created or provided by businessmen, and that such direct economic aid as the federal government gave in this emergency should therefore be limited to businessmen. He displayed no awareness of the fact that total national income must be so distributed as to be effective in the market place, that mass purchasing power must match mass productive power, if economic disaster is to be avoided. Adlai Stevenson laughed when someone, in a vulgar but remarkably apt metaphor, said that Hoover's economic policies were based on the theory of "feeding the sparrows by feeding the horse"—but he could not laugh at the effect these policies produced. And Hoover's was one of the examples he would have in mind when, in later public speech, he repeatedly inveighed against the dangers of stereotyped "political thinking," the "lazy preference" for "slogans" and "labels" and omnibus "isms" over the "rigors of rational thought" and direct, clear-eyed observation. As for himself, "I have no fixed principles by which every issue is to be *automatically* resolved. . . ." [4]

Nevertheless the Republican party, its Old Guard firmly in control, in June nominated Herbert Hoover for a second term and mapped a campaign strategy that stressed the international causes of the Depression and blamed the obstructive tactics of a Democratically controlled Congress for the administration's inability to act effectively in the growing emergency.

The Democratic National Convention met in the Chicago Stadium the last of June. The meeting was remarkably harmonious. Adlai Stevenson, who observed a good portion of the proceedings from the gallery, felt no such excitement and witnessed no such displays of acrimony as had marked his last Democratic convention (that of 1924), for there was not, this time, a really close competition among the top three candidates for the Presidential nomination.

Speaker John Nance Garner of Texas was one of the three, but the fact that he was William Randolph Hearst's choice indicated personal qualities that made him unacceptable to the decisive liberal wing of his party. Al Smith was still in the running, but could be nominated only if there was a deadlock between Garner and the front-running candidate. The latter was fifty-year-old Governor Franklin Delano Roosevelt of New York, who received a majority of the delegated votes on the first ballot and was nominated on the fourth, with Garner as his running mate.

Franklin Roosevelt at the time of his nomination was widely regarded as an amiable weakling, so eager to please everyone, so needful of being personally liked, as to be incapable of truly bold, decisive action. Of his personal charm, Stevenson had direct experience during the campaign. The Democratic candidate for governor of Illinois that year was Henry Horner, the probate judge of Cook County. Since much of the practice of Cutting, Moore and Sidley had been probate work, Stevenson had had many professional contacts with Horner and the two became good personal friends. They shared a passion for Lincolniana, of which Horner was an avid collector, and often discussed the role of Stevenson's maternal ancestors in early Illinois history. Particularly did they talk about Jesse Fell. Horner was intensely interested in the three-page autobiography in Lincoln's handwriting, now in the possession of Adlai's cousin Emmett Richardson, executor of the estate of Adlai's great-aunt Fanny Fell. Through Stevenson, Horner hoped to obtain the priceless document for the State Historical Library in Springfield—and perhaps it was in the nature of a "bribe" that Horner took Stevenson with him to call upon Roosevelt in the latter's campaign train that autumn.[5]

A long line of politically important men was passing through the car in which Roosevelt sat, and as Stevenson joined the line with Horner he expected no more than a perfunctory handshake from the candidate. Instead, Roosevelt recognized the young man as soon as Horner pronounced his name, recalling that F.D.R.'s father, James Roosevelt, had been a friendly acquaintance of the first Adlai Ewing Stevenson and that Lewis Stevenson had played important roles at both the New York and Houston conventions and in the drafting of agricultural planks that remained substantially unchanged in the platform of 1932. The zest and magnetism of the man seemed to Stevenson almost irresistible.

When election day came, Roosevelt's victory, though decisive, was less overwhelming than might have been expected under the circumstances, and during the four months intervening between election day and the inauguration of March 4, there was a rising tide of financial panic. A wave of banking holidays, declared by state governors, swept the country in February. Trade was reduced to a barter basis in hundreds of communities. A virtually complete economic paralysis, wholly unprecedented, wholly terrifying, gripped the country as the fateful month of March came on.

IV

Saturday, March 4, 1933. . . . That morning the banking system of America ceased to function. That morning the Democratic party—that loose collection of dissident elements, flawed by a score of self-contradictions—was to assume control of both the legislative and executive branches of government, for the first time since 1918. What would it do? What would the new President do? What could anyone do. . . ?

Adlai and Ellen Stevenson were in Washington that day. They had obtained tickets to the inaugural festivities through their good friend James H. Douglas, Jr., who in March of '32 had accepted appointment as fiscal Assistant Secretary of the U.S. Treasury, and through Senator J. Hamilton Lewis, Democrat and Stevenson friend from Illinois. Buffie and Ernest Ives were also in Washington. Ernest had completed his tour of duty in Africa and was to be stationed for several months in the capital between assignments abroad. Because Adlai was suffering from an ear infection, he dared not take his seat with the others on the great square, immediately below the flag-and-bunting bedecked platform at the Capitol's east front, for it was yet winter in Washington and exposure to the cold would be dangerous to him. Instead, he listened to the ceremony huddled beside a radio, like millions of his fellow Americans.[6]

Those millions were gripped by a fear as gray and chill as the sky above the Capitol dome. The oath was administered by Chief Justice Charles Evans Hughes. Then, in a ringing, confident, mellow voice, the new President of the United States addressed his fellow Americans.

First he said, "Let me assert my firm belief that the only thing we have to fear is fear itself—nameless, unreasoning, unjustified terror which paralyzes needed efforts to convert retreat into advance." What caused the present crisis? Not a blind impersonal force, but living and all-too-fallible men, said Franklin Roosevelt; the trouble flowed from the grasping actions of "the rulers of the exchange of mankind's goods." And such men, in control of government, had proved their inability to cope with the evils they had produced. "True, they have tried, but their efforts have been cast in the pattern of an outworn tradition. . . . The money changers have fled from their high seats in the temple of our civilization."

If necessary, the new President declared, he would not hesitate to ask the Congress for "broad executive power to wage a war against the emergency, as great as that which would be given me if we were in fact invaded by a foreign foe." The declaration rang in ears that, for three stagnant years, had heard mostly from government abstract moralistic reasons for not doing what the people wanted it to do. The people, this new leader said, "have registered a mandate that they want direct, vigorous action. . . . They have made me the present instrument of their wishes. In the spirit of the gift I take it."

Speech like this, in these circumstances, was itself action—passionate action! Adlai Stevenson had had a sense of this from the moment he set foot in Washington: there was a new excitement in the air, an electric energy, which made him long to have some part in the history about to be made. He had hinted as much to an old family friend, Harold Ickes, who was the new Secretary of the Interior, and had been surprised when Ickes pounced on the vague suggestion. The New Deal would need bright, eager, energetic young men—men able to plunge boldly into new, uncharted country. Like a magnet, the administration would draw such men to Washington. . . .

On Sunday, March 5, the banking holiday would be made national; the Congress would be called into an extraordinary session; and the export of gold and all dealings in foreign exchange would be prohibited. Thus the country would go part way off the gold standard—and this was but a slight shadow of coming events. Soon the country would go all the way off gold into a managed currency, which would be promptly inflated. In orderly fashion, and with no renewal of panic, the banks would be reopened, their individual deposits soon insured up to ten thousand dollars through a Federal Deposit Insurance Corporation.

Adlai Stevenson thereafter would live his life against a background of positive government, some of his life in the midst of that government.

CHAPTER ELEVEN

FOR Adlai Stevenson the Depression meant no sharp break in the continuity of his life but only the addition of another growth ring to his organically developing character. There was no radical difference of substance between it and the earlier growths. It was permeated by many of the same basic values, most of the same essential attitudes. Though there was inevitably a change of emphasis among them as his total self enlarged through experience, all his former selves remained alive in him, organically joined, including the well-behaved little child, the over-mothered schoolboy, the insouciant Princeton man, the Chicago man about town, the reluctant lawyer. The viability of these several selves widened the range of his possible reaction to stimuli. It provided him with multiple levels of response; and he would become able to shift from one to another of these with a smooth ease baffling to those who, knowing him well in some one of his aspects in the 1950's, believed that they knew *him*, totally, intimately. The latter knowledge, in so far as it could be achieved at all, depended upon an intimate knowledge of his ancestors and of their effects upon him—for his ancestors, too, remained alive in him. Especially Jesse Fell.

Hence the symbolic aptness of the fact that Jesse Fell's friendship with Abraham Lincoln provided one of the chief means of Adlai Stevenson's friendship with Henry Horner, who was inaugurated as governor of Illinois in 1933; and that this in turn led to a meeting with Franklin Roosevelt, whose historic role was to prevent that utter break with the American past that political upheaval might otherwise have produced. Historical tradition, personified by Jesse Fell, was vital to Adlai Stevenson. It was a main source of his innate conservatism, that moderation which, in the 1950's, would make him unacceptable to the "give 'em hell" type of politician in his own party. In the 1930's, coupled with his personal observations of the Soviet experiment in 1926, it prevented his seeking primary cues where so many American intellectuals were seeking them, in Moscow.

Not that he was wholly unsympathetic with the motives that prompted other young men—some of them in his own economic and social class—to don the red cap and the moujik blouse.* He might even honor those who suffered and died (brave and honorable young Americans did die in Spain in '36) for their belief that communism was infinitely preferable to fascism, on humane grounds, and was fascism's only alternative. But he was not himself tempted nor conscience-driven in that direction. No descendant and emulator of Jesse Fell, that firm defender of free speech in Bloomington during the Civil War, was likely to regard the sacrifice of essential civil liberties as a legitimate means to any political end; these liberties, he would say, *were* an end of government as well as a means. Nor would he admit, in the Depression's darkest hour, that the sacrifice was necessary to the cure of economic ills. On the contrary, he insisted then and always afterward that a full and free expression of all ideas, attitudes, even prejudices on public questions is an essential of political stability and progress in any society. Out of this freedom, as he clearly saw—out of this ferment of controversy—the

---

* The phrase is from Scott Fitzgerald's *Echoes of the Jazz Age,* published by *Scribner's* magazine, November 1931.

Roosevelt programs emerged, giving the lie to Marxist predictions of an immediate total collapse of American capitalism.

Thus the New Deal was, for him, a continuation of the American Way as envisaged by such diverse American leaders as Jefferson and Jackson and Lincoln, Bryan and Wilson, George Norris and La Follette. He watched its development with an avid interest after he returned from the inauguration, and the brief holiday following it, to a Chicago desk piled high with work. "The routine of life here quickly dispels holiday memories, and by this time I hardly feel I've been away," he wrote his ailing mother rather wearily in early April, "except for the children, who surprise me every night." The routine seemed to him particularly monotonous and dull after the excitement of Washington, an excitement that rose steadily higher as the Congress, applauded for doing so even by a good portion of the Republican press, rubber-stamped one after another of Roosevelt's revolutionary proposals.

True, Stevenson's own life continued very active through the spring. In early April he and Ellen believed they had found their future home—an old farmhouse, with barn and other outbuildings, on thirteen acres of the highest ground in Lake County; it was just four miles from the Lake Forest station, had a lovely view in all directions, and could be bought for approximately fifteen thousand dollars. (They were destined never to buy it.) During that same month, he concurred in Dave Merwin's decision to cut *Pantagraph* dividends by twenty-five percent, because of declining revenue, and advised his mother to reduce her expenditures accordingly. That winter he had been repeatedly tested as a chairman of meetings of the Council on Foreign Relations, and had not been found wanting by Clifton Utley and fellow members of the executive committee; as a result he was nominated for president of the council, and was elected in May.[1]

But these activities did not suffice to stifle his yearning for a part in what Ernest Lindley was soon to call the "Roosevelt Revolution." He hoped that Harold Ickes would not forget. As it turned out, however, he was brought to Washington not by Harold Ickes but by George Peek, whom the new Secretary of Agriculture, Henry A. Wallace, had called to the capital as organizer and first head of the Agricultural Adjustment Administration. Peek had taken with him a friend of Stevenson's named Wayne Chatfied-Taylor, of Chicago, with whom Stevenson had often discussed the farm problem—so when Peek began recruiting lawyers for the AAA staff, Chatfied-Taylor told him about Stevenson.

Thus, within four months after the New Deal's initiation, Adlai Stevenson was a working member of it. He obtained a leave of absence from the law firm—though Sidley warned that, upon his return, he might not be given the same position he then held. In the hot Washington July of 1933 he became a special assistant to the General Counsel of the AAA, with the formal title of Special Attorney and a salary (it seemed to him munificent) of sixty-five hundred dollars per annum, less the fifteen percent deducted by the Federal Economy Act of March. Ellen and the boys remained for the summer in the house Adlai and she had rented in Lake Forest, while Adlai lived as a bachelor with Ernest Ives and John Kennedy in the Kennedy home at 2121 Bancroft Place. (Mrs. Kennedy, the former Ellen Bruce Lee, who had undertaken to float Adlai in society during the youth's holiday visit with his family in Washington in 1918, was spending the summer at Gracelands, her family estate in West Virginia. Buffie was staying with Helen Stevenson at Charlevoix.) Immediately he was plunged into such a fever of work that he saw little of Ives and virtually nothing of Kennedy.[2]

"The work is complicated but interesting and vastly important," he explained in a letter to Ellen.

> In essence, we're creating (what amounts to) gigantic trusts in all the food industries, to raise prices and eliminate unfair competition, thereby increasing returns to the farmers ultimately. Everyone from flour millers to mayonnaise manufacturers are here and each day I hear all about the troubles of a different industry in conferences, then spend the night drafting a remarketing agreement to correct them. Then the objections begin to flow in from all over the country. Finally we hold public hearings, and at last the Sec'y of Ag. signs and approves the agreement, etc., etc.

Most of his work, which later involved a good deal of travel for the purpose of holding public hearings, had to do with special crops—particularly tree crops on the West Coast. Oranges were ripening in California's orange groves by the time the Agricultural Adjustment Act was signed into law: there was enormous pressure upon the legal division to execute swiftly the marketing agreements covering them; and Stevenson probably drafted more of these than anyone else. The work was so frenzied that he had no time for casual friendly intercourse with fellow staff members, one of whom was an attractive, thin-faced young lawyer named Alger Hiss. Felix Frankfurter had sent Hiss down from Harvard in 1929 to serve as secretary to the ancient and honorable Justice Oliver Wendell Holmes—the highest honor Frankfurter bestowed upon his students—and he now embarked upon a career in the federal service.

Ellen and the boys came to Washington in September ("and am I happy!" Adlai wrote his mother, now returned to Bloomington). They moved into rather too large a house in Georgetown. ("We may rattle a bit," wrote Adlai.) He continued to work ten-hour days. But it renewed him to come home at night to his family. Watching the daily growth, mentally and physically, of Big Boy and Squeak was literally re-creative.

As 1933 drew to a close, the emergency pressures upon the AAA legal staff slackened. By that time, however, a Federal Alcohol Control Administration was being set up to exercise control over liquor prices, production, and distribution quotas and to administer the distillers' code developed through the NRA. There was an immediate demand by the control committee (Joseph L. Choate, Jr., of New York was its director: Willard L. Thorp was among its other four members) for men to staff its legal division. Since the FACA was a subsidiary of the AAA, its staff could be most easily recruited through transfers from the AAA legal division, and Adlai Stevenson was asked if he would accept such a transfer. He said he would. So in January of 1934 he became assistant general counsel of this newest of the fifteen major special agencies thus far established by the Roosevelt administration—and was again working ten-hour days.

His tour of duty with the FACA lasted eight months, during which he had a good deal to do with establishing the administrative structure of the agency as well as with the application of controls to the industry. Perhaps the most pleasant episode of the period was an official trip to the Hawaiian Islands, where he organized the wholesale liquor dealers into a regional board to administer liquor codes. Ellen accompanied him on this trip. She was photographed with him as they were about to disembark from the *Lurline* for their nine-day stay. The photograph, printed in a Honolulu newspaper and later mounted in a family scrapbook, showed both Ellen and Adlai wearing leis and wearing, too, rather wan, sheepish smiles. . . .

He resigned his government position in September and returned to Chicago, resuming his work as an associate of Cutting, Moore and Sidley. A few weeks later he was appointed to two positions on governmental bodies. By the NRA, he was appointed government member of the code authority for the flour milling industry; by the FACA, he was appointed government member of the code authority for the wine industry. Stories and photographs of him appeared in the press, as the appointments were announced. He was rapidly becoming one of the best known young civic leaders in Chicago, and this fact was of course an asset to his law firm. It helped overcome whatever reluctance some of the partners may have had about accepting him as one of them, with the result that, early in 1935, small news stories in the Chicago press announced that Adlai E. Stevenson had become one of eleven partners (there were by then sixteen associates also) in the firm of Cutting, Moore and Sidley. He thereby gained not only added prestige in his profession but also a marked increase in his annual income: his share of the firm's profits soon amounted to between eighteen and twenty thousand dollars a year.

Soon after Adlai and Ellen returned with the boys to Chicago, in the autumn of 1934, Mrs. Helen Stevenson came there, moving into the Churchill Hotel at 1255 North State, just a block from the apartment where her son lived. She was unwell; her health had steadily deteriorated since her husband's death. Dr. Ed Stevenson, for one, was convinced that her physical ills were due in part to her state of mind, and certainly she was profoundly depressed.[3]

Now that both children were wholly independent of her, having outgrown even their need for her loving advice, they sometimes seemed actually to resent a little her attempts to advise them, help them. Restlessly she had moved about the country and gone abroad, seeking in vain for that vividness of experience she had formerly known. The world had gone stale—and she was tired. More and more she found herself turning toward the past, toward older members of her family who had known her parents and herself as a little girl. She strove to renew herself through these living repositories of the family tradition; sometimes she *was* renewed, but at other times, measuring herself against the past, she seemed more than ever diminished. She measured, she felt, so very small. "Who would ever think I was a Fell!" she wrote her aunt Rachel.

After a while she felt better. The doctors said it would not harm her to travel: her blood pressure was a little high, but not alarming, and though there were vascular changes, these were not alarming either.

She died very suddenly in November of 1935. She had been on a trip; she stopped in Milwaukee in order to be near Cousin Harriet Richardson.* There she became ill and went to a hospital. . . . Down in Bloomington a new building was being erected to house the *Pantagraph,* and one of Helen Davis Stevenson's last acts was to pen a public message to the newspaper, congratulating it on the laying of the cornerstone.

The funeral service, in Bloomington's Unitarian church, was preached by the Reverend Rupert N. Holloway, of Madison, Wisconsin. She was buried beside her husband in the Bloomington cemetery.

Yet in her son, much of her essential self lived on, helping him to grow steadily toward that recognized greatness she had long believed would be his. Her influence upon him was greater by far than any other person's had been, or could ever be. Though it seemed overly aggressive to some observers, the love she had given him was of a kind he apparently needed to ensure the inner security, the serenity of spirit, that was so strongly characteristic of him, enabling him in later years to bear with grace, with apparent gaiety even, strains and disappointments severe enough to break most men. There was a fortunate balance between reticence and expressiveness in his handling of emotions, and for this his mother's influence may have been largely responsible. She expressed, even extravagantly, her love for him, forcing him to respond in kind and thus keep liquid emotional assets which might otherwise have frozen in the reserves that seemed natural to him.

Again there was a balance of death with new life in Adlai's immediate family. On February 7, 1936, Ellen gave birth to her third son. He was named

* This was Harriet Fyffe Richardson whose *Quaker Pioneers* is mentioned in notes for chapters one and two of this work.

John Fell, after an English ancestor five generations removed from Jesse Fell, eight removed from Adlai Ewing Stevenson II.

The future seemed by then to be rushing into the present, ruthlessly shoving the past farther and farther back. Aunts, uncles, cousins in swift succession followed Lewis and Helen Stevenson into the grave. "Aunt Lizzie and Cousin Charlie passed away within a week of each other, and I wasn't able to get down for either funeral," wrote Adlai to Buffie early in 1937. "Our family is vanishing rapidly and it gives one a wistful, lonely feeling. But I suppose it happens to everyone and that we must realize that we've suddenly become the older generation now."

II

On January 1, 1937, the law firm became Sidley, McPherson, Austin and Burgess. ("Sounds like a trunk falling down stairs, doesn't it?" commented Adlai in a letter written to Buffie, who, with Ernest and Timmy, had just transferred from Algiers to Stockholm.) And, as a partner, Stevenson was given increasingly difficult and important assignments. He often complained, in brief and hurried notes to Buffie, that he was "on a day and night shift at the office," so that he saw John Fell but once a week, on Sunday, during most of his youngest son's first years. ("Ho hum!" he wrote in January of '37. "It's Saturday night and I'm still at the d—— office. John Fell thrives— tho I haven't been home in time to see him since last Saturday.") But his complaints were mild responses to extreme provocations. Actually the intense pressure of work upon him failed to crush his cheerful good humor; this continued to be one of the most attractive and remarkable things about him, his associates later remembered.

In the summer and fall of 1938, for instance, Commonwealth Edison Company, with some of its subsidiaries, including the Public Service Company of Northern Illinois, was preparing to issue over forty-two million dollars worth of debentures, some thirty-three million dollars of first-mortgage bonds, plus other series of bonds that brought the total new financing to approximately eighty million dollars. At that time the SEC was a recent development; there were few precedents to guide the performance of a huge, complicated job. Involved was the preparation of the prospectus and the registration statement that must be filed with the SEC. The latter was a lengthy document, one hundred or so typed legal-length pages, detailing the history of each company, its earnings, its organizational structure, and so on. The most scrupulously detailed accuracy was required, and the work had to be completed rapidly.

The law firm, representing the underwriters of the loan, assigned Adlai Stevenson to work on the project with Edward D. McDougal, Jr. (McDougal, a Princeton graduate of the class of 1918, had become a partner in the firm in 1930.) The two worked night and day with Willis Gale, who was then financial vice-president of Commonwealth Edison and its subsidiaries (in the 1950's he would be chairman of the board), in the Commonwealth Edison offices at 72 West Adams. They'd go down at midnight to Toffenetti's restaurant, for coffee and a sandwich and a breath of fresh air, returning often to work hours more. McDougal would remember that he became brusque and short-tempered under the pressure, and that Gale became even more so, but that Stevenson was unfailingly cheerful.[4]

Yet, despite his work load, his extracurricular activities continued. Along with Dutch Smith, he joined the board of directors of the Illinois Children's Home and Aid Society, a private corporation with an annual budget of many hundreds of thousands (the budget would be over a million by the 1950's) that cared for orphans and children from broken or impossibly bad homes, placing these in foster homes where their care was paid for by the society or, in many cases, arranging for their legal adoption. Adlai Stevenson became a vice-president (he was fourth vice-president, then third, then second), serving in this office from January of '45 and remaining on the board of directors into the 1950's. He also continued as a member of the Hull House board of directors into the 1950's.

At the request of Governor Horner, the Illinois State Liquor Commission, and State Senator James O. Monroe (Democrat of Collinsville), he drafted a bill that would separate wine and beer legislatively from distilled spirits, making the former subject to lower taxes and more liberal regulations of sale and distribution. There were several reasons why doing so seemed to Stevenson sound public policy and, drawing upon his experience with the FACA, he wrote the bill, which Monroe introduced into the state Senate the last of May and which was passed.

During the same spring Stevenson's name appeared for the first time in a major headline on the front page of a metropolitan daily. Above a by-line story by Charles N. Wheeler, political reporter, the Chicago *Herald-Examiner* placed the head:

DWIGHT GREEN POST MAY
GO TO A. E. STEVENSON

Walter J. Cummings Supports
Grandson of Ex-Vice-President;
Attorney for Utilities

Cummings was chairman of the board of the Continental Illinois National Bank and Trust Company and treasurer of the Democratic National Committee. The post for which he was reportedly supporting Stevenson was that of United States Attorney. Stevenson was identified as a "practicing Chicago lawyer" who "heretofore has not been identified with local politics," and it was deemed certain that the Cummings endorsement would carry considerable weight with the administration. However, "the political experts point out that [Stevenson] is connected with a Chicago law firm that represents the Illinois Bell Telephone Company, which Congress is about to investigate as a subsidiary of the A.T.&T." It was the "experts'" notion that "the government would not be likely to select its chief legal representative in Chicago from among lawyers close to the telephone company under present circumstances." At any rate, the post was not offered to Stevenson—and more than ten years would pass before his name was again linked, in headlines, with that of Dwight Green.

Shelby Singleton ("that grand old man," as Stevenson always called him) furthered the young lawyer's political education by persuading him into the Legislative Voters' League. The League's mission was "to promote good government through the agency of the State legislature." It watched the Illinois legislature with a critical eye. It prepared reports on the actions of individual members of the two houses and graded these according to its own high standards of government. It also endorsed candidates, though it was strictly nonpartisan.

When Stevenson became involved in it the organization was on the point of dissolution for lack of financial support (the Depression had hit it hard), but public announcement of this fact evoked what the Chicago *Daily News* termed (in November of 1937) an "overwhelming popular protest." In this crisis, when a man of prestige and vigor was required for the job, Adlai Stevenson was persuaded to accept the League presidency. He promptly initiated a fund drive which was sufficiently successful to enable the League to continue effective operation for a time.

This work with the L.V.L. undoubtedly helped Stevenson's political career later on; it gained for him the further respect and friendship of influential, public-spirited men. But it also proved to be, on occasion, a mild political embarrassment in later years. Some of the politicians attacked by the League while Stevenson was president of it were later key people in Stevenson's political campaigns.[5]

As if these activities were not enough, piled atop his law practice, he had other special assignments that drew heavily upon his time and energy. He became, in the late '30's, a director of the Personal Loan and Savings Bank. In January of 1937, when he was frantically busy with office work, he was coerced into acting as General Chairman of the President's Birthday Ball for Chicago. He was also involved, in '36 and '37, in attempts to salvage as much as possible for Ellen and Betty from the wreckage of certain Borden enterprises.

During the presidential campaign of 1936, when Governor Alfred M. Landon of Kansas was the Republican candidate, Stevenson served as finance director of the Democratic National Committee and state chairman of the National Council of Roosevelt Electors in Illinois. He also made his first major political speech, at Carlton College in Minnesota. Never in his life, he later confessed, did he work harder on a speech than he did preparing for this occasion. In terms of historical principle he developed what he believed to be a clear, unanswerable case for Roosevelt over Landon. The speech held the large crowd's attention and was well applauded. Afterward, Adlai, walking along a corridor of the auditorium building beside the college president, accepted the latter's congratulations in the rather smug belief that he had, indeed, earned them. In front of the two, however, walked a couple of students whose conversation they overheard. The students agreed that it had been a fine speech. "But," asked one of them, "could you tell which side he was *for?*" [6] After this, Stevenson could hardly believe that his effort was particularly helpful to Roosevelt, who, as a matter of fact, seemed not to need much help that year. The President was overwhelmingly re-elected, carrying every state except Maine and Vermont.

Repeatedly during these years Stevenson was requested to return to government service in Washington. In early May of 1937, for example, he was called to Washington by the Secretary of Labor, Frances Perkins, who offered him the position of Commissioner General of Naturalization and Immigration. He was then, and had for some time been, a director of the Immigrants' Protective League of Chicago. He was actively interested in the problems he would have handled as a commissioner, and the offer flattered him. He turned it down, however, without much hesitation. Thereafter, the trip was chiefly memorable to him because of a two-day tour that he and Ellen, who had accompanied him to Washington, made of the Charlottesville district of Virginia.

He had barely returned to Chicago from this trip when Senator J. Hamilton Lewis tried unsuccessfully to persuade him to accept appointment as Assistant Attorney General. A few weeks later he attended his fifteenth class reunion in Princeton.

In that crowded summer of '37 Ellen was looking forward eagerly to a trip to Ireland. Her great-aunt Lucy, Mrs. Kingsley Porter, owned Glenaeagh Castle in County Donegal, and the plan was that the Stevensons sail from New York on July 9, spend a week at the castle and another week motoring through southern Ireland, then sail home, returning to Chicago just one month after leaving it. Alas, when July 9 came, pressure of work forced Adlai to postpone sailing till July 23; when July 23 came, work pressure forced postponement till late August; and in early August Mrs. Porter cabled that she was renting the castle beginning August 5. There ceased to be any good reason for going to Ireland at all. Not until mid-August did he have his work enough under control so that he and Ellen could arrange a brief vacation in Bermuda, leaving New York on August 24, on the *Monarch of Bermuda,* and returning to Chicago September 11.

Despite occasional disagreements over his excessive busyness, he and Ellen were happy through those years. They delighted in their sons, but undoubtedly the happiest of their family activities was their development of a country home near Libertyville, only a few miles west from Lake Forest. They were delighted to find, one day, seventy acres of almost wild land on the Des Plaines River—gently rolling land dotted by the tallest, finest, oldest hard maples in all that region; land that could be reached then only by canoe up the river or on horseback. They bought the property and built upon it a flat-roofed house designed, mostly by Ellen herself, somewhat like a ship riding a gently rolling sea of grass. It had picture windows framing lovely views, second-floor porches like a ship's sun decks, and spacious rooms in which Ellen displayed her talent for interior design. Family heirlooms were moved up from Bloomington—relics of the Fells, the Osbornes, the Ewings, the Stevensons, which Adlai regarded as priceless. The house and adjoining garage-stable cost some thirty thousand dollars in what was yet a Depression year; there was an enormous amount of work to do around the place; but the investment of work and money was, they were convinced, more than compensated by dividends of happiness.

Then came catastrophe.

That autumn the Stevensons moved into town for a few months, and one evening, early in those months, the house caught fire. A disagreement between two local fire companies as to which was responsible for this new place delayed the arrival of the engines and promoted confusion among the crews when they did, at last, arrive. By the time Adlai and Ellen drove up their private roadway, the house of which they were so proud was beyond power of rescue. All that its owners could do was stand helplessly with their neighbors and watch the flames burst through windows and roof. Stevenson was heartsick, not so much because of the house itself, which was fully insured, as because of its furnishings, which were not. Especially was it agonizing for him to watch the destruction of family heirlooms. They were irreplaceable; he felt himself to be convicted of a breach of trust.

But when a neighbor came over to express his sympathy Stevenson merely shrugged, smiled ruefully, and stuck a cigarette between his lips. At that instant, a piece of burning debris arched through the air and landed at Stevenson's feet. Calmly he picked it up, lit his cigarette with it.

"Oh well," he said, "as you can see, we are still using the house." [7]

Within a few months the house had been rebuilt; it would remain, for all the years to come, his home, taking precedence in his affections even over 1316 East Washington, in Bloomington. "And it is very much home because I built it out of field and forest," he was quoted as saying in a Chicago newspaper in 1950. "I love it because I worked over every inch of it and so have my boys from their infancy."

III

In February, 1937, emboldened by the impotence of the League of Nations, demonstrated when Japan invaded Manchuria in '31 and contemptuously withdrew from the League at the first sign that sanctions might be imposed on her, Hitler reoccupied the Rhineland while France stood idly by. Mussolini had conquered Ethiopia. And there raged in Spain a bloody civil war which many recognized as a dress rehearsal for World War II.

Against the background provided by these dark events, the Council on Foreign Relations, of which Stevenson had become president in May of 1935, stood out more prominently every year as an important civic activity in Chicago. It was Clifton Utley's impression that Stevenson quite consciously used the Council presidency to develop himself, improving his techniques as a public speaker and as a leader in group enterprises.[8] As presiding officer, he was not, at first, outstandingly effective, but he quickly developed into an excellent public speaker, continuously called upon to address professional societies and businessmen's organizations. Thus the Stevenson style, which was to become nationally famous, became locally famous in the 1930's. A natural response to Princeton's double world, the style seems, at least in part, to have reflected the council's manner of conducting business. It *seemed* offhand. Actually it was carefully studied, as Utley well knew and as those who later disliked it (fearing and misunderstanding it) suspected. But it was a form of humility rather than egotism, being motivated by the conviction that it would be presumptuous of him, who was but a single fallible mortal, to present his wares to the multitudes as though they were solemn dicta from on high. Moreover, as Stevenson might have said, it is fallacious to assume that truth is always homely and honesty always blunt. It is an even greater fallacy to assume that inarticulate speech coupled with crude earnestness of expression is prima facie evidence of deep sincerity and noble purpose. To be earnest gracefully, to make an aesthetically pleasing gesture of the quest for truth—these are the marks of a truly civilized man.

But style was not all he learned from council work. He learned a great deal from the subject matter presentations of the famous speakers he introduced at public meetings, and even more from his personal conversations with them. Particularly did he learn from foreign correspondents of the Chicago *Daily News*. In those days the *News* had a brilliant foreign staff, and rarely did a correspondent return to Chicago without being called upon to address a council meeting. Thus, the meeting at which Stevenson was reelected to a second term as council president was addressed by Wallace R. Duell, who had just returned from two years in Berlin. Duell spoke that day on Hitler and Nazi Germany, stressing what he termed the "dangerous integrity" of the dictator.

Perhaps it was while Duell was speaking that Stevenson shaped certain of the ideas he expressed, in October of 1939, when he was principal speaker at the celebration of the eightieth anniversary of Bloomington's Unitarian church.

"There is nothing a jellyfish wants more than a rock," he said on that occasion, "and authoritarian political systems have gained a foothold in Europe because well-intentioned people had no program and little courage to carry a program through. In the Unitarian church we believe we can achieve necessary standards through free discussion and free inquiry." He remained sure that the totalitarian states, for all their seeming monolithic strength, must ultimately fail for lack of "wisdom." But he stressed the dangers which a questing, self-critical society faces when opposed by dictatorships. "Liberals tend to say we should suspend judgment until all the facts are in. The trouble with this attitude is that *all* the facts will never be in, and while 'good people' are withholding judgment the practical affairs of politics are taken over by those lacking social wisdom."

By the time he made this speech Stevenson was deeply involved with the problem of defending American civil liberties against the manifold pressures a war-racked world brought against them. As the year 1939 opened, he had accepted the chairmanship of a twenty-nine-member Civil Rights Committee of the Chicago Bar Association. "What is happening elsewhere in the world reminds us again of the importance of constant and vigilant protection of our own liberties," Stevenson had said in a public statement, as his chairmanship was announced.

It was as a result of this chairmanship that Stevenson first formed a working relationship with a young man who was to have a considerable role in the Stevenson future—a sandy-haired, lean-faced, rather dour-looking Scotch-American, thirty years old, named Carl McGowan.

McGowan had gone from the public schools in Paris, Illinois, to Dartmouth, graduating in 1932. After a year or so of odd-jobbing around his home town, he'd gone to Columbia Law School, receiving his degree in 1936. He'd then entered the law firm of Debevoise, Stevenson, Plimpton and Page, in New York—a young firm, two of whose senior partners, Francis Plimpton and William Stevenson, were old friends of Adlai Stevenson. When McGowan came to Chicago as an assistant professor in the Northwestern Law School, Stevenson, informed of McGowan's coming, asked him to lunch.

"He had forgotten, when making the date, that there was a Council on Foreign Relations luncheon that day, so when I showed up at his office he asked if I'd mind going there with him," McGowan would remember. "It was at the Palmer House, of course, and of course I did go with him." [9]

A little later Stevenson asked McGowan to help him with the civil rights committee work, preparing compendiums of the laws and the interpretations of the bill of rights in the various states.

On August 21, 1939, Adlai, Ellen, and their three boys were with the Dutch Smiths at Desbarats, Ontario. That day Stevenson, like virtually every other student of foreign affairs in the Western democracies, was stunned by the radio news that Hitler and Stalin had signed a nonaggression pact, hard on the heels of an announcement by the Nazi leader in Danzig that the hour of "deliverance" was at hand. One of the few constants in foreign affairs had been the implacable hostility of Nazi Germany and Communist Russia.

Ellen Smith would never forget how profoundly Adlai was disturbed by the news, nor how they all huddled beside the radio on September 1, listening hour after hour to news bulletins of Nazi bombs raining upon Warsaw and Nazi panzer units roaring across the Polish plains.[10]

On September 3, Britain and France declared war on Germany. Stevenson could at least be glad that Buffie, Ernest, and young Timmie were no longer in Europe. The year 1939 marked the retirement of Ernest Linwood Ives, after thirty years, from the Foreign Service of the United States. At a dinner in his and Buffie's honor in Washington, he was presented with a silver cigarette case engraved with the names of nineteen far-spaced stations at which he had served. They were ready for a settled life.

They would establish two homes. In the summers, thereafter, they would live at 1316 East Washington, in Bloomington, where Buffie would keep the house as it had been when she and Adlai were growing up—the same furniture, carpets, window curtains, color scheme. In the winters they would live in an early nineteenth-century log house, unpretentious but very comfortable and picturesque, on a 115-acre farm they purchased near Southern Pines, North Carolina.

CHAPTER TWELVE

I N September, 1939, Clark Eichelberger, director of the League of Nations Association and the Union for Concerted Peace Efforts, asked William Allen White to head a national Non-Partisan Committee for Peace through Revision of the Neutrality Law. The famous editor of the Emporia (Kansas) *Gazette* acceded to Eichelberger's request with some reluctance.[1] But he threw himself with characteristic energy into his task and was supported in this effort by two other leading Republicans, former Secretary of State Stimson and Colonel Frank Knox, publisher of the Chicago *Daily News* and Alf Landon's running mate in 1936. It can hardly be said that these three, or the committee as a whole, were particularly effective with Republican politicians (only twenty Republican House members voted for the revision; one hundred forty voted against it), but they were certainly effective with the country at large. The arms embargo was repealed, permitting exports to Britain on a cash-and-carry basis, and the move was supported by American public opinion in large part as a result of the White-Eichelberger enterprise. The experience encouraged these two, in April, 1940, to plan a new committee with wider terms of reference: they called it the Committee to Defend America by Aiding the Allies.

The need for it seemed urgent that month, as the Nazis occupied Denmark and invaded Norway; it seemed imperative in May, when the "phony war" ended on the western front with the lightning attack upon the Low Countries and France. A few days later White sent out dozens of telegrams from Emporia to influential men all over the country, asking for and receiving pledges of support for the new organization. Special attention was paid to Chicago, for it was clear that this city would be a major focus of the coming fight for public opinion, since it was the home of the archreactionary Chicago *Tribune* and the capital of Midwest isolationism. Quincy Wright, Clifton Utley, and Paul Douglas (he was then a city alderman as well as a professor of economics at the University of Chicago) agreed to serve, and strongly recommended that Adlai Stevenson be asked to become chairman of the committee's Chicago chapter.

Immediately both White and Utley called Stevenson, who, after consulting with his law partners, accepted the chairmanship. He then plunged into the most hectic and important public activity in which he had ever engaged up till then.

It was, to begin with, a big job of organization. Money must be raised, subchapters established, outstanding speakers obtained for giant rallies, and means developed for effective presentation of the committee's case through press and radio. Clifton Utley became the radio voice; the *Daily News* became the chief newspaper voice; and the Council on Foreign Affairs provided informed, dedicated, and highly prestigious leaders. Upon Stevenson's own energies and talents immense and often unexpected demands were made.

Not long after the fall of France, for example, while the Battle of Britain was being fought in the air, a public meeting was arranged in Mandel Hall at the University of Chicago by the Chicago student subchapter, with Edgar Ansel Mowrer, the famous *Daily News* correspondent, as speaker. Mowrer's name attracted a large crowd, but at the last moment some circumstance prevented his appearance. Stevenson, with no time to prepare, was called upon to pinch-hit.

"He was introduced that way, too—as a pinch hitter," recalled Walter Johnson, the student committee's faculty sponsor, years later. "The man who introduced him simply said, very flatly, that Mowrer couldn't be there, that Stevenson would speak instead. You could hear the sigh of disappointment from the crowd. Few of them knew much about Stevenson, most had probably scarcely heard of him. I can imagine no more trying situation for a speaker. But within three minutes he had that crowd's attention riveted on him. And he held it. He was magnificent! Afterward he was given what amounted to an ovation." [2]

The committee, during that hectic summer and autumn of an election year, did not take a merely general stand in favor of all aid short of war. It focused on specific issues. In mid-June, as France collapsed and Mussolini declared war, Stevenson and the Chicago chapter sent telegrams to Washington urging the government to release war planes to private manufacturers, who in turn would sell them to Britain and France. In late June Republican members of the Chicago chapter joined White in putting pressure on Republican Senators who threatened to deny the confirmation of Knox as Secretary of the Navy and Stimson as Secretary of War—appointments by Roosevelt which aroused great wrath among the G.O.P. Old Guard. The Chicago chapter joined other chapters in efforts to keep foreign policy from becoming a Presidential campaign issue. This end was largely achieved when the Republican National Convention at Philadelphia nominated Wendell Willkie and the Democratic National Convention, meeting in Chicago, nominated Franklin Roosevelt for a third term, with Henry A. Wallace as his running mate. White, Eichelberger, and Stevenson appeared before the Democratic platform committee and helped persuade it to write a plank pledging aid to the Allies. The committee also helped develop public support for Roosevelt's plan to exchange old-age destroyers for naval bases in British possessions in the Western Hemisphere, and for the Lend-Lease Bill a few months later.

"It was during this period," said Stevenson years later, "that Bill Blair first came into my life. He came in one day and volunteered to work for the committee." [3]

William McCormick Blair, Jr., then twenty-three, was a dark, slender, attractive young man. He was a cousin of Colonel McCormick (his father, a first cousin of the *Tribune* publisher, would be the colonel's closest surviving male relative by the mid-1950's). He had long been fascinated by politics; at the Groton School, in 1932, when he was fifteen, he had worked actively on behalf of Herbert Hoover. He had developed a serious sinus infection (he would deny that his efforts for Hoover had anything to do with it) which ultimately required several operations; it had prevented his enrolling in an Ivy League college. Instead, seeking relief for his sinus trouble, he had attended a succession of colleges in warm climates—the University of Hawaii, the University of California, the University of Arizona—receiving his A.B. degree from Leland Stanford University just a few days before he appeared at the Chicago White Committee office.

As a scion of one of the wealthiest, most distinguished, and most staunchly Republican families in the city, Blair's mere presence in the committee headquarters had a considerable persuasive value to the aid-Britain campaign. His joining the White Committee was construed by many as a direct and effective slap at Colonel McCormick, especially so since the *Tribune* publisher was one of the few politically active Republicans whom White openly detested and consistently opposed editorially, even in election years. ("He and his paper are a disgrace to American journalism," White used to say.) Young Blair himself may have been motivated, in part, by his own aversion to his Cousin Bertie.

Blair did much more than lend his presence to the cause. For two months he, with one helper, manned the headquarters at 86 East Randolph Street, serving a kind of apprenticeship for the role of facilitating officer and administrative assistant which he was later to play in the Stevenson organization. His dedication to the aid-Britain campaign was profound, and became all the more effective by reason of his urbane sophistication, his rare social charm. Everyone liked him. One of the first things he did was to go to a five-and-ten-cent store where he bought a number of toy model destroyers that he put on display in the headquarters street windows, with appropriate signs pointing up the need to support the destroyers-for-Britain plan.[4]

II

In Stevenson's view, during that summer of disaster for the Western democracies, the committee's most important job was to counteract the growing belief that Britain's cause was hopeless, now that she stood alone against overwhelming German and Italian might.

The battle for public opinion grew daily more bitter in Chicago, and personal attacks upon Stevenson, as local White Committee chairman, became numerous and venomous in the Chicago *Tribune*. Isolationist sentiment—though it remained a minority sentiment even in Chicago, according to a Gallup poll—was now well organized and richly financed through an America First Committee, headed by General Robert E. Wood of Chicago, president of Sears, Roebuck and Company.

Wood, Charles A. Lindbergh, and other prominent America Firsters insisted that their sole motive was to keep America out of the war; they claimed to be exclusively *national* patriots, and undoubtedly most of them were. Nevertheless, Lindbergh and others made speeches and wrote articles which seemed to contain an ugly strain of anti-Semitism—and there was no blinking the fact that many of the most vociferous America Firsters were openly sympathetic to Nazism and Fascism. Though America First publicly repudiated the support of the pro-Hitler German-American Bund, it did not reject the support of Father Coughlin's Christian Front, the American Destiny Party, the Ku Klux Klan (again resurgent), William Dudley Pelley's Silver Shirts, and the notorious publicist, George Sylvester Viereck. Strangely allied with these were American Communists (now that Stalin and Hitler were allies), Socialists, and Christian pacifists.

It seemed to Stevenson ominously significant that America First steadfastly refused to publish a list of its principal contributors. His own committee published such a list periodically, and announced that its books were open for inspection at all times. Nor could he fail to resent being dubbed, with his colleagues, a "cookie pusher," a "professional bleeding heart," a "warmonger," day after day in *Tribune* news and editorial columns (in Colonel McCormick's paper, news stories on political questions were really editorials) and from the platforms of America First rallies. He was finally goaded into writing a letter to the Voice of the People section of the *Tribune*, replying to one of the more virulent of that newspaper's attacks, in which he asserted that "the importance of the controversy warrants more sobriety" than was indicated by *Tribune* epithets, and went on to state the case of the committee whose local chapter he headed: "We think Hitler is a menace and detests democracy; he has said so. We think Britain is engaged in a death struggle to stop that menace. We think that, with our help, she can succeed. ... We know that no more aid for Britain would be great news in Berlin— and evidently in some quarters of our country."

The *Tribune* held the letter for eleven days before publishing under the heading, "From America Second." On that same day, its editorial was more viciously personal in its attacks on Stevenson than earlier ones had been. Four days later Stevenson had the dubious pleasure of seeing himself branded a coward by a *Tribune* letter writer who proved his own courage by signing his communication "Just a Veteran."

Thereafter Stevenson made no attempt to debate the issue in *Tribune* columns. He did accede to a request from the *Daily News*, in a front-page editorial, that he and the chairman of the Chicago America First Committee, Thomas S. Hammond (president and general manager of the Whiting Corporation), "get together behind the production program for a strong national defense." Hammond and he agreed that the United States must speed up its defense effort, and Stevenson seized the opportunity to plead that the whole foreign policy debate be kept on a high rational plane.

America does not want war, nor does it want Britain defeated. But Britain cannot win without our help on a tremendous scale. So we must decide in the critical weeks ahead how far we are going to help her, what risks we are willing to take. . . . I hope and pray that this issue can and will be presented to the people henceforth with the restraint and responsibility it deserves. Sincere, patriotic Americans can honestly disagree on this issue. . . . There has been too much suspicion, too many epithets, too little reason. The decisions we make this winter will affect our future for years, perhaps generations. Let us approach them in our best, not our worst, national tradition.

By the time he wrote this he had had a considerable education in the ways and means of influencing public opinion and in the hazards of controversy in areas where emotions grow strong. In early September he had helped arrange one of the largest public meetings ever held in Chicago—a giant rally of some sixteen thousand people (more than three thousand were turned away) in the Coliseum. It was held on Wednesday evening, October 18, with Stevenson presiding. As the crowd entered the great hall, it passed through lines of sign-carrying pickets: "Britannia Rules the Waves! Free Ireland and India," "Youth Needs a Job, Not a Gun," "Lest We Forget 1918 —40 Million Dead." Inside, the crowd heard itself characterized by Stevenson as a "decisive answer to Chicago's active minority, well intentioned and otherwise, of appeasers, defeatists, and foes of aid to Britain." They then listened to eloquent and impassioned pleas for British aid from Maury Maverick, former congressman and now mayor of San Antonio, Texas; Admiral William H. Standley, U.S.N., Ret.; Douglas Fairbanks, Jr., the motion picture actor; and Dorothy Thompson, author and newspaper columnist. They adopted, by roaring acclamation, a resolution calling for the extension to Britain of "all possible aid, compatible with our own defense requirements, to sustain her gallant resistance against Nazism and Fascism" and specifically urging "that 24 'flying fortresses,' as many other combat planes as can be safely released, and two mosquito boats be made available to Britain immediately."

A month later the Adlai Stevensons were hosts to Ambassador William C. Bullitt—envoy first to Russia, then France—when he came to address a Council on Foreign Relations meeting at the Palmer House. The crowd on that occasion, as on many others during these months, more than filled the hotel's Grand Ballroom and the adjoining Red Lacquer Room; hundreds who wished to attend had to be turned away.

"It was an exciting time," Stevenson himself recalled in a later year. "It was a knock-down-drag-out fight, really. The *Tribune* used to send photographers to photograph all empty seats, if any, in halls where we presented programs—and the *News* photographers photographed all the full ones. I'd be a dirty dog in the *Tribune* in the morning, and a shining hero in the *News* at night. . . ."

Nor was the fight always conducted according to the rules of fair play. As 1941 came on and advanced through spring into early summer, some America Firsters displayed an increasingly strong tendency to answer arguments with economic sanctions. Clifton Utley found his income reduced, his very livelihood threatened, through the cancellation of contracts by certain sponsors of his radio broadcasts. Adlai Stevenson himself suffered from pressures brought to bear upon him, and upon his law firm, by angry America Firsters. Fortunately for him, Donald F. McPherson, a senior partner of the firm, was president of the Council on Foreign Relations that year, and Sidley continued active in the council; but even so there were members of the firm who grumbled at the amount of time Stevenson was spending on committee work and over the withdrawal of business from the firm by clients who were bitterly hostile to the committee's activities. Moreover, some of the grumbling seemed, to Stevenson, justified. He offered to take a reduced share of the firm's profits for that year—an offer that Sidley refused.

Stevenson was hurt, too, by some of the things said to him, and about him, by men and women he'd always regarded as friends. One person said, "Adlai's trying to kill our sons." This cut him so deeply that years later, talking about those hectic months, he still cried out against it. "I was trying to *save* their sons!" he said. "I was convinced that aid to Britain was the only means, the only chance of our keeping out of the war."

III

Yet, almost from the moment he assumed his duties as committee chairman, he had been uneasily aware that he occupied an ambiguous position—and this sense of ambiguity had grown stronger as a result of his working relationship with William Allen White. Critical Kansans had long complained that White's great service to the state's political conservatism had been to focus liberal energies upon himself between elections in order to dissipate them at precisely the points (the polling booths in even-numbered years) where they might be truly effective—and he seemed determined to exercise this dubious leadership in the present moment of national peril.

The first instance of this occurred in the late summer and early autumn of 1940, when White was actively supporting Willkie for President while Clark Eichelberger supported Roosevelt.[5] Stevenson also supported Roosevelt. In September he contributed to the Chicago *Herald-American*, at that paper's request, a statement on "Why I'll Vote for Roosevelt" in which, while praising Willkie as a "sincere and forthright liberal," he condemned the isolationism of the candidate's "adopted party" (Willkie had been a

Democrat). A number of committee members, Stevenson included, wanted the organization to publish the voting records of incumbent isolationists running for reelection to the Congress. This seemed to them a logically necessary step, determined by the committee's *raison d'être*. White, however, flatly refused to permit it. To do so, he argued, would cause the committee to oppose nearly all the Republican members of Congress, destroying the committee's nonpartisan character! Thus balked, members of the committee's New York chapter formed a Non-Partisan Committee to Defeat Hamilton Fish, New York's notoriously isolationist if not actually pro-Hitlerian congressman. (Fish had organized a well-financed propaganda campaign against lifting the arms embargo, he had fought every measure of aid to the Allies, he had visited Germany and happily accepted the feting Nazis gave him there, he had asserted that German demands upon Poland were just demands.) White then wrote to Fish, October 18, disavowing every attempt to use the White Committee's name against him and adding, "I hope as Republicans we are united in our support of the Republican ticket from top to bottom in every district in every State." The letter, White made clear, was intended for publication—and Fish did publish it. But when the storm raised by this letter threatened to destroy the White Committee altogether, the Emporia editor wired Fish's opponents: "Our Committee is nonpartisan. As such we wish to see the Republicans and Democrats elected who support a program of aid to Great Britain. Our Committee naturally wishes to see appeasers, isolationists and pro-Germans defeated irrespective of party. You may make the widest use of this you wish." Whereupon Fish was reelected and continued to fight everything for which the White Committee stood.

In mid-November, White and Stevenson, with other Chicago chapter leaders, conferred on committee policy. They lunched at the Chicago Club and retired afterward to White's room for further discussion. Stevenson was deeply concerned by the rising rate at which British supply ships were being sunk by German submarines. So was White. But the older man hesitated to advocate the only step that could now be taken to help Britain at sea, namely the convoying of ships carrying American aid. It was, White said, another long step toward actual intervention. Stevenson argued that, unless this step were taken, the whole aid-Britain program might soon be rendered futile— and in this he was supported by Utley, Wright, and others of the Chicago group. White then agreed that a new national committee policy should be determined and went on to New York to shape it with Eichelberger and others on his national committee.

The new policy statement was issued on November 26, making front-page headlines in the nation's press. It asserted that, since the "life line between Great Britain and the United States is the sea route to the Western Hemisphere," the United States could "under no circumstances" permit it to be cut and "must be prepared to maintain it. . . ." It called for "a revision of

our international policy" through congressional action, including "a repeal
or modification of restrictive statutes which hamper this nation . . . when it
would cooperate with nations defending themselves from attack by nations
at war in violation of treaties with the United States." The implications were
clear. The committee favored American convoys to Britain and a repeal of
the Neutrality Act; and White, like all the others at the meeting, knew that
this was so. But he had barely returned to Emporia—weary and worried—
before he was wavering before the blasts of isolationists who charged him
with warmongering. Four weeks later, having been informed that the Scripps-
Howard newspapers were about to launch an attack upon him and the committee, he dictated a typical White letter to Roy Howard, head of the chain,
and, without consulting Eichelberger or anyone else on the White Committee, gave Howard permission to publish it. He flatly denied that he or
"our outfit are in favor of sending convoys with British ships or our own
ships, a silly thing, for convoys unless you shoot are confetti and it's not
time to shoot now or ever." He said, "It is not true even remotely that we
favor repealing [the Neutrality Act] to carry contraband of war into the
war zone. . . . If I was making a motto for the Committee to Defend America
by Aiding the Allies, it would be 'The Yanks Are Not Coming.'"

Stevenson read this in the papers with the same astonishment and dismay
that overwhelmed Eichelberger and the New York chapter. Rebellion against
this kind of leadership—a rebellion centered in New York but also widespread in other chapters—threatened to wreck the national organization.
Mayor La Guardia of New York personally denounced White for "doing
a typical Laval." White promptly tendered his resignation as chairman.
Stevenson and Utley took part in a four-way long-distance telephone discussion with Eichelberger in New York and White in Emporia, striving to
persuade White to reconsider. In vain. . . .

Twice in preceding weeks Stevenson had engaged in public debate with
Clay Judson of the America First Committee—once before the Hyde Park
League of Women Voters, once before the Chicago Bar Association. On
both occasions he had argued that the fall of Britain would inevitably mean
war for the United States. "You hear it said that this is not our war," he had
told the Bar Association. "I don't care whose war it is—the enemy is our
enemy, and if Britain can't stop, can't defeat that enemy now, then we can
confidently look forward to the day when, perhaps alone in the world, we
shall have to make a stand. . . . I do not think that with tyranny in four fifths
of the world, freedom can endure in one fifth. . . . Great Britain can win, but
I'm not sure that she will win—and she cannot win without us."

But his committee was vulnerable to precisely the attack Judson made
upon it—the one point in Judson's argument that deeply disturbed him.
Said Judson: "The question we must answer before it is too late is: 'Is this
our war?' If it is our war, then we should be in it without delay, even though

it will not be the comparatively simple job it was the first time we saved the world for democracy."

If this is our war, then we should be in it!

The point seemed to Stevenson unanswerable. And was not he himself arguing, with all the eloquence at his command, that this *was* our war?

One evening, as he rode a North Shore commuters' train toward the Deerpath station whence he would drive to his farm on St. Mary's Road, he read in the paper a "Letter to the Editor" that focused the matter so sharply that it probed painfully into his already aching conscience. The Committee to Defend America by Aiding the Allies continued to assert that its purpose and function were "to keep America out of war by keeping the war out of America." But this was palpably dishonest. So said the letter writer. The committee's real purpose and function were to condition American public opinion for full intervention in the war. To pretend otherwise was contemptible. For as matters now stood, the letter went on, there was no tenable "middle ground" between isolationism and outright intervention: one must choose one side or the other. . . .

And Adlai Stevenson, looking up from his paper, gazing out upon the greening April countryside, was forced to admit that, in his deepest self, he had made his choice long ago—as long ago as the fall of France. He was an interventionist. By the time his train came to a halt beside the tiny Deerpath station, he had decided that, at the earliest opportunity, whenever he could do so without letting down his committee colleagues, he would resign his position as committee chairman.[6]

The opportunity soon came.

He stood now at another critical point in his career. What mark had the decade left on his appearance?

At forty-one he had less hair on his head, for one thing; he had more flesh on his middle, for another. But he still had thin strands of hair atop his skull —a lonely-looking, obviously ephemeral wedge of hair—and his middle was by no means paunchy. He continued to bend upon the world an unusually bright, blue-eyed gaze, but in his latest photographs those eyes seemed darker, their gaze more narrowly lidded, than they had appeared to be in the early and middle thirties. His cheeks were perhaps a trifle fuller now than they had been then, and his lips no longer seemed to be twitching on the verge of a rather self-conscious smile. The aesthetic look of his earlier pictures remained, but it was coupled now with an appearance of firmness, self-assurance, poise.

Because he was aware of subtle shifts of atmospheric pressure in more realms of discourse than most men ever know, he was vulnerable to more and deeper hurts than most men in his external circumstances would be. But his heightened sensitivity was matched by a heightened capacity to withstand adversity and smile, and go forward without malice or self-pity along his chosen path. He was a prudent man, not prone to running un-calculated risks. He shied away from extravagance of emotion, or money spending, or self-expression in other forms, yet continued to admire in Ellen precisely these qualities and the spontaneity that goes with them.

His nervous and physical energy was almost limitless, and sometimes it moved him about, restlessly, from one activity to another. But for the most part it was a controlled energy. He walked very fast, but purposefully. He talked very fast, but always in complete sentences. His movements were quick, but precise. He could go at top speed, working under great pressure, yet relax instantaneously and completely when an opportunity for doing so presented itself. On planes or trains (latterly he had traveled mostly by plane) he was learning how to drop off to sleep in a flash, and awake in a flash, too, instantaneously alert as he opened his eyes from a seemingly deep sleep. A ten- or fifteen-minute nap seemed to refresh and restore him com-pletely after a period of strain that would push most men into a stupor of weariness.

Career decisions continued to be difficult for him, but they were less so than they had been a decade ago whenever their objects were of anywhere near the same size as they then had been. The trouble was that lately the ob-jects had not been the same size: they were much larger, they involved more factors. Indecision, however, was no longer as deeply rooted as it once was in doubts concerning his capacities. Experience had taught him that there were certain natural limits beyond which he could not go, but that these limits were fewer than he had once believed they were. For instance, he had once had none too high an opinion of his mental abilities; now he knew that these abilities (though he would never say so out loud) were superior and that they grew constantly through experience. He had once felt nervous, inadequate, as he faced the brilliant people who attended Council on Foreign Relations meetings; now, before such audiences, he felt perfectly at ease, provided he was prepared. He must be prepared, though; he was not, at this point in his life, a man who could stand up before an audience and give a good extemporaneous speech.

A dozen or so years before he had been by no means a social snob; he lacked wholly the malice that lies at the core of snobbery. But when he came to the city to live and work he was more impressed by wealth and power, more flattered by associations with the wealthy and powerful, than he now was. He was no longer as prone as once he had been to accept privileges as rights or to assume the prejudices, the exclusive attitudes of his own social class. Naturally his closest personal contacts and companions were all of the upper income group. This would continue to be so. But from now on this fact would be more a function of past circumstances than of con-scious personal choice.

BOOK FOUR

War and Its Aftermath

CHAPTER THIRTEEN

M AY, 1941 . . . Greece, who had been able to hold her own against
the Italians, has fallen swiftly under the onslaught of German troops;
shattered remnants of a token British expeditionary force have been rescued
from Greek shores in another, smaller Dunkirk. Still more frightening has
been the lightning conquest of Crete by German airborne troops.

After a bitter battle with Republican-led isolationists the administration
has been able to push the Lend-Lease Bill through the Congress (Republicans in the House voted 139 to 24 against it, in the Senate 17 to 10 against),
but Secretary of the Navy Knox is now well aware that Lend-Lease will not
be enough to prevent Britain's fall, even if the shipping gets through—especially so since American industry, in the absence of profit guarantees, continues naturally reluctant to convert itself to war production on anything like
the needed scale. Nor are the voices of isolationism noticeably muffled by
the impending Nazi-Fascist victory: on the contrary, they seem strengthened
by the fact that all Western Europe—with the dubious exceptions of Franco's
Spain, Salazar's Portugal, and Vichy France—is now a Nazi-Fascist empire.
The war, say such men as Lindbergh, is already virtually over. Hitler has
won. We should accommodate ourselves to that fact. . . .

On May 27, President Roosevelt proclaims that "an unlimited national
emergency exists. . . . Our patrols are helping now to ensure delivery of the
needed supplies to Britain," the President says. "All additional measures necessary to ensure delivery of the goods will be taken. *Any and all further
methods or combinations of methods which can or should be utilized, are
being devised.*" Surely this means that the President will soon appear before

the Congress to ask for a declaration of war against Germany. But does it? Next day at his press conference the President denies any intention of using the U.S. Navy for convoy duty or of asking the Congress for revision or repeal of the Neutrality Law....

Nevertheless, the proclamation can only mean further pressures upon the Navy and the Navy Secretary. Stocky, sandy-haired, sixty-seven-year-old Frank Knox is a strong and brave man. He has proved his physical courage time and again: as one of Teddy Roosevelt's Rough Riders in 1898 (Teddy remains his idol, upon whom he models himself); as a weekly newspaper editor crusading against vice and corruption in tough Sault Sainte Marie; as a private who became a major of field artillery in France during World War I (he is now a colonel in the reserves, ret.). He abundantly proves his intellectual and moral courage by being in the position he now occupies. All his mature life he has been the most rugged of rugged individualists, a laissez-faire economist who was outraged by the New Deal: he condemned the AAA, the Social Security Act, the Wagner Act, the federal administration of relief, and as Republican Vice-Presidential candidate in '36 he had fought Roosevelt far more effectively than Alf Landon had been able to do. His acceptance of a cabinet post under Roosevelt, therefore, had been an act of patriotism that cost him many long friendships and a terrific struggle with himself. Ever since, he has heard himself damned as a traitor and turncoat by Republican leaders he has long admired; daily he sees and hears himself vilified by isolationist newspapers and radio broadcasters. But he stands firm in his conviction that the republic is in mortal danger, having been "educated," as he himself admits, by the superlative foreign staff of the *Daily News*, which he had acquired in the early 30's.

A strong man ... yet the mounting pressures of his rapidly expanding job in the gathering crisis call for a strong and able personal assistant with legal skills and strong convictions. He knows, too, whom he wants as assistant. He wants Adlai Stevenson.

He had become interested in the work of the Council on Foreign Relations at about the time that Stevenson became president of it; besides sharing Stevenson's views, he had soon developed an admiration for Stevenson's quality of mind and leadership and a personal liking for him. This liking and admiration have grown since Stevenson assumed the chairmanship of the local White Committee. About once a month since becoming Secretary of the Navy Knox has been in Chicago, and on each occasion he and Stevenson have conferred. Occasionally, when Stevenson has had to go to Washington on committee business, Knox has given him a ride in his Navy plane and they have talked some more of dark events. He has told Hopkins and Roosevelt about this "young man, a terrific guy"—and it is only because the aid-Britain work has seemed so important that he hasn't demanded that Stevenson join his own staff.

"I go to all these meetings," Knox grumbles to Stevenson. "Every day, important meetings with important people. There sit Hillman and Knudson and Stimson, and the others—and every one of 'em has his own personal lawyer. Even Jim Forrestal has his own lawyer"—James Forrestal is Knox's Undersecretary—"and I don't have one. Why don't you plan to come down here and be my lawyer, so I won't feel so defenseless?"

But it is not until a day or so after the "unlimited emergency" proclamation that the request becomes specific. On an afternoon near the end of May he puts through a telephone call to Stevenson in Chicago.

"When are you going to be in Washington again?" he wants to know.

Stevenson says he has no definite plans for coming at all.

"Well, you'd better plan to come as soon as you can. Bring a big suitcase, and plan to stay." [1]

The public announcement of Adlai Stevenson's appointment as personal assistant to the Secretary of the Navy was made on July 6, 1941, two weeks after-German armies had invaded Russia. He accepted the appointment on a strictly temporary basis, having been granted a three months' leave of absence by Sidley, McPherson, Austin and Burgess—and when he arrived in Washington some ten days later, he came alone. Ellen and the three boys remained on the farm near Libertyville. If things worked out that way the family would join him in the autumn. He moved into the Hay-Adams House on Lafayette Square across from the White House, and was given an office next door to Knox.

A test of his usefulness soon came—and it was a major one.

At Kearny, New Jersey, in the huge shipyard of the Federal Shipbuilding and Dry Dock Corporation, some 16,000 employees worked on $493,000,000 worth of fighting ships for the Navy and merchant vessels for the Maritime Commission. It was of crucial importance to the national security that this yard's production be uninterrupted. When Stevenson arrived in Washington, however, a work stoppage at Kearny was imminent. Negotiations between the company and the CIO's Industrial Union of Marine and Shipbuilding workers were breaking down over a union maintenance of membership clause, which the union insisted must be in the contract in exchange for a no-strike pledge during the emergency. Under this clause, present and future union members would be required to remain in good standing as a condition of employment, though nonunion workers would not be required to join.

Stevenson sat in as Knox's assistant at meetings with the Defense Mediation Board, the Maritime Commission, and the Office of Production Management, during which the deepening Kearny crisis was discussed. It was decided by those agencies that the government must be prepared to take over and operate the shipyard if a strike occurred. Stevenson was asked to draft the plan devising the necessary legal machinery for carrying out this decision: it involved such matters as management responsibilities, contractual continuances, and other intricate and, for the most part, unprecedented problems. It also involved an executive order for the President's signature, for this would be the first seizure of a great private plant by the government in the interest of national defense. The assignment was by far the most important given Stevenson up to that time, and he plunged into the drafting and negotiating job with tirelessness and trepidation. He emerged days later, however, with plans and documents that the services, the Department of Justice, the Office of Production Management, and all others concerned found satisfactory.

On August 7, the union struck. The Kearny yard closed down. Again Stevenson sat by Knox's side, or as Knox's representative, at long and fateful meetings as the Mediation Board held negotiations with both the union and the management, but the company flatly refused to accept the Mediation Board's recommendation. After eleven days of shutdown it was deemed imperative for work to resume on the ships at once and for the President immediately to issue the executive order for seizure of the plant. To a feverishly excited Washington officialdom even another twenty-four-hour delay seemed fraught with mortal danger to the republic.

But the President was not in Washington. On August 9, British Prime Minister Winston Churchill on H.M.S. *Prince of Wales* and the American President on the cruiser U.S.S. *Augusta* had met at a secret rendezvous off Newfoundland. There they reached agreements concerning American aid to the Allies, now that Soviet Russia was one of them (Hopkins, just back from Moscow, was present), and drafted the Atlantic Charter with its historic pronouncement of the Four Freedoms as the basis of future peace. The President, therefore, would not be back on United States soil until August 16, when he would debark at Rockland, Maine. It was decided that Adlai Stevenson must fly out to meet the *Augusta,* brief the President, and secure his signature to the executive order. Hurried arrangements were made for his flight to Quonset Point, Rhode Island, whence a Navy seaplane would fly him to the cruiser at sea.

Just as he was about to depart, he was called again into Knox's office. A solemn-looking Admiral Chester Nimitz, then chief of the Navy Department's Bureau of Navigation, was there. Knox, too, looked solemn and worried.[2]

"The admiral has a message he wants you to take to the President and deliver to him in person," the Secretary said. "Go ahead, Admiral."

"You are to deliver this message to the President, and *to no one else!*" the admiral said with stern emphasis. "Tell him I have learned today, from a heretofore reliable source, that Stalin has opened negotiations with Hitler."

Stevenson stared, and gulped, as well he might. If the information were true, every plan based on the assumption that Russia, for weeks or months to come, would absorb much of Germany's offensive strength was rendered futile. Moreover Stevenson could see that both Knox and Nimitz were not dismissing the report lightly.

"May I write the message down, sir?" he asked.

"Better not!" the admiral said. "Better nothing on paper about this on your person."

Stevenson then repeated the message aloud, to make certain that he stated it correctly, and asked some questions about the source of the report. Again he was warned that the President *alone* must receive it, and as quickly as possible. He departed.

All the way to Quonset, Stevenson pondered the implications of his mission and the message he was carrying—and the more he pondered the more solemn and urgent his journey became. Germany would be free to turn westward again, perhaps in time to invade Britain in the autumn—and her westward-driving power would be greater than ever before because her eastern frontiers would be secure. That Britain could long withstand the onslaught seemed unlikely. She would have to stand alone. The United States was not ready to give aid on a scale large enough to be effective; she was even more unprepared psychologically. Another moment's delay at the Kearny yards seemed intolerable, for after Britain *we* were next.

At Quonset, Stevenson's trip began to take on nightmare qualities. Bad weather had closed in. All planes were grounded. Desperately he tried to impress upon the admiral in charge the crucial importance of time. Emphatically the admiral refused to permit his plane to take off in search of a cruiser at sea in weather like this. Hours passed. Finally the admiral agreed to permit a small plane to fly Stevenson to Rockland, Maine, though to do so was risky.

"You can get there by the time the President's ship docks," he said.

The plane got through to Rockland all right, but as it circled over the port, Stevenson looked down to see the *Augusta* already at the dock and a huge crowd gathered around a train alongside. The pilot, urged by Stevenson, set the plane down in a primitive grass field. Stevenson, lugging his precious brief case, ran to the highway and flagged down a car driven by an elderly lady. She was startled, even a little frightened, but Stevenson, turning on all his charm, reassured her; she kept a heavy foot on the gas pedal as she drove to town. There, six blocks from the station, they were halted by a traffic jam. Jumping from the car, Stevenson ran as hard as he could to the station. But as he drew near he could hear the shouting and see the puffing smoke above the housetops as the President's special train pulled out. Hitchhiking back to the airport, he and his pilot took off for Portland, which was the first stop the train would make—hours from Rockland by rail but a short distance by air.

In Portland, Stevenson nervously whiled away a couple of hours at dinner and in a motion picture theater, though he had difficulty keeping his mind on the picture. He then went to the Portland station where he discovered that a crowd had gathered which was many times larger than the Rockland crowd had been. Every approach to the tracks was blocked by a solid wall of humanity. Portland's policemen were wholly unimpressed by Stevenson's insistence that he had a message of crucial importance to deliver to the President personally. At last a slight acquaintance, Senator Claude Pepper, appeared, accompanied by two other gentlemen and two policemen. The gentlemen turned out to be the mayor and former governor, and, thanks to them, Stevenson stood at last in the front line by the station platform.

He explained to the senator the imperative importance of his getting on the train when it came: he had papers relating to the Kearny shipyard case which required immediate Presidential signature. (He did not, of course, mention the secret message.) Pepper promised to see what he could do. The train pulled in. Pepper and the others promptly boarded it. Stevenson, however, was held back by Secret Service men. For fifteen agonizing minutes thereafter he waited on the platform. At last General "Pa" Watkins, Presidential aide, came out the door of the Presidential car, spoke kindly to Stevenson, and asked him to hand over the necessary papers. The President, explained Watkins, was at dinner. Stevenson refused to hand the papers over; he insisted that he see the President personally. Watkins at last withdrew into the car—and for five more minutes, Stevenson, now red-faced with embarrassment before the snickering crowd, waited helplessly until Pa Watkins returned and said that the President would see him.

Roosevelt was still at the dinner table as Stevenson entered the car. With him were Marvin McIntyre, Harry Hopkins, Mrs. Roosevelt, and Grace Tully (the President's personal secretary).

"Well, Adlai," said Roosevelt, smiling, "I'm glad to see you again. Glad to hear you're working for Frank Knox."

Astonished by such a warm and personal greeting, Stevenson mumbled an incoherent reply, rushing on to say that he had emergency papers for the President's signature.

"Let's have a look at them," said Roosevelt.

Stevenson's own written account of what then transpired, an account he would always swear was literally accurate, follows:

> I opened up my brief case clumsily and fished out the Kearny shipyard papers. I explained the intricate situation as best I could, as the President's dinner got colder and the others more restive, and pointed out where he was supposed to sign the order. He looked it over for a minute and then said:
>
> "Well, now, Adlai, you just leave all these papers in your folder with me, and I'll read them over tonight. We'll have a meeting at the White House in the morning. You fly back to Washington and arrange it. Tell

Secretary Knox I'd also like to see him and Myron Taylor and the Attorney General at nine o'clock—and you be there, too."

"But Mr. President," I said, "these are supposed to be signed right now!"

"I think it will work out all right this way," said the President.

"Well," I said, "if you say so I guess it will be O.K.!" I marvel that I could have talked like such a fool but I was so nervous I hardly knew what I was saying—mostly, I suppose, because I hadn't yet said the really important thing—the message—and I didn't know how to deliver it with all those people sitting around. I could see he was waiting for me to leave, and I had to come out with something. The talk went about like this:

"I have something else to tell you, Mr. President."

"Do you, Adlai? What is it?"

"Well, Mr. President, it's a message from Admiral Nimitz. He said to tell you . . . alone."

"Oh, I think you can tell me here, Adlai."

"No sir, I can't." I had a feeling that everyone was doing his best to keep from laughing! I had an idea, just in time. "Can I write it down, sir?"

"Why, certainly."

I took the menu and I wrote on the back of it, "Admiral Nimitz has heard from a heretofore reliable source today that Stalin has started negotiations with Hitler."

Then I gave him back the menu. He read it carefully and then looked up at me.

"Adlai," he said, "do you believe this?"

That was too much! I didn't know what I thought. "Why, I don't know, Mr. President," I stammered.

"I don't believe it," said F.D.R. "I'm not worried at all. Are you worried, Adlai?"

I said I guessed I wasn't so much worried after all. Then, mission completed after a fashion, I took my departure, and in my embarrassed confusion, I wheeled around and crashed right into a closed door, thus bending my crooked nose some more. I flew back to Washington, woke Secretary Knox to tell him about the meeting at the White House, and we all went over there at nine o'clock. My crowning mortification was that the President hadn't even opened the envelope containing my precious Kearny shipyard papers. He pulled them out and settled the whole business in fifteen minutes and signed the Executive Order. As for the negotiations between Stalin and Hitler, the President was, of course, right, and the Admiral's source was unreliable that time.

Thus Stevenson's account, deliberately designed, it would seem, to create an impression of fumbling foolishness. Actually, of course, he had displayed courage, tenacity, and ingenuity, a fact well realized by Knox, and Roosevelt too, when the full story was known. Even at the time, the President expressed to Secretary Knox appreciation of the manner in which the critical Kearny case was handled. From that moment forward Stevenson's position as Knox's assistant was secure.

The seizure of the shipyards on August 23 (work resumed there on August 26) by no means ended the Kearny matter. The case was a test of the emergency powers granted the President, and there were all sorts of complicated problems whose solutions required creative and legal intelligence of a high order. "It was very tough," said Stevenson years later, "and I worked very hard on it off and on, all that fall of '41." He worked closely with Admiral Harold G. (Hal) Bowen, technical aide to the Secretary, who took over the management of Kearny and did, as Stevenson always said, "a really terrific job—I think of Hal Bowen as one of the great unsung heroes of the war." [3] In the end, the legal machinery through which the Kearny problem was solved became the pilot plan for scores of plant seizures that the war effort later made necessary.

But the Kearny matter was by no means the only one with which Stevenson dealt even in those early months of his new assignment. For many purposes he became, in effect, Knox's alter ego, intimately involved in problems of Navy administration, public relations, and relations with other departments. As Knox's assistant, often as his deputy, he attended virtually all the top-level policy meetings of the interdepartmental agencies which, as the defense effort grew, sprang up in bewildering quantity and variety. He himself had no small part in the shaping of executive policy, particularly in liberalizing the Navy's public relations in the interests of fuller disclosure of news about the Navy's infinite activities and problems. In labor relations and in enlarging opportunities for Negroes in the naval service, his liberalizing influence was especially apparent.

As time went on and their trials and travels together multiplied, Stevenson became an even closer and more intimate personal friend of Knox. The two complemented each other in many ways and learned from one another. Knox was bluff, hearty, forthright; he liked to think of himself as a tough, hard-driving, ruthless patriot and super-administrator. In actual fact, he was a simple, kind, and gentle man who enjoyed Stevenson's wit, respected his judgment, and admired mental qualities which he himself lacked. As for Stevenson, he more than admired Knox.

"I loved that man," he said, long afterward. "He was brave, and honest. And he made a very great contribution to his country in her hour of greatest need. It cost him a lot. I'm sure it shortened his life. He was no intellectual, God knows, but he was highly intelligent—which a lot of 'intellectuals' aren't, you know—and he knew his fellow man from a rough and crowded life. His loyalty to President Roosevelt, his political adversary in 1936, had a defiant quality, and his admiration and respect for his chief seemed to grow as the going got tougher. He had the ability to simplify complex problems. He and I saw eye to eye on foreign policy. On domestic policy we often disagreed pretty radically. But he never held that against me. We belonged to different generations, and I really think he became a lot more tolerant as a result of his Washington experiences. Although he continued to regard himself as violently anti-New Deal, of course, he liked to call me *his* New Dealer. He used to say, 'I have to have a New Dealer next to me to protect me from the New Dealers around here.' And he'd turn to me and say, 'Adlai, you're not letting any of 'em creep in here, are you?' Yet I can't recall that he ever vetoed an appointment I wanted made or ever asked me more than perfunctory questions about it." [4]

II

In early September, 1941, Mrs. Ellen Borden Stevenson—with Adlai, Jr., Borden, and John Fell—moved into a large old Washington town house, which her husband had rented furnished. It stood at 1904 R Street, just off Connecticut Avenue. According to a Chicago society reporter, "Washington society is charmed by Ellen's Greuze-like beauty and Adlai's witty sayings," and during the months that followed, Ellen's name and photograph continued to appear with frequency in the society sections of Washington and Chicago papers. The impression this may have given of a full social life was misleading, however, for Stevenson was working night and day and over the weekends all that autumn. He had little time even to be with his family and virtually none for parties that were not directly in the line of duty.

To his shipyard worries were added, in October and November, numerous other anxieties. He helped draft ideas for Roosevelt's annual Navy Day speech on October 27—the strongest speech the President had yet given on America's relation to the war. (It followed an attack on the U.S.S. *Kearny*, a destroyer, by a Nazi submarine, in which eleven Americans were killed, and a public statement by General Wood of the America First Committee daring the President to ask the Congress for a declaration of war.) He was involved in the stupendous logistical problems incurred by the granting of a one-billion-dollars Lend-Lease credit to the Soviet Union in November, insofar as these problems affected top policy-making levels. And then there were the endless committee and interdepartmental meetings about industrial production, controls, manpower, foreign trade, government information, and all the policy questions precipitated by the war that was creeping ever nearer. He was of course kept abreast of the situation in the Far East where Japan, according to British and American intelligence reports, was preparing to attack Indochina and the Dutch East Indies. He shared to the full Knox's concern over this: a Japanese conquest of these areas would forge a sword pointed directly at the throat of a United States whose hands now seemed tied more securely than ever behind her back by bonds of apathy, confusion, and isolationism. By the narrowest of margins, in early November, after the U.S. destroyer *Reuben James* had been sunk, the Congress permitted the administration to begin arming merchant ships. . . .

On Friday, December 5, Mr. and Mrs. Hermon Dunlap Smith arrived in Washington to spend the weekend as guests of the Adlai Stevensons. That evening they were the guests of honor at a dinner party in the R Street house. Among the other guests were Ted Weeks of the *Atlantic Monthly* and Henry S. Morgan, the banker son of J. P. Morgan, whom Dutch Smith had known since his Harvard days. Ellen was the same superb hostess she had always been, and her husband was as witty and stimulating as always before. After the other guests had left, Dutch and Ellen Smith planned with their host and hostess a picnic for the following afternoon. The Stevensons knew of a wonderful picnic spot some fifteen or twenty miles from Washington, along the Chesapeake and Ohio canal on the Maryland side of the Potomac.

When Adlai went to the office next morning, however, he found that new problems had arisen in the Kearny shipyard matter. The Smiths, with Ellen Stevenson and the three Stevenson boys, picnicked without him. They returned with glowing accounts of their afternoon.

Next morning, Sunday, December 7, the Smiths left Washington for Chicago. Adlai and Ellen Stevenson drove them to the Union Station, with Dutch sitting beside Adlai in the front seat and the two Ellens sitting in the back. In the back seat the talk turned to Washington life and Ellen Stevenson's dislike for it—a reaction, as Ellen Smith discovered, actually stronger than dislike—and to her feeling that she was being increasingly alienated from Adlai, who had no time for her. . . . In the front seat the talk turned to Illinois politics.

The old Horner group remained a major power in Illinois politics, despite Horner's bitter primary fight with the Kelly-Nash machine in 1936, his death in October of 1940, and the election of Dwight Green, Republican, to the governorship on a reform platform in 1940. Some of this group, Stevenson told Dutch Smith, were "after him" to run for the Senate against the Republican isolationist incumbent, C. Wayland (Curly) Brooks, darling of the Chicago *Tribune*, who was up for reelection in the fall of '42. The issue, of course, would be foreign policy, and on that issue Stevenson would be a strong candidate, according to the people who had talked to him about it.

On the train Smith reviewed his weekend with his friend, and it was then, as he said years later, that he first realized that Adlai Stevenson was becoming a great man.[5] He had sensed in his friend a greater weight and balance of judgment, a firmer grasp of problems, a wider and deeper vision than he had ever noticed in him before. He had always had a high opinion of his friend's abilities. He had admired him for his nimbleness of wit and loved him for his sweetness of character. But it had not occurred to him before that Adlai might play a major role in history.

On the way back to R Street from the station the Stevensons decided to go on a family picnic, to the same spot where Ellen and the boys had gone with the Smiths the preceding afternoon. They had one of their happiest times together. They picnicked on a high rock bank overlooking the Potomac. They canoed on the river. On the way back to Washington they stopped at the falls of the Potomac, a particularly beautiful spot, where Adlai romped with the boys for some time. They returned in the winter dusk to R Street where the maid informed them that the phone had been ringing constantly; beside the phone was a stack of messages requesting Adlai to call back. Undoubtedly it was the Kearny business again, he told Ellen; they could wait until he'd had a shower.

While he was showering the phone rang again, and Ellen answered. A newspaperman was on the line, an acquaintance of theirs. He demanded to speak to Adlai, overruling Ellen's objections to calling her husband at that moment. Of Stevenson he requested a statement for the press.

"About what?" Stevenson asked.

The newspaperman was at first irritated by what he deemed Stevenson's tasteless facetiousness, then astonished by the realization that Stevenson really didn't know what had happened. The Japanese had bombed Pearl Harbor; they were attacking the Philippines, Guam, Wake Island. . . .

Stevenson rushed to his office adjacent to Secretary Knox's. He spent most of that night by Knox's side as Admiral Stark, Chief of Naval Operations, and other senior officers came in for conferences and ominous tidings continued to roll in from the Far East.

Next morning, before a joint session of the Congress, the President of the United States asked for and promptly received a declaration of war against Japan, Germany, and Italy. Four days later Stevenson drafted and sent to Knox at Pearl Harbor a message that Knox signed and released to the press.

"The enemy has struck a savage, treacherous blow," the message said. "We are at war, all of us. There is not time now for disputes or delays of any kind. We must have ships and more ships, guns and more guns, planes and more planes, men and more men—faster and faster. There is no time to lose. The Navy must lead the way. Speed up—it is your Navy and your Nation."

The possibility of Stevenson's running for the Senate next fall was, of course, shelved if not actually forgotten. In November the egregious "Curly" Brooks would be reelected as Republican senator from Illinois.

The Stevensons had long planned to spend the Christmas holiday of 1941 with Buffie and Ernest Ives at Southern Pines. For many days following

Pearl Harbor it seemed impossible that Adlai could get away. He managed to do so, however, just for Christmas Day itself, taking a night train down from Washington on Christmas Eve and a night train back to Washington on Christmas night. Ellen and the three boys, who had grand times with Timmie Ives, remained for nearly two weeks.

To Buffie, as to Ellen Thorne Smith, Ellen Stevenson revealed her unhappiness in Washington, her dislike for the hectic Washington life with its demands and its constantly recurrent crises. Everyone was so full of self-importance, so sure that the fate of the world rested on his shoulders. She loved the quiet, the solitude, the freedom from plans; planning destroyed the element of surprise, it kept the planned things from *really* happening.[6]

III

During the war Stevenson traveled with and for the Secretary extensively. In three years he flew some two hundred thousand miles throughout the United States, into the Pacific theater, across the Caribbean, across the Atlantic to North Africa and Europe.

The longest of his numerous trips with Knox was an inspection tour made in January of 1943, covering the entire Pacific theater. It was not without its hazards. One of the engines of the big four-engine flying boat in which they took off from Pearl Harbor at dawn quit when the plane was barely seventy feet above the water. In the violent landing Admiral Nimitz's scalp was cut, and one wing went under the water. To right the plane the party had to crawl out of the hold through the escape hatch and out onto the high wing, a procedure somewhat complicated by the portliness of the Navy Secretary, who was squeezed through the narrow hatch by pulling from above and hearty shoves from the rear. ("To see the rotund Secretary pulling himself up that steep wing on his stomach followed by the commander of the Pacific Fleet is my most vivid and amusing memory of that memorable trip," commented Stevenson in a speech before the Maryland Council of the Navy League two months later.)

At Midway Island, which had been badly battered by the Japanese in the Battle of Midway, the plane in which they rode smashed a pontoon while landing, and their departure was delayed. At Espiritu Santo in the Solomon Islands the party slept on the decks of a Navy ship. Never before having bombed the site, the enemy chose the time of the Secretary's visit to send over a bomber, which missed the target but gave rise to the suspicion that enemy intelligence might be cognizant of the party's composition and itinerary.

During those years Stevenson wrote or edited most of the Secretary's public statements and formal speeches, and it was perhaps in this role of ghost writer that he earned Knox's most fervent admiration and gratitude. It cannot be said, however, that he succeeded in such attempts as he may have made toward tailoring his eloquence to Knox's natural style of public speaking. The speech drafts employed a longer period, a greater vocabulary range, and a much more intricate rhythmic balance than earlier writings bearing Knox's name had done. Their creator was embarrassed by the purple passages they contained when, a few years later, after the fever of the war had subsided, he reread them. Knox, he then opined, must have had the devil's own time giving some of them.[7]

He was also called upon by the Navy to give some speeches of his own—and if he never wholly mastered the art of writing a speech that sounded like Frank Knox, he became during these years a master of speeches that were uniquely Adlai Stevenson. He did not do so easily. Never a swift and facile writer, always pressed for time, he now found composition more painful than ever. But he knew that, in large part, the difficulty of his drafting stemmed from his refusal to accept easy ways. If he aimed for clarity and simplicity, he aimed also for an eloquence increasingly rare among the public speakers of his time, knowing well that a formal eloquence has its own message, enhancing the meaning of all that is said through it. Determined to do this work in the grand tradition, he must risk the ridiculous continuously in an effort to achieve the sublime—an effort that succeeded more and more often, as he learned through experience.

The style he was developing was not, in his own view, consciously influenced by any other one style. "My object," he would say, "has merely been to talk as well as I can—to honor the language and elevate the listeners if I could." Inevitably, however, whether consciously or not, he was influenced by others, notably Abraham Lincoln and Woodrow Wilson, with echoes of Winston Churchill.

In mid-February of '42 he electrified a large crowd at a Chicago Council on Foreign Relations luncheon in the Palmer House with a passionate, fighting speech denouncing complacency. Said a feature story in a Chicago paper next day: "The talk which Adlai Stevenson gave . . . was sufficient to make him one of the most celebrated men of the times." He spoke before the Princeton Club in New York, before the Real Estate Board in Chicago, before a huge Navy Day celebration in Bloomington, before a dozen other large audiences, and with each address his power as a speaker, he felt, was increased.

It was, he admitted to himself, a thrilling power; it was also a sobering one, counseling humility. One could become addicted to this kind of power. And one could misuse it to disastrously egotistical ends, as Hitler had done, if one let it slip the leash of logical rigor and moral responsibility. He therefore strengthened the leash. He began, more and more, to weave strands of humor into it—a wit that not only leavened his serious message, making it more palatable, but also illumined the points he wanted to make. It was himself he most often laughed at publicly. He presented himself in the role of Everyman, whose individual fate is tragic, certainly, since the grave inevitably awaits him, but who is also a comic character as he fumbles and stumbles along his path, striving to hide his woeful inadequacy behind a thousand ridiculous pomposities.

In May of 1943 Stevenson became involved in a legal problem that was even more difficult than the Kearny shipyard case had been. What's more, as the devoted assistant saw it, it was fraught with greater peril to Frank Knox's personal reputation.

It had to do with the naval oil reserve at Elk Hills, California—a focus of the greatest of the Harding regime scandals in the 1920's. The reserve contained approximately forty-three thousand acres, but not all of these were government-owned. Some nine thousand acres belonged to Standard Oil of California. Standard was under pressure to fill huge war orders for oil, but if the company operated its nine thousand acres independently of government control it would drain off oil that Congress, in the Naval Reserve Act as amended in 1938, had sought to guarantee as reserved. Accordingly, Knox had entered into a contract with Standard for unit operation of the pool by Standard under Navy supervision, in November of 1942. Soon there were published rumors that the contract was illegal and that graft and corruption were involved in it. Pressure developed in the Justice Department and in Congress for immediate condemnation of Standard's nine thousand acres.

It was at this point that Knox called in Stevenson and assigned him the problem. Stevenson's paramount consideration was to ensure uninterrupted production of the fifteen thousand barrels of oil a day that the war effort required of the Elk Hills pool. Only Standard, it appeared to him, could get the needed oil out. Accordingly he recommended to Knox that a temporary operating agreement be executed with Standard to remain in effect while the Navy Department drafted amendments to the 1938 Act for presentation to the Congress. Knox accepted this recommendation; the temporary agreement was signed on September 8, 1943, and was approved by the President and by Attorney General Francis Biddle.

Associated with Stevenson in this task was his younger friend Carl McGowan. Shortly after Pearl Harbor Day, McGown had written to Stevenson, asking if there were a spot for him in the Navy Department; Stevenson, having high regard for McGowan, said to come at once, and early in '42 McGowan had become a civilian lawyer in the Bureau of Ships. Out of their work together in the terrible urgency of wartime Washington, Stevenson and McGowan became close personal friends with a profound respect for each other's abilities. A foundation was firmly laid for their future working relationship.[8]

CHAPTER FOURTEEN

I N late 1943 and early 1944 Adlai Stevenson was taken from his duties
with Frank Knox by President Roosevelt to head an emergency mission
to Sicily and Italy for the Foreign Economic Administration. The assignment
was by no means an easy one; it was, indeed, "one of the most difficult"
possible under the prevailing circumstances, as an unnamed official of the
FEA (probably Leo Crowley, FEA head) was quoted in the national press
as saying. There were no real precedents for the job Stevenson had to do.

By late 1943 Allied forces stood on a bloody line reaching from sea to
sea just south of Cassino, less than a third of the way up the Italian boot,
their position made all the more difficult by the chaos, the human misery
behind them. Cut off from the industrial north and devastated by war, the
southern Italian economy was at a standstill, transport paralyzed, the people
hungry and demoralized, the specter of disease and famine looming over the
land. Stevenson's mission was to study and report on how relief should be
given the Italian people while the country was rehabilitated; the ways and
means by which a working economy might be reestablished; and the economic aspects of the problem of reestablishing local governments in areas
where every experienced administrator was *ipso facto* a Fascist or Fascist
supporter.

All this was difficult enough. It was further complicated by what seemed
to many close observers a hopelessly tangled administrative setup. The
Foreign Economic Administration had been created by Presidential edict in
late September in an effort to reduce interagency squabbles that were sadly
reducing the effectiveness of the whole economic warfare effort. In FEA
had been consolidated the Office of Economic Warfare, the Lend-Lease Administration, the Office of Foreign Relief and Rehabilitation, and other foreign economic agencies. But this nominal unification had not, in actual fact,
removed the causes of interagency strife: to some observers strife seemed to
be the very essence of the FEA; and it was even more severe in the Mediter-
ranean theater, at the end of long lines of communication, than it was in
Washington itself.

Abruptly and painfully he was introduced to the situation which had
frustrated other civilian missions in the war theater: the Army was indifferent if not actually hostile to such visitors. Not until Stevenson turned to
the Navy, where he was well known as the Secretary's confidential assistant,

did he obtain adequate transportation, shelter, and other facilities for his party. The naval commander at Palermo, Sicily, assigned him a command car and two bluejackets, sent word of his coming up the line, and from then on the mission proceeded relatively smoothly.[1]

In the command car, with blanket rolls, gasoline cans, and K rations, the party toured Sicily and Italy for six weeks, accumulating huge piles of notes on market, transportation, the agricultural situation, industrial destruction, housing, rehabilitation of all kinds, and the problem of reestablishing a maximum possible civilian control of local government. Stevenson's diary was filled with vivid impressions of the scenes and people he encountered. Typical were his jottings for December 23, when the party was near Nicastro:

> ... off without breakfast in a cold gray dawn. K rations on a deserted road in the country, but somehow the children showed up accompanied by a cheerful young philosopher driving a donkey who pointed to our car and said, "American car" and to his donkey—"Italian car"; to our shoes, "American shoes"—to his bare feet—"Italian shoes"; to our K rations —"American food," to a small crust of black bread in his shirt—"Italian food"—and then laughed merrily. He got his reward and I some phrases that summarized my whole experience in Italy—and also an uneasy feeling that such contrasts won't endure forever. But how is the American taxpayer to be persuaded that to help Italy at his expense is to help himself? "Perhaps his grandchildren. . . ."

In Naples, in a corridor of the headquarters building, he at last and by chance met Eisenhower. The two had a brief, pleasant chat and parted, not to meet again for many years.

Stevenson wrote later, in some desultory memoirs of the trip:

> I spent a day at the front. We stopped first at 5th Army headquarters in the great Bourbon palace of Caserta . . . ; then on to Capua and across the bloody Volturno River, past Nignano, 98 percent destroyed, and after a wild dash of several miles where the road to Rome was exposed to enemy fire . . . we climbed up a hillside into a pile of rubble that was once the ancient town of San Pietro. From there we had a fine view of Monte Cassino Monastery a few miles north. . . . That day our patrols were in the olive groves on the hillsides around Van Vittore. . . . I wish I could describe that mud that has to be shovelled off the roads like snow and the cold penetrating rain, the stench of those ruined towns with their unburied dead in the rubble, the condition in which the doughboys live and stand sleepless watch over their guns—and fight, up and down those stony rugged mountains, supplied by donkeys, with the Germans and their machine guns and screaming mortars always above you on the next hilltop.

On his return trip to the United States he stopped in Dakar, where Admiral Glassford suggested that before flying home he go down to Liberia for a quick look-see in connection with a port development and submarine base that the Navy was considering. Although some familiarity with the harbor at Monrovia, Liberia's capital, and a talk with some of the officials should be helpful back in the department, Stevenson's mission was behind schedule and he might not have made the trip (he took Wesley Sturges with him) if he had not long had a curiosity about this remote Negro republic. His great-grandfather, Dr. Lewis Warner Green, it will be remembered, had been one of the leading sponsors of the Liberia project in the decades immediately preceding the Civil War....

The official fruit of the FEA mission was a hastily prepared report of some one hundred and fifty printed pages which became a model of its kind. Not only did it provide a firm factual and interpretative basis for top-level decisions about Italy, it also served as a guide for the solution of similar problems in other liberated areas as the Allied armies forced the Nazi hordes back step by reluctant step into the bloody ruins of the Third Reich. Partly as a result of it, the effective coordination of economic, political, and military activities in the areas liberated by the Allies was greatly increased.

II

In the late summer of 1943 it had been decided that Ellen, who had gone to the Libertyville farm with the boys, would not come back to Washington in the fall.

Her dissatisfaction with wartime capital life had become a chronic unhappiness, and her conclusions as to how she wished to live had been confirmed for her by her experiences of what seemed to her the idyllic country life of the Iveses' in North Carolina. On one visit to Southern Pines, Ellen, Adlai, and the boys had stayed in a house owned by Struthers Burt, the novelist, just a little way from the Iveses' farm. When they returned to Washington, Burt wrote to Ellen in high praise of her poetry. "She *must* find time or *organize* her time to write more," Stevenson noted in his diary. "Her quality is so high and her output so low." At Libertyville she was free of schedules. She was free of servants, too, that year; she cooked and kept house and gardened, with the help of the boys. It was, she laughed, her "war effort," and she loved it. She wrote light verse and satires, including a playlet in verse which satirized the Great Books program developed by her friends Robert Hutchins and Mortimer Adler at the University of Chicago.*

* This playlet was later presented by Ellen and others at a meeting of the Friday Club in Chicago, where it made a great success. Mrs. Quincey (Louise) Wright, Executive Secretary of the Chicago Council on Foreign Relations, would remember that, though men seldom attended meetings of this club, Adlai slipped in at the back of the room and stood beside her as the playlet was presented. He enjoyed it hugely, and enjoyed too the success it had with the audience. "That girl is so clever!" he said proudly to Louise.

So from September into the spring of 1944, Stevenson lived in a small bachelor apartment above a bookstore in Georgetown, sharing it with his old Princeton friend, Francis A. Comstock, now a commander in the Navy. The apartment consisted of a small sitting room, a small bedroom, and a tiny kitchenette where Adlai sometimes cooked for his guests at dinner. Ellen came for infrequent visits during that winter and spring. Adlai came even more infrequently to Chicago, once on February 18, when he accepted on behalf of Frank Knox the 1943 Award of Merit of the Decalogue Society of Lawyers, presented to the Secretary of the Navy for distinguished service to the nation and "unselfish work for a better community." Knox had been unable to attend the great dinner honoring him because of ill health.

As ardent a devotee of the strenuous life as ever Teddy Roosevelt had been, Frank Knox had refused to admit in practice that, at seventy, he was not so fit and vigorous as he had been at fifty. He looked easily ten years younger than his actual age, and as he strode over the golf course he displayed a young man's strength and endurance. He laughed at the advice of friends to slow down. But on Sunday, April 23, he had a clear intimation of his own mortality. He had come to his old home in Manchester, New Hampshire, to attend the funeral of John A. Muehling, his publishing partner for forty years. There he suffered a mild heart attack. He treated this infirmity with contempt, returning to Washington on Monday and going to his office Tuesday morning, intending to hold his regular press conference. He was unable to do so, however; he became ill and was forced to go home and to bed.

He died at his home at 1:08 o'clock on the afternoon of Friday, April 28, 1944. Ellen, Buffie, and Ernest Ives were with Adlai in the Georgetown apartment when the news came. None of them would forget how profoundly the news affected him.

James V. Forrestal, then Undersecretary, was appointed as Knox's successor, and there was newspaper speculation that Stevenson would be named to succeed Forrestal as Undersecretary. Roosevelt, it was reported, wished to do so. Stevenson himself believed, however, that Forrestal should choose his own second-in-command and that Ralph A. Bard, an old Chicago friend of Knox, who had served as Assistant Secretary during the Knox regime, had earned the post—although Bard happened to be a Republican. Stevenson therefore decided to get out of the way and resigned his position in early June, returning to Chicago.

III

By that time he was deeply involved in an enterprise which might well have determined the whole of his future career, had it succeeded, removing him altogether from active political life.

Knox's funeral was at the Mount Pleasant Congregational Church in Washington, and virtually all of the key people of the Chicago *Daily News* were among the mourners. A group of them met with Adlai Stevenson to discuss with him the future of their newspaper. They wished to form a syndicate, with others, to purchase Knox's controlling stock from his estate; they wanted Stevenson to head the group and to be publisher of the paper once the property was acquired. By the terms of the will the entire estate was left to Knox's widow, Annie Reid Knox, who was named as one of the three executors, the other two being Holman D. Pettibone, president of the Chicago Title and Trust Company, and Laird Bell, Knox's attorney. These were given great powers of discretion; they could sell to anyone at whatever price they desired, though the will asked them to do all possible to perpetuate the personnel and policies of the paper. Knox had often indicated, orally, that he would like to have the paper become employee-owned when he died.

The idea was more exciting to Stevenson than any earlier career opportunity had been, awakening all those ambitions for a career in journalism which had formerly been so strong in him. He immediately had dreams of making the *Daily News*, then a distinguished paper, into one of the greatest newspapers in the world—dreams that were shared and embroidered by his old and dear friend, Paul Scott Mowrer, the famous foreign correspondent who was then the editor, and by another intimate and beloved friend and Libertyville neighbor, the celebrated critic and biographer, Lloyd Lewis. (The colorful Lewis, who had been the managing editor during the last year of Knox's life, would often say to Stevenson during this period: "We'll ride down the street, shooting the varmints as we see 'em from *both* hips!") [2]

Through the rest of that summer and fall of 1944 he devoted all his time and energy to the syndicate. He managed to "scrape up" (as he put it) almost two million dollars. A small part of this was money of his own and that of *Daily News* editors; the bulk of it came from Stevenson's friends and acquaintances. He had in addition a promise by Marshall Field, then publishing the morning Chicago *Sun* in competition with the *Tribune,* to make up whatever balance Stevenson needed for a fair, acceptable bid. Also, Jesse Jones, the Texas millionaire, who had been a wartime admirer of Stevenson's in Washington, had made it clear that he was available if needed. After elaborate professional appraisals, Stevenson felt justified in bidding twelve dollars a share for the 149,941 shares of common stock held by the estate. This bid, however, was considerably lower than those made by several others. One of the others approached him with an offer to make him publisher at a large salary if he would facilitate the acquisition of the property, an offer he promptly refused. As the executors wanted to give Stevenson's group another chance, he raised his bid to thirteen dollars per share after consulting his investors. This, he felt, was as high as he should go in view of his representations to the investors about value based on the appraisals. Actually he could legitimately have gone high enough to outbid the others had the money been available. Even at twenty dollars a share, as it turned out, the *Daily News* would have been a bargain. He could have outbid his competitors, too, if he had been willing freely to exercise Marshall Field's commitment to him, but he was uneasy about having a competitor, however friendly personally, with a large stock interest.[3]

If Mrs. Knox considered any other factor than her desire to obtain as much money as possible for the property, it may have been one that worked against the Stevenson group. As one Chicago paper's gossip columnist put it, "Mrs. Knox has indicated that she prefers to sell to a purchaser with Republican leanings." Laird Bell indicated that the Stevenson group should be preferred, even at some sacrifice in price which, after all, was within the executors' discretion. But apparently he felt he could not insist upon his view in the circumstances. The Stevenson bid was rejected.

It was a great disappointment to him, though he had had misgivings about the difficulties of management under a voting trust. Few if any career dreams had been as vividly desirable as this of a creative metropolitan journalism.

CHAPTER FIFTEEN

ADLAI STEVENSON was so immersed in the negotiations for the *Daily News* that he took little active part in the Presidential campaign of 1944. He watched from the side lines as the Republican party nominated Governor Thomas E. Dewey of New York as its Presidential candidate while the Democrats nominated Franklin Roosevelt for a fourth term, with Senator Harry S Truman of Missouri as running mate. This was the campaign in which Roosevelt, fearful that overconfidence would reduce the Democratic vote, made a talk to the Teamsters' Union about "my little dog, Fala" ("I am accustomed to hearing malicious falsehoods about myself but I think I have a right to object to libelous statements about my dog"), whereupon the campaign became, as some contemporary remarked, a "contest between Dewey and Fala." Fala won the contest, with Roosevelt picking up the winnings in November. The Democratic victory, though no landslide, was substantial.

In Europe, World War II was approaching its final phase. Germany was

being subjected to unprecedentedly powerful and continuous air bombardment focused on her factories, power plants, transportation centers—and
such air-power proponents as General Henry H. (Hap) Arnold, commanding general of the United States Army Air Forces, were claiming that
strategic bombing was more decisive of victory than any other part of the
war effort. Others had long asserted that air power alone, if adequately employed, could win the war. Were such claims and assertions valid? Precisely
how effective was strategic bombing in general, and in what particular areas
and respects was it most effective?

It was an attempt to answer such questions that called Adlai Stevenson
back into war service from his law office, whence he returned following the
Daily News affair. He became a member of the United States Strategic
Bombing Survey, conducted by the War Department to determine the
physical damage to the enemy, the psychological effect upon him, and the
aid given Allied ground forces by the massive air attacks. "The methods of
warfare may change," Stevenson explained to Bloomington friends when he
returned from his mission, "but the fundamental theories of both ground and
sea power remain the same. It is hoped that out of our experiences in this
war some basic theories of air power may be evolved." He spent two months
in England, France, and Belgium. He toured the western front from Eichs-
weiler in Germany to Metz in France, where he met General George Patton.
He was at General Courtney Hodges's First Army headquarters at Spa in
Belgium on the day before the Germans launched their last desperate attack
of the war, into the Ardennes forest. Ignorant of the fact that the Battle of
the Bulge had begun, he drove back to Brussels with an Air Force general
and flew from there to England in a Canadian Air Force plane, in weather
so bad that an emergency landing was made miraculously in a forbidden
field many miles from London. By this time the organization was established,
and since he was unable to do much survey work because of stubborn
German resistance, he left bomb-blasted London and flew back to America.
He arrived at his Libertyville farm on Christmas Eve.

Less than two months later he was again called into government service,
this time in a field for which he was unusually well prepared and upon
which his major interest had long been focused. On February 23, 1945,
Joseph C. Grew, Undersecretary of State, announced the appointment of
Adlai Stevenson as special assistant to Secretary of State Edward R. Stettinius, Jr. "He will work with Archibald MacLeish, Assistant Secretary of
State, in matters relating to postwar international organization," the announcement said. Actually his role was to assist MacLeish in pioneering a
popular education program being initiated by the State Department in an
effort to narrow the gap that had theretofore existed between ordinary citizens and professional diplomats. It was a job of particular importance at
that time because of the upcoming international conference at San Francisco

where the United Nations Organization was to be formally developed out of proposals originally made, months before, at Dumbarton Oaks.

Ellen Stevenson remained on the farm with the three boys when her husband departed for Washington. "She's seen a terrific lot of that farm these past three years since her husband has been in Washington and all over the globe besides," wrote a Chicago society columnist. "And after Mr. Stevenson was released from his job with the Navy Department last summer they were settling down, as they supposed, to the quiet life in the country. Now with the new State Department appointment, Adlai Stevenson is back in Washington, probably until the war is over." In Washington, until he went to San Francisco in May, he lived with his old friends, Mr. and Mrs. Benjamin W. Thoron, in their large old Georgetown house at 2900 N Street, N.W.

His office was next to MacLeish's in a first floor corner of the old State Department building, and in his daily contacts with the distinguished poet he cemented a permanent and mutually admiring friendship. It was, for him, a highly educative friendship. One of the things he learned was abundantly confirmed by his own later experience, namely that, in the political life of our time, *"dura est ovicipitum via"* or, freely translated, "the way of the egghead is hard." * The word "egghead" as a synonym for "intellectual" had not yet enriched the American language—it would be one of the products of Stevenson's future career—but MacLeish certainly belonged to the category it named. He suffered for it. "For some reason hard to fathom, the fact that he is a poet has been treated by hostile editorialists as though he had a record down at the Bureau of Identification," wrote Edwin A. Lahey, Washington correspondent of the Chicago *Daily News,* in his column of April 12, 1945. ". . . MacLeish is . . . a man's man, a World War I flier, a scholar, a distinguished journalist . . . who believes in what he is doing." What he was doing, "with the valuable assistance of Adlai Stevenson," was "making the people of this country State Department conscious." Lahey added that "letters of comment and inquiry have been coming to the State Department at the rate of 600 a day in recent weeks. . . . This kind of mail," he added, ". . . is no small tribute to the performance of MacLeish and Stevenson."

By the time this column was written MacLeish and Stevenson had been placed in a particularly unhappy position.

When the announcement of Stevenson's appointment was made President Roosevelt was on his way to Washington from the Yalta Conference, at which the British, Russian, and American heads of state had, among other things, endorsed the United Nations Conference, which was to assemble in

---

* The phrase was coined by Professor Madison Priest of Princeton University in reference to the political campaign of 1952 and was made famous in a nationally syndicated column by Joseph and Stewart Alsop.

San Francisco on April 25. On March 2, Roosevelt had addressed Congress in a bid for support of the Yalta Agreement, mentioning in passing that "it is not yet possible to announce . . . publicly" the terms of the voting procedure for the Security Council of the proposed UNO, but that the announcement would be made "in a very short time." Why could not the announcement be made now? people asked, suspiciously. Three days later, from Mexico, where the Chapultepec Conference was in progress, Secretary of State Stettinius made known the veto provision that had been agreed upon for the Security Council at Yalta—a provision that was immediately interpreted by many as a sellout to Stalin (though in point of fact the United States would have insisted upon it if Stalin had not done so). It began to look as though the true relationship between the three great powers was far different from that which the American and British leaders had represented to their peoples.

All of this complicated the task of preparing a knowledgeable popular support for the proposed United Nations Organization, but MacLeish and Stevenson went forward with an educational program emphasizing that Big Three solidarity was indispensable to the peace and that the basis for this had been well laid at Yalta. Particularly did they seek to scotch the rumor that unknown arrangements had been made for voting in the proposed UN's General Assembly. In printed materials and radio broadcasts they repeatedly emphasized the absolute equality of the UN voting procedure, giving small nations the same voting power as big ones within the Assembly. They did this in the perfect assurance that they spoke the truth.

One can imagine their dismay, therefore, when a leak to a New York *Herald Tribune* reporter revealed that an arrangement had indeed been made at Yalta whereby Britain and the United States would support Russia's request for three votes in the Assembly in return for Russia's support of the U.S.'s request for three votes, if the latter request were made. (It never *was* made, of course. The leak had come from a supposedly off-the-record meeting between Roosevelt and newly appointed members of the U.S. delegation to the San Francisco Conference.) Roosevelt was on his way to Warm Springs, Georgia, when this news was published; from there he planned to go to San Francisco to open the great conference. Harry Hopkins lay ill in a hospital at Rochester, Minnesota. Stettinius alone had to bear the brunt of public outrage and suspicion. Only the obvious fact that no Assistant Secretary had been informed of the Yalta voting agreement kept the pressure on MacLeish from becoming unbearable, and both he and Stevenson well knew that the effectiveness of their program was greatly impaired. Seeds of suspicion had been planted, which might grow into a jungle of reactionary isolationism.[1]

Then came the fateful day of April 12, 1945, a day whose event dwarfed to insignificance the MacLeish-Stevenson job anxieties. . . . On that April 12, the American Ninth Army reached the Elbe River in Germany, where, two weeks later, American and Russian troops would meet in a show of fraternal affection that would seem incredible before many months had passed. On the other side of the world, air bases were established on Okinawa just 325 miles from Japan, though bitter fighting would continue on portions of the island for many weeks to come.

In his cottage at the Warm Springs Foundation in Georgia, the President of the United States sat for an artist's sketches from which a portrait of him was to be painted. His spirits were buoyed up by the news of victory in war, his mind filled with hopes for victory in peace and *for* peace in San Francisco. Suddenly he felt great pain at the back of his head.

"I have a terrific headache," he said.

He collapsed into unconsciousness. It was one fifteen in the afternoon.

At four thirty-five he was dead. He had suffered, said his doctor, a "massive cerebral hemorrhage. . . ."

Archibald MacLeish was asked to write the official proclamation of the President's death, and he and Adlai Stevenson sat together in the State Department late and alone that hushed night. Stevenson's contribution, however, was a modest one, as he himself always insisted. It consisted of looking up proclamations that had been issued when earlier Presidents died in office. MacLeish did the actual writing.[2]

II

To millions of mankind, in that hour, it seemed that a rock indispensable to the foundation of world order had crumbled into dust. It still seemed so to very many when the delegates of fifty nations formally assembled at San Francisco on April 25 to write a charter for the United Nations Organization. Roosevelt, as everyone knew, had been his own foreign minister on every crucial matter; in his administration the Secretary of State had become increasingly an instrument rather than a maker of policy, and this had been particularly so since the retirement of Cordell Hull in the autumn of 1944. His successor, Stettinius, a rich and handsome man who had served as Lend-Lease Administrator, was ex officio head of the United States delegation in San Francisco; and it was soon evident that he lacked the prestige if not the natural ability to lead his own delegation with its large staff of experts, including as it did some very strong-willed and senior political leaders of both parties as well as the foremost international experts in the country. The U.S. delegation included John Foster Dulles and Harold Stassen; Senators Tom Connally of Texas, Chairman of the Foreign Relations Committee, and Arthur Vandenberg of Michigan, senior Republican member of that committee; and Congressmen Sol Bloom of New York and Charles Eaton of

New Jersey. Of these, only one was younger than the Secretary of State in years (Stassen had just turned thirty-eight; Stettinius was forty-five) and all were far older than he in governmental experience.

Particularly was it difficult to handle the group's public relations since it included so many conflicting prima donnas. Other delegations, notably the British, were clever at managing their press relations in such a way as to strengthen their hands in conference negotiations. They skillfully leaked to newsmen such items of information as would enhance their popular prestige and further their national policies. The United States delegation, on the other hand, could seldom agree on what to announce to the press and on who was to do it, with the result that it gave out little and that little was often garbled and soon contradicted.

American correspondents were reduced to getting much of their information about the conference from the members of other delegations, and as public pressures increased upon them—there was of course an avid popular interest in the historic conference—they grew wrathful. Editorials attacking the U.S. delegation's handling of news began to appear, notably in the Washington *Post*, whose publisher, Eugene Meyer, lived on the same floor of the Fairmont Hotel as Stettinius did. The *Post* editorial so enraged the Secretary of State that he and the *Post* publisher came close to blows one day when they met in a hotel corridor. It was at that low point that Adlai Stevenson was sent for, reportedly at the suggestion of Arthur Krock of the New York *Times*.[3]

"What are you doing here, exactly?" asked Louise Wright when she encountered Stevenson in San Francisco in early May.

"Why, haven't you heard?" Stevenson whispered, laughing. "I'm the official leak!" [4]

And this was precisely his function. It was, in his opinion, one of the most difficult assignments of his life—to keep the press as fully informed as his good judgment indicated and to educate the American press on the background of all the controversies—and do it unofficially and largely unknown to the delegation itself. He was assisted by Edward S. Miller, later Assistant Secretary of State of Latin-American Affairs, and Thomas K. Finletter, later Secretary of Air.* He quickly grasped the necessarily complex organization of the conference, defining the issues involved in the strategies and tactics of all the delegations. He attended all the meetings of the United States delegation—meetings closed to newsmen, of course—and thus kept himself intimately informed of what the U.S. was doing and trying to do,

---

* Thomas K. Finletter told me, in an interview on October 4, 1966, that he and Edward Miller originally established the "leak office" at the suggestion of Krock and James (Scotty) Reston of *The New York Times* and that Stevenson was outraged by the procedure when, newly arrived in San Francisco, he first learned of it. He quickly saw the necessity for it, however, according to Finletter.

and why. He established an unpublicized headquarters in Room 576 of the Fairmont, where the wholly new and very welcome departure for the State Department was dubbed Operation Titanic. He became the cheerful focus of the top correspondents' close attention. Inevitably he became a focus, too, for some criticism by some of the U.S. delegation members. When anything went wrong in the newspapers the delegates could conveniently disclaim both the accuracy of the report and responsibility for it, blaming him. But his arrival marked a turning point from impossibly bad to excellent press relations, and his methods established a precedent that has frequently been followed. The correspondents were grateful to him, and so, ultimately, were all the members of the U.S. delegation.

The conference ended on June 26, having drafted the United Nations Charter. The new organization was very far from being a world government of the kind many philosophers of history now deemed essential to a permanently peaceful world order, but in several respects it went farther in that direction than the League of Nations had done. Perhaps its greatest hope for the long run lay in the Economic and Social Council, with the attached agencies through which a closer, more fruitful international collaboration than ever before was provided in a number of fields of common interest.

Stevenson himself did not deplore, as many idealists did, the fact that national sovereignty was the stuff out of which the new edifice was being built. How could it be otherwise, in the prevailing circumstances?

"Everything depends on the active participation, pacific intentions, and good faith of the Big Five, and particularly the United States, Russia, and Britain," he admitted. "Everything we hope for depends on their collaboration in peace as in war; and I risk the estimate that in the United Nations Organization that collaboration is based on the most solid of all foundations —national self-interest."

He made these statements in an article contributed to the Bloomington *Pantagraph* just two weeks after the conference had ended, an article in which he asserted that the Charter represented a "long stride" toward world peace.

A few weeks later the crucial importance of that peace would be emphasized by the dropping (on August 6 and August 9) of atomic bombs upon the Japanese cities of Hiroshima and Nagasaki, swiftly followed by the surrender of Japan, the end of World War II.

With the San Francisco conference expired Stevenson's "term of enlistment" (as he called it) with the State Department. He agreed, however, to go back to Washington to help promote Senate ratification of the Charter, eager though he was to return to his family and the "business of earning a living." He continued for some weeks as special assistant to the Secretary of State, a post to which James F. Byrnes was appointed after Stettinius resigned in early July—and on July 7 he himself was publicly honored for his wartime service in the Navy Department. On that day, at a ceremony in the Navy Department, Adlai Stevenson was awarded the Distinguished Civilian Service Award, the Navy's highest civilian award.

Next morning the Washington *Post* illustrated its story of the award with a photograph of the first Adlai E. Stevenson in his last years. Mildly irritated, Stevenson clipped out the story and mailed it with a brief note to his friend Wayne Coy of the *Post*'s editorial staff. "Ho hum," he wrote, "I've a white mustache and a wing collar and I'm 70, and all the time I thought I was a young man and in the very mould of fashion. But then perhaps it's just as well we see ourselves as 'ithers see us,' and the resemblance would be very surprising to grandfather, dead these 35 years."

In late July, after Senate ratification of the UN Charter, he resigned his State Department post and returned to Chicago.

III

The Laird Bells loaned him a cottage they owned in Michigan's Huron Mountains, and Stevenson took Ellen and the boys there for a vacation—his first since 1940. While at the cottage he received separate phone calls from Secretary of State Byrnes and Stettinius. The latter had been named the chief American delegate to the Executive Committee of the Preparatory Commission of the United Nations Organization; he and Byrnes, and the President, too, wanted Stevenson to serve as Stettinius's deputy. The committee's work, they pointed out, was of major importance. Meeting in London, it would draft recommendations concerning the structure of the UN—"putting flesh on the bare bones of the Charter," as Stevenson would describe it—and on the location of UN headquarters. These draft recommendations would be acted upon by the Preparatory Commission as a whole, which would meet in London in November, to be followed by the first meeting of the UN's General Assembly in January.

The pressure they exerted overcame Stevenson's reluctance, but he flatly refused to be again separated from his family. Stevenson discussed the matter with Ellen. It was decided that she would follow him to England, bringing with her thirteen-year-old Borden and (as he would be on October 10) fifteen-year-old Adlai, III. The two boys would be entered as day students in the ancient and famous public school, Harrow. Nine-year-old John Fell, however, was considered too young to profit much from the months ahead, and Ellen disliked removing him from his school at Lake Forest. The problem of caring for him was solved by Buffie and Ernest Ives's agreeing to come to live on the Libertyville farm, with John Fell, until

Ellen and the others returned. "I'm so glad you can take [him] while we are away and I hope it won't be too inconvenient," Stevenson wrote Ernest Ives on the evening before he flew to Washington, en route to New York. "I hope he won't be too much of a burden for you. Please take care of his tuition, travel, etc., and I will repay you when I return."

Stevenson sailed on the *Queen Elizabeth* on September 5 with a party that included Secretary Byrnes, Charles Bohlen, Ben Cohen, and John Foster Dulles, as well as Ralph Bunche, Dorothy Fosdick, and other expert San Francisco veterans. Byrnes and his group were going to the first and far from successful meeting of the Council of Foreign Ministers in London. The others, assigned to the Preparatory Commission, met Stettinius in London. He was, they discovered, a sick man. By the time Ellen and the boys arrived in late September, doctors had diagnosed Stettinius's trouble as gallstones, and a few days later he resigned his post and flew back to the United States for the needed surgery. Stevenson was placed in charge of the American delegation, with its large staff of workers and advisers.

Said the Chicago *Tribune:* "Mr. Stettinius has pulled out of the conference of United Nations architects in Europe, leaving American interests in the hands of Adlai Stevenson, the boy orator of Bloomington." Said the Chicago *Daily News:* "This step brings an able man to a bigger job than he has previously held. . . . To date Mr. Stevenson has been one of those government servants 'with a passion for anonymity.' He has not been much in the public eye. Henceforth he may be."

The Stevensons, mission completed, expected to return by Christmas. As it turned out they did not do so until the spring of 1946.

When he took over as chief of the U.S. delegation, difficulties with the Soviet delegation, headed by Andrei Gromyko, were accumulating. One was a basic disagreement about the proper relationship of the Security Council, the General Assembly, and the Secretariat of the United Nations Organization. In the Soviet view the Security Council was the only really important organ of the United Nations, and to it alone should all real powers be reserved: the roles of the Assembly and of the Secretariat should be wholly secondary. To this end, Gromyko, supported by Czechoslovakia and Yugoslavia, pressed stubbornly for a departmental rather than a functional organization of the UN's Secretariat. In other words, the Soviets wanted a separate secretariat to be established for each of the UN's major departments—the Security Council, the Economic and Social Council, the Trusteeship Council, and the General Assembly—under the Secretary General. The United States and other Western powers desired a Secretariat that, under the Secretary General, was organized in terms of economics, social problems, trusteeship, legal operations, personnel management, and so on. Between these two positions there was no possibility of compromise; one side or the other must yield; and in the end it was Russia that did so. Other crucial problems arose from the Soviet delegation's iron concept of the world divided, like all Gaul, into three parts: Russian, British, American. The Soviet delegates insisted that Russia have one third of the total representation on every UN body. They shuffled around their satellites—Yugoslavia, Poland, Czechoslovakia, the Ukraine, and Byelorussia—like chessmen, displaying a profound contempt for the idea that each sovereign state should have one vote. To the Russians as (it must be admitted) to many others it seemed ridiculous that San Salvador and the U.S.S.R. should have an equal voice in the determination of any major UN policy.

Stevenson was chairman of the Executive Committee sessions in which the draft recommendations were finally acted upon. His general strategy was to avoid showdown votes on which the outcome was perfectly predictable, namely eleven to three against the Communist nations, since repeated defeats only made the Russians more stubborn. He tried constantly, during these trying weeks of night-and-day negotiation, to accent the areas of agreement. Someone remarked that while the world was falling apart at Lancaster House, where the Council of Foreign Ministers was meeting, it was being put together again at Church House, where the Preparatory Commission met—and for the latter, Stevenson was largely responsible. He was endlessly patient, and resourceful as a parliamentarian. But when firmness was necessary he was as stubbornly inflexible as Gromyko.

Newspaper correspondents covering the meetings (they included Herbert L. Matthews and Sydney Gruson of *The New York Times,* William H. Stoneman of the Chicago *Daily News,* Frederick Kuh of the Chicago *Sun,* and Carl W. McCardle of the Philadelphia *Bulletin*) were unanimous in their praise of Stevenson's overall operation. Said one observer, "I never saw a man handle the Russians like he did." *

He did so through patient personal negotiation and, in the committee sessions, by moral suasion, everlasting good humor, and a wit that relieved many tense moments. At one point, for example, Gromyko bitterly protested the form in which Stevenson, as chairman, had phrased a question for a vote. "I'm surprised at you," the Russian snapped angrily. Stevenson "politely but firmly" (as one reporter wrote) reminded the Russian that he was chairman. "I don't think we should alter our procedure item by item," he commented mildly. "At least I don't propose to do so while I am chairman." Gromyko then said quickly, "I have a very great respect for the chairman." And the difficulty was smoothed over.

* Clifton Utley told me in 1956 of visiting Stevenson in London during this period. He was impressed by the way Stevenson adapted his conversational technique to the temperament and point of view of the man with whom he talked. "His approach to the Russians was wholly different from his approach to the French, and his approach to the British differed from his approach, say, to a member of his own delegation," said Utley. "He changed his word choice, the structure of his argument—even to some extent his tone of voice. . . . It was a virtuosity I had not noted before."

The Executive Committee completed its agenda on October 27, having arranged for the full Preparatory Commission to open its session on November 23 and for the first United Nations General Assembly to convene during the first week of January, 1946. One of the things the committee had *not* done, however, was to prepare the way for the meetings of the full Preparatory Commission, beginning on November 24. "The Committee's last sessions were so rushed and were held in such an atmosphere of nervousness that no one apparently wanted to take the responsibility for smoothing the way for the Preparatory Commission," reported Herbert L. Matthews from London on November 15. "As Mr. Stevenson was the last chairman, he felt it incumbent on him to do something about it. Otherwise the . . . Commission would spend its first days wasting valuable time on purely procedural questions." Accordingly, Stevenson and Gladwyn Jebb, British general secretary of the committee, worked out proposals for the commission's agenda, election of president, and so on, calling a special meeting of the Executive Committee to pass on these. As a result, the full commission, with delegations from fifty-one nations, organized itself swiftly and with a minimum of disagreement within two days after its session opened.

The most newsworthy item on the agenda of the Preparatory Commission meeting was the location of the permanent headquarters of the United Nations Organization. Some twenty-two American cities had deputations in London, lobbying for their respective municipalities as UN sites. Chicago was among them. Early in the sessions, Stevenson, continuing as chief of the United States delegation, felt called upon to divorce these lobbying activities, publicly, from official U.S. delegation policy. In a strong statement issued through the American Embassy, he pointed out that the United States had consistently emphasized that she was not seeking the permanent UN home, though she would welcome it if the commission voted to locate in this country. The deputations from American cities were composed, he stressed, of private citizens who had come to London on their own initiative "with the best will" and whose arguments should be considered on their merits and in no sense as expressions of official American views.

This prompted a typically inaccurate Chicago *Tribune* editorial, entitled MR. STEVENSON VOTES FOR EUROPE. He did so, it said, by "gratuitously" informing his international colleagues "that this country is not seeking the world capital."

"It is easy to understand why he does not want the international capital in America," the *Tribune* went on. "He and his kind profess an interest in foreign affairs only because they wish to get away from America and associate with foreigners, to whom they pay fawning obeisance. . . . Mr. Stevenson . . . evidently is ashamed of the fact that his roots until recently were in such a typical American community as Bloomington, Illinois."

This was neither the first nor last of such items of journalistic intelligence and integrity focused on Stevenson by the *Tribune*—items of intemperance and deceit that would concern him less and less as time passed, though, as he later said, he "bemoaned the fact" that he lacked "both the calm and the vigor of Colonel Knox's contempt for that journal."

A Philippine delegate, Pedro Lopez, opened the debate on the UN home, asserting that "the best way to keep the United States in the United Nations is to put UNO's feet in the United States." The danger of American isolation was "as great today as ever," Lopez asserted. The United States "behaved like an elderly excited lady about to become a grandmother at San Francisco when she observed the birth pangs of the UNO," he continued. "She threw out her arms in hysterical hospitality to the delegates. . . ."

To this Adlai Stevenson made reply. He was, he said, "shocked" to hear his country referred to as an excited grandmother. He had always considered the U.S. position to be more similar to that of "an agitated, blushing debutante. . . . But the young lady is not sensitive," he assured the delegates, as gales of laughter swept the hall, "and she wishes you to converse as freely as possibly about her, in connection with the UN site—and not only about her, but about all the other ladies in the block." After days of debate and maneuvering, the commission voted 30 to 14 for the United States as the UNO headquarters, with the U.S. abstaining.

On December 20, 1945, after the Preparatory Commission meetings had ended, Stevenson gave a lengthy interview to C. I. Sulzberger of *The New York Times*, in which he expressed his sense of United Nations progress thus far and of the organization's possible future. America, he said, had become the "new center of world policy for peace" and by establishing its headquarters in this country, the United Nations Organization would learn much from the example of "vibrant democracy" presented by the U.S. Significant, in view of a basic developing issue of his time, was Stevenson's carefully worded comparison of the United Nations Charter, as an historic event, with the United States Constitution. The Charter "of course cannot go nearly as far as the Constitution did in the delegation of sovereign powers by the States," he said, and the analogy between Charter and Constitution "cannot be carried too far. . . . We are at a much earlier period of development in international organization, law, and government than were the thirteen colonies in the organization of a national government in the United States in 1787." The great problem now was to make the United Nations work so well within its present limitations that individual governments might be willing at some future time to cede to it more of their sovereign powers. His implicit recognition of the analogy was further expressed in his warning that the "members . . . must never permit the organization to be divided into two camps, as the issue of slavery divided the Federal Union before the Civil War."

The historic General Assembly opened its first session in Central Hall,

Westminster, on January 1, 1946. The U.S. delegates were Secretary of State James Byrnes, delegation chairman; Edward R. Stettinius, Jr., who had sufficiently recovered from his illness to assume this duty; Senator Connally; Senator Vandenberg; and Mrs. Eleanor Roosevelt. "Foreign diplomats were slightly surprised when Stevenson was made senior adviser to the American delegation to the Assembly, instead of being made a full delegate or an alternate," reported Stoneman of the Chicago *Daily News*. "Americans who had watched his work during earlier meetings were not only surprised, they were slightly disgusted." Nevertheless, Stevenson's role as probably the most effective member of the entire U.S. contingent did not go unrecognized as the Assembly proceeded. Nor was this recognition confined to his own compatriots: delegates from all the fifty-one nations, many of whom after the long weary weeks had become his fast friends, regarded him as a key figure in the total proceedings—intelligent, trustworthy, utterly dedicated to the cause of international organization.

Two and a half days after the Assembly's opening, its entire slate of important electoral posts had been filled, with a minimum of discontent and a wholly unexpected wealth of common agreement. "Taken as a whole," wrote Saville R. Davis of the *Christian Science Monitor* on January 14, "it was a remarkable achievement." And the "hero of the elections," wrote Davis, "is Mr. Adlai Stevenson. . . . In an unguarded moment, when he was being congratulated on his achievement, he said with a laugh, 'I guess I'm just a ward politician at heart.' This modesty wholly misrepresented his talents. Mr. Stevenson did virtually the entire job of preparing the election lists for the United States delegation, and negotiating with other delegations.

"He acted, with the support of the delegation, on the principle that he was seeking a democratic agreement rather than imposing big-power dictation," this reporter continued. "He drafted with great patience and skill a list which represented not what the United States wanted but, as nearly as possible, what all delegations and groups wanted. The result was a phenomenal electoral success."

All around them lay the devastation of war and the iron austerity (the meager rationing, the shabby living) that was the war's long aftermath in England. Their immediate environment pointed up the gravity of the work they were doing.

The Stevensons themselves lived in a small bomb-damaged house, converted from a stable, at No. 2 Mount Row just off Grosvenor Square. (Stevenson's office on the square, during the period he was head of the delegation, was the same one General Eisenhower had once occupied.) Ellen's total domestic staff consisted of an elderly cook. They were happy there together, happier than they had been for a long time, and the two boys were obviously and swiftly enriched by their experience. Ellen sparkled at diplomatic din-

ners and receptions, which are the inevitable and often excessive accompaniment of international conferences; there is no doubt that her scintillating
presence helped her husband in his personal negotiations with the representatives of other countries and in his relationship with the members of the
American contingent. She seemed not to feel, in London, that species of
claustrophobia which had afflicted her in wartime Washington.

In January she returned to the United States with the two boys, enrolling
them in school there for the second semester, then sailed back to England
to rejoin her husband. She arrived in London almost simultaneously with
tragic family news. At approximately three o'clock on the morning of January 31, a United Air Lines plane crashed into Elk Mountain, some sixty-
five miles northwest of Laramie, Wyoming. All twenty-one persons aboard
were killed. Among them was Robert S. Pirie, manager of the New York
office of Carson, Pirie, Scott and Company, whom Ellen's younger sister
Betty had married and by whom Betty had had two children, Robert, Jr., and
Joan.

For weeks thereafter Stevenson continued his behind-the-scenes role for
the American delegation, doing "much of the leg work and no small part of
the brainwork," as Stoneman of the Chicago *Daily News* put it. In early
March his mission, as he said in a letter of resignation to Secretary of State
Byrnes, was completed.

Secretary Byrnes replied: "I want to thank you on behalf of the President
and myself for the distinguished services you have rendered. . . . You have
helped greatly to get the United Nations started as a going concern."

By the time this was written, Adlai and Ellen Stevenson were on the high
seas, aboard the *Queen Mary,* en route for New York. In the second week
of March they were back upon the Libertyville farm.

CHAPTER SIXTEEN

THERE began for Stevenson an interregnum, during which his life
seemed to lack a clear direction. He was forty-six years old as this period
started. He had never flatly repeated himself from one year to the next. He
had done new things, larger things. Was this process of growth and widening activity now to end? Must he now begin repeating himself? Men did,
generally, at his age—or long before they reached his age. They got into a
quiet rut, with nearly all elements of their lives predictable, and perhaps

they were mostly happy there, raising their families, sending sons and daughters out into the world, making money, taking longer vacations, confining their ambitions within comfortable limits. He rode with such men on the commuter trains to the Loop each morning, from the Loop to Lake Forest each evening.

He returned to his law firm, now become Sidley, Austin, Burgess and Harper, where he strove conscientiously to resume the law practice he had relinquished five years before. Mrs. Quincy (Louise) Wright visited him there one day on business. She thought his office dismal and Stevenson himself unhappy, and not merely because he said things that indicated as much. "He always talks that way, deprecating what he's doing or himself for doing it," Mrs. Wright explained long afterward. "I wouldn't have based any conclusions on what he *said* if he hadn't somehow *seemed* unhappy." She sensed that he was bored with the law and the old routines, a readjustment not unfamiliar to many returning to private life from the turmoil of war.[1]

But he worked hard at it, and competently. On one case—it had to do with an extremely valuable piece of real estate in the financial district of downtown Chicago—he worked with a young man named J. Edward Day, who had joined the firm before the war, after having taken his law degree at Harvard and, in 1941, had married Mary Louise Burgess, daughter of senior partner Kenneth F. Burgess. He was acute and witty; he amused himself, and released tensions in times of pressure, by writing humorous topical verses. He was also a hard worker. He helped Stevenson with the brief for this case, and he was impressed by the skill with which Stevenson presented the argument in court before a judge (there was no jury). Stevenson won the case. Day and Stevenson had one thing in common, a rare thing in that office: both were Democrats. The younger man was destined to play a role of importance in the Stevenson future.[2]

II

If he drifted, as he sometimes felt he was doing, it was in no tranquil stream. Rather was it a whirlpool. His life, however lacking it might be in a clear direction during those months, certainly did not lack busyness.

He resumed his activities in civic affairs. He did a good deal of public speaking, writing out his speeches with painstaking care as always. In early June he was awarded an honorary Doctor of Laws degree at Northwestern University. A week later he gave the commencement address at the eighty-seventh annual Illinois Wesleyan University exercises in Normal, and he was there awarded another honorary degree. On weekends he worked happily in the yard of his country home, trimming trees, pruning shrubbery, making hay, and working in the kitchen garden. He played tennis with old friends on the court he had built years before in a little shaded grove not far from the house.

Sometimes he wandered along the clay bank of the Des Plaines River with his neighbor Lloyd Lewis, who lived a mile or so away in a house designed for him by his friend Frank Lloyd Wright. Lewis and his wife, Kathryn, had with the Stevensons a friendship that had deepened through the years, strengthened especially by the struggle the two men had made for control of the *Daily News*. It was now richly satisfying on all levels of companionship. Lewis was a vibrant, happy personality, beloved of all who knew him. He was a great outdoorsman—had been a short-time sheep rancher in the West, and loved to rough it in the western wilderness. He was a versatile journalist and writer—had been a sportswriter, a drama critic, and a political writer who found politics and politicians fascinating. He was one of the great raconteurs of his time. To his home came many famous personages— Marc Connelly, Alexander Woollcott, Oscar Hammerstein—and the Stevensons were always included in parties which Lloyd and Kathryn gave for such guests.[3]

Lewis's greatest literary interest was history, particularly Civil War history. The characters of our national tragedy—somber and gaudy, funny and sad, heroic and villainous—fascinated him as they did Adlai Stevenson. He had written *Myths After Lincoln; Sherman, Fighting Prophet*, and other books, and was now beginning a long biography of U.S. Grant.

What Stevenson could not but be aware of during this period was the fact that he and Ellen had been growing apart through the last several years. A gap had opened between them which now was rarely, briefly bridged, and in this widening gap lay a ground increasingly barren of sympathy and understanding. In earlier years each had *seemed* to take pride in the other. Ellen had helped him then; he had tried to help her. Freely he acknowledged the help she had given—though it is possible that (not being the demonstrative kind) he had not made her sufficiently aware of his gratitude, assuming, falsely perhaps, that she must realize it. Now, however, she seemed to take little satisfaction in his successes; she seemed almost to resent the honors and recognition that came to him.

Yet there were ties between them: legal ties and ties of affection and memory and family. These grew more painful as the two seemed increasingly determined to go separate ways, each refusing to yield to the other's direction. Ellen was seemingly impelled toward the arts, or the literary life, as strongly, as inevitably, as he was impelled toward public service. The pain came when impulse encountered external compulsion. Vital needs tugged against vital obligations, so that the ties that bound these two together cut ever more deeply into their separate spirits. Each became aware of self-divisions. Each became aware that the struggle was within as well as between them. Each feared the effects this might produce upon their sons. If worse came to worst, the boys might be torn asunder by divergent loyalties. During this period, the youngest son, John Fell, entering his teens, began to stammer quite badly.

Opportunities came repeatedly to Stevenson for government service abroad and at home. Embassies in South American countries were offered him. Trygve Lie, the Secretary-General of the United Nations, offered him the post of Assistant Secretary-General for Administrative and Financial Services. President Truman wanted to appoint him to the Securities and Exchange Commission, with chairmanship of that body as a sequel (he'd been recommended by the Investment Bankers Association). In September of 1947, George Marshall, then Secretary of State, urged him to consider the post of Assistant Secretary of State for Public Affairs. All these offers he refused.* A newspaper report said he had "expressed the feeling that he would like to retire to his private career as corporation lawyer"—and hints of one element of his inward turmoil, one major factor of his indecision, were contained in a newspaper columnist's assertion: "[Stevenson's] boys are growing up and he wishes them to live their impressionable years in their native environment."

III

But other calls to public service came during this period which he could not in good conscience refuse. President Truman named him one of five alternate United States delegates to the second part of the first session of the UN's General Assembly, meeting in New York from early September into December of 1946.

During this session, Stevenson, operating in the Hotel Pennsylvania, was in charge of liaison, which is to say that in New York as in London he kept in touch with other delegations and engaged in the personal behind-the-scenes negotiations on which so much of the outcome of the public sessions depended. He represented the U.S. on the committee dealing with economic and social affairs. He was Senator Warren R. Austin's alternate on the committee-of-the-whole that decided to locate the permanent home of the United Nations in New York. And he was often the United States spokesman in plenary sessions on major international political questions.

It was he who presented the United States position regarding the administration of international relief, a highly controversial and hence newsworthy item on the Assembly agenda. The United Nations Relief and Rehabilitation Administration (UNRRA) was soon to go out of existence, and the issue

---

* He told General Marshall that his wife had said flatly that she would divorce him if he ever again accepted a Washington post. This, he confessed, was a major reason why he could not become William Benton's successor as Assistant Secretary. Benton had urged his appointment upon Truman and Marshall.

before the Assembly was whether or not a new international organization should be created to handle UNRRA problems. On behalf of the United States, Stevenson opposed the formation of a new international relief and rehabilitation organization.

There followed a prolonged and vigorous debate with New York's Fiorello La Guardia, the head of UNRRA, who insisted that a new organization was needed and proposed a four-hundred-million-dollar international fund for emergency relief. Stevenson proposed, as an alternative, consultation among the producer nations and the nations still in need of assistance—a step which the New York *Herald Tribune* (agreeing with *The New York Times* and many other papers) deemed a "backward" one, since it meant a reversion to national settlements in place of international cooperation. This argument had weight, Stevenson privately conceded. He himself strongly believed that every practicable method by which international organization could be strengthened should be employed. The trouble with the present La Guardia position was that, in Stevenson's personal view and in the view of his government, it was impracticable. In the first place—as he openly stated—it would almost certainly complicate relief administration, thus delaying and perhaps reducing the actual transfer of food and goods from producer nations to hungry people. In the second place—as he could not openly state—Congress was much more likely to vote adequate foreign relief funds if these were administered directly and wholly by the U.S. Government.

Nat Barrows, Chicago *Daily News* correspondent, saw the La Guardia-Stevenson debate as a study in contrasts. "Stevenson is calm, dignified, and rational, appealing to the minds of his . . . colleagues. La Guardia is flamboyant, dramatically oratorical, and close to rabble-rousing, appealing to the emotions." In his final speech La Guardia looked across the oval table at Stevenson and shook his finger menacingly as he charged that the United States, supported by the United Kingdom, was "making a political football out of food." To this Adlai Stevenson next day made sober reply. There were indeed hungry people in the world, he conceded; they must and would be fed; but the situation now was very different from the immediate postwar emergency. It could be "best and most efficiently met by simple and direct means." After certain compromises had been negotiated, his view—the official U.S. view—was substantially accepted. Afterward he himself was never sure that the policy he had espoused was the best one possible. Perhaps it would have been better to handle the relief situation in such a way as to merge it with a continuing world food program, thus giving initial impetus to the UN's Food and Agriculture Organization. . . .

After the session had ended, Nat Barrows made acid comment upon the U.S. delegation's work. "OUR SIDE FUMBLED U.N. BALL, *Only Mrs. F.D.R., Stevenson Did Job*"—so ran the headline over Barrows' story. "Mrs. Roosevelt and . . . Adlai Stevenson measured up to their jobs excellently," the correspondent wrote. "They worked hard, thought clearly, tried to make sense out of muddled directives and inter-delegation confusion, and addressed their respective committees with ideas instead of oratory. They merit return to the 1947 delegation, with increased responsibilities. Otherwise, a realistic overhaul is necessary."

The Barrows view was widely shared, and was largely acted upon in July of 1947, when Truman appointed the delegation to the General Assembly session which opened in late September. Mrs. Roosevelt and Senator Austin were reappointed. General George Marshall, Secretary of State, was named a delegate and chairman of the delegation. John Foster Dulles was named a full delegate. So was Ambassador Herschel V. Johnson, Austin's deputy on the Security Council. Adlai Stevenson's appointment as an alternate was, as before, greeted with a chorus of editorial approval, with only the Chicago *Tribune* dissenting. During this session he represented the U.S. on the important Budgetary and Administrative Committee and also spoke for the U.S. on matters relating to the admission of new members.

When he returned to his home in December the anguished interregnum in his life was mounting toward its crisis as it approached its end. Caught up in a web of circumstances which he himself had helped to spin, he was forced toward the most important and difficult career decision he had ever made. . . .

BOOK FIVE

Politics in Illinois

CHAPTER SEVENTEEN

T HE web of circumstance had many strands. . . .

One of them—it had run as a minor recurrent theme through all the years of his Washington and foreign service—was a simple unorganized response to the fact that he came from a political family, bore a widely known political name, and had become in his own right, through demonstrated abilities, one of the best-known and most highly respected Chicagoans of his generation. It was this that had led to his being considered for the Senate, opposing C. Wayland (Curly) Brooks, as far back as the late autumn of '41. It had led also to an abortive movement to draft him as candidate for governor, opposing Dwight Green's reelection to a second term, in late 1943 and early 1944, though he himself had never taken this movement very seriously.

It was upon the Senate that he fixed whatever political ambitions he then entertained, and it was with the Senate in view, as a vague possibility, that he spun his own personal strand into the web of circumstance that ultimately enmeshed him. By temperament, knowledge, and past experience, he was well equipped for the national legislature in an age when foreign affairs were of paramount concern. He knew that he was—and the value he placed upon his own qualifications, the sense of public duty, which was naturally strong in him, could not but be enhanced by the sorry view he took of Curly Brooks's performance. Neither Brooks nor Brooks's master, the baron of the Tribune Tower, exhibited the slightest capacity to learn from direct political experience, much less from history. In every realm of domestic and foreign affairs they exhibited what seemed to Stevenson a willful obtuseness, a stubborn

177

preference for the worse over the better way, which might have been laughable had it not been joined to governing power.

But Stevenson's senatorial ambitions were certainly not very definite, nor did he implement them with any definitely planned strategy. He merely presented himself to the public gaze, when occasion offered, in such light as would most beautifully shine upon a senatorial toga; he chose for his public speech such subjects as would befit a chairman of the Senate's Committee on Foreign Relations.

When he pleaded for the reelection of Emily Taft Douglas (Mrs. Paul H. Douglas) as Democratic congressman-at-large from Illinois, in a statement issued in October of '46, he did so in terms of foreign policy. When he made a speech supporting Mrs. Olive Goldman as Democratic candidate for Congress from Illinois' Nineteenth District, in 1946, he asserted that "peace," not "meat," was the dominant issue in the November election and pleaded for support of a foreign policy "which recognizes the principle of compromise and rejects the compromise of principle." He told a University of Chicago Walgreen Lecture Series audience, in November of '46 (he flew back from the General Assembly session for this address), that many grave difficulties must be overcome before an international security force (a UN "army") could become a reality. He told a Central States Conference of the Investment Bankers' Association in March of '47 that there was no "plausible alternative" to Truman's policy of military and economic assistance to Greece and Turkey save "default," which would lead to "the isolation of the United States." At the opening of the annual Jewish Welfare Fund Campaign in Chicago in June of '47, he spoke in support of the "bold" and "realistic" Marshall Plan.

By that time, another strand of circumstance was becoming interwoven with the one he himself was spinning. In consequence his senatorial ambitions were becoming more definitely focused.

The spinning of this strand began with a dark, stocky, ebullient man named Louis A. Kohn, a Chicago lawyer, partner in the firm of Mayer, Mayer, Austrian and Platt.[1] In 1947 he was thirty-nine years old and was but one year released from the military service in the Pacific. When he returned to Chicago in 1946 it was with the determination to do what he could to improve Illinois' representation in the Senate. This positive aim had its negative requirement: Curly Brooks, and all that Brooks stood for in public life, must be repudiated at the polls.

Kohn had known Adlai Stevenson during the 1930's. As lawyers, the two had had many professional contacts; as fellow members of the Council on Foreign Relations, sharing common views on foreign policy, they had had many personal contacts. It now occurred to Kohn, who listened with growing excitement to Stevenson's public speech, that his old acquaintance would make an excellent senator. Others had had the same idea, but none other had devoted to it such fervent energy as Kohn at once applied. Encountering Stevenson in the Bar Association one day, he broached the idea and found Stevenson receptive to it. They lunched together. Thereafter Stevenson's candidacy became the chief (some complained it was the sole) subject of Kohn's conversation. He talked to Dutch Smith about it, at Stevenson's suggestion. These two discussed the matter through a long luncheon hour. Then he and Smith had lunch with Stephen A. Mitchell, senior partner of the law firm of Bishop, Mitchell and Burdett, who formerly had been chief of the French division of the Lend-Lease Administration and adviser to the State Department on French economic affairs, stationed in Paris and Washington. Mitchell, an Irish Catholic and a Democrat, was much wiser in the ways of politics than either Smith or Kohn; he was no less enthusiastic than they were about Stevenson-for-Senator.

It was with this triumvirate and this luncheon, in the late spring of '47, that the first real political boom for Adlai E. Stevenson began.

Kohn wrote letters by the score, to his own acquaintances and to Stevenson's friends. Dutch Smith got in touch with his friend Loring C. (Bud) Merwin, Stevenson's cousin and active publisher of the Bloomington *Pantagraph,* who in turn sent letters to twenty-five downstate newspaper publishers, presenting Stevenson's background and asking the publishers to "find out how well, if at all, Stevenson is known in your district and whether you think he might draw any substantial number of Republican or independent votes there in a race against Senator Brooks." These identical letters concluded: "Please be completely frank, as Mr. Stevenson is in no way seeking this job, and I suspect he might even prefer discouraging reactions to those which sound hopeful!" To most of these letters the reply was that Stevenson, though respected by all who knew him, was not well known downstate. In Chicago, where he was well known, the reaction was strongly in his favor.

Meanwhile the highly tentative Stevenson candidacy was receiving considerable newspaper publicity—largely, at the outset, as a result of the Kohn-Smith operations. The publicity was aided by the fact that one Martin H. Kennelly, successful businessman and alleged reformer, had been elected mayor of Chicago on the first Tuesday in April, 1947. Kennelly had run as a Democrat, with the full backing of Colonel Jacob Arvey and the powerful Democratic organization, and his landslide victory not only plowed into political oblivion his Republican opponent, Russell W. Root, but also markedly deflated what had looked like quite a promising presidential boom for Republican Governor Green, whose candidate Root was. Professional Democrats were naturally jubilant. It was clear, however, that Kennelly's triumph (he gained a plurality of 273,354 votes while eleven of nineteen Democratic aldermen went down to defeat in runoffs) could never have grown to such proportions had it not been fed by many Republican and nearly all independent votes—a conclusion underlined by the fact he had carried wards that had long been Republican strongholds. His triumph, then, was due in large part to his proven general abilities and to his shining personal reputation for integrity and independence. The lesson was obvious: Democrats had a chance to score further victories in Illinois in '48 if they made up a slate of high-caliber men whose past was untainted by machine politics. Into this suggested pattern Adlai Stevenson fitted perfectly, and several political writers said so in print within a few days after the Kennelly victory.

Another who perfectly fitted into the pattern was Paul H. Douglas, the professor of economics at the University of Chicago who had got into politics before America's entrance into World War II by winning election as city alderman. Douglas, though overage, had enlisted as a private in the Marines, had emerged an officer with a Purple Heart awarded for a combat wound in the Pacific, and was deemed by many the perfect opponent of Brooks, a World War I Marine who had used his distinguished war record effectively in his political campaigning. Douglas, however, was talked of for the governorship at least as much as he was for the Senate, and the most knowledgeable early speculation was that he would seek the former post while Stevenson sought the latter.

As always in politics, the picture was clouded with uncertainties, its outlines blurred by imponderables. For instance, there was the possibility that Senator Scott W. Lucas might decide, or be persuaded, to run against Green, though Lucas's term as senator was not up until 1950. When Stevenson went to Washington on June 5—partly on private law business, partly to try to facilitate congressional action on the pending bill to admit four hundred thousand displaced persons to the United States—he and Lucas lunched together, then took the same train for Chicago. Immediately a "Democratic team of Scott Lucas and Adlai Stevenson to run for Governor and Senator respectively . . . appeared a strong possibility," according to Griffing Bancroft of the Chicago *Sun*.

"There is no sense in being disingenuous about these things," Stevenson told Bancroft, with a smile. "My mind is open. Naturally I'm interested."

Thereafter the Stevenson candidacy was continuously in the news, being publicized in *The New York Times* and other out-of-state papers, in magazines, and in nationally syndicated columns to such an extent that by October, when Stevenson was in New York for the General Assembly session, Lou Kohn's pockets bulged with clippings, which he constantly pressed upon his acquaintances. On November 6, with Stevenson's blessing, Kohn, Mitchell, and Smith announced the formation of an Adlai Stevenson for Senator committee. A "vigorous campaign," including personal visits to hundreds of Illinois communities, would be waged, Mitchell said. Among those on the committee and prominent thereafter in Stevenson's political life were Mrs. Edison (Jane Warner) Dick; William McC. Blair, Jr., still a registered

Republican; Walter T. Fisher, a Winnetka lawyer; and Walter V. Schaefer, professor of law at Northwestern University.

Smith, meanwhile, was soliciting campaign fund pledges from his wealthy friends and acquaintances, achieving sufficient success to encourage continued efforts. Kohn was convinced that, once Stevenson's nomination was assured, they would have no trouble raising $250,000—and Stevenson himself was much more sanguine about money-raising possibilities than later events justified. (He relied excessively on "cocktail party promises" made in former years by wealthy Republican friends, according to Smith. "If you ever run for office, you can count on me to back you," such people said—and proved now that they hadn't meant to be taken seriously.) [2]

Up to this time, however, no professional politician had come out openly for Stevenson, and the problem of getting organization support was worrying Smith and Kohn and Mitchell.

It is a measure of the vast esteem in which Kennelly was then held that Stevenson's backers, and Stevenson himself, were particularly anxious to have the mayor's backing. "I have spoken to Mayor Kennelly several times about Adlai, and he asked me to arrange a meeting with him sometime," Smith wrote Bud Merwin on July 30. "That meeting is now scheduled for tomorrow afternoon, and although I do not expect any immediate results, it is obvious that the mayor could be a very helpful friend." He could have been—at that time and later. He chose not to be. He was courteous, he was mildly interested, he was aloof and noncommittal. So was George Kells, the Democratic state chairman. So were the other prominent Democrats; all wished to wait, they said, to see what developed. It became apparent that they waited, most of them, to see what Colonel Arvey, chairman of the Cook County Democratic Central Committee, would do.

Accordingly, one early November day, the leaders of the Stevenson committee called upon Arvey in the latter's Loop office. If the essence of humor is the juxtaposition of incongruous elements, that meeting had, certainly, its comic aspects. The Stevenson delegation was composed of North Shore socialites, nearly all of them lifelong Republicans and members of families that had been prominent and wealthy for generations. They were Ivy League college graduates. Their distaste for machine politics, their disdain of machine politicians, were cardinal articles of their political faith. Yet here they were, calling upon probably the most powerful big city boss then operating in America, and bidding for his support.

Arvey, however, was no such crude type as Hague of Jersey City or Crump of Memphis or old Tom Pendergast of Kansas City. Born of a poor Jewish family in Chicago's Twenty-fourth Ward, which was ninety percent Jewish, he had come up in the hard way traditional of bosses, working in his teens as a delivery boy for a tailoring firm and attending the John Marshall Law School at night. After being admitted to the Bar he became clerk in the law firm of John McInerary, an associate of Pat Nash and Ed Kelly, later the principals of the notorious Kelly-Nash machine. Of this machine, Arvey became in time a leading member—he was smart, he was hard-working, he was immensely likable—with a law firm of his own, which was naturally on the books of every company which wanted to stand in, or at least stand well, with the local political powers. As ward committeeman and absolute boss of the Twenty-fourth Ward, he regularly delivered ninety percent or more of the ward's vote to Kelly-Nash candidates. He did so even in 1936, when Horner was waging his bitter and successful fight for reelection against the machine—and this despite the fact that Horner was a coreligionist and personal friend.

But by the fall of 1947, when Arvey was fifty-three years old, he had gone through a widely advertised conversion to clean politics and good government for Illinois. Various motives of idealism and expediency were alleged. Some said that Arvey, who had served as judge advocate of the 33rd Division in the Pacific, had returned from the war a different man, having seen the dreadful cost of gangster politics practiced on an international scale. Others said that the elections of 1946, which swept Republicans into power, had convinced him that the kind of machine politics he had theretofore practiced had passed its point of diminishing returns. Whatever his motives —and they were undoubtedly mixed, as all men's are—he used the defeat of Kelly-Nash stalwarts, in '46, to persuade Ed Kelly (Pat Nash was now dead) to step down. Times had changed in Chicago, Arvey argued; Kelly's chances of winning reelection in '47 were too slim to justify taking them. Thus the city had been presented a choice for mayor between "Honest Martin" Kennelly and a Republican party hack who was but a pawn of McCormick and Green.

The results naturally encouraged Arvey's friendly interest in the mission of his callers, that November day. He greeted them cordially, and they looked on a man who certainly lacked the appearance of a tough city boss. Nearly all bosses are big men physically. Arvey was not. He stood five feet six inches high and weighed one hundred and fifty pounds. He had quick, shrewd, friendly eyes behind horn-rimmed spectacles, a bald head mottled with sun-darkened spots, and a wide genial smile which, joined to a gentle manner, disarmed his visitors as it had customarily disarmed his harshest critics whenever these came into personal contact with him. The smile, the gentleness, were obviously expressions of the inner man, and they were accompanied by slight nods of seeming agreement as Stevenson's virtues were extolled.

This, of course, was not the first time he had heard of Stevenson; he had long known of him in a general way. Nor were his present visitors the first to call Stevenson specifically to his attention as a political possibility. No less a personage than former Secretary of State Byrnes had done so as recently

as late July of that year, when Arvey was in Washington consulting with
Senator Lucas over the naming of a U.S. attorney for the Northern District
of Illinois. The Senate Secretary, Leslie Biffle, had given a luncheon that
Lucas and Arvey attended. Byrnes was there and, hearing talk of Illinois
politics, gave it as his opinion that "you people out there have a gold nugget
in the person of Adlai Stevenson; he is one of the smartest, cleanest, most
patriotic men I know."

Arvey, however, said nothing of this to his present callers, nor did he
indicate to them the depth of his real interest in Stevenson as a possible
nominee. He agreed, aloud, that Stevenson would make a very good senator.

"But to become a senator, you have to get elected," Arvey said, "and your
man is not as well known as Douglas, who worked all summer downstate.
I feel Douglas would make a better candidate."

The question was left open, however, as the callers departed.

A few weeks later Dutch Smith encountered Arvey in the club car of the
Twentieth Century Limited, en route to New York, and seized the opportunity to talk with him again about Stevenson. Arvey this time seemed somewhat more interested. He had been told, though, that Stevenson had gone
to Oxford, and if that were true it was a serious political liability, Anglopho-
bia being a disease spread widely through Illinois by Colonel McCormick's
Tribune. Smith promptly laid this bogy to rest (he obtained a telegram from
Stevenson, saying, "NEVER WENT TO OXFORD NOT EVEN ETON") [3]
and, discovering that he and Arvey were returning to Chicago a few days
later on the same train, arranged to meet Arvey then in the club car. On
this return trip Arvey asked about Mrs. Stevenson. Would she be an asset
in a political campaign? She certainly would, Smith replied; she was very
pretty, very friendly, a wonderful hostess. He offered to arrange a luncheon
at his Lake Forest home, where Arvey could meet the Stevensons.

This luncheon was held soon after Stevenson's return from the General
Assembly session. Arvey was favorably impressed by both the Stevensons.
Subsequently, as the Christmas season approached, there were other meetings between Arvey and Stevenson, all of them pleasant, each more friendly
than the last. By this time, several newspaper reports of slate-making Democratic meetings agreed that Stevenson was the probable senatorial candidate,
since Douglas had encountered labor opposition, though the strength and
nature of this opposition was never made clear. Others reported an increased
likelihood that Douglas would be run for governor. Douglas himself preferred the governorship; he had told many people privately that he did.
Kennelly, too, was considered for the gubernatorial nomination until December 17, when he told a delegation to his office, headed by Arvey, that he
definitely would not run. He declined to recommend a candidate but said,
in reply to a question, that he considered Circuit Judge Thomas J. Courtney "eminently qualified for any position"—a remark that caused some con-

sternation among party leaders since it hinted the possibility of a split between Kennelly and the Arvey group that would discard all slate-making
efforts thus far. Courtney, who had broken with Ed Kelly and Arvey to run
for governor in 1944, was cordially disliked by organization Democrats.

The climax came in late December. On the day after Christmas, a Friday,
Arvey, who had talked with Smith several times during the last week, announced to Smith a final decision. The organization slate for '48 was to be
finally decided by a thirty-man Democratic State Committee meeting in the
Morrison Hotel next week. At that meeting Douglas would be named the
candidate for senator. The candidacy for the governorship, however, remained open. Would Stevenson take it? Smith, dismayed and disappointed,
shook his head dubiously. He was almost certain that his friend would not
be interested. He suggested, however, that Arvey put the question to Stevenson directly. Next morning Arvey did so at a meeting of the three men in
Smith's office.

Stevenson's initial response was negative, as Smith had predicted.[4] His
experience had been almost wholly with the federal government. "I know
the Congress like a book," he said. He was qualified for the Senate; he was
interested only in the Senate. Douglas, on the other hand, was primarily
interested in the governorship. Why the switch? Jack Arvey (it is an interesting if insignificant fact that Jacob Arvey was never called "Jake") said
that there were reasons, not good perhaps from Stevenson's point of view,
but sufficient in terms of practical politics. There was Douglas's war record,
for one thing; a spellbinding orator, Douglas would be able to match Curly
Brooks "wound for wound and deed for deed" in campaign speeches. In
any case the matter was no longer debatable. Douglas was slated for the
Senate. Stevenson, if he agreed to it, would be slated for the governorship.

"What about my appointments, if I'm elected?" Stevenson asked. "Will
I be entirely free on my appointments?"

He would be, Arvey said.

"On your major appointments I wouldn't make a suggestion if you asked
me to," Arvey went on. "On minor appointments—there'd be scores of them
—you'd need help. Even there I wouldn't suggest names unless you asked
me to. My bet is that you'd ask me, as a practical matter, but it would be
your free choice."[5]

Stevenson pondered. Finally he said that he'd like to think it all over for
a few days. Arvey agreed, pointing out, however, that the final slate-making
session was early the next week.

For Stevenson there followed three and a half days of soul-searching. On
the one hand was the safety, the assured and secure comfort of an established financial lawyer with multitudes of interesting friends, a gratifying
community prestige, and no enemies. This he would at once have to renounce; he must sever completely his relationship with the Sidley firm on

the day he became a bona fide candidate. On the other hand were the hazards his dying father had spoken of—the hundred chances for public failure and humiliation, the thousand inevitable frustrations and injustices, in a career wholly dependent upon an erratic, often deliberately misinformed public opinion. To accept those hazards as a national legislator, a role for which he was well rehearsed, was one thing; to accept them as a great state's chief executive, a role that he had never seriously considered, was quite another. He was not wholly without large-scale administrative experience: he had learned much while with Knox in Washington: but for large-scale political administration he was, he feared, unprepared.

Ellen made no objection to Springfield; she would prefer Springfield to Washington. She told Dutch Smith so on Monday evening, December 29, when Smith called her. Arvey had phoned Smith, worrying because Stevenson's decision had not been made and wondering if Mrs. Stevenson were persuading Stevenson not to accept. No, she wasn't doing that, Smith now told Arvey, calling back, adding that he'd not been able to reach Stevenson himself. (Stevenson was attending a performance of the Princeton Triangle Club, but Smith feared that saying so would make the prospective candidate seem to hard-boiled politicians a hopeless "cream puff.") Well, said Arvey, his patience near an end, he'd give Stevenson until noon tomorrow to make up his mind. The slate had to be completed.

Through the corridors and suites of the Morrison Hotel that night confusion drifted and eddied thicker than the cigar smoke as Democratic politicians sought to do their work amidst repeated alarms and excursions. The evening edition of next morning's *Sun* had carried a scarifying story. John Pickering, interviewing Mayor Kennelly in his office at City Hall, had emerged with a direct quotation from the mayor: "Judge Courtney is my man for governor and I will campaign for him if necessary." As soon as they read this, the slatemakers recessed until the following morning, gathering in little gloom-laden groups to ponder the imponderable. They worried, too, about an announcement just made by former Vice-President Henry A. Wallace saying that he would run for President on a third-party ticket. Meanwhile a *Daily News* reporter called the mayor, who said he had been misquoted, though he again praised Judge Courtney, whereupon the slate makers, somewhat soothed by the dubious retraction, insisted that Stevenson be brought to them that night.

He came at midnight from the gay foolery of a college boys' musical comedy to a serious business conducted in the atmosphere of comic opera, and he told the slate makers what he had told Arvey on Saturday. His experience had been "largely in the Federal field" and he had "never thought of anything else than the post of senator"; he needed more time in which to "reflect."

At nine o'clock next morning Dutch Smith came to Stevenson's office.

He found his friend "in terrible shape," as he later recalled. He argued, as Stevenson had argued with himself, that it was "now or never" so far as a political career was concerned. "They need you this year," Smith said. "If you say no when they need you, they won't take you when they don't need you." Stevenson paced the floor, saying over and over, "I'm bothered, I'm bothered." Back of the decision he struggled to make, impelling him toward it, was the great inward weight of his family tradition, with all the moral obligation it imposed. Finally he said that, if he were to do it at all, he would have to have Kennelly's backing. Smith balked at that, arguing that Kennelly had "nowhere to go" except into the Stevenson camp, once Stevenson became the Democratic candidate.[6]

"He could hardly support Green, could he?" Smith asked.

"I want his active support, at least his announced support," Stevenson said stubbornly. "If I can't have it, I won't run."

So Smith tried to reach Kennelly through a mutual friend, Edward Eagle (Ned) Brown, chairman of the board of the First National Bank. Kennelly was in a City Council meeting and would not be out until after Arvey's deadline had passed.

"Well, you've certainly shown your respect for his opinion," Smith said to Stevenson. "He'll *have* to support you. He can't do anything else."

Stevenson shook his head. He knew that Kennelly might just sit it out, being so strongly committed to Courtney and so determined to be above politics, and he believed that this might utterly destroy what then seemed very slender chances for victory. (The event proved him right about Kennelly. Not until August 31, 1948, in a statement endorsing the entire Democratic slate, did the mayor publicly mention Stevenson by name.)

The clock hands moved toward noon.

"Well, I guess you're right," Stevenson said. "It's now or never." He sighed wearily. "I'll do it," he said.

II

If this career indecision was characteristic of Stevenson, his post-decision operation was no less so.* Once his mind was made up, he suffered no anxiety. He was a candidate for governor. He was utterly absorbed into that role. He was going to win if it were humanly possible, though he was realistic enough to admit, strictly in private, that it might not be possible.

For as the new year began it certainly looked like a Republican year

---

* Colonel Jacob M. Arvey writes in *As We Knew Adlai*, p. 54, "I am greatly amused at the stories that Adlai Stevenson was indecisive. He was not a superficial man. He insisted upon knowing everything about his subject. He did not do things impulsively. He . . . wanted to know every facet of a problem before he decided upon action."

nationally, what with Truman's inability to dominate his own party and Henry Wallace's third-party movement, which, at the outset, seemed likely to garner from five to ten million votes, nearly all of them from Democratic ranks. If the national Republican victory were of landslide proportions, it would be likely to ensure the election of a Republican governor of Illinois. Recognition of this probability, however, served only to increase Stevenson's campaign effort. Others might regard him as a sacrificial goat led to the slaughter by the cynical Arvey and the machine. Why, otherwise, they asked, would a man like Arvey choose men like Douglas and Stevenson as candidates? But Stevenson himself focused primarily on the weaknesses of his opponent, and would make increasing capital of these as they were more and more fully exposed. No one who watched him closely through the first nine months of '48 would ever have the illusion that this son of privilege, this society Ivy Leaguer, was not a tough man in a fight—tireless, resourceful, courageous.

On January 7 Stevenson and Douglas rode down on a train to Springfield with Arvey to accept formally the endorsement of the Democratic State Committee. Stevenson's brief acceptance speech, which he'd written in the club car on the way down, declared that Illinois had been richly blessed with almost everything but good government. "The crude, old-fashioned spoils politics of the State Administration cannot be veiled forever by virtuous pronouncements," he said. "The people don't like what they've heard, and they will like it less and less as they hear more and more about what's been done and what's not been done in the last eight years." Arvey and Spike Hennessey, the Democrats' publicity campaign manager, looked at one another with pleased surprise as they listened. Stevenson had an accent vaguely "British" or "Eastern" (actually it reflected his wide-ranging travel during his formative years and had as its chief quality a clipped precision), but it was pleasant to listen to, riding out as it did on a voice with singing overtones. The accent might be an initial political liability, but it might also become, ultimately, a definite asset, if Stevenson in other ways identified himself with his audiences. Instinctively the average American, listening to this voice, might think Stevenson above him, but if Stevenson expressed the hopes and aspirations of his listeners the latter might conclude that they *wanted* their elected executive to be superior.

On February 4, the eve of his forty-eighth birthday, Stevenson's withdrawal from the Sidley law firm was announced. That evening Democratic leaders in Chicago gave him a well-publicized birthday party. Thereafter he was a professional politician, though he continued to refer to himself for years to come as an amateur.

He opened campaign headquarters on the fifth floor of Seven South Dearborn, in a large room with cubbyhole offices, temporarily partitioned, at one side. Wooden floors clicked and clacked as women's hard-heeled shoes came down upon them. The bare walls and ceiling echoed the noise of typewriters and voices. The lighting was poor. As a working office the place's only virtue, dictated by necessity, was that it was cheap.

The campaign, from first to last, was run on a shoestring, with outgo often exceeding income in ways maddening to Stevenson, whose acute awareness of the value of a dollar had certainly not lessened with the years and who put into the campaign some thousands of his own money. So did Dutch Smith, who served as campaign treasurer and had often to issue hurry-up appeals to contributors in order to pay cash on the line for radio time, newspaper advertising, and billboards. Buffie put in at least two thousand dollars. Numbers of Smith's and Stevenson's personal friends, most of them Republican, made substantial contributions. But there were many others who should have contributed, Smith felt, if their deeds were to be consistent with their long-professed concern for good government and with their personal loyalty to Stevenson, yet who gave nothing. Of the $250,000 that Kohn had thought they could easily raise, less than $100,000 was actually obtained (Green's campaign received at least five times that much)— and some of this had to be raised after the election to pay off deficits.

The financial problem could have been easily solved, of course, if Stevenson had been willing to make deals. He wasn't. At one dark moment, when the treasury was virtually empty and Stevenson feared that his headquarters might have to be closed for lack of rent money, he wrote a long letter to Smith indicating possible money sources. It was a letter full of anxiety, but embedded in it was a casually matter-of-fact sentence: "I am, of course, trying to avoid taking any money which would leave me with any possible embarrassing commitments."

Nor was his aversion to deals limited to financial matters. Two powerful labor leaders called on him at the headquarters one day. Arvey was in the office at the time. The union men came directly to the point. They were prepared to support Stevenson, but they wanted it understood that he would appoint as labor director a member of their union. Arvey, they said, would be a witness to Stevenson's promise. As witness, Arvey's later testimony was far different from what the union officials had confidently expected.[7]

"I need your support," Stevenson said frankly. "But I haven't made any promises about appointments, and I'm not making any. I may or may not pick a man from your union. Jack, here, hasn't asked me for such commitments. If he doesn't, why should you?"

The campaign manager was James Mulroy, who, in the 1920's, while a reporter on the *Daily News*, had won a Pulitzer prize for uncovering the typewriter evidence that helped to convict Loeb and Leopold. He was a heavily built, ruddy-faced, excitable Irishman, utterly devoted to Stevenson and incredibly energetic, who had a decided flare for the dramatic moment and seemed to operate best in an atmosphere of crisis, which, sometimes, he himself created. Publicity was handled by a young man, a friend of Mulroy's, named William I. Flanagan, who had recently left a newspaper reporting job to head the Chicago office of a national press agency. Flanagan helped out at nights and on weekends at first, then worked full time for Stevenson until the impossibility of paying him forced his resignation. The chief secretary was Carol Evans, a tall blond woman, then in her thirties, whom Stevenson had known casually for ten years. She had been secretary to Paul Harper, senior partner in the Sidley law firm when Stevenson returned to his law practice in '46, and she had worked for Stevenson for a brief period in the late spring of that year. Soon thereafter she had left the firm to return to the University of Chicago, where, while working intermittently toward a degree, she had been secretary to Louis Wirth, the famed University of Chicago sociologist.

Necessarily, a great deal of work was done by unpaid volunteers whose dedication was often far greater than their professional competence. People from Lake Forest and other North Shore suburbs came down to help. There was frequent despair among the amateur politicians because the organization (it's always "the organization" when it's on your side, Bill Blair once declared, and "the machine" when it's against you) seemed to be doing nothing to help.

Cochairman of the women's division of the nonpartisan Stevenson-for-Governor Committee, formed in July, were Stevenson's long-time friend, Mrs. Edison (Jane) Dick, and Mrs. Eric W. Stubbs, wife of a Chicago businessman and long a leader in the Hyde Park League of Women Voters. Lloyd Lewis helped Stevenson with speech preparation, especially in the later stages of the campaign when the number of speeches he must make far exceeded the time and energy that any one man could give to their writing. Many others presented drafts of which portions were sometimes used.[8]

This first of the Stevenson campaigns, however, set a speech-writing pattern from which he seldom deviated, and then only under extreme pressure, in the campaigns which were to follow. By and large he wrote his own speeches—and he seemed to need a prepared address for every major gathering, particularly in these first months of his politician's life. Then, as later, his associates complained that he spent far too much time on his speech writing. Then, as later, he readily agreed that he did. But he seemed unable to help himself in this regard. Something in him—a stubborn integrity, a literary craftsman's respect for words—rebelled against the whole system of ghost-writing and public relations engineering whereby a manufactured myth rather than the real man is presented to the electorate's decision.

He formally opened his campaign on February 23, 1948, in Bloomington, with a reception in the Ives's home—his own boyhood home—at 1316 East Washington. The reception was attended by hundreds, among them Miss Kitty Cowles, Adlai's grade school teacher, and was very fully covered by the press. Scores of newspaper photographs showed Ellen standing beside her husband—very pretty, smiling happily; it was one of her few public appearances during what would be a very long campaign. Then, from March 1 through March 17, Stevenson toured downstate Illinois with Douglas in a Democratic campaign caravan, speaking at forty-one meetings.

At the outset he was no more than moderately effective as a speaker before political rallies. But he learned steadily and rapidly, and from the first the meetings were surprisingly well-attended.

His own view of the strange new experience he was having was expressed in one of his personal letters to Mrs. Dick, written on the stationery of a motel in the little town of Carmi in the midst of his first campaign tour.[9]

> It's Sunday morning. I'm in an automobile driving from Danville where we spoke last night to Decatur to resume this fantastic ordeal. We've driven 1350 miles since last Sunday, and I've spoken about 20 times, shaken hands with thousands of people, and slept all too little.
>
> It has been an amazing experience, and I've come to wonder how anyone can presume to talk about "America" until he has done some campaigning. Perhaps it's the secret, perhaps the curse, of American political success—the illusive business of finding your way to the heart of the average man—when there is no such thing—and, unhappily, the human heart is often an organ encased in a pocketbook, and not a Bible or a textbook.
>
> I've seen Illinois in a capsule—the beauty of the south, the fruit belt, the coal fields, the oil fields, the great industrial area around East St. Louis—and everywhere the rich, black fecund earth stretching away and away.... But I'm getting a little lyrical for a Democratic politician....

Thus his personal reaction, privately expressed. His public reaction took a wry, ironic form. When a Republican organization adopted a resolution saying that his Libertyville address was a phony one, that he actually lived in Vernon Township and claimed Libertyville as home simply because it was a "symbol of American freedom," he made a public speech that convulsed his listeners with laughter.

> People wiser in the ways of politics than I am say that it doesn't make any difference what you think or I think. The way I tie my necktie or whether I prefer jelly or jam can win or lose votes.... And of course whatever I say or don't say will be misinterpreted or misrepresented by the opposition.... Now they say I'm a fraud and imposter who doesn't even reside in Libertyville. In my innocence it never occurred to me to tell the U.S. Post Office Department its business or the correct address of my farm. I guess I am too naïve to be a good candidate....

Good or not, he was certainly different. Being so, he could not but con-duct a very different kind of political campaign. Political reporters admitted in print that they had never seen anything quite like it, and their glowing reports had an effect on Governor Green, who was taking a winter vacation in Florida. Green had let it be known that he would not bother to conduct a primary campaign, but he now cut short his vacation, returned to Illinois, and began his campaign with a speech at Fairfield on March 10. In this maiden speech he identified his opponent as "a man on leave from the striped-pants brigade of the Roosevelt-Truman State Department. . . . This candidate, whose chief claim to fame is a sub-author of the UN plan—the most dismal failure in the history of American diplomacy—seeks to hold up to ridicule the men and women who grapple with our State problems in the House and Senate at Springfield." To this, Stevenson made swift reply. "The governor has added two words to the lexicon of political damnation," said he, on the night following Green's speech. "One is 'striped.' The other is 'pants.' But, damned or striped . . . I will continue to talk Illinois, which is the business of the governor of Illinois. . . ."

Green repeated his striped-pants charge in later speeches, until *Daily News* reporters found in the files a photograph of the governor in striped pants and cutaway, and printed it with the comment that they had been un-able to find any such picture of Stevenson. Stevenson himself was not amused, though his responses amused voters. "He probably likes Easter parades," said he, and went on earnestly to identify himself with the cause of world collaboration. "How can any thinking man in the world today be anything but an internationalist?" he asked, intensely serious. "At this mo-ment, we are engaged in an ideological conflict throughout the globe in the interests of democracy and decency." He pointed out, however, that he was not running against Green for the Vice-Presidency of the United States—a statement of penetrating point since Green was, at that time, working hard for a second place on the national ticket.

He had good reason to be thankful for Green's vaulting aspirations, how-ever, for they led the governor into repeated and ultimately disastrous polit-ical errors. At the National Republican Convention in Philadelphia in late June, Governor Green made the keynote address. It might have been written by Colonel Robert McCormick, whose hatred of Governor Thomas E. Dewey of New York and the entire liberal wing of the Republican party was pro-found and vociferous. Isolationism in foreign affairs, black reaction at home —these were the twin themes of Green's performance, which branded him before all men as the "errand boy" (Stevenson used the phrase again and again) of the *Tribune* publisher. When Dewey won the nomination, Green's chance for a place on the ticket was gone with the wind that blew from the Tribune Tower, and his cause in Illinois was badly damaged.

Stevenson, on the other hand, helped his local cause and gained national political stature with his performance as a delegate to the National Democratic Convention, which also met in Philadelphia that year, in mid-July.

It is a measure of the depths to which President Truman's prestige had fallen that his renomination, in the spring of '48, seemed doubtful. Jack Arvey was among the astute politicians who were convinced that if Truman became the candidate, he would inevitably lead his party to disaster at the polls. He joined Mayor O'Dwyer of New York, the Americans for Democratic Action, Paul Douglas, and numerous others in an attempt to draft General Eisenhower as the Democratic Presidential candidate despite the fact that the general's politics, in so far as he had any, seemed vaguely Republican. Stevenson, however, declined to join the draft-Eisenhower movement. He genuinely admired Harry Truman as man and as President, critical though he was of both. He was convinced that Truman's handling of the great crises of his first term gave the President no small claim to historical greatness and an overwhelming claim to renomination.

Accordingly, on the train going to Philadelphia on July 10, Stevenson jumped into the Truman camp with both feet, saying to reporters that "Truman deserves our support in Illinois, and he will get it." Thus he anticipated the harmony that prevailed throughout a two-hour caucus held in Philadelphia next day, following which it was announced that all of Illinois' sixty votes would go to Truman on the first ballot. At that caucus Stevenson joined Ed Kelly in advising the delegates to "shake off the gloom about November" because "we're going to win"; he then invited the delegation to a cocktail party to "get more cheer."

Two days later, at the Stevenson party, "an incipient revolt against Arvey-Kelly direction flared into the open," according to one typical newspaper account. "Angry downstaters, distressed first at Arvey's ditch-Truman-for-Ike movement, now accuse him . . . of trying to substitute a New Dealer for Minority Leader Alben Barkley, the strong favorite of most of the Illinois delegation for the Vice-Presidential nod," this account went on. "Stevenson, who did not participate in the dump Truman efforts, also did not participate in the Barkley maneuvering." He admired Barkley: at seventy-one, the senator was one of the few political leaders who had served both Wilson's New Freedom and Roosevelt's New Deal: and Stevenson might even have some slight family feeling for the grand old man, since his paternal grandfather was a second cousin of Barkley's mother. After Truman had been nominated on the first ballot, Stevenson strongly supported Barkley for the Vice-Presidency, making a speech seconding the Barkley nomination.

He did this despite the fact that he and Barkley had been on opposite sides of one of the key issues of the convention. 1948 was the year of the Dixiecrat revolt against Truman's stand on civil rights, and, as a member of the credentials committee, Stevenson led the fight to bar from the convention the Mississippi delegation, which had announced in advance that it would not support Truman or any other candidate who stood for Truman's civil rights program. Having failed to carry with him a majority of the committee, Stevenson sought to carry the fight to the convention floor—and it was there he encountered, and was defeated by, Barkley. Barkley was chairman of the session, and when Stevenson, Arvey, and Kelly rose to protest the acceptance of the slim majority action on the credentials committee, he was "afflicted with temporary deafness," as newspaper accounts put it. He was also afflicted with temporary blindness, being unable to see the commotion among the Illinois delegation, whose standard was immediately in front of the speaker's stand. "Something must have been wrong with the microphone system," he later blandly explained.

The general public was, of course, neither as blind nor as deaf as Barkley seemed to be that day, and Stevenson's civil rights role received national recognition, reducing the effectiveness of later attempts to label him an appeaser of the South's institutionalized racialism.

Adlai Stevenson III, eighteen years old, had been graduated from Milton Academy that spring. His cousin, Timothy Ives, twenty, was a student at the University of Virginia. Both served as pages at the Democratic National Convention. "Little Adlai," as everyone called him, though he was in fact taller than his father, toured with his father and the sixteen-year-old Borden through the fervent Illinois summer. In September the two brothers left for school—Adlai to enter his freshman year at Harvard and Borden to enter his last year at his father's old school, Choate. Only John Fell then remained with his mother at the Libertyville farm. He was twelve and a student at the Lake Forest Day School, where he organized his friends into a kind of Stevenson-for-Governor committee, which reportedly addressed envelopes and distributed campaign literature.

"He keeps close track of my campaign," Stevenson laughed proudly. "He tells me my chances are very good."

III

Others did not think so. Betting odds against Stevenson's election had been reported at ten to one as the summer began; they reportedly stood at five to one in late July, after the national conventions had enhanced Stevenson's prestige while lowering Green's. Green still possessed perhaps the best-financed, most tightly organized political machine in all Illinois history, plus the inestimable advantage of an expected national Republican landslide. (To offset the latter, Republicans-for-Stevenson inserted newspaper ads urging support of a Dewey-Stevenson ticket—and most of the papers supporting Stevenson took the same line in their editorials.)

Certainly Stevenson himself did not underrate his opponent's strength. All through the August doldrums he concentrated on Green an unremitting fire—and after Labor Day this fire became even more intense. He had a twelve-point program for the state. Again and again he presented it in public speech. If elected, he would strive—

  —to improve Illinois' inefficient and inequitable taxing system;
  —to increase the proportion of total tax revenue going to cities;
  —to abolish the present flagrant corruption in state purchasing;
  —to call a constitutional convention for a complete revision of the constitution adopted in 1870;
  —to overhaul drastically the state's public welfare system, which had permitted state hospitals—particularly those for the mentally ill—to degenerate "into unspeakable horrors of sadism, inefficiency, and corruption";
  —to undertake an extensive long-term road-building program, and do away with "political engineering" in highway building and maintenance;
  —to establish a state Fair Employment Practices commission;
  —to strengthen the mine safety laws and take mine inspection out of politics;
  —to increase state financial aid to the common schools;
  —to increase the efficiency and economy of state administration;
  —to take the state police out of politics and use them *as* police rather than as politicians' errand boys;
  —to remove parasites, and the names of nonexistent employees, from state payrolls.

But he quite generally presented this positive program in negative terms, as an attack on the Green administration.

His campaign's effectiveness was vastly increased that fall by the fact that, of the state's most influential newspapers, only the Chicago *Tribune* yet bitterly opposed him. The *Daily News* and *Sun-Times* had supported him from the first. So had the Bloomington *Pantagraph*, which asserted that it did so "despite rather than because of" Stevenson's vice-presidency of the publishing company. (Editorially the paper explained that the Stevenson interest in the paper was a minority one and that he had nothing to say about management or policy.) So had the St. Louis *Post-Dispatch*, which had a great downstate readership and whose editorial page, under the editorship of Irving Dilliard, was perhaps the best written and certainly one of the most effective in the nation. Many another normally Republican paper deserted Green for Stevenson.

And all this support became of a crusading fervor when, in mid-campaign, a *Post-Dispatch* star reporter, Theodore C. Link, sent to Peoria to investigate the murder of one of the notorious Shelton gang, was arrested and criminally indicted by Green machine politicians. (The indictment was withdrawn immediately after the election.) It was then revealed that scores of downstate newspaper editors were actually on the payroll of the state, placed there by Green's machine in order to keep them quiet while the politicians shook down gamblers, formed working alliances with all kinds of grafters and racketeers, profited richly from kickbacks and payroll padding, and bought state materials at fantastically inflated prices in profit-sharing schemes. With freedom of the press thus raised as an issue, papers that usually made little effort to uncover or develop the news began to do so with a vengeance.

These scandalous revelations in the autumn augmented the moral outrage that had been inspired in the spring by revelations concerning a coal mine disaster in southern Illinois. On March 25, 1947, an explosion in Centralia No. 5 had killed 111 miners. In March of 1948, a long article by John Bartlow Martin, in *Harper's* magazine, had exhaustively reviewed the tragedy and the investigation into its causes, revealing an appalling looseness of mine safety laws and an even more appalling laxness in state mine inspection. Included were the facts that the Centralia miners had repeatedly complained that the mine was unsafe, that these complaints had been ignored by both the operators and Green's mine inspectors, and that the latter regularly solicited campaign contributions from the former. Extended excerpts from the Martin article had been printed in Illinois papers and numerous angry anti-Green editorials had been stimulated thereby. Stevenson himself quoted the article again and again throughout his campaign. . . .

On the afternoon of Tuesday, November 2, Adlai and Ellen Stevenson voted at Half Day, a tiny village near their Libertyville farm. They were photographed as they emerged from the voting booths. He was wearing a dark suit, rather rumpled-looking, with a white handkerchief protruding well beyond the fashionable tenth of an inch from his left breast pocket. Ellen was wearing a bright plaid suit with a long boxlike jacket. Unsmiling, he looked tense and tired. Smiling, she seemed relaxed and happy. That evening the Stevensons and Dutch and Ellen Smith dined as guests of Mrs. John Alden Carpenter, Ellen's mother, in town. Then they all went downtown to Seven South Dearborn. On the sidewalk before the headquarters a newsboy was selling the early evening edition of the Chicago *Tribune*. The eight-column front page banner headline proclaimed in huge type that Dewey had won a landslide victory over Truman. Dutch Smith glanced quickly at Stevenson whose face showed nothing and who said nothing.

The headquarters was crowded.[10] The Edison Dicks were there. Lloyd and Kathryn Lewis were there. Everybody seemed to be there. Newspapers had reported that the Stevenson campaign, roaring through its final week, had become an even-money bet for victory among the professional gamblers, but at Seven South Dearborn there was little optimism of even the cautious kind as the early returns, nearly all of them from Cook County, came in.

These early returns all showed Stevenson leading, but Cook County was Democratic country; he'd have to carry it by a huge majority to offset the expected Republican victory downstate. Many of those who had worked hardest in the campaign, and were now tired, let down, expressed the belief that the Cook County margin wasn't large enough—that the election was lost. Stevenson expressed the opposite view.

"I think we've won," he said quietly.

He went into his little corner office. The returns kept pouring in, with Stevenson's leadership margin steadily widening. "Don't let 'em leave the polls," Lewis kept warning Stevenson, referring to the Democratic poll watchers, for he knew well that ballots had been stolen in the past in Chicago and that this had sometimes robbed winning candidates of their victories. Stevenson knew this well, too. (In 1908, when his grandfather ran for governor, ballot boxes full of votes for Adlai E. Stevenson had found their way, somehow, to the bottom of the Chicago River and were never officially counted.)

By nine o'clock the initial apathy, streaked with despondency, had departed from the office. Stevenson was winning! *He was winning big!* The crowd grew noisily jubilant.

Stevenson sat quietly in his cubbyhole, with Lloyd Lewis beside him, rewriting his acceptance speech. (His habit of rewriting speeches up to the moment he gave them would become legendary.)

By ten o'clock it was clear that he had scored a landslide victory. Radio broadcasters were saying his margin might be as high as four hundred thousand when all the returns were in. He was leading his ticket, though Douglas was overwhelming Brooks and other Democrats on the state ticket were winning by substantial margins. More amazing was the fact that Truman remained consistently if only slightly ahead of Dewey, even after the national rural vote began to come in; nationally Truman was winning thus far! Copies of the early *Tribune* edition were gleefully displayed. . . .

Green conceded his defeat.

Stevenson spoke into a radio microphone, saying that he was "at once gratified and humbled by the size of the majority which has, today, called me to the state capital of Illinois."

Ellen, wearing a gray wool dress with fringed cuffs and a two-toned gray felt hat, came to sit beside her husband at photographers' requests. Flash bulbs flared. The resulting pictures showed Stevenson's face lighted from within by a radiant smile, white teeth gleaming as he talked into the telephone. Ellen's smile, in some of the pictures, was pleasant but withdrawn; in other pictures she wasn't smiling at all. She declined to answer newsmen's questions about herself, except to say that she was forty years old, that both she and her mother had expected her husband to win, but that the victory margin was wider than she had expected.

"I think when people have the facts they choose the best man," she said, "and I think my husband is made for this job."

"Will you enjoy the next four years?" she was asked.

She half smiled, half frowned, in reply. "What a question!" she said, with a slight reproving shake of her head.

When all the returns were in, it was found that he had won the governorship by the largest plurality in Illinois history—572,067 votes. Of these, 546,424 came from Cook County, but the really incredible thing was that he had also won downstate by 25,643 votes, carrying 48 out of 101 counties in an area as monolithically Republican, most years, as Kansas or Vermont. Truman had carried Illinois by only 33,612, some 539,000 votes less than Stevenson's margin. Stevenson, it appeared, had carried Illinois for the President whose victory was the most amazing upset and perhaps the greatest personal triumph in all American political history.

CHAPTER EIGHTEEN

B Y the evening of Sunday, January 9, 1949, every hotel, motel, and tourist home in Springfield was jammed to capacity. Some hotels had lined their corridors with cots, for each of which there were many bidders. The capital of Illinois had not had a full-scale inaugural celebration for eight years—Green's second inaugural, in the midst of World War II, had been a brief, perfunctory ceremony—and hundreds of Chicago Democrats, with almost as many hundred Republicans, came down on special trains for the occasion, many of them sleeping Sunday night in parked Pullmans.

The governor-elect, with an official party of some seventy members, arrived on Sunday evening in the last two cars of the Abraham Lincoln Streamliner. Heavy rain was falling upon Springfield when the train pulled in. Stevenson and his family were driven to the Hotel Abraham Lincoln, where they were staying, in the limousine of Governor Green, who had sent it to the station with his state police chauffeur. Stevenson remarked that this was the first time he had ever ridden in the state car with the number 1 license plate. As they entered the lobby they were greeted with cheers and applause by a great crowd.

At eleven o'clock next morning—a chilly gray morning through which a drizzling rain fell intermittently—the Stevensons pressed their way through an applauding crowd, which had long jammed the hotel corridors and lobby awaiting their appearance. They were driven directly to the ninety-three-year-old Executive Mansion—a plain, square, white-painted structure containing twenty-three tall-ceilinged rooms, set upon a low hill overlooking Springfield's downtown district. They were greeted in the blue-carpeted foyer by the Greens, who, with simple and gracious ceremony, gave them the keys to the mansion.

At eleven-fifteen the inaugural procession left the mansion. It was a cavalcade of thirty-eight cars, headed by eight white-gloved state policemen on motorcycles and followed by marching soldiers in white helmets. The slow ride through the business district to the National Guard Armory might have been an uncomfortable one for both the Greens and the Stevensons. It wasn't. Whatever bitterness the Greens felt was well hidden by a warm hospitality, and in appreciation of this the incoming governor decided to omit from his inaugural address a reference to "the last election in Illinois" that reflected upon his predecessor. The procession arrived at the armory, across the street from Illinois' tall-domed capitol, shortly before noon. Hundreds of people who had been unable to gain entrance to the jam-packed building stood on the sidewalks applauding as the Greens and the Stevensons entered.

Halfway through the thirteenth hour of January 10, 1949, Adlai E. Stevenson was formally installed as the thirty-first governor of Illinois—the fourth Democratic governor of that state since the Civil War.

Next morning, the new governor did not arrive at his State House office until eleven-fifteen. Smiling broadly as he strode in, he cheerfully greeted assembled newspapermen and sat for the first time in the big chair behind the executive desk.

He apologized for his lateness. This was his first morning in the Executive Mansion, he explained ruefully, and already a "major crisis" had occurred. His son John Fell and the eleven-year-old Edison Dick had gone upstairs to peek into the room where Carl Sandburg, who had spoken at the inaugural, slept late. They were fully aware that what they did was reprehensible, and when the poet stirred in his sleep they scampered into the mansion's automatic elevator, excitedly pushing buttons in such a way that the elevator got stuck between two floors. An hour passed before a repairman arrived to rescue them. . . .

A newsman was emboldened by this to tell the governor that the poll was not yet completed on his use of the word "proliferation" in the inaugural address as a description of the process by which state bureaus had become overlapping. Another newsman said he'd looked the word up and as far as he could tell it had something to do with the way coral spreads.

"That's good," Stevenson laughed. "Better than I thought."

Thus did this first of his press conferences set the tone prevailing through later ones, causing newsmen to speak with delighted surprise of "this strange new governor." His gaiety and wit did not hide from them the seriousness of his purpose nor the almost incredible energy he devoted to it.

Within his first twenty-four hours in office he was forced to take action on a reportedly dangerous situation at the state penitentiary in Pontiac. It was said that twice the normal number of prisoners were in solitary confinement there and that a riot was brewing as a result of maladministration by the Green-appointed warden, Arthur A. Bennett. T. P. Sullivan, State Public Service director and Bennett's superior, was a Green appointee who had "achieved an outstanding record" and whom the new governor planned to retain "indefinitely" as a cabinet member. He would resign a few months later, the target of considerable public criticism, but he now stood high in Stevenson's esteem, and when he recommended that Bennett be dismissed at once "for the good of the service," Stevenson issued the dismissal order, being careful to announce at the same time that this action did not affect the other wardens' positions. Bennett, informed of his dismissal by phone on the morning of January 12, protested to newsmen that he had had no chance to present his side of the case and that "someone had lied to the governor about me." "Charges that I collected campaign funds for Green at the prison are a damned lie!" he cried excitedly, adding that he was "going to try to see Governor Stevenson right away" because "I'm sure he doesn't know all the facts." He did try to reach the governor, but in vain. Two days later he was dead.

"The abrupt dismissal," said his grief-stricken widow, "broke his heart." He hadn't been able to understand why he was ousted without even the customary thirty days' notice; he had had no place to take his family. The coroner, with the widow's permission, performed an autopsy whose findings confirmed the attending physician's diagnosis: Arthur Bennett had died of a coronary thrombosis.

II

Every newly elected governor has a honeymoon period with the press of the state. Stevenson's was unusually ecstatic and unusually prolonged. For once, the correspondents of an overwhelmingly Republican press found themselves face to face with a Democratic chief executive whom they not only personally liked but of whom they could express their liking in print, since most of their publishers had supported him. They delighted in him, and the delight came through in the copy they wrote.

"The new Governor of Illinois is a curiosity," reported a Springfield newspaper. "Powerful politicians such as once gave orders from smoke-filled rooms are now taking orders from Mrs. Bricklayer, Mrs. Breadbaker, Mr. Farmer, Miss School Teacher, Mr. Butcher, Mr. Ditchdigger, and Mr. and Mrs. Everybody interested in good government."

"Governor Stevenson ordinarily looks out on the world with a humorous, good-natured air, which is one of the reasons so many people are drawn to him," wrote Marquis Childs in a nationally syndicated column. "Seated in the Governor's chair, surveying the horrendous housecleaning job to be done, he looks grim. The old habits, the old indifference, the familiar venality may be too deeply entrenched. But you know that here is a man who is going to do his damndest to end ancient evils that benefit the few and burden the many."

"This fellow Stevenson had better look out lest he wake up some fine morning and discover he's got no one with him other than the public." So wrote John P. Akers in the *Sun-Times*. "A Governor who tries to keep his campaign pledges; imagine that, this day and year in Illinois!"

Even the Chicago *Tribune* said surprisingly kind things for a number of weeks after the inaugural.

More correspondents than one found similarities between Stevenson and Lincoln, for all their obvious differences. According to John Dreiske of the *Sun-Times,* in the spring of 1949, Stevenson had "a literary flare and mode of expression that strikes many as being definitely along the Lincolnian line...." (Dreiske referred to the governor's "quotability" as a "refreshing breeze" and reported repeatedly, as a newsworthy item, that Stevenson "writes his own stuff.") Such public views of Stevenson as one who moved and had his being in the Lincoln tradition were enhanced by the governor's obvious love affair with Illinois history. One of his earliest acts was to establish direct and well-used lines of communication between his office and the Illinois State Historical Library, whose head, State Historian Jay Monaghan, was the author of widely read books on Lincoln and Illinois history. From the library he obtained a carefully selected group of books for his office shelves and oil paintings by Illinois artists to hang on the mansion walls. Out-of-town visitors to the mansion were almost invariably taken, either by the governor himself or by an appointed guide, to reconstructed New Salem, to Lincoln's tomb, to the house on the corner of Market and Eighth—and these visitors spread abroad tales of the governor's total immersion in Lincolniana and of his fondness for the company of such famed Lincoln scholars as Monaghan, Benjamin Thomas, then at work on his classic one-volume biography of Lincoln, and Carl Sandburg. He himself, in conversation with a Springfield physician, developed or accepted a theory about the causes of Mrs. Lincoln's notorious temper and of Lincoln's chronic melancholia—a theory he enjoyed expounding. Lincoln, he concluded, had a duodenal ulcer.

His close, widely publicized friendship with Lloyd Lewis further enhanced the public view of him as a man in the Lincoln tradition. In that year, and for some years earlier, Lewis was editor of the *Newberry Library Bulletin,* coming in from his farm home to this Chicago research library for a day or so each week. On April 21, 1949, on his way home from Chicago, he was stricken by a heart attack. A few hours later he died. In the book he was then working on (it was published the following year with the title *Captain Sam Grant*), he had got his hero only as far as Camp Yates on the outskirts of Springfield where, on June 28, 1861, Grant was colonel in command of the Seventh District Regiment of Illinois volunteers.

Stevenson came to Libertyville for the funeral. He was unexpectedly called upon to say a few words.* When he arose he spoke from a full heart, for he had loved Lloyd Lewis as he loved few people.

> I have been asked to share in these farewells to a friend. I think it is a good day for this meeting. It is April now and all life is being renewed on the bank of this river that he loved so well. I think we will all be happy that it happened on this day, here by the river with the spring sky so clear, and the west wind so warm and fresh. I think we will all be the better for this day and this meeting together.
>
> He was my neighbor. He was the neighbor of many of you. He was a very good neighbor; quick in time of misfortune, always present in times of mirth and happiness—and need. . . . I think it will always be April in our memory of him. It will always be a bright fresh day, full of the infinite variety and promise of new life.

III

The sorrow over the death of Lloyd Lewis was sudden, swift, leaving behind it a long ache of loss as well as sweet memories. There was, however, another sorrow in Stevenson's life that spring, which, all through those crowded months and through the fervid Illinois summer, grew in a crescendo of hidden anguish until, in late September, it burst at last its bonds of secrecy. It became, then, a too public sorrow, and in it there was no sweetness. Instead was an acid bitterness, which ate into the remembered past. The acid worked strongly in Adlai Stevenson's mind. It worked even more strongly in the mind of Ellen Borden Stevenson. It would keep on working, deeper and deeper. . . .[1]

On the day after the Springfield inaugural, Adlai III began his journey back to Harvard and Ellen accompanied her husband, with John Fell, to Bloomington for the Chamber of Commerce banquet at which Stevenson and Alben Barkley were featured. She then returned to the Libertyville farm. It was reported in the press that "Stevenson will lead a more or less bachelor

---

* Stevenson's words, later often quoted, were accurately recorded only because Louise Wright, with a rare sense of historical values, had arranged to have a stenographer present to take down all the spoken words in shorthand. Lewis was a Quaker and his funeral was in the tradition of a Friends meeting, where anyone is free to speak as the spirit moves him. His wife is a Roman Catholic.

existence during the next six months because his 12-year-old son, John Fell, is a student at Lake Forest Day School and Mrs. Stevenson wants to be close to him rather than live in the Executive Mansion in Springfield." The Chicago *Herald-American's* story added a cryptic sentence: "Mrs. Dwight H. Green's warning to Mrs. Adlai E. Stevenson that being the wife of the Governor of Illinois is not all everybody thinks it will be, already is being proved." It was said that Mrs. Stevenson planned to spend weekends at the mansion and to come down for "special occasions."

She spent, in fact, few weekends there. She accompanied her husband to the Truman inaugural. In early February her husband came to Libertyville for a celebration of his and John Fell's birthdays: his forty-ninth birthday was February 5, John Fell's thirteenth birthday was February 7, and Ellen, as in the past, split the difference, holding a joint celebration on February 6. She came to Springfield in late March to preside as hostess at the first and second of the series of dinner parties that the governor traditionally gave for members of the legislature. The legislators were invited, in alphabetical order, in groups of twenty-five or thirty. After the fifty Senate members had been dined, and before the series for the lower house began, she returned to Libertyville. At subsequent state dinners, and at other absolutely necessary social functions, Mrs. Ernest Ives was hostess, coming up for days at a time from Bloomington. Her husband moved into the mansion to be of what help he could to her brother in his terrible difficulties.

Inevitably there was a great deal of talk about the social situation at the mansion among legislators and Springfield residents, much of it sparked by a malice born of disappointment, for it had been forecast that Mrs. Stevenson, famed as a belle of the highest Chicago society, would bring to the mansion a glamorous social life such as the old house had not known since the Lowden administration, way back in the early 1930's. Instead, there was for many months virtually no social life at all. State senators and their wives complained, after the first of the two Senate dinners, that the affair had been coldly formal. A single cocktail was served before dinner and the guests were dismissed promptly at nine-thirty. (During the regimes of Horner and Green these dinners had lasted sometimes until well into the following morning.) Forewarned, several of the guests of the second Senate dinner took the precaution of pausing at the hotel bar on their way to the mansion, but even this added incentive to a festive mood failed noticeably to thaw (so several guests complained) a freezing atmosphere—and again the affair ended promptly at nine-thirty. Springfield gossips contrasted Mrs. Stevenson's polite reserve at the inaugural festivities with the elation and happy pride that Mrs. Ives had displayed, and they quoted frequently Mrs. Stevenson's remark about the "ancestor worship" in "Adlai's family." They also quoted remarks allegedly made by Chicago socialites at a luncheon in the Drake Hotel, shortly after the election—remarks that "Ellen has a mind of her own," and that "she's a positive personality" who would "never live in the state mansion."

Only to the Iveses, to those members of his staff who necessarily handled confidential detail in the governor's office, and to the most intimate of his long-time friends did Stevenson himself give any hint of the impending dissolution of his marriage. Even with these few he was extremely reticent concerning his personal feelings. Several times he indicated his pride in Ellen's wit and literary talents. One day he brought to the office, and proudly circulated, a "round-table discussion" of "Modern Woman" (years later, it was printed under that title in *Chicago* magazine), which Ellen had written. It was a dialogue in verse whose scene was "any intellectual parlor" and whose characters were Plato, Aquinas, Bacon, Voltaire, Freud—and Modern Woman.*

He also indicated a respect for Ellen's political opinions—though his most intimate friends believed he did so partially because he wanted so desperately to involve her in his new life, saving his marriage.

When school was out and John Fell no longer provided a convenient excuse for Ellen's continued absence from Springfield, the gossip, of course, increased. By this time several of Stevenson's intimates were aware that Ellen was determined to sue for a divorce. The reasons were as obscure to them as they were, perhaps, to Ellen herself, and to Adlai. She felt "smothered," she said; she suffered "a kind of claustrophobia" in her marriage; she had to live her own life, not a life as alien to her tastes as Adlai's now was. She had to be "free" in order "to write." A few intimates, mutual friends of hers and Adlai's, tried in vain to dissuade her. Wouldn't she at least agree to a separation without a divorce? She would not. It had taken her a long time to make up her mind, but now that it was made up there was no changing it.

Adlai, too, tried to dissuade her, pleading not just for himself but also for her own future happiness (he told a close friend that he was so terribly afraid of "what will happen to Ellen"), and then not for just the two of them but, especially, for their three sons. Ellen countered by saying that the three sons were virtually "raised"; Borden and little Adlai were away at school, and John Fell would enter Milton Academy in September (he would enter, as a matter of fact, a year earlier than had been planned originally). She agreed, however, that everything must be done to protect the *amour-propre* of the boys. To that end she would sue in Nevada rather than in Illinois where incompatibility was not acceptable as grounds for divorce and where,

---

* Some in the governor's office thought that Ellen's Modern Woman was her view of herself. Modern Woman's opening speech was:

They say I'm distracted and lost	*I emote with a speed supersonic.*
I think I'm impacted and bossed.	*My dissatisfaction is chronic.*
When I was a kid	*I envy the peace*
They ruined my id;	*Of the Ancients of Greece;*
So now I raise Cain when I'm crossed.	*O Plato, please make me platonic!*

in consequence, the judicial process was quite commonly corrupted by manufactured evidence. In public statements it would be emphasized that the parting was amicable. The boys would divide their holiday time equally between their parents, neither of whom would make any effort to alienate them from the other, and the Libertyville farm, which Adlai so deeply loved and which was his property, would remain his home.

On the last Friday in September, 1949, Stevenson made the formal announcement: "I am deeply distressed that, due to the incompatibility of our lives, Mrs. Stevenson feels a separation is necessary. Though I do not believe in divorce, I will not contest it. We have separated with the highest mutual regard." The press handled the story with rare restraint and sympathy. Said the Chicago *Daily News:* "Though news of the Adlai Stevensons' impending divorce was dropped on the general public like a bombshell last weekend, friends of the couple sensed a smouldering fuse months ago.... Mrs. Stevenson never made any secret of the fact that she considered a political campaign disrupting of home life and that she found political banquets boring."

On December 8 a Chicago *Herald-American* reporter managed to get in touch with Ellen in Las Vegas, Nevada, where she had lived for the five preceding weeks, establishing her residence. Early in the following week she would file petition for divorce. "What will the grounds be?" she asked. She replied: "I really can't say, but aren't they usually mental cruelty out here?" She was very cheerful. She had been "doing a lot of things I never seemed to have time to do before." She'd rented a typewriter and written at least fifty letters. She had read at least twenty books she had been planning to read for years. She was living in a ranch house about three miles from town. "There is a piano in my room, and I entertain myself a lot by playing it. Then I take long walks, sometimes hiking the three miles into town. I chose this spot because it's quiet, restful, and the weather is so nice. Why, right now while I'm talking to you—" she was interviewed by phone—"I can see the roses blooming outside my window." She planned to spend Christmas with the three boys at Libertyville, and then would try to obtain an apartment on the near North Side in Chicago.... The *Daily News* reported that "Mrs. Stevenson made it very plain there was no use asking any questions about her husband and what led to her decision to seek a divorce." Her standard reply to such questions was, "Of course you know I can't talk about that."

In the years that followed she engaged in a number of literary activities. She worked, intermittently, on a book. She wrote light verse. She became president of the Modern Poetry Association, which published *Poetry* magazine, founded by Harriet Monroe in 1912. In the 1950's she established in her childhood home, now owned jointly by her and her sister, a new club devoted to the arts, calling it the 1020 Arts Center (from the address at 1020

Lake Shore Drive). She worked hard to make this club a success, displaying again her talent for interior decoration, providing for excellent service and excellent food and drink, scheduling first-rate art shows and chamber music recitals by such stellar organizations as the Fine Arts String Quartet, arranging for lectures by such literary lights as W. H. Auden and Dylan Thomas. By the mid-1950's, this club absorbed most of her time and energy.

But by that time, too, the acid bitterness had worked very deeply into her, poisoning, it seemed, most of her life. Formerly she had seemed to resent the success and public acclaim that had come to her husband: it was not the limelight she disliked, said some of their mutual friends, but the fact that the limelight was not focused on her. "Everyone pays so much attention to Adlai!" she cried out, once, after a meeting of the Modern Poetry Association directors in the Newberry Library. "Why doesn't someone pay attention to me!" She laughed as she said it—but it was not a happy laugh. And her resentment of her former husband seemed to grow in direct proportion to his fame, as though this fame were for her a public humiliation. Certainly, if she felt she had made a mistake, if she suffered a sense of vital loss, the knowledge of the mistake and of her loss was inescapable: everywhere she turned she would encounter her former husband's face and hear his voice— in the press, on TV, over the radio, in newsreels.

Most of the friends she and Adlai had shared remained friends of his, and for that reason were repudiated by her as time went on. She began to make public statements that seemed obviously designed to hurt him, and she made malicious remarks about him at private affairs—remarks that were, of course, widely circulated. "The divorce," she now said, "was not just because of politics in general, as they said at the time...." In 1952 she told reporters that she was supporting her former husband's political opponent, and issued a weird statement that seemed intended to foster the most pernicious and nearly unanswerable of all false whispering campaigns. To Adlai himself she sent a message: "I am a Democrat but I will vote Republican. All good wishes to you personally."

She did succeed in hurting him, again and again, striking at the very roots of his pride, though he gave no outward sign of his hurt and made no public reply. She struck at him until some who loved him were driven into an actual hatred of her, and newsmen ceased to print the news she strove to make. She was, such people thought, an utterly selfish woman, a spoiled little rich girl who had never grown up and couldn't bear the knowledge that, measured against the man she had married, she now measured small. He had kept growing, they said, whereas she remained fixed in the Fitzgerald era, and she continued to believe that the fashionable, insouciant, not-very-important young man whom she had first met at parties was the real Adlai Stevenson and that all the other larger selves that now enveloped this first-known Adlai were phony. Such people pointed gratefully to the fact that Mrs. John Alden

Carpenter, Ellen's mother, and Lady Spears, Ellen's aunt, publicly demontrated their loyalty to Stevenson.

He developed, at last, a kind of protective callus over those portions of his spirit where she had repeatedly hurt him, but he never ceased to care for her as a human being, nor to worry, helplessly, about what was happening to her. Particularly did he care what happened to her as it affected the boys; he was scrupulously careful to say and do nothing that would destroy their love and respect for her. He insisted, too, that they pay their respects to her, that they not neglect her. And close observers of him and his sons became convinced that his strategy in this respect was successful. He was, such observers agreed in later years, a remarkably successful father of three remarkably fine, strong sons.

But in the immediate aftermath of the divorce he was convinced of his own failure. He worked incredibly hard for incredibly long hours all during the divorce period. He worked compulsively, as if afraid to stop—as if work were a pain-killing drug which, if it wore off, would leave him in unbearable agony.

One midnight Buffie went down to his basement office in the mansion to plead with him to go to bed. He'd been working into the morning hours every night that week; he'd collapse if he kept it up.

He looked at her through eyes that were dark with weariness and pain. He shook his head stubbornly, and made, unwittingly, one of his rare revelations of his hurt and of his excessively conscientious response to it.

"I've failed as a husband," he said. "I've failed as a father. I will succeed as governor!" [2]

CHAPTER NINETEEN

THAT good government requires good people in government had been a cardinal point of Stevenson's campaign. He had promised to improve the quality of the state's personnel. And on no phase of his administration did he spend more painstaking care than on the selection of personnel.

The problems the new governor faced, in this respect, were typical of American government. For the most part they stemmed from the fact that the salaries paid key officials were pitifully small when measured against the responsibilities those officials must shoulder. Consider his own salary, for example. He was paid twelve thousand dollars a year. In addition he received a house, a car and driver, and an expense allowance so modest that he constantly had to augment it from his own private income. Yet he was responsible for an enterprise directly employing some thirty thousand people and with a proposed budget, for the biennium beginning July 1, 1949, of some $1,055,000,000. Moreover, his performance of his assigned duties, his efforts toward a genuinely creative administration, were hampered at every turn by an archaic constitution, hostile political pressures, and public apathy. Much the same thing, if in different degree, was true of the key appointive officers.

It is a general rule of personnel management that if you pay less than the going wage you'll get, on the average, less than you pay for, whereas if you pay more, and can choose your employees from among many competing applicants, you're very likely to get more than you pay for. Failure to apply this general rule to public administration is by no means due wholly to popular ignorance. It is due also, and perhaps equally, to the fact that certain elements have a vested interest in corrupt, inefficient government. There are men who shout loudly for economy in government, bitterly opposing every effort to pay truly adequate government salaries, precisely because they profit personally from a system that virtually ensures mediocrity and venality among public servants. In few if any other states, historically, has such a system operated more effectively than in Illinois.

To fill his top appointive offices with first-rate men, therefore, required of Stevenson a great persuasive talent and administrative ingenuity. In nearly every case the man he wanted could accept appointment only at a considerable financial sacrifice—and he felt himself to be partially responsible, in a personal way, for the sacrifices these others made. He sought to discharge this responsibility by making cash gifts at Christmas time to those whose services and sacrifices were greatest. For this he used his own money in part. He used, too, some thousands that remained in his personal campaign treasury (as a result of postelection fund raising) after all his campaign debts had been paid. But most importantly he used a fund of ten thousand or so which had been made up, on their own initiative, by Dutch Smith and others of his well-to-do Chicago friends. ("He's down there fighting to give us decent government, using some of his own money to do it," said Dutch to his friends. "We have an obligation to help him out.") [1]

The core of Stevenson's immediate staff—those personally associated with him in his daily work—was formed at the outset by people who had worked closely with him during the campaign. Carol Evans became the governor's personal secretary (she took the job on a six-month trial basis; twelve years later she'd still be his secretary). Margaret Munn became her co-worker. James Mulroy, the campaign manager, became the governor's executive secretary, the only man close to Stevenson whose role might be compared to —though it was also very different from—that of Jim Farley in the early

Roosevelt years; it was Mulroy who dealt directly with lawmakers and lobbyists in behind-the-scenes negotiations essential to the political process. Lou Kohn, taking leave of absence from his law firm, served as administrative assistant handling appointments for the first few months, returning then to his law practice.

Joseph Knight, who as a very young man had been named to the Commerce Commission by Governor Horner and who had been active in the Stevenson campaign, became administrative assistant in charge of patronage. He seems in this position to have made more enemies among the politically powerful than Stevenson could afford and was soon switched to a State Insurance Department position. He was replaced in the patronage job by Lawrence E. Irvin, then thirty-eight, of Bloomington, a former Red Cross fieldworker and business manager of the Illinois State Normal University. A plump-faced, smiling man, he was tactful, adroit, and firm; patronage problems became immediately less thorny as he handled them. William I. Flanagan, who had served as press relations man during the campaign, became the governor's press secretary, with the high-sounding title of Superintendent of the Division of Department Reports.

The legislative assistant, a man of crucial importance to the administration, particularly in its first months, was Walter V. Schaefer, on leave from the Northwestern University Law School, where he was a professor. Stevenson had known him since 1934, when both were members of the legal division of the Agricultural Adjustment Administration in Washington. He was a quiet, scholarly, yet eminently practical man of fifty-one, chiefly responsible for translating the candidate's campaign promises into definite legal proposals for presentation to the legislature. After the first term of the legislature had ended, he returned to his Northwestern law professorship until he was appointed by the governor to fill a vacancy in the Supreme Court of Illinois. Subsequently Stevenson assured Schaefer's nomination and confirmation for a full nine-year court term despite acute pressures for the appointment of a party faithful.

Carl McGowan assumed Schaefer's role on the staff, becoming the most important member of the governor's inner circle during the remainder of the term. McGowan, who had returned to Northwestern's law school faculty after the war, was one of the first men Stevenson asked to come into the administration, but he had not felt free to do so until the school term ended in June of 1949. He then moved into a room in the mansion, living there until June of 1950 when his wife and family moved down into a rented house.

J. Edward Day, Stevenson's friend and associate in the Sidley firm, joined the initial group on March 3, 1949. As administrative assistant, he worked closely with Schaefer, and later McGowan, on the legislative program; he also helped to choose personnel and acted as general adviser. Not the least of his contributions was the exercise of his talent for light verse, which not only brightened the lives of his associates but also made excellent copy for newspapers, helping to fill out the public picture of the Stevenson operation as a remarkably light-hearted and nimble-witted reform administration. In June of 1950 Day resigned as administrative assistant in order to accept Stevenson's appointment of him as Director of the Department of Insurance, succeeding Harry Hershey, a highly respected lawyer of Taylorville who had been Horner's choice for governor in 1940 and would become a member of the Illinois Supreme Court in later years.

It was Day's resignation which led Stevenson, one early June morning, to place a call to William McC. Blair, Jr., in Chicago.

After his summer of work for the White Committee in Chicago, in 1940, Blair had returned to the University of Virginia Law School. Immediately after Pearl Harbor he enlisted in the Army and served as intelligence officer in the China-Burma-India theater, headquartered for a time in Calcutta and for a time in China. Released from the Army as a captain (he'd be a major in the Reserves in the 1950's) in December, 1945, he returned to the Virginia Law School, completed his work there, and was admitted to the Illinois Bar in the fall of 1948, entering one of the best of Chicago's law firms.

The law, however, bored him—not so much the actual law work as the commuting rut into which the law might put him. He had a horror of an increasingly dull and repetitious social life, a smothering of individuality in the homogenized culture of a fashionable suburb, a slow atrophy for lack of exercise of his capacity for excitement and innovation.

By March of 1950, thoroughly fed up with the life he was leading, he resigned from his firm and went on an extended trip through Latin America. While in Mexico, he received a wire asking him if he would head the Chicago office of the Hoover Commission. The job sounded interesting, having political overtones; he accepted it. He had been in the commission's Loop office precisely one hour and a half when the call from the governor came.

"I'm in need of an administrative assistant," Stevenson said. "If you're interested in the job, I'd appreciate your coming down this evening so that we can talk it over."

Blair did so and took the job, though he felt more than a little guilty about leaving the Hoover Commission in the lurch. A few days later he moved into the mansion and began a close working association with Stevenson, which would last for more than a decade.

Another who became a member of the immediate entourage, after the administration had run half its course, was Richard J. Nelson, a heavyset man who, though only in his mid-thirties, had wavy gray hair. A stellar student of Schaefer's at Northwestern University Law School, where he'd taken his degree in 1949, his interest in politics was matched by political talent; in June of 1950 he was elected president of the Young Democratic Clubs of America. As administrative assistant, Nelson often accompanied the governor on speaking trips, particularly those outside the state.

Yet another administrative assistant—the only one inherited from the preceding regime (a tribute to his abilities)—was T. Don Hyndman, who had served in the executive office since 1944 and was in his late thirties when Stevenson took office. A former newspaperman, Hyndman's job under Green had been to write nonpolitical statements and proclamations, verbal productions that must be graceful, if possible substantial, yet politically innocuous. He continued in this role under Stevenson and served also, loyally and effectively, as general adviser.

II

Stevenson chose his cabinet slowly, carefully, presenting for Senate confirmation only six of thirteen code-department directors when he took office; the other seven were Green holdovers to be removed when and if he found better men to replace them. One of these, Dr. Roland R. Cross, had been director of the Department of Public Health since October, 1940—a holdover from the Horner regime, whom Green had retained and whom Stevenson would keep throughout his administration.

Occasionally the new governor could obtain a good man with little effort. On the day after his election, he received some 250 telegrams urging him to appoint one Leonard Schwartz of Edwardsville to be director of the Department of Conservation. This aroused suspicions of a political deal, but when Stevenson investigated he found that the wires came from sportsmen's clubs and that Schwartz was a nationally known writer for outdoor magazines, an organizer and former president of the Illinois Federation of Sportsmen's Clubs, and had helped to raise hundreds of quail and pheasant each year for Illinois hunters. The appointment was made and Schwartz did an excellent job.

Generally, however, appointment making was an arduous process during which the governor drew heavily upon the advice and good will of his long-time friends.[2]

He was, for example, particularly anxious to obtain an outstanding man to serve as chairman of the Commerce Commission, which regulates public utilities and common carriers. No state agency is subject to greater pressure than this one, and none had fallen, deservedly, to a lower popular esteem during the Green administration. Man after man, approached by Stevenson, turned him down. Finally, just a few days before his inauguration, he took his problem to Laird Bell. Without real hope, he asked if Walter T. Fisher, a partner in the law firm of Bell, Boyd, and Marshall, might be persuaded to take the job. He was surprised when Bell replied that Fisher just might be; certainly Fisher had long been interested in problems of public utility regulation and had the best possible background for the assignment.

"Except that he's a Republican," Bell said, smiling.

That made no difference, Stevenson replied. He wanted outstanding men, regardless of party affiliation; besides, he well knew that Fisher's Republicanism was so liberal as to slide all the way over into political independence during election years.

The interview took place in a Loop hotel where Stevenson stayed some of the time between election and inaugural days.[3]

At fifty-seven, Fisher was a tall, thin-faced, gray-haired man wearing rimless glasses through which clear gray eyes looked out with acute perception upon the world. His financial resources were such that he could afford the luxury of public service if he chose so to indulge himself. He had also a highly principled, philosophic mind, and it was stimulated by this interview to reflect long upon the psychology and character of the man with whom he dealt.

Stevenson made his proposal and the two "kicked it around" for a while (the language was typical of Stevenson men). At one point Fisher said, "Ought I to do this, Adlai? Do you really think I should?" Stevenson's response took Fisher aback. "Well," said the governor-elect, "trade with me about it." From one point of view—the view Fisher initially held—this response was a kind of rebuff. Stevenson was refusing to join with Fisher in the making up of a mutual mind. He would not share in a joint decision. He remained isolated and kept Fisher isolated from him. But from another point of view—the view Fisher ultimately held—this was not a rebuff at all. On the contrary, it was an expression of respect for Fisher as an individual person who must make up his own mind, being responsible for his own character and acts.

Fisher took the job. He was one of three commissioners appointed at that time, the other two being Democrats. Two Green appointees were held over, giving the commission temporarily a Republican majority, a fact much commented on by the press. As chairman, Fisher's salary was eight thousand dollars. "What a sacrifice you are making!" people said to him, intending praise. Fisher shook his head in reply, insisting that no sacrifice was involved. Some of his friends maintained yachts on Lake Michigan; these were expensive; yet no one regarded such expenses as sacrifices. He, Fisher, chose to recreate himself through service on the Commerce Commission, a service that gave him compensations far more important to him, in his circumstances, than money could possibly be.

Another position for which the new governor was particularly anxious to find an outstanding man was that of director of the Public Welfare Department, by far the largest of all departments in Illinois government. He turned for advice to Dutch Smith, who was vice-president of the Community Fund of Chicago and a member of the executive committee of the Chicago Community Trust.

"The best possible man you could get," said Smith, "is Fred Hoehler."

Stevenson immediately agreed. Hoehler, a short, gray-haired man of fifty-five, was executive director of the Community Fund and had long been recognized as one of the outstanding professionals in his field. He was spectacularly well qualified for the state job.

There were, however, serious obstacles to his taking it. In the first place, his salary from the Community Fund was eighteen thousand dollars, whereas his salary as Illinois welfare director would be only eight thousand dollars—and Hoehler, unlike Fisher, was not a wealthy man. In the second place, Hoehler's health at that time was not good. It was largely for this second reason that he at first declined the offer Stevenson made to him. Both Stevenson and Smith continued to press him, however, until finally, one Sunday afternoon, he yielded to Stevenson's telephoned request that he at least agree to take the job for three months.

"That'll give me time to find a permanent director," Stevenson said.[4]

But of course the governor made no effort to find another director. Hoehler, as Stevenson had obviously expected, became so strongly committed to the state job that he stayed for the full term, writing during that period some of the brightest pages in the Stevenson gubernatorial record.

The Welfare Department, with a biennial budget of some $125,000,000 and a payroll of nearly twelve thousand people, had in its jurisdiction children's hospitals, mental hospitals, correctional institutions, sanitoriums, schools for the deaf and blind—twenty-four institutions in all. These cared for some fifty thousand persons and had theretofore been staffed in many professional positions by political appointees. Hoehler changed this. He insisted that Public Welfare should be a career service staffed by professionals who were chosen and promoted on the basis of professional competence. Stevenson agreed and gave Hoehler full backing, despite loud protests by certain Democratic politicians who felt themselves to be robbed thereby of the fruits of party victory. These outcries were not lessened when Hoehler fired payroll parasites, eliminated what had been standard graft in the department's purchasing system, and canceled construction contracts where the costs were revealed, by investigation, to be from five to ten percent too high. He brought in out-of-state professionals to reorganize purchasing, rewrite specifications, and supervise the awarding of contracts.

Illinois' mental health program was one of the worst among the forty-eight states when Stevenson took office. Within three years it had become very close to the best, enthusiastically praised by such world-famous psychiatrists as Dr. Karl Menninger of the Menninger Clinic, Topeka, Kansas. Hospitals that had been overcrowded and understaffed, often with incompetents, were expanded and staffed with first-rate people, their morale kept at a high level not only by Hoehler's inspired leadership but also by Stevenson's intense and knowledgeable interest in what they were doing.

In connection with the Peoria State Hospital the first center devoted entirely to psychotic children in any state hospital in the country was opened in 1951. Basic research into the causes and treatment of mental illness was begun; an ambitious program of research into geriatrics was launched; research into special therapies for Mongoloid children and epileptics was conducted; and there was special research into the use of an ultrasonic-ray method of destroying brain tumors. A program for using special therapies on so-called incurables and senile patients was also begun.

When a Chicago civic organization awarded Governor Stevenson a citation for outstanding public service, it did so primarily because of his attraction of outstanding men into top state positions. Walter T. Fisher and Fred K. Hoehler were specifically mentioned. The citation would not have been awarded, however, if these two had been wholly unique among the Stevenson appointments. They were, on the contrary, typical of the high-caliber personnel he sought and often succeeded in obtaining—men like Henry F. Tenney, a civic-minded and wealthy lawyer (he was a friend and neighbor of Walter Fisher in Winnetka), whom he appointed to the Illinois Public Aid Commission, and women like Maude Meyers, an outstandingly capable career public servant whom he appointed to the Civil Service Commission.

His first Director of Revenue was Richard J. Daley, a former member of the legislature who was destined to become mayor of Chicago (with Stevenson's influential support) in 1955. Daley served as revenue director for some eighteen months and aided the new governor greatly, particularly with the legislative program, having learned the ropes thoroughly during his service in earlier sessions of the General Assembly. Daley was succeeded by Clifford E. Halpin, a career public servant who had served in the department since 1933.

George W. Mitchell became Stevenson's first director of finance, responsible for budget, purchasing, printing, and accounting controls. Mitchell, an officer of the Chicago Federal Reserve Bank, was a former president of the National Tax Association and had edited an eight-volume work on the organization and financing of local government. He did an outstanding job and Stevenson fought hard, though vainly, to keep him in the state government after his leave of absence from the bank was terminated. Mitchell, however, helped Stevenson to persuade Joseph Pois to come in as his successor. Pois, who had done consulting work on budgetary and taxation problems for the states of Michigan and Kentucky, was treasurer and member of the board of the Signode Steel Strapping Company of Chicago.

Closely allied with Pois in the elimination of graft and the increase of efficient and economical state operation was the state purchasing agent. The latter's job was one on which politicians focused eager attention and which they would have been glad to help Stevenson fill. Instead, the governor turned for advice to acquaintances in the business world whose firms employed topflight purchasing men. Among these, strangely enough, was General Robert E. Wood, chairman of the board of Sears, Roebuck and Company, who as head of the America First Committee had been bitterly opposed to Stevenson in the early 1940's. Wood told the governor that Sears' own purchasing agent, Carl Kresl, was retiring and might be persuaded to take the state job. Stevenson persuaded him.

Another state agency subject to great pressures and frequently corrupted by them in the past was the Parole and Pardon Board. He was able to obtain as chairman perhaps the best-qualified man in the country: Joseph D. Lohman, world-famous sociologist specializing in criminology.

The three-man Illinois State Liquor Commission, as Stevenson learned somewhat to his surprise, was yet another agency in which a certain kind of politician, and numerous other unsavory characters, took an inordinate interest. He discovered that there were abundant opportunities for commissioners to earn graft from the issuance or revocation of liquor licenses and that these opportunities had been abundantly realized in the past. Accordingly, he was determined to find a man whom he knew absolutely he could trust, and the man he ultimately found, W. Willard Wirtz, was to play a major role in the Stevenson story during the years ahead.[5]

Then thirty-eight, Wirtz was a native of De Kalb, Illinois, a graduate of Beloit College in Beloit, Wisconsin, and had taken his law degree at Harvard Law School in 1937. At Harvard he had known J. Edward Day. From Harvard he had gone to the University of Iowa as a law school faculty member (the dean there was Wiley Blount Rutledge, later an associate justice on the U.S. Supreme Court, whom Wirtz profoundly admired), and from Iowa he had come to Northwestern. At Northwestern, before the war, he had formed a close friendship with his law faculty colleague, Carl McGowan, who became a neighbor of his in Winnetka.

At a party in Wirtz's home one evening a few months after Stevenson took office, McGowan mentioned the difficulty of finding good men for state jobs. "Maybe that's because you don't ask," Wirtz said, half joking, yet serious, too, for he had long been interested in politics and was perhaps a trifle envious of the exciting experience his friend was having in Springfield. A week later Wirtz received a call in his law school office from McGowan, who told him that the governor would like to see him at 160 North La Salle, the State Office Building in Chicago. Wirtz went down and met Stevenson for the first time—this was in February of 1950—in a Finance Department office that the governor used as his Chicago headquarters until the penthouse atop the building was remodeled for his use. With no ado, Stevenson asked if Wirtz would accept appointment to a six-year term on the Liquor Commission.

"But I don't know anything about liquor control," Wirtz said.

"What we need, and find hard to get, is somebody who'll just keep his hands out of other people's pockets," Stevenson said, with a rueful grin. "That's the chief qualification."

Wirtz grinned, too. "If that's so," he said, "I'm not likely to deny that I'm qualified."

He took the job, whose duties were of modest proportions. He would attend from two to five meetings a month and there decide simple questions. For this, and being honest, he would be paid six thousand dollars a year.

He had barely returned to his office when his phone rang. It was Stevenson. The Liquor Commission was, by law, a bipartisan one, he said, and he had neglected to ask a key question: "Are you a Democrat?"

"Is it necessary that your appointee be a Democrat?" Wirtz asked.

"It is."

"Then I'm a Democrat," Wirtz said. "As of now."

Other code-department heads were Roy E. Yung, Agriculture; Joseph K. McLaughlin, Aeronautics; Walter Eadie, Mines and Minerals; Michael F. Seyfrit, Public Safety; Charles P. Casey, Public Works and Buildings; Noble Puffer and C. Hobert Engle, successively heads of Registration and Education; and Frank Annunzio, Labor.

Of these, only Annunzio proved an embarrassment to the administration. Though Stevenson during the campaign had refused to permit labor organization leaders to name his labor director, the appointment of Annunzio to the post was interpreted, and with justification, as the payment of a political debt to the C.I.O., whose leaders (Annunzio had been one of these) had supported his candidacy, whereas several A.F. of L. leaders had been Green supporters. When Annunzio was asked to resign, Stevenson replaced him with Fern R. Rauch, formerly assistant director.

And even the Labor Department, whose initial top administration was certainly no worse than it had been in the past, profited in its lower echelons from Stevenson's talent for personnel recruitment, a talent which was of a piece with his social charm.

At a party given by the head of the *Time* magazine bureau in Chicago, a year or so after the war, Stevenson had met for the first time Mrs. Stanley (Betty) Pargellis, wife of the librarian of Chicago's Newberry Library. In the course of their conversation ("He has a talent for drawing people out," Betty Pargellis later said, "listening with such obviously genuine interest to what people have to say") he learned that Mrs. Pargellis, an active member of the League of Women Voters, was deeply interested in the women's and children's aspects of Illinois government labor policy.[6] A year later young Marshall Field gave a party for his mother—a very large, social affair. Betty Pargellis was there. Stevenson came up to her and introduced himself again, saying, "I don't suppose you remember me." Of course she did remember him—by that time he was being talked of for senator—and then and there, in the midst of a "very posh chit-chattering affair," the two held a long and animated discussion of the Women's and Children's Division of the State Labor Department. Political appointments of women inspectors were being made—such appointments were among the few patronage spots for women —and Betty Pargellis was emphatic in her statements about the evils of this practice.

When Stevenson was elected governor he wrote to Betty Pargellis, among others, asking for personnel recommendations for the Labor Department, particularly of women. She recommended Miss Martha Ziegler, who'd been in such work in the federal government, to head up the Women's and Children's Division; she recommended Miss Florence Klever as Ziegler's second-in-command. Others confirmed these recommendations, and the appointments were made. The Ziegler-Klever team was a fortunate one for Illinois, despite the fact that much of its work, like much that Fred Hoehler's department did, was swiftly wiped out by the Republican administration which succeeded Stevenson's.

III

It was a concomitant of the kind of man he chose for government that Stevenson himself, as man and as administrator, should become the object of close study and penetrating observation by his associates.

Walter Fisher, for example, found the governor a fascinating human being. The Stevenson mind, from Fisher's point of view, was a lawyer's mind —and Fisher contrasted it with the businessman's mind or the mind of a general of armies.

A general or a business executive, facing the need for decision, consults his staff, who present him with factors to be considered in solving a problem. These are presented and dealt with as though they were definite, static entities; and in business or military operations they often are relatively static, relatively definite. But sometimes—and almost always in politics—the factors are fluid and essentially indefinable: they flow into one another as processes instead of remaining distinct and separate things. In such cases the problem cannot really be solved in engineering terms, and when the chief executive of the military or business type says, "We'll do *this*" (he is likely to say it with a great show of force), the decision is an act of will rather than of intellect. Quite generally he has proceeded on hunch or impulse, his basic motivations remaining obscure to him. Of such a man it cannot be truly said that he has a decisive *mind*—though of course it often is said of him. He is more likely to have a vague, confused mind, which has never really been made up, which shifts with shifting external pressures, and which has terrifying capacities for self-deception since its possessor has not heeded Socrates's urgent admonition to "Know Thyself."

Stevenson's lawyer mind proceeded very differently from this, in Fisher's view. Faced with the need for decision, Stevenson shaped a tentative hypothesis and then tested it against opposing arguments. To superficial observers, this might appear to be hesitation and vacillation, indicating an incapacity to decide. Fisher was convinced it was the precise opposite. People tend to confuse action with decision, whereas it is quite possible to act *without* deciding. Stevenson's acts (so Fisher concluded) were truly decisive, the proof of this being that they were "very firm"; they "stood up" against the pressures that were inevitably brought against them. In the Stevenson administration there was no backing and filling, once a decision was made.

To all this, Jane Dick added an observation with which Fisher thoroughly agreed. Mrs. Dick did not retire wholly to private life once the gubernatorial campaign was ended. She was persuaded to accept an appointment as one of the five-man State Board of Public Welfare Commissioners, from which vantage point she (in her own words) "kept an eagle eye on the Stevenson administration for the next four years." It was her observation that Stevenson, as a part of the process of decision, always examined his own motives with scrupulous care and utter candor.

"He keeps asking himself, 'Why am I doing this?'" she said. "'Am I doing it because it's the right thing to do, or because it's the expedient thing?' He often acts on grounds of expediency, of course. Every politician has to. But when he does, he *knows* that he's doing it. He doesn't pretend to himself or anybody else that he's expressing in action some noble principle." [7]

Perhaps Stevenson's working relationships with his immediate staff provided the deepest insights into his character as executive and human being. Significantly, the men closest to him were sharply distinguished from one another as personalities.

McGowan and Blair, for example, were actual contrasts in several respects. Blair disliked the law as a career; McGowan loved the law, was fascinated by its intricacies and challenged intellectually by its problems. Blair had a relaxed easy charm, the manners of a polished hedonist of the aristocracy, and a smiling warmth in his human relations. This caused people to like him at once, but it also caused many to underrate him as a mind and character; it was not until one knew him well, having observed him in action, that one realized the breadth as well as the acuteness of his intelligence and the seriousness of his purpose. McGowan, on the other hand, gave to many people an initial impression of rigidity and coldness. He seemed a stern Scotch-Presbyterian type—craggy, humorless, and intolerant of human frailties. Yet as one knew him better, this initial impression was modified by one's experience of the real human warmth of his nature, the concern he had for the welfare of those around him, so that this very sternness became an element of the attraction he had for people. Close observers spoke of McGowan, in Springfield, as "Stevenson's conscience"—and Stevenson himself often said that McGowan and he "thought alike" and that never before had he met a man whose moral judgment so perfectly agreed with his own. When McGowan said, "There are things more important than winning an election, even an election to the Presidency of the United States," he expressed not only his own nature but also that which Stevenson regarded as best and highest in himself. The honest expression of such sentiments therefore (and there was no doubt that McGowan meant what he said) could not fail to enhance Stevenson's respect for his subordinate's moral judgment and essential attitudes.

Blair became appointments secretary, personal facilitating officer, and the governor's most constant companion. He had always loved travel, and he was so relaxed on long trips, so eminently useful, that the governor seldom traveled without him. He knew how and when to keep silence. "I don't talk to him much, unless he wants to talk," Blair once explained. "I don't even sit with him on a plane or train—unless he has some work to get done, as he often does, and wants me there as a kind of buffer. He needs privacy and solitude, he gets so little of it; and when he wants companionship, it does him good, refreshes him, to see new people." [8]

As the months passed, Blair also became Stevenson's chief personal political agent and adviser, concentrating on the things Stevenson personally should do in order to advance his political fortunes. Yet this role was never specifically assigned to him. The fact is typical of Stevenson's relations with his immediate staff, and significant of his general administrative style. Blair was required to assume his role, creating it in the process of assuming it— and it was never openly acknowledged by Stevenson himself. On the contrary, in later years Blair had often to proceed *despite* Stevenson, or even against the latter's stubborn resistance, in order to accomplish what he knew, deep down, to be his mission—the mission that Stevenson himself wanted Blair to perform.

Legendary among Stevenson associates would become Blair's bravery and skill as he entered what seemed to some a lion's den, there to persuade, and cajole, and often laugh the governor into doing something he'd flatly refused, at the outset, to do. At such times Blair was suave, even-tempered, firm, endlessly patient, quick to see openings through which he might thrust home his sword of persuasion; he was also adept at using Stevenson's own wants and commitments against himself in a kind of mental and moral jujitsu. Politicians learned that it was often better—and perhaps generally so—to deal with Blair than with Stevenson directly on matters involving the governor's personal activity.

Typical was an episode which occurred some years later. Blair, having consulted with Stevenson (he never made such decisions without consulting him), committed the governor to a speech in Detroit, having been persuaded by the Michigan Democracy, and by his own sense of values, that this was of importance to the welfare of Stevenson Democrats. Sometime later, when Blair was out of town, the Michigan people telephoned the Stevenson office, asking for Blair. The call was referred to the governor by a new employee who had not been warned of the governor's penchant for seizing such opportunities to get out of commitments, claiming afterward (to Blair) that he had "forgotten" he had agreed to them. On this occasion Stevenson told the Michigan people that his schedule was overcrowded (as indeed it always was) and that he just couldn't make the speech. That evening, walking along Jackson Street to his commuter's train, he told a friend of his "horrid afternoon"; the Michigan state Democratic chairman and the Michigan national committeeman had been on the phone with him for forty minutes.

"Forty minutes!" Stevenson said. "I timed them." He felt a little guilty about "pulling the rug out from under Bill," he went on. He was sure Bill had made the commitment in good faith and for what seemed to Bill good reasons.

"You're not going to do it, then?"

"I am not!" he said, with emphasis.

A few weeks later he flew to Detroit and made the speech. Why, then, the initial resistance? Why his frequent reluctance to do things that he knew would serve his interests and were, indeed, necessary to the advancement of his political fortunes?

Such questions never ceased to intrigue, when they did not actively annoy, Stevenson's close working associates. Part of the answer doubtless lay, part of the time, in the surface irritability produced by the constant, galling pressures upon him. The more acute among his close observers were convinced, however, that the ultimate answer lay deep in Stevenson's character. Some wondered if the answer might not be related to the terrible accident of 1912, the accident in which the boy Adlai had been the inadvertent agent of Ruth Merwin's death. He seemed to punish himself. He seemed to feel that it was somehow *wrong* for him to succeed easily.

"He has to do it the hard way," one close observer said, "the hardest possible way."

If this were true—and it was a very tentative hypothesis—Bill Blair's role might come close, at times, to that of whipping boy. It would be up to him to help Stevenson, despite himself, toward success, and in the process to absolve the governor of the guilt of success. Stevenson himself, in later years, was inclined to assign to Bill Blair, in conversation, the responsibility for many of his self-promoting activities. "Bill made me go there," he would say. Or, "Bill says I have to do this." Of a quip of which he grew fond (and he grew inordinately fond of some of them), he would say wistfully that "Bill won't let me use it any more."

But it must not be assumed from this that he ever really regarded himself as, in any sense, Blair's puppet or any other man's, to be manipulated toward ends that he himself did not perceive. Certainly Blair himself never made that mistake. He neither manipulated nor was manipulated. There were occasions when Blair wholly failed to overcome an initial resistance, and if these failures were relatively few, it was only because Blair generally knew when this resistance was a false front, or an outer bastion which would not be strongly held. The inner citadel was impregnable, and he never knowingly attacked it.

Blair dealt with what Stevenson might regard as merely "formal" matters (at Springfield he was deemed the "handyman"), whereas McGowan certainly dealt with substantive matters. McGowan's work had to do directly with administration policy: he handled a great deal of Stevenson's official correspondence, he often served as Stevenson's alter ego in policy meetings or in the handling of administrative problems, he helped in the preparation of major speeches and formal messages to the legislature, including the veto messages through which Stevenson's philosophy of law and government was revealed almost as completely as Justice Holmes's was in the famed dissenting opinions on the Supreme Court.

But if the roles of Blair and McGowan could be thus contrasted, they were in yet another respect essentially similar. By the time Blair came into the administration, McGowan had long assumed his particular role vis-à-vis Stevenson—and had created it in the process of assuming it—just as Blair found he had to do.

When McGowan first came to Springfield he took his problems into Stevenson's office somewhat as one might do who was assistant to an orthodox executive. But he discovered that Stevenson's tendency was to take over the problem in such cases. If, for example, McGowan brought in a letter concerning which he had some question, Stevenson was likely to keep it, saying, "I'll handle it." It quickly occurred to McGowan that he could hardly be of much help to Stevenson if this became a standard pattern of operation. He began to handle more and more matters on his own, including matters of considerable importance but concerning which he was certain of Stevenson's position. As he did so he demonstrated a rare sagacity, both in his understanding of his chief and in his grasp of state problems.

"I tried to determine what I'd want as an assistant if I were in the governor's spot," McGowan explained, some years later. "I'd had an opportunity to observe how Stevenson worked for Knox during the war and it seemed to me that he'd now want me to work for him in the same way. It also seemed to me that, if I were Stevenson, I'd probably never spell out in any detail what I wanted from an administrative assistant. I'd probably not even know, in advance of problems, precisely what I wanted. But I'd certainly be grateful to my man if he handled things as much as possible on his own, and lightened my burden—even if he took risks, sometimes, and made mistakes. Stevenson had a crushing burden down there, you know. He worked terrifically hard for from ten to fifteen hours a day *every* day!"

Stevenson, McGowan added, was definitely a small-staff man. ("I do dislike having a lot of people bustling around me all the time," the governor himself said. "A measure of solitude and tranquillity is surely necessary to any man who would reflect upon his problems and solve them through concentrated thought.") He liked to handle things himself, being very much his own man and tacitly insisting that others be similarly self-possessed and inner-directed.[9]

IV

Though Stevenson professed to be an admirer of Governor Thomas E. Dewey's streamlined efficiency in New York (when a former top member of Dewey's administration visited Springfield, Stevenson questioned him at length about the manner in which Dewey organized his personal staff and worked with it), his imitations of Dewey's administrative methods, in so far as he made them, were too slight to be recognizable. He might be intellectually convinced of the value of a standardized order and method in the handling of his office's enormous work load, and that an efficiency expert could help him achieve it. But this intellectual conviction could make small headway against his deep, seemingly instinctive aversion to organization charts and the organization-chart mentality.

It was as if he felt, deep down, that there is a vital loss, unjustified by an increase of external efficiency, in any system that rigidly confines a man to a particular staff function, hedging him about with precise terms of reference (a detailed job-description) and placing him as a static item in a chain of command. One can gain predictability of operation by doing so, he might have said, but by that same token one loses creativity. Moreover there is grave danger that decisive responsibility will be shifted from the individual person to the system if the latter becomes too slickly efficient, with consequences destructive of human freedom and productive, over the long run, of disastrous errors. Politics, in his view, was an art rather than a science, and of politics his immediate staff operation was a part.

The great defect of blurred delegations of authority, of course, is that they foment personnel discords. Status anxieties and power conflicts are likely to spring up as weeds on a ground uncultivated by a sharply defined authority. And to some extent this happened in the governor's office. "Adlai's a little like Roosevelt as an administrator," said one veteran of the Springfield days, years later. "If a man isn't working out quite right, Adlai'll often put another man in approximately the same spot without getting rid of the first one. That causes a lot of trouble, sometimes. And because his assignments of authority were so vague, there was a lot of jockeying for position in Springfield—people trying to get close to the throne." Stevenson very seldom used the governor's executive suite in the State House. He established his personal office in the basement of the Executive Mansion, and one result of this was a considerable jealousy between that portion of the immediate staff which worked in the State House office and that portion which was in daily contact with the governor in the mansion.

Opinions varied as to Stevenson's own awareness of the anxieties and subtle conflicts that often swirled around him. Some people believed that status envy was so foreign to his nature, so alien to his personal experience, that he didn't recognize it for what it was when he encountered it; this meant that a self-promoter might advance himself beyond his deserts or abilities. Others believed that Stevenson was perfectly cognizant of what went on around him and that his seeming unawareness was, in part at least, a useful pose. "He believes in giving a man plenty of rope," one former associate said, contradicting the Springfield veteran quoted above, "but he knows damned well when that man has hanged himself, and he doesn't keep the dead body around the office too long." Yet others believed that Stevenson's whole administrative strategy was like Franklin Roosevelt's in more ways than one, having in it certain elements of craft and even of ruthlessness whereby his aides were tested and stimulated to do their best.

That Stevenson was beloved of his staff no man could doubt who talked to his staff members about him. "There is such *sweetness* in him," said one of these. "Oh, he's irascible at times. Who wouldn't be with the pressures he's constantly under? He says hurtful, cutting things at times to those who work intimately with him. But underneath, as a constant thing, there's the real sweetness of the man." Arthur Schlesinger, Jr., the historian, later regarded Stevenson as "approximately the most beguiling, seductive individual I've ever known." [10] Yet another, who worked with the governor in Springfield, was convinced that Stevenson was as John Mason Brown once described him, "That rare, almost forgotten creature, a Christian gentleman."

Gaiety and wit, a youthful zest permeated by idealistic purpose, characterized the weekly staff meetings over which the governor presided. "Skull practice," these sessions were called, and they were swift and searching reviews of all manner of current state problems and of underlying policies. They were held with a rigid regularity, largely because Carl McGowan insisted upon it. "I knew that if I didn't insist, the governor, buried in work, would cancel them every so often," McGowan later explained. "Soon we'd be holding none at all—or holding them too infrequently." Regularly present were McGowan, Blair, Irvin, Day, Nelson, Flanagan, Hyndman, and Mulroy until his work relationship with Stevenson ended, as we shall see, tragically.

Something of the flavor of these sessions is revealed in a verse Ed Day read to one of the earliest of them. State Senator Roland Libonati of Chicago had introduced a bill which required that every room in every public building in the state be equipped with at least one cuspidor. On the floor the bill was amended, after solemn debate, to except public school houses, and was then passed by the Senate. This provoked a hilarity not unmingled with exasperation in Stevenson and his staff. Wrote Day:

> *A bill has passed the Senate*
> *About which some are skeptical:*
> *It would give a legal mandate*
> *To a rather crude receptacle.*
> *For those among the public*
> *Who may not approve of this,*
> *We point out that good government*
> *Should not be hit or miss.*
> *We recommend approval*
> *For Libonati's legislation;*
> *We feel sure it will live up*
> *To our best expectorations!*

On another occasion Johnson Kanady, the Chicago *Tribune's* Springfield correspondent, wrote in a typically snarling dispatch that "Stevenson's policy toward press conferences has always been to have aids carefully question newspapermen on what questions will be asked," and that this "accounts for his quick wit and ready answers." Howls of derisive glee were provoked by this among other Springfield correspondents as well as among Stevenson's staff. Ed Day's comment upon it was widely published. Wrote he: "This conjures up a rather improbable picture of the ebullient Stevenson occupying himself, amid mounds of paper work and lines of callers, in company with a group of 'aids,' drafting and redrafting impromptu bon mots to fit all possible questions at an approaching press conference."

CHAPTER TWENTY

G OVERNOR STEVENSON presented to the Sixty-sixth General Assembly of Illinois the most extensive and ambitious legislative program that any governor of that state had ever tried to enact in a single session. Jack Arvey was convinced the program was too ambitious, and said publicly that the new governor, had he been more experienced, would not have attempted it. Stevenson himself was inclined to agree with this judgment after the arduous session had ended. "But," he added, "I think campaign talk should be more than sweet, deceitful words. It's easy to talk big and act small when the responsibility suddenly falls on you like a ton of coal." Moreover, he was encouraged to believe that his proposals would be more likely to pass a Democratic House and a Republican Senate that were still enthralled by his tremendous electoral triumph.[1]

In an unusually candid Report to the People, broadcast over forty-eight Illinois radio stations after the term's end, Stevenson pointed out that approximately two thirds of the legislation he had particularly recommended had been enacted. This legislation took the state highway police out of politics; upped state aid to schools from the $66 million for 1947–49 to $112 million for 1949–51 (he was forced to cut this by ten percent after the Senate blocked new revenue bills); increased unemployment compensation from a $20 to a $25 a week maximum, and extended eligibility to pregnant women, while reducing employers' contribution tax rates; improved mine safety equipment and took mine inspectors out of politics; increased from $50 to $65 a month the ceiling on pensions for the aged and the blind, with an escalator provision by which the ceiling went up or down in accordance with cost of living indices issued by the federal government; created a county superintendent of assessments for every county excepting Cook and St. Clair; and increased the salaries of all elective state officials, to be effective in 1953, and of all heads of departments and commissions, to become effective immediately. Simultaneously, he cut padded payrolls, greatly increased the efficiency of executive agencies, and effected economies in purchasing and the use of materials which would save millions of tax dollars during his term.

These were substantial victories for any new governor to achieve in his first General Assembly. They measured relatively small, however—in the public mind and for a time in Stevenson's own—against the defeat of proposals on which the governor had placed major emphasis. The three principal ones of these were (1) a referendum on calling a convention to revise the state's 1870 constitution, (2) a series of bills issuing from the Chicago Crime Commission and designed to speed and improve criminal justice; and (3) a bill to establish a Fair Employment Practices Commission to reduce job discrimination based on race, color, or creed.

The FEPC law, modeled on New York's, was introduced to both houses in mid-February of 1949. It was the first such administration-sponsored bill in Illinois history, and was strongly supported by ministers, the Illinois C.I.O., the Chicago Mayor's Commission on Human Relations, racial and religious minority organizations, and a few individual employers. It was fervently opposed by the Illinois Chamber of Commerce, the Illinois Manufacturers Association, the Illinois Small Business Association, the Chicago Retail Merchants Association, and other employer groups as well as by leading newspapers, including the Bloomington *Pantagraph*, which asserted that the bill would prevent the hiring of people on the basis of ability and would subject employers to "nuisance lawsuits" for "shakedown purposes." A storm of controversy was aroused. A bulletin widely circulated by the Small Business Association asserted that the bill was "class-legislation . . ." whose "motivating force" was "Communism."

Stevenson replied that the bill was in line with the Republican party's 1948 platform on civil rights and that in other states, like New York, New Jersey, and Connecticut, "which have adopted more stringent FEPC laws under Republican governors, these laws have not caused any important difficulties for employers. . . ." In a radio Report to the People, he cited the argument that the answer to racial and religious discrimination is to be found, not in legislation, but in education. "There is," said he, "no conflict between legislation and education in our quest for economic justice."

The measure came to a vote in the House in mid-May, and was passed by that body. Sixty-eight Democrats and thirteen Republicans voted for it; three Democrats and forty Republicans voted against it; twenty-eight Representatives didn't vote. The Senate vote was originally scheduled for June 15, but was postponed when Stevenson, having summoned Democratic leaders to his office, learned that he apparently had one less vote for his measure than was necessary for passage. That night he and his aides worked hard to gain votes. Next morning, after a bitter three-hour debate in which Republican leaders termed FEPC the "worst bill" in the session, one which "would put us back economically 25 years," the final vote was taken. With twenty-six votes needed for passage, the measure received twenty-three, with twenty-five votes against it and two senators not voting. Sixteen Democrats and seven Republicans voted for it, twenty-four Republicans and one Democrat voted against it. Stevenson, deploring the fact that Republicans in the "State of Lincoln" had defeated the measure, and this despite the 1948 national Republican platform, promptly pledged that the bill would be reintroduced to the next General Assembly. It was, but died in committee.

The resolution calling for a constitutional convention, which was immediately dubbed "Con-Con," was introduced to the legislature on February 2, 1949, after a night meeting of Democratic chieftains called by the governor at the Executive Mansion. It provided that the people be permitted to vote in the regular election of November 1950 on whether to call a convention in 1951 or later. Joined to it was a so-called "party circle" bill, designed to ease the adoption of a new constitution. This called for a revision of the ballot law so that political parties, at their conventions, could endorse the calling of a constitutional convention, the endorsement then to appear at the top of the election ballot under the party's circle. A straight ticket vote in the circle, for all party nominees, would also be a vote for the calling of the convention. Split-ticket voters would be able to vote "yes" or "no" specifically on the constitutional question.[2]

This was the number one item on the new governor's legislative program and the lines of battle over it were drawn even before the measure was introduced. In the vanguard of the supporting forces was the Illinois League of Women Voters, who had made an extensive study of the 1870 constitution and were convinced that it was, as Stevenson said, an almost insurmountable "roadblock to good government." Much more strongly organized was the opposition, consisting of powerful labor, farm, and manufacturing pressure groups, plus a bloc of downstate lawmakers who feared that convention delegates would approve legislative reapportionment on an actual population basis, giving Cook County control of the legislature. There were fears by businessmen that a new constitution might pave the way for a state income tax (none was permitted under the 1870 constitution), fears by some labor leaders that a new charter might wipe out labor's recent legislative gains, fears genuine or synthetic, but loudly proclaimed, that the bill of rights might be jeopardized, and protests that the proposed convention would cost from five to ten million dollars and would probably fail to produce an acceptable charter.

All these arguments were answered in extended public speech by administration supporters and by Stevenson himself, who pointed out that the risk of constitutional reform was the calculated risk of democracy, since democracy rests upon a faith in the people's judgment and capacity for self-government. A free society which refuses to take that risk, when changed circumstances demand it, is assured thereby of stagnation and ultimate death.

The measure came to a vote in the House on April 14. Two thirds of the House, or 102 votes, were required for passage, and Revenue Director Daley, who served as the governor's contact man with the legislature on this item, believed that he had them, though he knew that the predicted victory margin was paper thin. After a stormy seven-hour debate, during which two Democrats who had been brought from sickbeds were excused after being allowed to record "aye" votes, the roll call ballot was taken on a resolution to approve the measure. This failed of passage by what would have been a five-vote margin had Democratic Speaker Powell stepped down from the rostrum to cast his favorable ballot. Ninety-six votes (76 Democrats, 20 Republicans) were cast for the resolution, 48 votes (46 Republicans and two Democrats) were cast against it. Only adroit floor management by Stevenson forces prevented a vote, then and there, to kill the measure completely. Thus the measure was kept alive for another attempt at passage.

Stevenson promptly announced that the attempt would soon be made, and he and his supporters began to exert all the pressure at their command, offering, as a concession, to drop the party circle proposal in return for Con-Con votes. As they did so, they themselves were offered a proposal that would almost certainly have assured passage of the measure.

The two House Democrats voting against the measure were members of what was known as Chicago's West Side Bloc, whose other members included four Republicans. All came from the city's "tough wards" and they voted in concert against whatever anti-gambling and anti-racketeering bills were proposed. They now made it known to the governor that they would support Con-Con the next time around if the governor would withdraw his active support from the Crime Commission bills. There were five of these latter, introduced to both houses almost simultaneously with Con-Con in early February, and they were of course adamantly opposed by Chicago's politically organized hoodlums.

Stevenson was profoundly discouraged. His legislative program was in serious trouble. He had been presented with an opportunity to put through an act of fundamental importance to Illinois' progress; he could have done it by scuttling an item of somewhat smaller importance. But if he chose the lesser of two evils—as it might appear to be—he gave a decisive power, in this one instance at least, into the hands of the worst political elements in the state. He flatly refused to do so.

And then another deal was offered him. A bill to permit dog racing in Illinois was before the General Assembly, and he had been assured of West Side Bloc support for Con-Con if he would merely promise not to veto this bill if it passed. Since its chance of passage through both houses was slight, he might argue that he could make the desired promise without seriously jeopardizing the general welfare. He rejected the argument, however. He refused the promise. Once again he acted on principle, out of a conviction that ends and means, or effect and cause, are no more discontinuous in politics than they are in physics.

Con-Con came to its second vote on May 4 and received, this time, only

89 of the 102 votes needed for passage, despite the fact that Stevenson had ordered tabled the party circle item in his bid for supporters. Seventy-three Democrats and 16 Republicans voted for the measure; 52 Republicans and the two West Side Bloc Democrats opposed it. As for the Crime Commission bills, they passed the Senate but were lost by a narrow margin in the House when they came to a vote in June.

A major factor reducing Con-Con support was a proposal by Republicans for a so-called "Gateway Amendment" to the constitution, as a substitute for the Stevenson measure. This would render more easy the amending of the 1870 constitution. It provided that an amendment could be adopted by two thirds of all those specifically voting on the question instead of by a majority (virtually impossible to obtain) of all those voting in a general election as had theretofore been required. There were reasons for believing that this Senate Republican proposal was cynically made. "They are attempting to nail down the lid on Con-Con!" cried Democratic Representative Paul H. Ferguson of Decatur. "They know that the Gateway Amendment proposal lost five times, but they are trying it again. Most of them don't even want constitutional reform." With this Stevenson agreed.

It occurred to him, however, that the Republicans had placed themselves on a rather small rug spread upon a very slick floor. The rug might be pulled out from under them. Moreover, by doing so, he might salvage something from what then appeared to him the crumbling ruin of his legislative program. Accordingly, as it became increasingly apparent that he hadn't enough votes for Con-Con, he prepared an alternative move, and immediately after the final Con-Con vote he issued a statement supporting the Gateway plan because, as he said, "we cannot wait forever for the most urgent constitutional reforms. . . . I doubt the sincerity of the 'Gateway proposal,'" he said, with a tinge of bitterness. "It looks like an effort to dodge responsibility for blocking much-needed changes." He doubted that the constitution could be effectively revised piecemeal. "But in spite of my misgivings, I feel it is better to have something than nothing," he went on. ". . . I will urge the Democratic party to join the Republican party in an all-out nonpartisan effort to secure ratification of the Gateway Amendment by the voters in 1950."

The Republicans, taken by surprise, were helpless to prevent what ultimately impressed itself upon the public mind as a Stevenson administration victory. Gateway passed the Senate almost unanimously. It passed the House by a vote of 138 to 2. It was presented to the voters on a separate blue ballot in 1950 (Stevenson supported the "blue ballot" bill in the legislature) and was adopted.

Stevenson also had budget trouble with the Sixty-sixth General Assembly.

On April 10 he delivered his budget message, calling for the expenditure for the biennium of $1,273,400,000, the largest two-year budget in the state's history. For additional revenue he proposed the removal of the service exemption from the state's two percent sales tax, thus extending this tax to the building and construction industries and raising an additional twenty-five million dollars annually. He proposed that this money be used to aid cities, schools, and tuberculosis hospitals, providing needed relief from mounting local property taxes. Lobbyists of the affected industries reacted immediately, violently, effectively. The proposal was clearly in line with the legislative intent of those who first put through the sales tax in Illinois, and had been recommended by a Green-appointed tax-study commission of which seven Republicans still in the legislature were members. It was a disillusioning but educative experience for Stevenson when five of these seven actually voted against the Stevenson proposal—against, in other words, their own recommendation! The bill was defeated.

Small wonder that, a few weeks after the General Assembly session had ended, Stevenson told a cheering crowd at a Democratic rally that he "didn't know whether I love you so much after all. . . . But I guess," he added, "I'm like the everlasting optimist who fell off the skyscraper. As he passed the twentieth floor the horrified spectators in windows heard him shout, 'So far, so good!'" By that time, however, he had had time to assess profit and loss from his dealings with the legislature, and found reason to believe that what in late June had seemed the total ruin of his legislative program contained, after all, a number of new and solid structures. More importantly, he seemed to have retained if not enhanced his prestige with the general public, a fact that should produce Democratic gains in the election of 1950 and smooth the path toward his goals in the second session, especially so since he had learned a great deal about what to do and what not to do in his handling of legislators and of legislation.

II

Paradoxically it was during the crucial month of June, when he himself was sickened by a sense of failure, that his hold on public respect and affection became strongest. Courage, in the famous Hemingway definition, is "grace under pressure," and it was this kind of courage that Stevenson seemed to personify, in the public view, during weeks when every possible provocation toward partisan bitterness and personal animosity was given him. He fought hard for his program, but always in terms of principle, never in terms of personalities. He blasted "fiscal irresponsibility," not the Republican Senate leader, Wallace Thompson, who seemed bent on practicing it in government. He did not wash his hands of all responsibility for his defeats, as Mayor Kennelly seemed inclined to do; he gave no hint that he regarded Illinois politics too hopelessly dirty for him to engage in; he refused every temptation to slam the door on possible future cooperation with the men who now baited and frustrated him. Instead, "I blame myself," he said, for naïvely believing that Republican Senators would practice what they preached. "I thought they really believed in conservative financial management," he told the people in a radio report, and he was grateful that "some of the Republican Senators would not follow their leaders" in attempts to discredit him at the expense of the state's welfare.

"I think you people want legislators who do not put some small party advantage, real or fancied, over courage, intellectual integrity, and public responsibility," he asserted. ". . . I don't think most people even care much about party labels any more. What they want is honest, sincere, courageous performance. And what's more, I think the sooner politicians realize that that's the best politics the better it will be for them and for the people."

A few days before the General Assembly's end, he issued a statement in which he condemned Republican senators for approving sixty-five million dollars' worth of expenditures for which no budget provision had been made. Of this total, fifteen million was for township roads and fifty million for a city-aid program that conflicted with the one the governor had backed.

"The people will not be misled by false generosity," he declared. "If the appropriations voted exceed the revenue provided, I will be obliged to make reductions, by amendment or veto, in the aid programs I have recommended for education, health, and local governments. If these programs go out, local tax rates must go up or adequate local services won't be provided."

The Republican Senate (the Republicans had a 32 to 18 edge there) chose to regard this as a direct challenge. Its response was perfectly in line with its earlier actions. Customarily the Illinois General Assembly ends its session on June 30—and since it passes most of its bills during the session's last days, the governor can exercise his veto without fear that his action will be overridden. But if the governor was determined to use his veto to balance the budget, the Republicans were determined to unbalance that budget again, if possible, by overthrowing his vetoes; at the very least, impassioned appeals for worthy programs would embarrass an executive who struck those programs from the list of enactments on the ground that no money was available for them. The Republicans could do this, however, only if the legislature remained in session. Accordingly, on the night of June 30, when the legislature ordinarily adjourned *sine die* (that is, without date), the Senate voted to adjourn until July 18. Simultaneously the Democratic House voted to adjourn as usual, *sine die*. The official clocks had been stopped at midnight to permit the General Assembly to work into the morning of July 1.

The governor spent that night in his office on the second floor of the State House. Microphones in the two legislative chambers on the third floor picked up the floor action, which blared through special loudspeakers mounted on the governor's office walls. When it became evident that the two houses disagreed on when to adjourn, a faint memory was stirred in Stevenson's mind. Way back in 1863, Illinois' Civil War governor, Richard Yates, had had to deal with a legislature torn by bitter party wrangles. Then, as now, the two houses had disagreed about adjournment. Yates had finally prorogued the legislature—that is, he had ended the session by executive order. The term "prorogue" and the device it named was an ancient one, referring originally to the ending of a session of Parliament by order of the Crown.

"Doesn't a governor still have that power?" Stevenson asked Walter Schaefer, who kept the nightlong vigil beside him.

"I was thinking precisely the same thing," said Schaefer. "I'm sure you *do* have the power. But let's see."

In a copy of the 1870 constitution he found what he wanted. He read aloud Article 5, Section 9: it said in effect that when the two houses cannot agree on when to quit, the governor can adjourn the Assembly until "such time as he thinks proper."

"It's a complicated procedure, though," Schaefer said. "We'd have to time everything perfectly, and it'd never work if the Republicans got wind of it."

"Let's do it," Stevenson said.

Schaefer, Day, Mulroy, and other Stevenson aides hurried back and forth between the executive office and the legislative halls, explaining the strategy to floor leaders and directing tactical moves. At five o'clock in the morning Stevenson gave the signal. A few minutes later, when only ten minor bills were left on its calendar, the House was suddenly presented with a resolution saying there was disagreement between it and the Senate regarding adjournment. The resolution was promptly passed by voice vote. Then Walter Schaefer handed Speaker Paul Powell a proclamation from the governor. Powell ordered the clerk to read it. At 5:30 A.M. Powell brought his gavel down.

Lieutenant Governor Sherwood Dixon, presiding officer of the Senate, and Senator Wallace Thompson, Republican Senate majority leader, were both in the House chamber as the clerk began reading. The two raced one another to the Senate chamber, Dixon carrying the governor's proroguing proclamation in his hand. Just as Dixon mounted to the presiding officer's chair, to take over, Thompson managed to get the floor from which he moved, breathlessly, that the Senate adjourn until ten o'clock Friday morning. If passed, this motion would render ineffective the governor's order, since the Senate would not be in session to receive it—and it is of course a basic rule of parliamentary procedure, incorporated in the Illinois Senate rules of order, that a motion to adjourn is not debatable and may not be tabled. Nevertheless Dixon promptly recognized Democratic Senator Kent Lewis, who moved to table the Thompson motion. Angrily Thompson shouted his protests. Lewis shouted back.

And while this shouting was going on Dixon read the governor's order, from which no appeal was possible, and brought his gavel down. At five thirty-two in the morning of July 1, 1949, the Sixty-sixth General Assembly was ended. Thompson, white-faced with anger, was still shouting.[3]

III

A special session of the General Assembly was called by Governor Stevenson in the summer of 1950, chiefly to pass a rent-control bill made necessary by the Korean War, but also to provide more state aid for Chicago, which was in grave financial difficulties. The latter was wrecked against Republican opposition.

That autumn it appeared that the governor had lost every chance to put his program through the second of his regular General Assembly sessions, for in the November elections, contrary to his expectations in the summer of '49, the Republicans won control of the House, 84 to 69, while retaining control of the Senate, 31 to 20. Two factors influenced this result, neither of them under Stevenson's control. One was the entrance of the Chinese Communists into the war between North and South Korea, requiring the drafting of American youths into the armed services. The other was a widely publicized investigation of crime in politics conducted by a Senate committee headed by Estes Kefauver, Democrat of Tennessee. Both increased the Republican vote.

However, Stevenson had a greater success with this Republican-controlled legislature than he had had with the divided one of 1949. No doubt one cause of this was that one-party control meant one-party responsibility, with the result that Republican lawmakers became somewhat more concerned with the general welfare and somewhat less susceptible to petty partisanship. This cause would not have been as effective as it was, however, if Stevenson had not made it so through his own operation. His handling of the Sixty-seventh General Assembly was masterful, with the result that, at the session's end, he signed into law several bills he had vainly struggled to push through in 1949.

How did he do it?

His general method can perhaps be best defined by contrasting it with the method President Truman employed during those years. Truman's relations with the Republican Eightieth Congress had been of war, with no quarter asked or given. In the campaign of 1948 he attacked this Congress as the "worst" in history and castigated individual members of it unmercifully. When he won his amazing victory that year, he was confirmed in his belief that his brand of "give 'em hell" campaigning was the best if not the only kind for a Democrat to conduct and that the language of coercion was the proper executive language for communications with a recalcitrant legislature. Stevenson, campaigning for a Democratic legislature in 1950, hurled no charge of "worst" against the Republican Senate of the Sixty-sixth General Assembly; never did he attack his opponents by name; so that when his bid failed (and he was convinced it failed despite rather than because of his campaign style) he was not required to pay a ruinous forfeit to the victors. He had been reasonable and conciliatory. Before the bar of public opinion, therefore, he could plead convincingly for reasonableness and a conciliatory attitude on the part of his opponents.

His general method, in other words, was that of nonviolence—and the frequent result, in power-political situations, was the overthrow of his opponent from within, through a kind of moral subversion. The opponent's conscience was likely to become a Fifth Column which fought on Stevenson's side. Not that he depended wholly on moral suasion. He learned to employ with skill the traditional devices of political reward and punishment: the smile that prospers another's career, the frown by which that career is blighted, the patronage that can strengthen or weaken a legislator's hold upon his constituency. But in general he conceived his executive function to be the encouragement and facilitation of that desire for goodness and honor that he believed to be embedded in all men. The path of honor might never be as delightful to the senses as the primrose path, but there was no moral reason, in Stevenson's view, why it should not be made as smooth and easy to follow as possible.

Doing so required of him a quantity and quality of hard work that amazed his closest observers. He seemed determined to master every detail of the state's business, a task analogous to Thor's effort to drink up the sea and one whose hopelessness aroused protests from his associates. Once an aide found Stevenson at his desk late at night, engaged in a close study of the specifications for pipe insulation in a state hospital.

"Why do that?" the aide asked. "You don't know anything about insulation."

"That's why," the governor replied.[4]

Always his presentations to the legislature were thoughtful, knowledgeable, and clear. Being armed himself, he armed his legislative leaders with such a wealth of factual argument that the artful dodgers of special interest had difficulty overcoming them. Moreover, through his press conferences and regularly scheduled reports over the radio, and through public speech in which he communicated to all kinds of audiences his passionate concern for good government, he mobilized public opinion behind his proposals in such a way that many legislators who could not otherwise have gone along with him without risking their next election were enabled to do so. Finally, he displayed, as he had done in London, an unsurpassed talent for face-to-face negotiation. By exercise of that talent he not only persuaded others toward the goals he defined but also committed them to him personally.

All this—his careful preparation, his mobilizing of public opinion, his negotiating genius—was effectively employed in his handling of highway legislation during the second of his regular legislative sessions. In the early 1920's, if at a cost excessive to taxpayers under the Republican regime of the execrable Governor Len Small, Illinois had built one of the first and best state highway systems. During the 1940's this system had been required to bear unprecedented burdens with inadequate maintenance. The result was that by 1948, like the Wonderful One-Hoss Shay, the highways began to fall apart all at once. Stevenson therefore proposed a ten-year building program to cost one hundred million dollars, financing it (as he had proposed in '49, and proposed again in '51) by increasing the gasoline tax from three to five cents a gallon and increasing the license fee for trucks and busses. Vehicles were to be taxed on a ton-mile basis, so that heavy vehicles paid their fair share of the highway cost instead of shifting much of their proper burden to passenger cars doing relatively little damage to roads.

Inevitably, well-heeled lobbyists descended in droves upon Springfield to prevent both the gas tax and truck license fee increase. They found their activities greatly hampered by the campaign of popular education on the highway crisis that the governor had conducted. Important segments of every legislator's constituency vehemently supported the governor's program. Newspaper support was almost unanimous—which meant that the lobbyists must pursue their ends in an unaccustomed and decidedly inhibiting glare of publicity. Their only hope was to create disputes among legislators as to how the increased revenue was to be distributed, playing off Chicago (whose motor clubs wanted arterial highways) against downstate residents (who wanted township roads), and special interest against special interest, in such a way that a hopeless deadlock resulted.

This strategy came very close to success. It would certainly have succeeded if Stevenson had not called the leaders of the contending groups to the Executive Mansion for a well-publicized night meeting in late June and exercised there his talent for negotiation. He proposed compromise solutions. When the meeting broke up at three o'clock in the morning, solid agreements had been made. Next day the necessary amendments of the bills were introduced. The amended bills passed.

After the 1949 General Assembly, Stevenson had established a Commission to Study State Government, with Walter Schaefer as chairman. In the 1951 Assembly session 166 bills were introduced to carry out proposals of this commission, and of these 78 were passed, in addition to approximately a dozen other bills growing out of the commission's findings.

He suffered defeats, too, of course. His FEPC law was rejected. So were several bills designed to improve law enforcement. When Congress passed a law forbidding the shipment of slot machines in interstate commerce, Stevenson proposed a law prohibiting their manufacture in Illinois where, as a matter of fact, practically all slot machines were made. The legislature said no. He also proposed to strengthen the powers of the Liquor Control Commission, to halt gambling wherever liquor was sold. Again the legislature said no.

But in general his legislative leadership scored successes, and while doing so the executive branch continued to make a remarkable record of economy. It was remarkable in that the economy was achieved, not by reducing needed services, but by increasing administrative efficiency and eliminating waste.

IV

For weeks following the end of each General Assembly, Stevenson with his legal aides (Schaefer and Day in 1949, McGowan, Blair, and others in 1950) worked late every night over the more than eight hundred bills, which were deposited by departing legislators on the governor's desk. Approximately ten percent of them were vetoed, and perhaps two percent more were permitted to become law without the governor's signature.

The veto messages were carefully prepared. They revealed not only Stevenson's principles of government but also salient features of his character, notably his humor, his profound respect for the English language, and his equally profound contempt for all efforts to intimidate him. Some of them became famous.

Widely reprinted, for example, was his veto of a bill promoted by Illinois bird lovers and passed by both houses in 1949:

> I herewith return, without my approval, Senate Bill No. 93 entitled, "An Act to provide Protection to Insectivorous Birds by Restraining Cats." This is the so-called "Cat Bill." I veto and withhold my approval from this bill for the following reasons:
>
> . . . I cannot agree that it should be the declared public policy of Illinois that a cat visiting a neighbor's yard or crossing the highway is a public nuisance. It is in the nature of cats to do a certain amount of unescorted roaming. Many live with their owners in apartments or other restricted premises, and I doubt if we want to make their every brief foray an opportunity for a small game hunt by zealous citizens—with traps or otherwise. I am afraid this bill could only create discord, recrimination and enmity. Also consider the owner's dilemma: to escort a cat abroad on a leash is against the nature of the cat, and to permit it to venture forth for exercise unattended into a night of new dangers is against the nature of the owner. Moreover, cats perform useful service, particularly in rural areas, in combatting rodents—work they necessarily perform alone and without regard for property lines.
>
> . . . The problem of cat versus bird is as old as time. If we attempt to resolve it by legislation, who knows but what we may be called upon to

take sides as well in the age-old problems of dog versus cat, bird versus bird, even bird versus worm? In my opinion, the State of Illinois and its local governing bodies already have enough to do without trying to control feline delinquency.

Stevenson's conception of free enterprise and his commitment to logical consistency were exemplified in his veto of the so-called "Sunday Car Bill," sponsored by a great majority of Illinois used-car dealers who wished to restrain a minority from staying open on Sundays and thereby forcing all to stay open. The bill would have made it a criminal offense for any person to sell a motor vehicle on Sunday. Having cited an opinion of the Attorney General that the bill was unconstitutional, Stevenson's veto message went on to say:

> I cannot forbear to add that this is one case in which the constitutional objection and sound public policy clearly coincide.... If such a restriction on Sunday trade is sound for automobiles, why should it not be extended to newspapers, groceries, ice cream cones and other harmless commercial transactions? Carried to its logical extreme, any business group with sufficient influence on the legislature can dictate the hours of business of its competitors. And if hours, why not prices?
>
> Under our free enterprise system government should not interfere by regulatory or prohibitory laws in the business field except (1) where the activity in question is directly related to the public health, safety, morals, or welfare or (2) to *enforce* competition. Traffic in automobiles does not qualify under the one, and, so far as the latter is concerned, its only purpose and effect are to restrain competition.

Also vetoed, on the grounds that government should be as local in character as possible, was a bill for state regulation of trailer camps. The veto message recognized that trailer camps had created a genuine public health problem requiring public regulation but condemned the bill as "another example of the constant migration of local responsibility to higher levels of government."

But by far the most important of his vetoes, and the one most widely and heatedly discussed, was his veto of the final Broyles Bill. The bill had a lengthy title:

> An Act to protect against subversive activities by making it a crime to commit or advocate acts intended to effect the overthrow of the Government of the United States or the State of Illinois or of any political subdivision thereof by violence or other unlawful means, or to attempt or conspire so to do, by defining subversive organizations and making them illegal, by establishing procedures to insure the loyalty of candidates for public office and of public officers and employees, and providing for the enforcement of the provisions of said Act, and providing penalties for the violation thereof.

It was, of course, fervently promoted by its author, Republican Senator Paul Broyles, by the Illinois Department of the American Legion, and by such champions of reaction as the Chicago *Tribune* and *Herald-American*. It was inadvertently promoted—or so one assumes—by the tactics and testimony of one Claude Lightfoot, the top Illinois Communist, who opposed the bill with such violence that he had to be removed from a committee room by the sergeant at arms. It passed the Senate by a vote of 35 to 15 and the House by 87 to 15.

Said Stevenson, in his veto message:

> That the Communist party—and all it stands for—is a danger to our Republic, as real as it is sinister, is clear to all who have the slightest understanding of our democracy. No one attached to the principles of our society will debate this premise or quarrel with the objectives of this bill.
>
> Agreed upon ends, our concern is with means. It is in the choice of methods to deal with recognized problems that we Americans, in and out of public life, so often develop differences of opinion. Our freedom to do so is a great source of strength and, if not impaired by mistakes of our own, will contribute greatly to the ultimate confusion of the enemies of freedom.
>
> The issue with respect to means raised by this bill has two aspects. One is the question of the need for it in relation to existing weapons for the control of subversives. The other is whether this addition to our arsenal may not be a two-edged sword, more dangerous to ourselves than to our foes.

He then reviewed existing legislation, federal and state, dealing with treason and subversion, in support of his contention that no new legislation in the field was needed and would, indeed, do harm by increasing the already great legal confusion.

"But it is in the enforcement provisions that I find this bill most objectionable," he said. These provisions required the state attorney general to appoint a special assistant attorney general "who must assemble and deliver to the State's Attorney of each county all information relating to subversive acts within such county." The local state's attorney was then required to present this matter to the Grand Jury. The assistant attorney general in Springfield was to maintain complete records of such information, which might, with the permission of the attorney general, be made public. "I know of no precedent of any such interference with the normal discretion accorded to a public prosecutor," said Stevenson, and "... I can see nothing but grave peril to the reputations of innocent people in this perpetuation of rumors and hearsay." He also objected to provisions "intended to assure the loyalty of the employees of the State government and its political subdivisions" by requiring special loyalty oaths and ordering all governmental agencies to "establish procedures to ascertain that there are no reasonable grounds to believe that any applicant for employment is committed, by act or teaching, to the overthrow of the government by force or is a member of an organization dedicated to that purpose." Thus both applicants for employment and those already employed would be required to prove their loyalty—a radical departure from the basic principle of Anglo-Saxon justice whereby the burden or proof rests on the accuser rather than on the accused.

By such provisions as these, irreparable injury to the reputation of innocent persons is more than a possibility, it is a likelihood. If this bill becomes law, it would be only human for employees to play safe and shirk duties which might bring upon them resentment or criticism. Public service requires independent and courageous action on matters which affect countless private interests. We cannot afford to make public employees vulnerable to malicious charges of disloyalty. . . .

Does anyone seriously think that a real traitor will hesitate to sign a loyalty oath? Of course not. Really dangerous subversives and saboteurs will be caught by careful, constant, professional investigation, not by pieces of paper.

. . . I know full well that this veto will be distorted and misunderstood, even as telling the truth of what I knew about the reputation of Alger Hiss was distorted and misunderstood. . . . But I must, in good conscience, protest against any unnecessary suppression of our ancient rights as free men. . . . [We] will win the contest of ideas . . . not by suppressing those rights, but by their triumph.

v

The deposition regarding Alger Hiss's reputation to which Stevenson referred had been taken in May of 1949. It would be repeatedly used, and had already been used, to convey the impression that Stevenson was "soft" on communism in government, that he had joined in an attempt to white-wash Alger Hiss, and that at the very least he was, as Republican Senator Richard Nixon of California would say over and over again, guilty of "poor judgment"—so guilty, indeed, as to cast serious doubt upon his capacity to exercise governing power.

It will be recalled that Stevenson first met Hiss in 1933 when both men were members of the AAA's legal division. Both had worked on marketing agreements, but since they dealt with different agricultural commodities their association was not close. From then on until 1945, when Stevenson became Archibald MacLeish's assistant in Washington, the two men did not meet at all. In the spring of the latter year they met occasionally at intra-departmental meetings in Washington. They met again a few weeks later in San Francisco, where Hiss was secretary general of the United Nations

Conference and Stevenson was attached to the United States delegation. The two had no working contacts there but met now and then at official social functions. In July, 1945, in Washington, Stevenson had conferences with Hiss regarding preparations for the presentation of the United Nations Charter to the Senate for ratification. The two did not then meet again until January, 1946, in London, during the First General Assembly of the United Nations. They had offices close to one another in London. They met frequently at staff conferences and delegation meetings. Again in 1947, during the United Nations General Assembly in New York, they met in a business way.

By then Alger Hiss was president of the Board of Trustees of the Carnegie Endowment for International Peace. He had been elected in December, 1946, by a board whose members included John Foster Dulles. A few days later Dulles had been warned by a Detroit lawyer that Hiss had a "provable" Communist record. Said Dulles, in a reply dated December 26:

> I have heard the report which you refer to, but I have confidence that there is no reason to doubt Mr. Hiss's complete loyalty to our American institutions. I have been thrown into intimate contact with him at San Francisco, London and Washington.... Under these circumstances I feel a little skeptical about information which seems inconsistent with all I personally know and what is the judgment of reliable friends and associates in Washington.

It will be recalled that Stevenson worked on the UN budget during this 1947 General Assembly. He was called upon once or twice by Hiss, for conference on budget matters, in Stevenson's office—and these were the last occasions on which Stevenson had seen Hiss.

In December of 1948 Whittaker Chambers, a senior editor of *Time* magazine, testified as an admitted former Soviet agent before the House Un-American Activities Committee. He asserted that in the 1930's he had worked with Alger Hiss, who, he said, was also a Communist party member at the time and had passed to him forty-odd confidential State Department documents for transmittal to a Soviet secret agent. One day that month Chambers led agents of the investigating committee to a hollowed-out pumpkin on his Maryland farm, where some of the documents allegedly passed by Hiss were found. Two weeks later Hiss was indicted by the Federal Grand Jury in New York on two counts of perjury, he having denied Chambers' charges under oath.

On May 24, 1949, the U.S. District Court in New York—the court before which Hiss was to be tried in June—directed the U.S. commissioner in Springfield to put certain questions to Stevenson on behalf of the Hiss defense, and certain cross-questions on behalf of the prosecution. This order was issued upon motion of Hiss's attorneys, who had, of course, ascertained in advance that Stevenson would make replies which did not damage their client. Hiss's attorneys had asked the governor to come to New York but he had declined, pleading press of duties. On June 2, Stevenson's deposition was taken at the mansion. (On that same day, at the Hiss trial in New York, Chambers admitted that he had committed perjury when, though then a Communist, he had taken an oath to defend the Constitution of the United States while accepting a federal job in 1937.) In response to the questions, Stevenson reviewed his past relationships with Hiss. The key testimony follows:

Q. No. 7. *Have you known other persons who have known Mr. Alger Hiss?*
A. No. 7. Yes.
Q. No. 8. *From the speech of those persons, can you state what the reputation of Alger Hiss is for integrity, loyalty, and veracity?*
A. No. 8. Yes.
Q. No. 9 *(a) Specify whether his reputation for integrity is good or bad?*
A. No. 9 (a) Good.
Q. No. 9 *(b) Specify whether his reputation for loyalty is good or bad?*
A. No. 9 (b) Good.
Q. No. 9 *(c) Specify whether his reputation for veracity is good or bad?*
A. No. 9 (c) Good.

In the cross interrogation in behalf of the United States of America, "complainant in said cause," the following testimony was taken:

Q. No. 1. *Were you ever a guest in the home of defendant Alger Hiss at any time in 1935, to and including 1938?*
A. No. 1. No, I have never been a guest in Mr. Hiss's home.
Q. No. 3. *Did you, prior to 1948, hear that the defendant Alger Hiss during the years 1937 and 1938 removed confidential and secret documents from the State Department and made such documents available to persons not authorized to see or receive them?*
A. No. 3. No.
Q. No. 4. *Did you, prior to 1948, hear reports that the defendant Alger Hiss was a Communist?*
A. No. 5. No.

In 1950, after Hiss had been convicted of perjury in his second trial (the first ended with a hung jury), Everett Dirksen, the Republican candidate for U.S. senator from Illinois, repeatedly attacked Stevenson for having given this deposition.

"What would Dirksen have said?" asked Stevenson. "Would he have told a lie?" The Chicago *Tribune* then editorialized that Stevenson could have avoided giving the testimony, that by giving it he had "arrayed himself willingly beside Alger Hiss." To this Stevenson made no reply at the time. But on March 30, 1952, he would be interviewed on a nationally broadcast radio and television show, "Meet the Press," and would be asked about his Hiss testimony. He would tell, factually, how he had come to give it, then add:

> And I would say this—I am a lawyer, and I think it is the duty of all citizens and particularly of lawyers, it is the most fundamental responsibility of lawyers, to give testimony in a court of law, honestly and willingly. And I think it will be a very unhappy day for Anglo-Saxon justice when a man in public life is too timid to state what he knows or has heard about a defendant in a criminal case for fear that defendant would be ultimately convicted. That is the ultimate timidity.

On October 23, 1952, in a campaign speech in Cleveland, Ohio, Stevenson would reply directly to Senator Nixon's charge that he had exercised bad judgment in making the deposition. " 'Thou shalt not bear false witness,' is one of the Ten Commandments, in case Senator Nixon has not read them lately," Stevenson would say. "And if *he* would not tell and honestly tell what he knew of a defendant's reputation, he would be a coward and unfit for any office." Stevenson would also point out that General Eisenhower was elected to the Board of Trustees of the Carnegie Endowment at the same meeting at which Hiss was reelected president and Dulles chairman of the board. Stevenson would continue:

> After he had been indicted by the Grand Jury, Hiss tendered his resignation as president and trustee of the Carnegie Endowment. The Board of Trustees, of which General Eisenhower was a member, declined to accept his resignation and granted him three months' leave of absence with full pay so that he might defend himself. The General was not present at the meeting, but I do not find that he ever voiced disapproval of this concrete expression of trust and confidence. In May of 1949, the month in which I gave my deposition, and again in December, 1949, after the first trial of Alger Hiss, the Board of Trustees, of which General Eisenhower was still a member, again voted to reject Hiss's resignation. ... I bring these facts to the American people not to suggest that either General Eisenhower or John Foster Dulles is soft toward Communists or even guilty of the bad judgment with which (I am charged). I bring them out only to make the point that the mistrust, the innuendoes, the accusations which this "crusade" is employing, threaten not merely themselves, but the integrity of our institutions and our respect for fair play.

CHAPTER TWENTY-ONE

T HE successor to the Capone gang of the 1920's in Chicago was a genuinely subversive organization as mysterious to ordinary citizens as it
was sinister, and as corrupting to Illinois' governing processes as it was
profitable for its members. Known as "The Syndicate," it was a firm yet
shadowy working alliance between crime and politics whose agents were
everywhere: no governor was able wholly to overcome it. Crucial portions
of Stevenson's legislative program had been destroyed by it. Human beings
high in the Stevenson administration were also destroyed by it.

One of these was Jim Mulroy.

Mulroy was the Stevenson staff member who did most of the political
"horse trading," in bars and hotel rooms, on which so much of legislative
success depended. In the late spring of 1949 he was asked by the House
Majority Leader Paul Powell if he would care to "take a flier" in the stock
of Chicago Downs, a harness racing association which had been legalized
by a unanimous vote of the legislature a few weeks before. Chicago Downs
did its racing at Sportsman's Park, generally deemed a syndicate operation
and located in Capone's old home town of Cicero at the west side of Chicago.
Mulroy had been ill a great deal; he was frequently in the hospital after
he'd gone to Springfield. He needed money. He bought a hundred dollars'
worth of the stock—one thousand shares at ten cents a share. A few months
later each of those shares yielded a dividend of $1.65, which meant that
Mulroy made $1,750 on his hundred-dollar investment.

In the late summer of 1951 Senator Kefauver's Senate Crime Committee
turned a publicity spotlight on Chicago Downs. It revealed that some of
the stockholders were close associates of members of the old Capone gang,
that several Illinois legislators had been employed by the association, and
that a very select list of politicians and state employees had been offered
the ten-cent stock. Inevitably the spotlight focused with a special intensity
upon stockholder Mulroy. He had done nothing illegal; he argued that the
stock offer had been made *after* the legalizing bill had passed, so that the
offer could not have been an effort to buy his influence; but few knowl-
edgable people could doubt that the stock offer had, in fact, been an influ-

ence-buying operation, whether Mulroy realized it at the time or not. There were some who asserted, without evidence, that Mulroy had helped to pass the Chicago Downs legislation smoothly through the legislature in the assurance that a stock offer would be his reward.

Stevenson himself was convinced his aide had been guilty only of thoughtlessness and impetuosity. For weeks, while public criticism mounted and other staff members insisted that Mulroy be fired, the governor refused to act. But in October he sadly told a mutual friend of his and Mulroy's that "Jim will have to go." He had talked to Mulroy about it. The interview had been heartrending. Stevenson felt that he owed Mulroy a great deal (others pointed out that Mulroy also owed Stevenson a great deal), and he told Mulroy so, but he had an obligation to the people of Illinois, which must override any merely personal loyalties.[1]

Less than six months later Mulroy died suddenly of a heart attack. His widow and close friends were convinced that his public disgrace, which he brooded over in black depression, had killed him.

Different from Mulroy's tragedy, but equally hurtful to the Stevenson administration, was the affair of Frank Annunzio, director of labor. In early 1951 he had been named Democratic ward committeeman in Chicago's First Ward (the Loop) and had been ordered by Stevenson either to resign that position or his position in the cabinet. He had resigned the former. At the same time he resigned as president of an insurance agency called Anco, Inc., and sold his stock interest in that firm. Anco had been formed by Annunzio, early in '51, in partnership with John D'Arco, a member of the West Side Bloc in the 1949 legislature who had helped to kill the crime bills and Con-Con. D'Arco was vice-president of the firm, whose other officers included a man who had been convicted of vote fraud in 1928 and had been wounded in the gang wars of the Capone days. The enterprise, though legal, was a highly dubious one for any cabinet officer to engage in.

Annunzio's connection with Anco became widely publicized during the investigations following the assassination of one Charles Gross, a Chicago ward committeeman, in February of 1952. The fact that Annunzio had sold his stock failed to convince the public, or Stevenson, that the cabinet position had not been compromised and with it the prestige of the whole administration. The governor promptly asked for and received Annunzio's resignation.

Far more serious than either the Mulroy or Annunzio affair was a scandal involving Charles W. Wray, the superintendent of Foods and Dairies in Roy E. Yung's Department of Agriculture.

Soon after his election Stevenson was warned by the kind of political pressures brought upon him that the Foods and Dairies superintendency was an office in which certain unsavory social elements took an excessive interest. He had therefore rejected every name pressed upon him and had hand-picked Charles Wray, a Lake County farmer who had been active in local politics, whose reputation for ability and honesty was high, and whose selection was approved both by farmers and food industry men. Of this appointment Stevenson had been particularly proud. It was therefore inconceivable to him that Wray could be in any way involved in the scandal, which began to develop in the summer of 1951 when Director Yung of the Agriculture Department first heard reports that horse meat was being used to adulterate hamburger in Illinois and that this was being done with the connivance of state meat inspectors. Wray, who had charge of the inspectors, was ordered to conduct an investigation. He found nothing wrong.

By December of 1951, however, investigators for the Federal Office of Price Stabilization reported to Stevenson that something definitely *was* wrong. They were certain that specified meat packers were selling horse meat as beef. They were certain that some state inspectors were being bribed to overlook it. They had a list of the inspectors they suspected. Stevenson in January of '52 turned the matter over to Carl McGowan, whose handling of it enhanced the governor's opinion of his judgment. All the meat inspectors were called to Springfield and questioned by two assistant attorney generals. Wray was called also. At the end of two days, Wray, faced with incriminating evidence, confessed to McGowan that he himself was involved, that he had taken thirty-five hundred dollars from one Joe Siciliano, who operated a packing plant in Lake and Henry counties and who was indeed selling horse meat as beef for use in hamburgers. He was fired, his statement turned over to the Lake County state's attorney. He was later indicted in Lake County on charges of bribery and conspiracy, though the charges were finally dismissed on a technicality.[2] Joe Siciliano, however, was tried and convicted. (When he was arrested, his bond was set at thirty thousand dollars. "Thirty thousand!" cried Siciliano. "They must think I ground up Man O'War.")

No event in Stevenson's administration struck harder at his confidence in human nature than this one. His immediate response was stern. He pressed for a thorough investigation of the inspectors who had served under Wray, with the result that a dozen of them were fired or suspended. He appointed a former FBI agent to be his special personal investigator. He called his department directors to his State House office and there lectured them on their responsibility for the wrongdoing of their subordinates in so far as they failed adequately to supervise those subordinates. He said flatly that the "calm confidence" he had theretofore had in the men under him was being replaced by "an eager persistent surveillance." Thereafter, as his close associates noted, his faith in the essential decency of human beings was qualified by a greater awareness of human weakness.

There was yet another major scandal during the Stevenson administration, but Stevenson was convinced that it was not an *administration* scandal. Rather was it, in his view, an administration triumph.

In 1951 Stevenson was informed that some Chicago wholesalers were cutting cigarette prices to an extent which would have been impossible had they paid the state tax on them. His response was prompt and highly effective. He instituted his own secret investigation, securing the appointment of a Chicago lawyer as a special assistant attorney general and employing a firm of private detectives. It was found that the cut-rate cigarettes bore counterfeit state tax stamps printed on the packages by stolen tax meter machines for which new plates had been made. There was no doubt that the whole lucrative business was a syndicate operation. When sufficient evidence had been gathered, Stevenson ordered state police raids on ten wholesale firms in greater Chicago. Several wholesalers were indicted and one was sent to the penitentiary. Stevenson also ordered an investigation of Department of Revenue employees, with the result that the head of the Chicago office of the cigarette tax collecting division and two inspectors there were fired. A third inspector resigned. They had refused to sign waivers of immunity.

II

Other disastrous events having political repercussions occurred during the Stevenson regime. One was an ugly race riot, which broke out in Cicero in the summer of 1951 when a Negro family attempted to move into an all-white community. The other was an explosion in a coal mine at West Frankfort, which killed 119 men on December 21, 1951.

Local law enforcement broke down completely during the Cicero riots and the governor ordered in five National Guard companies to restore order. Some 109 rioters were arrested on charges of unlawful assembly, but the handling of their cases by Cook County State's Attorney John S. Boyle so disgusted the governor that he was instrumental in having Boyle removed from the Democratic slate for reelection in 1952. During the '51 General Assembly Stevenson had put through a measure transforming the Illinois Interracial Commission into the Illinois Commission on Human Relations, broadening its responsibilities to include "the promotion and encouragement of interfaith and interracial harmony and good will." To the first meeting of this commission on October 11 of '51, Stevenson said:

> Deep beneath the Cicero disorders . . . lie the fears, the alarms, the pressures, the tensions of the continuously critical housing shortage. . . . Large numbers of the low income groups, and among these large numbers of the so-called minority groups, are inadequately housed, rigidly segregated and confined to slums and deteriorated residential areas. The demoralising effects . . . are placing a severe strain upon the whole

range of State and municipal welfare services. This is . . . the grim reality underlying the tension and violence that accompany the efforts of minority group members to break through the iron curtain which confines so many of our fellow citizens.

One of the successes of the governor in the 1949 legislative session had been the reorganization of the Department of Mines and Minerals. This, however, was but the first step of the journey Illinois had to make toward the goal of maximum practical mine safety. The governor therefore had called upon Dr. Harold Walker, head of the Department of Mines at the University of Illinois, to revise the patchwork mining code, assisted by the state mining department, by the governor's own aides, and by the Legislative Reference Bureau. On January 10, 1951, the resultant draft bill was submitted to the Mine Investigation Commission for review and comment. Examined by members of the commission and by representatives of the mine operators and the unions, the bill was unanimously rejected. (It was one of the distressing facts of Illinois politics that the mine operators and the union leaders were as one in their opposition to needed mine reforms.) Stevenson then had a breakfast at the mansion, to which he invited all the senators from the mining areas. These recommended that the bill not be introduced until the mining industry had had further time to consider it.

"Hence I am unable to make good my promise to present such legislation at this session," said Stevenson in a public statement issued May 16, 1951. "I hope the industry will bring in such further safety legislation as it can agree upon at this session. . . ." In that same statement he remarked that "currently our safety record is very good" but that "that situation could be sharply altered at any moment."

A little over seven months later the West Frankfort mine blew up. The Republicans attempted to tag Stevenson with responsibility for this disaster as Green had been tagged with responsibility for Centralia, but in order to do so they had to ignore or falsify a great many facts. John Bartlow Martin's long, authoritative article in *Harper's* magazine on the Centralia tragedy had played a part in the 1948 campaign. In 1952 Martin reported that the Centralia and West Frankfort tragedies were very different. Wrote he:

> The cause of the Centralia disaster was clear and avoidable; the cause of West Frankfort was not clear. Many warnings had been given that the Centralia mine was dangerous; the West Frankfort mine was considered a "model" mine. Centralia miners had repeatedly asked the Department of Mines and Minerals to make the company comply with the law and once had appealed to Governor Green; no such steps had been taken at West Frankfort. Investigation after Centralia disclosed that mine inspectors had been soliciting political campaign funds from operators; no such evidence was adduced after West Frankfort.[3]

III

In striking contrast to the seamy side of politics, with which Stevenson the governor had now and then to deal, was the life in the Executive Mansion of Stevenson the man.

From the earliest possible moment in the spring until late in the fall he dined in the garden behind the house. In good weather he had his breakfast and luncheon upon the porch, save on days when he was so pressed for time that he lunched from a tray at his desk or had so many guests that luncheon was served in the dining room. Almost always people were with him—guests, or family, or staff members.

Certainly no one rendered more valuable personal service than Ernest and Buffie Ives. Ernest had stayed with him in the mansion through most of the hard spring and summer of 1949, when, amid the intense and novel pressures of his office, he'd tried so hard to save his marriage. Ernest's was a soothing presence: in the most literal meaning of the word, he was a gentleman—courteous, kind, self-effacing, devoted. He had lightened a grievous burden; he continued to do so. Unobtrusively, anonymously, he served in a hundred ways, taking care of family matters, helping entertain visitors, performing all manner of needed if inglorious chores, and above all providing relaxing companionship. Ernest knew how and when to keep silence. And Ernest was a good companion. The warm affection everyone had for him was a great asset to the mansion, helping often to smooth out personnel difficulties, which inevitably arose among those who lived and worked there.

Buffie came and stayed for long periods, to serve as the governor's official hostess while Ellen remained in Libertyville. She lived there most of the time after the divorce, when Adlai rented his Libertyville farm to Marshall Field, Jr. At the same time she ran her homes in Bloomington and in Southern Pines. It was she who managed the mansion's domestic arrangements, working with Mrs. Van Diver, the housekeeper whose husband, a state police captain, was the governor's chauffeur; and with Gertie Dent, the cook.[4]

Buffie loved the stately house. There were twenty-eight rooms in it. The so-called "basement," where the governor and his secretaries and personal aides had their offices, was really a ground floor, being level with the top of the knoll on which the mansion stood. The first floor, with the tall ceilings typical of its architectural periods, consisted largely of "official" rooms, used not only for formal entertaining by the governor but also by Springfield's women's clubs and auxiliaries for special teas and the like. The two front parlors had long windows, reaching to the parquet floor across which spread shaggy white rugs; mirrors rose to the ceilings above the mantels. From the ceilings hung crystal chandeliers whose teardrop prisms sparkled in the light. Adjoining each parlor was a long room with a bay window; one was the living room, the other the music room. Behind the music room was the state dining room whose beautiful paneling had been painted white and whose wallpaper was of a dogwood pattern; here was a complete silver service for eighteen, which came originally from the battleship U.S.S. *Illinois* and bore the seal of Illinois. Behind the living room was the family dining room, and adjoining this was a sunroom which had been originally a side porch.

It was in the sunroom on the west side of the house that Stevenson and the Iveses gathered before dinner and where they spent most of their informal moments. Occasionally Stevenson stretched out for a few moments before dinner on a long sofa there. The sofa and the armchairs had been newly slipcovered by Buffie in colors that harmonized with the green tile floor. One side of the room was lined with bookshelves that were entirely empty when Stevenson moved in and which he filled with books loaned by the historical library. Gradually these shelves became filled with books he received as gifts, particularly after it became generally known that he wished to establish a permanent library for the mansion. Many of these books were autographed, "To Governor Adlai E. Stevenson, and to be left in the Executive Mansion."

Above the impressive entrance hall, with its curving stairway, painted ivory-white with mahogany handrail, was a skylight of multicolored glass through which sunlight fell in rainbow hues. Buffie enthusiastically seconded, and helped to implement, her brother's desire that oil portraits of past governors be hung upon the downstairs walls, as permanent reminders that this was a house of history and tradition.

Upstairs were the bedrooms, the larger of which had fireplaces in them. One of these was transformed by Buffie into a memorial room to the early occupants of the mansion, a project in which her brother took a special pride. It began when Mrs. John Pickering, granddaughter of the Civil War governor, Richard Yates, gave to the state her grandfather's bed, bureau, and armoire. These pieces were supplemented by other period pieces and by pictures, vases, figurines. The room became as beautiful as it was historically fascinating, and Buffie and Ernest, and Stevenson, were grieved when the next administration abandoned the project and sent the room's furnishings into storage.

The house was well kept, and as thriftily as circumstances permitted. Buffie naturally would have liked to buy a few handsome pieces, but she respected her brother's conviction that the house, filled with flowers and pictures, should do as it was.

Soon after Buffie's arrival for her first extended visit in the mansion, she and Ernest persuaded the governor to take a walk one chilly evening with them, and Artie, the Stevenson dog. (Artie's full name was King Arthur. He was a melancholy Dalmatian whose wanderings through Springfield's streets, in defiance of the law, became famous in Illinois. People were always calling up the mansion to report that the governor's dog was at such and such an address, and could someone come fetch him?) Returning from the walk, Stevenson was horrified to see the mansion ablaze with light; electricity burned in a dozen empty rooms. "I never want to see that again!" he told Buffie, with emphasis. "I keep preaching economy in government—and it's up to us to set an example."

He quite agreed that something should be done about the soiled, food-stained Scalamandré silk on the chairs in the state dining room, but he could not bring himself to approve the expenditure of two thousand dollars (the upholsterer's estimate) for that purpose. So Buffie had the silk removed, cleaned, and dyed gold. She had then slipcovered the gold silk of the chairs in the family dining room.

She strove mightily to please him, and he found her "indispensable. . . . I couldn't get along without her," he said.

She reminded him of what he had been, of what they both had been, in their childhood and youth. Some intimate observers felt that she occupied in his life a place somewhat analogous to that his mother had occupied long ago. She was so utterly committed to him, so profoundly convinced that he had greatness in him and could do no wrong. He needed that, an unwavering faith in him, during those trying years. Partially through Buffie he renewed friendships with Springfield people he had known in his teens, including Jim Patton, Mrs. Logan Hay, and the former Mary Douglas ("Dougie") Hay, who had been his favorite girl when he was a student in Springfield High and who was now Mrs. Donald Funk, wife of the chairman of the board of the Sangamo Electric Company.

When he went to Centre College in Danville, Kentucky, to receive an honorary degree and give an address, Buffie helped make the trip memorable for him. Together they explored the old college of which their great-grandfather Lewis Warner Green had been president and where Adlai Stevenson I had been a student. Together they visited Waveland, the brick mansion built in 1797 on the Wilderness Road by their great-great-grandfather Willis Green, now the homestead of a large dairy farm. Such vivid contacts with his own family traditions renewed and strengthened him. And to Buffie it seemed that he must draw upon that serene strength on their return flight from Danville in the governor's two-engine Beechcraft, for they flew into a terrible storm during which Buffie fervently prayed, while her brother calmly read official documents and made notes on them. (As an air traveler, Stevenson was notoriously brave to the point of rashness, and had sometimes to be overruled by his pilot, Major Dan Smith, when he wanted to make landings which radio control towers ruled unsafe. Smith had to land by radar control in Chicago, on the return from Danville, because the Springfield airport was closed off.)

But it was not only the family past that gave him strength and serenity; it was also the family future, manifest in his three sons and in his strikingly handsome nephew, Timothy Ives. "I have always tried to live on a contemporary basis with my sons," he was quoted as saying in *Look* magazine in 1956. "We have an easygoing relationship. I've tried to set an example for them and trust that they defer to me out of respect rather than authority. I believe in being patient with them. In the future, I would want them to be satisfied that they are giving rather than getting. I'd like to see them in teaching or law or business. Givers are needed in the business world, so I would like to see one of my sons go into it."

Of all the hurtful charges Ellen had hurled at him during the period of their marriage's dissolution, the one that had most deeply hurt was that, by entering public life, he was betraying and even "ruining" his sons. In solitary anguish he had examined that charge, striving with the objectivity characteristic of him in such concerns to determine whether it was true or false. And as he looked now upon his sons, and upon his relationship with them, he concluded that the charge was not true.

Each boy was a distinct personality. Adlai III seemed most closely to resemble his father; he was reflective, affable, a great reader, and interested in politics. Borden, the second son, believed himself to "take after" the Borden side of the family, but his father could see in him traces of the boy he himself had been. Borden was perhaps more the type of the "Princeton man" than the type of Harvard, where he would become a student; he was often baited—overbaited in fact—for being so little a scholar, so much a playboy, and he developed an inferiority complex wholly unjustified by his innate abilities. John Fell was yet too young to have formed any clearly defined career ambitions, but it seemed unlikely that he would ever be interested in a political career. He was very shy—and very lovable. He had also what some described as a "monkey's curiosity." (Buffie once said that he had the lively curiosity of Kipling's Elephant Boy, though, as she promptly added, this was "not the best simile for the son of a Democrat.")

Every Christmas season there was a reception in the mansion and at least two big evening parties, one for the staff and one, a formal dance, for the Stevenson boys and Timothy. To the latter were invited young people from Chicago, from Lake Forest, from all over the state. The governor, and Buffie too, moved into the servants' quarters to make room for the guests, many of whom stayed overnight in the mansion, with the overflow quartered in a hotel where Ernest chaperoned them. Among the festivities was a solemn ritual which the governor never failed to honor: he took his young guests up into the attic of the mansion to view the mansion ghost. This was a mannequin which he had carefully placed in a corner with just enough light upon it to make it gleam palely through the gloom, with eerie effect. John Fell was fourteen when the first dance was given and he attended it, his own first dance, donning one of his father's dinner jackets whose shoulders were so wide for him that whenever a girl placed her hand upon his arm, the coat slid down. John Fell was unperturbed; he was wearing, he explained, the new "off-the-shoulder fashion."

During the holidays, too, the governor and the boys always managed to crowd in some trapshooting.

All the boys, like Stevenson, loved the out-of-doors, and particularly the western mountains. In the summer of 1951 the three Stevenson sons and Adlai had a vacation at the Jackson Hole wilderness south of Yellowstone Park.

Among the warm friendships that Stevenson formed during his Springfield years was one with the Reverend Dr. Richard Paul Graebel, pastor of the First Presbyterian Church. This was the church which Abraham Lincoln, never a church member, occasionally attended during the 1840's and '50's. It was rich in historic tradition, and none could have made this tradition more effective of good in the mid-twentieth-century community than Dr. Graebel.[5]

Of German ancestry, a fair Nordic type physically, Graebel was yet a young man who, wherever he went, generated an electric excitement. During the 1948 gubernatorial campaign he had earned the wrath of the Chicago *Tribune*—a wrath displayed in front page headlines—by arraigning the Green regime in his sermons for graft and corruption. Simultaneously, of course, he had earned the respect and gratitude of Adlai Stevenson.

The two, however, did not become close personal friends until February of 1950. There was in Springfield an organization known as the Midday Luncheon Club, which every year held a banquet in honor of Lincoln's birth. The banquet commemorating the 151st anniversary was held on a Sunday evening in the Centennial Auditorium. A great crowd was there. The club president, George C. Hoffman, introduced Adlai Stevenson, who, in turn, introduced with grace and wit Dr. Graebel, the principal speaker of the evening. Graebel's address, "Lincoln and the American Dream," was a powerful and moving one. (During it he paid tribute to Lloyd Lewis and was distressed to see, as he did so, that a woman in the audience wept; later he learned that she was Kathryn Lewis.) It made a profound impression upon Stevenson.[6]

Thereafter the two men were often together. They enjoyed one another immensely in a social way but they also were often very serious together, talking over questions of ultimate faith, ultimate meaning. Some of the tone and temper of their talk was revealed, a few years later, when Stevenson made a recording for Edward R. Murrow's "This I Believe" broadcast over the CBS network. Stevenson, while preparing his statement, talked it over with Graebel, and in it he fused his Unitarian convictions with a religious feeling absent from any earlier one of his public statements.

At eleven o'clock every Christmas Eve, a candlelight carol service was held in the First Presbyterian Church. It was a beautiful service, and Adlai Stevenson, with his sons and the Iveses', never failed to attend. They sat in the Lincoln pew, listening with rapt attention as the minister, standing alone, sang in German, in his rich warm voice, "Silent Night . . ."

BOOK SIX

Triumph and Defeat

CHAPTER TWENTY-TWO

FROM the moment of his gubernatorial victory in 1948 Adlai Stevenson had been talked of for President. The talk had increased in urgency and volume while he made his record as governor and other Democratic candidates of commanding stature failed to arise. He was stimulated by this talk to examine closely not only himself and his obligation to Illinois but also the contemporary national political scene. Both examinations fed his reluctance to heed the call to national duty.

In the field of foreign policy, the most crucial of all fields of government during the Truman regime, the administration had been, on the whole, courageous and creative. The United Nations had been firmly supported and its congeries of specialized agencies now pursued their quiet labors on behalf of international cooperation and understanding largely because the United States participated fully in them and gave them, at the outset, the bulk of their financial support. Under the leadership of Secretary of State Dean Acheson, the containment policy vis-à-vis the aggressive Communist nations had been pursued with boldness and considerable success, particularly in Greece, the Middle East, and western Europe. The Truman Doctrine, the Berlin Airlift, the Marshall Plan, Point Four, NATO—all these stood as monuments to tough executive decisions intelligently made and effectively implemented. Though firm, foreign policy had been flexible, swiftly adapting itself to changing circumstances.

There had been failures. China had been lost to the Communists, and this was a defeat for the West of as yet incalculable historical significance to the world. But if China was a major defeat, Korea, in Stevenson's view, was a victory, when viewed in the proper historical perspective. He said so in an article he wrote in November of 1951, which was published in the April, 1952, issue of *Foreign Affairs*. "When North Korean forces invaded the Republic of Korea on June 25, 1950, with the full support of Peking and Moscow, most of us knew what was at stake," he said. "One of the men who took part in the long anxious meeting at Blair House gave the simplest explanation of the decision: 'This attack on South Korea is like Hitler's reoccupation of the Rhineland.'" He quoted the speech Senator William Knowland, California Republican, made on the floor of the Senate in immediate support of the President's announcement and reminded his readers that only one member of the Congress had opposed the Korean action and he, Representative Vito Marcantonio of New York, had been defeated for reelection.

Since the article had appeared, there had been a rising criticism of the conduct of the war—particularly of the removal of General Douglas MacArthur from his Korean command after he had repeatedly tried to defy his commander-in-chief. The immediate objective, namely, to drive the North Koreans beyond the 38th parallel, had been achieved; the physical and psychological defenses of the West, and Western prestige among the uncommitted peoples of the Far and Middle East, had been immensely strengthened; there was every evidence that this tough demonstration of collective security had deterred the Soviet Union from other plotted conquests. Yet the war dragged on (it was limited mostly to air action in 1952) and was now dubbed, by certain Republicans, "Mr. Truman's War." The sobriquet seemed to Stevenson as palpably unfair as the repeated assertions that Truman and Acheson were "soft" on communism, and it was significant that both charges, despite their somewhat contradictory nature, were quite generally made by the same people. "There is, of course, no tidy solution to the Korean problem," Stevenson wrote, "precisely because it is only a part of the whole Soviet imperialist drive.... For that reason, the full settlement of the Korean problem is likely to take a long time and to wait upon the settlement of many other issues."

He had reason to know, that spring, the human anxieties, the angry impatience, that the military stalemate bred in a million families. His nephew, Timothy Ives, was training as a jet pilot in the U.S. Air Force at Byram Air Base and would soon go to Korea, there to fly scores of combat missions. His son, Adlai, Jr., would enter the Marines in June to train at Quantico and ultimately become a Marine lieutenant. It was a hard thing to say that the sacrifice of such young men was necessary to the prevention of a greater sacrifice. Yet Stevenson did say it. "[The] meaning of our experience in Korea as I see it is that we have made historic progress toward the establishment of a viable system of collective security," he asserted.

"To deprecate our large and decisive share in that undertaking as 'useless' is both mischievous and regressive."

But if he could approve, on the whole, our foreign policy, he had reservations as he viewed the domestic scene. The latter was not, in all respects, an edifying one—and some of the most unedifying portions of it might strike an honest mind, looking at it in historical perspective, as due in part to twenty years of one-party control of the federal executive. During so long a tenure of power a political party's organization is likely to become fused almost to the point of identity with the institutions of government. These may then become as barrels of apples from which the few bad apples are unculled: corruption spreads through a process of secret deals and agreements until the public office which should be a public trust provides instead a currency for the payment of private debts and the satisfaction of strictly private desires.

Particularly this is likely to happen in the absence of an intelligently critical, morally responsible party opposition. History must record that little such opposition had been provided by the Republican party since 1932. During two decades of unparalleled national peril, when the country was threatened from within by economic collapse and from without bv a rising tide of totalitarian imperialism, Republicans in the Congress, with few exceptions, had fought every measure of social and economic reform, every measure to strengthen Britain when she stood alone against the Nazi terror, almost every measure (at the outset) to develop an adequate military establishment. Small wonder that the Republicans had lost persuasive influence with a majority of Americans. Small wonder that their cries of wolf were largely ignored, since the wolves they had named in the past had so often proved to be the friendliest, most useful of hounds. The fact might embolden real wolves until a formidable pack of them roamed the forests of bureaucracy.

Had this happened? Adlai Stevenson would never believe that the wolf pack was anywhere near as large or as ravenous as Republican politicians proclaimed it to be, but he saw evidence that it was large enough. Quite large enough. So did millions of others.[1]

Senator Kefauver's committee investigations, pursued before TV cameras, had stimulated popular disgust with the sordid alliance of crime and politics in many a big-city political machine. Though none dared allege that President Truman had ever been personally involved in such corruption, the Republican press and Republican politicians had not failed to reiterate the fact that he had begun his political career as a protégé of Tom Pendergast, whose Kansas City machine had been one of the most notoriously corrupt in the country during the 1920's and 30's. The doubts thus raised were repeatedly encouraged by disclosures of wrongdoing by men close to Truman, men whom he clung to with a machine politician's loyalty when he should have repudiated them out of a statesman's loyalty to the national welfare.

There was a wave of such disclosures in late '51 and '52. The President himself, to his credit, admitted in practice that things had gone very wrong in the Internal Revenue Bureau, for he ordered a sweeping reorganization of that agency in early January, one which the Congress approved in March. A federal grand jury indicted E. Merl Young, former RFC examiner, charging him with giving false testimony to the grand jury. A House Appropriations subcommittee revealed that some eight millions of tax dollars had been lost through Commodity Credit Corporation operations whereby government buildings were rented and then leased back for up to twenty times the amounts paid the government by private contractors, the buildings being used for grain storage. And all this followed revelations of influence peddling, whereby minor governmental figures were corrupted with "gifts" of mink coats and deep freezes.

An honest mind, remaining committed to Democratic principles, might wonder, as he surveyed the domestic scene, whether a continuance of Democratic control of the executive was really in the best interests of party or country. Perhaps a respite from power would give the party an opportunity to find new leadership, cleansing itself, whereas an assumption of power by the Republicans would force them to become realistic and responsible to a degree they had not been during two powerless decades. There is no clear evidence that Stevenson had such explicit thoughts during those months, but there is a good deal of evidence that such wondering was part of the current of feeling that permeated his political thought.

It is true that an old broom sweeps poorly, whereas a clean sweep is easy with a broom that is new. The question, as always in politics, was one of alternatives. If the alternative to the old Democratic broom was the old Republican one, then the historical evidence was that the former would do a much better sweeping job. Like the Bourbons, the Republican Old Guard seemed to have learned and forgotten nothing during a world depression and a world war. Its leader was Senator Robert A. Taft of Ohio, who, judging from his voting record and public speech, would return the country to isolationism and big-business domination to precisely the extent that he was given the power to do so. In his now desperate ambition to become President, he seemed even to have lost his former firm commitments to essential civil liberties, for he now loaned his support to Senator Joseph R. McCarthy of Wisconsin. One shuddered to contemplate what would happen to individual liberty in America and to the painfully wrought system of collective security against Communist aggression abroad, if Taft occupied the White House, McCarthy had a free rein in the Senate, and the devotees of special privilege had again in hand the guardianship of the public weal.

But was this the only alternative?

As Stevenson often said, the G.O.P. elephant was a two-headed beast. One head was the Old Guard, the other was the so-called liberal wing, which seemed willing to hold most of the social gains made under the New and Fair Deals and to prevent a retreat into isolationism in foreign affairs. The latter group, since the days of Alf Landon, had been uniformly successful in its efforts to dictate the Republican presidential nominee: Willkie in '40, Dewey in '44, Dewey again in '48. It now appeared that the liberals had found a champion who could not only capture the nomination but might even reform the party, lopping off the head of reaction and enabling the party as a whole to take a new, more hopeful direction.

The champion's name was Dwight David Eisenhower.

Stevenson in early 1952 may not have shared to the full the popular enthusiasm for the general as a potential political leader, but his admiration for Eisenhower as man and soldier was certainly great.[2] This was one of the roots of his own reluctance to become a candidate that year.

Who, after all, could fail to admire the Eisenhower who had made of SHAEF an unique instrument of international cooperation, imbuing it with his own warm human qualities, his own strength and tolerance and sunny good will? Who could fail to admire the Eisenhower who seemed quite consciously to have made himself a symbol of Western unity, using his prestige to solidify American public opinion behind a foreign policy that might otherwise have split the people between an irreconcilable isolationism and internationalism? Like nearly all Americans, Stevenson believed he saw in the general a quality of moral goodness, an earnest desire to do good in the world, an innate human decency in which was rooted an apparently instinctive ability to make the proper public gesture on important occasions. The governor in late '51 and the first months of '52 might contemplate without serious qualms the possibility of the general as President.

Not until later would he wryly regard, as all too typical of the postwar Eisenhower, the manner in which the general had at last entered the Presidential campaign.

Senator Henry Cabot Lodge, Jr., Massachusetts Republican, having just returned from a visit in Paris with Eisenhower, then commanding NATO armies, had told a press conference on January 6, 1952, that the general was a Republican, that the general would accept the Republican nomination if it were offered, and that this statement would not be denied by the general. On the following day Eisenhower, besieged by reporters, made his reply. In it he did not flatly state that he was a Republican; he said that Senator Lodge's announcement "gives an accurate account of the general tenor of my political convictions and of my Republican voting record." He did not clearly approve the political movement on his behalf; he said that "of course there is no question of the right of American citizens to organize in pursuit of their common convictions." He did not even clearly say that he would accept the nomination; he said that Senator Lodge and associates had a right to "attempt to place before me next July a duty that would transcend my present responsibilities" but that "in the absence... of a clear-cut call to political duty, I shall continue to devote my full attention and energies to the performance of the vital tasks to which I am assigned."

The only thing wholly unequivocal in the entire Eisenhower statement was his assertion that "under no circumstances will I ask for relief from this assignment in order to seek nomination to political office and I shall not participate in the preconvention activities of others who may have such an intention with respect to me." Whereupon, in the late spring, he did seek relief from his assignment, returned to America, and engaged in an intense preconvention campaign against Senator Taft.

On July 13, 1952, this campaign was crowned with success. At the Republican National Convention in the International Amphitheater in Chicago, following a bitter contest over delegates during which Taft supporters were charged with deliberate dishonesty in their attempt to claim the Texas delegation, Eisenhower won 585 votes on the first ballot, compared to 500 for Taft, whereupon the nomination, by floor motion, was declared unanimous.

II

Simultaneously there was the campaign to secure the Democratic Presidential nomination for Adlai Stevenson. Far different was its history. Not only did Stevenson refuse to "participate in the preconvention activities of others," on his behalf, he opposed those activities so consistently and effectively that by the late spring of '52 they had collapsed into seeming utter futility. If some of his motives for doing so were never explicity stated, his dominant motive was proclaimed to the world again and again: he wanted another four years as governor of Illinois.

On Sunday, January 20, Stevenson, with Bill Blair, flew to New York, where, on the following evening, in the grand ballroom of the Waldorf-Astoria, he delivered an address to the annual banquet of the National Urban League, an address which had been scheduled in November. It dealt with the harmful effect of racial discrimination in the United States upon our relations with other countries, particularly with Asian lands, and Stevenson had prepared it in the knowledge that it would be used as a news peg on which *Time* magazine, then edited by his old Princeton friend T. S. Matthews, would hang a cover story dealing with his record in Illinois. The speech was enthusiastically received by its immediate audience and next morning at breakfast Stevenson and Blair were gratified to see that it was well covered in the New York press. The *Herald Tribune* had an editorial lauding it.

Less gratifying was the information that all planes were grounded that morning by lowering, drizzling skies, for Stevenson and Blair were scheduled to fly down to Washington, where the governor was to confer with Secretary of the Interior Oscar Chapman and John L. Lewis of the United Mine Workers concerning a proposal to place mine inspection under federal rather than state control. The weather failed to improve, so Blair and Stevenson took the noon train to Washington. They had planned to stay at the Metropolitan Club, but when they arrived there shortly after four o'clock they discovered that all rooms were taken. Reservations had been made for them at the Roger Smith Hotel, the Metropolitan clerk told Blair, handing him some telephone messages. One of these, the two men noted with surprise, was from Blair House, where the President of the United States was living while the White House was being renovated. When Stevenson answered this call from his Roger Smith room, he learned that the President wished to see him that evening.

Truman, in his *Memoirs*,[3] has given his version of the meeting with Stevenson:

> I told him that I would not run for President again and that it was my opinion he was best-fitted for the place. He comes of a political family ... had served the country in the State Department and the United Nations ... had made an excellent Governor of Illinois. When I talked with him, I told him what I thought the Presidency is, how it has grown into the most powerful and greatest office in the history of the world. I asked him to take it and told him that if he would agree he could be nominated. I told him that a President in the White House always controlled the National Convention. Called his attention to Jackson and Van Buren and Polk. Talked about Taft in 1912, Wilson in 1920, Coolidge and Mellon in 1928, Roosevelt in 1936, 1940, 1944. But he said: No! He apparently was flabbergasted. ...

And Stevenson might well have seemed so to such eyes as Truman's. Certainly he was flattered, and even astonished, by the President's request. He was convinced that Harry Truman—despite his Supreme Court appointments, his predilection for unfortunate off-the-cuff remarks, his sometimes dubious personal loyalties—would go down in history as one of America's strong chief executives. Few if any Presidents had displayed a greater personal and political courage than he in his great campaign of '48, one of whose consequences had been an unprecedentedly swift advance of American Negroes toward their full rights as citizens of the United States. This gave to Truman's request a weight of honor to which Stevenson responded with gratitude.

Stevenson pointed out, however, that as an announced candidate for reelection as governor, he had an obligation to the people of Illinois, and particularly to the good people who had invested their talents, energy, and money in his campaign and administration on the assumption that he would see the job through to the end. He mentioned, also, his obligation to his three sons. Borden and John Fell were yet very young: a pitiless light of publicity would focus upon them if he ran for national office; they would be exposed to pressures and temptations which could warp their lives. Four years from now, he said frankly, the story would be different as far as his personal availability was concerned. By then he would have completed his job in Illinois in so far as it was possible for him to do so, and his youngest son would by then be a college student. He also, by then, would be better equipped for the Presidency; as of the present moment he had doubts about his capacity to fill the job. No, he was deeply moved, greatly honored, profoundly grateful, but he just couldn't do it.

Thus the words between these two men.

But beneath and beyond the words was a deeper, wider communication, flawed by misunderstanding. Because of it, this meeting took on (in subtle ways) some of the aspects of an encounter whose reverberations, echoing against those augmented by subsequent events, would be heard throughout the land four years later.

These were two very different men—different in temperament, experience, attitudes, mind—and the difference was such that it was easier for Stevenson to appreciate Truman at the latter's full value than it was for Truman to appreciate Stevenson. That Truman misunderstood and underrated the man on whom he sought to bestow the nomination seems evident from the notes quoted above, written by the President soon after the meeting occurred. Stevenson—for all his outward deprecation, his seeming eagerness to defer to others—was not a man who could be "told" in this fashion; neither could he accept, easily, a gift of the nomination. His instinct for freedom, coupled with his obscure but powerful need to do everything the hard way, required that he earn whatever glory came to him and remain, always, his own man.

His arrival at Blair House and his departure a little less than two hours later went unnoticed by White House news correspondents. But shortly after he breakfasted with Senator Paul Douglas next morning, the Presidential visit was front page news in the national press, having been released by the President himself. By nightfall Stevenson had been the focus of a dozen news cameras, the target of a score of pointed news questions, the subject of many a nationally syndicated columnist. And on the following day, Thursday, *Time* magazine with its cover story about him appeared. *Time* had shifted its news peg from the Urban League speech to the Blair House visit, saying: "Whatever the truth behind the rumors, this much was evident: in a cold season for the Democrats, Adlai Stevenson is politically hot, and Harry Truman feels the need of a little warmth."

Stevenson himself, having conferred on Wednesday with Chapman and Lewis concerning the mining law, continued to devote himself to Illinois business. On Thursday morning he breakfasted at the Metropolitan Club with a stocky, dark-haired, brown-eyed young man (he was then twenty-six) named Newton Minow, a graduate of the Northwestern University Law School, who was now the law clerk of Chief Justice Vinson of the U.S. Supreme Court. Minow had told McGowan he was interested in coming to Springfield as a Stevenson aide, and the breakfast conversation (a most congenial conversation, for the two liked one another immensely) dealt exclusively with that proposal and with state problems. Minow then drove the governor from the Metropolitan to the Roger-Smith.[4] An hour or so later Stevenson and Blair boarded a plane for Chicago.

Thereafter, the movement on behalf of Stevenson for President grew swiftly to boom proportions. In early February an Illinois Committee of Stevenson for President was organized in Chicago by a group of directors and former directors of the Independent Voters of Illinois, an Americans for Democratic Action affiliate. Of this Draft Stevenson Committee, Walter Johnson, professor of history at the University of Chicago, and George Overton, lawyer, were co-chairmen.[5] Neither Stevenson nor anyone close to him had anything to do with organizing this committee nor with its work once it was organized—work that included mailing out literature and buttons (the latter said merely "Stevenson" so that they might be used in the gubernatorial campaign if the presidential movement collapsed), buying advertisements in newspapers, and in general focusing and keeping alive through doubtful times the draft movement. By spring the Illinois committee had become a national committee.

By that time, too, Stevenson was so far ahead of the other candidates for nomination that his selection on the first or second ballot seemed a certainty, if only he gave a word of encouragement to the movement on his behalf. He gave no such word. On the contrary, he refused to permit his name to be entered in any primaries (when it was entered without his permission in Oregon and could not legally be withdrawn, he urged Democrats to vote for Kefauver, the only other Democrat entered). Over and over again, to reporters, to visitors, and in answer to thousands of letters, he reiterated that he was a candidate for governor of Illinois and for that office only. "One does not treat the highest office within the gift of the people of Illinois as a consolation prize," he said in 1953, summarizing what he had told people in the preceding spring. "Moreover . . . I had little time to go around the country campaigning for an unwanted nomination to an unwanted office— an office, moreover, of such appalling difficulty and responsibility in the year of grace, 1952, that I felt no sense of adequacy." He urged Jack Arvey, national committeeman from Illinois, to do nothing on his behalf, and he urged this so persistently and consistently that Arvey did, in fact, nothing.

Meanwhile the campaign launched by Kefauver on the day following Stevenson's Blair House visit plodded through primary after primary, beginning with New Hampshire, where he inflicted a humiliating defeat upon the President, and ultimately winning the delegates of eight other states, plus half of Ohio's and part of Florida's. He also won the Pennsylvania Presidential preference primary.

It was not such a campaign as Stevenson himself would have conducted. Launched with a criticism of Truman's alleged laxness in cleaning up governmental corruption, continued through the use of coonskin caps and an implacable handshaking folksiness, it seemed designed to advance the candidate at the expense of the party organization. One could not but admire Kefauver's courage and his indefatigable energy. Stevenson did so. But he was convinced that in the American political system good government depends very largely upon strong, effective party organizations, and he deplored the debilitating effects the Kefauver campaign seemed to be having upon one of these. There seemed to him no necessity to conduct the battle against dishonesty in government in such a way as to weaken the party at its every level, from precinct and ward to the state and national committees. On the contrary, one should battle for governmental integrity in such a way as to *strengthen* the overall party organization, thus exercising—as he and Jack Arvey were doing in Illinois—a necessary political art.

A future historian might find that Stevenson himself was giving a remarkable demonstration of the essential political art as he dealt, that spring, with the Presidential movement on his behalf. The "pressure changed" somewhat, he wrote in early '53, as this movement proceeded. The question asked him was no longer, "Will you be a candidate for nomination?" but, "Will you accept the nomination?"

> This was more difficult. If I said, "No," how would it reconcile with all my preaching about public service and politics? How could I foretell then, long before the convention, what manner of deadlock and bitterness might develop to the lasting damage of my party? And, finally, could anyone in good health and already in public life refuse the greatest honor and greatest responsibility in our political system? So I concluded to keep still and say nothing more to anyone, contenting myself with confidence that no one could in fact be drafted by a modern convention against his often-expressed wish.[6]

In early March Stevenson and Truman again met in Washington to discuss the Presidential nomination. According to Truman's *Memoirs*,[7] this meeting was requested by Stevenson. According to Stevenson and his closest aides, he went in response to a call from the President. In either case, the governor was at great pains to make the trip in secrecy since a public knowledge of it could only feed the Presidential boom he wished, or believed he wished, to discourage. He was driven in a car with unofficial license plates to the St. Louis airport, where he boarded a commercial airlines plane with a ticket issued to him in the name of William McC. Blair, Jr.

The plane stopped at Louisville, Kentucky, where Stevenson visited briefly with Barry Bingham of the Louisville *Courier-Journal,* an old friend who had been asked to meet him there. He wanted advice, and Bingham was full of it. "I argued, with as much force as the brief period allowed, my conviction that he should not fight against a fate which seemed to have settled upon him," Bingham told Walter Johnson in the spring of '54. "I did not urge him ... to make himself a candidate, or to promote his availability in any way at all. I only pleaded that he should leave himself uncommitted, so that a genuine draft could have an opportunity to develop.... As to his personal qualifications, I urged that the Democratic delegates and the people of the country in general should be allowed to judge for themselves on the basis of the public record.... He was modest, friendly, deprecating, seeking advice and yet protesting that he could not bring himself to take it. As we parted, he laughed and said: 'Well, you certainly haven't been much help to me!' " [8]

In Washington he repeated to Truman what he had said in January. Reelection to the governorship of Illinois was the full measure of his ambition; he could not be a candidate for any other office.

On the evening of Saturday, March 29, Stevenson was again in Washington, in the National Guard Armory, as one of fifty-three hundred Democrats gathered for the annual Jefferson-Jackson Day Dinner. The President was the speaker of the evening, and near the close of one of his typical "give 'em hell" addresses he announced, as if casually, that he would not be a candidate for reelection nor would he accept a renomination. The chorus of protest had scarcely died before newsmen were jammed around Adlai Stevenson, asking him the same old questions with more urgency than before. Next day he was interviewed before TV cameras on the "Meet the Press" program, acquitting himself so well in answers to deliberately needling questions * that his stock received another boost in the political market. To the key question about his political future, he made his by then standard reply: "I must run for governor. I want to run for governor. I seek no other office. I have no other ambition." Said Lawrence Spivak: "Governor, doesn't this large studio audience give you any indication of how some people of the country feel about that?" Stevenson surveyed the audience with a smile. "It's very flattering indeed," he said, "and I suppose flattery hurts no one— that is, if he doesn't inhale."

In the days immediately following, however, he was convinced that the flattery he was receiving was hurting him—if, indeed, it was flattery. The key question was asked him in a hundred forms, and he kept repeating his answer to it, with growing weariness and rare flashes of exasperation.

---

* One of these concerned his Alger Hiss deposition.

At last, on April 16, eight days after he received his formal nomination as Democratic candidate for governor of Illinois, he felt compelled to issue a statement that would, he thought, end any chance of his nomination. On April 17, a great Democratic fund-raising dinner was to be held at the Waldorf in New York, with W. Averell Harriman, then Mutual Security Director, as guest of honor. All the leading contenders for the presidential nomination were to be present, and for that reason Stevenson at first declined to attend: he was not a contender, and by appearing at the banquet and speaking there, as he was asked to do, he would be automatically classified as one. His initial refusal, however, raised an outcry among party leaders, who pointed out that, whether he liked it or not, he was the crowd getter, the publicity getter, and the party needed all the money and all the publicity it could raise. In response, Stevenson agreed to appear, but as he entered the plane for New York he issued the following statement, in order that his appearance would not be misconstrued:

> I have been urged to announce my candidacy for the Democratic nomination for President. . . . Others have asked me merely to say that I would accept a nomination which I did not seek. To state my position now on a prospect so remote in time and probability seems to me a little presumptuous. But I would rather presume than embarrass or mislead. . . .
> I have repeatedly said that I was a candidate for Governor of Illinois and had no other ambition. To this I must now add that in view of my prior commitment to run for Governor and my desire and the desire of many who have given their help and confidence in the unfinished work in Illinois, I could not accept the nomination for any other office this summer.

And that, it appeared, was that. Stevenson "seems effectively to have closed the door to his nomination," said The New York Times, adding that "many people will regret Mr. Stevenson's decision, for he is the type of man that either party should be proud to have for its leader." Political commentators agreed that Stevenson was now definitely out of the race, ensuring that the Democratic convention would be wide open for the first time in twenty years. Yet the very papers which carried such comments also carried news stories about the hit Stevenson had made with his speech at the Harriman banquet, stories that kept alive (if feebly through the next weeks) the hope that, somehow, he would become the nominee after all.

III

Six days later Harriman formally announced his candidacy, and in the following weeks several others, overtly or covertly, took steps to advance their candidacies, among them Senator Richard Russell of Georgia, Senator Robert Kerr of Oklahoma, and Vice-President Alben Barkley.

The Walter Johnson committee, though discouraged, continued its operations. Its members drew what comfort they could from the fact that Stevenson had not said he would not accept the nomination but only that he could not, thus suggesting that the decision was a function of circumstances rather than an expression of private will. Circumstances might change.

In late April and in May, Stevenson spoke in Texas, Oregon, and California, filling engagements he had made in early January after he'd announced for governor and before the Presidential boom had begun. Everywhere he was enthusiastically received. Everywhere he was hounded by reporters, and by partisans who insisted that he must run. Pressed in Portland, Oregon, to say whether or not he would accept a draft, he replied: "I cannot speculate about hypothetical situations. But I don't believe there ever has been a genuine draft of an unwilling man for the presidential nomination by either party.* I doubt if such a thing is possible." But suppose it happened? reporters kept asking him. Was he "afraid" to run against General Eisenhower? No, he replied in California, adding with a smile: "I don't think Ike is afraid of me." A few weeks later, when he visited the Illinois National Guard encampment in Wisconsin, a fervent supporter followed him around all day, pursuing him even to the airport, and as the governor climbed the steps to the plane's door, the man called out: "Well, what'll you do if we nominate you anyway?" Stevenson turned in weary exasperation. "Guess I'd have to shoot myself," he said, and entered the plane. (Later, Republicans spread the story that Stevenson had threatened to commit suicide if he were nominated, thus revealing that he was mentally unstable.)

On June 30, at the annual Conference of State Governors, he again told reporters that "without such participation on my part I do not believe [a] ... draft can or will develop," but this time he added: "In the unlikely event that it does, I will decide what to do ... in the light of conditions then existing." The latter remark kept alive the flame of hope in such men as Walter Johnson.

Others—professional politicians—fully shared the view of Jack Arvey and Stevenson that such a draft would be a miracle. They were no strong believers in miracles. Some of them remembered only too vividly what had happened to them when, in 1948, they had participated in the movement to draft Eisenhower on the Democratic ticket.

Frank McKinney, chairman of the Democratic National Committee, repeatedly urged Stevenson at least to make his availability known covertly and became convinced that, in the light of the governor's attitude, the cause was hopeless. He and Harry Truman therefore turned their attention to other candidates, eliminating one after another of these as unsuitable for one reason or another. Dick Russell was impossible because of the race issue;

---

* James A. Garfield was drafted against his will in the Republican convention of 1880, as Stevenson was soon reminded.

Kerr was impossible because he had represented oil and gas interests in the Senate, introducing a bill on behalf of these which Truman had vetoed; * Harriman, who had served well in supremely important federal posts, had never run for elective office; Barkley was an old man, and there was doubt that labor would support him.

Nevertheless it was on Barkley that Truman and McKinney finally settled, two weeks before the convention opened. At a meeting in the White House, Truman told the Vice-President "that up to that time Stevenson had refused to run and if he [Barkley] was serious about wanting the nomination we would support him." [9]

CHAPTER TWENTY-THREE

THERE were three national news foci in Chicago during the week which began Friday, July 18. One was the International Amphitheater, vacated by the National Republican Convention a week before and now redecorated and refitted for the Democratic convention, which opened on Monday, the twenty-first. A second was the Conrad Hilton Hotel, where the aspirants to the Democratic Presidential nomination had their headquarters and where many of the convention delegates stayed and held their caucuses. The third was a large and handsome three-story brick house at 1416 North Astor Street, the home of Bill Blair's father, William McCormick Blair, Sr. Into this house, that Friday, moved Adlai Stevenson, with Carl McGowan and Bill Blair, an event that abruptly transformed this normally quiet neighborhood of the wealthy into a scene of hectic, crowded activity. Five phone booths were set up along the sidewalk to accommodate hordes of reporters who trampled into mud the walled garden between Chicago's suddenly famous "Blair House" and the house to the north where Bill's grandmother, Mrs. Joseph T. Bowen, lived. The crowds soon grew so large that the police were forced to close off the block.[1]

On the fifteenth floor of the Conrad Hilton, on Wednesday the sixteenth, the National Stevenson for President Committee, with Leo Lerner now serving as a co-chairman with Johnson, had established an unique campaign

* Wrote Truman on p. 494 of Vol. II of his *Memoirs:* "I have always felt that any man who goes either to the Senate or the House to represent a special interest in his own state and who sponsors legislation to help that special interest forfeits any claim to national leadership in the Democratic party. Historically, the Democratic party is not a special-interest party."

headquarters. Like the headquarters of other candidates, it distributed buttons, literature, and free soda pop. Like the others, it was a scene of incessant noise and excitement as delegates came and went and crucial tactical conferences were held morning, noon, and night. But, unlike any other, this headquarters, manned by volunteers, had no contact, direct or indirect, with the candidate it sought to nominate. Johnson and his colleagues went to great lengths to avoid such contacts: when Bill Flanagan, the governor's press secretary, appeared there, he was asked by Johnson to leave; when John Fell and Borden came on Saturday afternoon, curious "to see the people who were trying to make . . . father do what he said he did not wish to do," [2] the headquarters was thrown into consternation, and the boys were asked not to come back. It would have been fatal to the committee's strategy if the impression had got abroad that the reluctant candidate was merely another coy one. The draft that Johnson and the others sought to arrange must not only *be* genuine, it must also *seem* so.

On that oppressively hot Saturday the committee's primary concern was to make sure that Stevenson's name was put in nomination, and under conditions most favorable to his candidacy. In this it was greatly aided by a meeting called by Kenneth Anderson, National Committeeman from Kansas, in his headquarters at the Palmer House. Anderson and John Young, the Democratic state chairman from Kansas, were the first bona fide delegates to come out strongly and definitely for a draft of Stevenson, and though the Palmer House meeting broke up without clear-cut decisions having been made concerning nomination strategy, it initiated a process by which the Stevenson movement grew like a snowball rolling downhill—a simile peculiarly attractive to sweating delegates on that fervid day. Thereafter, Anderson, Young, and Anderson's youthful assistant, Milo Sutton, were ceaselessly active, getting in touch with other delegations, stimulating caucuses, and obtaining committed votes.[3]

On that same Saturday an important meeting was held with members of the Pennsylvania delegation at the Morrison Hotel, a meeting at which Johnson and the leaders of the Pennsylvania group agreed to work together. One of the Pennsylvania delegation was an old Princeton friend of Stevenson's, Lewis M. Stevens, now a member of the Philadelphia City Council. Another, a man who would be of crucial importance to Stevenson's political future, was James A. Finnegan, president of Philadelphia City Council, who up to that time had never met the governor and would not meet him for some time thereafter. A key question, maddening under the circumstances, was: "Will Stevenson accept a draft?" (They could not know that Stevenson had decided he must do so: he had told McGowan and Blair that he would, though he continued to believe that a draft was a remote possibility and he continued to do all he could to discourage it.)[4] By the time the meeting broke up, the Johnson group was fairly certain that the Pennsylvania caucus next day would produce a substantial number of Stevenson votes and that delegates emerging from that caucus wearing Stevenson buttons would produce a significant impact on the convention as a whole.

Meanwhile, on the second floor of Blair House, Stevenson worked with McGowan on the welcoming speech he would make to the delegates on Monday. On Sunday morning he attended services at the Fourth Presbyterian Church (the church in which he had been married), where his friend, the Reverend Harrison Ray Anderson, preached a sermon quite obviously aimed at him entitled, "How Men Know God's Will." When he left the church reporters asked him what he thought of the sermon. It was "superb," he said; the minister had "helped" him.

Later that day he attended the caucus of the Illinois delegation, of which he was a member. The meeting was closed to reporters, but those enterprising gentlemen lay down on the floor with their ears to the crack beneath a sliding partition. They heard Stevenson insist again, with now-desperate sincerity, that he did not want the nomination. Of the Presidency he said: "I do not dream myself fit for the job—temperamentally, mentally, or physically. And I ask therefore that you all abide by my wishes not to nominate me, nor to vote for me if I should be nominated." Emerging from this meeting, he was asked by reporters if he would yield to a draft if the convention became deadlocked. "Show me the deadlock first," Stevenson replied. The reporters already knew that he had done all he could to discourage the placing of his name in nomination. When he arrived in Chicago he had been told that either Governor Henry F. Schricker of Indiana or Archibald Alexander, a young friend of Stevenson's who was a candidate for senator in New Jersey, might make the nominating speech on his behalf. "I shall do all I can to prevent that," he promptly replied. And he did so. "I called them both by phone and asked them not to," he later said.[5] "Alexander agreed, but my esteemed friend, Governor Schricker, rebelled...."

Next morning, Monday, July 21, two determining events occurred. One was a breakfast given by Vice-President Barkley for sixteen labor union leaders, in which he bid for their support and was refused it.* The other was Stevenson's speech of welcome. A spontaneous six-minute demonstration followed the governor's appearance on the rostrum, and only his departure from the rostrum ended the wild applause at the speech's close. For fifteen minutes the delegates and the nation listened to a politician like none they had heard before.

---

* Said Harry Truman, on p. 495 of Vol. II of his *Memoirs:* "[In] one essential respect Barkley failed to follow our suggestions to him. In meeting with the leaders of labor to enlist their support, we told him to be sure to see the leaders one at a time.... We knew that they would never commit themselves in a crowd, and all that came of this meeting ... was a unanimous turndown. I am of the opinion that if Barkley had been advised by a manager skilled in dealing with labor this rejection would never have occurred and Barkley would have been the Democratic nominee."

He said, in part:

> Here, my friends, on the prairies of Illinois and of the Middle West we can see a long way in all directions. . . . Here there are no barriers . . . to ideas and to aspirations. We want none; we want no shackles on the mind or the spirit, no rigid patterns of thought, and no iron conformity. We want only the faith and the conviction that triumph in free and fair contest.
>
> As a Democrat perhaps you will permit me to remind you that until four years ago the people of Illinois had chosen but three Democratic Governors in a hundred years. One was John Peter Altgeld, whom the great Illinois poet, Vachel Lindsay, called the Eagle Forgotten. He was an immigrant. One was Edward F. Dunne, whose parents came from the old sod of Ireland, and last was Henry Horner, but one generation removed from Germany. John Peter Altgeld, my friends, was a Protestant, Governor Dunne was a Catholic, Henry Horner was a Jew.
>
> And that, my friends, is the American story, written by the Democratic party here on the prairies of Illinois.

He reviewed the Democratic era that had been ushered in, there in Chicago, with the nomination of Franklin Roosevelt. Then his wit sparkled and crackled, sending his audience into gales of laughter:

> But our Republican friends have said that it was all a miserable failure. For almost a week pompous phrases marched over this landscape in search of an idea, and the only idea they found was that the two great decades of progress in peace, and of victory in war, and of bold leadership in this anxious hour, were the misbegotten spawn of bungling, of corruption, of socialism, of mismanagement, of waste and of worse. They captured, they tied and they dragged that ragged idea here into this hall and they furiously beat it to death for a solid week.
>
> After listening to this everlasting procession of epithets about our misdeeds I was even surprised the next morning when the mail was delivered on time. . . . But we Democrats were by no means the only victims here. First, they slaughtered each other and then they went after us. And the same vocabulary was good for both exercises, which was a great convenience. Perhaps the proximity of the stockyards accounts for the carnage.

But he also spoke soberly, calling for a "sober understanding of the breadth and depth of the revolutionary currents in the world," and closed with a solemn exhortation:

> And let us remember that we are not meeting here alone. All the world is watching and listening to what we say, what we do and how we behave. So let us give them a demonstration of democracy in action at its best—our manners good, our proceedings orderly and dignified—and, above all, let us make our decisions openly, fairly, not by the processes

of synthetic excitement or mass hysteria. Let us make them as these
solemn times demand, by earnest thought and prayerful deliberation.

And thus can the people's party reassure the people and vindicate and
strengthen the forces of democracy throughout the world.

Even before that fateful Monday, the political columnist, Doris Fleeson,
had written (on Sunday evening, the twentieth): "It now looks as though
Gov. Adlai Stevenson will be dragged protesting to the Presidential altar by
the Democratic party. His shrieks are growing fainter, his suitor more im-
portunate." On Monday evening Barkley issued a bitter statement in which
he charged "certain self-anointed labor leaders" with forcing him to "withdraw my name from the consideration of the convention." On Tuesday, Anne
O'Hare McCormick said in *The New York Times*: ". . . In one day . . . all the
confused and unchanneled currents seemed to converge upon the shrinking
figure of Governor Adlai Stevenson as the one and only, the almost automatic choice of the convention. Nothing but action by the President could
alter the picture, and the general feeling here is that even that would now
be too late. . . ." By that time, too, a firm coalition of the Draft Committee
with the delegates of Pennsylvania, Kansas, New Jersey, Indiana, North
Carolina, and Washington had been formed; Governor Schricker was at
work on his speech nominating Stevenson; and former Senator Francis J.
Myers of Pennsylvania was operating, despite Stevenson's public request
that he not do so, as floor leader of the pro-Stevenson forces.

On Thursday afternoon the nomination speeches began. By late afternoon
the names of Russell, Kefauver, Kerr, Senator J. W. Fulbright of Arkansas,
and Averell Harriman had been presented to the convention with the usual
demonstrations. Then Governor Schricker arose (Delaware having yielded
to Indiana for the purpose) to speak for twelve and one half minutes, concluding: "Ninety-two years ago, the nation called from the prairies of Illinois
the greatest of Illinois citizens, Abraham Lincoln. Lincoln, too, was reluctant.
But there are times when a man is not permitted to say no. I place before
you the man we cannot permit to say no, Adlai E. Stevenson of Illinois."
There followed a wild demonstration which left no doubt that Stevenson was
the convention's majority choice. Other names were then placed in nomination: Governor G. Mennen Williams of Michigan; Senator Hubert Humphrey of Minnesota; Governor Paul Dever of Massachusetts; Barkley; and
Federal Security Administrator Oscar Ewing. But these were clearly anti-
climactic.

On Thursday evening there was a bitter floor fight in the convention over
a loyalty pledge aimed at the Southern Democrats who, as Dixiecrats, had
bolted their party in revolt against Truman's civil rights program in 1948.
A resolution adopted on Monday required all delegates to sign a pledge that
they would support the convention's nominees. Virginia, Louisiana, and

South Carolina refused to do so. The floor fight then developed over the seating of the Virginia delegation, a resolution by Maryland to do so being vehemently opposed by supporters of Kefauver and Harriman, who hoped thus to halt the Stevenson draft. The resolution was finally adopted by a vote of 650½ for to 518 against—and the nomination of Stevenson, in the view of most observers, was assured. Even if the resolution had been rejected, that nomination would have been virtually certain.

One can imagine at least some of Truman's feelings as he read such comments as Mrs. McCormick of the *Times* had made Tuesday morning and as Roscoe Drummond published in the *Christian Science Monitor* Tuesday evening: "... This convention is jelling so speedily, the prospect is that President Truman will have no opportunity to determine the presidential nominee—even if he could. ... They say that Mr. Truman, who can recognize a trend as well as the next politician, is ready to give his favor to Governor Stevenson. The view here is that if he does not do so shortly, he will be waving at a bandwagon which has passed by." The President, it appeared, had been neatly cut off from power, and it must have been as salt upon the resulting wound to have Stevenson call him, on Thursday, July 24, to ask if it "would embarrass" the President if he, Stevenson, "allowed his name to be placed in nomination."

Stevenson meant this to be a courtesy call, but Truman's response to it clearly revealed the President's sense (an unadmitted sense) that party control had slipped from his hands. Wrote Truman of this telephone conversation: "I replied with a show of exasperation and some rather vigorous words and concluded by saying to Stevenson, 'I have been trying since January to get you to say that. Why should it embarrass me?'" *

II

During those historic days Stevenson emerged only twice from Blair House: to make his welcoming speech Monday morning and, on Friday morning, to breakfast in attempted secrecy with Averell Harriman at Ed McDougal's apartment on Lake Shore Drive, where Buffie and Ernest Ives stayed during the convention.[6] He watched the proceedings intermittently on TV. When it became evident that his name would be placed in nomination in such circumstances as to make his selection likely, he began to write an acceptance speech, working in a second-floor bedroom on the north side of the house, with windows overlooking the walled garden. He wrote, as always, on a ruled yellow tablet, in longhand, slowly, painfully, conferring

* Harry Truman, *op. cit.* p. 496: He added: "Actually, if Barkley had not withdrawn when he did ... I would not ... have been able to tell Stevenson that I would support him, and Barkley would have been the Democratic nominee."

often with Carl McGowan, passing the written sheets to Carol Evans, who worked on a typewriter set upon a card table in the next room. After Governor Schricker's nominating speech Stevenson issued a brief statement: "I had hoped they would not nominate me, but I am deeply affected by this expression of confidence and goodwill."

On Friday afternoon he received a phone call from Frank McKinney, asking him to dine that evening with President Truman, who had just flown in from Washington. With thanks and regrets, Stevenson declined. He explained that by dining with the President he might appear to be promoting his chances for the nomination, in contradiction of all he had done and said before with regard to it. He did not say what was of course true, namely that by dining with Truman he would have given the public impression that he was Truman's man, restoring to the President some of the party power and prestige which had been lost through the course of recent events. To the precise extent that Truman's power was increased, under those circumstances, Stevenson's would be reduced.

As the convention moved toward the balloting session, it became evident that he did not, in fact, have a clear choice between the governorship of Illinois—which he certainly did want—and the nomination for President. If he rejected the latter he might be defeated in his pursuit of the former. Obviously he was the strongest Presidential candidate the Democrats could run against Eisenhower—the only candidate, people kept telling him, who had a chance to win against the popular military hero. And if Eisenhower won a landslide victory he might well carry into office the Illinois Republican gubernatorial candidate, William G. Stratton, a personable young man who bore a name well known in Illinois politics—and this despite Stevenson's record. . . . Stevenson may also have been reminded that the situation now facing him on the national level was similar to that which had faced him on the state level in late 1947, when he had been reluctant to run for governor. Dutch Smith had told him then that if he failed to run when the party needed him he would probably not be permitted to run when other conditions were more to his liking.

The balloting took place on Friday afternoon. Of the 615½ votes needed for nomination, Kefauver received 340 on the first ballot. Stevenson was second with 273, Russell third with 268, and Harriman fourth with 123½. The other votes were scattered among ten candidates, led by Kerr, who received 65. On the second ballot Kefauver still led, having increased his vote to 362½. Stevenson's vote had increased to 324½, an increase which did not seem significantly large to many observers, but which clearly indicated to convention insiders that the governor would be nominated on the third ballot with votes which had been committed for two ballots to other candidates. The convention then recessed for dinner (the time was six-fifteen).

When the convention reassembled, the crucial third ballot was taken; it required a long time, for there were many switches. The final official tally gave Stevenson 613 votes, two and a half less than needed for nomination. Utah then switched its twelve votes to Stevenson, Kefauver and Russell yielded to him, and thus, early in the morning of Saturday, July 26, he became the Democratic Presidential nominee for 1952.

He had not yet said publicly that he would accept the nomination. But after the balloting ended he crossed to the steps of Mrs. Bowen's house and made a short speech for TV and to the crowd in which he indicated he would accept. Then he left for the convention, where he joined President Truman in the Stockyard Inn for the short walk to the hall.

Meanwhile, at the International Amphitheater, Buffie Ives was taken to Mrs. Truman's box, where she sat beside the First Lady, with Perle Mesta, Secretary of the Treasury John Snider, and other distinguished people. "I felt in a haze as hot white lights flashed on us," she later said, "and above my head floated one small balloon lettered 'KEFAUVER.'" [7] Mrs. Truman explained that her husband would present the nominee to the convention. In the box assigned to Adlai Stevenson were his aunt Letitia, the Edison Dicks, Dutch and Ellen Smith, Mrs. Harriet Welling, and Borden and John Fell, who had all but lived there throughout the week. That night, though, the Dicks and some of the others were at Blair House, watching on TV.

Time passed. Weary, restless, the great throng waited. The organ played, again and again, "Don't Let Them Take It Away," the campaign song.

There was a stir at last, then a hoarse roar as the President of the United States strode briskly to the rostum, with Adlai Stevenson beside him.

The roar died.

The President—that familiar jaunty figure with the flat Midwestern twang in his voice echoing, it seemed, almost nostalgically, out of an age already past and swiftly receding—the President spoke a fighting speech, as he had done in '48. Then he presented Adlai Stevenson. He lifted Stevenson's hand high as the convention rose to its feet, wildly cheering, its placards swinging as the organ boomed out again the campaign song.

And then, at what might have been a long moment of deflating anticlimax, came from Stevenson what to millions at that time seemed the voice of the future, but a voice that sang with a lyric sense of the past.

"I accept your nomination—and your program," he said.

"I should have preferred to hear those words uttered by a stronger, a wiser, a better man than myself," he said.

"None of you, my friends, can wholly appreciate what is in my heart," he said. "I can only hope that you may understand my words. They will be few."

And millions, listening that dark early-morning hour with a kind of awed astonishment, believed they understood. Many of them listened again next morning, in company with additional millions, as the "few words" were rebroadcast.

He said:

> I have not sought the honor you have done me. I *could* not seek it because I aspired to another office. . . . I *would* not seek your nomination for the Presidency because the burdens of that office stagger the imagination. Its potential for good and evil now and in the years of our lives smothers exultation and converts vanity into prayer.
>
> I have asked the Merciful Father—the Father of us all—to let this cup pass from me. But from such dread responsibility one does not shrink in fear. . . . So, "If this cup may not pass from me, except I drink it, Thy will be done." *
>
> . . . And now, my friends, that you have made your decision, I will fight to win that office with all my heart and soul. And, with your help, I have no doubt that we will win. . . .

He praised the conduct of the convention. He praised the platform that had been adopted. He strove to allay the fear that a continuation of Democratic control of the government would mean the death of the two-party system. It had seemed to him that the Republican party "looked brutally alive a couple of weeks ago, and I mean both Republican parties!" Nor was he afraid that the Democratic party was "old and fat and indolent"; it could never become so "as long as it looks forward and not back, as long as it commands the allegiance of the young and the hopeful who dream the dreams and see the visions of a better America and a better world." He said:

> . . . When the tumult and the shouting die, when the bands are gone and the lights are dimmed, there is the stark reality of responsibility in an hour of history haunted with those gaunt, grim specters of strife, dissension and materialism at home, and ruthless, inscrutable and hostile power abroad.
>
> The ordeal of the twentieth century—the bloodiest, most turbulent era of the Christian age—is far from over. Sacrifice, patience, understanding and implacable purpose may be our lot for years to come. Let's face it! Let's talk sense to the American people! Let's tell them the truth, that there are no gains without pains, that we are now on the eve of great decisions, not easy decisions, like resistance when you're attacked, but a long, patient, costly struggle which alone can assure triumph over the great enemies of man—war, poverty and tyranny—and the assaults upon human dignity which are the most grievous consequences of each.
>
> . . . Better we lose the election than mislead the people; and better we lose than misgovern the people. Help me to do the job in this autumn

---

* Stevenson soon regretted, as a serious lapse of taste, his use of this sentence from Christ's prayer in Gethsemane (Matthew, chapter 26, verse 42); it seemed to identify his plight with Christ's agony. Thousands deemed it sacrilegious.

of conflict and of campaign; help me to do the job in these years of darkness, doubt and of crisis which stretch beyond the horizon of tonight's happy vision, and we will justify our glorious past and the loyalty of silent millions who look to us for compassion, for understanding and for honest purpose. Thus we will serve our great tradition greatly.

Saturday morning . . .

Though he had had little or no sleep for twenty-four hours, the Democratic candidate for President seemed as fresh and cheery as always to Newton Minow, who had arrived at the governor's Loop office on the preceding Monday wearing a big "Stevenson for President" button, earning thus a frown of disapproval from Carl McGowan. (Minow was an innocent in this; someone had pinned the badge upon him as he entered the building.) On Saturday Minow went to Blair House to confer with Bill Blair, and as the two talked, he saw Stevenson with Averell Harriman in the next room. Then Stevenson came out. "Why, hello, Newt!" he said, shaking hands. "I heard you were in town. I'm sorry I haven't had an opportunity to discuss things with you." Minow averred that the governor may have been a mite busy the last few days. Stevenson nodded. "I'll see you in Springfield," the governor said. "Glad you're going to be with us." [8]

Buffie Ives, that morning, was awakened from two hours of sleep by phone calls. Three highly important calls from highly important people came to her, for transmittal to her brother, who seemed to them barricaded behind an interminable busy signal. She dressed and hurried over to Blair House, delivering her messages to Bill Blair. Then she rode in the back seat of a car, between Stevenson and Harriman, to the convention hall. Harriman and Stevenson discussed the chairmanship of the Democratic National Committee; Truman was exerting tremendous pressure to ensure the continuance of Frank McKinney in that office and Stevenson was, as yet, noncommittal. (Desperately he strove to think of someone with whom to counter Truman's pressure, but it was not until ten days later that, lying awake one night, he suddenly thought of Stephen Mitchell, the lawyer who, with Lou Kohn and Dutch Smith, had launched the Stevenson political career in 1947.) There was no talk about the Vice-Presidency, for this matter was settled the night before. Truman, Stevenson, McKinney, and Sam Rayburn of Texas had met in a private room behind the stage and there agreed upon Senator John Sparkman of Alabama.

At the convention hall, soon after the Stevenson party's arrival, Senator Sparkman was nominated. He and Stevenson stood together on the rostum, smiling and waving to cheering thousands. They turned this way and that to face a hundred cameras.

Sunday . . .

Stevenson rode south from Chicago by train. A cheering throng awaited him at the Bloomington station, where the train paused. He saw the faces

of scores of boyhood friends. Alverta Duff presented him with a floral horse-
shoe as the crowd laughed and applauded. "If you can't get a good cup of
coffee at the White House," said she, "just send for me." Twenty-five thousand people awaited him at Springfield. The ovation he received there
deeply moved him, more so than any other of those last hectic days. He
spoke to the vast crowd with tears in his eyes—a rare thing with him: seldom
did he reveal his deepest feelings. He spoke in the shadow of the courthouse,
on the square Abraham Lincoln had known so well.

Monday night . . .

The hour approached midnight as Bill Blair entered the governor's basement office in the mansion.

"The caretaker has been alerted," Blair said.

"Thanks, Bill," Stevenson replied, rising. "Don't let a hint of this get
out, will you not?"

"Not a hint," Blair said.

Stevenson slipped furtively out a side door of the mansion and down a
dark side street to the corner of Eighth and Market. He paused for a second
or two, looking up at Lincoln's home. Then he hurried up the short walk
to the door, where the caretaker admitted him. For an hour he sat alone
in Lincoln's rocking chair. What did he think, feel, as he sat there? He would
never tell anyone; perhaps he could not if he would. But a great calm was
upon his spirit when he left that house and walked again the darkened
side street. He had come to some sort of terms with the stupendous, the
incredible thing that had happened to him.[9]

III

He had promised to "talk sense" to the American people. He proceeded,
in early August, to map out a campaign which would do so, a campaign
which would stimulate a "reasoned and precise debate" on the great issues
emerging from the "ordeal of the Twentieth Century." He interpreted General Eisenhower's hard-won victory in the Republican convention as a
"victory of the constructive and progressive men in the Republican Party
over its bitter and reactionary elements." The entire campaign might therefore mean the elevating of the "national political dialogue" to a higher plane
than any it had occupied, perhaps, in the whole of our national history. He
realized that his views and he, personally, were little known in the country.
He therefore planned in his early speeches to set forth his position as clearly,
as unequivocally as possible upon such matters as agricultural policy, foreign
policy, labor, natural-resource conservation, inflation, governmental corruption, and so on. These initial statements would, according to his plan,
occupy the first half of the campaign. October, or the second half of the

campaign, would be reserved for "amplification and rebuttal" and for dealing with "the exigencies and opportunities that were bound to develop as the campaign progressed." [10]

His chief consultant and partner in this planning was Carl McGowan, and McGowan was largely responsible for the hasty recruitment of a research and writing staff whereby the substantive aims of the campaign would be implemented. As a principal writing aide, Stevenson himself called in Arthur M. Schlesinger, Jr., Harvard historian and author of a Pulitzer prize-winning book, *The Age of Jackson*. Also called in were McGowan's old friend, W. Willard Wirtz; David Bell, who had served as a Truman speech writer in the White House and who returned to Springfield with Stevenson after a conference with Truman in Washington on August 12; Robert Tufts, who had been a member of the State Department's Policy Planning Division; John Bartlow Martin; William Reddig, editor of an Olathe, Kansas, newspaper and formerly literary editor of the Kansas City *Star;* and Sidney Hyman, who had been closely associated with Harry Hopkins and Robert Sherwood in wartime Washington. With this core group was associated a group of in-and-outers—men who contributed as much of their time and energy as their other obligations would permit them to do. Among them were Kenneth Galbraith, Harvard economist; Jack Fisher of *Harper's* magazine; David Cohn, then closely associated with Senator Fulbright of Arkansas; Eric Hodgins of the Luce publications, author of the best-selling *Mr. Blandings Builds His Dream House;* and Bernard De Voto, historian of the American West and a conservation authority.

This group was dubbed the "Elks Club" because it headquartered in a large and noisy room on the third floor of Springfield's Elks Club.[11] At the back were four bedrooms where some of the writers slept. They proved to be a congenial group, fortunately so in that they had to engage in concentrated mental effort under frantic circumstances with six hours or less of sleep a night for many weeks. Contact with the governor was maintained through McGowan. The organization was as loose, as informal as it could possibly be, but Schlesinger functioned as its head, with David Bell as a kind of second-in-command, performing most of the duties of office manager. Writing assignments were made virtually automatically in terms of the special subject-matter competencies of the man, one or two of whom— different ones at different times—traveled with the governor and served as pipe lines back to the Club.

All of them became convinced, if they were not at the outset, that Stevenson was a far better writer of Stevenson speeches than any of them could ever be. Most of them were initially perturbed by the fact that the final drafts of speeches generally bore little resemblance to the drafts they had painfully prepared, but whatever resentment they may occasionally have felt was submerged in the pride they took in a political candidate who was so fine a master of their own profession. With pride and truth they could proclaim that the speeches as Stevenson finally gave them—speeches that would be gathered into a best-selling book months after the campaigning had ended—were very much Stevenson's own.

Nevertheless, none in the campaign organization, save the governor himself, bore more of the health-breaking brunt of that campaign than did the Elks Club members (including, of course, McGowan), most of whom collapsed into a hospital bed at some point during the ordeal. None contributed more, save the governor, to that which would make the campaign memorable and perhaps unique in American political history. They were indispensable instruments of that extraordinary clarity and eloquence with which Stevenson discussed issues between mid-August and election eve.

There was one issue, however, on which neither they nor the governor prepared even an initial statement, one on which the governor's personal stand was not wholly unambiguous. That issue was President Truman and the portion of the administrative record which had been dubbed, in the Republican press, "Trumanism."

Stevenson stood firmly by the major domestic and foreign policies of the Democratic administration; he defended vigorously the overall record President Truman had made; but at the same time, in Truman's own words, he seemed to give "the impression that he was seeking to dissociate himself from the administration in Washington, and perhaps from me." [12] He did so by replacing Frank McKinney with Stephen A. Mitchell as chairman of the Democratic National Committee (according to Truman he "fired" McKinney) and by establishing his campaign headquarters, not in Washington where the National Committee headquartered, but in Springfield. The two acts were of a piece: had he not had his own man as national chairman, the problem of cooperating with the national Democratic organization would have been insoluble. As it was, it was so far from perfectly solved that some, even in Stevenson's organization, wondered if the G.O.P.'s "two-headed elephant" wasn't being matched against a two-headed donkey in several respects.

There were other grave disadvantages to headquartering in Springfield. Travel in and out of the town was much more difficult than travel in and out of Washington would have been, and Springfield was deficient in mass-communications facilities. The latter complication was enhanced by the apparent fact that Bill Flanagan, whom Stevenson retained as his personal press secretary, seemed not to enjoy the candidate's full confidence. When newsmen asked Flanagan questions to which, they felt, he should have immediate answers, Flanagan was likely to reply that he didn't know, he'd try to find out. For this, and various foul-ups in news facilitation, the unfortunate Flanagan was soon very much in the doghouse with reporters. The situation was considerably improved when the White House loaned to Stevenson one of the President's principal assistants, Clayton Fritchey, who had had a brilliant newspaper career (he'd been editor of the New Orleans *Item,* managing editor of the Baltimore *Post,* and won a Pulitzer prize for reporting while on the Cleveland *Press*) before coming to Washington in 1950 as assistant to General Marshall, then Secretary of Defense.

Fritchey and Bell, however, were the only men closely associated with Truman and the national organization who became closely associated with Stevenson during the campaign. A large red brick house a half block from the Executive Mansion was rented, and some thought it significant of the whole campaign effort that the sign on the front porch identifying this house as "Stevenson Campaign Headquarters" was so small ("I want it small," Stevenson had insisted. "Nothing gaudy!") that many who sought the house failed to notice it. Soon this headquarters was vastly overcrowded with what many old-time Democrats regarded, disgustedly, as amateurs—so much so that considerable space was rented in Springfield hotels.

The chief amateur was Wilson Wyatt, whom Stevenson asked to become his personal campaign manager. Actually Wyatt, however green some might think him to be about national politicking, was certainly no stranger to public life. A successful lawyer, he had been mayor of Louisville, Kentucky, in the early 40's; had served with the Board of Economic Warfare in North Africa for a time in '43; and had been National Administrator of Housing, in Washington, immediately after the war. He was a good friend of Barry Bingham and Mark Ethridge of the Louisville *Courier-Journal* and of Carl McGowan, whom he had known in Washington during the war. Wyatt's chief assistant as campaign manager was Stevenson's old and close lawyer friend, George Ball. Dutch Smith and Jane Dick served as co-chairmen of the national Volunteers for Stevenson.

Bill Blair continued as Stevenson's personal facilitating officer and appointments secretary, proving under intense fire his good judgment and evenness of temper, his efficiency, his remarkable talent for human relations. Richard Nelson, the governor's aide who was president of the national Young Democrats that year, was another close assistant. Carl Evans and Margaret Munn continued their secretarial duties on the tours. Nearly all the others personally associated with him during those strenuous days were long-time colleagues and personal friends. As always, he seemed to need people immediately around him with whom he could relax and through whom he could keep in touch continuously with his own past, his own personal tradition. Thus Ernest and Buffie Ives traveled on the campaign trains and planes with him and so, part of the time, did John Fell, Borden, and Aunt Letitia Stevenson. Adlai, Jr., on leave, joined the party in Boston briefly.

Inevitably Truman took a sour view of much of this operation. The President was unpersuaded by Stevenson's explanations that the Presidential candidate customarily chose his own man as National Committee head and that the campaign headquarters must be in Springfield since Stevenson continued to be governor of Illinois. In actual fact, of course, Stevenson was very seldom in Springfield during the whole of the campaign and the executive power was transferred to the lieutenant governor, Sherwood Dixon. He, however, had taken Stevenson's place as candidate for governor in Illinois, and was busy with his campaign, so that much of the work in the governor's office devolved upon Newton Minow, who served as Stevenson's deputy in the mansion office.

The only major item of state business that Stevenson personally handled from August to November had to do with an ugly prison riot at Menard in late October. Stevenson was campaigning in Pennsylvania at the time. Back in Springfield, Minow struggled to handle things in such a way as to make the governor's return unnecessary, especially since the governor's intervention might look like a grandstand play. But the rioting convicts, some 339 of them, held seven guards as hostages in the east cell block and, after two days had passed, Sherwood Dixon felt compelled to put through a call to Carl McGowan on the campaign train.

"I immediately made the arrangements for the trip back," McGowan later recalled. "I knew that Stevenson had the same close feeling for the state police I did—a force he had taken out of politics and built up—and I knew he would want to be with them. When I told him of the plans he approved, without a flicker of hesitation. We also thought that, when the rioters knew the final authority was there on the spot, they would feel there was no more room for delay and bargaining, and that it might well help to prevent bloodshed." [13]

Stevenson spoke on Thursday evening, October 30, before a great crowd in Hunt Armory in Pittsburgh, then slipped away to fly with McGowan, Blair, and several news correspondents (the latter, covering his every move, could not be left behind), to Chester, Illinois, where the prison was located. He arrived at four o'clock in the morning, conferred with Dixon and others until dawn, then issued an ultimatum calling for immediate release of the hostages, "or the police will enter and use any force necessary to restore order." Shortly before noon the hostages were released unharmed and Stevenson personally entered the east cell block, with police, in what observers regarded as a demonstration of physical as well as moral courage, which was decisive. One or two shots were fired, one rioter was killed by a ricochet bullet, and it was all over. Stevenson returned to his plane and flew to New York.

There were, Truman complained, "two campaigns being waged by the Democrats" that year, for Truman, at Stevenson's request, was vigorously campaigning in defense of his record, giving the Republicans "hell" in the style of '48. There was between the two campaigns "overlapping and confusion," to use Truman's words. There was also a measure of bad feeling.

The latter focused particularly upon Stevenson's answer to a letter written him by a Portland, Oregon, newspaper editor who was considering endorsing the Stevenson candidacy. In this letter the editor asked, among other things, how the candidate proposed to deal with "the mess in Washington." In his reply Stevenson referred to this phrase as a means of identifying a specific point he meant to answer, without conceding either the accuracy or the propriety of the phrase itself, and the public impression became that Stevenson had promised to clean up the mess. Truman, naturally, was outraged and personally hurt.

"How Stevenson hoped he could persuade the American voters to maintain the Democratic party in power while seeming to disown powerful elements of it, I do not know," Truman would write in his *Memoirs*. But of course the President sensed that it was precisely by seeming to do this that Stevenson hoped to persuade independent voters into his camp. Whether Stevenson was practically, or morally, right in this strategy is an unanswerable question. Truman himself was convinced that Stevenson would have received at least three million more votes than he did if he "had accepted in good faith the proposition I made to him on January 30, 1952, and enabled us to make the proper build-up. . . ." [14]

A few months later, Stevenson recorded some of his personal impressions of the "exacting ordeal" of a Presidential campaign:

> You must emerge, bright and bubbling with wisdom and well-being, every morning at 8 o'clock, "just in time for a charming and profound breakfast talk, shake hands with hundreds, often literally thousands of people, make several inspiring "newsworthy" speeches during the day, confer with political leaders along the way and with your staff all the time, write at every chance, think if possible, read mail and newspapers, talk on the telephone, talk to everybody, dictate, receive delegations, eat, with decorum—and discretion!—and ride through city after city on the back of an open car, smiling until your mouth is dehydrated by the wind, waving until the blood runs out of your arm, and then bounce gaily, confidently, masterfully into great howling halls, shaved and all made up for television with the right color shirt and tie—I always forgot—and a manuscript so defaced with chicken tracks and last-minute jottings that you couldn't follow it, even if the spotlights weren't blinding and even if the still photographers didn't shoot you in the eye every time you looked at them. . . .
>
> But the real work has just commenced—two or three, sometimes four hours of frenzied writing and editing of the next day's immortal mouthings so you can get something to the stenographers, so they can get something in the mimeograph machines, so they can get something to the reporters, so they can get something to their newspapers by deadline time. . . . Finally sleep, sweet sleep, steals you away, unless you worry— which I do. [15]

Actually, as his associates noted with awe, he had a remarkable capacity to relax and nap at odd moments, and his powers of recuperation, his resilience, were amazing. As the campaign ground toward its close, and others were breaking down around him, he seemed to grow stronger, as though he thrived on the incredible strain. As he himself recorded, he "gained weight on it" and that extra weight around his middle was "as tenacious as a campaign deficit."

He did so despite the disillusionment he increasingly suffered as he studied and sought to counter the tactics of his Republican opponents. He, who had "believed that an educational and elevating national discussion would result" from Eisenhower's Chicago victory, recorded with rare bitterness in late October [16] that this was "not a campaign by debate" but "a systematic program of innuendo and accusations aimed at sowing the seeds of doubt and mistrust." Nixon had set the pace. "Next Monday, I'm informed, the junior Senator from Wisconsin (Senator Joseph R. McCarthy) is going to make a highly advertised speech—the man who said last week that, if he were put aboard my campaign train with a club, he might be able to make a good American out of me." During that same week, nettled by charges that the Old Guard had captured him, General Eisenhower said emphatically that the decisions in the Republican campaign "have been and will be mine alone," and had added: "This crusade which I have taken to the American people represents what I, myself, believe."

"Crusade indeed!" cried Stevenson. . . .

But what, then, did it signify, this hard-fought campaign?

CHAPTER TWENTY-FOUR

S ELDOM in the history of American Presidential campaigns have the two candidates been more different in character and personality, in background and education, in style and taste, in approach to historic issues, than were Stevenson and Eisenhower.

Raised as one of six sons of a humble family on the wrong side of the tracks in Abilene, Kansas—a town whose most famous citizen had been Wild Bill Hickok—the boy Eisenhower was soaked through and through with Abilene's Wild West tradition, so much so that even after he became world famous his favorite reading for relaxation was Western pulp magazines. He was passionately interested in athletics, particularly in football and baseball, and his courage as a fist-fighter was notable even in a town where kid fights were brutal affairs. In school his grade record was no more distinguished than Stevenson's. His teachers remarked in him, however, a quick retentive mind, one concerned with facts rather than theories. His natural bent was pragmatical, in the manner of the old Western frontier, though qualified to some undetermined extent by the religious idealism of his parents, both of whom came of Mennonite stock (the Eisenhowers were River Brethren from Pennsylvania).[1]

His education as a whole was highly specialized. At West Point he received a thoroughly technical training without being exposed to the humanities in any such way as to make them attractive to him in the absence of a natural interest. He was popular with fellow cadets and teachers; he demonstrated, indeed, what amounted to a genius for popularity, in that he achieved it without apparently aiming to do so. And this genius served him well throughout his Army career, coupled as it was with an iron self-control and fortitude, the kind of swift calculating logic employed by an expert bridge player, and the ability to use this logic in situations whose very vastness breeds in most men a species of superstition.

As a professional soldier he had been outwardly apolitical through most of his life; he had seemed to his intimates to have no strong political convictions. And as a candidate for President he remained curiously apolitical, a universal hero rather than a partisan candidate. He maintained this role by being (or so his opponents believed) essentially passive. He evidenced no resistance to strong-willed men who wished to use his prestige to achieve their aims, even when their aims were at odds with those of the men who had done most to advance him. At the very outset of the campaign, he issued with Taft a joint statement in which he conceded, it appeared, every point of difference between his liberal Republican supporters and Taft's Old Guard. (Said Stevenson, "Taft lost the nomination but won the nominee.") Campaigning in Indiana, he embraced Senator William E. Jenner of that state both figuratively and physically—the same Jenner who, on the floor of the Senate, had called Eisenhower's greatest benefactor, General Marshall, a "living lie." When urged to remove sentences praising Marshall from a speech to be given in Milwaukee, because the sentences would displease Wisconsin's Senator Joseph R. McCarthy, he protested but did so. He then gave rather more than tacit support to McCarthy's campaign for reelection by saying that he and McCarthy were agreed as to "ends," only differing as to "methods." When his running mate, Senator Nixon, got into trouble over a large sum of money given directly by ten or so California businessmen, he prudently waited until Nixon had won popular support with a national TV broadcast, then gave him such public support ("Dick, you're my boy!") as a proud father might publicly give a son who had won a closely contested athletic event. Neither publicly nor privately did he protest or try to modify Nixon's efforts to convince the public, mostly through sly innuendo, that the Democratic party was infiltrated with Communists and that Adlai Stevenson had testified in defense of Alger Hiss.

Nixon did not directly charge that Stevenson, too, had a "secret fund" for the advancement of his political ambitions, but he acquiesced in the strategy which created that impression. This was the one Dutch Smith and a few other public-spirited Chicagoans had presented to Stevenson and which Stevenson used to supplement the salaries of men whom he had persuaded into Illinois government at financial loss to themselves. It was in no way analogous to the fund which had been given directly to Nixon for Nixon's personal use. So said Allan Nevins, the Columbia University historian, and several of his colleagues, in a public statement issued at the time. The donors of the Stevenson fund remained anonymous; they had no means of influencing, directly or indirectly, the official acts of those to whom Stevenson made his Christmas "gifts"; so that while the procedure might be deemed unwise in terms of effective personnel management (it could easily lower rather than raise employee morale), it could not be deemed unethical. The episode ended when first Stevenson and Sparkman, then Eisenhower, made public their income tax returns for the last several years,* by which time it seemed clear that the whole affair had hurt the Stevenson campaign far more than it had the Eisenhower one.

II

Stevenson, who had begun his campaign with such high hopes for an honest, probing "national dialogue," was soon distressed and disillusioned. Only three specific issues developed during the whole campaign on which the general's position could be defined against Stevenson's with much sharpness or clarity, and even on these the general seemed, in his opponent's view, to waver a good deal.

One issue had to do with foreign policy. Stevenson defined as an aim of foreign policy the creation of a balance-of-power system whereby Soviet Russia and the West could maintain a peaceful if competitive coexistence until such time as a firmer world cooperation could be achieved through the United Nations. He said that Formosa must not be permitted to fall to the Chinese Communists after the Korean War was ended.

---

* Senator Sparkman's returns showed an income of $89,497 for the last eight years. He had never had a personal campaign fund, he said, but had employed his wife as office receptionist. Stevenson's personal income for 1942-51 had totaled $500,046, of which $211,980 went for taxes. These disclosures were made on September 15. Eisenhower published his returns on October 14, revealing that his personal income since 1942 had totaled $888,303, including $635,000 for rights to his book, *Crusade in Europe*. He paid $217,082 in income and capital gains taxes during this period.

He had decided, as his closest aides knew, to go immediately to the Far East if he were elected, visiting not only the fighting front in Korea, where his visit would raise the morale of our troops, but also Japan and India. Upon the teeming revolutionary masses of those far lands rested, he was convinced, the fulcrum of any workable balance-of-power system. Here, with the "uncommitted third" of the peoples of the earth, lay the center of gravity of a world caught up in a torrent of history. And Stevenson not only wanted firsthand information about these peoples but also wanted them to know that America proposed to be their friend. But he was adamantly opposed to any public disclosure of this plan of his. To publish it in the midst of an election campaign would, in his view, amount to an attempt to buy votes in the coin of others' sacrifices, and at the expense of the general welfare. It could dangerously complicate negotiations then proceeding on the Korean question, it could conceivably prolong the war, and it would certainly raise hopes of an early peace, which might prove false, thus weakening the popular will to do what, in Stevenson's view, must be done to secure the peace.

Eisenhower, addressing the national convention of the American Legion on August 25, urged that the United States help the people of Communist-controlled countries to "liberate" themselves from "Soviet tyranny," a proposal which, Stevenson later asserted, cruelly raised false hopes among oppressed peoples and was "far more frightening to our friends than our foes." The immediate and vociferous response of America's allies was one of alarm and protest. Did Eisenhower propose, if elected, to promote violent revolutions in the Communist countries and give them active American aid? If so, World War III would come inevitably and soon, in the view of London and Paris. Two days later, John Foster Dulles, the Republican foreign policy adviser, was forced to explain that the general did not mean what he had seemed to mean; the general did not advocate a violent revolution in the satellite countries but, instead, "peaceful methods" (what they would be remained unsaid), which would lead to the "internal collapse" of communism.

Thereafter Eisenhower made no major statement on foreign policy until October 24 when, in Detroit, barely a week before the election, he pledged that if elected he would "go to Korea" to seek "an early and honorable" end to the war there. (On June 5, in Abilene, Kansas, he had said that he had no plan for ending the Korean War and that the United States should stand firm and try for a "decent armistice.") Stevenson, within hours, made public reply, saying that the general's proposal for a "slick, quick" way out of Korea risked a "Munich in the Far East" and increased the possibility of World War III. The root of the Korean problem, he indicated, lay not in Korea but in Moscow.

A second issue was that of state versus federal ownership of submerged oil lands off the shores of California, Texas, and Louisiana. The Supreme Court had ruled that, under existing laws, the federal government had the paramount interest in these submerged lands, that they were as much a part of the national public domain as the national forests, the national grazing lands, and the other public lands which, though lying within state boundaries, belonged to all the people. When Congress had adopted a joint resolution transferring ownership to the states, President Truman vetoed it. During the controversy Senator Lister Hill of Alabama had suggested legislation that would have earmarked the federal money received for these oil rights to be used for aid to education, alleviating the shortage of classrooms and teachers that was becoming increasingly desperate as the population swiftly grew. Eisenhower came out for legislation giving the states title to the off-shore lands. Stevenson complained that Eisenhower's precise position on the matter was difficult to define and that he took "at least three separate positions on the ... question." ("I lack the versatility of my opponent," he added.) But the general's overall position was clear enough; he favored the legislation Truman had vetoed. The issue, he said, was one of "States' rights." And this was as music in the ears of the managers of giant oil corporations whose headquarters' offices were in New York, whose interests extended to South America and the Middle East, and whose effective influence on state governors and legislatures was immensely greater than it could normally be upon the President and Congress of the United States.

Stevenson came out unequivocally for retaining federal ownership of the off-shore lands. He did so against intense political pressure to take an ambiguous stand upon this issue, or none at all. In late August, Governor Allan Shivers of Texas called upon him in Springfield, personally to urge this course of action. Shivers never explicitly promised his support if Stevenson did as Shivers wished, nor did he threaten to support Eisenhower if Stevenson refused, but both threat and promise were implicit in the visit itself. Stevenson replied that in his view, the Supreme Court's majority opinion was a valid statement of the public interest. He would say so forcefully during the campaign, "regardless of the possible effect upon electoral votes." And he chose to do so, not before an audience in New York, say, which would have been sympathetic to his stand, but to an audience in New Orleans, which was hostile to it.

The third issue was of a different order from those described above. It had to do with humor in the campaign. The general was against it.

In this, Eisenhower stood by a well-established tradition in American Presidential politics—a tradition which said that candidates for President must, in their speeches, be solemn as an owl. If they were not, if they indulged an ironical wit or even a storytelling humor, the electorate would write them off as smart alecks and lightweights. In contrast, Stevenson's gift for laughter was remarkable and he dared to exercise it freely before an electorate whose intelligence he respected. It is an open question whether this actually cost Stevenson votes, but it is certain that his immediate audiences were so much more responsive and enthusiastic than the general's that the general's camp grew worried and the general himself was irked. There was nothing funny in the Korean War, high taxes, inflation, and governmental corruption, Eisenhower said—as if these were matters that Stevenson treated lightly.

Stevenson's reply was to laugh all the more. He noted that "in the midst of the terrible years of the Civil War, Abraham Lincoln—and the Republican party still claims him—at least at election time—said of humor: 'If it were not for this occasional vent, I should die.'"

He averred that G.O.P. must now stand for "Grouchy Old Pessimists" and that the general had chosen Cromwell as the "model" for the "crusade," chiefly because Cromwell could never be "accused" of having "cracked a joke." However, he added, "to be surrounded by the Republican Old Guard night and day would be a melancholy fate . . . and I can understand why it is no laughing matter for the general." [2]

Nor was his humor confined to written speeches. It was sparked instantaneously by the unexpected. When a freight train roared by while he was speaking from his campaign train in Canandaigua, New York, he said, when he could resume, that "it must have been a Republican train—but don't worry —all the guys on it are for us." When he spoke in a town square and heard his voice tossed back at him in a disconcerting echo, he said, "I think what I am saying is worth listening to, but it's certainly not worth listening to twice." At Springfield, Massachusetts, he spoke from a railroad embankment high above the crowd. "I have often been accused of talking over the heads of the people," he said. "Thank goodness, at last you have given me an opportunity to do it."

Consistent with this style of humor, and indicative of the Stevenson frugality, was the most famous photograph taken of the candidate during his campaign. It showed him on the platform at Flint, Michigan, his legs crossed, a large hole in the sole of one shoe, and it was awarded a Pultizer prize next spring. (Stevenson would learn of the award while in the Far East and would send a post card to the photographer: "Congratulations. I'll bet this is the first time anyone ever won a Pulitzer prize for a hole in one.") [3]

But he was forced to admit in restrospect that in the '52 campaign—as in many Presidential campaigns in the past—the discussion of issues was largely irrelevant to the campaign's outcome. The mood of the country was in several respects similar to that which had prevailed in the America of 1920. Weary of war and politics, weary of the burdens of self-government in an era of seemingly endless crisis, disgusted with the mess of communism and corruption that they were persuaded prevailed in Washington, Americans seemed eager to believe in a hero who would take these burdens from them, leaving them free to pursue their private interests without guilt feelings and without being called upon for great decisions. In terms of this mood, the "Great Crusade," as Eisenhower labeled his campaign, was shrewdly designed to win votes.

Republican strategists transformed the contest largely into one of synthetic personalities: Eisenhower as hero, Truman as villain, Stevenson as "eggheaded" clown. To do so they employed new public relations techniques on an unprecedented scale. The Republican treasury, as always, was far larger than the Democratic one, which meant that Republicans could make much greater use of radio and, especially, of the new and expensive medium, TV. In the closing days of the campaign, they employed saturation TV in some crowded areas, presenting through Eisenhower's image, in that endless reiteration with which commercial products are sold, the twin appeals to a revulsion against the high cost of living and to a revulsion against the sending of "our sons" to Korea. Obviously aimed at women voters, the appeals would seem, in the event, to have been influential.

To the greater space and time that the Eisenhower forces could buy from America's mass communications agencies was added the immense advantage derived from the ownership of those agencies by Republican businessmen. Every influential mass-circulation magazine supported Eisenhower. A total of 993 daily newspapers with 40.1 million readers supported Eisenhower. Only 201 dailies supported Stevenson, and they were on the average papers of smaller circulation, having altogether only 4.4 million readers. Eisenhower received support from major papers in every state of the Union whereas in at least nine states—Delaware, Maine, New Hampshire, South Dakota, North Dakota, Rhode Island, Utah, Vermont, and Kansas—not a single daily supported Stevenson. Moreover, as Stevenson remarked in a speech on "The One-Party Press" in Portland, Oregon, nearly all these papers "rushed to commit themselves" to Eisenhower in the spring of '52, "long before they knew what [he] . . . stood for, or what his party platform would be, or who his opponent was, or what would be the issues of the campaign."

Truman had faced much the same situation in '48 (Roosevelt never faced a press so solidly committed to an opponent), but Truman at that time was President and his opponent was a man personally unpopular even among important segments of his supporters.* Under the circumstances Stevenson faced, press coverage became a major decisive factor—and it was but slender comfort for him to know that a majority of the journalists working for Republican publications were personally for him.

---

* It was often alleged that the Roosevelt-Truman victories proved the press ineffective in a political campaign, but who could tell what the margin of victory would have been had Truman and Roosevelt been given a fifty-fifty break in the press?

III

On Saturday, November 1, 1952, the Stevenson campaign train rolled through Ohio and Indiana toward Chicago. During the day the governor gave eight rear-platform talks, the last one at Gary, Indiana, shortly after five o'clock in the afternoon. That evening he spoke at a giant rally in the Chicago Stadium. He exuded confidence. "My friends of Chicago," he said, "it has not only been a great campaign for me—it's also a winner. There has been an electric feeling of victory in the air all the way home." He then flew to Springfield, where he slept again in the mansion. Next morning, Sunday, he, with Buffie and Ernest Ives and a friend, Art Moore, drove from Springfield to Bloomington where they attended services in the Unitarian church. He lunched at the Iveses' home, his own boyhood home, and napped afterward in the room that had been his as a boy (Alverta Duff tiptoed in to pull down the blinds and place a blanket over him). He was awakened, refreshed, an hour later to ride in a motorcade through a hailstorm to a reception at the Bloomington armory. He spoke there and returned to Springfield.

On the following day he went again to Chicago where he made, that night, his election-eve address. "Anyone who runs for office wants to win," he said. "I want to win, of course, but win or lose, if I have kept faith with myself during the campaign, then I can await tomorrow—and the day after—and all the days after that—in good temper and sober contentment.... Tomorrow you will make your choice.... If your decision is General Eisenhower and the Republican party, I shall ask everyone who voted for me to accept the verdict with traditional American sportsmanship. If you select me, I shall ask the same of the Republicans—and I shall ask Our Lord to make me an instrument of His peace."

He voted, next morning, at Half Day, near his Libertyville home. He talked informally before the school building, which was the polling place, to children assembled there. "I would like to ask all of you children to indicate, by holding up your hands, how many of you would like to be Governor of Illinois, the way I am," he said. Nearly all the children raised their hands. "Well, that is almost unanimous. Now I would like to ask all the governors if they would like to be one of you kids." He raised his own hand.

He spoke, then, soberly to the children:

I don't know whether you understand what is going on here this morning very well. I am not sure I do myself! But what you see here is something that does not happen everywhere in the world. Here are a lot of your parents and your neighbors going over to the schoolhouse there to cast their vote. That means they are deciding for themselves who is going to lead them—who is going to be their leader.... It is not everybody in the world who can do that. These are the things you read about in the history books, that your ancestors have been struggling for for generations—not only to get the right to govern themselves but to keep it....

He flew back to Springfield and was in the mansion by noon.

That day, Stevenson, Blair, and a few others on the governor's personal staff formed a pool to bet on the outcome of the election. Each contributed five dollars; each wrote his guess as to the distribution of the electoral votes on a slip of paper which was then initialed, folded, and sealed in an envelope. No man bet that Stevenson would lose, though Blair had a strong suspicion that he would. Blair, as a matter of fact, had renewed his passport on October 27, in the expectation of a trip abroad after the election—a clear indication of his dubious state of mind—and both Blair and McGowan shrewdly appraised the potency of Eisenhower's popularity combined with the people's longing for a period of peaceful quiet. Nevertheless, Blair estimated an electoral vote of 270; only one guess in the pool was lower, a guess of 267, the narrowest possible margin of victory. Stevenson's own initialed slip, which Blair would keep as an item of some historic interest, recorded his belief that he would receive 381 electoral votes—a landslide victory! [4]

The election-night party was held in the ballroom of the Leland Hotel, where a giant scoreboard was erected on which votes were recorded as the totals came in. There was a great crowd, including many celebrities, in the room. An even greater crowd was outside wanting to get in; and the "ins" had red stars stamped on their hands so that they could move in and out at will. Carl McGowan cautioned staff members, who had worked so hard, "Now, don't get your hopes up too high. The news may be bad, you know." And from the first, the news, recorded on the giant scoreboard, was bad. People began to drink too much and to break down into tears. [5]

Adlai Stevenson sat that night in his basement office at the mansion, working on items of state business as he listened to the returns through a small portable radio. He remained there, listening alone, much of the time, to the news that what he had offered the American people had been overwhelmingly rejected. "But I don't *have* to be President!" he had said often during the campaign when someone had urged a course of action which might gain votes but with which he disagreed. He had said it, then, stubbornly. Could he now say it to himself serenely?

Bill Blair came into the office sometime around nine o'clock.

"Well, Bill," said Stevenson cheerfully, being perfectly aware of the answer, "which is it to be—'A' or 'B'?" He referred to statements he had written out, one an acknowledgment of victory, the other a concession of defeat.

Blair answered, "I'm afraid it's 'B,' Governor."

"Okay," Stevenson said. His tone was casual. His face was calm.

Nevertheless he delayed his announcement for several hours because Steve

Mitchell, calling from Washington, pointed out that it could have adverse effect on local candidates by causing Democratic poll watchers to cease watching the counting.

Buffie came in while he revised, as he always did up to the last moment, the statement he was to give. Borden came in.

"I'm conceding," the governor said cheerfully. He read the telegram he was sending to General Eisenhower in the Commodore Hotel in New York: "The people have made their choice and I congratulate you. That you may be the servant and guardian of peace and make the vale of trouble a door of hope is my earnest prayer. Best wishes. Adlai E. Stevenson."

"I'll be broke for a year after I pay my election bets," said Borden gloomily.

They all drove over to the Leland Hotel. Stevenson passed through a crowd whose members, many of them, wept as they cheered his appearance. He spoke to those immediately before him whose lives, especially during these last weeks, had been bound by the strongest ties of affection and interest to his own and who had spent so much of themselves in behalf of the cause he represented. He spoke, through microphones, to the American millions:

> General Eisenhower has been a great leader in war. He has been a vigorous and valiant opponent in the campaign. These qualities will now be dedicated to leading us all through the next four years. . . .
> I urge you all to give to General Eisenhower the support he will need to carry out the great tasks that lie before him.
> I pledge him mine.
> We vote as many, but we pray as one. With a united people, with faith in democracy, with common concern for others less fortunate around the globe, we shall move forward with God's guidance toward the time when His children shall grow in freedom and dignity in a world at peace. . . .

He read to the silent, teary-faced crowd the telegram of concession he had sent. Then, looking out upon his friends and fellow workers, he added: "Someone asked me, as I came down the street, how I felt, and I was reminded of a story that a fellow townsman of ours used to tell—Abraham Lincoln. They asked him how he felt once after an unsuccessful election. He said he felt like a little boy who had stubbed his toe in the dark. He said that he was too old to cry, but it hurt too much to laugh."

Few in that room that night were too old to cry. Many sobbed aloud. . . .

Through the dark streets of midnight along which Abraham Lincoln had so often walked, Adlai Stevenson drove back to the mansion. Close friends were gathered there. His laughter spread over them, dissolving gloom. He called for champagne with which to toast "our defeat."

When at last his friends had gone and he was alone in his room Buffie came in to wish him good night.

"How are you?" she asked, trying to sound matter-of-fact.

He smiled a trifle wearily. Oh, he was "all right," he said, adding that he hadn't asked for "any of this." He had done the best he could.

He who had believed he would win by an electoral vote of 381 to 150 had been defeated by a vote of 442 to 89. He had carried only nine states, none outside the South, and of the Solid South he had lost Virginia, Florida, and Texas, as well as the normally Democratic border states of Oklahoma and Tennessee. His opponent had received 6,626,068 votes more than he, out of an unprecedented total of 61,637,951. He might draw some comfort from the fact that he had polled the third largest vote of any Presidential candidate in history, a total of 27,312,217. Aside from Eisenhower, only Franklin Roosevelt in 1936 had surpassed, and by less than 165,000, the popular vote Stevenson received in 1952. Moreover, on a proportionate basis Eisenhower's had not approached the majorities received by Franklin Roosevelt in 1932 and '36, by Harding in 1920 or Hoover in 1928. Stevenson might conclude that, in the circumstances, his defeat was by no means disgraceful.

All the same it was overwhelming, and during the two months following election day, as he busied himself with the completion of his term as governor and with a mountainous correspondence that climbed beyond the possibility of his scaling it, he told his friends he would cheerfully accept the usual fate of a defeated candidate, making way for another choice at the next Democratic convention.

He revealed a good deal of his state of mind in a hilariously funny speech he gave in early December before the Gridiron Club in Washington. This club, composed of newspaper writers and publishers, held annually a banquet at which members produced musical skits ridiculing the public figures of the day. At each banquet held after a national Presidential campaign it was customary for the winner and the loser to make brief humorous talks at the close of the evening's entertainment—talks strictly off the record. Stevenson's speech, however, was reprinted in pamphlet form following the dinner, in violation of the Gridiron rule, by one who heard it and felt it should be shared with a larger public. None who heard or read it could fail to be convinced that Stevenson in his own mind was through as a political figure. "A funny thing happened to me on the way to the White House!" he began. "Let me tell you something about it all." The general had run "so far ahead we never saw him. . . . I was happy to hear that I had even placed second." Stevenson wondered if he were not "entitled to some kind of record. . . . Did anyone starting from scratch ever enter our public life with such widespread approval, and then leave, with such widespread approval—all in the space of four years?" he asked. "Frankly, I think the chroniclers of our times have overlooked the meteoric beauty and brevity of my political career."

He laughed, he made others laugh with him, but it was a laughter not far removed from tears. This fact became clear when, a month later, on January 8, 1953, he made his farewell report as governor to the people of Illinois. The lieutenant governor, Sherwood Dixon, who had taken Stevenson's place on the Illinois ticket, had been defeated by the Republican William G. Stratton. Much of Stevenson's farewell address dealt with the unfinished business of his administration, which he hoped the Stratton administration would complete: with the highway program, public schools, welfare services, the renovation of the constitution, the improvement of mine safety and labor laws, and so on. But at its close he expressed, in phrases reminiscent of Lincoln's farewell to Springfield, some of his own feelings as he left office, and as he did so he nearly broke down before his audience—a display of emotion so rare as to be virtually unique for him. He had wanted, so terribly much, to finish the job.

"Illinois, where my family have lived and prospered for a century and a quarter, means a great deal to me," he said, "and I am humbly thankful for the opportunity that has been mine to serve it. I leave my high office content in one respect—that I have given it the best that was in me. It has been a richly rewarding experience, and the satisfactions have far outweighed the disappointments. To the people of Illinois who have honored me so generously, and to the associates in this great undertaking whose friendship and loyalty have meant so much to me, I shall be eternally grateful."

His gaze swept the audience before him. In a choked voice he spoke his final words: "And now, with a full heart, I bid you all goodbye."

BOOK SEVEN

A Second Defeat

CHAPTER TWENTY-FIVE

ON February 7, 1953, Adlai Stevenson basked in warm sunlight upon the green shores of Barbados in the British West Indies, enjoying another afternoon of his first extended vacation in many years. It had not been a time wholly free of work; another, in fact, might have found it a time of arduous labor, whose fruits, as he lolled back in a canvas lounge chair, lay in forty or fifty ruled yellow sheets of paper upon his knees. His fingers ruffled those pages, filled with his neat small script—an introduction to the book of fifty of his campaign speeches, which a New York publisher would issue in the spring—as he rested his eyes upon the immense blue vistas of the Caribbean Sea.

But he had written those pages far more easily than he usually wrote, as he told of why he was a Democrat, how he had happened to become a politician, what the campaign had meant to him.

"Did I talk over people's heads?" he had asked. And his reply had been, "No—and that's about the only aspect of the campaign I am sure of!" He conceded that radio, television, and press create the means of mass manipulation and the "sale" of political ideas and personalities. He conceded that "many of us may be taken in now and then by professionalized emotionalism, showmanship and huckstering." But, he had added, expressing perhaps more confidence than he really felt, "I am not much troubled by that danger." [1]

His confidence was sustained by his review of the thousands of letters that had recently come to him. Letter after letter, he recalled, had expressed an almost pathetic gratitude for his effort to talk sense to the people—to speak, in other words, not as a front man for a collection of interests, not as a corporate personality whose brain was a board of directors, but as an individual human being who represented his party best by being true to his own values and his own sense of realities. Implicit in letter after letter had been the recognition that if the individual man is to be free he must, first of all, *be* an individual, with enough space around his essential self to define him as an unique person. He must have integrity.

One chief determinant of all in his mind was the fact that he remained —and would remain for nearly four more years—the titular head of the Democratic party. "In our country this rule is a very ambiguous one," he would write in a later year.[2]

> The titular head has no clear and defined authority within his party. He has no party office, no staff, no funds, nor is there any system of consultation whereby he may be advised of party policy and through which he may help to shape that policy. There are no devices such as the British have developed through which he can communicate directly and responsibly with the leaders of the party in power. Yet he is generally deemed the leading spokesman of his party. And he has—or so it seemed to me— an obligation to help wipe out the inevitable deficit accumulated by his party during a losing campaign, and also to do what he can to revive, reorganize, and rebuild the party.

The Democratic party's deficit, at that time, amounted to some eight hundred thousand dollars. Taking account of these things, he resolved to play out the role assigned to him with more planned consistency than most, if any, of his predecessors in that role had done.

He must, of course, earn money, and for this purpose he would eventually return to the practice of law in Chicago—but he also resolved to develop, informally but effectively, a staff of advisers (they must nearly all be unpaid volunteers) who could keep him informed on public questions and help him become a responsible critic of the Eisenhower administration's policies and actions. He resolved to emulate Wendell Willkie by journeying around the globe, at a more leisurely pace than Willkie had been able to do, to see for himself the people and the concrete problems of the world in which his country had so much power and therefore so much leadership responsibility. He resolved that, upon his return, he would revisit his own country to see it from coast to coast in the perspective of a world traveler and, in the process, help raise money, through fund-raising dinners, which would not only wipe out the campaign deficit but also build up treasury funds for the future. He further resolved that in the congressional campaign of '54 he would devote his full energy to his party's cause, as he himself would define it, for as many weeks as he could spare from his law practice.

Thus his plans.

II

And, in the event, he carried out those plans. With a contract for articles from *Look* magazine, he set out on March 1 of '53 for the Far East, accompanied by Bill Blair, Walter Johnson, William Atwood of *Look* magazine, and Barry Bingham of the Louisville *Courier-Journal*. He had honestly believed that he could tour the world as a private citizen, albeit as one with special advantages for seeing and learning, but was abruptly disabused of this notion when a huge crowd greeted him at the airport in Tokyo. Thereafter, his world tour was almost as hectic as his '52 campaign had been, so much so that by the time he reached England on his way home he felt "numb." But during those nearly six months of incessant sightseeing and absorbed discussion he learned an immense amount about the psychology, the problems, the history of other lands, developing a yardstick for the critical measurement of the American performance in the field of foreign policy.[3]

In January of '53 he had opened an office at 11 South La Salle Street in Chicago, consisting of a reception room and four small offices. It was not then, nor for nearly two years afterward, a law office but a personal office, staffed with Carol Evans, Phyllis Gustafson, Florence Meadow, and Juanda Higgins, all of whom had remained with him after the governorship ended. Bill Blair remained, too, as Stevenson's assistant. Here, after his return from the round-the-world tour, Stevenson wrote the many speeches he must give; wrote articles for magazines; struggled to make a book out of the *Look* pieces, finally abandoning the project for lack of time; prepared the Godkin Lectures he gave at Harvard in 1954, lectures on world affairs published in book form under the title *Call to Greatness;* and dealt with a veritable flood of correspondence. That office, and Stevenson's Libertyville farm, became major centers of political intelligence in the country.

Headed by Thomas K. Finletter, former Secretary of the Air Force, an informal advisory group met at irregular intervals, sometimes in New York, sometimes for a weekend in Chicago or at the Stevenson farm, to discuss issues and present suggested position papers. Its membership was fluid, but its core was composed of Finletter; Arthur Schlesinger, Jr.; Seymour Harris, Harvard economist who concentrated on fiscal policy; John Kenneth Galbraith, Harvard economist who concentrated on agricultural policy; Chester Bowles, former governor of Connecticut and former ambassador to India, who concentrated on foreign policy; and W. Willard Wirtz. Governor Harriman of New York often met with the group.

An increasing purpose began to dominate Stevenson's life during this period.

Through the first year and a half of the Eisenhower administration, when Republicans controlled both houses of the Congress, Stevenson watched with growing disapproval what seemed to him a failure of the President to function effectively either as chief executive or as party leader. Eisenhower's primary concern, it sometimes appeared, was to maintain intact his personal popularity by remaining above the battle, at whatever cost to the general welfare, though Stevenson would concede that this concern might be motivated in part by a belief (mistaken in Stevenson's view) that the Republican party could in this way be unified and made, ultimately, an effective instrument of conservatively liberal or liberally conservative government. Occasionally the President proposed legislation that moderately extended the programs of the New and Fair Deals, but he seemed content to let the Congress dispose of it without active intervention on his part. As a result, his key measures were often defeated, and in most cases received more support from Democrats than from Republicans in the Congress. Meanwhile there was formed, behind the smiling façade of Eisenhower popularity, what Stevenson regarded as a "hard coalescence" of big business, the executive bureaucracy, and the press, whereby the public domain was increasingly opened to private exploitation, creative intelligence in government was increasingly replaced by a stagnant mediocrity, and freedom of conscience and speech were increasingly threatened.

Emboldened by the apparent willingness of the White House to have his witch-hunting used as a partisan political weapon, Joseph McCarthy, Wisconsin's junior senator, embarked upon a program designed to brand Democrats as a party of pro-Communist traitors, asserting (on Lincoln's Birthday in 1953) that the regimes of Roosevelt and Truman had been "Twenty Years of Treason." Nor was McCarthy alone in his efforts to sow the seeds of suspicion, fear, and hatred in psychological ground prepared by the Cold War. The Attorney General of the United States, Herbert Brownell, joined in the enterprise by publicly charging President Truman with having harbored in government a "known traitor" in the person of Harry Dexter White. The White House itself joined in by releasing figures on the number of security risks removed from government jobs (2,427 of them, the President finally announced), doing so in such a way as to indicate that the great bulk of these were "subversives," "spies and traitors," "Communists," as Governor Dewey, the Postmaster General, and Herbert Brownell openly said they were. This "numbers game," as Stevenson called it, was continued even after an administration spokesman was forced to admit that, out of more than two million federal employees, only one alleged active Communist had been found. Ultimately it was discovered that the overall figure included not only people removed for a great variety of causes having nothing to do with loyalty but also some who had resigned their posts in blissful unawareness that they had ever been regarded (if, indeed, they ever had) as risks.

It was this rending assault on individual liberty, combined with what seemed to him a potentially disastrous foreign policy of "bluff and back-down" dictated by the business community's desire to cut taxes, which most outraged Adlai Stevenson. If the processes were permitted to continue, he asserted, the "end result" would be "a malign and fatal totalitarianism." He made this assertion in a fighting speech at Miami Beach, Florida, on March 7, 1954—a speech in which he pleaded for a restoration of honesty and human decency to a party which had become

> half-McCarthy, half-Eisenhower. . . . Perhaps you will say that I am making not a Democratic but a Republican speech; that I am counseling unity and courage in the Republican party and administration. You bet I am!—for as Democrats we don't believe in political extermination of Republicans, nor do we believe in political fratricide, in the extermination of one another. We believe in the republic which exists to serve, and we believe in the two-party system which serves it—that can only serve it, at home and abroad, by the best and noblest of democracy's processes. . . .

In that same speech he criticized the doctrine of "massive retaliation" to Communist agression, which had just been announced by Secretary of State John Foster Dulles.

> We are told, and I am quoting the words of Secretary Dulles, that we have rejected the "traditional" policy of "meeting aggression by direct and local opposition." We have taken the decision, he says, "to depend primarily upon a great capacity to retaliate instantly, by means and at places of our choosing.". . . Is this a "new look" or is it a return to the pre-1950 atomic-deterrent strategy which made some sense as long as we had a monopoly of atomic weapons together with a strategic air force? Yet even then it didn't deter attack, and brought us to the brink of disaster in Korea where atom bombs were useless. . . . But, you say, we did not use the bomb against Russian and Chinese targets for fear of enlarging the war. Exactly: and if we should now use them in retaliation that way it would certainly mean World War III and atomic counter-retaliation. For the Russians [also] have massive power of retaliation. . . .

Thus were stated the twin themes—the assault on civil liberties at home, the inflexible either/or policy abroad, implemented by tactics of vacillation, that wove through the campaign Stevenson waged on behalf of his party during the congressional elections of '54.

Shortly after he gave this speech, however, it appeared that he might play no role in the approaching campaign, nor any role in public life again. After "nineteen years plus" during which he had "never missed a day's work because of sickness," he suffered a serious illness. One day that spring he was abruptly doubled over with an agonizing pain in his abdomen. He was taken to the Passavant Memorial Hospital in Chicago. There, on April 20, he underwent surgery for the removal of a kidney stone lodged in his urethra. But in ten days he was out of the hospital, the only permanent consequences of his misfortune being his adherence thereafter to a low-calcium diet (he who had formerly drunk milk even at breakfast now drank no milk at all) and his giving up smoking (he had formerly smoked a pack of cigarettes a day).

By the time the '54 campaign began he was as strong, as remarkably energetic as ever, his zest for the contest increased by the fact that his principal opponent was Vice-President Nixon, a "plausible young man" of "flexible convictions," for whom his contempt was profound. Demonstrating to the full his skill for scoring debater's points through innuendo and insinuation, Nixon sought to convey the impression that President Truman had been guilty of "treason" (his actual words were that the President had been a "traitor" to the "high principles" of his party, but the context was such that disloyalty to the nation was clearly implied) and that the Democratic party itself was soft on communism. In the autumn, aided in no small degree by Stevenson's efforts (he made eighty speeches from coast to coast and from North to South during the campaign), Democrats won a number of new governorships as well as control of both houses of the Congress—an unprecedented accomplishment for an opposition party during a popular President's first term.

It was a victory, Stevenson came to realize, which did little to aid the prosperity of his personal political fortunes. With the removal of McCarthy and other right-wing Republicans from key committee chairmanships, with the restoration to power of Democrats who would support measures opposed by a majority of Republicans during the first two years of the administration, and through Eisenhower's continued exercise of his genius for popularity, the President again looked good in the eyes of those who had begun to doubt him. To a remarkable degree he was absolved of blame for his own party's deeds, even those of Vice-President Nixon, whose '54 campaign had outraged liberal minds while earning the public thanks of the President himself and who became, increasingly, the President's apparent first choice as successor. Senate Majority Leader Lyndon Johnson of Texas, House Speaker Sam Rayburn of Texas, Senator Walter George, who became chairman of the Senate Foreign Relations Committee—these and other conservative Southern Democrats who led the Congress—declined to attack Eisenhower effectively on issues, while the press surrounded him with what Stevenson called a "reverential hush." Never before, complained the titular head of the opposition, had a President been so protected against legitimate criticism.

"And I have become convinced through rather sad experience," Stevenson added in a later year, "that real issues cannot be developed, nor even effectively presented, during a political campaign. They must be sharpened and clarified largely through the legislative process *between* elections. In the campaign itself, about all a candidate can effectively do is present alternative courses of action."[4]

III

But though an increasing purpose dominated Stevenson's life during this period—though his personal opposition to Eisenhower's leadership grew steadily harder and deeper—he had by no means decided that he himself would become a candidate for the Presidency in 1956. This decision, he believed, should be the party's rather than his own. He was available. Through words and deeds he let it be known that he was. But he would become an active candidate only if he had firm assurance that the party wanted him.

On December 4, 1954, in New Orleans, a Democratic National Committee conference was held. There Paul Butler was chosen to succeed Stephen Mitchell as national chairman. In the evening a dinner was held at which Stevenson was the principal speaker, addressing his audience on "The Challenge of Political Maturity." He deplored the "cruel, unjust, and foolish things" that had been said during the campaign, the fact that "patriots were slandered, evil motives imputed, parties traduced and defamed." The campaign had imperiled the "essential harmony" which, "especially in the conduct of our foreign policy," was a "necessity for our survival." "There is a relation between legitimacy of power and responsibility," he said. "The insecurity of knowing that power must be gained by tricks and deception breeds dynamic words coupled with irresponsible action. But power which comes legitimately ... can be responsibly exercised with reason, patience, prudence, and wisdom. It is only from that sense of security that wisdom can be joined with innovation and that new paths can be explored...."

In his pocket as he spoke was a handwritten statement, which he had shown to no one save his immediate staff, because he wished to avoid the arguments that would be raised, he knew, against his presenting it. When his prepared address was completed he fished the statement from his pocket.

Now that we are off the air, let me add a final, personal word.... As in the past I have no political ambitions.... For more than two years I have sought as best I could to discharge my obligations to the Democratic party which had honored me, and to the millions of my fellow Americans who have given me their confidence.... But now I must devote more time to my own concerns. So if henceforth I cannot participate in public and party affairs as vigorously as in the past, I hope you will understand and forgive me, and I assure you that it reflects no lesser interest in our party's welfare and no ingratitude for the inspiration and encouragement you have given me in such abundance.

In later years he would express surprise that this statement received virtually no attention in the press. He would speak of it as though it were an announcement of his intention to withdraw from political life. Actually, of course, it was no such thing. What it did do was give party leaders an opportunity to withdraw their support from him, should they choose to do so, while encouraging his supporters to express their wishes.

More than four months passed before he again made a public speech.

By the beginning of 1955 he had come close to paying off single-handed the deficit his '52 campaign had accumulated—a feat, said John Mason Brown, "as revealing of his drawing power as of his probity," [5] since he achieved it by speaking at dinners ranging from fifty to a hundred dollars a plate. By that time, too, he had formed his law partnership with Bill Blair, W. Willard Wirtz, and Newton Minow. It was a firm that practiced a good deal more law than the general public believed it did, though the political pressures on Stevenson continued to be such that the firm rejected far more clients than it accepted. Both Minow and Wirtz were impressed by Stevenson's professional competence as a lawyer. He personally handled few cases, but those he did were handled unusually well. "He sees things differently than most lawyers," Minow would explain. "He's quick and thorough, and sees implications and connections that most men don't see." And Wirtz would say that Stevenson went into "every facet" of a problem, was "ingenious in the development of strategy and argument," and obviously enjoyed the "challenge of a problem." [6] The firm, soon after it was formed, moved to Suite 887 at 321 South La Salle Street—the Continental Illinois Bank Building—just across the hall from the law firm of Stevenson's '48 political opponent, Dwight Green.

During the Chicago mayoralty campaign in the spring of 1955 Stevenson gave active and probably decisive support to his former state director of revenue, Richard J. Daley, who defeated young Robert Merriam, a former Democratic alderman become a Republican. And while that campaign was being waged he lunched, one blizzardy March day, with Bill Blair and an out-of-town friend, to whom he spoke of his personal career indecision. He still had not made up his mind, he said, whether or not to become an active candidate in '56. He spoke of the "subtlety" of issues in this mid-twentieth century. "They are no longer black and white, or not to anything like the extent they were in the 1930's," he said. "The contest is no longer so clearly one of the haves versus the have-nots. The issues are there. They are very real. But they are difficult to define now—and I must say the present administration does everything it can to blur and obscure them." They seemed to him to be more "philosophical" than they had formerly been, having to do now with "spiritual" values at least as much as they had to do with economic ones. He referred also to the operation he had had the year before.

"I'm not going to run again just for the exercise," he said emphatically. "I've had all that kind of exercise I need. Another race like the last one and I will *really* have had it."

Bill Blair smiled. "He always talks that way, as though he were about to collapse into his grave," Blair explained. "Don't believe a word of it. The last physical examination showed him to be in perfect condition." [7]

A few weeks later a crisis developed in the Far East which contained grave threats of global conflict. Telephone calls, letters, and telegrams poured in upon Stevenson urging him to address the nation on this crucial matter, and on April 11 he did so, speaking over a national radio hookup. The President had just asked for and received from the Congress a "blank check" on which to write his will, should Communist China attack, as she threatened to do, the tiny islands of Quemoy and Matsu which, as Stevenson said, "lie almost as close to the coast of China as Staten Island does to New York," which had "always belonged to China," and to which neither the U.S. nor the Nationalist China government on Formosa had any legal claim. That the President at this juncture should require the Congress to underwrite in advance any decision he might make seemed to Stevenson to set a dangerous precedent. Under the Constitution the President, as commander in chief of the armed forces, already had the right and responsibility to defend national interests against foreign aggression; by turning to Congress, Eisenhower diminished the power of the President's office. Said Stevenson:

> Having loudly hinted at American intervention in Indo-China just a year ago, and then backed away; having forced General Chiang Kai-shek to evacuate the Tachen islands when the Communists made menacing gestures just a couple of months ago, we now face the bitter consequences of our government's Far Eastern policy once again: either another damaging and humiliating retreat, or else the hazard of war, modern war, unleashed not by necessity, not by strategic judgment, not by the honor of allies or for the defense of frontiers, but by a policy based more on political difficulties here at home than the realities of our situation in Asia.
>
> Given these unhappy choices it appears that President Eisenhower will decide what to do if and when the attack comes, depending on whether in his judgment it is just an attack on these islands or a prelude to an assault on Formosa. While our President has great military experience, perhaps it is not improper to ask whether any man can read the mind of an enemy within a few hours of such an attack and determine whether, at some later date, the enemy plans to go further and invade Formosa. Is it wise to allow the dread question of modern war to hinge upon such a guess?

Moreover, he reiterated, we stood at this juncture alone, our policy strongly opposed by our allies. Our Formosa policy was firm; it had been established five years ago when Truman sent the Seventh Fleet to defend that island from attack; but Quemoy and Matsu were in no sense essential to the defense of Formosa. Clearly the administration had placed the world in grave peril through Eisenhower's appeasement of the extremists in his own party, his refusal (it was of the essence of his genius for personal popularity) to take a firm and definite stand against those "inflammatory" elements who put forward a "defensive war" against Communist China. "If the best hope for today's world is a kind of atomic balance, the decisive battle in the struggle against aggression may be fought not on the battle-fields but in the minds of men, and the area of decision may well be out there among the uncommitted peoples of Asia and Africa who look and listen and who must, in the main, judge us by what we say and do."

As it turned out, the Chinese did not, that spring of '55, attack Quemoy and Matsu. The administration and its apologists were quick to say that this was due to the administration's "deterrent strategy." While not denying that the threat of war may indeed have deterred the Chinese at that moment, others remained convinced that the risk we had run had been a needless one and that the returns were by no means all in on the policy we had pursued. Quemoy and Matsu, fortified by the Chinese Nationalists with American approval and assistance, remained as irritating pinpricks in the flank of a huge and awakening dragon—and who could say but what that dragon merely waited, while Chiang's already overage army grew steadily older and weaker, until the time seemed ripe for a swift surprise seizure of the islands? What would we do if and when that time came?

IV

The weeks that immediately followed were unusually crowded for Stevenson, even by his own unique standards. He made a trip to Africa, partially for business reasons but also to visit a part of the world he had not seen before: Kenya, Rhodesia, the Belgian Congo, the Union of South Africa, the Gold Coast, Swaziland. At the last place he had a wonderful time, particularly during his visit with the king. He returned from Africa in May, having prepared an article on Africa for *Look* magazine, and then made several long-scheduled speeches: before the General Federation of Women's Clubs in Philadelphia, where he protested against the rising tide of anti-intellectualism in America; at Oberlin College in Oberlin, Ohio, where his old Princeton friend, Bill Stevenson, was president; at the dedication of the New York-Bellevue Medical Center in New York, where he outlined a national health program; at the Smith College commencement in Northampton, Massachusetts, where he stressed the value of nonconformity of mind in a free society; before the annual meeting of the National Education

Association in Chicago, where he presented a national educational policy outline.

The latter address was on July 6. He would never forget the date. In the morning he was terribly ill with fever, his voice so hoarse he could barely speak, and his doctor told him he must go at once to bed. "I have to speak," said Stevenson stubbornly. "Prop me up so I can do it." The doctor, with pills and hypodermics, managed to do so—though barely—and after an agonizing hour before the huge throng in the Chicago Stadium ("I never felt more miserable") Stevenson virtually collapsed and was taken to the Passavant with what, in an earlier year, might have been a fatal case of virus pneumonia. But in a few days he was fit again.

On August 12 the Governors' Conference was held in Chicago, and while it was going on the Democratic governors removed whatever doubts may have remained in Stevenson's mind concerning the party's wishes for his candidacy. Some twenty governors called upon him at his Libertyville farm, including Governor Harriman of New York, and most of them thereafter issued statements paralleling Harriman's "I'm for Stevenson all the way." Stevenson's own mind was then made up: he began to lay definite plans for a campaign. While in Desbarats, Canada, with the Hermon Dunlap Smiths during the following August days, he hired at least one major staff member and made decisions concerning others.

A few weeks later he went to Haiti and Jamaica on behalf of a law client, taking with him his son Adlai III and his daughter-in-law, the former Nancy Anderson of Louisville, Kentucky, a very attractive girl of nineteen whom young Adlai had married in June. He asked his eldest son for opinions on whether or not he should run again. Adlai III, examining the matter as a problem in the methodical way characteristic of him, favored his doing so. Then Stevenson talked to Borden by phone, Borden being then stationed in Hawaii as an Army lieutenant. Borden was not sure that running again was best for his father, but whatever his father thought best he wanted his father to do. John Fell, when his father talked to him, was, as Stevenson described it, "passively acquiescent."

Thereafter the only question about Stevenson's entrance into the campaign was one of timing. When should he announce formally? Truman, among others, believed he should announce at once. Stevenson himself thought he should delay the announcement as long as possible and tentatively decided to make it on November 19, at a huge Democratic National Committee dinner which was to be held in the International Amphitheater in Chicago and at which Stevenson was scheduled to make the principal address.

CHAPTER TWENTY-SIX

THE campaign of 1956, as Stevenson and his staff conceived it in the early autumn of 1955, was to be different in several important respects from that which he had waged in '52. Then he had been a reluctant candidate, doubtful of his personal qualifications for the Presidency. Now he was a determined one, convinced that no available person was better qualified than he for the highest office. Then his role had been that of defender and apologist. Now his role would be that of critic and prosecutor. Then he had had to do everything at once, for he had started unprepared and little known; necessarily he had engaged in improvisation that was often frantic. Now he was a figure of world renown and was perhaps better prepared than any earlier Presidential candidate had been.

The campaign he foresaw would be a long one, but it could be carefully planned and wholly focused on the opposing party, since he then appeared to be the inevitable and virtually unchallenged choice of the Democratic party. Already, with the aid of the Finletter advisory group and through a massive correspondence, he had accumulated much of the factual data and interpretative material he would need for attacks upon the administration and for the development of his own positions. Already he had gathered around him several of the key people of his campaign staff. These included, as a core group, his three law associates. Bill Blair, whose constant prodding had had no small part in keeping Stevenson's political aspirations alive, was the candidate's executive assistant. Newton Minow handled most of the law work in the firm while his colleagues became absorbed in politics, but he also served the candidate as a valued special assistant. W. Willard Wirtz began to function as head of the growing research and writing staff. Characteristically, this role, played in '52 by Carl McGowan, was not specifically assigned to Wirtz by Stevenson at the outset. The younger man assumed it and was even forced sometimes to defend it in subtle power struggles against newly recruited men who, being themselves without clear and definite status, sought to make places for themselves close to the throne.

The campaign plan called for the development, in the months immediately ahead, of a "reservoir of words," a reservoir which could be drawn upon at will and need during the late summer and the fall of the following year. It would contain not only full speech texts on all the basic issues, but also "appropriate language" for all manner of special occasions.[1] Thus would be avoided the nerve-racking travail through which speeches had been born in the nick of time all through the campaign of 1952. Thus would be promoted the Stevenson concept of campaigns as "democratic dialogues," processes whereby the public was educated in the public's business and the final choices were made, not between competing personalities ("A Presidential campaign ought not to be a popularity contest," said Stevenson repeatedly), but between the principles and proposals that the candidates expressed.

The major targets of Stevenson fire had already been selected. They radiated like spokes from a wheel whose hub was the alleged domination of government by big business. It was the business community that determined the nation's fiscal policy, which in turn affected national defense, which in turn influenced the bluff-and-backdown diplomacy. It was the business community's hostility to public power, its primary commitment to personal monetary profit, that determined the administration's view of the TVA as creeping socialism, incited the give-away (as Democrats called it) of natural resources in the public domain, and caused the government to make haste very slowly indeed in the development of atomic energy for productive uses. It was the business community's faith in the automatic beneficence of a free market—provided this market was not defined in such a way as to reduce protective tariffs drastically or to produce effective trust busting—that determined the administration's apparent indifference to the plight of the family-sized farm. It was the business community's awareness that its concepts of government would prove vastly unpopular, if frankly stated, that determined the duplicity of the administration's public relations —its substitution of vague slogans for clear ideas, its constant effort to manipulate rather than inform public opinion—and it was the business community's domination of the means of mass communications that made this duplicity effective. In general it was the business community's self-centered conservatism—its unwillingness to recognize new problems of government or to explore new paths into the future—that must cause the Eisenhower years to be regarded in history as an era of missed chances for greatness, of lost opportunities to make giant strides toward a world of material abundance and permanent creative peace.

The process was encouraged by the fact that there were still two Republican parties, the Old Guard and the so-called liberal wing. Eisenhower was the symbol of the latter, but in actual practice he continuously appeased the former, with the result that virtually every proposal, particularly in foreign affairs, was flawed by inner contradictions that made it ineffective if not actually dangerous to the general welfare.

So it was that the Stevenson men defined their political targets, and these were the terms by which their political ammunition was shaped. But it must be reiterated, as Stevenson himself reiterated, that the central theme of the proposed campaign was in no sense a hostility to the business community per se. Far less than some of his advisers was Stevenson inclined to attack big business as in itself a force inimical to our free institutions. What he did deplore, with increasing insistence, was the tendency to fuse big business and big government in such a way that business interests became the principal if not the sole determinant of major federal policies. He deplored the basic assumptions from which this tendency proceeded. In an article entitled "My Faith in Democratic Capitalism," published in *Fortune*, October, 1955, he said that a great respect for "the concept of 'rugged individualism' (usually incorporated) is no warrant for the illusion that modern America was *created* by businessmen." Rather was it created "in a complex collaboration whereby the Federal government offered to individuals the best soil and nurture for enlightened capitalism ever devised." A vast program of internal improvements, paid for by taxpayers, had opened the frontier and moved it westward; tariffs had protected infant industries and now subsidized established ones, if generally to the detriment of world economic health; cheap public power had stimulated private enterprise in the Tennessee Valley and the Northwest; federal irrigation projects had transformed deserts into privately owned farms; and "much of the newspaper and magazine industry is carried by the taxpayer through the government's massive subsidy of second-class mail." Clearly there had always been an "interaction" and there must in our technological age be an ever closer "interdependence" of business and government, but for that very reason we must, said Stevenson, be careful not to confuse the functions of business with those of government. He suggested that we "think in terms of a doctrine of 'separation of powers' in this area of business and government relations—a separation resembling the constitutional differentiation between the executive, the legislative, and the judicial in the government itself. . . . Although commercial interests and national interests can and usually do walk a certain distance hand in hand, no full identity between them can ever be forced, and any attempt to force it would be apt to end in misery, or disaster, or both—and for both."

Addressing a University of Texas audience in late September of '55, he spoke of twentieth-century America as a "unique partnership between governmental and private enterprise, a mixed economy which is the despair of doctrinaire reactionaries as it is of doctrinaire radicals. . . .

Slowly, sometimes painfully, [he went on] most of us have come to realize that mass production implies mass consumption, and that mass consumption in a free economy requires mass purchasing power. . . . To achieve a market whose demand keeps pace with an ever-expanding supply, we have used the power of representative government in several creative ways. Through graduated income taxes, through public works, through encouragement of labor unions and collective bargaining, through slum clearance and public housing, through the protection of the public domain, through the policy of equal treatment for the farmer —through these and other public measures we have helped to make our way to our present power and abundance. . . .

But as party politician Stevenson was not loath to point out, little of the creative partnership he praised had been achieved under Republican administrations. The great gains had been made under Democratic admin- istrations—those of Wilson, Roosevelt, Truman; during the 1920's, when key figures in the Republican administration openly proclaimed that govern- ment's primary purpose was to aid business, federal policies had contributed largely and directly to the most dangerous economic collapse in our history. "The Republican party has stood traditionally for an isolationist foreign pol- icy, high tariffs, and other business subsidies," he asserted in an address to the Democratic State Convention in Green Bay, Wisconsin, October 7, 1955. "It has opposed most efforts of government to regulate business abuses, to conserve natural resources, to assure the growth of cooperatives, the develop- ment of cheap power, and the growth of organized labor." The reason for this was that the Republican party, which in Lincoln's day had been "the party of a single, compelling moral idea" had become "essentially the party of a single economic interest. . . . The Democratic party, on the other hand, has grown from many different groups and interests" and of it "there has been no dominance by any single interest." The nature of Democracy required that "the shaping of party policy" be "a process of reconciling dis- cordant and often contradictory interests," with the result that the party had "an extraordinary record of accomplishment, of doing things for the first time, of serving . . . the general welfare."

This Green Bay speech was illustrative of the manner, the attitudes with which Stevenson then faced the approaching campaign. Its central theme was farm policy, and during its preparation Stevenson was under severe pressure to endorse a return by the federal government to rigid high-price supports for basic crops, thus repudiating the flexible supports adopted by the administration.

The administration argument was that high supports added to the mount- ing farm surplus and for that reason must reduce rather than increase farm income over the long run—but behind this argument lurked the belief that, due to the impact of technology on agriculture, there were now too many farmers and that a reduction in the farm subsidy, a greater reliance on the allegedly free market, would have the beneficial effect of reducing the number of farm units while increasing their average size. Both the stated argument and the unspoken belief were challenged by some of Stevenson's advisers. There was no clear evidence, they argued, that high supports were in any way responsible for the farm surplus, but there was considerable evidence that a reduction in support payments meant a further reduction in farm incomes at a time when those incomes, amid a booming industrial economy, were already dangerously low. No doubt this would further reduce the number of farmers, and perhaps this reduction might be justified if one's sole criterion of value was economic (though of this last there was no firm assurance). But was cold economics the sole valid criterion? Were not aesthetic and moral values concerned in the preservation of the family farm? Might not a considerable farm subsidy be justified on the ground that the family farm—farming as a way of life—was a strand of diversity we needed to retain in an increasingly uniform cultural pattern?

Thus the arguments and counterarguments, thus the opposing value judgments, that played upon Stevenson's mind. Concerning them, his mind was by no means made up. He was very sure that high rigid supports provided no real solution to the farm problem. He was unsure of their effect on surpluses, prices, and incomes. He had as yet no creative agricultural proposals of his own to make. He therefore resisted the pressures toward even a tentative and temporary endorsement of rigid supports. Instead, at Green Bay, he criticized the method "by which prices have been supported in the past, and which the Republicans adopted. . . ." He said that "we must explore new techniques" and mentioned "such devices as production payments" and the "temporary or permanent withdrawal" of some land from grain production, not only to reduce overproduction but also to conserve soil. Many of Stevenson's political advisers fumed. Why, in these circumstances, ignore the one clear vote-getting issue the Democrats then possessed? The odds against Stevenson's victory over Eisenhower seemed great enough without adding to them through a misguided perfectionism.

In reply, Stevenson counseled patience. The election was more than a year away. There was time enough to prepare a full-length exposition of the farm problem, with reasoned conclusions concerning it—an exposition giving full weight to those moral and aesthetic values which his materialistic-minded opponents seemed wholly to ignore.

II

Indeed, the definition of these latter values, not only in the farm problem but in every other political issue of our time, might well prove to be the central, unifying theme of the campaign Stevenson then foresaw. Perhaps he could develop the basic philosophic issue, which he had vaguely mentioned to an out-of-town friend the preceding March.

Certainly a nagging sense of this issue, a felt need to clarify it, permeated all his thinking about specific, practical matters that autumn. "Technology, while adding daily to our physical ease, throws daily another loop of wire around our souls," he wrote in his *Fortune* article of October. "It contributes hugely to our mobility, which we must not confuse with freedom. The extensions of our senses, which we find so fascinating, are not adding to the discriminations of our minds, since we need increasingly to take the reading of a needle on a dial to discover whether we think something is good or bad, right or wrong." He had no doubt that America's material standard of living would continue to rise. "But spiritually, morally, and politically, I don't think we are doing too well." We need "a renewed understanding that the essence of our material power is a moral commitment whose maintenance against hostile outside pressures, and against our own inward corruption by the very power we wield, is our greatest mission as a people," he said at the University of Texas in late September.[2]

But as he thought along these lines, he might come to recognize, as others who closely watched him recognized, a profound irony of American history —an irony in which his own career was involved and by which his ultimate political fate might be determined.

Here was a country that had been born of revolution and dedicated to the proposition that all men are created free and equal. It was a country committed to the belief that the individual human life is sacred and is the center and measure of all value. Its central political documents asserted over and over again, in various forms, that individual human beings are (in Kant's phrase) to be considered always as ends, never as means; and its political vocabulary centered on such words as "liberty," "freedom," "private enterprise," "self-reliance," "individualism." Yet as one surveyed the history of this country, one seemed to discern its dominant economic genius as a flat contradiction of individualism. It was a genius for planning and administering vast organization in which the individual played a sharply defined and limited role—a genius, one might say, for mass production and mass consumption—and as such its natural tendency was to regard the individual as *always* a means, *never* an end.

In his Texas speech Stevenson referred to the inventive career of Eli Whitney as a kind of portrait-in-little of the process by which American enterprise, believing itself to be rooted in "rugged individualism," generated an economic environment in which such individualism became impossible. Having contracted to supply ten thousand muskets to the United States Government within the unheard-of period of two years, Whitney proposed (as he said) "to substitute correct and effective operations of machinery for that skill of the artist which is acquired by long experience." He proceeded to do so in the armory he established near New Haven. "And so," said Stevenson, the system of manufacturing standardized interchangeable parts through a division of labor and the use of machines came into existence, to be followed by the assembly-line techniques of mass production which men like Henry Ford later applied with such huge success to industry in general. . . . Since the success of Whitney's armory, individual human skills, whether manual or mental, have become steadily less important to the actual work of producing goods. Machines took over. Organization took over. Routine took over. And they continue to take over with a frightening speed as we move into the age of automation—an age in which accounting and even the administration or direction of work is increasingly usurped by electronic brains.

The America which Whitney foreshadowed and helped to create, Stevenson went on, was one in which "the shoemaker, the ironmonger, the gunsmith, the miller, the butcher, the merchant, was with increasing frequency not an individual but a corporation whose 'personality' was a legal fiction."

And surely a dangerous ambiguity was compounded by this application of the concepts and vocabulary of individual liberty to giant institutions and organizations! Surely only a species of totalitarian tyranny could result, ultimately, from the notion that the Declaration of Independence applied to U.S. Steel and General Motors, guaranteeing to these the fundamental human rights of "life, liberty and the pursuit of happiness"! Such a tyranny might come silently, imperceptibly, through the gradual growth of a single-minded control over industry, merchandising, and the agencies of mass communication. The communications control might then be used to transform human persons into bundles of conditioned reflexes, drowning their unique integrities in a dead sea of statistical averages. Consistent with this would be the rise of a new kind of ideal human—the "well-adjusted personality" perfectly balanced on dead center, whose "mind" was a barometer of social pressures, whose "decisions" were yieldings to such pressures, and whose appetite for economic goods was insatiable.

Neither Stevenson nor any responsible contemporary historian would argue that America had as yet come all the way to this sorry pass, but they might agree that there was a strong tendency in this direction. Stevenson had protested against it in his address at the Smith College commencement in early June. He deplored the theory of education which had as a "paramount aim" the production of citizens "who can fit painlessly into the social pattern. . . . While I am not in favor of maladjustment," he went on, "I view this cultivation of neutrality, this breeding of mental neuters, this hostility to eccentricity and controversy, with grave misgiving. . . . [We] need not just 'well-adjusted,' 'well-balanced' personalities, not just better groupers and conformers (to casually coin a couple of fine words) but more idiosyncratic, unpredictable characters (that rugged frontier word 'ornery' occurs to me). . . ." [3] In this as in other addresses he reiterated his belief that human freedom was, ironically, threatened by the very progress that had resulted from a resurgence of human freedom during the Renaissance. By promoting an ever narrower economic specialization and an ever closer interdependence of specialities, an advancing technology drove hard "toward that extreme of machine state in which individual freedom is wholly submerged." The drive could be halted only by a renewed emphasis upon, and perhaps a new definition of, the ends—the human, personal, spiritual ends—that all eeonomic devices should serve.

Nor could Stevenson be unaware that he was far from alone in regarding the essential political issue between himself and Eisenhower to be precisely this of human freedom. To many thoughtful observers the very contrast between the two men as personalities seemed to define this issue. Stevenson, the heir of a family tradition intertwined with American history, was essentially an historical person; Eisenhower was the product wholly of his time and immediate experience, essentially ahistorical. Stevenson's formal education had been classical and general, with a major emphasis on the humanities; Eisenhower's had been highly specialized, a technical training through which he had no effective exposure to the humanities. Stevenson was, in philosophic bent, an idealist who tested the truth of an idea by its consistency with other true ideas; Eisenhower was a pragmatist whose test of truth was whether or not an idea worked toward some practical end in the immediate situation which called it forth. Stevenson's natural tendency was to view each moment as part of a continuous flow of time from past into future, and to deal with it in terms of a planned pattern of action and principle; Eisenhower in his farewell to the students of Columbia University, in January of 1953, had advised his hearers not to "plan anything too carefully" because "in this life, you don't know what's around the corner." (More important than a plan, said he, was an attitude of "confidence— confidence that you can meet the problem of the day as it comes up.")

The issue thus defined in mid-twentieth-century America was consistent with that which had divided Jefferson and Hamilton at the very beginning of our national experience, but it differed from this not only in the concrete terms in which it was expressed but also, and primarily, in its psychological mood. In one real sense, the basic issue of 1952, and of the upcoming campaign as then discerned, seemed actually to be psychological in that it was an opposition of that which was active to that which was passive in the American spirit. It seemed to present a choice—an as yet far from clear choice—between a major emphasis on the values derived from physical sensation and a major emphasis on values derived from inwardness. One party seemed to insist that Americans must be "otherdirected," * the other party seemed to insist that Americans be "inner-

* The phrases "other-" and "inner-directed" were made famous by *The Lonely Crowd*, David Reisman (Yale University Press, 1950).

directed," and John Mason Brown, in an unusually perceptive essay on the '52 campaign,[4] remarked how this difference was expressed in the very phrases that the two Presidential candidates used "automatically" in their speeches, and even in the hand gestures that the two made toward their audiences. Stevenson, noted Brown, was constantly saying in his speeches, "This reminds me," or "I am reminded by," while Eisenhower "when making a serious point, was apt to say 'I am told' or 'Someone told me.'" When Eisenhower waved to crowds he made sweeping gestures, his arms held straight out; Stevenson "tended to keep his elbows at his sides and to make tentative, half-finished gestures." Brown further noted that the center of the famous Eisenhower smile was his mouth whereas the center of Stevenson's smile was his eyes.

But though the issue of human freedom seemed to Stevenson real and basic, though he longed to clarify and present it concretely, he was well aware of the difficulty of translating it into effective vote-getting terms.

Once an adviser submitted to him a memorandum arguing that a major full-length speech should be addressed to the "new suburbia," whose citizens were notoriously civic-minded without being in any sense politically minded, who depended wholly upon the standard agencies of mass communication for their national and international information, and who (mistakenly, as the memorandist said) identified their political interests with those controlling the Republican party.[5] A rather smug materialistic complacency seemed to mark the people of suburbia, but beneath this, the memorandum argued, lay a deepening discontent—vague but powerful. These people had more and more leisure time and more and more gadgets with which to kill it, yet their lives, as they themselves felt in their moments of reality, were strangely empty of purpose and meaning. They were "spiritually unemployed...."

The phrase interested Stevenson. Economic unemployment had been the great problem of the 1930's. Was spiritual unemployment the great problem of the 50's? "By all means write that speech," he said, "and we'll see what can be done with it." It might fit well into the "New America" theme, which was vaguely shaping itself in his mind and through which he hoped to stir the imaginations and arouse the highest aspirations of his countrymen.

III

Then, with that total unexpectedness which (in Eisenhower's view) militated against planning anything "too carefully," there occurred an event that drastically transformed the nature of the coming campaign, setting at nought all of Stevenson's pre-convention plans.

On Friday, September 23, 1955, the President of the United States, on vacation in Denver, Colorado, played twenty-seven holes of golf at a Denver country club. That night, or early in the morning of Saturday the twenty-fourth, he suffered a heart attack and was taken from the house of his mother-in-law, Mrs. John S. Doud, to Fitzsimmons General Hospital. Major General Howard McC. Snyder, the White House physician, diagnosed the attack as a coronary thrombosis or blood-clot injury to the heart tissues.

The immediate and virtually unanimous conclusion of politicians and the general public was that Eisenhower, though he might complete his first term, would certainly not seek a second one. A concomitant of this was the probability that a Democrat would be the next President of the United States and that his party would score decisive victories in the '56 congressional and gubernatorial races. Certainly the financial community was convinced, in the immediate aftermath of Eisenhower's illness, that the President's political career had come to an end and that without him their party could not retain control of the executive branch. On Monday, September 26, the stock market broke with a computed loss of more than $12 billions—a loss second only to that of October 28, 1929.

It might be thought that this turn of events—apart from the natural human sympathy for a dangerously ill man—would cause secret jubilation in the Stevenson office. On the contrary, it caused a considerable measure of consternation and not a little dismay, particularly among those who were concerned with campaign research and writing. Every strategic calculation was thrown awry; every tactical concept must be revised. There was even a feeling, expressed by Wirtz among others, that the President's illness, if he made a satisfactory recovery from it, might prove to be of a piece with the famous "Eisenhower luck," since it would remove him, for months at least, from the area of effective critical fire. For the time being, no direct attacks could be made upon him. "And just when we were getting him within our sights!" said Wirtz.[6] Stevenson himself had looked forward to a sharply defined battle and deplored the fact that this new event must aid Republican strategists in the obscuring of real issues, the divorcement of the President from responsibility for the unpopular elements of his administration. As for the possibility of any deep philosophic exploration of the historic issue, this too, it soon appeared, was drastically reduced if not actually destroyed.

For it was soon clear that Stevenson's relationship to his own party had been changed. Theretofore he had been assured by mutual friends of his and Kefauver's that the Tennessee senator would probably not seriously challenge his candidacy, while Harriman had placed himself solidly, unequivocally in the Stevenson camp. But soon Harriman was saying, with that slyness that caused some to dub him "Honest Ave the Hairsplitter," that while he was still "for" Stevenson, he was not necessarily "for him for President." ("What does he think I'm running for, county coroner?" asked

Stevenson, who, though he laughed, was wounded by this defection of a man whom he had regarded as among the firmest of his political friends.) Soon Harry Truman was letting it be known that he favored an "open" convention. Whereupon it appeared that Kefauver would again become an active candidate, laying plans for a formal announcement and a campaign for pledged convention delegates through the state primaries, such as he had waged in 1952.

It is possible that Stevenson, had he anticipated the intraparty struggle that now loomed, would have made a decision concerning his own candidacy different from that he had made a few months before. He indicated as much to Newton Minow when the two flew back from Texas following the university speech there on September 28. "Lyndon Johnson has been telling me I'll have to enter some primaries," Stevenson said. "What do you think?" Minow gave as his opinion that "of course" Stevenson would have to do so, now that the Democratic nomination was so obviously a prize any politician might covet. Stevenson shook his head and looked out the plane window upon the vast land he aspired to govern, and said, half sighing, that he certainly hadn't counted on this.[7]

He had been at great pains to make sure that he was the dominant choice of his party before he definitely committed himself to the battle. The kind of campaigning required of candidates in Presidential primaries seemed to him demeaning of the candidates and unworthy of the high office toward which the campaigns aimed. The lack of uniform primary laws among the states (only nineteen states chose convention delegates in primaries), plus the effective presence of local factors unrelated to the national situation, seemed to him to make the primary results virtually unintelligible as guides to convention action. Moreover, in the present situation, Stevenson had everything to lose and nothing to gain by what would certainly prove to be a long, hard struggle, as expensive of his physical and mental stamina as of his campaign treasury. The governor of New York, Harriman, could justly say that he was unable to engage in a primary struggle; having made known his availability, he might stand on the side lines and pick up the prize, painlessly, effortlessly, if Kefauver succeeded in fighting Stevenson to a standstill.

But at this juncture Stevenson was no longer a free agent in the political arena. Hundreds of people had already invested money, time, and effort in his cause, numerous staff commitments had been made, and he could not in honor forsake them even if he would. Nor would he have done so had the possibility of doing so been wholly honorable. Though a peaceable man, he had never shrunk in fear from a fight and his fighting spirit was roused by allegations that he wanted glory handed to him on a silver platter. He remained convinced that of all available party leaders, he was best equipped to win the prize and use it in the service of the general welfare—and though he would never say so, he must have been convinced that he had earned the nomination, if anyone in the party had done so, through the effort he had made in '52 and the victories he had helped to gain in '54. Accordingly, albeit reluctantly, he revised his strategy and changed his posture to face the new situation. A first instance of this occurred in mid-October when, to counteract the effect of a forthcoming speech of Harriman's in Des Moines, he issued a statement favoring price supports of basic farm crops at ninety percent of parity. He did so only after it became clear that the rights and interests of many other people to whom he felt obligated would be harmed by his failure to do so; and he flinched a bit, displaying an irritable resentment toward some of his staff, when the opposition promptly hurled at him the charge of cheap political expediency.

Far more in character for him was the long-scheduled address he delivered a few weeks later, on November 11, during a Woodrow Wilson Centennial celebration at the University of Virginia. It would be the last, for many months, of the kind of foreign policy review, on historical principles, he liked best to make. Subsequent events would bestow upon it an historical interest.

He referred to the violence that for five years had been "mounting ... along the armistice lines" between Israel and her hostile Arab neighbors. "Unless these clashes cease there is danger of all-out war developing while we debate which side was aggressor," he said, insisting that a "major effort of statesmanship is required if we are to avert ... disaster in this troubled area." Vital interests of the United States, the structure of the Western alliance against communism, the very existence of the United Nations were threatened by the "recent arms deal between Egypt and Russia," together with our failure to assure Israel of "an equitable balance of armed strength"— for the "Middle East has long been an area of Russian ambitions." While "we do not want to see an arms race in this area," neither side should feel "that it lives by the grace of its none-too-kindly neighbor. ... We must help, if need be, to counteract any Soviet attempt to upset ... [a] balance, and we must make it emphatically clear that the status quo shall not be changed by force."

But this was only the negative side of his proposal. It seemed to him that "we have shown little initiative within or outside the United Nations in devising measures to prevent these clashes," and this despite the fact that one device for doing so was clearly indicated. "After years of experience it would seem evident that the only way to avoid bloodshed and violence along the border is to keep the troops of these antagonists apart," he said. "And I wonder if United Nations guards could not undertake patrol duties in the areas of tension and collision. Certainly both sides would respect United Nations patrols where they do not trust each other."

Writing these sentences, Stevenson had had high hopes that his suggestion, striking fire from American imaginations, would spark the administration into a realistic, clearly defined Middle Eastern policy. It did cause some excitement among those who were convinced that a minimal world government was indispensable to genuine world peace. A long step might be taken in that direction, these people felt, if UN troops could be recruited, not as national units, but as individual volunteers owing allegiance only to the UN flag, and in numbers sufficient to enforce UN laws in areas where those laws were violated. But in general, as Stevenson ruefully admitted a few weeks later, his idea dropped quietly into the pool of national complacency, disappearing with scarcely a ripple.[8] Far from facing the realities of the Middle Eastern crisis, the administration continued to address the Egyptian dictator, Colonel Nasser, in a language of threat-and-bribe that was self-defeating, while Israel, Britain, and France—acutely aware of the meaning of Soviet Middle Eastern penetration—grew daily more desperate.

As for Stevenson, he was by then in no position to lead a loyal opposition to policies which, as he told his friends again and again, were creating a dangerous power vacuum in the Middle East. By then he was engaged in an intraparty fight for his political life.

IV

To reassure himself as to his fitness for the coming ordeal, Stevenson early in November had entered Passavant Hospital in Chicago for a comprehensive physical examination, supervised by Dr. Leander W. Riba. As if to counteract the politico-medical reports then issuing in a steady stream from Eisenhower's physicians, Dr. Riba told a reporter that Stevenson, upon examination, proved to be "in perfect health" with "far better than normal endurance for a man at his age." Heart, blood pressure, lungs, urinary tract, nervous system—all these were in excellent condition. His weight was "entirely satisfactory at 180 pounds." Stevenson had, said his doctor, a tremendous chest expansion—"nearly five inches between inspiration and expiration" —and had "legs on him like an ox." His arms were "well-muscled, too. . . . His health is better than at any time during the three years I have known him," the doctor concluded. "I was very agreeably surprised at how far within normal limits his tests fell."

The candidacy was formally announced on November 15. "In partnership with our friends and allies, with confidence born of strength and influence born of magnanimity, we must work to uproot the causes of conflict and tensions and to outlaw the very means of war in this atomic age," said Stevenson's announcement statement. "The task of the Democratic party is to make 'peace and prosperity' not just a political slogan but an active search for a better America and a better world. I am ready to do what

I can to that end either as a worker in the ranks or at the top of my ticket if my party sees fit so to honor me." Next day, at a press conference in Chicago, he announced several major appointments to his staff.

The campaign manager was to be James A. Finnegan, an early adherent of the initial "draft-Stevenson" movement in '52. A short, gray-haired Irishman born in Philadelphia in 1906, Finnegan had been administrative assistant to former Senator William J. Myers and had been chairman of the Democratic County Executive Committee of Philadelphia from 1948 to 1952, during which time Philadelphia elected its first Democratic mayor in sixty-seven years. He was president of the Philadelphia City Council and secretary of the Commonwealth of Pennsylvania. Stevenson found him hard-working and efficient, "politically adroit and sophisticated, unusually effective in his handling of local politicians but with sound, informed judgment, too, on overall issues." A man of gentle manner and even temper, he was greatly liked by the staff.

Finnegan's second-in-command was the executive director of the campaign committee, Hyman B. Raskin, a law partner of Stephen Mitchell's and a former deputy chairman of the Democratic National Committee. Born in 1909, Raskin was a big man with prematurely white hair, who worked well and effectively with Finnegan. Harry Ashmore, editor of the Arkansas *Gazette*, was a special assistant who played an important role during the primary campaign, particularly during its early weeks, returning to his newspaper in June of '56, after the last primary had been held. Mrs. Edison Dick and Barry Bingham served as co-chairmen of the National Stevenson for President Committee, with Archibald S. Alexander as that organization's executive director; their task was to recruit, organize, and direct the activities of Volunteers for Stevenson. Roger Tubby, former press officer of the Department of State and assistant press secretary in the White House for President Truman, became Stevenson's press secretary, a fact which initially caused widespread newspaper comment, since Tubby resigned from Harriman's staff in Albany, New York,* to accept the Stevenson assignment. Tubby's assistant was C. K. McClatchy, a young man who proved unusually efficient as facilitating officer to newspapermen who followed the primary campaign.

Stevenson, at this first press conference, also said he would call upon Stephen Mitchell and Wilson Wyatt for "continuous advice and counsel." He then made headline news by announcing his entrance into the Minnesota primary, to be held March 20. This, he said, was the only "firm decision" he had made with respect to primaries. "The others we will consider as we come to them."

During the question period he was asked if he expected Eisenhower to

* Tubby's Albany assignment was in public relations for the New York Commerce Commission, but he had close working contacts with the governor's office.

be his opponent. "I hadn't thought so," he replied, "but I read in the papers that his recovery is rapid and encouraging, and that there are those who believe that he may be fit to be a candidate again. That I just don't know. I can't speculate." He was asked whether, in his view, he was a "middle-of-the-road Democrat." In his reply he laughed at some of Eisenhower's favorite political slogans. "I am not one of those who believes that you can characterize a philosophy on public issues by slogans," he said. "I have never been sure what progressive conservatism means, or was it conservative progressivism? I have forgotten. And I am not sure what dynamic moderation or moderate dynamism means. I am not even sure what it means when one says he is a conservative in fiscal affairs and a liberal in human affairs. I assume what it means is that you will strongly recommend the building of a great many schools to accommodate the needs of our children, but not provide the money."

His hostility to sloganeering of course did not prevent the use of it against himself and his campaign. During his address to the Democratic National Committee dinner, a hundred-dollar-a-plate affair on November 19, he arraigned the administration for single-interest government, stressing the farm, public power, and foreign policy issues. Truman promptly termed it the "best fighting New Deal speech" he had ever heard Stevenson give. But in the midst of it Stevenson said: "I agree that it is a time for catching our breath; I agree that moderation is the spirit of the times. But we best take care lest we confuse moderation with mediocrity, or settle for half-answers to hard problems." Next day Governor G. Mennen Williams of Michigan assailed Stevenson's "policy" of "moderation." Governor Harriman promptly announced that there "is no such word as 'moderation' or 'middle-of-the-road' in the Democratic vocabulary." Whereupon Truman discovered that he, too, was a champion of immoderation, or at least was opposed to "moderation," and had lost his initial enthusiasm for Stevenson's speech.

Thus it was made evident that Stevenson would not only have to fight for his nomination but also that, as front-runner, he faced serious problems. He who had repeatedly attacked the G.O.P. elephant as a two-headed beast now found himself the titular head of a party whose division might become as great, and as hampering to decisive government, as that separating the Republican Old Guard from the so-called Eisenhower wing. He must establish and hold firm positions from which he could withstand fire from the left of his party, directed by Northern liberals, and fire from the right, directed by Southern conservatives, and he must do so in ways which would recommend him to the great mass of independent voters upon whose decision depended the outcome in November. The only alternative to this was a decision to write off the South, as Truman had done in 1948, and run as a candidate of the Northern Democracy. The latter alternative was that chosen, in effect, by Harriman-Kefauver supporters, and it was here that the real issue lay between them and Stevenson in the struggle for control of the convention.

The split between the two regions had been greatly deepened by a unanimous decision of the U.S. Supreme Court, on May 17, 1954, declaring racial segregation in public schools to be unconstitutional. It had not been lessened by a decision on May 31, 1955, which assigned local authorities the task of integrating the schools and instructed federal courts to enforce "a prompt and reasonable start" toward integration, with the proviso that "additional time" be allowed where required by local conditions. "Good faith" was to be a major test of compliance with the law. In six Southern states this ruling was openly defied by officials who denied that the Supreme Court had the authority to make it, and the violent disagreement on this point exacerbated every other difference between Southern conservatives and those liberals who were convinced that Southern congressional leadership since 1954 had played directly into Eisenhower's hands, immensely strengthening the administration as it approached the new election.

On December 16 Estes Kefauver announced his candidacy, promising a "vigorous campaign" through the primaries—and as the Christmas season came on, Stevenson knew that he could not avoid a head-on collision with the Tennessee senator in at least one primary and probably in several. His decisive defeat in any of these could, and probably would, cost him the nomination.

To his political concerns that Christmas was added a tragic personal concern.

On the morning of December 21 a car driven by nineteen-year-old John Fell Stevenson, on his way home from Harvard for the holidays, was struck head on by a truck on a railroad overpass near Goshen, Indiana. With him were three Harvard friends, two of them Chicago boys who had been intimates of his since childhood. These two, William S. North, III, and William C. Boyden, Jr., were instantly killed, while the third youth, riding in the back seat, suffered minor injuries. John Fell himself suffered a shattered kneecap which was subsequently removed, lost a number of teeth, and was badly cut and bruised. Adlai Stevenson learned of this when he arrived in his office that morning, his greatest relief from the pain of that dark hour being the firm assurance that his son was in no sense to blame for the accident: the truck had been passing another and its driver was soon indicted for reckless driving and involuntary homicide. Stevenson promptly flew to Goshen in a chartered plane, returning in an ambulance to Passavant Hospital in Chicago with his son.

One of the first of the sympathy messages that poured in upon him was from the President of the United States, and to this Stevenson replied in longhand: "I am deeply grateful for your most thoughtful and kind message about John Fell; and he was at first incredulous and then profoundly impressed and grateful too!" John Fell joined in the thanks, said Stevenson, "with all the emphasis a cracked jaw permits!" He spoke of the grave concern they all felt for the parents of the dead boys, and it was to this that he referred most emphatically in the form reply he was at last forced to prepare as the inpouring messages became a flood. Wrote he: "Your message of sympathy for John Fell was very kind and very helpful. While his body is recovering rapidly, the spirit will be slower to mend. But faith and love are healing powers, and there is a great reservoir of both in the world. . . . Our greater anxiety is that the families of his beloved friends will be given the strength to live through and beyond this tragedy."

Inevitably Stevenson was reminded of the great tragedy of his own childhood, the death of Ruth Merwin. In early January he drove with a friend from his farm to the Deerpath station. The friend asked how John Fell was getting along.[9]

"Oh, fine," Stevenson replied. "He's been released from the hospital."

"Will he have a permanent limp?"

"No, he won't be crippled at all. It looked at first as though he would be, but the doctors say he'll make a complete recovery." Then Stevenson glanced away and went on, in a different tone, "That is, a complete physical recovery. Of course—a thing like this, it leaves scars on the spirit. They'll always be there."

CHAPTER TWENTY-SEVEN

IF a man's character is his fate, it becomes so in terms of the environment through which it must express itself, and in the politics of the Eisenhower years the dominant environmental condition seemed to be a fog of ambiguity whereby men and issues became badly blurred. They were blurred not only in the popular view but also in themselves, as though the fog dissolved all essential definitions.

Such, it might seem, was one lesson demonstrated by Stevenson's struggle in 1956 for the Presidency of the United States. Four years before, as a drafted candidate of the party in power, he had projected a public image of himself which was true to his essential character. He had gone down in defeat. In 1956, as a challenged candidate of a party out of power, he seemed required by the spirit of the times to present to the public a new Stevenson, one that blurred the image he had projected theretofore. Having suffered a nearly disastrous reverse as the "Old" Stevenson, he scored a series of tactical victories in his new form, but in the end he went down to a defeat worse than that of 1952 and one for which the blurring of his image seemed in some part responsible.

Some among his immediate staff would assert that this new Stevenson was wholly a public relations myth invented by correspondents. Stevenson in '56 did nothing that he had not done in '52, they would claim; newsmen simply shifted their emphasis as they reported his activities, stressing in '56 elements they had largely ignored in '52.[1] But no close objective observer would be likely to agree with this. Stevenson himself seemed to shift emphasis sufficiently to create a new public self as an overlay of the old.

He did not do so easily. Only with great reluctance, and only a step at a time, did he abandon his dream of a '56 campaign which would be in every way an improvement, as a contribution to the "democratic dialogue," over that he had conducted four years before. Particularly was he reluctant to abandon those attacks upon the administration's conduct of foreign affairs, which he had conceived to be a principal element of his struggle for power; he was convinced that foreign policy was by far the most crucial of the real issues facing the American people, one fraught with the gravest dangers to the republic and to the world. As late as November 17, James Reston of *The New York Times* was reporting "talk" of Stevenson's "going abroad early in 1956 so that he can study some of the problems first hand and keep his campaign stocked with fresh themes."

At that time the Minnesota primary, as we have seen, was the only one Stevenson had definitely decided to enter, and it seemed unlikely that Kefauver would challenge him there, since Senator Hubert Humphrey, Governor Orville Freeman, and a Democratic farmer-labor organization which was reputedly one of the most effective state organizations in the nation were solidly supporting the Stevenson candidacy. Subsequently it became clear that Kefauver could hurt Stevenson's chances merely by making a good showing in Minnesota (no one, Kefauver included, thought he had a chance actually to defeat Stevenson there), whereupon Kefauver filed. Thus was scheduled the first of three major battles between the senator and Stevenson, the other two being the Florida primary on May 8 and the California one on June 5.

Even then Stevenson made no serious effort to match Kefauver's expenditure of time and energy in Minnesota. He had a personal distaste for the kind of folksy, handshaking, coonskin-cap campaigning that Estes Kefauver so assiduously practiced. This was not because he had a contempt for the average voter and disliked to associate with him. On the contrary, it was precisely because he had so high a respect for people as individuals, so high an opinion of the intelligence of the electorate at large, that he hated to deal with them as mere elements in an emotion-ridden mass of flesh. He wanted to communicate with people as individuals, each with a mind of his own. Assembly-line handshaking seemed to him a travesty of this process: surely one who aspired to the highest office in the world should be primarily concerned to touch minds rather than flesh. Hence, in those early weeks, he confined himself for the most part to large meetings before which he could present prepared addresses.

In one of these addresses, given in February, he reasserted those principles which had animated his '52 campaign and whose half-defiant, rather self-righteous expression seemed to some of his advisers unfortunate in his present circumstances. "I shall try in these coming months to fool no one, including myself," he said, "—not with slogans or false promises or easy answers to hard problems. . . . I must add frankly to what I've said about myself that it is quite possible that I would not be the best candidate for you, if winning is the first objective of any political race, because I have an allergy for false promises. . . . I am told that promises . . . are indispensable to victory and that keeping them is far less important than making them. Well, I don't agree." When he prepared these remarks he was campaigning more arduously in Minnesota than he had originally planned to do, but far less arduously than Finnegan wanted him to do—and a campaign manager might be forgiven for believing that, no matter what the candidate said, the first objective of the race *was* victory and that victory was by no means as certain as the candidate seemed to believe.

Not until the New Hampshire primary of mid-March did Stevenson have a premonition of disaster. Though he was not entered in that primary and had not campaigned there, whereas Kefauver was formally entered and had shaken most of the Democratic hands in the state, Stevenson was encouraged by his supporters to expect a large write-in vote for himself. When this vote was not forthcoming, Stevenson confessed to his staff that he now "worried" a little about Minnesota.

On the evening of March 20 he had as his dinner guest at Libertyville his long-time friend, George Ball, who had been associated with him in the Sidley law firm, was now a partner in a New York and Washington law firm, and would serve after the convention as Stevenson's director of public relations. After dinner the two men sat before the fireplace in the living room, listening to the Minnesota returns. A few hours later they were joined by Mr. and Mrs. Willard Wirtz, Mr. and Mrs. Edison Dick, and Archibald Alexander. These latecomers found a Stevenson who was "fighting mad," though his anger was of a nature peculiarly his own in that it contained remarkably little personal bitterness.* He was being licked in Minnesota.

---

* It is interesting to compare this authentic account of that evening in Libertyville, and of Stevenson's apprehensions concerning Minnesota, with the account published in *Time* magazine, April 2, 1956, under the heading "Minnesota Miracle." Said *Time:* "At his country home in Libertyville, Ill., he, Stevenson, had planned a victory party on primary night. It was to be just the kind of political gathering Stevenson likes: a black

Indeed, his defeat there was of crushing, humiliating proportions. Of Minnesota's thirty delegates Kefauver captured all but four while piling up a lead of some sixty thousand votes over Stevenson out of a total vote of a little over three hundred thousand. It seemed at once evident, and subsequent analysis proved it to be true, that Kefauver's margin of victory was largely made up of Republican votes, for Republicans were permitted by Minnesota law to vote in the Democratic primary and were encouraged to do so by Republican strategists, Eisenhower being virtually uncontested in the Republican primary and Stevenson being (as the Republican strategists believed) by far the strongest candidate the Democrats could run in November. Nevertheless Stevenson was abruptly removed from his front-running position. He must, it seemed, drastically revise his campaign strategy and tactics.

He cheerfully admitted as much next day at a large press conference, while denying emphatically that he was "through" or had any intention of withdrawing from the race. "When something like this happens, I don't feel bitter, or that an injustice has been done," said he. "I feel simply that I have failed to communicate, and that I must try harder." Asked if he now planned to shake more hands, he replied with a grin that apparently "a certain identity *is* established between shaker and shakee" when a hand is shaken.

Thereafter he ran, as he said, "like a singed cat." Gone from his prepared talks were the witticisms that had sparkled from his speeches of '52; gone was the evident reluctance to campaign for the presidency as though it were a popularity prize. The new Stevenson was bussed by pretty girls in California, donned cowboy boots in Arizona, carried a stuffed alligator and thumped a bass fiddle in Florida, and everywhere shook hands by the hundreds, the thousands. He traveled continuously from coast to coast, and into the South, giving hundreds of talks to small groups and numerous prepared addresses before large audiences.

At first he betrayed a certain self-consciousness in this unwonted role, but as time went on he gave every outward appearance of thoroughly enjoying himself. He even managed, by the manner of his playing it, to make the role at least consistent with, if not truly expressive of, his essential self. His handling of the stuffed-alligator episode was typical. The alligator was thrust unexpectedly into his hands by one of the crowd around him on a Florida

---

tie dinner (he wore a red tartan dinner jacket), with only his really good friends invited—the wealthy, intellectual, aristocratic amateurs. Among the guests were Washington lawyer George Ball, Louisville Editor (*Courier-Journal*) Barry Bingham, Chicago industrialist (duplicating machines) Edison Dick. By the time that Stevenson's sister and biographer (*My Brother Adlai*), Elizabeth Ives, arrived, Stevenson was beginning to get the news from Minnesota. 'It's lousy,' he said. 'It's just awful.' " In fact, no dinner party had been planned and Stevenson wore no dinner jacket but, instead, an old red jacket he often called his "Christmas jacket." *Time* described the press conference next day as "grim."

street. He laughed, but his laughter was a bit forced and his aides could see that he was annoyed. "What am I to do with this thing?" he muttered in an irritable aside. But as he went on down the street, he began to make extravagant gestures with the alligator, fumbling with it to indicate how it embarrassed him, laughing at the absurdity of his predicament, until, soon, the crowd was laughing uproariously in sympathy with him.

And his tactics, it seemed, paid off. Forced to play Kefauver's game, he played it with a vengeance, to the delighted astonishment of his own staff, scoring a series of minor but significant victories in Alaska, the District of Columbia, New Jersey, Illinois, and Oregon on his way to Florida, where Kefauver was reputed to have the advantage. Stevenson won Florida, too, if narrowly. And in the crucial California primary on June 5, he scored an overwhelming victory, gaining some 1,100,000 votes to 627,000 for Kefauver. In early August the Tennessee senator withdrew from the race and, resisting the blandishments of Harriman forces, threw his support to Stevenson. He also made a handsome public apology for certain unfortunate remarks he had made about his opponent in the heat of the campaign, an apology that Stevenson, who had himself said some harsh things he regretted, gratefully accepted.

Thus was Stevenson restored, on the eve of the convention, to his position as front-runner for the nomination. And thus was it decided once and for all, or so it seemed, that the Democrats would enter the Presidential race as a united party of North and South rather than of the North alone.

During this primary struggle, only two issues of national import were developed in such a way as to impress strongly the public mind. In February, before a Negro group in California, Stevenson opposed (a) the use of federal troops to force compliance with the Supreme Court's school desegregation decision and (b) an amendment to the pending school-aid bill denying federal aid to any segregated school. In so doing he used the term "gradualism" to characterize what seemed to him the proper approach to a problem with deep historical roots and one imbued with passionate prejudice. This "gradualism," in his view, should be characterized by "all reasonable speed," but the term was one particularly hated by Negro leaders, who had learned from bitter experience that it generally meant the maintenance of the status quo. Stevenson was soon impelled to issue a prepared statement in which he asserted his strong personal agreement with the Supreme Court decision while pointing out that the Court itself had

> recognized that we cannot by a stroke of the pen reverse customs and traditions that are older than the Republic. . . . Instead of establishing a fixed time limit for compliance with its decrees it has established the test of good faith as the measurement of progress in cases pending before the district courts. . . . We will not . . . reduce race prejudice by denying

to areas afflicted with it the means of improving educational standards of all their people. Certainly we will not improve the present condition or future prospects of any Negro citizen by coercive federal action that will arm the extremists and disarm the men of goodwill in the South who, with courage and patience, have already accomplished so much.

Subsequently he called repeatedly for "positive leadership" by the White House to alleviate the dangerous situation in the South, where white citizens' councils were organized to defy the Court order and where state governments embraced a doctrine of "interposition" indistinguishable from Calhoun's Union-destroying "nullification." He suggested that the President call a conference of white and Negro leaders to work out means of implementing, in fair and orderly fashion, the "law of the land." The suggestion fell on deaf ears. The President even declined to say explicitly that he personally favored the Court's decision. It didn't matter what he personally thought, said Eisenhower; the Constitution was as the Court said it was, and he was under oath to uphold the Constitution.

In April, before the American Society of Newspaper Editors, Stevenson suggested that the United States ban the further testing of hydrogen bombs, and announce the fact to the world. Such tests, he pointed out, were poisoning the earth's atmosphere with deadly strontium 90, and while there was some disagreement among scientists as to the immediacy of the danger (there were scientists who claimed that the tolerance point was being rapidly approached), there was none at all that the ultimate effect, if the tests continued, would be race suicide. Moreover, this was a disarmament move that the United States might make unilaterally, without serious risk to our national security: scientists had means of knowing immediately when and approximately where a massive atomic explosion occurred, so that if Soviet Russia tested a bomb we could promptly resume the tests ourselves if we wished to do so. In any case, the risk of the proposal was small compared to the gains the United States might make from it in the esteem of all the peoples of the earth and as a contribution to peace and sanity. But this suggestion, too, fell on deaf ears in the administration, and was initially opposed by Kefauver, though a majority of the nation's physical and biological scientists seemed to favor it strongly. Indeed, key administration spokesmen treated the proposal with contempt, indicating that it was presumptuous of Stevenson to make it to the greatest military leader of the age.

II

Meanwhile, it had become apparent that the President's heart attack, far from being a hazard to his reelection, was probably a political asset. Having passed through the valley of the shadow of death, he was now a greater hero, more beloved of the populace than before. In large part this was due to his personal qualities—to the perfection with which he expressed the dominant mood of the country and to the warm affection he personally inspired. But it was also due to a triumph of public relations engineering unprecedented in American political history, as several writers on political affairs pointed out at the time.

While the President yet lay part time in an oxygen tent, Dr. Paul Dudley White, an eminent specialist from Boston, had joined White House Press Secretary James Hagerty in a massive "Operation Candor" to publicize every phase of the sick man's recovery. Within days Dr. White announced that he saw "no medical reason" why Eisenhower should not run for reelection. When the sick man, on September 30, initialed a couple of documents, the fact received banner headlines in the nation's press. This gesture was followed by others in ever closer succession, all of them immensely publicized to indicate that the President, though he still had a long way to go for full recovery, remained in effective control of all his essential duties. On November 11, seven weeks after his attack, he was flown to Washington. November 11 happened to be Veterans' Day; parades and crowds were on Washington's streets in memory of martial events in which General Eisenhower had played so conspicuous a part. Grinning broadly and waving to the crowds, providing visible evidence of his returning health, the President announced that, according to his doctors, he would have to "ease" rather than "bulldoze" his way into a full exercise of his responsibilities, but that he felt fine. He then proceeded to his Gettysburg farm where he convalesced for several weeks, working part time in a headquarters established in the town's post office.

Long before he had returned to the White House, nearly all the nation's press and all Republican politicians were praying in chorus that he run again. And by early spring, when he announced that he would indeed run, though he might have to transfer some of his nonessential functions to his "associates" during a second term, his physical fitness for the office seemed no longer an issue of even the silent kind in the minds of most voters; public-opinion polls continued to show him the overwhelming choice of the electorate.

Whatever slight doubts may have remained concerning his health were presumably removed by a comprehensive physical examination in Walter Reed Hospital May 10 to 12. "His general condition continues good," said the vastly publicized medical report. "He is physically active and mentally alert." Among the special examinations was one of his digestive tract. "The X-ray examinations of the gastro-intestinal tract with barium studies showed a normally functioning digestive tract," the report concluded.

It was through his digestive tract, however, as the culmination of what one doctor said was an ailment of long standing, that the sixty-five-year-old

President was struck down on June 8 by his second dangerous illness within nine months. Rushed to Walter Reed Hospital, he underwent emergency surgery at two fifty-nine on the morning of June 9 to relieve obstruction of the ileum, or lower part of the small intestine.

Here, surely, was an ultimate test of Republican public relations skills. But within hours, or so it appeared to knowledgeable observers, a successful strategy had been decided upon. This strategy was to minimize the seriousness of the President's affliction and to refuse to admit that it could have any effect upon his candidacy. Eleven hours after the operation began, Major General Leonard D. Heaton, who had performed the surgery, told a jampacked news conference that he saw no medical reason why the President should not run again. A "rapid and complete recovery" was anticipated. The President should be able to resume the "full duties" of his office in four to six weeks and to play golf again by mid-August. OKAY FOR IKE TO RUN SAY DOCTORS was the standard banner headline in the nation's press that afternoon.

Thereafter, in marked contrast to the tactics following the heart attack, no press conferences at which reporters could question the doctors were held. Embarrassing questions concerning the recurrence rate of ileitis were brushed off by Press Secretary Hagerty. One Republican leader after another indicated that of course the President's decision to run remained unchanged. And while he was yet in acute misery, with a tube running through his nose, Eisenhower was reported to have "personally decided" (Hagerty stressed it as a *personal* decision) that American military leaders should not visit the Soviet Union as the Soviet government had invited them to do. Thereafter, his physical recovery was almost as rapid as Heaton had predicted while his popularity with voters, according to the polls, remained undiminished. A Gallup poll in early August showed Eisenhower to be favored by 61 percent of the voters as against 37 for Stevenson.

Awesome to all, gratifying to most, dismaying to the few who believed that a complacent and ill-informed America drifted in a dangerous world was this renewed evidence of Eisenhower's tremendous appeal to the average citizen. His popularity seemed to tower like a rock above the political seas. Every adverse argument, every citation of adverse evidence, seemed to break futilely against it. Stevenson and his supporters must realize that he, if nominated, must run not only against a man but also against a myth. The man was formidable enough to make his defeat difficult. The myth was sustained by so powerful a will to believe, so firm and skilled a control of mass media, as to make its defeat nearly impossible.

III

Nevertheless, the Democrats who began to gather in Chicago during the week of August 5 in preparation for their national convention, which would open August 13 in the International Amphitheater, were by no means downhearted.[2] All that the Presidential polls indicated, in Democratic opinion, was that the American people had not yet begun to take the election seriously. The people were being asked to reelect a President whose principal recommendation, in the Democratic view, was an amiable personality, who in good health had been the opposite of vigorous in the discharge of his responsibilities, and who was now both average and in failing health. Surely they would take a good hard look at actuarial figures, if at nothing else, and would decide that a vote for Eisenhower would be, in all probability, a vote for Vice-President Nixon as President. Few Democrats doubted that this decision, if widely made, would be fatal to the Republican ticket. It was a cardinal article of their faith that the average American disliked Nixon as much as they did, and in this faith they were not wholly alone. At that very moment, Harold Stassen, one of the President's principal advisers, was leading a dump-Nixon movement which, though it would doubtless fail in the Republican convention, dramatized the views of many an independent, many an Eisenhower Republican.

There was no denying, of course, that the Republican slogan, "Peace, Progress, Prosperity," was a potent one in the prevailing circumstances. It would remain so, however, only to the extent that it obscured what, to Democrats, seemed the plain facts. In fact, there had been no progress in government but instead a retreat in several areas. In fact, the peace was a precarious armed truce during which Russia profited hugely from the administration's incredible bungling. In fact, the much-vaunted prosperity, in so far as it was affected by governmental action, was determined by inherited Democratic policies, had been damaged by every departure the administration had made from these, and now contained several soft spots, notably in agriculture and closely related industries. And did not Democratic victories in every recent election show these facts to be realized by an increasing number of Americans? Did not the very polls that predicted an Eisenhower landslide predict that Democrats would increase their number of governorships and their majorities in the Congress? In view of all this, what reason was there to assume that even the Ike myth was invulnerable? After all, in four years of politics Eisenhower had faced less hostile fire than Truman and Roosevelt had faced in an average month, and who could say that he would not swiftly wither in the heat blasts of a fighting campaign?

But it must be a fighting campaign, led by a fighting Presidential candidate committed to New and Fair Deal principles. So said Averell Harriman, who, at last formally announcing his candidacy on the weekend of the President's ileitis attack, proclaimed himself precisely the fighter the situation demanded. So, too, said Harry Truman who, having thus far declined to say whom he favored for the nomination, dominated the preconvention scene from the moment of his arrival in Chicago. The ex-President would, he told a press conference, "let the people know for whom I stand before the convention meets," and then dropped broad hints (he was "no bandwagon fellow," he had no faith in political polls, he had no use for Presidential primaries) that his choice would be Harriman.

The probability, combined with an earlier event of that hectic week, struck more dismay into the heart of the Stevenson camp than any other development since the Minnesota primary. This earlier event was a curbstone TV interview in which Stevenson had said that, in his opinion, the party platform "should express unequivocal approval of the [Supreme] Court's decision" on school desegregation. Southern delegates, who theretofore had seemed firm Stevenson supporters, had reacted promptly and wrathfully against him. There now loomed the distinct possibility that Harriman, aided by concerted Southern favorite son votes, could prevent Stevenson's nomination on an early ballot, deadlock the convention, and ensure the victory of a dark horse compromise candidate. To the eyes of many an outside observer this possibility came close to becoming a probability when, on Saturday, August 11, Truman announced that his choice was indeed Harriman. The New York governor, said Truman, had "the ability to act as President immediately upon assuming that office, without risking a period of costly and dangerous trial and error." The ex-President then made it clear that he personally would fight with every ounce of his strength to stop Stevenson.

But by that time Stevenson and his staff had carefully assessed the probable effect of Truman's move and, though they remained acutely concerned, were no longer dismayed. The move, they believed, had been made too late. Truman, they were convinced, mistook his personal popularity with the delegates for persuasive power over them, whereas in fact his popularity had waxed to almost the precise extent that his power had waned. They conceded that it might now be impossible for Stevenson to win on the first ballot, but they were confident, if far from overconfident, that he would win on the second or third.

Thus did Stevenson pay a final installment on the preconvention and campaign strategy he had followed, partly from conscious choice and partly from character-determined necessity, in 1952. He was aided greatly to do so by the fervent support of Mrs. Franklin D. Roosevelt. All that weekend Stevenson, his staff members, and leading supporters went from caucus room to caucus room in Loop hotels, working for new pledges and for the reaffirmation of old ones. Nor did the pace slacken after the gavel came down opening the convention on Monday. While the convention struggled toward adoption of a civil rights platform plank which rejected "all proposals for the use of force to interfere with the orderly determination" of desegregation matters in the courts and which asserted the Supreme Court decisions to be "the law of the land" (other planks called for repeal of the Taft-Hartley Law, international control of the Suez Canal, arms for Israel, and high rigid supports of farm prices), the battle for delegates went on. By Wednesday it became clear that Stevenson had won it despite Truman's increasingly harsh strictures upon him. (On Tuesday night a stubbornly defiant Truman, seemingly bent on ruining what he could not rule, asserted that Stevenson was a "conservative" who follows the "counsel of hesitation" and "lacks the kind of fighting spirit we need to win.") At two-thirty that morning, most of Michigan's forty-four delegates, led by Governor Williams, voted to support Stevenson. A few hours later, New Jersey's thirty-six votes were pledged to Stevenson when Governor Robert Meyner, a Stevenson man from the outset, absolutely refused to stand as a favorite son. It was more than enough to ensure a first-ballot nomination. . . .

On Wednesday evening Stevenson, his name having been placed in nomination a few hours before by youthful Senator John F. Kennedy of Massachusetts, sat in his office at 231 South La Salle. During the preceding weeks he had come to a decision which he planned, later that night, to announce to the convention, and he revised his statement of it as he sat there. He paid scant attention to the telecast of the convention's balloting session where the Stevenson vote grew steadily toward the 686½ votes needed for nomination. He was watching, though, at approximately ten o'clock when TV cameras focused on a jubilant governor of Pennsylvania rising to cry his delegation's vote into the microphone. "Pennsylvania casts seven votes for Harriman . . ." shouted Governor Leader, pausing dramatically before adding, ". . . and for Stevenson, enough to put him over the top—sixty-seven!" Stevenson watched pandemonium break loose on the convention floor, then walked from his office into a glare of TV lights and an explosion of photographers' bulbs, smiling a trifle wanly. "I feel fine," he said, ". . . relieved and happy."

He went down to the Clark Street entrance of the bank building and into the limousine waiting for him there. He drove the miles southward to the Amphitheater in precisely twelve minutes, escorted by police cars and motorcycles whose sirens screamed through the warm summer night, arriving at the Stockyards Inn, adjacent to the convention hall, at about the time the conclusion of the roll call showed Stevenson's total vote to be 905½.

While the convention, by thunderous voice vote, was making his nomination unanimous, Stevenson himself was engaged in heated argument. The move he planned to make was strongly opposed by Sam Rayburn, Lyndon Johnson, and Paul Butler, none of whom had had prior inkling of it. It would, they claimed, "deadlock the convention." The move was supported, however, by Jack Arvey, Dick Daley, David Lawrence of Pittsburgh, and Governor Abraham A. Ribicoff of Connecticut, none of whom had had any inkling of it either. For fifteen minutes tempers flared into harsh words, until at last Sam Rayburn, the convention chairman, said that, under duress, he would do as Stevenson wished.

"Are you absolutely sure this is what you want to do?" asked Rayburn.

"It's what I want to do, Sam," replied Stevenson, his face somewhat flushed but his voice calm.

Then, facing the roaring hall, the TV cameras again, and the newsreels and the flashing bulbs, he announced in a brief statement his unprecedented decision, one shrewdly designed to serve not only the political interests of the immediate present but also, he was convinced, those of the future. The choice of his running mate, he said, would be the convention's alone; he himself would have no part in it. "The American people have the solemn obligation to consider with the utmost care who will be their President if the elected President is prevented by a Higher Will from serving his full term," he explained. "It is a sober reminder that seven out of thirty-four Presidents have served as the result of such an indirect selection. The responsibility of the Presidency has grown so great that the nation's attention has become focused as never before on the office of the Vice-Presidency. The choice for that office has become almost as important as the choice for the Presidency." For this reason he wished to depart from the custom of having the Presidential candidate choose his running mate for reasons of geography, political expediency, or personal liking. "Until tomorrow night," he concluded, "my heartfelt thanks, and may God be with you."

The convention's stunned surprise had not passed before Senators Humphrey, Kefauver, and Kennedy had become active Vice-Presidential candidates—and all that night the Loop hotels were scenes of frenzied activity as the intense campaigns for delegates went on. Stevenson himself, having downed a glass or two of champagne at a party in his suite at the Sheraton-Blackstone and appeared briefly at a party for his staff and volunteers in the Conrad Hilton, slept peacefully. Next day he received a phone call from Harry Truman offering to come down from his suite two floors above Stevenson's in order to congratulate the nominee. "Don't do that," said Stevenson. "I'll come to see you." And he did, staying for approximately three minutes with the man who had so bitterly fought him, who had said things that would plague Stevenson throughout the campaign, and who now offered to do whatever the candidate wished him to do in the struggle for election. Stevenson thanked the ex-President but was frankly dubious as to what Truman could now do to help. He then went to 231 South La Salle where he put finishing touches on his formal acceptance speech and thereafter watched, on TV, the convention's most exciting afternoon. Humphrey's candidacy, damaged by the Minnesota primary results, swiftly waned. The

Vice-Presidential race was between Kefauver and Kennedy, with the South
—out of dislike for Kefauver rather more than love for Kennedy, whose
Catholic religion was a handicap among Southern agrarians—fervently supporting the latter.

Stevenson himself remained scrupulously neutral, outwardly at least, im-
pressing upon staff members that they must not, by word or sign, indicate
a preference. While the roll-call vote on the convention floor seesawed between Kefauver and Kennedy, he worked calmly in his office on the speech
he was to give that night. Occasionally Bill Blair, in whose office the TV set
was located, came in to tell Stevenson the latest development; once or twice
Stevenson came into Blair's office to watch the screen for a few moments.
And whatever his secret preference may have been, Stevenson was certainly
not dismayed when, on the second ballot, Kefauver emerged the victor by the
narrowest of margins. His respect for the Tennessean's senatorial role was
great, and whatever dislike he had had for the man had been overcome by
the events that followed June 5. Certainly no one could doubt that Kefauver
would be an indefatigable campaigner on the national ticket. Moreover he
would have one important advantage over Kennedy as candidate: the Massachusetts senator had voted against the Democratic high rigid farm price-
support bill a few months before and would, it appeared, have been unable
to make a strong bid for the farm vote, whereas Kefauver's popularity with
farmers was notable.

In the nature of things, Stevenson's acceptance speech that night could
not be as dramatic, as full of surprise, as that he had made four years before,
and there were some among his supporters who regretted that it was not
more clearly organized, more sharply focused on a few central issues. It
was eloquent, however, stimulating no less than fifty-three bursts of enthusiastic applause as he proceeded.

History, he proclaimed, had brought us to the threshold of a "new America." "I mean an America where poverty is abolished and our abundance is
used to enrich the lives of every family. I mean a new America where freedom is made real for all without regard to race or belief or economic condition. I mean a new America which everlastingly attacks the ancient idea
that men can solve their differences by killing each other." On his way to
these shining generalities, he arraigned the Eisenhower administration in
terms highly pleasing to his supporters. The men around the President, said
he, had dealt "the ultimate indignity to the democratic process," by attempting to "merchandise candidates like breakfast cereal." They "cynically cov-
eted" Eisenhower as candidate but "ignored" him "as leader." And indeed
Eisenhower had shown little desire or capacity for leadership. His major
talent, Stevenson indicated, was for *mis*-leading the people. For instance, the
President had proclaimed that our prestige abroad "has never been higher,"

when the blunt truth was that "it has probably never been lower." We were, said Stevenson, "losing the cold war."

The following week, in San Francisco, the Republican National Convention renominated Dwight Eisenhower and Richard Nixon in a session enlivened only by the expulsion from the hall of an irreverent Nebraska delegate who—apparently in an excess of boredom with the prevailing Ike adulation —sought to place in nomination a mythical "Joe Smith."

Thus, for the first time in fifty-six years, the two major-party Presidential candidates were the same men who had faced each other four years before. The last time this had happened was in 1900, when McKinley ran for reelection against Bryan, and on that occasion the Democratic Vice-Presidential candidate had been Adlai Ewing Stevenson I.

The fact could not but stir in the present Adlai Stevenson a renewed sense of that family tradition, of history as a family process, which had been a central theme of his growth. Both family past and family future seemed to meet among the events that had crowded around him during the last two weeks. Buffie, with Ernest Ives, had been close beside him. His sons, John Fell and Adlai III, had been there too, and young Adlai had worked hard and effectively for his father among the delegates during Truman's effort to black the Stevenson candidacy. Borden was still with the Army in Hawaii (a typical photograph showed him sitting at ease, clad in gaudy sport shorts, listening to convention reports on the radio), but soon he would be discharged and would join his father in the later phases of the campaign. It was with pretty, twenty-year-old Nancy Anderson Stevenson, however, young Adlai's wife, that the family future lay. She had been one of the most photographed and televised personalities at the convention, being a wonderfully alive girl whose wholehearted reactions to the convention's abundant stimuli were delightful to behold, and all the world now knew that she carried the unborn first grandchild of the Democratic nominee. Moreover, this grandchild would be born, the doctors said, on or very near election day. . . .

IV

In retrospect it would appear that Stevenson, making his acceptance speech on August 17, stood at the apex of his political career. He had fought his way over one harsh obstacle after another on his way to party dominance, displaying in the process a rare courage, gaiety, intelligence, and integrity. His example had persuaded into active party work thousands of idealistic and energetic young people who would not otherwise have thought of entering practical politics, and his labors had contributed directly to the financial health of the party and to the victories it had scored at the polls since '52. No man could have earned in harder ways the public glory that was wrapped about him, in roaring acclaim, as he stood that night in the spotlight, behind the lectern and the microphones. He, of course, faced great odds as he again entered the lists against Eisenhower. Those who cheered him that night knew it. But they knew, too, that he had faced great odds before and had overcome them through the exercise of theretofore unsuspected strengths and talents. They were convinced he had a fighting chance, and this might be all that was needed by so shrewd, valiant, and experienced a warrior, armed as he now was with a battle-tested staff whose headquarters this time were in Washington, D.C., and whose organization was much more efficient than it had been before.

The campaign strategy, as worked out by the astute Finnegan, with Paul Butler and others, had two major tactical phases.[3] One was a pinpoint tactic whereby Stevenson would focus on those states, and even on those counties and wards, where a relatively slight shift of votes would transform an Eisenhower victory into a Stevenson one. The other tactic, one that was indeed required by pinpointing on so vast a scale, was a public display of energy and stamina which Eisenhower could not match, indicating, as mere words could never do, the contrast between a relatively young man in the full tide of vigorous health and an aging man whose health was waning. Great reliance was placed on the apparent fact that the Democrats were the majority party; Stevenson, by being thoroughly identified with his party, might therefore gain as much as Eisenhower would lose if somehow the President could be identified, in the popular mind, with *his* party. In this strategy Stevenson had concurred. He was dismayed, however, when he saw what it actually entailed. The travel and speaking schedule that had been worked out for him was, he vehemently protested, worse than grueling; coming as it did atop the primary and convention struggles, it was a "man-killer." He wouldn't have a minute's relaxation from mid-August through election day; he'd have no solitude in which to ponder his problems and shape for them creative solutions.

And indeed, or so it would appear in restrospect, the advantages gained by this incessant activity were outweighed by the effects it had upon the candidate himself. Every other error of the campaign was rooted in this initial one, Stevenson later believed, though he could not and would not blame anyone but himself for this. When the strategy was planned he had not realized how near to nervous exhaustion (though his physical condition remained excellent) the long struggle for the nomination had brought him. Nor did he realize, other observers would assert, how badly this struggle had blurred his popular image, how greatly it had contributed to a disillusioned view of him as just another politician who would do anything to gain votes —and this during a period when Ike adulation was mounting, or being carried, to unprecedented heights. If the Democratic party had united solidly behind Stevenson in the fall of '55, devoting its every resource to a carefully planned build-up of him, it probably could not have matched the Eisenhower build-up through those months. As it was, major portions of party strength had been devoted to tearing down Stevenson, and Republican campaign orators had been provided thereby with an ammunition they would now use gleefully against him.

But the chief blame, if blame there was, attached to a failure by Stevenson's staff and by Stevenson himself to take sufficient account of his essential character and temperament. The staff had assumed, and he himself had at least tacitly assumed, that the new Stevenson could do what the old one had never been able to do, namely delegate absolutely to trusted lieutenants nearly all the brainwork—the actual writing of speeches and policy statements—leaving himself free to concentrate wholly on public appearances and personal politicking. His inability to do this, he had long realized, was a serious handicap. In private conversation, not many months before, he had spoken of it. He had two roles to play, he had said; one was the "executive thing," the other the "creative thing." And he had deplored the fact that, though he felt he could play either role adequately, he could not play them simultaneously or shift easily, instantaneously from one to the other as a few "geniuses" (he had mentioned Arthur Schlesinger, Jr.) seemed able to do.

"What I ought to do is what everybody tells me to do—delegate the 'creative' thing (which is what I *like* to do, it's the fun of my life) and concentrate on the 'executive,'" he went on, "because so much of the latter is stuff that just can't be delegated. There are so many people who have to be dealt with on the top level, you know. They have to see *me*, or talk to *me*, and nobody else. And there are decisions to make, operating decisions, which nobody else can make."

The man to whom he spoke had replied that he understood all that, but added that millions of people over the country were hoping and praying that he would not become "just another candidate," that he would be able to retain the "high-level" approach he had made in '52.

"I know," Stevenson had said. "I just hope they realize what I'm up against. There's a limit to what any one man can do." [4]

This limit was reached and passed in the two and a half months following the convention. In effect, Stevenson attempted to conduct simultaneously *two* campaigns, either of which was sufficiently arduous to absorb all his energies. One was the campaign Finnegan had devised with Stevenson's concurrence. The other was the campaign Stevenson himself had envisaged in the weeks preceding Eisenhower's heart attack. Actually he made somewhat fewer public appearances, and fewer set speeches, than he had made in '52. Bill Blair could prove this by comparing the schedule followed in the earlier campaign with that being followed in this one, and he did so when Stevenson complained bitterly that the present ordeal was the "worst" he had ever endured. But the candidate was now much more tired than he had been before, and certainly the demands made upon him were severe enough. He traveled incessantly. He made as many as five talks in a single day. He was constantly meeting and mingling with local Democratic groups and appearing with local candidates. (In the event, it would appear to many that this helped local Democrats far more than it helped him; certainly he gathered for these larger crowds and more publicity than they could have gathered for themselves, while enabling his opposition to picture him as hanging ignominiously upon the coattails of these same candidates.) He also gave dozens of full-length addresses, supplementing these with five policy statements averaging ten thousand words each, in which he spelled out his "New America" program for "Older Citizens," "Education," "The Nation's Health," "True Economics," and "Natural Resources."

Thus the total brainwork required in '56 was probably in excess of that required in '52. The staff he had to perform it, however, was smaller than it had been four years before. Headed by Wirtz, the writers included Arthur Schlesinger, Jr.; John Bartlow Martin, who had joined the staff during the primary campaign; and Robert Tufts. Incidental help was given by Kenneth Galbraith, John Hersey, and William Lee Miller, among others. As in '52, most of the writers suffered breakdowns from overwork before the campaign ended (Wirtz was ill for three weeks after election day), and as in '52, or even "worse" than in '52, in the opinion of Bill Blair, Stevenson wrote and rewrote constantly in moments when he might otherwise have had some relaxation from the extreme tensions of his days. Nor was he as much at ease with the products of these labors as he had been with the speeches of '52. Though their intellectual content was at least as high as that of his earlier speeches, though many of them were wholly successful, they were in general less direct expressions of himself than former speeches had been and gave evidence, at times, of the haste, amid crowding distractions, in which they had been composed. He lacked the time in which to absorb them completely into his consciousness before he gave them; he had often not so much as five quiet and solitary minutes in which to get hold of himself before he went again before the multitude, under the floodlights and the staring camera eyes.

In consequence of all this, the image of him projected on TV screens was, very often, precisely the opposite of that intended when the campaign was planned. He often appeared tired, driven, harassed, his delivery stumbling and awkward as it had never been before. Moreover there were, now and then, incredible production failures, notably at Harrisburg where he made his kickoff speech over a nationwide hookup costing a quarter of a million dollars and where the teleprompter, on which he had been urged to rely, failed to work properly. Such mistakes were not likely to plague Eisenhower, whose campaign was much less arduous. Indeed, Eisenhower on TV, carefully made up and staged by such production experts as the actor Robert Montgomery, often appeared actually younger, at once more vigorous and more relaxed, than his opponent—an irony far from amusing to Stevenson's supporters.

But though these things were apparent at the time, they did not assume the relative importance given them here until after the event. Even then they would not appear to have been, of themselves alone, decisive of the outcome. Every losing campaign appears in retrospect to have been a succession of errors, just as every winning one appears to have been a triumph of intelligent planning. Republican strategists would later claim that the outcome had been determined by their decision, in early March, to conduct the "briefest" campaign in history—a five-week TV campaign in which they would capitalize on Eisenhower's personality and on the mistakes Stevenson must "inevitably" make. The fact that Eisenhower began to add trips and speeches to his itinerary in September and October was due, they would explain, merely to the fact that "Ike loves crowds." They would not admit what to the Stevenson camp seemed true, namely that there had been three distinct phases of the struggle during which there were major shifts in voter sentiment, and in all save the last of these the shifts had been away from Eisenhower and toward Stevenson.

The first phase, in the Stevenson view, began with the dramatic last day of the Democratic convention, whose color and excitement stood out in marked contrast to the performance of the Republicans in the following week. Stevenson took off on a flying three-week regional tour during which he presented his farm program to a responsive audience in Iowa and made, there and elsewhere, a series of hard-hitting attacks on the administration's domestic policies. The polls immediately showed a gain in Stevenson's strength, particularly in farm states whose normally Republican ground Kefauver assiduously cultivated. And the gains continued for some time, so narrowing the gap between Stevenson and Eisenhower that political dopesters who theretofore had spoken of an "Ike landslide" as a "sure thing" began to forecast a "close race." It was at this point that Eisenhower began to add speeches and appearances to his itinerary.

There followed, in the Stevenson view, a leveling-off period of some weeks during which the Democratic candidate, having seemingly provoked his opponent into a more active defense, failed to make gains and may even have lost ground. He was a little worried about this personally. He spoke of it to Jane Dick, who was immediately reassured by Senator Lehman of New York. This happened in every campaign, Lehman said, and it was well to have it happen in the middle of the struggle. "He'll come up again," predicted Lehman confidently.

And he appeared to do so. There were signs that his candidacy had been given a boost among Negro voters and among Northern independents when, before a pro-segregationist crowd in Little Rock, Arkansas, he said that he personally regarded the Supreme Court's desegregation decision to be morally "right." Some of his staff had sought, rather desperately, to dissuade him from this and were immensely relieved when the audience, in apparent admiration of his courage and honesty, actually applauded the statement. (Eisenhower, during a brief swing into the South, failed to mention the desegregation problem.) There were further signs of gain when Stevenson, having earlier said little about foreign policy because his staff was convinced, and the polls showed, that there was little public interest in it, began a series of slashing attacks upon Republican efforts to label itself the "peace" party and the Democrats the "war party."

Peace, said Stevenson, could not be defined as merely the absence of overt hostilities; it involved the "building of a community"; and the Republican administration, far from trying to build a world community, was weakening the foundations for such a structure through its vacillation between threats and appeasement vis-à-vis the Communists and through its reckless disregard of the opinions and feelings of our allies. (Replied Eisenhower: "But why this anguished cry of some politicians that we have no peace? Do they think they can make America's parents and wives believe that their sons and husbands are being shot at?") Again and again Stevenson scored the Republicans for "misleading the people" concerning our foreign affairs, for proclaiming "peace" when there was no peace, for asserting (as Eisenhower did in mid-October) that there was "good news" from Suez, where world crisis then centered, when in fact the news was all bad.

It was at the opening of this phase of the campaign that Stevenson made what his Republican opponents regarded as major errors. Stevenson's own supporters thought it a serious tactical error when their candidate, in the midst of a speech on the West Coast to an American Legion convention, said that the time had come to take a "new look" at our defense establishment and to consider the possibility of "ending the draft" as a means of assuring adequate military manpower. He did so in part because he was advised that Eisenhower planned to call for an end of the draft at the last moment of his campaign, in a move similar in its intent to the "I will go to Korea" statement of 1952. It was well known that influential voices in the Pentagon said the draft was wasteful, inefficient, wholly unsuited to the manpower needs of the armed services in this age of technological warfare. The defense services should be "career services," and the draft was no way of obtaining these. It would be far cheaper and more effective to employ higher pay and other attractions to recruit volunteers who would make careers of the military. So said Stevenson some days later, when he spelled out in detail his "end-draft" proposal. But by that time the damage had been done by his one-sentence statement so far as vote getting was concerned. The initial pronouncement had made the headlines and reaped a harvest of hostile Republican editorial comment; the exposition of it seemed defensive and was relatively unpersuasive.

The second so-called error, deliberately committed by Stevenson against the advice of the professional politicians on his staff was a renewal, with some changes, of his H-bomb proposal. The professionals warned him that this was not a vote-getting issue and might well be a vote-losing one, Eisenhower being the number one military hero of the country. Stevenson agreed. But he was convinced that what he had to say desperately needed saying, that it might open the way toward ending the threat of nuclear warfare, and that he had therefore a moral obligation to press the proposal with all the persuasive power he could muster, regardless of its effect upon his personal political fortunes. Eisenhower's initial response to both the end-draft and end-H-bomb-tests proposals was to dismiss them contemptuously. Both the draft and the tests must be continued in order that the United States could "negotiate" from a "position of strength rather than weakness," he said, and in a press conference in the second week of October he responded with a show of irritation to questions about the proposals. He had "said my last words on these subjects," he announced. Stevenson had not done so, however, and neither, it soon appeared, had Eisenhower.

On October 15, in a nationwide TV address from Chicago, Stevenson said that, if elected President, he would make an effort to achieve world agreement on the ending of H-bomb tests "the first order of business." He reminded his listeners that he had proposed last April that the United States take the initiative on this matter. Since then, both the Soviet Union and Great Britain had declared their willingness "to join us in trying to establish the kind of policy I have suggested." He reiterated that "little danger to national security" was involved, "because if another power conducts further tests we would know it and, as I have said, would have no choice but to resume such tests ourselves." Pending the agreement, the United States should proceed, he now said, with the production of hydrogen weapons and with further research in this field. That night and next day, a flood of telegraph and telephone messages poured in upon the Stevenson office, in support of his proposal. One was from Dr. Henry deWolfe Smith of the Institute for Advanced Studies in Princeton, N.J., who endorsed Stevenson's stand as "transcending the partisanship of the current campaign." Five nuclear scientists from the Argonne National Laboratories in Lemont, Illinois, telegraphed Stevenson that "nuclear physicists firmly believe your plan, far from being 'catastrophic nonsense,' is workable, wise, and in the best interests of the United States." ("Catastrophic nonsense" was the epithet Nixon had applied to the Stevenson proposal.)

In Portland, Oregon, three days later, Eisenhower found that he had, after all, quite a few more words to say on this subject. Stevenson's call for an end to H-bomb tests, said he, was a compound of "pie-in-the-sky promises and wishful thinking," presenting to the nation a choice between this and "hard sense and experience.... We reject any thought that we will say: We are going to disarm and we hope that you will too one day," he went on, as if this were what Stevenson had actually proposed. ("Along with other Democrats, I have been doing all I can to keep the Eisenhower Administration from slashing our defense establishment during the last four years," replied Stevenson some days later. "It ill becomes the President to talk about dropping our guard when his Administration has consistently put dollars ahead of defense. I want to see our defenses strengthened, not weakened, and there is nothing in my H-bomb proposal inconsistent with this object.") Subsequently the President ordered the preparation and release of a "history" of the H-bomb and a statement of why the tests should be continued. This document Stevenson branded a "campaign pamphlet" which "even as a political paper is remarkable for misstatements and distortions." He answered it, on October 29, with a point-by-point analysis of the President's argument. By then the scientific public was convinced (as, indeed, it had been from the outset) that Stevenson had by far the better of the scientific argument, but the politicians, including those in Stevenson's camp, were convinced that he had had by far the worse of the question's political argument.

The latter was in part due to a letter Premier Nikolai A. Bulganin of the Soviet Union had seen fit to address on October 21 to President Eisenhower and to publish in Moscow before it had been translated and delivered to the White House. In it Bulganin had taken cognizance of the fact "that an election campaign is being conducted in the United States, in the course of which the discussions of various questions of international significance ... acquires the form of polemic." However, "we fully share the opinion recently expressed by certain prominent public figures in the United States concerning the necessity and the possibility of concluding an agreement on the matter of prohibiting atomic weapon tests and concerning the positive influence this would have on the entire international situation." He accused Secretary of State Dulles of "obvious distortion of the policy of the Soviet Union concerning the above-mentioned questions.... As far as the Soviet Government is concerned," he asserted, "it is prepared to conclude an agreement with the United States of America immediately for discontinuing atomic tests. We proceed, of course, on the basis of the assumption that other states having atomic weapons at their disposal will likewise adhere to such an agreement." The President's prompt response was a stern reprimand of the Premier for unwarranted interference in the United States's domestic affairs. The statement concerning Dulles, he said, "is personally offensive to me." The Soviet Union had consistently opposed every system of international inspection and control of armaments, including Eisenhower's "open-skies" proposal. "However, though disappointed, we are not discouraged," Eisenhower went on. "... We will close no doors which might open a secure way to serve humanity."

"I share fully President Eisenhower's resentment at the manner and timing of Premier Bulganin's interference in the political affairs of the United States," said Stevenson in a statement released October 22, adding that Bulganin earlier had said he hoped that Eisenhower would run for re-election. . . .

> But the real issue is not Mr. Bulganin's manners or Russian views about American politics. The real issue is what we are going to do to save the world from hydrogen disaster. Viewed from the standpoint, not of politics, but of peace, I think the President's reply is unfortunate.
>
> There are two possibilities. One is that the Bulganin offer [to stop tests through agreement] ... is made for propaganda purposes only. . . . If that is true, it should be exposed for all the world to see. The other possibility is that the Russian offer, ill-timed as it is, reflects an opportunity to move ahead now toward a stop to the further explosion of hydrogen bombs. In either event, there seems to me only one course to follow. That is to pursue this opening immediately and all the way.

But no reasoned argument could now undo the damage the Bulganin statement had done to Stevenson. As a residue from the era of McCarthy and the Nixon campaign of '54, there was a widespread belief that the Democrats were not only a war party (witness Korea) but also a party of Communist appeasers (witness Yalta), and the fact that the two views were flatly contradictory did not prevent their effective exploitation in '56 by Dewey and Nixon. The latter's talent for sly innuendo and plausible distortions of truth remained, in the Democratic view, his principal campaign weapon. In tones of sorrow rather than anger, Nixon the Statesman rebuked Stevenson the Politician for having walked into a "Communist mousetrap," risking the national security in order to gain votes. He was enabled to do so the more effectively by the fact that the Bulganin letter had appeared amid the most dangerous international crisis since World War II.

v

The whole campaign had been conducted in the deepening shadow of this crisis, whose explosion into bloody violence on October 29 determined the final, decisive phase of the American political campaign. And it was the ultimate irony of the campaign that this explosion, which seemed to prove in blood and terror the truth of Stevenson's strictures upon the Eisenhower foreign policy, actually increased hugely Eisenhower's strength at the polls.

Thus there was a sense in which the outcome on November 6 was partially determined by a Middle Eastern policy decision taken by the Eisenhower administration more than three years before. In 1953, when Major General Mohammed Naguib was the newly installed Premier of Egypt, the Eisenhower administration, perhaps more strongly motivated by American oil interest in Arab countries than the preceding administration had been, began to court Arab friendship while de-emphasizing the friendship for Israel and the determination to help the latter country defend herself against armed aggression. This represented a major shift in American policy, and it was dramatized when Secretary Dulles presented to Naguib, as a personal gift from the President, an automatic pistol. Israeli leaders at once protested vehemently, warning that the real power in the new Egyptian regime was Colonel Gamal Abdel Nasser and that the colonel, far from being a moderate, was a fanatic Arab nationalist whose ambition was to lead an Arab bloc in a war of extermination against Israel. Britain and France, too, were dubious; the new regime seemed to them intransigent in its anti-Westernism.

Nevertheless, the Eisenhower administration persisted in its pro-Nasser policy even after the colonel, having taken over the premiership in 1954, made in 1955 his deal with Moscow to obtain heavy arms from the Soviet bloc in return for commitments to Russia whose scale and scope would remain secret a year later but whose nature was revealed in the anti-Western propaganda which the Egyptian leader immediately increased in volume and violence. The U.S. arms that Israel requested, with British and French support, were refused—a decision which, as we have seen, was roundly criticized by Stevenson at the time. A reluctant Britain was persuaded to join the United States in the offer to Nasser of a massive economic-aid program, including (in December of '55) help in building the $1.3 billion Aswan dam on the Nile, the prime object of Nasser's domestic program. Significantly the colonel did not accept the offer. Instead he considered it while, throughout the early months of '56, he organized a neutralist bloc of Arab states, worked to undermine the British position in Jordan, challenged Britain's control of vital oil fields on the Arabian coast, and gave active aid to nationalist Arabs fighting against the French in North Africa. He also financed, trained, and equipped anti-Israeli commandos who stepped up their raids across the Israeli border while he built up his regular forces for war. Israel warned Washington, with increasing desperation, that the stockpile of Communist arms was mounting to terrifying heights. So did Britain and France, again urging the United States to send arms to Israel in order to restrain Nasser. The Eisenhower administration refused to do so.

But in July of '56, in a typically abrupt reversal of policy, the administration withdrew its offer of help with the Aswan dam, doing so in a way calculated to be most humiliating to Nasser personally and most damaging to his prestige in the Arab world. Nasser's predictable response was a prompt seizure of the Suez Canal, whereupon Britain and France demanded that the canal be internationalized—by force, if necessary. They were restrained by Dulles, who proposed, as an alternative, a "users association" to operate the canal. When Britain and France agreed to this, Dulles, faced by angry Nasser threats, "weakened" the proposal "out of all recognition," as the normally pro-American London *Times* bitterly complained.

By October, Britain and France were convinced that Nasser planned to bar their use of the canal (vital to them), take over their Middle Eastern bases, and cut off their oil supplies. Israel was convinced that, soon, he would attack her. All three were convinced that no reliance could be placed upon the United States for help in what, to them, seemed a crisis of survival.* On Monday, October 29, Israeli armor and paratroops thrust deep into Egypt's Sinai Peninsula. Within two days after that, British bombs had fallen on Egyptian airfields, Israeli troops had sealed off the Gaza Strip, and Anglo-French landing forces were moving toward Suez. . . .

Stevenson would point out with some bitterness, in private conversation, that the Eisenhower administration had not seen fit theretofore to work through the United Nations in the development and implementation of its Middle Eastern policy. The economic-aid program, for example, might conceivably have been offered through the UN in such a way as genuinely to serve the people of the Middle East, making peace between Israel and her neighbors and solving the Arab refugee problem. Instead, the Aswan-dam offer had been handled in crude power-political terms, and with no intelligent consideration of Nasser's problems, psychology, and power-political resources. It was only now, on the brink of World War III, that Eisenhower suddenly discovered that the UN was responsible for making and keeping the peace.

And on Friday, in the UN, the United States found herself strangely allied with the Soviet Union against her own long-time friends and allies, demanding a cease-fire which, on the following day, was rejected by Britain, France, and Israel. The United States then increased her pressure for a withdrawal, though Eisenhower had promised—with a flatness that seemed to Stevenson unfortunate for peace, if effective as a vote getter—that no U.S. troops would be sent into the Middle East. Period. Ultimately the withdrawals were made after the Russians, encouraged no doubt by Eisenhower's "no-troop-involvement" pledge, had threatened to use "volunteer" troops on the side of Nasser and had "warned" Paris and London that their countries were vulnerable to Soviet atomic attack.

* It was on October 12 that Eisenhower, in a carefully staged television campaign show, said that he had "the best announcement that I think I could possibly make to America tonight"; namely that progress in settling the canal dispute had been "most gratifying" and that it looked as though "a very great crisis is behind us." The statement was given streamer headlines in the nation's press.

(Concurrent with these developments had come, that summer, the first really serious break in the Iron Curtain across central Europe. A rebellious Poland had been granted important concessions from Moscow in return for continued acceptance of a Polish Communist government. Soon thereafter, actual and initially successful revolution had flared in Hungary. For these events, Republican orators at first took credit, claiming that they stemmed from the Eisenhower administration's "liberation" policies. They claimed no responsibility for the disaster, however, when Russia, taking advantage of the break in the Western alliance, moved in with tanks and troops to drown in blood the Hungarian bid for freedom.)

For a few days after the Israeli attack, it appeared to Stevenson that the event must greatly reduce his opponent's vote and ensure his own victory. Surely the American people must now see the truth of his criticisms, though he regretted that he had not launched these more specifically at the Suez crisis earlier in the campaign. (He had refrained from doing so, as he had publicly announced, because he wished to do nothing that might weaken Eisenhower's hand in the dangerous situation.) Surely they would see that Nasser, with our open aid, had been built up into a most formidable foe of American interests and a most dangerous threat to world peace; that Russia, with our inadvertent aid, was now established as a major power in the Middle East, an object she had long pursued in vain; and that the Western alliance, largely through our fault, was seriously if not fatally wounded. Surely they would conclude that to continue in office an administration capable of such blunders would be to invite even worse disaster. He was swiftly disillusioned. By midweek he had begun to realize that the great majority of Americans were seeing what they had been long conditioned to see. "Ike is a great military hero and a Man of Peace; he loves you; he knows best. Have faith in Ike." This had been the burden of Republican propaganda, echoed and amplified by an unprecedentedly adulatory press, for four long years. And in this time of trouble, it was to Ike that millions turned who might otherwise have voted for Stevenson.

The irony was bitter to the Democratic candidate, moving from the East toward Chicago through that final crucial week. Had he, after all, overrated the critical intelligence of the electorate? His draft and H-bomb proposals, deliberately distorted by his opponent into proposals for unilateral disarmament; the Bulganin episode; the long image-distorting battle for the nomination; even the wit and gaiety that had formerly made him so appealing to civilized minds—all these now combined with the father image of Ike to work disastrously against him. In one of the most effective speeches of the campaign, he soberly analyzed the crisis, tracing the steps through which it had developed. The speech was well received, but it could not command any such attention, in the circumstances, as Eisenhower's moves to save the world from the catastrophe for which (in Stevenson's view) he was so largely responsible. Thereafter, Stevenson began to raise his voice in an effort to be heard above the tumult of foreign war. His denunciations of the administration became more harsh than any he had made before.

In Minneapolis, on the morning of Monday, November 5, he reminded his listeners that Nixon, who "has put away his switch-blade and now assumes the aspect of an Eagle Scout," had said not long ago in that very city, "There will be no war in the Middle East." He also reminded them of President Eisenhower's role in the making of our Middle Eastern policy. . . .

In February of this year, the Eisenhower administration started to send a shipload of tanks to Saudi Arabia. This was at the time that we were declining to send arms to Israel. When protests mounted, the administration first embargoed the shipment. And while it was trying to decide what to do, where was the President of the United States? On February 17, he played golf. On February 18, he shot quail. On February 22, when the ban was finally removed, the President shot eighteen holes of golf. . . . Toward the end of March, as the situation grew worse, Prime Minister Eden sent the President an urgent message about the Middle East. But some days later the President, when asked about it in a press conference, said, "I can't recall how long it has been since I have had a letter from the Prime Minister." On April 9 the White House announced: "The President and the Secretary of State regard the situation (in the Middle East) with the utmost seriousness." On the same day the President began a golfing vacation in Georgia.

When Egypt took over the Suez Canal in July, the President was at Gettysburg. On August 4, when *The New York Times* called the Suez impasse the "gravest challenge to the West since Berlin and Korea," the President played golf. On August 11, when Britain rejected Communist proposals for a Suez conference, the President played golf. As the crisis mounted toward the end of August the press reported that the President, now at Pebble Beach, California, golfed happily at one of America's toughest and most beautiful courses. . . . And even when we have been forewarned, we have still failed to act. Our government knew about the impending arms deal between Egypt and the Communists a full month before President Eisenhower met with the Russian leaders at Geneva. Yet our President made no protest of this action. . . . If there had been less hearts and flowers and more firm talk at Geneva, the Communists would never have dared to arm Egypt. . . .

The last four years have presented America and the free world great opportunities to exploit the weaknesses in the Communist ranks and advance the cause of peace. But this administration has failed to take advantage of them. The death of Stalin caught us off-guard. The uprisings in East Berlin caught us off-guard. The uprisings in Poznan caught us off-guard. The most recent revolts in Poland and Hungary obviously caught us off-guard. . . . And America reached the summit of foolishness when Mr. Nixon hailed the collapse of our alliance [with Britain and France] as "a declaration of independence that has had an electrifying effect through the world."

That night, in Boston, he reiterated in substance these foreign policy criticisms before proceeding to deal, in unprecedentedly frank terms, with the issue of the President's health. "[Distasteful] as the matter is, I must say bluntly that every piece of scientific evidence we have, every lesson of history and experience, indicates that a Republican victory tomorrow would mean that Richard M. Nixon would probably be President of this country within the next four years." The statement of course called down upon Stevenson's head wrathful charges of "dirty tactics" and "bad taste," and there were many among Stevenson's supporters who regretted that it had been made. However valid as a statement of probability, it seemed a poor note on which to end what had been, take it all in all, an extraordinarily gallant and high-minded campaign against overwhelming odds.

VI

He was originally scheduled to make his election-eve speech in Chicago. But on Sunday afternoon he had received a jubilant message from Adlai III, who had returned to the Harvard Law School in September: Nancy Anderson Stevenson, in Boston's Lying-in Hospital, had given birth to a baby boy whose name was Adlai Ewing Stevenson. Immediately the candidate had revised his schedule. From Minneapolis next day he flew, with John Fell and Borden beside him, to Boston.

Sirens screaming, police cars and motorcycles escorted him from the air-field to the hospital on whose third floor, in the late afternoon, he gazed down happily upon his plump, brown-haired, one-day-old grandchild. Flash bulbs popped. "He doesn't seem to mind at all," laughed Stevenson as the baby slept on undisturbed. "He must be a born pol." He then said he would "punch in the nose" anyone who said the baby looked like him. The baby, reporters laughingly agreed, was much better-looking. And this family happiness sustained him as, numb with weariness, he returned from his Boston speech to Chicago.

On Tuesday he voted at Half Day. That evening, in the President's Suite of the Sheraton-Blackstone in the Loop, he shared a buffet dinner with his family and close friends, some twenty people in all. Buffie and Ernest Ives were there, and John Fell and Borden. The Edison Dicks were there, and Bill Blair. The atmosphere reflected the candidate's outward mood: he was tired but smiling, a bit rueful yet gay, expecting the worst but by no means conceding it. Nor did this atmosphere noticeably change as, after dinner, they all watched the election returns on TV. Stevenson lounged back in an easy chair, sometimes shaking his head a little as, one by one, his enfeebled hopes were crushed to death, but not for a moment did he lose, outwardly, his good cheer.

At nine o'clock, by which time it was already clear that he was losing, he left his party to confer in another room with Jim Finnegan and Bill Wirtz concerning the timing of, and general arrangements for, his concession. He then went into his bedroom to write out the statement whose general form he had already well in mind. He would use in it a quotation from Fra Giovanni's Christmas Letter of 1513, and another, from Proverbs, which he had memorized from his mother's lips when he was a child. By the time he emerged, the proportions of his defeat were revealed as overwhelming. There would be no surprises for him on the morrow when he learned that he had won only 73 electoral votes compared to Eisenhower's 457, and 25,897,841 popular votes compared to Eisenhower's 35,500,000. He had carried Missouri and six Southern states. He had lost Oklahoma, Texas, Louisiana, Florida, Virginia, Kentucky, and Tennessee, of the states deemed solidly Democratic. Clearly he had come to the end of the road he had entered upon just eight and a half years ago; he could not but feel, deep within him, the gnawing pain of disappointment and failure. There seemed to be, in so crushing a defeat, a large measure of personal humiliation. Yet he smiled at Buffie, at Ernest.

"It's a pathetic night," Buffie said. . . .

He shook his head at her, still smiling. Someone had asked him once what he considered to be his greatest personal asset as a candidate. "Well, I should say, serenity of spirit," he had replied. "I can contemplate in tranquillity the distinct possibility that I will never be President of the United States. I can see many reasons for not wanting to be President during the next four years, for everything is likely to start unraveling within the next year or two. Of course," he had added, "I shall do my best to win." Well, he was, now, quite serene—and certainly he had done his best.

At twelve-twenty on the morning of Wednesday, November 7, he emerged from the Sheraton-Blackstone, with John Fell at his left arm and Borden at his right, with Buffie and Ernest behind him. He crossed the street to the Conrad Hilton where, in the Grand Ballroom, a tearful crowd of some twenty-five hundred supporters awaited him. And there, for those who saw him in the room and for millions who watched him over TV, he came again sharply into focus as the Stevenson of old, the gallant, urbane, witty man, sensitive and gay, whom they had long loved. He smiled and waved to the crowd upon whose faces, for the first time that evening, broad smiles appeared.

He said that he had sent a telegram to President Eisenhower. He read it: "You have won not only the election but also an expression of the great confidence of the American people. I send you my warm congratulations.

Tonight we are not Republicans and Democrats, but Americans. We appreciate the grave difficulties your administration faces, and, as Americans, join in wishing you all success in the years that lie ahead."

Stevenson paused and looked out over the crowd. "And now," he went on, "let me say a word to you, my supporters and friends, all over the country."

First, I want to express my respect and thanks to a gallant partner in this great adventure—Estes Kefauver. I wish there was some way I could properly thank you, one by one. I wish there was some way I could make you feel my gratitude for the support, the encouragement, the confidence that has sustained me through these weeks and months and years that I have been privileged to be your leader. Thanks to many of you, I have twice had the proud experience of being selected by the Democratic Party as its nominee for the most exalted office on earth. Once again I have tried hard to express my views and make clear my party's hopes for our beloved country.

To you who are disappointed tonight, let me confess that I am, too! But we must not be downhearted, for "there is radiance and glory in the darkness, could we but see, and to see, we have only to look."

For here, in America, the people have made their choice in a vigorous partisan contest that has affirmed again the vitality of the democratic process. And I say God bless partisanship, for this is democracy's life blood. But beyond the seas, in much of the world, in Russia, in China, in Hungary, in all the trembling satellites, partisan controversy is forbidden and dissent suppressed. So, I say to you, my dear and loyal friends, take heart—there are things more precious than political victory; there is the right to political contest. And who knows better how vigorous and alive it is than you who bear the fresh, painful wounds of battle?

Let me add another thought for you who have traveled with me on this great journey: I have tried to chart the road to a new and better America. I want to say to all of you who have followed me that I am supremely confident that our cause will ultimately prevail, for America can only go forward. It cannot go backward or stand still.

But even more urgent is the hope that our leaders will recognize that America wants to face up squarely to the facts of today's world. We don't want to draw back from them. We can't. We are ready for the test that we know history has set for us.

And, finally, the will of our society is announced by the majority. And if other nations have thought in the past few weeks that we were looking the other way and too divided to act, they will learn otherwise. What unites us is deeper than what divides us—love of freedom, love of justice, love of peace.

May America continue, under God, to be the shield and spear of democracy. And let us give the administration all responsible support in the troubled times ahead.

Now I bid you goodnight, with a full heart and fervent prayer that we will meet often again in the liberals' everlasting battle against ignorance, poverty, misery and war.

Be of good cheer. And remember, my dear friends, what a wise man said: "A merry heart doeth good like a medicine, but a broken spirit dryeth the bones."

His smile broadened as, to his prepared statement, he appended a typical "Adlaiism": "Let there be no tears for me. If I have lost an election, I have won a grandchild."

The crowd laughed, and cried, and cheered him while, for a last time, the floodlights poured down and the flash bulbs popped and the camera eyes focused upon him. The photographers, as always, called upon him to turn first this way, then that. Amidst the frenzy, Borden grasped his father's right hand and lifted it high in the traditional gesture of victory.

BOOK EIGHT

A Prophet and His Prophecies

CHAPTER TWENTY-EIGHT

BITTERNESS remained from that campaign for both Presidential candidates.

Eisenhower revealed his personal feeling through an impulsive gesture on the night of election day.[1] He sat then with Nixon and a few others of his personal and official family watching the election returns on television in the suite assigned him in New York's Park-Sheraton Hotel. His joy in victory was not unconfined. Anxieties beset him. The Egyptian crisis remained acute; and beyond its peaceful resolution, if it were so resolved, must remain a greatly augmented Communist threat to the whole of the Middle East. Soviet armor continued to patrol the streets of bleeding Budapest; and America's helplessness in the face of this barbarity was personally embarrassing to one whose public speech, in 1952, had encouraged the Hungarians, among others, to believe they would receive active American support if they moved to liberate themselves from Soviet tyranny. Moreover, he must continue to deal with a Congress dominated by the opposition party, for it was early evident on election night that his personal popularity had not been sufficient, or was not of the kind, to effect the election of other Republican candidates in significant numbers.

A spirit so troubled was peculiarly vulnerable to rancors from the campaign just ended, especially to those born of harsh strictures upon the administration's conduct of foreign affairs—and these rancors fed Eisenhower's impatience as, for long hours after the outcome of the election was obvious, he awaited his opponent's concession of defeat. Finally he decided to go to the hotel's main ballroom, regardless, to claim his victory. He was about to do so when Stevenson appeared at last on the television screen. Abruptly Eisenhower removed his glasses, thrust them into his pocket, and got to his feet.

"I haven't listened to that fellow yet," he said emphatically. "I'm not going to now!"

And stalked from the room.

Stevenson's bitterness was of a different order. If Eisenhower's TV image gave him no great pleasure, neither did it arouse guilt feelings in him nor any kind of fear-tinged spiritual unease. His bitterness was focused, not on the man, but on the Eisenhower administration as, in his view, at once an author and an expression of ignorant, witless national complacency. The campaign's outcome had been determined by no popular consideration of real issues. Of this he was convinced. In a statement to the press in Chicago two days after the election he asserted that the electorate had gone to the polls in almost total ignorance of the errors that had produced the Suez crisis: had they known, had they understood, they would have repudiated Eisenhower. And he was now deeply disturbed lest Dulles and Eisenhower, and peoples abroad, should interpret the election result as an endorsement of disaster.

He reiterated this theme a few days later when, in his La Salle Street office, he was interviewed in depth by John B. Oakes of *The New York Times*.[2] Amidst the "euphoria and complacency so vigorously cultivated by the administration and the press," he said, the electorate was generally uninformed or misinformed on the most crucial issues, and especially on issues of foreign policy. He regretted that he himself had not laid more stress on these during his campaign. (This was his only serious regret, he added; he did not regret at all his test-ban stand or his stand on the draft.) His advisers had insisted there was no political gain for him in a discussion of foreign affairs; in this area, the voters cared only for peace, and the peace label had been too deeply impressed upon the smiling father image of Ike to be removed, or even much blurred, by anything Stevenson could say. Nevertheless, he believed he and Kefauver were beginning to get their message through when the Suez crisis intervened.

The failure of his campaign, in other words, had been one of communication, and he was convinced that it was by no means total. There would be long-range effects. "What endures from all this," he said, "is the extent to which one can penetrate the minds of people and influence our generation. If I can't win, I at least want to impress some ideas on the thinking of our times.... I think I have done that during the past four years, and while I have lost the election, I have no doubt at all that many of the views and ideas I have tried to express will ultimately prevail."

II

They would not prevail automatically, however. They must be continuously and persuasively advocated before as large a public as possible. Somehow, activating descriptions and judgments must be beamed through the prevailing "euphoria and complacency" into a now-slothful public mind. The problem of doing this was the first to engage Stevenson's attention in the immediate aftermath of the election.

One of his sorrows during the closing days of the campaign had been the fatal illness of Marshall Field, III, who on October 22 had undergone brain surgery for removal of a blood clot and who, on November 6, died in the New York hospital where the surgery had been performed. Field and his wife, the former Mrs. Ruth Pruyn Phipps, had become personal friends of Stevenson's during the months of 1944 when Stevenson was involved in the attempt to buy the Chicago *Daily News;* the friendship had grown during and since Stevenson's years as governor; and among the few happy anticipations that had sustained the candidate as he plunged toward the campaign climax had been that of a November holiday on Field's 20,000-acre estate in South Carolina. The anticipation was not disappointed by the death of his prospective host. Ruth Field, the widow, insisted that her husband would have wanted the vacation plans to be carried out—and so they were. Stevenson went down to the Carolinas in mid-month for days of lazing in the sun, of shooting and hiking and riding in the pine woods.[3]

But these were not his sole activities there. All the while that he was in South Carolina he was collaborating with Tom Finletter and others on plans for his activities during the next four years as a leader of responsible opposition to the administration.

The plans were made in terms of lessons learned from the late campaign. He held himself partly to blame for the failures of communication that had defeated him. But he was not exclusively to blame, nor even chiefly, in his own view. For one thing, as he had often said, bitter experience had taught him the futility of attempts to develop issues during a Presidential campaign; issues can only be presented at that time. They *should* be developed during the legislative process in the years separating elections, shaped by tensions between the Executive and Congress, but during the Eisenhower years this hadn't happened. Stevenson had repeatedly complained to associates, as he planned the battle of '56, that Senate Majority Leader Lyndon B. Johnson and, to a lesser degree, House Speaker Sam Rayburn were denying him those sharp definitions of issues which the party's Presidential candidate had to have to win. They did little or nothing to reduce the political potency of Ike. On the contrary, they seemed often to go out of their way to protect the man (sustaining the myth) against the consequences of his own ineptitudes. They, too, "liked Ike." And under their leadership, Southern conservatives continued to team up with Republicans, as they had for decades, to frustrate the party's, and the nation's, liberal impulses.

Nor was there any sign that Johnson and Rayburn, in the new Congress, would change their basic legislative strategy. On the contrary, they planned as before to wait until the Republican Executive submitted a legislative program, and then act upon it, yea or nay, as seemed to them best. Such good-natured passivity in the face of a notoriously passive Chief Executive irked a group of liberal Democratic senators. They interpreted the election result as a popular endorsement of the liberal 1956 party platform and proposed to implement specific platform planks with a sixteen-point minimum program of liberal Democratic action. However, they were a minority group within their own party's Congressional delegation; they could hardly hope by themselves to have large influence upon the Congressional leadership.

And in any case, Constitutional arrangements made it impossible for any senator or representative to speak and act altogether as a *national* Democrat. He must speak and act for a limited consituency. For the most part he must be at one with his constituency in prevailing attitudes and ideas on public questions, especially where these differed from those of other areas, else he could not have been elected in the first place. On those occasions when his conceptions of the national good ran counter to his constituents' strictly private local interests, or to such regional passions as the Southern white man's guilty fear of the Negro, he must sometimes subordinate the former to the latter in order to remain in office.

Clearly, then, and especially in the prevailing circumstances, it was a mistake to permit the party's Congressional members to be the only effective spokesmen of national party policy. There must be a "broader base," as Stevenson later explained in a statement to the press; Democratic mayors and governors, and other Democratic officials and workers throughout the land, must be "informed about party activity at the national level." There was need for a new device.

The device now finally decided upon, unique in the history of national party politics up till then, was a committee of advisers appointed by the fourteen-member Executive Committee of the Democratic National Committee and authorized to issue party policy declarations during the four-year interval between national conventions.[4] It was formally proposed to the Executive Committee by three of its members who were among Adlai Stevenson's firmest political supporters, Jacob M. Arvey of Illinois, Paul Ziffren of California, and David L. Lawrence of Pennsylvania, all of them representative of Northern urban Democracy. Most rural Southern Democrats, and conservative Democrats elsewhere, were against the proposal which, nevertheless, was adopted. On November 27, National Committee Chairman Paul Butler publicly announced in Washington the establishment of a Democratic Advisory Council, with Adlai Stevenson, as well as Harry Truman, Averell Harriman, and Mrs. Eleanor Roosevelt among its principal members. (Mrs. Roosevelt refused her invitation because she felt its acceptance would compromise her work as a newspaper columnist, but her refusal was nominal; she actively served as "consultant" and later chaired a committee.) The organization meeting of the new body was to be held in Washington on January 4 and 5, 1957, simultaneously with the opening of the new Congress—a planned coincidence whose possibly inadvertent effect might be to point to substantial differences between the party's "Presidential wing" and its "Congressional wing," to use the phraseology of James MacGregor Burns.[5] Certainly one intended effect of the Council was to strengthen the former relative to the latter; Council meetings would provide major occasions for public speech, and for the exertion of intra-party influence, by the party's titular leader.

But could Stevenson play his role as liberal opposition spokesman with maximum effectiveness so long as he continued to aspire to the Presidency, or was widely believed to do so? Tom Finletter didn't think he could. Neither did Marietta Tree (Mrs. Ronald Tree), another of Stevenson's close friends, who was at that time a guest on the Field estate, nor did Clayton Fritchey, a long-time newspaperman who had been deputy chairman of the Democratic National Committee in 1952, an occasional writer for Stevenson that year, and a good friend ever since (he was on the Stevenson campaign staff in 1956). These argued that their friend's persuasive power must inevitably be reduced to the extent that his disinterestedness was doubted. And Stevenson only too readily agreed. "The responsibility of being the Chief Executive of this country is humbling and frightening," he had said to John B. Oakes. "I have often wondered how a man can presume to seek from his party so exalted a position. . . . To say to your party. . . , 'I am the best man to be President' seems to me inconsistent with the grandeur of the office, and I've never quite made the reconciliation in my mind. But, of course, to say that my party—its philosophy, its record, its program—is better than the other one is a different matter. And about such a contest I have felt strongly."

Accordingly, on December 4, he issued through the Democratic National Headquarters a statement of withdrawal from Presidential politics. His interest in the party continued undiminished. He would be "of whatever help I can," he said, calling attention to his acceptance of a place on the Advisory Council. Above all, he wanted to help "bring home to the American people the facts about our situation and to warn them against complacency and a false sense of security." But, he said flatly, "I will not again run for the Presidency."

III

The statement seemed, on the face of it, an absolute renunciation. Was it? If so, what precisely did it renounce?

At the time, less than a month after he had suffered one of the most overwhelming and personally humiliating defeats ever inflicted upon a Presidential candidate (he had run so far behind his party!), the question his statement purported to answer seemed almost absurdly academic. His chances of winning, if he tried again for his party's top nomination, seemed infinitesimal by any realistic calculation. A chapter of his life—probably the climactic chapter—was now closed; and as in his Gridiron Club talk of 1952, so now in his remarkably revealing interview with Oakes (though this time without laughter) he publicly sounded a note of farewell and retrospection. To a question as to how he felt about his "whole experience" of public life he replied that he counted himself "among the most blessed of men. Win or lose," he went on,

> there are not many of my generation who have played such a part in the life of our times. First, my experience of government during—even before—the war; then at the peace councils of the nation here and abroad; then Governor of a great State; then twice Democratic candidate for President—and all this in a few years, starting from scratch. I wasn't a war hero like Eisenhower, nor did I have a deeply rooted political experience like F.D.R. And besides, I've had enormous satisfaction in going around the country and meeting innumerable fellow Americans who have told me they are taking an active part in politics for the first time as a result of my influence. This gives me a hell of a kick.

He had come to an ending. Asked about his plans for the future, he replied that he was "going to forsake the hot debate" for awhile "and go out under the stars and listen."

But there is reason to believe that in the deepest recesses of his mind, even as he made his seemingly absolute renunciation, there remained a seminal hope for the 1960 nomination, accompanied by a very general conceptual scheme for bringing the hope to fruition. Actually, he did *not* "forsake the hot debate," even for a little while; in the weeks immediately following the election he was intensely engaged in strategy planning for the national dialogue of the next four years. And the strategy decided upon, though it faithfully served both party and national interests as he saw them, would also serve, as none other could have done, whatever secret lingering ambition he may have had for the Presidency. Certainly his circumstances, if he would pursue such ambition, required the adoption of what Liddell Hart has called "the strategy of the indirect approach." A direct frontal attack, wherein he openly requested a third chance from his party after his two decisive defeats, would violate his own as well as the general public's sense of fitness. It would almost surely fail. If a third chance were given it should be freely given by a convention which, having considered the bids of the active aspirants, turned to one whose public philosophy and personal quality were already well-known. The most that he himself should do in the service of his ambition was to see to it that he was not forgotten, that his character and ideas were continuously impressed on the public mind, while at the same time he carefully avoided any indication of personal preference among those who openly sought the office.

What his withdrawal statement renounced, then—and all that it absolutely renounced—was an active intra-party campaign for the nomination.* Never again would he form an organization to promote his candidacy; never again would he engage in a fight through the primaries for convention delegates. And this renunciation cost him nothing of spiritual anguish. On the contrary, it was a relief to him, a release from anxiety. Since neither conscience nor ambition required him to do other or more than he now planned to do, he could live at peace with himself as he engaged in precisely the kinds of private and public activity best suited to his desire, his temperament, his talents.

IV

He returned to Libertyville—to his farm with its towering maples, its wide lawn sloping down to the Des Plaines, its fenced meadow where Suffolk sheep grazed placidly during the green seasons. He returned to no such loneliness and heartache as had so often marked his solitudes in the months after the 1952 defeat. Scar tissue had formed over the wound Ellen had given him, and he who was intensely a "family" man soon had family again around him, a constant, deeply satisfying reminder of his past and that his line would continue after him, with honorable distinction.

His eldest son Adlai III, and Nancy, with the grandson he had "won" while losing the election, lived in Chicago after young Adlai had completed (in June, 1957) his last year at Harvard Law School. He saw them often during the week; almost every weekend that he was home they spent with him on his farm. He was delighted with the way young Adlai was develop-

---

* Thomas K. Finletter, Carl McGowan, Newton Minow, W. Willard Wirtz, and others with whom I talked were agreed that Stevenson continued to hope for the Presidency. Judge McGowan indicated in discussion with me that Stevenson was consciously "making a gamble" for the Presidency from quite early after the 1956 defeat. The analysis of his strategy is my own, seeming to me an obvious logical inference from his words and acts, then and later. He himself never admitted that he had a campaign strategy, but neither did he pretend in his dealings with Finletter and others of equal intimacy that he did not want the Presidency. He wanted it.

ing, who had formerly been much less outgoing, much more solitary than Stevenson himself had been at the same age. People now told him that young Adlai reminded them of him as a young man, which greatly pleased him, for his son seemed to him to possess more poise and sweet reasonableness than most and, if as yet incipiently, a first-class talent for the political career to which he frankly aspired. There were dangers, of course. Some intimates sensed (or believed they sensed) a covert struggle of wills between young Adlai and Nancy and feared that Nancy, with her strong and vivid personality, her immense vitality, and her wholehearted zest for life, might blot out her naturally quiet and rather retiring husband and become, over the years, the dominant one of the two. But if the threat was real it was also recognized, and was therefore not likely to become an actuality; and certainly Nancy, with her rare charm, could be for her husband an invaluable political asset.

The father also took pride and pleasure in his two younger sons. Borden, during the first year after the election, was still in the Army, but his letters to his father were frequent and full of things that the father proudly showed or read to his sister and brother-in-law and to intimate friends. ("You know," said Stevenson, "Borden is the best writer in the family.") Borden, when honorably discharged from the Army, continued to manifest playboy tendencies and gave occasional signs of having been more badly hurt by the divorce than either the eldest or youngest had been. He continued to underrate his abilities. But there was no reason seriously to doubt that he would ultimately find himself, and meanwhile he was a most pleasant companion, handsome, and with perhaps a greater natural charm (he was gregarious and easy and full of fun) than either of his brothers manifested. John Fell, the youngest, was making the predicted total physical recovery from the ghastly automobile accident in which his two best friends had been killed. If psychic wounds remained, they were not of the sort to incapacitate him for effective living. He remained very shy, very lovable. He was doing well at Harvard.

Thus sustained in his private life, Stevenson entered now upon what he and his close associates would later remember as probably the happiest time of his life since the early days of his marriage.[6] He was tremendously busy as always, and as always he often inveighed against the pressures upon him and spoke of his yearning for a quiet life, away from the hurly-burly. But woe be it to the hostess who, having him as a houseguest on vacation, took him at his word! For no more than a few hours, a day or so at the most, could he bear to be alone and still, relaxed, doing nothing. He had to act, he had to be with people. He was driven (he had always been driven) by a surplus of electric energy, and to this was now joined, it seemed, in consequence of his political experience, a craving for crowded hectic activity that was like a drug addict's craving for a drug. Hence the pressures he complained of were very often of his own making; they were the result of occupations he enjoyed and from which he derived large spiritual rewards.

Immediately after the election, he and his staff had to cope with a flood of letters pouring into his office—approximately forty thousand of them by the end of December. He insisted that all of them be answered, most of them (necessarily) by his hard-worked staff but hundreds of them by himself personally. Though a heavy labor, it was not dull. There were letters of condolence, letters of disappointment and anger over felt injustices, letters of hope deferred but still defiant, letters (like those following the '52 campaign, though not so many as then) explaining apologetically why the sender had not voted for him, letters with suggestions for what must now be done, letters motivated solely by a deep affection and admiration for him as the writers believed him to be. To read a fair sample of them was to look into the very heart of the America he had tried so hard to represent; they lifted his own heart with their expressions of commitment to the ideals, the goals he had set for a new America.

While this work was going on he entered into complicated negotiations with a hugely successful New York law firm, negotiations aimed at establishing mutually profitable connections between it and his own Chicago firm. Public announcement of the final arrangement was made in the spring of 1957. Stevenson, with the approval of the New York City Bar Association, became a partner in the firm of Paul, Weiss, Rifkind, Wharton and Garrison, at 575 Madison Avenue, while remaining a citizen of Illinois. (He was formally admitted to the New York bar in May, 1958.) No change was made in the name of the New York firm, but the name of his Chicago office became Stevenson, Rifkind and Wirtz, and two new partners were added, his old friend Edward McDougal and a younger man, John Hunt. A Washington office was established under the name of Stevenson, Paul, Rifkind, Wharton and Garrison. The new arrangement was congenial and mentally stimulating to him.

His legal paper work continued to be done almost exclusively in his Chicago office. Again he proved to be a highly competent lawyer, different from most in that he saw any given legal problem in a larger context than most and so dealt with it in terms of connections and relevancies that most lawyers ignored. Wirtz, who had long ago learned that most of his partner's complaining about "pressures" was not to be taken too seriously, now noticed that Stevenson did genuinely resent interruptions (an inevitable frequent consequence of his continued public role) once he had become truly interested in a case. And he *did* become interested. Congeniality and mental stimulation were not all that derived from the new arrangement, either. Stevenson now made far more money than he had ever made before; his annual income, before taxes, climbed into six figures.

Yet he was by no means narrowly confined to an office. His major contribution to the firm's prosperity had little to do with legal technicalities; it had much to do with his immense world-wide prestige. He engaged in what an enemy might have described as legalized influence peddling. He was valuable to Reynolds Aluminum, for example, because he had entrée to the ruling powers of Jamaica and the rising young nations of Africa. He was valuable to the Authors League of America because, of all Americans, he was most likely to succeed (though in fact he did not) in an attempt to persuade the Russian government to pay royalties in dollars to U.S. authors whose works that government had published in translation. And the service of such interests, along with contracts for the publication of his writings in newspapers and magazines and books, enabled him to combine business with the educative pleasures of travel abroad.

He did a great deal of world traveling. In the late spring of 1957 he left Chicago by plane for an extended business and sightseeing tour of Europe and Africa, returning to New York in mid-August. In the summer of 1958 he was again in Europe, visiting the Brussels World's Fair and the Scandinavian countries before making a four-week, seven-thousand-mile tour of the U.S.S.R. (his sons Borden and John Fell accompanied him) climaxed by a probing, wide-ranging two-and-a-half-hour conversation with Premier Khrushchev.

Academic honors came to him, at home and abroad. Most pridefully pleasing to him was the honorary degree he received in May, 1957, from Oxford, where, as the symbols of his honor were handed him, students, and faculty gave him an ovation unprecedented, so far as anyone knew, in that ancient university's history. (He opened his hour-long address with a reference to Oxford as the "reputed home of lost causes" and to the fitness of his presence there since he was "probably the greatest living exponent of the Lost Cause." He received another ovation at the speech's end.) Some of his friends suspected that he thereafter accepted academic honors (a Chubb Fellowship at Yale, doctorates from McGill and Michigan State, among others) in part so that he could march in academic processions wearing the scarlet robe and square black cap of his Oxford honor.

Whether at home or abroad, he lived an intensely active, brilliant social life. A stream of famous visitors from all over the world came to him at Libertyville, and he accepted a far higher proportion of the party invitations proffered him in great quantity than most men would have done, or could have done without detriment to their daily work. "But you forget, I'm only a country boy from Bloomington," he laughed to Barbara Ward when she protested that he was overdoing the social life—and indeed some such self-feeling is indicated by the fact that, as Marietta Tree has said, "he couldn't bear to miss a party, a concert, a meeting, a trip that he heard others discuss." [7] He was invariably the life of the party in the best, most literal sense. Never boring, he was generally a fascinating conversationalist, flattering his listeners with his unfeigned interest in what they had to say and sharing with them, which was also highly flattering, his own rich experience among the exalted of the earth. His rare zest for life was highly contagious; he made everything and everyone around him come alive. And laughingly alive. His hilariously funny self-deprecation seemed to increase with his years and disappointments. (A typical later anecdote he loved to tell was of his return from a 1956 campaign trip to be greeted at the Chicago airport by a placard-carrying crowd in whose forefront was an enormously pregnant lady. Her sign proclaimed that "STEVENSON IS THE MAN.") [8] He thoroughly enjoyed the company of pretty, intelligent women. They thoroughly enjoyed his. His women friends were so numerous and devoted (he had a genius for making each feel that she was a very special person in his life) that some among his masculine friends spoke a bit acidly, perhaps enviously, of "Adlai's harem." Yet even those who used this phrase knew that its implications were untrue. Most of them were women of wealth and social position whom he had known for many years: Mrs. Edison (Jane) Dick, Mrs. John P. (Harriet) Welling, and Mrs. Walter ("Pussy") Paepcke, in Chicago; Doris Fleeson (Mrs. Dan Kimball), Mrs. Nan McEvoy, Mrs. Philip (Kay) Graham, and Mrs. Eugene Meyer (Kay Graham's mother), in Washington; Mrs. Ronald (Marietta) Tree, Mrs. Marshall (Ruth) Field, Mrs. Mary Lasker, Mrs. Vincent Astor, Mrs. John (Jane) Gunther, Mrs. Dan (Babs) Caulkins, Mrs. Orville E. (Marian Sulzberger) Dryfoos (now Mrs. Andrew Heiskell), and Alicia Patterson (Mrs. Harry Guggenheim), in New York; and Barbara Ward (Lady Jackson) of England, who spent much time in the United States. Of these (and the list is by no means exhaustive), the one in whom he seems to have been most seriously interested romantically was Alicia Patterson whose death, in 1963, he took very hard—but at various times the press reported rumors of his impending marriage to Mrs. Field or Mrs. Lasker, whose husbands had died. On at least two occasions he, in public speech, proposed marriage to Mrs. Eleanor Roosevelt, not seriously, of course, but with a gracefulness and obvious deep affection that delighted her. There was less jealousy and competition among his women friends than might have been expected; for the most part, because he insisted upon it, the feeling he had for each of them became a bond of friendship between them, forming a warm community of spirit. And he was no less loved by men of power and intelligence, and by a great many men and women of only ordinary attainments who had personal contact with him.

v

Neither private business nor private pleasures detracted from the strategy decided upon for his public life, however. Often, indeed, they were made to serve this strategy.

His foreign travels were well publicized in ways that identified him with definite stands, definite points of view on international and domestic affairs. There was always a press conference on the eve of his departure and another upon his return; there were always frequent press interviews and occasional full-scale press conferences while he was abroad. Nor was this the only influential publicity he garnered from his travels. He wrote travel articles in series for *Look* magazine and *The New York Times;* those he wrote of his Russian tour were published in a book entitled *Friends and Enemies* in 1959.

Other books by and about him kept his name and ideas before the reading public, the country's principal opinion makers. In the summer of 1957 a selection of his 1956 campaign speeches and position papers was published under the title, *The New America.* In that same summer the first full-length biography of him appeared.[9] If neither volume made much immediate impact in that season when popular interest in him was at its lowest ebb since his emergence as a national figure, both provided source material for later, more widely read writings. And by 1959, when his Russian book appeared, the interest in him had revived and was indeed approximately as great as it had been four years before. *Friends and Enemies* sold well. So, for its kind, did a collection of articles and speeches published in early 1960 under the title given the most important of them, "Putting First Things First," a long critical essay on American foreign policy, which was first published in *Foreign Affairs* for January, 1960.

But the principal vehicle of his political energies, the chief means of his contribution to the "national dialogue," was (as had been planned) the Democratic Advisory Council.

When Stevenson came to Washington in early January of 1957 for the organization meeting of the Council he attended the opening session of the new Congress. He sat in the diplomatic gallery, where his presence created such a stir that a somewhat flustered Lyndon Johnson, as Majority Leader, called attention to him from the floor, twice referring to him as a "distinguished Senator" before correcting this to "distinguished American." Stevenson, rising in his seat, bowed in acknowledgment of hearty applause from Republicans as well as Democrats. But reporters noted that his appearance at that time and place dramatized differences between the liberals with whom he was largely identified and the "centrist" and conservative

Democrats who dominated the new Congress. The latter's dominance was demonstrated later that same day when an effort by liberal senators to effect a rules change limiting debate, to prevent the filibustering to death of civil·rights legislation by Southerners, was defeated.

It was also noted that Lyndon Johnson and Sam Rayburn, along with House Majority Leader John W. McCormack and Senate and House Democratic Whips, Mike Mansfield and Carl Albert, refused invitations to become members of the Council. They did so on plausible legal grounds: as elected officials of government, they said, they could not properly share policy-making functions with any organization outside the government. Moreover, they joined Council members in a great show of party harmony and good will at a two-hour breakfast tendered them by the Council on January 5. But their antipathy toward the new organization was thinly veiled and helped to incite attempts, in February and again in May of 1957, to strip the Council of its authority by vote of the National Committee as a whole. Both attempts failed.

Not all senators shared either the ostensible or actual motives of Congressional leaders for non-participation in the new body. Senators Kefauver and Humphrey joined at the outset and former Senator Lehman became a member at large a few weeks later. Senators Kennedy and Stuart Symington finally joined in November, 1959, their decision obviously motivated by the Council's proved effectiveness as a moulder of public opinion. Thus, when the next Presidential election was less than a year away, all the senators having Presidential aspirations that rivaled Johnson's were participants in a body that Johnson continued covertly to oppose.[10]

Ultimately the Council had thirty-odd members, including five governors (G. Mennen Williams of Michigan, Orville L. Freeman of Minnesota, Foster Furcolo of Massachusetts, Stephen L. R. McNichols of Colorado, Edmund G. [Pat] Brown of California), and one big city mayor (Raymond Tucker of St. Louis). To advise the Council in specific subject-matter areas, a half-dozen auxiliary committees were eventually appointed. Those dealing with foreign policy and economic policy, established in the summer of 1957, were headed by Dean Acheson and John Kenneth Galbraith, respectively.

Ultimately, too, the Council developed a formidable operating apparatus including an executive director (Charles Tyroler, II), a general counsel, a three-man administrative committee, a five-man steering committee of which Stevenson was a member, and a finance director. The latter post, that of fund-raiser (the Council financed its work for the most part with solicited private contributions), was initially and unofficially filled by Tom Finletter, who, in March of 1958, persuaded his friend Robert Benjamin to accept an official appointment to it. The choice was a fortunate one, not only for the Council *per se* but also for the advancement of Stevenson's Presidential aspirations. Benjamin, who had previously donated $10,000

of his own money to the Council, was a brilliant lawyer and business executive who, as Chairman of the Board of United Artists, had helped to make
that corporation "the great success story of the movie industry" in the postwar years, to quote a letter from Tyroler to William Benton. Energetic,
imaginative, ebullient, selfless, a superb salesman of ideas and enthusiasms,
he was among those who had never participated actively in politics until
drawn into the 1952 campaign by his admiration for Stevenson. He remained
a fervent Stevenson man. He became a key member of what came to be
known as the "New York group," a wholly informal and unofficial group
(others of it were Finletter, Marietta Tree, Senator Lehman, William
Benton, Mrs. Eleanor Roosevelt, Mrs. Eugene Meyer, though she lived in
Washington), who hoped as early as 1958 to engineer a Draft-Stevenson
movement that would sweep the 1960 Democratic Convention.

And by the time Benjamin accepted his Council post, this hope seemed
no longer absurd. A quite remarkable transformation of Stevenson's political
image had occurred within a year after his withdrawal from active contention for the Presidential nomination. "STEVENSON BACK IN THE
LIMELIGHT" was the heading of an article in *The New York Times Magazine* for December 22, 1957. Under it, John Oakes reported increasing
"speculation that Stevenson may again be the Democratic nominee. A few
months ago this would have been unthinkable," Oakes went on. "Now it
is at least thinkable." The other contenders, he said, tacitly recognizing
that Stevenson (despite disavowal) remained a contender, "may knock
themselves out."

VI

How had this transformation come about? It had come in large part by
means of the Advisory Council. Stevenson took his Council duties with
utmost seriousness; none among his activities during Eisenhower's second
term had for him a higher priority. And of all Council members he did the
most, through his press conferences and speeches and writings, to publicize
the Council's policy views. He also made full use of the opportunities that
Council meetings provided for a public expression of his own views, as had
been anticipated when initial plans for the new body were made.

His were the major headlines at the time of the Council's first meeting in
early January, 1957. The President had at that time just asked Congress for
a Joint Resolution authorizing his use of economic and military power "if
necessary" to counter Soviet aggression in the Middle East, the definition
of "aggression" being unspecified—though in point of fact no such Congressional action was required: the President as Commander in Chief already
possessed the necessary authority. (What Eisenhower strove for, typically,
was a propaganda effect. A "greater effect could be had from a consensus

of Executive and Legislative opinion," he told House Majority Leader McCormack.) [11] Stevenson, in his press conference, pointed out that barely two months had passed since Candidate Eisenhower had said flatly that "there will be no [U.S.] involvement in present hostilities." Now, as President, he requested a "military blank check to fight in the Middle East," evidently trying "frantically to fill the vacuum his own policies helped to create before Russia does." But "if the result of the Suez disaster is to jolt us into recognition at last of the bankruptcy of our Middle Eastern policy and the hypocrisy of the campaign, it may yet do some good," added Stevenson pseudo-philosophically.

His were the major headlines, too, when the Council held its second meeting and issued the first of its policy statements—this in San Francisco, in mid-February of 1957. Addressing a fifty-dollar-a-plate Democratic fund-raising dinner, Stevenson anticipated these formal statements by harshly criticizing the Eisenhower administration's conduct of foreign affairs, especially in the Middle East (he demanded an end to "rock and roll diplomacy" wherein "vote-catching boasts" were almost invariably followed by disastrous reversals), and by calling upon Congress to "pass civil rights legislation in this session with overwhelming Democratic support and without a filibuster or parliamentary harassment." He cautioned the party against "overconfidence in '60." It was dangerous to believe that "when Ike retires it will be easy to capture the White House." Continuously vigorous and vocal opposition was needed. "The Democratic Party must pick its issues and stand by them, fight for them, not only in the lobbies and cloakrooms of Congress, but everywhere and all the time and by all of us. . . ." Otherwise there would be no effective criticism of the administration. Certainly the press would not provide it—would on the contrary do all in its power to protect Eisenhower and the administration against it. "As far as the press is concerned, Mr. Eisenhower's dead-end kids don't know what the word 'paddle' means. But I don't mean to be facetious about this," he went on; "indeed I solemnly assert that immunity from criticism from a large segment of the press, combined with massive and skillful use of propaganda and advertising, have brought us to a crisis in the honest political communication on which an informed electorate must depend."

A current instance was provided by the Federal budget for fiscal year 1958. As proposed to Congress in mid-January, this budget was moderately liberal, seemingly designed to implement that Modern Republicanism of which Eisenhower had vaguely spoken in his victory statement on election night. (". . . as we look ahead at the problems in front," he had said, "let us remember that a political party deserves the approbation of America only as it represents the ideals, the aspirations and the hopes of Americans. . . . Modern Republicanism looks to the future. . . .") [12] The budget contained moderate increases for welfare programs, natural resource development, foreign aid, and defense; it added Federal aid for school construction; and it bore a price tag of 72 billion dollars—the highest in peacetime history up to then and some 12 billion dollars above the ceiling proposed by Taft and Eisenhower in 1952.

But all this had been presented by the Executive to the Legislative branch in an unprecedentedly, astoundingly equivocal fashion. On the very day it went to Congress, Secretary of the Treasury George Humphrey issued a prepared statement, approved by Eisenhower, regretting the budget's size, following this with a press conference in which he predicted "a depression that will curl your hair" unless reductions were made in "the terrible tax we are taking out of this country." He said there were "a lot of places in this budget that can be cut" and that he would be happy "if Congress can find ways to cut." As for Eisenhower, asked in his next press conference whether the budget should be cut, he replied, "if they can, if Congress can, their committees, it is their duty to do it." [13]

This seemed to Stevenson outrageous—and outrage was compounded by press treatment of the episode. "Instead of explaining and defending" the budget in his capacity as the administration's chief fiscal officer, said Stevenson in San Francisco, the Secretary of the Treasury denounced it with the President's blessing, "called upon a Democratic Congress to cut it, and then . . . went off quail hunting with President Eisenhower. . . ." And did the press castigate the two for this incredible flouting of duty and logic? On the contrary, it actually "applauded them for criticizing their own handiwork!"

Press coddling no doubt protected Ike in this instance against the reduction of his personal popularity that might otherwise have resulted from his middle-of-the-road (both-ends-against-the-middle) strategy. His power to influence Congressional action on the budget was certainly reduced, however. He continued to back and fill on budget matters throughout the 1957 Congressional session, siding sometimes with budget-attackers, sometimes with budget-defenders, while Congress, lacking firm Executive guidelines, played partisan as well as (often) strictly local-interest politics with authorization and appropriation bills. And it was a typical irony of the Eisenhower years that Stevenson and the Advisory Council, whose avowed role was to lead a vigorous opposition to the administration, perforce gave far stronger support to key elements of the administration's legislative program for that year than did the administration itself.

A further irony was the gap that widened, as the year wore on, between the authorized policy-making body of the Democratic party and that party's Congressional leadership. The "overwhelming support" of civil rights legislation that Stevenson and the Council had called for in the first Council policy statement was not provided by Congressional Democrats. A small majority of House Democrats (118 out of 225) voted for the Civil Rights Bill when on June 18, 1957, after prolonged parliamentary harassment, it finally passed the lower chamber in approximately the form proposed. In the Senate, a majority of the Democrats voted for deletions and amendments that rendered the voting rights portion of the bill totally ineffective, then joined with the Republicans to pass the enfeebled measure 72 to 18. On the day it passed, August 6, Stevenson in a New York press conference (he had just returned from his tour of Africa and Europe) spoke with frank bitterness of this performance.

He also spoke bitterly that day of the fate of the administration's school construction bill, killed by the House three weeks before. In large part because of an anti-segregation rider tacked on by a strange alliance of liberals (who believed in it) and economy-minded Republicans (who counted on it to defeat the bill), only 97 of 223 Democrats had voted for a measure whose failure to pass constituted, in Stevenson's words, a "criminal neglect" of the educational needs of children. But the margin of defeat was narrow— a mere five votes (203 for, 208 against, with 77 of the latter Republicans). It could have been wiped out, in Stevenson's opinion, if the Chief Executive had not encouraged the budget parers and, in this particular instance, had not tried as usual to steer a middle course between "two extremes," one of which vehemently approved of school construction and the other of which vehemently opposed it. "I wish President Eisenhower had talked as loudly to the Republicans in Congress [on this issue] as he did to the voters last year," said Stevenson in New York.[14]

A few weeks later, pressure from thoroughly aroused Negro and civil rights organizations and from that general public which the Democratic Advisory Council represented forced a Senate compromise (engineered with his usual skill by Lyndon Johnson) on the voting rights provisions of the Civil Rights Bill. It then passed the House by a vote of 279 to 97 and the Senate by 60 to 15, despite a twenty-four-hour, one-man filibuster by Senator Strom Thurmond of South Carolina. On September 9, 1957, President Eisenhower signed into law the first civil rights measure to pass the Congress in eighty-five years. It was, however, far less comprehensive, with far weaker enforcement features, than the national situation demanded, in the liberal view, and no liberal Democrat could be proud of the overall contribution that his party's Congressional delegation had made to its substance or its adoption.

Thus the efforts of Stevenson and the Council failed in terms of their immediate objective, that of influencing current legislation. They admirably succeeded, however, in terms of Stevenson's personal prestige, as well as in terms of the general welfare as Stevenson defined it. Not only did these efforts continue and even strengthen Stevenson in his position as the leading national Democrat, the leading national spokesman of political liberalism (he repeatedly called for a "reaffirmation of the liberal faith"); they also kept strongly alive in the Democratic party a liberal tradition which would certainly have been drastically enfeebled amidst the smothering mental fogs of

Eisenhower "moderation" had its care been entrusted altogether to Johnson, Rayburn, and their Congressional colleagues of the "center."

But the Council was not the only institutional means whereby Stevenson's political image had been transformed. Of equal importance to the process were institutional means provided him by the Eisenhower administration itself—provided, indeed, by precisely that portion of the administration to whose policies Stevenson was most bitterly opposed, namely, the State Department of John Foster Dulles!

VII

On October 4, 1957, the Soviet Union shot into orbit the world's first man-made satellite—an object twenty-two inches in diameter, weighing 184 pounds, and carrying two radio transmitters for continuous signal communication with earth. Its Russian name, *sputnik* (for "traveling companion"), became immediately one of the most-used nouns in the English language, while its implications regarding the relative standings of the U.S. and Russia in science, technology, weapons, and education abruptly dissipated much of that smug complacency, that lazy indifference to public affairs, which had characterized the national mood since the eclipse of Joe McCarthy. The administration, frankly surprised by the Russian achievement, was even more surprised by what Eisenhower later described as "the intensity of public concern." So intense was it, in fact, that soothing syrups theretofore used with great effect by the administration now failed to work at all. When Eisenhower told his press conference that he had never considered the U.S. and the U.S.S.R. to be engaged in a space "race" and that the satellite "does not raise my apprehensions, not one iota," he did less to soothe the public than to raise doubts about his own sense of realities, his own capacity to rise to great challenges with brave and active leadership. When Presidential Assistant Sherman Adams indicated that he found it absurd for the public to be so wrought up over "an outer-space basketball game" he provoked anger not untinged with contempt.

Adlai Stevenson, in this instance, was more inclined to agree with Eisenhower's public words than with the more extreme and frightened of the administration's critics. He was frankly glad for the widespread doubts being raised at last about the intellectual and moral quality of that America which Eisenhower so perfectly personified. He agreed with other Eisenhower critics that the absence of decisive leadership from the White House in this era of enormous rushing change might open the way to world disaster. But he deplored the prevailing tendency to view all space achievement solely in terms of an international competition having distinctly warlike overtones. He measured by other terms; he took a longer view. Speaking on November

12 at a dinner held under the auspices of the National Council of Christians and Jews in New York's Waldorf-Astoria Hotel, he asserted that the "basic issue" was not the supremacy of one nation over another but the "supremacy of man for good or evil, for survival or suicide." *Sputnik*, therefore, should be viewed as a "call to decision" rather than a "portent of disaster."

As he spoke that evening, he was well aware of one effect *sputnik* was then having on the administration, for he was personally involved in it. Greatly enhanced was the administration's sense of the importance of a NATO conference to be held in Paris in mid-December. This would be the first NATO meeting to be held since the Suez disaster; it would also be the very first in which the member nations were represented not by their foreign ministers but by their heads of government. It was to be a NATO "summit," attended by Eisenhower personally. In view of this, the immense dark shadows cast by tiny *sputnik* on the American mood made the administration particularly anxious to muffle so far as possible, in advance of a conference failure which then seemed distinctly possible, that single voice most persuasively critical of the administration's conduct of foreign affairs. The voice, of course, was Adlai Stevenson's.

Accordingly, Secretary of State Dulles, speaking, he said, for the President as well as himself, had approached Stevenson in early November to ask that the Democratic party's titular head participate to the fullest extent in the formulation of the U.S. position for the forthcoming meeting. Indeed, the words Dulles used could be interpreted to mean that Stevenson, if he accepted, would be responsible for drafting the new American position, which would then be passed upon by the President and Secretary of State. Further, Stevenson was asked to come to Paris as a member of the U.S. delegation, wherein he would be outranked only by Eisenhower and Dulles. The appeal (for it had that quality) was couched in terms of patriotic duty: at this juncture, a "bipartisan" approach was of the utmost importance.

Stevenson, nevertheless, was wary. He was not unmindful of the disadvantages he would suffer and of the advantages his political opposition would gain if he were tagged with public responsibility for final policies with which he might or might not agree. He therefore suggested for himself a much more modest role, that of mere adviser or "consultant." Thus his publicly assigned responsibility for the event would be no greater than his actual authority to determine it, and his freedom to criticize, if criticism seemed needed, would be unimpaired. But before this point was settled, that genius for "image-making" which played so determinative a role in the administration had seized upon the opportunity to make Stevenson appear once again to the general public as indecisive. It was announced in Washington (November 11) that Eisenhower had asked Stevenson to accompany him to Paris "as the third man in charge of U.S. efforts to revitalize Allied opposition to Soviet expansion"; it was further reported that Dulles was "concerned about

Stevenson's delay in making up his mind." White House Press Secretary Jim Hagerty, questioned on this, suggested, "Why don't you ask Mr. Stevenson?" When reporters did so, Stevenson, then in New York for his November 12 speech, referred them back to the White House, or Dulles, but (without permitting himself to be directly quoted) saw to it that his reasons for hesitancy were reported in next morning's papers. Later on that same day, November 12, the administration announced in Washington that Stevenson had accepted the role of "consultant." Whether or not he would accompany the President to Paris remained an "open question."

Five days later, Stevenson arrived in Washington to assume his consultant duties. Reporters greeted him and he talked freely with them. The United States must rebuild mutual confidence with her Allies in the Atlantic Pact, he said, and must, in concert with her Allies, develop a more flexible military posture. The danger of naked Soviet aggression in Western Europe, resulting in general war, had receded while that of "brush-fire" wars in various parts of the globe had increased. To deal with this latter threat the U.S. was militarily ill-prepared, having placed her emphasis on "massive retaliation" with nuclear arms. But Stevenson's primary concern was not with exclusively military matters. He was worried by the possibility of "a Communist economic breakthrough" in underdeveloped areas, among uncommitted ex-colonial peoples—and to deal with such problems, and at the same time take steps toward the organization of a peaceful world order under world law, he hoped that NATO might become more than an international military organization. He would like to see closer political ties among its members; he would like to see greater attention paid to social and economic matters....

It cannot be said that Stevenson's three-and-a-half-week stint in the State Department had much if any influence on U.S. policy at the conference. From the first he was treated with coolness by the White House. An announcement had been made that he would confer with both Eisenhower and Dulles as he entered upon his duties, but Eisenhower left town for a golf-and-work vacation in Augusta, Georgia, shortly before Stevenson arrived and conveyed his regrets by letter, along with a promise of future conference. (One of the most famous of Herblock's political cartoons, published at this time, showed a cherubic Ike on the golf links outside an office building wherein a sweating, shirt-sleeved Stevenson toiled over a stack of papers. Above hovered a flying saucer in which one Martian asked another, "How did you say their election came out?") Sherman Adams said publicly a few days later, with obvious reference to Stevenson, that some of the advisers the administration had taken on in its anxiety over NATO were of "dubious quality." Dulles and the State Department, on the other hand, treated Stevenson with the greatest courtesy and even with a measure of cordiality. They assigned him the prestigious "ambassador's suite" as his office in the department building; they did all in their power to facilitate his work; they gave the most respectful attention to his recommendations. But it was clear at the outset that the gulf between Stevenson's and Dulles's conceptions of foreign policy was far too wide to be bridged by any amount of personal good will.

Dulles, presented with Stevenson's proposals for closer political and economic collaboration among the Western Allies, countered with the view that an excruciating "dilemma of choice" was here involved. The suggested collaboration, he feared, would cost the United States that support of Asian and African States which she was trying so hard to obtain. This was so because of the wide divergence of national interests, as regards Africa and the Middle East and the Far East, between the United States and the ex-colonial powers of Western Europe. Consider, for example, the Middle East, where the U.S. had recently stood firm against the efforts of Britain and France to impose their will by force upon a people who had once been part of the British Empire. If the U.S. modified her policy in this area to the extent required for an accommodation with Britain and France she must, in the process, alienate ex-colonial peoples everywhere. Thus the Dulles view. Stevenson profoundly disagreed. ". . . I do not believe that we have interests in the Middle East and in Asia which differ materially any longer from those of our NATO partners," he wrote in a memorandum to Dulles on November 29.[15] "I doubt whether our interest in the survival of a democratic India is any greater or any less than Europe's. Collapse of the Western position in the Pacific would be as fatal to Europe as to us. Who can say whether we or our NATO partners have been more seriously damaged by the deteriorating situation in the Middle East? Our differences with our allies have not been so much differences of interest as differences in judgment as to the wisdom of actions." He strove mightily to persuade Dulles that NATO members should cease to place top priority "on launching pads and missiles," as he later put it to Theodore H. White, and should instead place it "on the concert of our resources to help the emerging nations." The "main threat is *not military aggression*, but subversion by propaganda, economic bribery and political penetration," he wrote in the November 29 memorandum, and he wanted to know whether the Atlantic Community had "any common plans to counter such ambiguous aggressions?" He also wanted to know whether "an experimental plan to stabilize some raw material prices which is so important to the underdeveloped areas" was "beyond the capacity of a league of the principal industrial states like NATO." He strove in vain. His arguments had no perceptible effect upon the position papers that were finally drafted.

Stevenson failed, too, in his effort to persuade the administration to take an affirmative attitude toward proposals put forward by Premier Nikolai A. Bulganin of the U.S.S.R. just as Stevenson was coming to the end of his work as consultant. He had anticipated some such Soviet move. "We must be ready for new Russian proposals which may be extremely effective as propaganda," he had written in his first memorandum to Dulles. "I have often said that suspension of nuclear testing with suitable monitoring posts to safeguard against violations should not be made conditional on cessation of production of nuclear materials. [Eisenhower had repeatedly refused to consider test suspension without production suspension.] It would be an important first step; it would break the deadlock and halt or slow down the dangerous race which at best leads only to stalemate and a balance of terror." What Bulganin now proposed, in a letter to the President, were talks between the two Governments aimed toward outlawing war, ending hydrogen bomb tests, and establishing a "new security system" for Europe. No doubt this communication on the eve of the Paris conference was designed to influence discussions there—State Department spokesmen said as much to reporters even before Eisenhower had read the letter—but Stevenson felt that the formal U.S. reply should take advantage of the opportunity to assure the world of our own commitment to the peace goals that Bulganin avowed while leaving the door open to further Russian moves in this direction. Instead, Dulles published his disinclination to engage in any bilateral talks with the Soviet Union on questions in which other countries were concerned, and Eisenhower's later formal reply to Bulganin was politely negative. "You renew the oft-repeated proposal ... [that nuclear bomb tests be suspended, but] you defer to the indefinite future any measures to stop production of such weapons," said the President in a letter to the Soviet Premier on January 13, 1958.[16]

The administration, in short, was not disposed to review critically its foreign policies and programs, much less change them. It was easy for Stevenson to conclude, as indeed he had suspected from the beginning, that the administration sought to use him primarily as "window dressing."

But it was equally easy for him to frustrate this design and turn it to his own purposes. In early December, Eisenhower, having returned from his Georgia vacation, accorded him a brief interview—the first face-to-face meeting of the two men in four years. The atmosphere was chilly. Immediately thereafter, Stevenson announced his decision not to go to the Paris Conference "unless there are compelling developments," since official membership on the U.S. delegation would put him in a position "without authority" yet "necessarily identified with decisions I might not always agree with and could not publicly oppose." Simultaneously, he let reporters know that he had been prepared to go if the President had urged him to do so but that, instead, Eisenhower had merely "suggested" that if Stevenson *wished* to be present he, Eisenhower, would welcome his presence. (Two days later a widely quoted *New York Times* story said that "high officials of the State Department" were distressed by Eisenhower's failure to issue that "hearty invitation" which Dulles, in his anxiety to obtain bipartisan support from Congress, had urgently recommended.) Stevenson also let reporters know, upon the completion of his assignment, what the general nature and some of the particular items of his disagreement with Dulles had been, information that was prominently featured in newspapers, news magazines, and newscasts.

The upshot was that he emerged from his otherwise futile labors with his personal prestige greatly enhanced. It was chiefly his State Department role that now brought him "back in the limelight," inciting the Oakes *New York Times Magazine* piece among much other favorable publicity. And the limelight found him clothed in dignity. The administration itself had draped over his plebeian garb as "politician" the patrician robes of "statesman."

CHAPTER TWENTY-NINE

T HE course of events through 1958, and Stevenson's responses to them, did nothing to reduce his prestige. They did much to heighten the speculation that the Presidential nomination of 1960 might, after all, be his.

The President's budget for the fiscal year 1959, presented to Congress in January of 1958, was far less liberal, far more restrictive, than the one George Humphrey had sabotaged the year before. Indeed it expressed, with remarkably few concessions to political expediency in a midterm election year, Humphrey's profound conviction that the greatest danger facing America was an amalgam of Federal spending, deficit financing, rising tax rates, and an allegedly consequent, ultimately uncontrollable inflation. No new starts on power, flood control, and reclamation projects; no Federal aid for school construction; severe restrictions upon urban development and welfare programs and on Federal aid for hospital construction; provisions for defense and space that were dangerously meager in the opinion of many knowledgeable observers—these characterized the new budget. Its single merit, which more than offset all its deficiencies in the administration view, was that its total expenditures of 73.9 billion dollars would be matched by the year's Federal revenues, or very nearly so, according to Budget Bureau estimates.

And in sharp contrast to his behavior of the year before, Eisenhower was unequivocal, even fervent in his support of the new budget.[1] He was now wholly converted to Humphrey's orthodox economic faith; the budget's basic premise should be, in his opinion, the central issue of the 1958 election campaign. ("... I ... decided to hammer away on one overriding theme [during the campaign]," he writes in his memoirs: "my conviction that the deficit-producing, inflation-inviting, irresponsible-spending proposals of self-described liberal Democrats in the Congress had to be combatted at every turn.")[2] Thus the battle lines were clearly drawn for a change: Stevenson and the Council, wielding weapons of opposition, could fire at targets that remained visible and in place instead of wavering from one side to the other in a fog of ambiguity. Moreover, events now provided them with far more effective ammunition than they had possessed the year before.

One such event was *sputnik*. The "public concern" whose "intensity" had surprised Eisenhower was further intensified when a second *sputnik* carried a dog into orbit while a much-publicized first attempt by the United States to orbit a satellite failed spectacularly (the Vanguard that was to take it aloft caught fire two seconds after lift-off and crashed to earth). Loud, and more widely persuasive than ever before, were criticisms of the administration's fiscal emphases—its alleged subordination of national security to the business community's special interest in reduced Federal spending and low tax rates. Loud were demands for a greater national effort in space technology and missile-weapons systems, and for stronger Federal support of education and scientific research. Nor were the voices making these demands much muffled by the successful launching of three U.S. satellites within eight weeks early in 1958; it remained obvious that Russian rockets had far greater thrust than any the U.S. had yet been able to make.

Another event that provided political ammunition for Democrats was the major economic recession of which the first signs appeared almost simultaneously with the first *sputnik* and which, by April of 1958, had become the steepest and deepest economic decline since World War II. Factory production was down nearly fourteen percent. Nearly five and a half million workers were unemployed. Corporate profits were down almost twenty-five percent. There was an ominous reduction in new investments for business expansion. And from all this Eisenhower could not even derive the negative comfort of relief from anxiety over inflation since the overall decline was not reflected by a decline in consumer prices; on the contrary, consumer prices continued to rise. By midsummer they were 2.6 percent higher than they had been when the recession began. To Eisenhower, the recession, by greatly reducing tax revenues, made it more urgently necessary than before to limit government spending in order that the budget might be kept near balance. To Stevenson and economists of the Advisory Council the recession had precisely opposite policy implications: there should be more rather than less government spending in order to stimulate the economy and prevent a loss of total income that must otherwise far exceed the cost of such spending. Sound policy in general, by their view, demanded government action to divert a larger portion of the total national income from the "private" to the "public sector" of the economy where it could be used for urban renewal, education, scientific research, and other public needs. The absolute size of the national debt, however great, was not *per se* dangerous, they further argued. What was important was the quantitative relationship between this debt and the gross national product. Only when the latter waned while the former waxed were grave anxieties justified.

Thus the circumstances (what with the fears born of *sputnik*, the hard times born of recession) were unpropitious, to say the least, for any such Budget Message as the President had sent up to the Hill that January. Seldom had the public mind been less susceptible to arguments that gave budget-balancing top priority in a list of governmental goals. Yet Eisenhower, with unwonted fortitude and consistency, clung to his position all through the spring, resisting (successfully) attempts by many Republicans to achieve a tax cut and (with somewhat less success but far more fervor) attempts by many Democrats to increase spending. "Happily, there was still enough common sense in controlling places in the Congress to prevent the most outrageous [spending] bills from reaching my desk," say his memoirs, in veiled tribute to the Congressional leadership of Rayburn and Johnson, though he complained to George Humphrey in the summer of 1958 that, denied the power to veto separate items within appropriations bills, he had been forced in several instances to sign measures that imposed "unwarranted drains on the Federal Treasury." [3] (For fiscal 1959, in point of fact, the budget was out of balance by nearly 13 billion dollars.) And by early autumn he might and did feel that his firm stand, his refusal to "panic" (as he himself described it), was being justified in the event. In June and July an upward trend began that continued through the remainder of the year. The event, however, did little to brighten Republican prospects for November. There was no such surge of returning prosperity as might have wiped active memories of recession from the public mind. And Stevenson and the Council, among others, were quick to stress the cost of what they termed a "needless" recession in terms of lost production, lost Federal revenues, reduced personal incomes, and, for many, acute economic distress.

Yet other events, these in Stevenson's chosen field of foreign affairs, produced political liabilities for administration Republicans and political assets for Stevenson Democrats that summer and early fall. On May 8, 1958, Richard M. Nixon, Vice-President of the United States, a symbolic personage as he and his wife made a good will tour of Latin America, encountered no good will at San Marcos University in Lima, Peru. There his party was booed and shoved and its cars were stoned by a mob of angry anti-American demonstrators. Five days later, in Caracas, Venezuela, an even larger and uglier mob closed round the car in which Nixon rode, smashing it with stones and clubs and threatening its occupants with bodily injury. (Eisenhower at once ordered a thousand U.S. troops to be flown to Puerto Rico and Guantánamo Bay in Cuba, whence they could be whisked to Venezuela to rescue the Nixons if necessary.) On that same day, anti-American rioters burned two American libraries in Lebanon and there were ugly anti-American demonstrations in Algeria and Burma. All this, seen by the administration as proof of the world-wide threat of communism, aroused widespread concern over the erosion of America's world prestige, a concern that Stevenson, convinced it was more than justified, did all he could to encourage and to blame upon what he regarded as the Executive's fumbling, deceitful ineptitudes. He inveighed against the administration's total failure to understand and adjust to what Harlan Cleveland had called the "revolution of rising expectations" among the great masses of the underdeveloped areas of the world; he bitterly condemned a continued reliance by the administration upon brinkmanship in international crises that could have been avoided if creative thought and action had been applied to their causes.

Two alarming instances of brinkmanship, as Stevenson saw it, swiftly followed.

In July, 1958, Eisenhower filled out and cashed that blank check for military action in the Middle East which he had requested and received from Congress six months before. He landed some fourteen thousand American troops in Lebanon (the entire Lebanese army numbered nine thousand), after having induced the Lebanese Government to request U.S. military aid. There was no Communist revolt in Lebanon, nor any serious threat of outside Communist aggression. There was only a threat of civil strife because a pro-American and Christian President was, with good reason, suspected of conniving in an attempt to assure himself a second term by amending the Constitution, which forbade it. This incited Moslem dissidents, some of whom formed armed bands, and the Lebanese Government hesitated to order out its own troops because so many of them, being Moslem, might have gone over to the other side. But this strictly internal trouble had as its international context the recent formation under Nasser's leadership of a United Arab Republic comprising Egypt and Syria—and the Eisenhower Administration *now* suspected that Nasser was secretly a Communist, eager to absorb Lebanon into his Communist "empire." Hence a show of American force which appeared absurdly exaggerated in the eyes of informed observers, with the attendant grave risk of provoking a countermove by Soviet Russia. (Eisenhower himself, in his memoirs, tells of the visit to Washington a year later of the leader of the Lebanese rebel forces, Rashid Karami, who had become Lebanese Premier. When Eisenhower mentioned the U.S. landings, "Mr. Karami said with a laugh that it would have been better had the United States held off sending troops but merely sent Mr. [Robert] Murphy. . . ." Eisenhower of course disagreed but "could not completely smother the thought that if our visitor's statement had been true, every one in my administration would have been saved a lot of anxious hours." [4])

Stevenson was touring Soviet Russia as U.S. troops made their wholly unopposed landing near Beirut. He was a personal witness to the anger aroused in Moscow by this new act of United States "aggression"; he was impressed by the fact that the extreme hostility that the Soviet Government and Russian people expressed toward his country on this issue did not prevent their giving him personally a warm, friendly reception. He perforce made no public comment on Lebanon at that time. But on his way to Russia in late June he had held a press conference in Paris during which he expressed the hope that whatever action was taken in Lebanon would be taken through the United Nations. "Anything else," he said, "would be unthinkable."

Simultaneously with the Lebanese crisis came the development of a new crisis in the Far East. As in January of 1955, and largely in consequence of the administration's decision at that time, along with the dangerously permissive relationship with Chiang Kai-Shek the administration continued to maintain, the crisis centered on the tiny island groups of Quemoy and Matsu just a few miles off the Chinese mainland. Its evident provocation was the build-up of Chinese Nationalist troops on these islands by Chiang through the first half of 1958 until, by summer, a full third of all his ground forces, or approximately 100,000 men, were stationed there. Since Chiang's avowed purpose was to reconquer mainland China, and since his capacity to wage even a strictly defensive war depended wholly upon U.S. naval, air, and matériel support, it was inevitable that his troop dispositions would arouse suspicion among the Red Chinese that a U.S.-supported attack upon them was being prepared. Why otherwise would the U.S. have permitted so massive a movement into so advanced a position? Actually, the administration's failure to prevent this troop movement was but another instance of Executive passivity. The Nationalist Chinese had been advised that their excessive concentration in the offshore islands seemed "militarily unwise"—and that was all.

On August 23, having built up their local strength opposite the islands, the Communist Chinese initiated a massive artillery bombardment, firing some twenty thousand rounds into Quemoy and Matsu. They continued for weeks thereafter to fire approximately eight thousand rounds a day, repeatedly strafed Quemoy from the air, established a blockade of the islands, and all the while broadcast in the harshest terms their determination to "liberate" not only the offshore islands but Formosa itself. Taken literally, the Communist broadcasts meant that the President, by the terms of the Formosa Resolution, which he had asked for and obtained from Congress in January of 1955, *must* order U.S. military intervention if the Red Chinese actually attempted to occupy Quemoy-Matsu. Thus the world was brought again to the fearful brink of World War III. Chiang of course did his best to make war between the U.S. and Communist China. He asserted that the defense of Quemoy-Matsu was hopeless unless he were permitted to take strong aggressive action against the mainland, and he demanded a categorical pledge that the United States would fully support such action. Eisenhower refused. Instead he ordered convoy protection for Nationalist shipping to the three-mile limit of Quemoy-Matsu, issued a statement combining firmness of intent to defend the islands with willingness to negotiate toward a permanent settlement, and in general acted with commendable prudence in the situation his policies had done so much to create. A stalemate resulted. In the end, in the autumn, the Communist Chinese reduced and then ceased the shelling, Chiang was induced to withdraw some of his forces ("... but not to the extent I thought desirable," says Eisenhower in his memoirs [5]), and the former precarious truce was restored.

All through the crisis, influential voices, some of them referring to Stevenson's Quemoy-Matsu speech of 1955, inveighed against permitting our Far Eastern policy to be made by Chiang, an aging island dictator whose incapacity for decent government had been a principal cause of his being driven from the mainland. Stevenson himself had watched developments with growing anger and dismay. He was convinced that, in any rational American foreign policy, Quemoy and Matsu would have been deemed expendable. Of what conceivable use could they be to us save as landing stages for Chiang's return to the mainland? And what person in his right mind could regard such a return as even a remote possibility? Surely, then, the 1955 crisis had presented the United States with a rare opportunity to open communications with the Red Chinese, to initiate negotiations that might have gone far toward stabilizing the whole Far Eastern situation. The negotiations would have had to be delicately handled, of course—but their conclusion could well have been our withdrawal of Chiang's ridiculously provocative forces from the offshore islands and a relinquishment of these islands to the mainland from which they were so narrowly separated, this in return for Peking's agreement to a plebiscite in Formosa and to a renunciation of the use of force in the settlement of disputes. The neutralization of Southeast Asia might well have followed. A way would then have been opened toward the fully responsible involvement in world affairs of a nation whose population numbered one-fourth of the human race, whose capacity and willingness to wage war were evidently rapidly growing, and whose continued exclusion from the family of nations was therefore the height of perilous folly. But instead of seizing this opportunity the administration had stood firm; the islands had been fortified, the dangers perpetuated if not augmented. The lost opportunity constituted, in Stevenson's later words to Theodore H. White, "one of the greatest political crimes of our times." [6] And now, in 1958, the crime was repeated. The stated willingness on our part to negotiate was not expressed in terms sufficiently concrete, nor with sufficient urgency, to invite any real hard bargaining with the Chinese. And so the evils were compounded. The only good Stevenson could see in the episode was a possible further decrease in public confidence in the Republican administration's conduct of foreign affairs, with a consequent reduction of the chances of Republican candidates at the polls. It was a highly problematic good, in the prevailing state of mass communications.

There was nothing problematic, however, about the political effects of another and very different event as it developed through that troubled summer. This was the sad case of Sherman Adams.

A former governor of New Hampshire, Adams was a taciturn Yankee of the Cal Coolidge type, singularly devoid of social graces and much given to moral pronouncements wherein the vulgarity, graft, and corruption of Truman's Washington were compared with the dignity and the ethical purity of Eisenhower's Washington. He had been delegated great personal power as, in effect, Deputy President of the United States, and had wielded it in such manner as to make few personal friends and many personal enemies. Right-wing Republicans, who thought him too liberal, and virtually all Democrats disliked him intensely. They were therefore wickedly, secretly gleeful when investigators of the House Subcommittee on Legislative Oversight discovered that Adams had several times elicited special information from government regulatory agencies for a long-time friend, Bernard Goldfine, a New England industrialist whose tangled and dubious business operations were under probing Congressional scrutiny; that Adams had accepted expensive gifts (a vicuña coat, an Oriental rug) from Goldfine; and that Goldfine had paid hotel bills to the amount of more than $3,000 for the Adams family in Boston and Plymouth, Massachusetts.

When the earliest of these disclosures were made, in early June of 1958, Stevenson was preparing to depart for his visit to Europe and the U.S.S.R. At a Chicago press conference on Friday, June 13, the eve of his departure, he made harsh comment on Adams's "holier-than-thou self-righteousness" and "pious preaching" and wanted to know if Goldfine had written off the gifts and hotel bills, on his tax returns, as business expenses. At almost precisely the same time, in Washington, Eisenhower at his press conference was reading a carefully prepared statement expressing liking and respect for Adams and an absolute confidence in Adams's "personal and official integrity," while admitting "the lack of . . . careful prudence in this instance." He added a plaintive note. "I need him," he said. But it was soon revealed that the ineffable Goldfine had indeed listed the Adams gifts and hotel bills as business expenses and that he had long had an unsavory reputation in the business world. Adams's continued presence in the White House now became an acute personal embarrassment for Eisenhower, an intolerable political liability for Republican candidates, and in September, after the Maine elections had resulted in the crushing defeat of that state's Republican governor (he, also, had had disclosed dealings with Goldfine), Adams was induced to resign.

The damage, however, joined to that inflicted by recession and (possibly) by repeated brinks of war, was irreparable in the few weeks remaining before the national elections. Eisenhower sought in vain to arouse in the general public the anxiety he felt over what he called "reckless public spending" by the wing of the Democratic party (the "stronger wing") dominated by "political radicals," as he put it in a Los Angeles campaign speech. On November 4, Republicans suffered, overall, a resounding defeat in the Congressional and gubernatorial races. In the new Congress, Democrats outnumbered Republicans 283 to 153 in the House and 64 to 34 in the Senate.

II

The event narrowed somewhat the gap between Democratic Congressional leadership and the Stevenson-Advisory Council wing of the Democratic party. Among the new faces in House and Senate were Democrats whose entrance into politics had been stimulated by Stevenson's example, whose election would probably not have been possible in the absence of that example, and who were more than willing to accept Advisory Council policy statements as legislative guidelines. Their active presence had, inevitably, its effect on the Rayburn-Johnson leadership. But the net result was no surge of liberal legislation. On the contrary, the 1959 Congressional session was more barren of such legislation than the 1958 session had been.

The reason for this was the emergence of a so-called "new" Eisenhower in the months that followed his party's election defeat—a development that more than offset the election's liberalization of Congress, so far as legislative effectiveness was concerned. The departure of Sherman Adams had the effect of requiring Eisenhower to exercise personally some of the Presidential powers that Adams had formerly exercised in his name. The election results, by his own view, required him to take strong, bold action against what he called "the central danger of the 1959 legislative session," which consisted of "soaring spending proposals from the overwhelming Democratic majority." In his press conference on the day after the election he frankly conceded that the "spender-wing" of the Democratic party had greatly increased its Congressional strength, but he refused to concede in advance the legislative defeat of his own fiscal policies. "I promise this," he said, "for the next two years, the Lord sparing me, I am going to fight this as hard as I know how." [7] And he *did* fight, surprising political friend and foe alike with his tenacity of purpose and tactical skill.

He submitted to Congress for fiscal 1960 a budget of (in his words) "Spartan-like economy" (it was considerably more restrictive even than his proposed budget for 1959) balanced at 77 billion dollars. He exercised party leadership as he had never done before to assure a cohesive voting bloc among Congressional Republicans in support of his program; this, with the aid of conservative Democrats, denied to his Congressional opposition the two-thirds majority they needed to override his vetoes—and he used the threat as well as the act of veto with consistent effectiveness. Simultaneously he stimulated a grass-roots campaign to convince the general public of the dangers of inflation, the necessity for a sound dollar, the iniquities of deficit financing. To counter the persuasiveness of Democratic Advisory Council pronouncements he followed a suggestion made to him by Arthur Burns: he had the Budget Bureau estimate the "total cost of the various high-sounding programs put forward," as he says in his memoirs, and was "delighted" when the Budget Director, Maurice Stans, "deluged the Cabinet and—when possible—the public with statistics that made truly fearsome ogres of the gaudily garbed promises of the spenders." [8] He won this battle. The budget was balanced; indeed, the end of fiscal 1960 found Federal revenues exceeding expenditures by more than one billion dollars.

But the victory was achieved at the expense of the consensus that maintained Eisenhower sacrosanct, above the battle. And among those whose political fortunes were affected thereby was Lyndon Johnson.

From the beginning of the President's second term, Stevenson's partisan political speech had been characterized by direct attacks upon Eisenhower by name—a consistent, continuous insistence that the man who occupied the White House bore personal responsibility for the failures of his administration. Lyndon Johnson continued to employ an exactly opposite strategy: he continued to do all he could to protect the politically potent image of "Ike" against the consequences of the President's acts or failure to act. When Clare Booth Luce was named Eisenhower's Ambassador to Brazil and won Senate confirmation despite the vehement opposition of Oregon's Senator Wayne Morse (he was Chairman of the Latin American Subcommittee), she promptly displayed her peculiar talents for diplomacy by remarking to a press conference that her "difficulties of course" went back "some years when Senator Wayne Morse was kicked in the head by a horse." The ensuing furor forced her resignation—but not before Johnson had phoned the White House, indicated his sympathy with Eisenhower's dislike of Morse, and suggested a statement Mrs. Luce might make to undo the damage she had done herself and the administration.[9] When Eisenhower's defense policy, as defined by his budget for fiscal 1959, was being most strongly opposed by Stevenson, the Council, and Missouri's Senator Stuart Symington, Johnson as Chairman of the Senate Preparedness Subcommittee worked hard to obtain Republican concurrence in a unanimous report on the state of the nation's defenses. He had hoped thus to remove the issue from partisan politics. He was more than irritated by the Council's policy statement of February 1, 1958, asserting that the country faced "unlimited dangers which it is unprepared to meet."

For, in truth, that bland mental climate of moderation which the administration sought to perpetuate by every means of mass communication and which Stevenson found so distasteful personally, so unhealthy for the body politic (in one draft statement for the Council, Stevenson defined moderation of the Eisenhower type as "a disposition for meeting adequacy halfway")—this climate was neither uncongenial to Johnson's temperament nor incompatible with his political pragmatism. It was positively stimulating to the growth of his Congressional powers, to the fruition of his Presidential ambitions. If it was a climate of fogs wherein the precise shapes of public men and issues were indiscernible and through which loomed only large (and often false) appearances, it was also for that very reason a climate perfectly suited to the nurture of the Eisenhower consensus. And Johnson wanted to maintain this consensus virtually intact. He profited from it in the present; he hoped to inherit it, or the bulk of it, in the future. He could not but regret, therefore, that the climate was changing as the 1959 Congressional session got underway. Thanks in no small part to the unremitting efforts of Stevenson and the Council, the fogs were being lifted here and there in the heat, the light of public controversy.

They continued to be dissipated (though large foggy patches remained) during the months that followed. The new Eisenhower, colliding head-on with the new economics, became increasingly identified in the public mind with one side of a basic issue, and the less popular side at that. He had never been so identified before. He had been hoarding his vast hero's prestige all of these years, it seemed, so that he would have it to spend in the closing months of his administration upon an object of supreme historical importance—and the object that now presented itself was fiscal soundness as defined by nineteenth century economics and expressed through a balanced budget! In this new crusade he invested all the fervor, the vital energy he had so carefully withheld from the struggles over McCarthyism, school desegregation, civil rights, disarmament, and the like. He made this investment, moreover, at a time when the orthodoxy he espoused, long discredited on theoretical grounds by leading thinkers, was being thoroughly discredited in practice by the successful application of Keynesian principles to the economies of Western Europe.

The consequences were distressing. So said Stevenson and the Council over and over again as they made pointed comparisons between the American economy and the economies of France, the Low Countries, West Germany, and Scandinavia. The Federal budget, they said, ought to be purposefully used as an instrument of economic growth. Instead, under Eisenhower, it was being used to stunt growth and prevent adequate spending for imperative needs in the public sector of the economy. As a result, the nation had been kept in recession half the time since 1953 and its growth rate had been held to less than half what it should have been. "Since the Republicans took over," said a Council policy statement issued in October, 1958, ". . . we have lost more than 100 billion dollars' worth of potential production which we should have enjoyed." And these arguments, in the face of Eisenhower's obduracy, were persuasive to an increasingly large segment of the general public, thus preparing the way for a major shift in governmental fiscal policy in the years immediately ahead.

The overall effect upon the Republican party was a strengthening of its right wing at the expense of both the center and the left. The reduction in the strength of the latter was drastic. Governor Nelson Rockefeller of New York, chief personification of the Republican left, was sincerely concerned over the dangers that (in his as in Stevenson's view) were bred by the administration's reckless conduct of foreign affairs joined to its (in his view) reluctant and niggardly defense spending. No doubt these policies would be continued by Richard Nixon, front-runner for the nomination, if Nixon were elected, for he ran as Eisenhower's choice, and in the Eisenhower manner (projecting an image of confidence and wisdom while blurring real issues), insofar as it was his nature to do so. Hence Rockefeller, in the fall of 1959, at no small financial cost, actively and exhaustively explored his own chances for the nomination should he decide to campaign for it.[10] He found that his chances were nil. He was far too liberal for the big business executives who were the party's financial mainstay and the chief determiners of its character; he was too independent for the party professionals whom the executives properly regarded as their political servants. These men wanted Eisenhower's fiscal views to be maintained; they had relatively little concern for anything else in government. Richard Nixon was their man. Accordingly, in the closing days of 1959, Rockefeller announced his withdrawal from the race, leaving Nixon a clear field. Later, when untoward events in the spring of 1960 stimulated anew his anxieties over the Eisenhower policies, he would announce his availability for a convention draft and would strive desperately, publicly, to impose his policy views on Nixon and the Republican platform writers. This would provoke an angry, covert opposition from Eisenhower himself, whose personal vanity and political convictions were alike outraged by it. Against such opposition, Rockefeller's attempt was doomed to total failure.

The overall effect upon the Democratic party was precisely opposite that upon the Republicans. The Democratic left wing was strengthened at the expense of the center and right. Adlai Stevenson emerged as more than ever the champion and spokesman of the liberal tradition, both in domestic politics and foreign affairs—and it was increasingly evident that the party's 1960

Presidential nomination must go to a man who operated within this tradition. It was also increasingly evident that the national desire for rest, comfort, and recreation after years of strenuous idealism, of gigantic risks and labors—that desire to which the Eisenhower "crusade" of 1952 had so strongly appealed—was now more than satisfied. It was satiated. There was actual revulsion against it in many formerly acquiescent quarters, a growing disbelief in easy promises and soothing words, a growing disgust with the intellectual sloth and moral shoddiness that characterized so much of the current regime. Stevenson spoke for a multitude when, in a speech late in January of 1960, he said that the administration was seeking "to lead us gently and expertly into an unreal, delightful, trivial world without veracity, without dignity, without humanity, and without purpose—except, of course, the purpose of balancing the budget." And for many his words were given added point by their appearance in next morning's newspapers side by side with the news that the President of the United States was again on a golfing vacation, having just flown to Palm Springs, California, in a 707 jet of the Military Air Transport and, from the airport, in a Marine helicopter. (The guest of millionaire George E. Allen, formerly identified in news stories as Truman's "court jester" but now always identified as "a New York and Washington businessman," Ike was accompanied by millionaire Freeman Gosden of "Amos and Andy" radio fame and millionaire Charles Jones, president of the Richfield Oil Company. On the day of Stevenson's speech, Ike golfed at Palm Springs's El Dorado Country Club with Gosden, Allen, and millionaire William E. Robinson, board chairman of the Coca-Cola Company.)

Lyndon Johnson perforce yielded, reluctantly, to the change of temperature, the shift in prevailing winds. So did Senator John F. Kennedy, if to a lesser degree, since his general political position had been somewhat to the left of Johnson's to begin with. A revealing test case was provided by Eisenhower's recess appointment of Admiral Lewis A. Strauss as Secretary of Commerce in late October of 1958. As Chairman of the Atomic Energy Commission, Strauss's arrogant and authoritarian temper, his strongly conservative Republican views, his high-handed methods of handling such matters as giant contracts with private power firms, his hostility to every effort toward nuclear disarmament (when it was said that an H-bomb test ban would reduce international tensions he replied that he was "not sure that the reduction of tensions is necessarily a good thing")—all these had made him anathema to New Mexico's Senator Clinton Anderson, Chairman of the Joint Committee for Atomic Energy, to Senator Kefauver, and to every other senator of liberal views. Their feeling toward him personally, as well as their disapproval of his policies, received effective expression when his nomination went at last before the Senate for confirmation in the spring of 1959. Lyndon Johnson could in former years have been counted upon to vote for the confirmation. Eisenhower counted upon him to do so now. Instead, Johnson hesitated until just before the vote was taken, after long and almost unprecedentedly acrimonious hearings. He then announced his intention to vote *against* confirmation. As for Senator Kennedy, he was reported to have assured Strauss, while the hearings were underway, that he would vote for the confirmation—and Arthur Schlesinger, Jr., has written in this connection of Kennedy's "belief . . . that any President was entitled to considerable discretion in naming his cabinet." But Schlesinger also records that it was "politically essential for Kennedy, as a liberal Democratic Presidential aspirant, to vote against Strauss." [11] This is what Kennedy finally did. Strauss's nomination was rejected by the close vote of 49 to 46.

III

It was not as critic, however, but as prophet that Stevenson came increasingly to be honored in his own country after his two overwhelming election defeats. His negative criticisms could not have been as effective as they were had they not been accompanied by positive proposals against which the administration's performance could be measured. Nor were his proposals themselves without practical effect. ". . . I have no doubt at all that many of the views and ideas I have tried to express will ultimately prevail," he had said in the dark immediate aftermath of his 1956 defeat. And indeed the number which had prevailed and the extent to which his own efforts had *caused* them to prevail upon a hostile administration were both impressive and surprising to those who studied closely the trend of current affairs.[12]

During the primary battles of 1956 he had called in vain for "positive leadership" by the President toward alleviation of the crisis arising from the Supreme Court's desegregation rulings and the organized resistance to their implementation in the South. In sharp contrast to Eisenhower's refusal to commit himself, he had left no doubt as to his own opinion of the Court's actions. "I think that these rulings are correct interpretations of the Constitution and of the conscience of the nation," he had told a press conference in Chicago. ". . . the Supreme Court has decreed what our reason told us was inevitable and our conscience told us was right," he had said in a campaign speech in Los Angeles. And in the city square of Little Rock, Arkansas, in a campaign address to an overwhelmingly segregationist crowd, he had said: "The Supreme Court . . . has determined unanimously that the Constitution does not permit segregation in the schools. . . . I believe that decision to be right." His concrete proposal, many times repeated, had been that the President exercise the "great moral influence and great prestige" of his office "by calling together white and Negro leaders from the areas concerned in the South to explore ways and means of allaying these rising tensions."

Such a conference, he had said, "would strengthen the hands of the thoughtful and responsible leaders of both races" and it should be called "before the situation gets any more serious." It was not until the situation had grown much more serious, however, through nearly two years of rising tension and occasional ugly acts of violence, that the White House called a conference of Southern governors. This was after Governor Orval Faubus of Arkansas, in the fall of 1957, called out units of his state's National Guard to prevent compliance with a court order to integrate Little Rock's Central High School—an act of rebellion that forced the President to order Federal troops to Little Rock, there to protect Negro children against a white mob. (Even then Eisenhower refused to say whether or not he personally approved of school desegregation.) The long-delayed White House conference, therefore, attempted to lock the door of a barn from which most of the horses were already stolen, and stolen at immense cost to America's prestige and influence among the teeming rising millions of Asia and Africa.

Stevenson's suggestion that the military draft was a recruitment method outmoded by technological developments and might therefore be ended in the foreseeable future had been derided by Eisenhower and the bulk of the press when first made during the 1956 campaign. His stubborn reiteration and expansion of it, against the urgent advice of most of his staff, provoked yet more derision (Eisenhower said the proposal was "incredible folly" which would "lead down the road to surrender") and undoubtedly contributed something to the magnitude of his defeat that November. Nevertheless, shortly after the election, Eisenhower's Secretary of Defense appointed a special advisory committee whose terms of reference were precisely those Stevenson had called for when he said that "we ought to take a fresh and open-minded look at the weapons revolution in connection with the whole problem of recruiting and training military manpower." The committee, composed of civilian and military personnel experts, was headed by Ralph J. Cordiner, president of General Electric. In May, 1957, it issued a report entitled *A Modern Concept of Manpower Management and Compensation* which, to quote Stuart Gerry Brown, read "from beginning to end ... like a documented elaboration of Stevenson's proposals." [13] Professor Brown points out that the Cordiner Report carefully avoided using the word "draft," substituting for it the word "compulsion" in evident deference to Eisenhower's sensitivities, but the emphatic conclusion was that the kind of manpower needed in today's armed services could not be obtained through the draft or short-term voluntary enlistments. ("Today there is a tremendous outflow of effort to train a stream of transient personnel to a journeyman level of competence without a reasonable realization of skilled service in return," said the report. "... The quality and degree of retention of skilled manpower required by the Services cannot be secured by compulsion in a democratic society at peace.") The armed services must become career services whose participants received "a reasonable measure of the prestige and benefits they could otherwise achieve in civil pursuits in the mainstream of the economy." The report was effective of policy. True, the draft was extended by Congressional action in 1959, when Russia was making new threats over Berlin, but less and less reliance was then being placed upon it and "it was clear to everyone," as Professor Brown writes, "that the only real purpose it served was to provide cheap common labor for the Army." [14] Other Cordiner recommendations were put into effect one by one, and very quietly; every effort was made to obscure the fact that the civilian candidate for President had been right, the great military hero had been wrong on a military matter of basic importance.

Even more harmful to Stevenson's candidacy in 1956 than his draft suggestions was his advocacy of a suspension by the United States of H-bomb tests. His argument, it will be recalled, was that the United States could safely suspend such big bomb tests unilaterally, simultaneously calling upon the Russians to do likewise, for if the Russians continued to test anyway we would instantly know it (big bomb tests anywhere in the world are immediately detectable by scientific instruments). We could in that case resume testing ourselves if our security required it. His conclusive reason had been that this dramatic act would not only reduce the danger of atmospheric poisoning with strontium 90 but would also be a first long step toward total nuclear disarmament. The proposal, later modified somewhat to meet technical objections, had of course been categorically and contemptuously rejected in all its forms by candidates Eisenhower and Nixon, and by nearly all the press. Most of the scientific community applauded it, however—and Stevenson by no means dropped the matter following his election defeat. In *Look* magazine for February 5, 1957, he restated his case and gained front-page publicity for it by asserting that he had "reason to believe that the National Security Council itself *between September 5 and September 19* [Stevenson had made his original proposal in April] had voted 'unanimously' in favor of a similar super-bomb proposal"—a decision that was "set aside for obviously political reasons...." Asked about this in his next press conference, Eisenhower said cautiously that Stevenson had "of course" been given intelligence briefings "all during the campaign and I don't know exactly what information you might say auxiliary to intelligence may have been given him"—an uncertainty on Eisenhower's part that might well have been sufficient reason for his refusal either to "deny or affirm" what Stevenson had said. The stated reason, however, was that "I make it a practice never to give a hint of what is a National Security Council conviction." In any case, he concluded emphatically, the Council was a purely advisory body. "I make the decisions and there is no use trying to put any responsibility on the National Security Council—it's mine." The decision Eisenhower with Dulles continued to make was *against* any suspension of bomb tests unless agreed to by the Russians as "part of a general system of ... controlled and inspected disarmament," to quote his press conference of June 5, 1957.[15] In other words, the test-ban proposal was part of a package deal; the Russians must buy all or none of it.

But by that time there were signs that this posture of frozen rigidity (Dulles always maintained such a posture against the Communists unless forced to modify it) was being thawed somewhat in the heat and light of controversy that Stevenson, more than any other man, continued to focus upon it. A few weeks before, Atomic Energy Commissioner Willard F. Libby had obliged the administration by saying again as he had said before that the "present rate of testing," if continued indefinitely, would not result in a dangerous concentration of strontium 90 in the human body. It was a conclusion with which other equally reputable scientists disagreed, even at current test rates—and of course there was a strong probability that the rates would soon be multiplied unless the tests were banned and international action taken to halt the proliferation of sovereign nuclear powers. Stevenson had called attention to this scientific disagreement when he appeared on a "Meet the Press" broadcast, on May 5. He had indicated that he himself was unpersuaded by the AEC statement. He had again deplored emphatically the continuation of tests by the United States, saying they threatened the rest of the world with "contamination without representation." Much of the rest of the world had by then expressed through Government channels a rising concern over the continued testing, as had Pope Pius in Rome. By the end of May, reputable Washington newsmen were reporting rumors to the effect that the United States was seriously considering a test limitation proposal as a first step toward general disarmament. And Eisenhower himself, in his June 5 reiteration of what had long been the official U.S. position, was something less than adamant about it. He had prefaced his policy statement with a defensive reference to the "authoritative document" issued by the National Academy of Sciences in 1956, adding that "on the other hand, here is a field where scientists disagree."

He had reason for cautious statement. Among scientists, the width of disagreement on this matter was being reduced as the area of general agreement was being widened that spring and summer—and the agreed conclusion, insofar as one was reached, had policy implications at odds with the administration position. A report of hearings conducted by the Joint Congressional Committee on Atomic Energy was issued in late August. It incorporated a report of a meeting of scientific experts in Washington in late July whose conclusion was that a dangerous radioactive fallout *would* develop if nuclear weapons testing were continued *at the same rate* as during the preceding twelve years. Though the conclusion differed significantly from that announced by the AEC during the 1956 campaign and by Willard F. Libby again in the spring of 1957, Libby concurred in it and so did the chief of the AEC's division of biology and medicine. In that same summer, Dr. Albert Schweitzer added immensely to popular pressure against the administration position with a public letter, appealing to the conscience of mankind, calling for an end to the tests; newspapers that had sneered at Stevenson's presumption in making his proposal in a nation presided over by a great military authority gave editorial approval of Schweitzer's stand. (Shortly after the letter was published, Stevenson, on his African tour, visited the letter's author at Lambarene, French Equatorial Africa. "I am in complete agreement with my old friend, Doctor Schweitzer, on the question of suspending hydrogen bomb tests," he said to the world's press as he boarded a plane at Brazzaville.) And Stevenson applied yet more pressure, perhaps more effectively (as to this the evidence is far from clear), while serving as State Department consultant in preparation for the NATO summit of December, 1957. Meanwhile, the Russians continued to score propaganda points with appeals for an end to testing and for a drastic overall reduction in armaments (they had in May of 1956 announced a reduction of their armed forces by 1.2 million men)—appeals that were initially categorically rejected by the administration because they contained no promise to halt the production of nuclear weapons and no specific suggestions for inspection.

But gradually, reluctantly—while disarmament negotiations dragged on, first in London, then in Geneva—the administration shifted its ground. In April, 1958, Eisenhower proposed and Khrushchev agreed to a meeting of technical experts from Western and Communist countries to work out the technical requirements for a nuclear weapons control and inspection system. Opening in Geneva in July and concluding in August of that year, the meeting produced a plan that was recommended for adoption by both Soviet and Western conferees. Eisenhower then proposed negotiations toward an implementation of the expert recommendations and announced his country's willingness to suspend nuclear tests for a period of one year after the date on which such negotiations began, unless Russia tested in the meantime. (The suspension would be after the U.S.'s current series of tests in the Pacific, code-named HARDTACK, was completed.) Khrushchev agreed to the negotiations and the U.S. test suspension went into effect when these negotiations formally opened on October 31. Soon, however, the negotiations foundered on a Russian refusal to accept the expert recommendations, evidently because of a fear that the proposed on-site monitoring system might expose the Soviet Union to an unguardable espionage danger. Yet even after an excessively suspicious Khrushchev had rejected Eisenhower's proposal of a ban only on atmospheric tests (which is what Stevenson had had in mind when he made his original proposal), Eisenhower maintained the U.S. test suspension in effect (which is what Stevenson had suggested).

Finally, in April, 1959, precisely three years after Stevenson had made his initial proposal—years during which the Russian success with rockets indicated their probable possession of an intercontinental ballistic missile that the U.S. still lacked and that offset much of the potency of our foreign-based bombers and our Polaris submarine—Eisenhower sent Khrushchev a letter stating in Stevensonian language the position Stevenson had originally urged: "The United States strongly seeks a lasting agreement for the discontinuation of nuclear weapons tests. We believe that this would be an important step toward reduction of international tensions and would open the way to further agreement on substantial measures of disarmament." He proposed an agreement to be put "into effect in phases beginning with a prohibition of nuclear weapons tests in the atmosphere," the first phase to be established while "our negotiators . . . continue to explore with new hope the political and technical problems involved in extending the agreement as quickly as possible to cover all nuclear weapons testing. Meanwhile, fear of unrestricted resumption of nuclear weapons testing with attendant additions to levels of radioactivity would be allayed." Thus the turnabout was complete; Stevenson's proposal had at last been adopted in the form in which he had originally proposed it, as Professor Brown points out.[16] The long delay, however, and the obviously reluctant and piecemeal manner of its adoption, had cost the United States most of that beneficent effect which the proposal would otherwise have had upon this country's moral prestige and consequent persuasive power among the peoples of the world.

IV

The test-ban proposal was only a part, if a highly important part, of a general approach to disarmament and a peaceful world order made by Stevenson, in public speech and published writings, during these years. On February 1, 1958, in an address to the Tenth Annual Roosevelt Day dinner given by the ADA at New York's Waldorf-Astoria, he urged a "new kind of effort" by the United Nations to end the disarmament deadlock. The UN Secretary General should "select a group of private citizens from all over the world," he suggested, to study and evaluate all present disarmament proposals and develop proposals of their own, presenting these to the UN in an advisory report. The private citizens would be "top men of affairs and science," and they would work in private. Two things would be accomplished: *first,* the issue would be removed from "the realm of competing propaganda;" *second,* non-nuclear countries would be given "some degree of responsibility in breaking the vicious circle." In a commencement address at Michigan State University on June 8, 1958, his call for an end to nuclear testing was joined to a plea for an "acceptance by the West of

Soviet equality of power." For, he went on, if "both sides accepted power-equality, rivalries could become fruitful competitions in science, education, and economic development."

Nor was it only peaceful international competition he sought; he sought also (and more so) for international cooperation. One of his suggestions—this, too, in the Michigan State speech—was for an International Medical Research and Health Year on the model of the International Geophysical Year then underway, a highly successful international effort having governmental support and, to that extent, hopeful political implications. Other suggestions, made at various times, were for a joint commission with the Soviet Union to solve the problems of the world's great deserts, including the desalting of sea water; for establishing permanent international commissions in vital fields of medical research as a follow-up of the worldwide medical year; and for the creation of an international outer space commission. In all these, as in his suggestion for divorcing disarmament talks from competing propaganda, he evinced his awareness of the need to translate as much as possible of the dialogue between East and West from the emotionally charged vocabularies of politics to the neutral vocabulary of science in order to establish firm bases of agreement. In terms of ideological vocabularies, agreement was difficult, perhaps impossible; the same words had such widely different meanings for those who use them. But agreement in terms of the scientific vocabulary, to the extent that this vocabulary could be used, was ultimately inevitable. And such agreement must necessarily imply, sooner or later, a degree of international political collaboration that would moderate ideologies in the interests of practical efficacy and so reduce the differences between them.

Thus two medical scientists, insofar as one remains a Marxist and the other a Jeffersonian, must forever differ in their definitions of the nature of man and human liberty, but they can hardly fail to see the same thing when they look at a test-tube culture or a slide under a microscope, nor can they fail to draw (ultimately), in terms of the design of their experiments, the same logical inferences from what they see. They must by this process be led far toward agreement about the international institutional devices—projects of the UN's World Health Organization, for example—needed for the practical application throughout the world of the knowledge so gained. And the effect of these devices, wherein definitions are made in terms of objective fact, must be to render increasingly irrelevant to the actual work and values of the world those ideological disputes that are now so dangerously joined to the competing interests and patriotic passions of national sovereignty. Stevenson saw great significance in the fact that Communist and Western technical experts had little difficulty in reaching agreement upon the control system needed to insure compliance with a nuclear test ban; they readily drew up a detailed plan for such a system and recommended its adoption by their respective governments. ("This was surprising," writes Eisenhower in his memoirs. "We had expected the Soviet technicians to be more politically oriented and negative than they turned out to be." [17]) Not until the politicians took over did insuperable difficulties arise. . . .

Along the same lines of thinking was Stevenson's insistence upon the need, the urgent need, to divert the energies of all countries from negative militarism to positive economic development. While in Washington as State Department consultant he had tried in vain to force an active consideration of economic as well as military matters upon the U.S. delegation to the Paris NATO Conference. "We must make it clear that in the American view the military defense of Europe and the winning of the economic battle for improvement of the conditions of life of the uncommitted peoples are not alternative imperatives for the NATO countries—they are both necessary," he had written in his memorandum to Dulles of November 29, 1957. "Moreover, the tasks of military policy are negative and an insufficient expression of the common aspirations of our peoples and of peoples throughout the Free World." He had followed this with a list of specific recommendations, none of them adopted in the final position papers. At Michigan State he called for appointment of a "committee of experts," as had been done in preparation for the Marshall Plan, to lay the groundwork for a "broad program" to meet an alleged "creeping paralysis" of the "free world economy." These experts would devise joint measures for assuring sustained economic growth, joint negotiations for a low tariff and free trade area, joint undertaking of a long-term aid and investment program, joint agreement to provide adequate working capital for world trade and convertibility. The United States, he asserted, "must be firmly prepared to assume the creditor burden which Britain and France are laying down."

His concern was enhanced by the threatened split of Western Europe into two mutually exclusive economic blocs. In March, 1957, the European Economic Community (or Common Market) was formally established, comprising France, West Germany, Italy, Belgium, the Netherlands, and Luxembourg—the Six, as they came to be called. This immediately worked so well for its members, to the disadvantage of the economies of Britain and other neighboring nonmembers, that these last were forced to form, in late 1959 and early 1960, a competing but much looser organization, the European Free Trade Association, comprising Britain, Austria, Denmark, Norway, Sweden, Portugal, and Switzerland—the Outer Seven. Thus Western Europe was said to be "at Sixes and Sevens" with itself economically, a development having possibly disastrous effects upon the Atlantic Alliance, upon the evident gradual emergence (a hopeful emergence) of what amounted to a United States of Europe, and upon programs of economic aid to underdeveloped countries. The last, in Stevenson's view, was a particularly urgent need in order to prevent the misery and chaos that breed wars and invite communism. Stevenson spoke of this to Theodore White in June, 1960, saying that "we can't let Europe subdivide" in this way, "we can't let the old nineteenth century equalization of trade operate again ... We have *got* to reorganize Europe's resources for the major cold war conflict or it can be extremely disadvantageous for us." He deplored the fact that for six years there had been "no evidence of our moving in that direction." [18]

But he added that he thought Douglas Dillon, who had become Undersecretary of State in 1957, "has been moving correctly recently." He referred to Dillon's efforts to organize within NATO an economic assistance program of the kind Stevenson as State Department consultant had vainly tried to urge upon Dulles. (Dulles, mortally ill of cancer, resigned as Secretary in April of 1959, was replaced by Christian Herter, and died a little over a month later.) These efforts, joined with others, produced in late 1960 what Stevenson had aimed for in 1957, namely, the Organization for Economic Cooperation and Development (OECD).

Underlying all his foreign policy proposals, informing them and binding them into a unity of purpose, was a general conception that was most explicitly stated by him, perhaps, in an address to a Conference on World Tensions, jointly sponsored by World Brotherhood, Inc., and the University of Chicago, held on the University Campus in mid-May of 1960.

"... we are irreversibly part of a world-wide human community," he said on that occasion.

> But it is not a community that enjoys the structure or the safeguards of a civilized society. At home we live under law. We play our part in promoting the general welfare. We share some sense of national purpose. These are surely the minimum conditions of a truly civil life, or of a life in society that deserves the name of human. But all are lacking in our international world. Should not, therefore, the introduction of such fundamental institutions be the first aim of our world policy? Can we tolerate a world in which everything changes—every measurement, every distance, every material prospect—and only civic life remains unchanged to founder in an environment for which it was never designed? The main aims of our foreign policies by-pass this central issue. We do not pursue the general welfare. We pursue our separate national interests and hope that the selfish good of the part will add up—against the witness of all history—to the wider good of the whole. We do not urgently seek a world under law. Primarily we seek national security or, in simpler terms, to stop the Russians. As for policies which attempt to articulate some common purpose for a threatened humanity, they occasionally get a brief run in our rhetoric. But they do not occupy much of our planners' time. So I would suggest that a first need of our international policies

is to be clear about our fundamental aims. We are trying to construct a civilized world for the genus man. We are trying to create for the whole human family institutions, obligations, decencies and traditions which will enable it—with planetary suicide in sight—to avoid disaster and build for itself a saner, comelier life on earth.

Thus, somewhat obliquely, in a language whose cautious vagueness was obviously influenced by his immediate political circumstances but which did not obscure his essential message from those who had eyes to see, Stevenson spoke for an end to unlimited national sovereignty, with the international anarchy it necessarily implies, and for the beginning of world law effective through a world government that expresses and protects and promotes world community in all its creative diversity. "... our Western peoples must speak ... for man and for the human city." This, he said, should be the ultimate goal, hence the major premise, of all American foreign policy.

BOOK NINE

To the End of Ambition

CHAPTER THIRTY

W HAT were the political circumstances in which Stevenson found himself by the spring of 1960? In general they were circumstances he had anticipated in late 1956 and early 1957. To a considerable degree they were circumstances of his own conscious choice and making.

He had always been a remarkably shrewd politician. The fact had been obscured from the public at large, and even from many of the most worshipful of his admirers, by his pursuit of goals different from those of most politicians. He had never regarded personal power as an end in itself, nor even as a particularly desirable possession. Often in politics he had deliberately sacrificed a sure present and personal gain in order to achieve a future and possibly permanent social effect. Often, as a result, he had been deemed politically naive. This had been especially so during his two Presidential campaigns. The fact nevertheless remained that he was a canny judge of the strengths and weaknesses of the men with whom he dealt, that there was craft in his handling of men without *seeming* to do so, and that he was acutely sensitive to prevailing popular moods and knew how to play upon them to produce calculated responses. To this was added a rare sense of the long-term trends of history as well as of the direction and overall shape of immediate events, and an ability to regard his public self quite objectively as a factor in the historical situation, an active agent of history. This enabled him to develop public issues in such a way as to make many of his prophecies self-fulfilling; when pronounced at the proper times and places, his prophetic statements became themselves a cause of their coming

397

true. His exercise of these political arts and crafts had brought him far toward the achievement of his Presidential ambitions as the election year opened.

There were at that time four generally recognized candidates for the Democratic Presidential nomination. Lyndon B. Johnson had become an "unofficially" declared candidate at a Dallas press conference called by Sam Rayburn in October of 1959. Senator Hubert Humphrey of Minnesota had formally announced his candidacy on December 30, 1959. Senator John F. Kennedy of Massachusetts, who had been openly, actively, and expensively seeking the nomination almost from election day of 1956 and who was now clearly the front-runner, announced formally on January 2, 1960. Senator Stuart Symington, though he was not formally to announce until March of 1960, was nevertheless known to want the nomination and to be quietly working for it; he was strongly supported by his fellow Missourian, Harry Truman.

The widely differing characters and special circumstances of these candidates had determined different preconvention strategies.[1] Only two of the four, and these the closest in style and intellect to Stevenson, planned of necessity to enter state primaries in quest of pledged convention delegates and (more importantly) national vote-garnering prestige. Humphrey planned to enter five of the sixteen primaries, Kennedy planned to enter seven, and in Wisconsin and West Virginia the two would meet in a head-on and decisive collision. Each had developed a campaign organization geared to the needs of this battling, though Humphrey's organization was skimpy and slap-dash indeed compared to the huge, lavishly financed, and expertly run machine of the very rich Mr. Kennedy. The other two candidates based their strategy, one of gathering organized strength through a period of watchful waiting, upon the possibility that Humphrey would knock the present front-runner out of contention by winning either Wisconsin or West Virginia in the primaries or that, having survived the primary battles, the front-runner would enter the convention with insufficient strength to be nominated on the first or second ballots. In that case, even his early strength would begin to fade; the convention would become deadlocked. There would follow a hectic time of hard bargaining and dealing in back rooms, among professional politicians, from which either Johnson or Symington might emerge as the party's choice. Johnson, in that case, counted upon his long and masterful exercise of Congressional politics to furnish him with major support from key men for whom he had done favors. Symington, in that same case, counted upon Johnson's being eliminated by organized labor's strong opposition to him while his own candidacy profited from his appeal to big city Democratic bosses and a consistently liberal voting record. He less than Johnson would be hurt by the changes in mental climate and in the nature of the Democratic party for which Stevenson was so largely responsible.

Thus the strategic planning. It was done, however, in the shadow of a question that no active aspirant could either answer or ignore. What were Adlai Stevenson's *real* intentions, and how would he react to the pressures upon him to run again? What Stevenson repeatedly said on the subject, beginning with his renunciation statement of December, 1956, seemed clear enough; but there were subtle changes in the *way* he said it as the months passed—changes whose implications were especially disquieting to John F. Kennedy.

In early May of 1957, on a "Meet the Press" broadcast, he said flatly that he would not again run for President, though he did not rule out the possibility that he might run again for governor of Illinois or for some other office. But that was the last time he made his public renunciation in the form of "I will not run." Three months later, at a press conference in New York upon his return from Africa and Europe, he said he could "conceive of no circumstances" that would induce him "to seek the Presidency again." And he then added, in response to a question, that Lyndon Johnson was certainly one who must be considered for the 1960 nomination. He declined to name any others. This was disturbing to the Kennedy camp. Did it presage a "stop Kennedy" coalition of Johnson and Stevenson forces? In a press conference in Helsinki, on his way to Russia in July, 1958, Stevenson was specifically asked his opinion of Kennedy for President. He replied merely that "Mr. Kennedy is a capable, competent man," quickly adding that "there are a lot of competent, capable men in the Democratic party." Concerning his own immediate future, his public reply to the inevitable question now took the form of an objective prediction—a statement, not of what he would or would not do, but of what would happen. "I will not be the nominee," he told reporters, typically, in mid-June of 1959. In early December of that year, on a "College Press Conference" TV broadcast, he said he was "not leaning toward anyone" among the Democratic Presidential aspirants but strove instead "to maintain an attitude of vertical neutrality." Privately he continued to assure the active candidates that he was not in the running and would do nothing prior to the convention to help or hinder any of them.

But as the election year opened and advanced into spring, the form of the question changed. A national "Draft Stevenson" movement was under way and gaining momentum as the energies of fanatic Stevenson cultists (there were at least as many of these as there had been in 1952 and 1956), as well as of growing numbers of more sober and responsible Stevensonians, were increasingly harnessed to organized effort by politically experienced leaders.

The first steps toward an organized draft effort had been taken nearly a year before in Madison, Wisconsin, by James Doyle, a prominent lawyer and former Wisconsin Democratic State Chairman. He had communicated with numerous political friends over the country to determine if a Stevenson draft were possible and had become convinced that it was. In July, 1959, Joseph Smolen, a labor representative in Madison, had called upon Doyle to urge that volunteers be actively involved on an organized basis to promote the draft, and by the end of the year considerable progress had been made toward this end. In December, 1959, national press coverage was given a Doyle interview in which he denied that he headed a "formal organization" but admitted that his group spearheaded an "informal drive" for a Stevenson draft. (It was the country, not Stevenson, that deserved "another chance in 1960," he said.) By then, or soon thereafter, the Doyle group was receiving its major financial support from Stevenson's Chicago friends and was attempting to keep track of the spontaneously rising volunteer groups over the country to prevent their doing anything, in their excessive zeal, that might seriously damage their cause.

By then, too, a loosely organized but highly effective survey and planning activity was secretly under way in New York, under the name "Russel B. Hemenway and Associates," Hemenway being a well-heeled young man active in reform politics. It had an office in the Squibb Building on Fifth Avenue and was supported and directed by the "New York group," including Tom Finletter, Ruth Field, Marietta Tree, Bob Benjamin, Arthur B. Krim (president of United Artists), Roger Stevens, and (financially for the most part; she attended few meetings) Mrs. Agnes Meyer of Washington. In Washington, Stevenson's long-time close friend, George Ball, with his young law partner, John Sharon, collaborated with Senator A. S. Mike Monroney of Oklahoma and Monroney's assistant, Tim Finney, Jr., to develop what became in effect the strategic center of the whole draft movement. On the West Coast, in Los Angeles, Dore Schary of the movies headed another loosely organized group, highly effective as fund raisers. (Los Angeles had been selected as the 1960 convention city, and no other choice could have served so well the purposes of the "Draft Stevenson" movement. Los Angeles was Stevenson's birthplace, and fervent Stevensonians dominated the local Democracy there.)

Hence the question for Stevenson now became what it had been prior to the convention in 1952: would he accept a draft? And his answer now was formally much the same as then. On the TV broadcast in which he expressed his earnest desire to maintain a "vertical neutrality," in early December of 1959, he declined to say he would refuse a draft. Two months later, in a press conference, he deprecated the possibility of a draft but added, pointedly, that he had never said he would *not* serve if drafted. "I hope I will always do my duty to my party and my country," he said. In March he told reporters that a draft was "a bridge I will cross when

I get to it—and I don't expect to get to it." Nobody "has ever been drafted twice in the United States." In April, a politically sophisticated reporter asked him if he would accept the nomination in case a deadlocked convention turned to him. He answered carefully. "If I told you I would accept a draft, I would appear to be courting a draft, which is the same dilemma I was in in 1952," he said. "And if I said I would refuse a draft, I would be a draft-evader. So I just don't say anything at all."

II

But if his public statements on this matter were much the same as they had been in 1952, the spirit in which he made them was far different. There was now present an element of disingenuousness that had formerly been absent.

In 1952 his personal desire and his assessment of the national need had coincided to prevent his doing anything at all, deliberately, to achieve the Presidential nomination. He had then sincerely wanted a second term as governor in order to complete the job he had begun; he had then sincerely believed that General Eiesnhower represented a liberalizing influence at work within the Republican party. Having no compelling reason to doubt that the general was qualified for the Presidency, he had seen several reasons for wondering if a loss of the White House for a term or two might not have a wholesome, chastening effect upon the national Democracy. In 1960, however, no such tolerance of Republican leadership or doubt concerning his own party was operative in Stevenson's mind. It was obvious that the Vice-President would become the Republican candidate, and Stevenson's personal aversion to him was as strong as it had ever been, if not a good deal stronger. Indeed he, though temperamentally disinclined toward personal animosities, actually loathed and despised Richard Nixon as he did none other in public life. He also feared him. He contemplated with nothing less than horror the possibility that this sly, slippery, plausible, ruthless, thoroughly unprincipled politician (for so it was that Stevenson saw him)[2] might become President of the United States. Moreover, he believed that he himself, of all possible Democratic candidates, could run the strongest race against Nixon and would, if nominated, win decisively. His two defeats would of course be counted against him. But in retrospect it seemed clear that no man could have defeated Eisenhower in the circumstances that prevailed in 1952 and 1956 (though Stevenson was not alone in the belief that the outcome *might* have been different in '56 if a Democratic Advisory Council had operated during the first Eisenhower term as it did during the second), and the circumstances now were far different. Thanks in no small part to his own example and efforts, these circumstances were far more favorable to the Stevenson personality and campaign style than they had ever been before. He had in effect been "courting a draft" for the last three years. To the extent that he now gave a contrary impression, he was dissembling.

He was kept informed of the plans and activities of the draft movement leaders. "I always told him exactly what we were up to," said Finletter in a later year. "He made no objections." [3] James Doyle conferred with him in Washington on a weekend in January, 1960, and returned to Madison to work with renewed vigor. Stevenson was in constant touch with George Ball and the others in Washington, and in frequent contact with Schary and the others in California. If he for the most part merely listened to what they had to say, if he made no personal commitments nor suggestions about tactics, it may well have been because their basic strategic concept was precisely the same as his own while the activities with which they sought to implement it, though recognized by him as necessary to his success, involved a degree of guile uncomfortable to his normally guileless nature. He would rather not know about them in any detail.

The basic strategy, of course, was simple. "Stop Kennedy" became its necessarily covert watchword. This meant in practice the encouragement of Humphrey's primary race. For if Humphrey won this race, or even if he merely reduced drastically the margin of Kennedy's victory, he would prevent Kennedy's nomination without insuring his own. Not a few ardent Stevensonians therefore worked for Humphrey in Wisconsin and West Virginia, and a considerable portion of Humphrey's total campaign fund (it amounted to but a fraction of Kennedy's) came from New York Stevensonians. Thus far the interests of Stevenson, Johnson, and Symington were the same; the preconvention activities of their supporters were mutually reinforcing. For the convention itself, however, the plans diverged widely. The Stevensonians counted relatively little upon back room deals and bargains to put their candidate over, once the hoped-for deadlock had occurred. They counted much upon popular pressure from all over the country (Stevenson's popular following was far greater than that of any other Democrat) —a pressure made manifest by communications (wires, phone calls, letters) to the delegates, by mass demonstrations outside the convention hall, and by packed galleries within the hall itself. Their hope was to stampede the convention in much the same way as the Willkie amateurs had stampeded the Republican convention of 1940.

As for Stevenson himself, he now and again revealed inadvertently that he was not wholly at ease in a situation of unwonted (and unwanted) ambiguity. On the "College Press Conference" broadcast of early December, he became visibly flustered when David Dulles, a Harvard law student who was a nephew of John Foster Dulles, asked him if he had ever refused a proffered position, such as head of a large corporation, because his acceptance would preclude his running again for President. He hemmed and hawed before saying, finally, "Maybe so—but they were mostly academic, not business." Why his confusion? Was it because his admission seemed to contradict his public pose whereas his denial would have been untrue? Certainly his capacity for self-deception was small whereas his dislike of subterfuge, of deliberate false impression, was very large. And at that very time, as he gave to the public an impression of personal detachment from the battle, he was persuading his friend William Attwood of *Look* magazine, one of his companions on the 1953 round-the-world tour, to take a leave of absence from the magazine in order to devote full time to preparing Stevenson speech material. Attwood, working in close touch with Finletter and Ball and Monroney, among others, was to produce drafts for some four major addresses which Stevenson was scheduled to deliver in the spring—addresses certain to make large headlines and boost Stevenson for President provided they said the right things. Nor was this all. Attwood was further to prepare speech material for use in the Presidential campaign itself—"just in case," as he himself later put it.[4]

Stevenson's public role nevertheless continued in the pattern he had consistently followed since 1956. Though he sometimes said, in response to questions about a draft, that lightning never strikes twice in the same place, he well knew that lightning repeatedly strikes an object sufficiently prominent. He proposed to be sufficiently prominent when the storm of the convention broke around him. Meanwhile he must scrupulously refrain from doing anything openly to advance his interests. He must publicly dissociate himself from the activities of his promoters, especially during the primary battles of Kennedy versus Humphrey. And this need was served by (if it did not help determine) his decision to be out of the country from early February to mid-April.

III

He went to Latin America. He had legal business there on behalf of Reynolds Aluminum and Encyclopedia Britannica, Inc. (a Spanish edition of the encyclopedia was in preparation), but as he told the press in early January he also went "for my own education." He departed by plane for Mexico City from Chicago on February 9, four days after he had celebrated his sixtieth birthday anniversary with the usual hilarious party of his long-time intimates, at Libertyville. He was accompanied by Bill Benton, Bill Blair, his son John Fell, and Dr. Carleton Sprague Smith, director of the Brazilian Institute of New York University, who served as his Latin American expert.

During the next nine weeks he visited in turn Mexico, Guatemala, Costa Rica, Panama, Colombia, Ecuador, Peru, Chile, Argentina, Uruguay, Brazil, and Venezuela; he engaged in the ceaseless daily round of activities (formal

dinners, formal luncheons, conferences, speeches, sightseeing) that characterized all his travels and, on this trip as on others, exhausted his companions;
and in each country, he served with rare effectiveness the purposes of an
ambassador of good will who, though without office, was known to have
large influence upon public policy in his own country. "The entire journey
was a personal triumph for Governor Stevenson," wrote Benton years later.
". . . More popular than any motion picture star, he was besieged everywhere
by admiring crowds seeking autographs, handshakes, waves and smiles." [5]
And in his private talks with government officials as in his public appearances he used his popularity, his prestige, his sympathetic concern for human
welfare to counteract, so far as he truthfully could, the ugly image of an
exploitive Uncle Sam that had been impressed upon the mass mind of Latin
America by long decades of dollar diplomacy. He publicly recognized the
need for U.S. concern over the widening gap between the high prices paid
by Latin Americans for U.S. exports and the low prices paid by the U.S. for
Latin American raw materials. He publicly recognized that a major contributing force to Latin anti-Yankeeism had been his own government's con-
ciliation of dictators like the bloody-handed Trujillo of the Dominican Republic. He repeatedly stressed the need for social responsibility of the rich
in countries where the rich refused to pay either taxes or decent wages while
great masses lived in abject poverty. And he repeatedly urged Latin Americans to "take the initiative in disarmament and set an example for the rest
of the world," saying he was "distressed by the amount of money being spent
in Latin countries in arming against each other when they need money so
badly for education and other social purposes."

Only twice did he comment publicly on U.S. politics. Neither comment
was likely to please Kennedy. In Costa Rica he spoke of the amount of
money being spent on Kennedy's campaign. It was, he said, "phenomenal,
probably the highest amount spent on a campaign in history—and I'm not
sure Kennedy planned it that way." His personal disapproval was obvious. In
Argentina, responding to a reporter's question, he spoke of the effect of
Kennedy's Catholicism at the polls as a campaign imponderable. Some would
deem it an advantage, others a disadvantage, but "on balance it is hard to
say." He quickly added his regret "that religion ever had to be mentioned
in a United States election" and refused to say whom he personally favored
among the contenders. "If I start picking horses in that race I had better not
go home."

But upon his return to the United States, the current campaign became
the chief subject of reporters' questions at his large press conference in New
York, and he answered the questions freely. (He did try to turn to other
matters, asking plaintively at one point if no one there was interested in
Latin America.) This was on April 11, just six days after the Wisconsin
primary.

Kennedy had won over Humphrey in Wisconsin. But he had won less decisively than had been predicted (he gained six pledged convention delegates to Humphrey's four instead of the expected eight, or even all ten), and analyses of the voting patterns in a state in which nearly a third of the population was Catholic left unanswered the question of what effect, if any, the religious issue might have upon a Kennedy race against Nixon. Thus the stage had been set for a showdown battle between Humphrey and Kennedy in overwhelmingly Protestant West Virginia where, to the extent that the religious issue was operative, it could be expected to work against Kennedy. Great bitterness was engendered in the Kennedy camp by Humphrey's refusal to withdraw at this point, and much of this bitterness, as Theodore White has reported, was directed against Stevenson's supporters because some of them encouraged Humphrey's move and helped finance it. Evidently the Kennedy people regarded this as dirty politics. At the same time, as White also reports, "some forms of pressure" put upon Humphrey by Kennedy's men to force his withdrawal "were so vile as to amount to blackmail." (White absolves Kennedy himself of all blame for this; the "vile" pressure was exerted "by men unauthorized to speak for Kennedy yet assuming to speak in his name. . . .") Also Kennedy's organization moved with swift ruthlessness to cut off what little money was flowing into Humphrey's campaign coffers—a mere trickle compared to that pumped into West Virginia by the Kennedy family. According to White, Stevensonians in New York were bluntly warned by Connecticut's Governor Abraham Ribicoff, acting on Kennedy's instructions, that if they continued to send money to Humphrey "Adlai Stevenson would not even be *considered* for Secretary of State" in a Kennedy cabinet. Former Connecticut Senator Bill Benton, who had contributed $5,000 to the Humphrey campaign a few weeks before, was told by Connecticut's Democratic boss John Bailey "that if he continued to finance Humphrey . . . he would never hold another elective or appointive job in Connecticut as long as he, Bailey, had any say in Connecticut politics. . . ." [6]

Nor was negative pressure the only tactic employed. Shortly before the Wisconsin primary, Kennedy had carefully explained to Arthur Schlesinger, Jr., that he was certain he could win both Wisconsin and West Virginia but would greatly prefer to avoid the latter contest with all it must involve in expenditures of time and energy and money. Hence, if Humphrey were to withdraw prior to West Virginia and come out for Kennedy, he would become the logical choice for Vice-President. Would Schlesinger mention this to Humphrey? Schlesinger had done so. Humphrey had replied that he was firmly committed to going into West Virginia no matter what happened in Wisconsin; he had, moreover, no desire for the Vice-Presidency. [7]

While all this was going on, Louis Bean had carefully planned and quietly conducted a poll to determine Stevenson's chances against Nixon if Stevenson became the Democratic nominee. Bean was the statistician (formerly of

the U.S. Department of Agriculture) who, alone among pollsters, had precisely predicted the fact and the margin of Truman's defeat of Dewey in
1948. He had done so by means of a special technique of scientific sampling,
and in early 1960 he had begun to wonder if this technique might not assess
more accurately than currently published polls seemed to him to be doing
Stevenson's actual vote-getting strength relative to Nixon. ". . . my historical
studies suggested that without Eisenhower as a 1960 candidate his (Stevenson's) rating should have been higher . . ." Bean wrote years later in a letter
to graduate student Donald Murray.[8] "This led me to suggest to Stevenson
people here (in Washington) that they . . . make it possible for me to arrange for conducting the polls. . . ." Bean had then been hired for the job
by "Russel B. Hemenway and Associates" and, in February and March of
1960, had conducted 1800 interviews in four carefully selected cities: New
York, Pittsburgh, St. Louis, and Los Angeles. He found that 21 of every
100 who had voted for Eisenhower in 1956 said they would vote for
Stevenson in 1960 whereas only 3 of each 100 who had voted for Stevenson
in 1956 said they would vote for Nixon. Projected nationally, this indicated
a net gain of 6.7 million votes by Stevenson and a landslide victory of 54
percent for him to 46 percent for Nixon.

Stevenson, informed of the poll result while in South America, had made
"jocular" comment upon it, according to Hemenway (quoted by Donald
Murray), but had nevertheless been, obviously, "impressed." The draft organization had then made arrangements to leak the poll result to reporters
in various parts of the country for publication simultaneously with Stevenson's return to the United States.

Also simultaneous with Stevenson's return was press announcement of the
formation of a Stevenson for President Committee of New York, with offices
at 929 Madison Avenue, under the chairmanship of David Garth, a television producer. (Initially wholly separate from Russel B. Hemenway and
Associates, the Garth and Hemenway offices soon coordinated their activities.)

In this context it is not surprising that the reporters in New York evinced
only slight interest in Stevenson's views on Latin America and great interest
in his views on American politics. Asked what in his opinion were the major
issues between Republicans and Democrats in 1960 he listed, in order of
priority: "First, peace; secondly, disarmament; thirdly, allocation of resources." He reiterated the familiar theme of Democratic Advisory Council
economists to the effect that a larger portion of the total economic effort
should be diverted from consumer goods to the public sector. Asked how
he would respond to a deadlocked convention which turned to him, he made
the draft-evader statement already quoted. An excessively earnest reporter
then spoke at length of the immense and immensely complex problems with
which the next President must deal in a world "which might be exterminated

at any moment," this as preface to the inevitable question as to whom Stevenson would like to see as the next President. Stevenson shook his head ruefully. "It might seem irreverent," he began, "if I suggested——" and stopped when his audience burst into laughter. "Short of that," he went on, "I should like to say, 'any of the Democratic candidates who are competing for the Presidency or appear to be.'" He was convinced, he said, that any Democrat could beat Nixon, because there was increasing "public awareness of the failures" of the Eisenhower Administration. He emphasized that, having no favorite candidate himself, he was opposed to any stop movement against anybody.

Next day he was in Charlottesville to deliver the Founder's Day address at the University of Virginia. The speech he took with him—as usual, the product of several minds while bearing everywhere the impress of his own—had had an unusually interesting genesis. A first draft, beautifully designed to please an academic audience, had been produced by Professor Julian Boyd, the famous Jefferson scholar. It had been extensively revised by Attwood to give it what Attwood called "political punch." Attwood had then flown with it to Barbados where Stevenson had paused for a few days, purportedly for rest and relaxation, on his way back from South America. Arthur Schlesinger, Jr., was there with Stevenson and the three men "used up a couple of yellow pads producing a version that would satisfy Stevenson and the scholars without sparing Nixon," as Attwood later put it.[9] And the speech as Stevenson finally gave it did please the scholars in its immediate audience and did have national political impact, being prominently reported in the press under such headlines as: "STEVENSON BLASTS REPUBLICANS," "ADLAI FLAYS IKE ADMINISTRATION." It contained one sentence remarkable for its length (at 216 words it was probably the longest sentence in modern American political oratory) and for the succinctness with which it summarized Eisenhower's failures as liberals saw them:

> The people have a right to know why we have lost our once unquestioned military superiority; why we have repeatedly allowed the Soviets to seize the diplomatic initiative; why we have faltered in the fight for disarmament; why we are not providing our children with education to which they are entitled; why—nearly a century after the Fourteenth and Fifteenth Amendments—all of our citizens have still not been guaranteed the right to vote; why we spend billions of dollars storing surplus food when one-third of humanity goes to bed hungry; why we have not formulated an economic development program geared to the world-wide passion for economic growth; why we have failed to win the confidence and respect of the billions of impatient people in Asia, Africa, and Latin America; why millions of Americans live blighted lives in our spreading urban slums; why we have fewer doctors per capita than we did forty years ago and pay more for our medical care than ever before; why we

spent more money last year on tranquilizers than on space exploration, and more on leisure than on learning; why the richest nation in the history of the world cannot support the public services and facilities we must have not only for world power but for national growth and opportunity.

The calculated effect was an enhanced awareness of Stevenson as potential Presidential nominee—and it is Schlesinger's role in this enterprise that imparts to it its special interest, psychological as well as historical.

For Schlesinger was at this time torn by conflicting loyalties. Since Kennedy and Humphrey were both friends, the bitterness of the battle they now waged against each other was personally painful to him.[10] Stevenson, too, was a personal friend, and one whom he knew intimately enough to suspect (at least) the deep game of strategic indirection that was being played—a game whose object was a convention draft. Yet of the three men, Kennedy (with Jacqueline Kennedy at his side) was the one who most charmed him. He and Kennedy met on many common grounds. Born in the same year (1917), they had both grown up in privileged social and economic circumstances and in the same locale (Boston and environs), had had from their earliest years many mutual acquaintances, had much the same educational background (both were Harvard graduates), and had in fact been casual friends for more than a decade. Schlesinger, like other liberals, had deplored young Senator Kennedy's failure to take a public stand against Joe McCarthy at a time when Kennedy's Catholicism and authentically heroic war record made him less vulnerable to McCarthy's smear tactics than almost anyone else in the Senate. He had found this hard to forgive in one who had written a book of biographical sketches entitled *Profiles in Courage*. But he had become recently convinced of Kennedy's sincere if limited conversion to liberalism; and he, who had himself so often felt his elders' resentment of his brashness in daring to display talents superior to theirs, was fascinated by the poise, the urbanity, the self-assurance, the single-mindedness with which this young contemporary pursued the most powerful elective office on earth. Hence, as between Humphrey and Kennedy, the latter had the stronger claim upon his personal allegiance; it was from Kennedy to Humphrey that he came bearing initial messages, not the other way around.

And it was from Kennedy to Stevenson, too, that he came. Pursuing a Kennedy suggestion, he told Stevenson in Barbados that Kennedy would naturally feel "under certain obligations" to any major Democratic leader who came out for him prior to West Virginia.[11] Knowing his man, Schlesinger said no more along this line. Stevenson replied that he was pledged to neutrality during the preconvention campaigning and intended to keep his pledge. He also said his great concern was to prevent a party split. This last implied a wish to hold himself in reserve as a candidate upon whom the party could unite if none of the others could win a convention majority—an implication not soothing to Kennedy's anxieties nor (amidst diverging political and personal loyalties) to Schlesinger's own.

In the weeks that followed, Stevenson became, in Schlesinger's words, "more and more the critical figure in the Kennedy calculations." [12] The West Virginia primary battle was waged with almost unparalleled ferocity during the last weeks of April and the early days of May. Religious bigotry fought on Humphrey's side, though he did all he could to prevent it; for a time, public opinion polls showed him ahead by a wide margin; and this fact seemed to the Kennedy people to justify as well as require ruthlessness and an expenditure of money and man-hours on their part far beyond that spent in any other primary in history. While Franklin D. Roosevelt, Jr., invidiously compared Humphrey's war record with Kennedy's as he toured the state on the latter's behalf, the state's electorate was overwhelmed with Kennedy billboards, handbills, rallies, doorbell ringers, and (most importantly) hugely expensive TV productions in which Kennedy frankly and boldly faced the religious issue, reiterating his personal commitment to the Constitutional separation of church and state. And on May 10, primary election day, Kennedy eliminated Humphrey from the Presidential race once and for all by winning approximately sixty percent of the votes cast. (A few days later Humphrey, at a vacation spot in the Caribbean, told Massachusetts publisher Alden Johnson of the Barre Press that his experience of the primaries proved one thing: never again could a poor man become President of the United States.) [13]

But so far as Kennedy's anxieties were concerned, this triumph was offset by the continued growth of the Draft Stevenson movement—a growth which now became almost explosive in consequence of a world event that was reported in the same newspapers as carried the results in West Virginia.

IV

Stevenson at Charlottesville had asked why the Eisenhower administration had "repeatedly allowed the Soviets to seize the diplomatic initiative." One outstanding instance of this, as he saw it, had been the Berlin crisis of 1958 and '59, engineered by the Russians to force a summit negotiation of such matters as the nuclear test ban, disarmament, and (above all) a permanent settlement of the German problem.

The crisis had begun with the abrupt announcement by Khrushchev in November of 1958 that the Soviet Union intended to sign a separate "peace treaty" with East Germany (itself a puppet Soviet State) at an early date and thus, according to the interpretation he put upon the original Berlin agreement, end all Allied rights in West Berlin. A little later, Khrushchev had set a time limit; the treaty with the East Germans would be signed in six months, or in late May of 1959. The United States had of course responded with an announced intention to stand firm, refusing to yield to force, and to this extent had been sustained by her Allies. Stevenson, too, had approved. "When the President says he will not give in to force he speaks for all of us," said Stevenson in a Boston speech in March, 1959. But the British had been much more willing (Prime Minister Harold Macmillan was even anxious) to arrange a summit conference than Dulles had been, and on this point Stevenson had been more inclined to agree with the British position than with the all-too-typical rigidity of Dulles. In the same speech in which he had called for "unity behind the President," Stevenson had expressed the hope "that we shall not show too much unwillingness to negotiate at the summit or any other level." Two weeks later, Prime Minister Macmillan had come to the United States to confer with Eisenhower at Camp David, a retreat in the Cacoctin Mountains, whence had been issued a joint message to Khrushchev proposing a foreign ministers' meeting to be followed by ("as soon as developments justify") a summit conference. The Soviets had then initiated an ease of tensions: Khrushchev agreed to the foreign ministers' meeting, which opened in Geneva on May 11, and allowed the date he had set for the signing of his East German treaty to pass without action. He had never intended to present the West with an ultimatum, he now said.

But in June, when the Geneva foreign ministers' conference was foundering on Soviet Foreign Minister Gromyko's obviously instructed refusal to permit it to accomplish anything, the Soviets had abruptly heightened tensions again by announcing that Western rights in Berlin would be terminated precisely one year hence (or in June, 1960) when all access routes in that city would be placed under East German control. There had followed a three-week recess at Geneva. Before the meeting was reconvened, in the third week of July, Khrushchev, balancing his threat with blandishment, had announced in Moscow his willingness to visit the United States. He had also said that a visit by Eisenhower to the Soviet Union would, he believed, be beneficial to Soviet-U.S. relations. And to this diplomatic initiative, too, the administration had responded as if a puppet on Moscow strings. Eisenhower promptly offered the invitation Khrushchev had solicited. He would later claim that he had intended the invitation to be contingent upon definite progress at the reconvened Geneva meeting, but, if so, he failed to make this intention clear to Robert Murphy, who issued the invitation on his behalf through Soviet First Deputy Frol R. Kozlov. (Kozlov was returning to Moscow from a visit to this country where he had formally opened a Russian Exhibition in New York; Vice-President Nixon later opened a United States Exhibition in Soloniki Park in Moscow where he engaged in a much-publicized debate with Khrushchev.) At any rate, the Geneva meeting soon collapsed in utter futility. Khrushchev nonetheless came to the United States in mid-September as an invited guest of the Government. ". . . this caused me some chagrin," confesses Eisenhower in his memoirs: "I now had to meet Khrushchev and allow him to tour our country in spite of the fact that he had deliberately engineered the breakdown of the foreign ministers' meeting." [14]

In the United States, Khrushchev made two speeches in New York (one of them at the United Nations) and a ten-day trip coast-to-coast during which a generally favorable impression of him was received by the American public. He presented himself as a blunt, salty, humorous, outgoing, and vividly vigorous personality, tough yet likable, and on the last day of his conversations with Eisenhower at Camp David he suddenly agreed to remove the time limit he had placed on the East German treaty signing. Eisenhower, who deemed the Soviet Chairman's action a "reversal" of position brought about by Eisenhower's own "firmness," then agreed to a four-power summit meeting in the spring of 1960, following which he would pay his personal visit to the Soviet Union.[15]

And so, through their exercise of the diplomatic initiative, their ruthless play upon the world's fear of nuclear war, the Soviets had won every point of their game thus far. They had obtained precisely what they set out to obtain, namely a summit conference, while forcing the United States to retreat step by reluctant step from her original position.

There had followed months whose wintry chill was mitigated by a so-called "Spirit of Camp David"—a relatively warm, friendly spirit whereby, it seemed, the icy hostility of the Cold War was being somewhat thawed. The spirit still prevailed when Stevenson spoke at the University of Virginia. The hopes of the world were fastened on the forthcoming summit conference now scheduled to open in Paris in mid-May.

Then came disaster. . . .

On May 5, 1960, amidst a long speech to the Supreme Soviet, Khrushchev abruptly announced that a United States reconnaissance plane had just been shot down deep within Russian territory. He made the announcement in the same tone of angry outrage and threatful belligerence as an American political leader would have employed had a Soviet spy plane been brought down in the American Midwest. A shudder passed through the world. A few hours later the State Department, with Eisenhower's approval, issued a statement referring to an announcement made two days before by the National Aeronautics and Space Administration (NASA). This announcement was that a "NASA U-2 research airplane, being flown in Turkey on a joint NASA-USAF Air Weather Service mission, apparently went down in the Lake Van, Turkey, area at about 9:00 A.M. (3:00 A.M., EDT), Sunday, May 1" after the pilot had reported on emergency radio frequency "that he was experiencing oxygen difficulties." The State Department suggested that the plane Khrushchev referred to was this missing plane: "It is entirely possible that having failure in the oxygen, which could result in the pilot losing consciousness, the plane continued on automatic pilot for a considerable distance and accidentally violated Soviet airspace. The United States is taking this matter up with the Soviet Government, with particular reference to the fate of the pilot."

Next day, a coldly scornful Khrushchev sprang the trap he had baited. He electrified the world and spread consternation through the American government with a second announcement, again before the Supreme Soviet: the uninjured civilian pilot of the reconnaissance plane, one Francis Gary Powers, was in Soviet hands; he had confessed that he was engaged in aerial photographic espionage; and much of the equipment he had used, captured intact, was also in Soviet hands. Pictures of Powers and of his wrecked plane were released in Moscow. By all this, the original U.S. lie was of course thoroughly exposed. Nevertheless, again with Eisenhower's approval, the State Department issued another statement repeating the original falsehood (the U-2, it insisted, had been engaged in weather research and had accidentally strayed), but tacking onto it a sentence asserting or admitting the necessity for intelligence-collecting activities. The effect of this last was to reduce still further, if that were possible, the statement's credibility.

Not until the following morning did the State Department decide that the government of the United States might as well tell the truth, since the truth was already known to everyone. Secretary of State Herter so informed Eisenhower. And Eisenhower of course agreed to this as he had to every other recommendation by his associates regarding the U-2 since the moment, back in 1954, when the proposal to build thirty of these highly specialized aircraft was first presented for his approval. And so, on May 7, a truthful statement was at last issued, after having been edited by Eisenhower in order "to eliminate any phrase that seemed to me defensive in tone," as he later put it in his memoirs.[16] Thus the public was informed that the U-2 was a plane of extremely light construction and with a relative huge wingspread, enabling it to operate at heights (70,000 feet) far beyond the reach of any known Soviet fighter-interceptors. It had been used from 1956 on, whenever weather permitted, to spy upon Soviet territory; Powers had in fact been thirteen hundred miles inside the Soviet Union when an engine flame-out * brought his plane down. (Neither he nor his plane was supposed to survive after such an event—the high pay he and his colleagues received from the Central Intelligence Agency for their flights was premised upon the assumption of fatal risks—but obviously, for whatever reason, Powers had not lived up, or died down, to his implicit bargain.) The public was further told that specific overflight missions had not been subject to Presidential approval. Eisenhower, in other words, had not *specifically* authorized the flight which had ended with Powers' capture.

* Actually, Powers was shot down by a surface-to-air missile (SAM) of the type the Russians later installed in Castro's Cuba.

It was in this context that Adlai Stevenson, on May 12, presented to the Conference on World Tensions at the University of Chicago his argument for an American foreign policy based on a recognition of the world-wide human community and aimed toward the development of an effective world law. He prefaced his argument with a reference to the U-2 incident. "In spite of all the rhetoric of the past few days, no one questions the necessity of gathering intelligence for our security," he said. "The Russians, of course, do the same, and they have a great advantage because of their addiction to secrecy, while our countries are virtually wide open to all the world's spies. But our timing, our words, our management must and will be sharply questioned. Could it serve the purpose of peace and mutual trust to send intelligence missions over the heart of the Soviet Union on the very eve of the long awaited Summit Conference? Can the President be embarrassed and national policies endangered at such a critical time by an unknown government official?" [17]

This last was of course an inference drawn from the State Department's sentence to the effect that prior Presidential approval had not been required for each U-2 overflight. This same sentence enabled Khrushchev, on the eve of the summit meeting for which he had pressed so hard, to offer Eisenhower an "out." He suggested that Eisenhower might not have been responsible for these outrageous violations of Soviet frontiers and security, that the flights might have been made without his knowledge. But the implication that Eisenhower was not in actual fact the Chief Executive—that he was not even kept informed of governmental activities of crucial importance—struck Eisenhower as personally insulting. He reacted promptly and strongly against it. He *was* responsible, he publicly insisted; he had authorized the overflights. Nor would he so much as hint to Khrushchev that he regretted what had happened. ("I felt the opposite of apologetic," say his memoirs.[18]) He even intimated that, because of Soviet secrecy and espionage in our own country, and because our security required it, the overflights would be continued! To this Khrushchev made the only response possible for a man in his position: the overflights were deliberate acts of aggression intolerable by a sovereign power; their continuation would mean war.

Meanwhile, final preparations for the Paris summit were completed, with Eisenhower categorically rejecting any suggestion that he avoid or postpone to a more propitious time a direct confrontation with Khrushchev. ("For me, the attendance had become a duty," he writes. "It might prove unpleasant, but I had no intention of evading it. Indeed, I welcomed the opportunity to uncover more Soviet hypocrisy." [19]) He left for Paris on May 14. By then he had belatedly issued orders that the U-2 flights over Soviet territory were *not* to be resumed, but he made no public announcement of this fact. Immediately upon his arrival in the French capital he was presented with a copy of a message Khrushchev had sent to both Prime Minister Macmillan and French President Charles de Gaulle. It demanded that the President denounce the U-2 flights as acts of "inadmissable provocation" against the U.S.S.R., punish those who were responsible for them, and renounce all such acts in the future. If the President did this, Khrushchev as head of the Soviet government would do all he could to make the conference succeed; if the President did not do it, then "I cannot be among the participants in negotiations when one of them has made perfidy the basis of its policy toward the Soviet Union." Eisenhower promptly told Macmillan and de Gaulle that there was no possibility of his apologizing or punishing anyone. And a few hours later, on the night of Sunday, May 15, he ordered (or acquiesced in the order of) a world-wide alert of U.S. combat forces!

Next morning, the inevitable happened.

At the opening of the first scheduled session of the conference, Khrushchev demanded the floor, was given it by de Gaulle (who presided), and then, speaking from a prepared text, which he later released to the press, delivered himself of a bitter indictment of the U.S. aggressions against the Soviet Union. Angrily and at length he revoked the invitation he had tendered Eisenhower to visit his country. It was now utterly impossible for him to participate in conference negotiations, he said. Eisenhower made brief reply. As at the height of the Quemoy-Matsu crisis, he displayed a prudence and conciliatory spirit that, earlier displayed, might have prevented the crisis and gone far toward insuring conference success, with all that might have meant to the peace and prosperity of the world. He announced that the overflights had been suspended and would not be resumed. He regretted the necessity for international espionage. "I have come to Paris to seek agreements with the Soviet Union which would eliminate the necessity for all forms of espionage . . . ," he said. He indicated his willingness "to undertake bilateral conversations between the United States and the U.S.S.R. while the main conference proceeds." [20] But it was now too late. Only an outright apology, which it was impossible for Eisenhower to make, would now have enabled Khrushchev to enter into negotiations without a politically disastrous loss of face. He and the other Soviet delegates arose and stalked from the room.

And so, with a President of the United States personally humiliated before the eyes of the world as none other in that office had ever been, the Paris summit collapsed even before negotiations had begun.

v

Adlai Stevenson was in Washington on the Monday of May 16, 1960.

In the five days since the West Virginia primary he had been under heavier pressure than ever before to endorse Kennedy's candidacy. Schlesinger had talked to him again on Kennedy's behalf, asserting that Kennedy now needed only 100 votes or less to win convention nomination and that a Stevenson endorsement could supply him with these from California and Pennsylvania. The great object, said Schlesinger, was the nomination of a liberal candidate and Kennedy, who wanted to be the liberal candidate, might in the absence of Stevenson help feel forced to turn to Southern conservatives for support. Kennedy himself, on his way back from campaigning in the Oregon primary, stopped at Libertyville a day or so later. He came prepared to deal. He asked Newton Minow, who with Bill Blair had met him at the airport, if he should offer Stevenson the post of Secretary of State. Minow had replied with an emphatic "No!" Stevenson, Minow knew, would resent any such proposition; he would regard it as an attempted bribe.[21] Nor was Stevenson immune from Kennedy pressure even in his own office. Wirtz alone among the three long-time Stevenson law partners remained wholly submissive to the senior partner's openly expressed wish; he alone acted on the suspicion that the expressed wish was but the outward sign of an inner wish to be available, and in the most favorable position, for a draft. Blair and Minow, having taken Stevenson at his word when he said he was not and would not become a candidate, had long been fervent Kennedy supporters. (Both, and Minow especially, were close social friends of the Sargent Shrivers, Shriver being then president of the Chicago Board of Education—and Mrs. Shriver [Eunice] was a sister of Kennedy.) They, too, now urged Stevenson to come out for Kennedy before it was too late.

Blair, in fact, had been urging this for nearly a year. All during the Latin American tour, he and Bill Benton had poured opposing arguments on the subject into Stevenson's ear. "Be realistic," said Blair. "Come out for Kennedy. He's going to win anyway. He'll make a good President and you'll be Secretary of State." "Do *not* come out for Kennedy," argued Benton with even greater vehemence. "It is *not* certain he'll be nominated unless you make it so. Hold yourself in reserve." [22]

To all these urgings, Stevenson had made the same reply as before. He was pledged to neutrality; he could not agree that the outcome in West Virginia, though it seemed to assure Kennedy of the nomination, did anything to justify a violation of his pledge. On the contrary, if he now endorsed Kennedy he would obviously be "jumping on the bandwagon" for his own advantage; he would be "angling for a job" and (as he said to Schlesinger) "I can't do that sort of thing." [23] He publicly reiterated his earlier statements when a *New York Times* reporter interviewed him by telephone shortly before he left Libertyville to board his plane for Washington on Sunday the 15th. Monday morning's papers carried the story. Stevenson had "no intention to support any one candidate at this time," and this, the reporter added, "serves in effect to keep the door open for Stevenson's supporters to draft him."

And indeed, though the West Virginia results were a blow to its leaders, the Draft Stevenson movement had by then become formidable. It remained unofficial. It was, however, guided now by experienced political hands from a national headquarters established in April at 100 Indiana Avenue in Washington—a headquarters provided (largely through the fund raising efforts of Bob Benjamin in New York and the Schary group in Los Angeles) with enough money to do a professional job of trend analysis, delegate checking and persuading, advertising and publicity. In dozens of states, too, Draft Stevenson organizations were either formed or in process of formation.

But it was not in connection with any of these activities of his supporters that Stevenson had come to Washington on this fatal Monday. One of the spots he scrupulously avoided in the capital was the Letter-Carriers' Building at 100 Indiana. He had come instead to testify before a Congressional committee on a proposal he had made in a widely-discussed article recently published in *This Week* magazine.[24] In that article, he deplored the "circus atmosphere" in which Presidential campaigns had been so largely conducted in the past and suggested as substitute the use of national TV for a great debate by candidates of the two major parties "conducted in full view of all the people." Such a debate, he had written, "would end the tendency to reduce everything to assertions and slogans." Congressional action and TV network cooperation were required for the implementation of this proposal; the radio-TV rule of equal time for all candidates, including those of tiny minority parties, would have to be modified, for one thing. And Stevenson, pleading for such action, had said that "in the long run it may turn out that the direction we give to political television is one of the great decisions of the decisive decade of the 1960's." The necessary action (actually a resolution) had been promptly introduced, and Stevenson was in the midst of his testimony upon it when announcement was made in the hearing room of the Paris summit collapse.

"This is terribly sad news," he said.

But within hours he had reason to know that the sad news might be deemed good if measured solely in terms of his personal ambition. When he left the hearing room at the close of his testimony he was followed by most of the crowd that had filled every seat. A mob of hundreds closed around him in the hall outside and he had literally to push his way through it to reach the office of Senator Monroney, where he took refuge. Monroney himself has told how Stevenson, after the crowd had departed, was taken "to a private room where he met with Lyndon Johnson and received a stern warning that he might yet be the nominee of the Democratic party." He also joined Johnson, Speaker Rayburn, and Chairman Fulbright of the Senate Foreign Relations Committee in drafting and sending a cable to Khrushchev via the U.S. delegation urging the Russian Premier to reconsider his action and permit the summit to proceed.* Back in Monroney's office, he met with some of the leaders of the draft movement on his behalf who also spoke sternly to him, laying stress upon his duty, his moral obligation; and there he promised that he would "provide the voice of leadership for the Democratic party" and would "do nothing to handicap our effort to secure his nomination. We asked for more," Monroney goes on, "but to these two [requests] he agreed." [26]

He fulfilled the first of the two promises just three days later with a hard-hitting political speech before a fund raising Democratic dinner in Chicago. The Republicans were making their inevitable demands for uncritical national unity behind the President in an hour of crisis. And this time the demands were unusually strong: national honor was involved; silence was a patriotic duty if its only alternative was criticism of a President who had been personally insulted by the head of a hostile state. Stevenson's reply, in Chicago, revealed his disgust with this latest attempt to suppress dissent.

While all Americans must "resent deeply and bitterly the gross affront to the President and his office," he said, far too much was at stake to permit us "to sweep the whole sorry mess under the rug in the name of national unity." Instead, it was the clear duty "of responsible opposition . . . to expose and criticize carelessness and mistakes . . . in a case of such national and world importance as this." He said: "Premier Khrushchev wrecked this conference. Let there be no mistake about that. . . . But we handed Khrushchev the crowbar and the sledge hammer to wreck the meeting. . . . Let there be no mistake about that, either." He swiftly reviewed the "incredible . . . series of blunders" which must inevitably have impressed "suspicious Russians" as a "deliberate effort to break up a conference we never wanted anyway." Though "nothing . . . can justify Mr. Khrushchev's contemptuous conduct," the Russian's anger "was predictable. . . . How would we feel if Soviet spy planes based in Cuba were flying over Cape Canaveral and Oak Ridge? And also we could predict with certainty his effort to use the situation to split the Western Alliance and intimidate the countries where our bases are situated. . . ." Stevenson then called upon "all thoughtful, concerned citizens

---

* According to Eisenhower's memoirs, the "curious telegram" was delivered to him on the evening of May 18, nearly forty-eight hours after it was sent! "This was a somewhat awkward attempt, I thought, to interfere with the day-to-day conduct of foreign relations," he writes. He ordered his staff "to reply that the conference had already broken up" and, whether the cable was delivered to Khrushchev or not, he "was leaving Paris early the following morning." But when Secretary of State Herter phoned Johnson of Eisenhower's "decision" (the word is Eisenhower's own), he asked if Johnson and the others still wanted the cable delivered—and Johnson said they did. "Why, I've never known," writes Eisenhower, "but the message, as I recall, was delivered by a staff officer to the Soviet Embassy in Paris." [25] Thus even this last and admittedly forlorn hope of retrieving something from the wreckage was frustrated by the administration. But the Soviets were at least informed, or reminded, that Democratic leaders were truly anxious to negotiate and would have handled matters differently.

to help retrieve the situation and to face the hard, inescapable facts: that this administration played into Khrushchev's hands; that the administration acutely embarrassed our allies and endangered our bases; that they have made successful negotiations with the Russians—negotiations vital to our survival—impossible so long as they are in power."

No other speech he ever gave aroused so great a storm as this one. Most of the press and all conservative politicians, including several of his own party, bitterly condemned him for a disruption of national unity akin to treason in the circumstances. James A. Farley did so. Lyndon Johnson indicated that, though the administration had indeed made mistakes, he felt Stevenson's indictment to be too harsh and sweeping. Stuart Symington, whom Truman favored over Stevenson for President in part because (as the former President had just said in a magazine article) Stevenson was "indecisive," responded to reporters' insistent questions with a statement so equivocal it indicated nothing save Symington's regret at being asked for an opinion. But there was approval, too—strong approval from an influential minority of the press, including the St. Louis *Post-Dispatch,* the Milwaukee *Journal,* the Louisville *Courier-Journal.* And John F. Kennedy publicly approved. He was the only one of the three declared Democratic candidates to do so. He indicated his belief that Eisenhower should have made some kind of conciliatory gesture toward Khrushchev before it was too late.

But if Kennedy publicly approved what Stevenson had said, he could not but privately deplore its effect upon the race for nomination. His published comment upon it brought down upon his boyish head the kind of vote-denying criticism hardest for him to counter: both Nixon and Lyndon Johnson told the public he had suggested an abject apology to Khrushchev, a recommended appeasement that evinced his lack of necessary toughness as well as of mature judgment. And indeed the terrors of the U-2 incident caused a great many Democrats to question, as they had not before, whether the nation's destinies could be safely entrusted to a young man who looked even younger than his years and who lacked executive experience. Stevenson's Chicago speech caused these same Democrats to look closely again at the man who had been twice their standard-bearer, whose moral and intellectual quality had transformed the party, whose world prestige was higher than that of any other American in political life, and whose earlier public statements had been so often prophetic, so often productive (despite the administration) of sound national decisions. The Kennedy bandwagon faltered. Until late May, every recent week had seen a solid gain in the number of votes pledged to Kennedy on the first convention ballot. There was no such gain in the week before Memorial Day; and the reason for this, as the Kennedy people well knew, was the movement toward Stevenson—a "convulsive movement," as Schlesinger has written.[27] Kennedy was worried.

And the Stevensonians were correspondingly cheered. Coldly realistic calculations of delegate voting strength, those made in the Kennedy camp as well as at 100 Indiana Avenue, were agreed as June opened that Kennedy lacked *at least* 100 of the votes needed to win nomination. Monroney and Sharon estimated his deficit at considerably more than this; Kennedy, they believed, lacked by well over 150 the 761 votes comprising a convention majority. They estimated Johnson to have somewhere between 400 and 450 votes, nearly all from the South and West with a scattering over the Midwest, while Symington, though he seemed no longer to regard himself as a serious contender, was believed to have somewhere between 100 to 150. As for Stevenson, despite his avowed non-candidacy, he was assured of at least 45 and possibly 50 first ballot votes, to which some 30 could be added with but slight effort on his behalf (whereas great effort would in fact be expended) before the convention opened in Los Angeles in the first week of July. Everything would then depend upon decisions taken by five states whose votes were pledged to favorite sons—the States of Iowa, Kansas, Minnesota, New Jersey, and California—and by Illinois and Pennsylvania, whose delegations were uncommitted. If all the favorite sons refused to release their delegates on the first ballot, and if a substantial portion of the Pennsylvania and Illinois delegations was denied Kennedy on that ballot, then a deadlock would be, it seemed, inevitable. For it was now more than ever apparent that Kennedy had to win on the first ballot or come very close to it if he were to win at all. He was unlikely to gain many if any votes on a second ballot; he would surely lose votes on a third and still more on a fourth. And these votes, most of them, would go to Stevenson, in whose image so much of the Kennedy candidacy had been fashioned—or so the Stevensonians believed. The popularity and high prestige of Stevenson in almost every part of the national Democracy would then be felt as a rising pressure upon the convention floor. The stampede to Stevenson would be on.

To prepare the way for this happy (as they saw it) conclusion, Monroney and Sharon, from the last week of May to the end of June, traveled incessantly about the nation—and "if there was a stop-Kennedy movement rolling," writes Theodore White, "it rolled wherever Sharon and Monroney moved." [28] They visited such long-time Stevensonians as David Lawrence of Pennsylvania, Governor "Pat" Brown of California, Col. Jack Arvey of Chicago, and Mayor Daley of Chicago. (It was known, however, that Daley had been under heavy pressure from Joseph P. Kennedy, the candidate's father, whose rich Chicago real estate holdings included the vast Merchandise Mart, and that the Mayor had probably already committed himself, along with the Cook County portion of the Illinois delegation, to young Kennedy.) Everywhere Monroney and Sharon visited with leaders of the Stevenson volunteers, encouraging and helping to organize a descent upon Los Angeles by many hundreds of Stevensonians to demonstrate with banners and placards for their champion when the convention opened. Meanwhile, James Doyle was moved from Madison to 100 Indiana in Washington where, in early June, he at last officially announced an organized Draft Stevenson movement and worked to stimulate further draft organizations on a state basis. (There were forty-two state organizations by the end of June.) Prepared news releases went out from the various headquarters in a swelling stream, paid spot announcements began to be made on local radio and TV broadcasts, and full-page advertisements for a Stevenson draft, signed by scores of influential citizens, began to appear in leading newspapers.

The persuasiveness of these efforts was aided by a continuing series of reverses for U.S. foreign relations, reverses that made Stevenson's strictures upon the administration's conduct of foreign affairs over the years, and his recommendations of alternative actions, seem prophetic and wise indeed.

In Geneva, a ten-nation disarmament conference, convened under United Nations auspices in March of 1960, came to a futile end when the Soviet delegation withdrew from it in June. In Turkey, a pro-American government was seriously threatened by left wing rioting and only precariously survived. In Korea, Syngman Rhee, long supported by the United States despite his addiction to a one-man rule sustained by police terror, had been overthrown by a student revolt; the country remained in political turmoil under a caretaker government as free elections were being prepared. In Cuba, Fidel Castro made military alliance with Khrushchev, who threatened war with the United States if the latter invaded the island; soon Soviet arms and technicians would be moving in, a breach in the Monroe Doctrine which the United States seemed helpless to close. Most immediately shocking of all, the President of the United States, for the second time within a month, was personally humiliated before the eyes of the world. Eisenhower had been originally scheduled to follow his Russian visit with one to Japan, arriving in Tokyo on June 19 after a flight across Siberia. When his invitation to visit Russia was revoked, he decided to keep his Tokyo date anyway, preceding it with visits to the Philippines, Formosa, and Okinawa, and following it with a visit to South Korea. But Japanese Communists and left wing Socialists were quick to exploit the fearful anger aroused in millions of Japanese by the U-2 incident, an anger directed toward the United States and Eisenhower personally; and when the President's advance party, including White House Press Secretary Hagerty, attempted to go by automobile from a Tokyo airfield into the city on June 10, it was immobilized by a stone-throwing, club-wielding mob. It had finally to be rescued from possibly fatal danger by a U.S. helicopter. A few days later, Eisenhower, in Manila, was informed that the government of Japan had withdrawn ("postponed") its invitation to him because his personal safety in Japan could not be guaranteed. . . . There was trouble in the Congo, too—grave trouble, as Africans unprepared for self-government were abruptly released from an unenlightened Belgian colonial rule and required to set up as a sovereign state; the danger of a Communist takeover there was acute.

Limned against this dark forest of troubles, wherein the future lurked as a dragon grown huge on the errors of the last seven years, Adlai Stevenson appeared to myriads of Democrats as more than ever a knight in shining armor.

CHAPTER THIRTY-ONE

BUT what was Adlai Stevenson's view of himself? It was this (the fact, for instance, that it was utterly impossible for him to regard his pudgy, balding, diffident self as any kind of shining knight) which now became decisive.

He found himself in almost precisely the position he had hoped by this time to occupy on the national scene. He had not, however, anticipated such a campaign for the nomination as young Kennedy had waged. Not a few Stevensonians who watched this campaign had been disturbed by the spectacle of so hard, so coldly calculated, so lavishly financed a thrust for power on the part of a young man who obviously knew exactly what he wanted and whose outer acts seemed never to be inhibited by questions as to *why* he wanted it or whether, in the total scheme of things, he really *ought* to have it. By instinct and on principle, Stevenson himself distrusted such manifestations of pure will in democratic politics. On the other hand, Kennedy was (or had been) personally attractive to him—a charming, witty, highly intelligent young man whose tastes, interests, and ideal commitments *seemed*, at least, to be much the same as Stevenson's own. . . . At any rate, there Kennedy was, in a position further advanced toward convention victory than Stevenson had counted on. And because he was there, Stevenson must, it seemed, revise his own strategy if he were to achieve his ambition, forsaking the indirect approach to the extent of taking a step or two toward his goal and then reaching out his hand to grasp the prize now dangling just out of reach. He should act. So others told him and so, intermittently, he told himself.

Once in the late spring, pressed by Tom Finletter to make a direct bid, he angrily blamed Finletter for his predicament. "*You* made me put out that damned statement," he said, referring to his 1956 announcement that he would not again run. "Now you want me to break my word." [1] But of course he knew Finletter was right to insist that that statement was no such solemn pledge of honor, binding for all eternity, as Stevenson now pretended. No one held against Eisenhower in 1952 the fact that he had issued, four years before, a renunciation statement much stronger than Stevenson's. Consistency in politics, and especially in matters of this sort, does not require a stubborn refusal to change with the times; indeed, political consistency actually *is* a congruity between one's general principles, one's stated present position, and the situation as it is *now*. Stevenson could hardly deny that the relevant situation had drastically changed since 1956. It was different even, in mid-June, from what it had been when he made his promise of "neutrality" to the active candidates. The U-2 incident had not then occurred. There had not then been the urgent popular demand for Stevenson's leadership which the U-2 incident had generated and which had been increased by subsequent foreign policy reverses. There had not then been such conviction as there now was in the arguments of Monroney, Ball, Finletter, and the others that of all Americans in political life he and he only could provide the kind of national leadership called for by the desperate times. Surely these changes in circumstance justified, if they did not require, a change in his own stance.

Theodore H. White tells in *The Making of the President, 1960* how he sat with Stevenson on the lawn of the Libertyville farm on a golden afternoon in early June, listening to his host's brilliant wide-ranging survey of domestic and world problems facing America in this election year. Stevenson was incisive and deeply probing in his diagnoses, decisive and creative in his prescriptions—"the clear voice for which Americans in search of leadership were aching." But then the phone rang, a long-distance call from New York demanding (Mrs. Roosevelt was going to publish the demand in her column or in an open letter) that he state publicly whether or not he sought the nomination. He returned to White "annoyed, angered," with his "clear voice" replaced by a muffled querulous one. Why did people refuse to understand and accept the position he had defined over and over again? he asked. Far from being indecisive, he adhered firmly to this position; he had done so ever since his statement of December, 1956. All the same, White was impressed by the contrast between the coldly decisive assurance with which Stevenson had dealt with public issues and the flustered way in which he now dealt with problems of his personal career.[2]

As for pressures from the other side, Arthur Schlesinger, Jr., tells in *A Thousand Days* of Stevenson's visit to his, Schlesinger's, Cambridge, Massachusetts, home a week after Memorial Day, 1960. Schlesinger again urged Stevenson to come out for Kennedy, repeating his argument that the beneficiary of Stevensonian votes withheld from Kennedy would be a conservative candidate. Stevenson made the same reply he had made so often before, but added this time he did not "preclude the possibility of coming out for

Kennedy" if he could do so without "letting down" Johnson, Symington, and his own supporters whom he had assured he would "stay out of this." Then, "in a worried way," writes Schlesinger, he said that "if his support became necessary to put a liberal over, this might change things." [3]

William Attwood lived much of that June on the Stevenson farm at Libertyville, where he continued to draft speech material and position papers on current issues. Several times he came to the University of Chicago to go with Walter Johnson to the offices of various faculty experts on subjects concerning which Stevenson needed to be briefed. One day in the second week of June, having spent the night in Johnson's home, he asked Johnson to come back with him to Libertyville and there try to talk sense into Stevenson concerning preconvention strategy. Attwood was exasperated by the failure of his own efforts along this line. Johnson did as Attwood asked. And in a conversation lasting many hours that afternoon Stevenson reviewed his dilemma more frankly and fully, perhaps, than he had done before in talk with others. [4]

Of the three declared Democratic candidates, Kennedy, he felt, though bright and able, was too young, too unseasoned for the Presidency. He pushed too hard, was in too much of a hurry; he lacked the wisdom of humility, and that wisdom, so necessary to the judicious exercise of executive power, would not be encouraged by success in his current campaign. Both Kennedy and the nation would profit from a postponement of his ambition. This feeling, Stevenson believed, was widespread among the electorate and would weaken Kennedy as a candidate against Nixon.

Symington, in Stevenson's view, was simply not qualified for the White House, nor could he be counted upon to wage a sufficiently vigorous campaign against Nixon. He was too easy, too safe. He seemed blandly indifferent to many of the most crucial national and world issues while vastly exaggerating the importance of national defense, and especially the technical details of air and missile strength, in the total scheme of things.

Lyndon Johnson seemed to Stevenson too regional a candidate to be a strong contender against Nixon; he had great abilities but they were those of a skilled political tactician rather than of a top policy-making statesman and he certainly could not, on the record, be deemed a dedicated liberal. He had bitterly (if covertly) opposed the Democratic Advisory Council and his candidacy was bitterly opposed by Walter Reuther and, in general, by the liberal wing of the party.

There remained Stevenson himself....

"Look, Governor," pleaded Walter Johnson, "since you feel the way you do about the other candidates, it seems to me it's beholden upon you to lift the telephone, call Dave Lawrence, call Mike Monroney, invite them to fly to O'Hare [then a new Chicago airport, with little traffic] and bring them here secretly. Tell them that you really want to do this thing, that you're not going to campaign for it but you do want it. Let them take it from there."

But Stevenson stubbornly refused to regard what he had said as an argument for decisive action on his part. It was instead, as Johnson soon realized, an argument for his being drafted. And he could not be moved from this position by Johnson's insistence that the kind of draft that had occurred in 1952, a draft in which Johnson himself had played a leading part, was utterly impossible in 1960. The Kennedy bandwagon, seemingly stalled on Memorial Day, was rolling again by the second week of June, with Kennedy in the process of taking away from Lyndon Johnson in the Western states the pledged delegate votes on which Johnson had been counting to force a convention deadlock. There would be no deadlock now, and hence no possibility of a Stevenson nomination, *unless* Stevenson did more than merely indicate that he would serve if called. Only if he clearly said that he *wanted* to be called would it be possible for the Stevensonians, now hamstrung by his seeming reluctance, to rally and organize the support they needed to prevent Kennedy's nomination on, probably, the first ballot. His failure to take this step had already cost him important support, but it was not yet too late. Walter Johnson was convinced of this: a forthright indication by Stevenson of his real opinions and wishes could still make him the nominee.

But Stevenson shook his head.

"No," he said. "No, I can't do that."

He continued to insist, in his most private conversation and correspondence as in his more public statements, that his law partners and all others who had committed themselves to him in earlier campaigns were now perfectly free to support any candidate of their choice and would suffer no loss of his affection or esteem by so doing. Yet it is significant that some of those who took him at his word and declared for Kennedy felt uneasy about it, as if a certain disloyalty were involved.

Thus Schlesinger tells in *A Thousand Days* how, just forty-eight hours after Stevenson's visit to Schlesinger's home in early June, newspapers announced that Schlesinger, Galbraith, Allan Nevins, Henry Steele Commager, and a dozen other liberal intellectuals, all fervent Stevenson supporters in 1952 and 1956, were preparing an open letter endorsing Kennedy—a fact Schlesinger had not seen fit to mention to Stevenson when the latter was his houseguest. (Schlesinger explains that the news release was premature: the statement had not yet been written when news that it was in preparation was leaked to a reporter. One suspects the ruthlessly efficient hand of the Kennedy organization, determined to risk no change of mind.) Schlesinger speaks of this as "the *defection* [italics mine] of old friends" which "could not but have . . . hurt" Stevenson.[5] And the wording of the letter itself, when finally formally released on June 17, betrays a certain unease, a certain defensiveness. "The purpose of this letter is to urge, now that Senator Humphrey has withdrawn from the race and Mr. Stevenson continues to stand aside, that the liberals of America turn to Senator Kennedy," it said in part. ". . . all of us supported Adlai Stevenson in 1952 and 1956 and hope that he will be a leading foreign affairs figure in any new Democratic administration. But he insists that he is not a candidate in 1960, and Senator Kennedy, a man of whom liberals can be proud, is an active candidate who has proved his appeal to men and women of all ranks and creeds."

The letter aroused a storm of angry protest from Stevensonians, much of it focused on Schlesinger who, of all the signers, had been most prominently and closely identified with Stevenson in the past. He and his fellow letter-signers were dubbed "turncoat opportunists," "prophets of a bought convention," and climbers onto a "well-oiled bandwagon at a time when the bandwagon can be stopped." It was the latter point that many Stevensonians found most infuriating. Timed as it was, the letter seemed to them a calculated betrayal of a cause not yet lost but whose loss the letter greatly encouraged and whose victory the letter-signers could have done much to assure if, instead of treasonably defecting, they had called with equal publicity for a Stevenson draft. Schlesinger's wife, Marian, evidently sympathized with, if she did not actually share, this view; she promptly announced in the press that her candidate for President remained Adlai Stevenson.

As always when absorbing blows, Stevenson kept his feelings well hidden. He could recognize the event as the realization of a risk inherent in his long-term strategy. Outwardly he remained serene. (". . . he never spoke a word of reproach," writes Schlesinger, "and our relations suffered no permanent damage.") [6] Yet he *was* hurt. He knew that such men as Galbraith and Schlesinger must sense, if they did not actually know, what he hoped for; their action, therefore, was a personal repudiation of him. They did not choose Kennedy because Stevenson was unavailable; they deliberately chose Kennedy *over* Stevenson; and part of their reason for doing so was revealed (their exasperation with Stevenson's posture was hinted at) by the sentence that compared Stevenson's avowed non-candidacy with Kennedy's being "an active candidate who has proved his appeal. . . ."

Obviously, Stevenson seemed to them to want to be begged.

II

On the evidence, the deepest root of his refusal to act did not lie in the kind of self-mistrust that his detractors seemed (or pretended) to discern. He knew as well as anyone that, if the wisdom of humility is necessary to the judicious exercise of power, a certain kind of rock-hard self-confidence is necessary to the decisive exercise of it at ultimate moments. He did not lack this kind of confidence. He had faith in his capacity to govern. For all his awe of the "grandeur" of the office, he truly believed he could be as successful a President of the United States as he had been a governor of Illinois. No, it was not his capacity to *be* President that he doubted; it was instead his right to *become* President through any egoistic assertion that violated (as he had said over and over again) his pledged word.

"We told him that his word given to trusted friends was unimportant when measured against the public need," writes Senator Monroney. "He understood better than we that ambition finds excuses that conscience cannot accept." [7]

And the Stevenson conscience was Presbyterian, Calvinistic, despite his intellectual rejection of Calvinistic dogma. Joined to it was a sense of fate, of destiny, that somewhat resembled the predestination of Presbyterian theology. What would be would be, so far as the Presidency was concerned. He had gone as far as he felt he could to satisfy his private ambition within the bounds of justice and fair play and public duty; he now resigned the event into the hand of God. Which is to say that others, as instruments of the Almighty, must now decide his personal fate.

Though basic, this may not have been the whole explanation of his refusal to act, however. Inertia worked in favor of his continuing along the lines already laid down. He had determined his present course at a time when calm reflection and judgment were possible; he might doubt the wisdom of changing course at a time when irrational drives within himself were vastly encouraged by outer pressures. And beyond this inertial doubt may well have lain another, a reasonable doubt that had nothing to do with his moral scruples but was born instead of a thoroughly hard-headed, pragmatic assessment of his chances. He may well have asked himself whether the action urged upon him by his supporters would actually achieve their (and his) end in view.

His supporters assumed that Kennedy's initial convention votes would, in case of deadlock, come to him in sufficient quantity to assure his defeat of Johnson. But would they? Especially would they if he himself, by his open avowal of his candidacy, became responsible for the deadlock?

The notes of warm generosity and selfless idealism had not thus far been strongly sounded in young Kennedy's known character. He would not have come so far so fast if he (or his family as a whole) had not advanced his career with a calculated and occasionally ruthless use of the power great wealth gave him—the power to threaten and promise, to punish and reward in highly tangible ways. Nor had he conspicuously displayed thus far a disposition to forgive and forget; it was said of him that he could drive down a Boston street and point out which stores had displayed his campaign posters and which had refused to do so ten years before. One might reasonably doubt, therefore, that a Kennedy made coldly furious by the denial of his ambition would, out of sheer devotion to liberal principles, permit the prize to go to the man who had thwarted him. And in a deadlocked convention his permission would almost certainly be necessary. He would almost certainly retain enough voting strength to enable him to decide the contest between Johnson and Stevenson—and Johnson would be his likely choice. (Actually, Kennedy had told Minow in mid-May, no doubt for tactical reasons, that if he could not have the nomination himself he favored Johnson.) All this led to the conclusion that Stevenson, at this juncture, could best serve his Presidential ambition by continuing the strategy he had followed for so long. By this reasoning, it was not merely that he wanted to be begged, wanted to be drafted; he *had* to be if he were to be nominated at all.

But—alas for the success of such pragmatism, assuming that Stevenson consciously espoused it—Kennedy was fully capable of recognizing it for what it was and of being more antagonized by it (for it seemed to him sneaky) than he would have been by an openly avowed Stevenson candidacy. His father, the redoubtable and reactionary Joseph P. Kennedy, had consistently and profanely asserted in the Kennedy councils that Stevenson (whom he designated by an insulting epithet) was running and had in fact been running without a moment's letup since 1956.[8] Young Kennedy now acted as if he agreed, recognizing Stevenson as the only serious obstacle to his nomination. Hence, whether Stevenson chose to admit it or not, he was engaged in a battle with Kennedy for the highest power-stakes in the world, and the bitterness of the fight was not mitigated for the participants by the covertness with which it must be fought.

III

On Saturday, July 9, 1960, Adlai Stevenson flew from Chicago to Los Angeles. Among the forty or fifty people with him on the plane were Buffie and Ernest Ives, Adlai III and Nancy, his nephew, Timothy Ives, and Timothy's wife, Adrienne, the Edison Dicks, and Marietta Tree. His arrival was delayed by an unscheduled fuel stop at Las Vegas, but when he finally emerged from his plane at Los Angeles' International Airport, late in the afternoon, he received a tumultuous, soul-stirring welcome from a crowd of 10,000—the largest demonstration in the airport's history—which was witnessed by the whole country via television and had its impact upon the assembling delegates. He made a brief, graceful statement that answered no questions about his candidacy. ("I never thought this convention was rigged," he said in part, referring to charges that National Committee Chairman Paul Butler, a fervent Kennedy supporter, was giving the Massachusetts senator preferential treatment in all convention arrangements, "until I was put down in the middle of the Nevada desert in 100-degree heat this afternoon.... You're probably the most heat-resistant bunch of supporters anyone ever had. Apparently in Los Angeles they like their eggheads hard-boiled.") He was then driven to his hotel, the Beverly Hills—a relatively quiet, pleasant hostelry whose distance (eight miles) from convention headquarters in the Biltmore, and from the Sports Arena where the convention would assemble, seemed to emphasize his personal aloofness from the campaign being waged on his behalf.

But of course he could not remain aloof. The campaign came to him; it swirled in gusts of excitement through the lobby and corridors of his hotel that Saturday night. And next morning it began to take hold of him personally—began to catch him up into its swirling energies and make him its puppet.

Tom Finney, Jr., and James Doyle came to his hotel suite that morning to review for him in detail the activities on behalf of his candidacy now underway in Los Angeles. He was surprised and disturbed, and could not help but be flattered, by the scope and intensity of these.

Advance parties of draft movement workers had been in the city for more than two weeks, facing and solving one difficult problem after another. The first and most serious had been Paul Butler's refusal to assign adequate space to the draft organization in the Biltmore. The two small conference rooms on the mezzanine to which he limited them had been dubbed "Butler's Pantry" by embittered Stevensonians (the rooms happened to be adjacent to a banquet kitchen); to reach them, reported Stan Opotowsky of the New York *Post*, one must "march past huge ballrooms set aside for Kennedy, Johnson, and Symington forces and then finally up two flights, turn left, knock and say, 'Paul sent me.'" But the Stevensonians had triumphantly surmounted this obstacle by renting an abandoned six-story office building—the Paramount Building, which was in the process of being condemned—across Pershing Square from the Biltmore. Decorated by a 107-foot STEVENSON FOR PRESIDENT banner, it was now crowded with activities, among them the daily preparation of a four-page convention newspaper, *America Wants Stevenson*, of which 5,000 copies had been distributed Saturday and whose circulation was destined to reach 15,000 by Tuesday, July 12. A rudimentary communications network was being established, with two phone lines from the convention floor to a trailer outside the hall and two from the trailer to the Biltmore.[9]

Literally thousands of people had already come to the city from all over the country for the sole purpose of securing his nomination. More were arriving every hour. Their enthusiasm, their energy, their commitment were boundless, and his airport reception was but a mild taste of the demonstrations that would be conducted on his behalf. These would remain spontaneous, impromptu, and extemporaneous, but they would not be wholly unplanned, unorganized. The Stevensonians who now descended upon Los Angeles came not as a gathering mob but as an army of volunteers, loosely disciplined to do battle in a sacred cause.

Nor was the cause yet lost; far from it. Finney, Ball, Finletter, Monroney were agreed on this. It was simply not true that Kennedy had the nomination sewed up, as he and his organization had claimed for weeks past. Despite the gains he had made in the Mountain States and the Midwest since early June, Kennedy still could not count *absolutely* on more than 600 votes on the first ballot. He still needed 161 more; he still must gain them from the favorite son states of California, New Jersey, Kansas, Iowa, and Minnesota, and from the uncommitted delegations of Illinois and Pennsylvania. Kennedy himself was now convinced that he *had* to win on the first ballot; intelligence gathered by Stevensonians from the adversary's camp clearly revealed as much. The persuasive contacts of Stevensonians with individual delegates, the more formal arguments by Stevensonians before key caucuses, along with the popular demonstrations on Stevenson's behalf, must inevitably influence votes. Delegates would soon be receiving wires and phone calls from home as the excitement over Stevenson was impressed by mass communications on the public mind. All that Stevenson had to do to make his nomination certain was to say he would heed the call to serve, he would permit himself to become a candidate.

Thus Finney. And thus Monroney, in the early afternoon of that Sunday.

But Newt Minow came to Stevenson with an entirely different story. Shortly after arriving in Los Angeles, he dined with two old friends, one of whom worked for Kennedy and the other of whom worked for Johnson. From these he obtained an allegedly absolutely accurate list of committed delegates, and it convinced him that Kennedy was in fact assured of nomination. So when he, entering Stevenson's Beverly Hills suite, found Stevenson seated on a divan with Monroney and another supporter seated beside him, both arguing vehemently that Stevenson must now make his move, Minow broke in. He asked if he might see the Governor alone for a moment. The two went into the toilet, which was the only place where complete privacy was possible, and there Minow told Stevenson emphatically that his candidacy hadn't a chance of success. He reviewed the information he had obtained.

"Furthermore," he went on, "the Illinois delegation is caucusing this afternoon and they are going to come out for Kennedy. What you ought to do is go before the Illinois delegation [Stevenson was a member of it] and throw your support to Kennedy. Now is the time."

But Stevenson doubted the accuracy of Minow's prediction about the outcome of the Illinois caucus. "The Governor couldn't believe it," said Minow later.[10] And he refused to budge from his long-held position. He felt now more than ever at the mercy of events beyond his control: he could neither advance, as Monroney urged, nor withdraw, as Minow urged, without doing violence to conscience and honor.

A few hours later, however, he made his closest approach to a public declaration of his candidacy—a highly equivocal approach, revelatory of inner turmoil. He appeared on CBS's nationally televised "Face the Nation" program. He was asked if there were "any way" in which his supporters could make him say he would be a candidate. He replied: ". . . let me put it this way . . . : that while I am personally not a candidate, and I don't believe you can persuade me to be a candidate, and I do insist on being consistent about it, I think that these supporters of mine have converted me into a candidate. That is, I am their candidate, the candidate, I dare say, of a great many people around the country who signed these petitions. They have moved me very deeply. . . ." But he was *not* saying and *would* not say to these people, "Follow me." "If they want me to lead them, I shall lead them. I have indicated that many times. I don't see why it is so complicated . . . for one to say he will not seek nomination, who has enjoyed the greatest honors that his party can accord to anyone, not once but twice, to step aside and say, 'Now it is time for someone else,' and likewise to say that if called upon of course I will serve."

This encouraged the political professionals among his supporters to believe he was beginning to yield to their pressures and might soon declare his availability in a way that would enable them to exert tangible pressures on delegates, engaging in the kind of hard tit-for-tat trading that is an inevitable part of elective politics.

By Sunday night, however, some twenty-odd hours before the convention formally opened, knowledgeable reporters were filing stories saying that Kennedy's victory was now practically certain. Minow's information concerning the Illinois caucus had by then been proved correct. Mayor Richard Daley of Chicago announced in the late afternoon that 59½ of Illinois' 69 votes would go to Kennedy; of the remaining 9½ votes, one remained uncommitted and 6½ belonged to Symington. Only 2 of the delegates from Stevenson's native state, of which he had been governor, would vote for him! Nor was this all. Both Governor George Docking of Kansas and Governor Herschel C. Loveless of Iowa had declared for Kennedy (which seemed to assure Kennedy of 52 more votes, since both states operated under the unit rule) and so had Governor Brown of California. It appeared that Kennedy's absolute voting strength had climbed from 600 to more than 700 since Sunday morning. "The clincher," said *The New York Times* dispatch, "could come tomorrow from Pennsylvania's 81-member uncommitted delegation headed by Governor David L. Lawrence. That State could give 45 to 60 of its votes to Kennedy if Lawrence so decides."

And it was known that Lawrence was under heavy pressure from the Kennedy people so to decide. He had been met by John Bailey when his plane landed at the Los Angeles airport on Saturday evening. Bailey had driven him from the airport to the Biltmore, no doubt arguing the case for Kennedy through every one of the many miles. No doubt, too, Bailey had pressed Lawrence to accept an invitation from Kennedy for a private chat next morning. At any rate he did visit Kennedy in the latter's Biltmore suite at eleven o'clock Sunday morning and spent a half-hour alone with him.[11]

But Lawrence remained in heart and mind a Stevenson man. He was convinced that no other man in political life was as well qualified as Stevenson to be President in these dangerous times, and he loved Stevenson as a man. He therefore readily agreed when Stevenson supporters urged him to talk with Stevenson privately before making up his mind regarding Kennedy. He did so late that Sunday night in the Beverly Hills Hotel. Precisely what was said between the two men, when they were alone together, was unrecorded and (now that the two principals are dead) is unremembered, but all the evidence indicates that Stevenson, at this decisive moment, when he might have stemmed the tide toward a Kennedy victory and done much to insure his own, said nothing in contradiction of his public position. He was not an active candidate; he had not and he could not openly seek the nomination. Lawrence undoubtedly spoke of the pressures upon himself, from both within and outside his delegation, to go for Kennedy—pressures that Stevenson's passive attitude did nothing to alleviate. For two long hours the conversation continued; it was well after midnight when Lawrence at last took his leave.[12]

The Pennsylvania delegation caucused next morning, Monday, July 11, in its Pasadena hotel. It decided, under Lawrence's chairmanship (though it is said he wept at the decision), to give 64 of its 81 votes to Kennedy and 8 to Stevenson, with the remainder scattered among other candidates. And Lawrence's announcement of this result did, indeed, seem to be the clincher. Kennedy's first-ballot strength, it appeared, was now definitely sufficient to nominate him—and Stevenson was being urged not merely to withdraw but to make the speech placing Kennedy in nomination, as Kennedy had done for Stevenson four years before. Kennedy certainly wanted him to do so; it would help assure him of the active Stevensonian support throughout the country that he had to have if he were to defeat Nixon; and Bill Blair and Minow were among the close friends of Stevenson who favored this action.

But Monroney and the other leaders of the draft movement were not yet ready to give up. They doubted that Kennedy's actual strength was as great as it appeared to be on paper. They sensed a rising resentment among delegates of the unremitting pressures put upon them by the Kennedy organization, and particularly of the often intimidating tactics of Bobby Kennedy, the campaign manager. New Jersey was an example. That state's

Governor Robert Meyner * had been infuriated by Joseph P. Kennedy's pressurized wooing of northern New Jersey's political bosses on behalf of his son through the spring of 1960; it had created internal dissensions that threatened the governor's control of Democratic state machinery. Meyner, therefore, was flatly refusing to release his delegation from its pledged first-ballot support of him as favorite son—a release that would have given Kennedy a large majority, perhaps 30, of the state's 41 votes.[13] Monroney spoke with disgust of the wholesale manner in which Kennedy's people were using the promise of a Vice-Presidential nomination to bribe leaders whose support they sought. (Even so obviously unsuited a man as Kansas's Governor Docking was calculatedly mentioned in the press as a "Vice-Presidential possibility." Said Monroney: "If they called a meeting of all the people to whom they've promised the Vice-Presidency, they couldn't find a room in Los Angeles large enough to hold it in.") [14] There was, further, the distinct possibility of revolts against their leaders in state delegations that had been, by these leaders, committed to Kennedy. For instance, there were clear signs by Monday afternoon that the Kansas and Iowa delegations (the Iowa unit vote had gone to Kennedy by a mere half-vote) might so revolt, reverting to support of their favorite sons on the first ballot and thereby denying Kennedy their 52 votes. Such revolts, such defections, were certain to be encouraged by the massive demonstrations for Stevenson that were timed to begin when the convention was formally opened that Monday evening. The whole trend of the convention might then be reversed.

"Stand firm," said Monroney to Stevenson. "If you can't declare your candidacy, at least maintain your present position."

Stevenson did so.

And before Senator Frank Church of Idaho had completed the convention's keynote speech that evening, the first effects of the Stevenson demonstrations were being felt by the delegates. Through the doors and windows of the Sports Arena, as Church spoke, came the sounds of a vast crowd excitement outside, a rhythmic roar that grew louder as time passed. The hall was completely encircled by marching thousands of people—some in work clothes and others in business suits, some women pushing baby carriages and others leading their children by the hand—carrying Stevenson placards (FACE THE MORAL CHALLENGE—STEVENSON; A THINKING MAN'S CHOICE—STEVENSON; NOTHING LESS THAN THE BEST—STEVENSON), endlessly chanting as they marched: "We want Stevenson! We want Stevenson!" When the convention adjourned that night, the delegates and gallery spectators, no matter what their door of exit, had

---

* Meyner in January, 1957, had married Helen D. Stevenson, daughter of Dr. and Mrs. William E. Stevenson. Doctor Stevenson was a Princeton classmate of Adlai Stevenson and Mrs. Stevenson was a distant connection of Adlai's by marriage. He had been a guest at the Meyners' Oberlin, Ohio, wedding.

to push their way through the rhythmically roaring, placard-waving picket line.

Next day, Tuesday, July 12, 1960—though no name had yet been placed in nomination upon the convention floor, nor would any be until late the following afternoon—was actually the convention's day of decision. When the day opened, it appeared to the watching world that Kennedy's nomination was a foregone conclusion. When the long day closed, it appeared to the world that Kennedy was losing his grip on the convention and that Stevenson's nomination was distinctly possible, perhaps even probable. Both appearances were false. And for the reality they obscured, Stevenson himself—what he did and refused to do, what he said and refused to say— was to no small extent responsible. On that day, writes Monroney, "they 'thrice presented him a kingly crown, which he did thrice refuse.' " [15]

Among the first events, obviously influenced by the rising tide of popular excitement over Stevenson, was a revolt of two state delegations against leaders who had committed them to Kennedy. After heated caucuses, both Iowa and Kansas announced they were going to vote for their governors on the first ballot, whether Loveless and Docking wanted them to or not.

And while this was going on, Minnesota also caucused. There had developed over the long weekend a growing resentment, in this delegation, of the pressure tactics employed by the Kennedy forces, and especially by Bobby Kennedy. There had developed overnight, in this delegation, a strong Stevenson sentiment, fed by the belief that Stevenson might, after all, become an active candidate. This belief, encouraged when it became known that Stevenson was moving from the remote Beverly Hills to a suite in the nearby Sheraton West (the move seemed to manifest an increased availability), seemed virtually confirmed when, in response to urgent pleas, Stevenson agreed to speak to the caucus in person, as Kennedy and the other candidates had done the day before. He was preceded by Monroney. The Oklahoma senator's talk was at once a slashing attack upon Kennedy's campaign tactics and an eloquent statement of the case for Stevenson, and it had raised its audience to a fever pitch of excited anticipation when, at its end, the door opened and Stevenson entered.

He was greeted with a standing ovation and wildly cheered. He could not but sense, as he stood before this crowd, that its spirit was incandescent with enthusiasm for him and required from him but a breath of affirmation, of inspiration, in order to burst into flame. He refused to give it. He made no appeal to the emotions. He avoided any word that could have ignited his audience and started a conflagration which might well have swept the convention. He spoke instead of the Eisenhower administration's long list of foreign policy errors and, concerning himself, was wholly uncommittal.

The crowd spirit glowed less brightly when he left than when he entered the room.[16]

Thus his first refusal that day of the kingly crown.

In the afternoon, California's delegation, for whose allegiance the Kennedy forces had made immense expenditures of time and energy and money, met in a stormy three-hour caucus during which Governor Brown's leadership was angrily challenged. Brown had definitely promised Kennedy that a large majority of the state's 81 votes would go to him on the first ballot, and the Kennedy forces "entered the caucus abrim with confidence," as a newsman reported. But Jim Doyle had been hard at work on individual delegates who were known to have a personal preference for Stevenson. Mrs. Eleanor Roosevelt had impressed the delegation as a whole in an earlier secret caucus when she pleaded with the members not to "desert what your heart tells you to accept" but to "fight to the bitter end."[17] And Brown himself wavered, seeming at times to favor the Stevensonians, for he believed in his heart (and had admitted to Monroney in the spring) that Stevenson was the man in America best qualified to be President. The caucus results were announced shortly before the second formal evening session of the convention was opened, and it sent a shock wave through the assembling delegations. California had split wide open: 31½ votes would go to Stevenson on the first ballot, only 30½ would go to Kennedy, with the rest scattered.

As the delegates came into the Sports Arena that evening they had to make their way again through a marching, yelling picket line of Stevensonians, seemingly swollen to twice the size of Monday's. At a little after six o'clock Stevenson himself crossed that line, having been persuaded by his supporters (after much pro and con discussion among them) to come onto the convention floor and take his seat as a member of the Illinois delegation. A good deal of persuasion had been required. When Stevenson protested his distaste for "making a spectacle" of himself, Bill Blair reminded him that he had come to Los Angeles, after all, as an official delegate and had, therefore, a delegate's obligations. Blair might also have reminded him of the long-established tradition against a candidate's showing himself upon the floor of the convention prior to the balloting (Kefauver had done so in 1952, with consequences unfortunate for his ambition); in view of this tradition, Stevenson's floor appearance could be interpreted as emphasizing his non-candidacy.

At any rate, he did come—reluctantly, with grave misgivings.[18] And no single act in all his public career was more revealing of his moral fastidiousness and compulsive disdain of easy ways than his response to the emotional storm that swept the hall as soon as he was seen, reaching hysterical heights as he was dragged and pushed through a howling mob toward his seat.

He had expected to be noticed and applauded, of course. But he had expected nothing like this, nor had anyone else, not even those of the draft movement who had alerted reporters and TV cameramen to assure a maximum possible coverage of the event. His reactions were curiously mixed. To those closest to him he seemed at first to be in a state of shock. His face flushed crimson and was soon bathed in perspiration, and the fixed smile upon it was replaced, now and then, by a "scared expression," as one reporter noted. Later, as the wild demonstration continued after he had arrived at his assigned seat, he seemed to those next to him to become calm, almost detached. The smile on his face remained wooden. Finally the convention chairman, helpless to restore order, summoned him to the podium.

It took him twelve long minutes to get there through the crowd that pressed around him (from the galleries came in rhythmic roar: "We want Stevenson!') but when at last he did, the noise died down almost instantly. (He had "succeeded in doing something no one else had managed to do since the convention started—get the hall quiet in a brief thirty seconds," reported *The New York Times*.) All were tensely anxious to hear what he would say. The Kennedy forces were full of apprehension, the Stevensonians full of hope, for (though some Kennedy people would later deny it) it seemed to almost everyone at the time that to start an avalanche of Stevenson sentiment which no one could have stopped he had only to indicate a rapport with his audience, a willingness to do what so many so obviously longed for him to do. Any formula of words along the lines of "never have I been so moved" would have done it, in the opinion of Tom Finney, Jr. Almost any three-minute talk would have done it, according to the volunteer organization's press secretary, Tom Morgan.* Instead, Stevenson spoke three short sentences, each of them flatly out of tune with the mood of his audience. He thanked the delegates for their welcome, but in a strangely cool way, as if he felt they had rather made fools of themselves and was trying politely to overlook it. Then he said: "After getting in and out of the Biltmore and this hall, I know whom you are going to nominate. It will be the last survivor." The tasteless quip stirred a gust of laughter and applause, followed by futile cries of "More! More!" And that was all. The audience letdown was terrific....

Thus his second refusal of the kingly crown.

The third came a few hours later. It was preceded by Stevenson's appearance before a group from the New York delegation carefully selected by Senator Herbert H. Lehman and Stanley H. Lowell, former Deputy Mayor

---

* Both the Finney and Morgan statements were made to Donald Murray, an instructor at Brooklyn College of the City University of New York, as he gathered interview material for a master's thesis on the Stevenson convention effort. The story of the meeting in Benton's suite, which follows, is told in an as-yet unpublished draft of this thesis.

of New York City, as potential Stevenson supporters. Attended by some sixty-five people of whom only 22 or 23 were delegates, this meeting was held around midnight in Bill Benton's Ambassador Hotel suite. Stevenson spoke to it for perhaps fifteen minutes, saying nothing new. (Having been twice accorded his party's highest honor, he would not, he said, "be so immodest as to ask for it again.") He then went to a much larger and more important meeting—some 250 delegates and alternates assembled in the Lafayette Room of the Sheraton West Hotel by the draft organization leaders. They were all in an excited, expectant mood; they had been encouraged to believe that, persuaded by popular demand, he would at long last say (as Monroney again urged him to say), "I seek your nomination, I need your help." He didn't say it.

The few words he spoke were this time moving words, warm and eloquent and in perfect key with his listeners' emotions. He closed with a quotation from the most enigmatic of Robert Frost's poems, "Stopping by Woods on a Snowy Evening":

> The woods are lovely, dark and deep,
> But I have promises to keep,
> And miles to go before I sleep,
> And miles to go before I sleep.

Not a few of his listeners assumed this meant that he had finally decided to fight for the nomination and would, as Attwood writes, "spend the night rallying support for his cause." He was wildly cheered as he left the room. "But when I went up to his suite a few minutes later," adds Attwood, "he was already in his pajamas." [19]

IV

In retrospect it is obvious that, by the dawn of Wednesday, July 13, 1960 —the day on which the nominations would be made and the balloting begin —the convention's decision had already been made. Stevenson might have changed it had he indeed spent the dark early morning hours in an open personal campaign for votes. The delegation from North Dakota, a unit rule state belonging to Kennedy by a mere half-vote, had split in a late Tuesday night caucus; there was at that time an apparent shift of Mountain State delegates from Kennedy to Stevenson or Johnson on the first ballot (Idaho could be counted upon by Kennedy only so long as its governor believed himself to be favored by Kennedy for the Vice-Presidential nomination); the Stevensonians could have picked up more votes in California (they were assured of at least 45 California votes on a second ballot); and there remained lucrative unexploited possibilities in New York, as evinced by the fact that the Tammany boss, Carmine De Sapio, had asked (and been profanely refused) Bobby Kennedy's permission to shift 30 New York votes to Johnson on the first ballot with a guaranteed return of them to Kennedy on the second. But instead of acting, Stevenson had slept, if fitfully. When he awoke early next morning, his last chance was gone.

And it is a psychologically revealing irony that only then—after Kennedy was absolutely assured of 740 first-ballot votes and could confidently count upon enough switches to bring his first-ballot total above the needed 761— only then did Stevenson personally make a direct move to secure his nomination. He attempted to call in (much too late) the large political debt owed him by Chicago's Dick Daley for the probably decisive support Stevenson had given in the 1955 mayoralty campaign. He put in a phone call for Daley that morning, a call Daley didn't answer until the convention session had opened late in the afternoon, and only then because Colonel Jack Arvey (at Stevenson's request) had pressed him to do so. On the phone, Stevenson said that, while he had not actively sought the nomination, his name *was* going to be placed in nomination. He wanted Daley to know that his refusal to campaign for the nomination did not mean that he would not campaign against Nixon with utmost vigor if he were nominated. He wanted to know from Daley if the meager 2 votes out of 69 that the Sunday Illinois caucus had given him was the full measure of his home-base support. It was, replied Daley curtly. Moreover, he went on (evidently to indicate that his political debt had been long ago paid in full), there had been no real support for Stevenson in the 1956 Illinois delegation either; only as a result of his, Daley's, efforts had the State gone for its former governor in that year's convention. . . . [20] The click of Daley's telephone receiver was as a slap in Stevenson's face. . . .

Three hours later he sat with Bill Blair, George Ball, Buffie Ives, his sons and nephew and their wives, and a few others of his intimates in his Sheraton West suite, watching on television the proceedings on the convention floor. (Lying on a side table were evening papers proclaiming in banner headlines: KENNEDY TIDE EBBS; KENNEDY BANDWAGON FALTERS.) Sam Rayburn's nomination of Johnson had been followed by a large but rather mechanical demonstration. Orville Freeman's nomination of Kennedy had been followed by a larger, more enthusiastic demonstration. Relatively small and altogether perfunctory had been the demonstration for Symington. At 7:56 P.M., the convention chairman, LeRoy Collins, recognized Wilson Wyatt of Kentucky, who promptly yielded to Senator Eugene McCarthy of Minnesota. There was a sudden visible, audible stir of excitement in the Arena, there was abrupt tension in the Stevenson suite, as McCarthy emerged from the door to the chairman's office at the back of the stage and made his way to the podium.

McCarthy then gave by far the best speech of the convention, one of the great nominating speeches of all time, reviewing in a voice that throbbed with emotion Stevenson's record of prophecy through eight years "ruled by ... false prophecy," stressing the gallantry and courage and honor with which he had fought the campaigns of 1952 and 1956 and "made us all proud to be called Democrats," reminding his listeners of Stevenson's call to greatness. "He did not say he possessed it. He did not even say he was destined for it. He did say that the heritage of America is one of greatness. And he described that heritage to us." McCarthy closed with an almost desperate plea: "Do not leave this prophet without honor in his own party. Do not reject this man. ... I submit to you: Adlai E. Stevenson of Illinois." [21]

Stevenson, relaxed in an easy chair, watched and listened with that detachment from his public image which so often surprised and puzzled his associates. He murmured, as if commenting on an artist's performance, "Magnificent!"

And as he did so he saw wild tumult break out upon the convention floor, such a convention demonstration as had not been seen in twenty years, not since Wendell Willkie's supporters stampeded the Republicans in Philadelphia in 1940.

The convention management had limited the number of seats assigned Stevensonians at the convention even more severely than it had the space assigned them at the Biltmore. But through careful organizational planning—by individual ingenuity whereby they had gained gallery seats in the earlier sessions by posing as supporters of Kennedy and other candidates, by gathering in unwanted tickets assigned large campaign donors, by luring away one of the door guards and replacing him with a Stevensonian clothed in a guard uniform—the Stevensonians had managed to pour into the hall. They came through and from Stevensonian picket lines that by late afternoon had become so swollen and excited (their "We Want Stevenson!" became an ominous roar) that the police, fearing an attempt to storm the hall, called for large reinforcements. They pressed now by the thousand onto the Arena floor, waving their placards in time to their Stevenson chant and adding to them one state standard after another as they passed the state positions. They made a seething sea of people above which bounced, in rhythm with "We Want Stevenson!", a huge papier-mâché ball.

It was an uncontrollable outburst of crowd emotion, and it went on and on and on. When LeRoy Collins's plea for order went unheeded, Eugene McCarthy tried for it. In vain. Finally the Arena lights were turned off, and all was blackness on Stevenson's TV screen save where spotlights shot out their long slender arrows of light. (Meanwhile leaders of the Johnson and Stevenson organizations were making an effort to obtain a convention adjournment, postponing the balloting until next day. Sam Rayburn wanted Collins to declare adjournment from the chair, but Collins refused and, for

some reason, no formal motion to adjourn was later made from the floor.)
And then, at last, the tumult and the shouting died.

Slowly, with much difficulty, the floor was cleared. . . .

The balloting began. Stevenson watched, outwardly serene, laughing frequently and joking with his friends, while on the convention floor everything now went smoothly for the Kennedy forces. By the time Washington was reached in the roll call of states, Kennedy's total neared 700, and Washington brought him up to 710. Wisconsin made it 748, and the TV cameras focused on the Wyoming delegation, with youthful Teddy Kennedy, youngest brother of the candidate, very busy in its midst. Wyoming could clinch it. Wyoming did. All 15 of its votes went to Kennedy, giving him two more than were needed for nomination.*

Stevenson got to his feet. He had reached the end of a long road and the end of his ambition. He would never be President of the United States. It was probable he would never be Secretary of State.† But he gave not the slightest sign of hurt or disappointment. Indeed, some who were with him that night thought he seemed relieved as, grinning, he remarked that the time had again come for "some purple prose" and, with George Ball, went into another room of his suite to compose a statement. . . .²²

Next day, to the astonishment of everyone (including Kennedy himself at the outset), and to the initial angry dismay of party liberals, Lyndon Johnson, tentatively offered the Vice-Presidential nomination, quickly accepted it. The event seemed to put the seal on the end of the Stevenson era of the party, marking a major shift of direction; it increased the anger and bitterness toward Kennedy which, despite Stevenson's efforts to remove it, remained in the hearts of a multitude of Stevensonians as they took their departure from Los Angeles. Stevenson himself, before he left, had a serious, friendly private talk with Kennedy during which he gave campaign advice that surprised the young nominee with its hard-headed practicality. He promised to make ten campaign speeches on Kennedy's behalf in September and October. He also suggested that Kennedy, who would necessarily be out of touch with foreign affairs (then in so perilous a state everywhere in the world) during his months of absorption in the campaign, should have prepared and ready for his perusal immediately after the election an authoritative review of foreign policy problems. Kennedy, accepting the suggestion, asked if Stevenson himself would be willing to write the report; Stevenson said he would.²³

* By the first ballot's end, Kennedy received 806 votes, Johnson 409, Symington 86, Stevenson 79½, and all other candidates together 140½.

† Kennedy, in his informal acceptance speech to the convention an hour or two later, referred by name to Johnson, Symington, and the "favorite sons," but pointedly made no mention at all of Adlai Stevenson.

A few hours later, as the sun went down on Friday, July 15, 1960, Stevenson stood up before a crowd of 80,000 in the Los Angeles Coliseum to introduce John F. Kennedy for the formal nomination-acceptance speech. "He is a man whose passion for peace was bred in the agony of war.... His devotion to the ideals of liberal democracy assures our nation swift and steady progress toward the full promise of our American heritage.... He will lead our people into a new and spacious era, not for us alone, but for our troubled, trembling world...." Then Stevenson stepped into the background and sat down to listen attentively to Kennedy's call for "pioneers" on a "new frontier—the frontier of the 1960's, a frontier of unknown opportunities and paths, a frontier of unfulfilled hopes and threats...."

Stevenson left Los Angeles on Saturday. "I don't know why you are all so sorry," he said to the obviously mournful supporters who swarmed around him as he passed through the hotel lobby. "I had no expectation of being a candidate again. You made me one, and it was a very happy, happy experience." The important thing now, he indicated, was to secure a Democratic victory in November. Someone thrust into his hand a miniature golf club and an oversized golf ball, telling him this was a "do-it-yourself politician's kit." Stevenson turned back, laughing. He said: "In Teddy Roosevelt's day, it was 'Speak softly and carry a big stick.' Nowadays it's become, 'Don't talk, I'm putting.'" The crowd roared with delight as Stevenson, broadly smiling and with a wave of his hand, went out into the hot sunlight, entered his limousine, and was driven away.

BOOK TEN

To the End of Life

CHAPTER THIRTY-TWO

As the world knows, the Presidential campaign of 1960 was decided in favor of John F. Kennedy and Lyndon B. Johnson by almost the narrowest possible margin. In the national popular vote, Richard M. Nixon and his running mate, Henry Cabot Lodge, trailed the victors by just 118,550 out of a grand total of 68,335,642, or by a mere 0.1 percent, while carrying twenty-six states to the victors' twenty-three.* It was only because, by small majorities, he carried certain big states that Kennedy won a substantial electoral college victory—303 to 219; a switch of fewer than 25,000 votes in five closely-contested states lost by Nixon would have reversed the verdict.

In an election so close, any one of a great number of causal factors may be deemed decisive. But it is probably true that, aside from the two candidates themselves, no one man deserves more personal credit for the outcome than Adlai E. Stevenson. It was Stevenson who had created the style and intellectual tradition in which Kennedy campaigned and who (more than anyone else) had defined for the public the basic campaign issues. It was Stevenson, perhaps mindful of his great-grandfather Jesse Fell's proposal of the Lincoln-Douglas debates, who initially and most persuasively proposed a great debate on TV between the rival Presidential candidates—a debate which Nixon early agreed to in mistaken self-confidence and which removed once and for all Kennedy's greatest handicaps, namely, his being less well known than Nixon and his alleged boyish inexperience contrasted with

---

* Mississippi was so disgusted with both candidates that it elected unpledged electors who cast their ballot for Senator Harry F. Byrd of Virginia.

Nixon's maturity and competence. It was Stevenson and only Stevenson who, by personal example and effort, could finally persuade into activity on Kennedy's behalf myriads of disgruntled Stevensonians who had done yeoman's work for the Democrats in 1952 and 1956 but, in the bitter aftermath of Los Angeles, were prepared to "sit this one out."

These disaffected Stevensonians generally subscribed to sentiments expressed by Eric Sevareid in a famous syndicated column published soon after the Republican convention. Both candidates were business junior executive types, in Sevareid's acid view, with little to choose between them. They were the "first completely packaged products" of the " 'managerial revolution' (which) has come to politics"—"tidy, buttoned-down men" incapable of dreaming great dreams or of true compassion or of a deep emotional commitment to anything beyond self-advancement. It was in harmony with this view that chapters of the Americans for Democratic Action (ADA) throughout the country, whose members had been almost religiously devoted to Stevenson in his two campaigns, were reluctant even to endorse Kennedy. They had to be talked into it, with much difficulty, by the ADA's National Board at the end of August, at which time (which was late) the only effective argument with them was more negative than positive: it was no strong attraction to Kennedy but rather a strong aversion to Nixon that decided them.

Both Schlesinger and Attwood called Kennedy's attention to this marked lack of enthusiasm for him in a segment of the electorate whose persuasive influence far exceeded its numbers and whose support, in what promised to be a close race, Kennedy had to have if he were to win. Attwood, who had joined Kennedy's staff as speech writer in August, suggested at the month's end that he could do the candidate more good if he left Kennedy's campaign entourage and traveled instead with Stevenson.[1] Kennedy agreed. And so, from early September until just before election day, Attwood, Bill Blair, and Bill Wirtz toured the country with Stevenson who, at Kennedy's request, greatly expanded his speaking schedule and ended up making not ten, but eighty-four campaign talks.

A few of these, especially his address to a $100-a-plate dinner of New York Citizens for Kennedy and Johnson at the Commodore in mid-October (Bob Benjamin arranged it) were nationally reported. (In this speech of twenty-five minutes, during which he was interrupted five times by cheers and applause, he followed a slashing attack upon Nixon's "deceitfulness" with a call for a reexamination of our China policy, indicating it might be well to admit Red China to the UN, if she would subscribe to the charter, and thereafter let the UN rather than the United States alone guarantee the independence of Taiwan [Formosa].) But for the most part the talks received only local coverage in newspapers and broadcasts, being aimed specifically at targets of disaffection from the national ticket among formerly ardent Stevenson supporters, especially in California, Minnesota, and Illinois. The speeches were generous in their praise of Kennedy. Their principal impact, however, was as a reiterated indictment of the administration in general and Nixon in particular.

They were effective. California, where Nixon as a native son with powerful press support had great advantages, went Republican, but by a paper-thin margin which would certainly have been much wider in the absence of Stevenson's campaign there. Illinois and Minnesota were very narrowly won by Kennedy—Illinois by fewer than 9,000 out of nearly 3,000,000 votes—and would certainly have gone the other way but for Stevenson's efforts.

Meanwhile work had gone forward on the foreign policy report which Stevenson had promised to prepare for Kennedy. Pressed for time when his campaign speaking schedule was abruptly expanded, he had called for help from George Ball who, with John Sharon, wrote a first draft and gave it to a travel-worn Stevenson at Libertyville just three days before the election. Stevenson revised it carefully during the next week and wrote a cover letter to Kennedy in which, typically, he apologized for the report's "infirmities" of excessive length and mistaken emphasis (it concentrated more on NATO and the sharing of the "nuclear deterrent" and less on the underdeveloped countries and on measures for alleviating East-West tensions than Stevenson would have liked). In mid-November, Sharon presented the report in person to the President-elect at Palm Beach, Florida, where Kennedy, after reading it and asking questions about it, told him it was "terrific" and "just what I wanted." [2]

But if this revived Stevenson's hopes of being named Secretary of State, a post for which he frankly yearned and was obviously eminently well suited, these hopes were soon dashed.

Kennedy could not feel he owed Stevenson any huge debt of gratitude for services rendered during the campaign. They seemed to him no greater, as he indicated to his associates, than he had rendered Stevenson in 1956 when he'd campaigned for the nominee in twenty-six states. As for Stevenson's decisive wooing into activity of theretofore doubtful and passive liberals, it would not have been necessary if Stevenson had not himself promoted or at least permitted the liberal disaffection by the posture he had maintained before and during the convention. Surely Kennedy's anxieties would have been greatly reduced and his victory margin greatly widened if Stevenson had declared for him after West Virginia and then made the nominating speech for him in Los Angeles. Surely it had been made sufficiently clear that the State Department would be Stevenson's reward for this *truly* valuable service. Stevenson had refused the tacit offer.

Moreover, there was a notable lack of rapport between the two men. The circumstances of their relationship had caused each to see and overemphasize in the other qualities that, by his own standards, were the least admirable. And there is evidence that at the same time each, paradoxically, aroused guilt feelings (if vague, unadmitted) in the other.

Stevenson seemed to see in Kennedy a coldly calculating ambition, a lust for power, a willingness to use other people as a means to his ends, a lack of profound commitment to ideals whose realization (in Stevenson's view) was essential to that world order whose only alternative was world destruction. Attwood has told of dining with Kennedy in the latter's Georgetown house in mid-June of 1960 when, with some heat, Kennedy had protested Stevenson's failure to come out for him. Stevenson, he had said, would soon find he had made "a big mistake." Then, pointedly, knowing the conversation would be reported to Stevenson, he had asked Attwood whether Stevenson or Chester Bowles should, in Attwood's opinion, be named Secretary of State. Stevenson's face had mirrored his distaste as Attwood repeated this to him. "How could I ever go to work for such an arrogant young man?" he had asked.[3] And perhaps because Kennedy sensed this attitude of Stevenson's, he was never wholly comfortable in the older man's presence and, prompted by the imp of perversity which is in us all, displayed more arrogance of manner in his dealings with Stevenson than in his dealings with most others. "That young man!" said Stevenson to journalist Mary McGrory a few months later, as he came from a White House meeting. "He never says 'please' and he never says, 'I'm sorry.'"[4]

It is clear from his remarks to close associates that Kennedy saw in Stevenson a personal indecisiveness, a fussiness over small details at the expense of larger aims (as in the endless rewriting of speeches up to the moment of their delivery), and a lack of candor even with himself, which (in Kennedy's view) had characterized Stevenson's drive for the 1960 nomination. He had been more than irritated by what seemed to him Stevenson's false pose of lofty indifference to personal advancement in 1960, compared to which Kennedy's frank and open pursuit of his ambition had been made to seem at times unbecomingly egoistic; and by Stevenson's sly stratagems (Kennedy saw them so) for gaining without personal risk or effort the prize Kennedy had so arduously earned with his primary victories. What in fact was Stevenson's compulsion to do everything the hard way, so far as the realization of personal ambition was concerned (his diffidence, his habitual self-deprecation), seemed to Kennedy a penchant for easy ways: it seemed to manifest a finicky aversion to the sweat and grime of practical politics, a deficiency of will power, a certain overall softness of character. And of course Stevenson, sensing and resenting the younger man's attitude (the contempt in it grated harshly on Stevenson's inner wounds), was perversely led to exaggerate in Kennedy's company the very traits that Kennedy found most exasperating. He would in any case have found it hard to come hat in hand to one almost young enough to be his son who, having borne but little of the heat of battles in which the older man had repeatedly risked his political life, now profited from their consequences.

In view of all this it is not surprising that Kennedy, who had been more than willing to offer Stevenson the State Department in return for support before or even during the convention, never seriously considered doing so as President-elect. He returned from Florida to his red brick eighteenth century Georgetown house at 3307 N Street, N.W., Washington, in the last week of November. He had an unpublicized talk with Stevenson—an interview that was far from easy for either man but harder for Stevenson. Kennedy pointed to the narrowness of his election victory; he had in fact run behind many of the Democrats who had won Congressional seats and who therefore owed him nothing for their victories. It was obvious that the old coalition of Republicans and conservative Democrats would again be in a position to frustrate liberal legislation. Kennedy could not afford to limit further his already severely limited persuasive and coercive powers over the legislative branch. For Secretary of State, therefore, he needed a man not already tagged by controversial stands on a great number of public issues and thereby hampered from the outset in his dealings with the Congress. Stevenson could hardly be considered such a man. He was, however, the best qualified man in America to serve as U.S. Ambassador to the United Nations, where he could render an immense service not only to his country but to the world. Would Stevenson accept this post? Obviously emotionally jarred (for he had continued to hope for State, in spite of everything), Stevenson hesitated, then replied with a question of his own: Who, then, was to be Secretary of State? That choice had not yet been made, Kennedy replied. Well, then, said Stevenson, he must defer his own decision: he would have to be assured that the Secretary was one who had confidence in him, and in whom he had confidence, before he could make up his mind.

Kennedy, according to Schlesinger, "was nettled at this reaction and strengthened in his belief in Stevenson's indecisiveness"—but it seems in perspective to have been wholly reasonable and the very opposite of "indecisive."[5] Kennedy *had* to find a prominent place for Stevenson in his administration. He was being bombarded by wires and letters urging him to do so, and, though members of his immediate staff were almost unanimously hostile to Stevenson, others among his most important supporters were vigorously pressing Stevenson's case in conversation with him. James MacGregor Burns, the Williams College political scientist, describes a typical instance. Burns visited Kennedy within a day or so of the Stevenson interview, arriving at the Georgetown house just as the President-elect was announcing a cabinet appointment from the front stoop before assembled reporters, photographers, and TV cameras. The narrow sidewalk across N Street was jammed with onlookers despite the coldness of the day, and as Burns watched and waited "a woman cried out in a voice of anguish, 'Jack, what about Adlai Stevenson for Secretary of State?' "[6] To ignore pressures of this sort was not politically feasible, and both Kennedy and Stevenson knew it. Hence Stevenson's hesitancy, far from being an expression of indecisiveness, was actually a tactic of decision-making, as was so often the case with Stevenson. He was using his prestige to influence Kennedy's actions, insofar as these pertained to him, forcing Kennedy to meet to some extent his terms. No doubt it was *this* that truly "nettled" the youthful President-elect.

On December 8, immediately after having talked for the first time with Dean Rusk, who was then president of the Rockefeller Foundation, Kennedy publicly announced that he had offered Stevenson the post of UN Ambassador, with full cabinet rank. (In the meantime, surprisingly enough, Kennedy, through Bill Blair, had sounded out Stevenson on the possibility of his entering the cabinet as Attorney General and had been told that Stevenson was not interested—that, indeed, he preferred the UN post.) [7] The announcement, as had by then become customary, was made from the front stoop of the Georgetown house with sufficient forewarning to permit the gathering across the street of a considerable crowd—a predominantly pro-Stevenson crowd, including many Georgetown University students, two of whom held placards calling for Stevenson's appointment as Secretary of State. Kennedy's announcement was greeted with cheers and applause, interspersed, here and there, with expressions of disappointment.

But Stevenson himself, to Kennedy's increasing irritation, still deferred a final decision "pending resolution of 'some unknown factors,' " as *The New York Times* put it. Not until Kennedy was able to announce in Palm Beach four days later that Dean Rusk had been offered and had accepted the appointment as Secretary of State, with Chester Bowles as Undersecretary, could he say that Stevenson had agreed to the ambassadorship. Rusk was acceptable to Stevenson: living in Scarsdale, he had been chairman of that wealthy New York suburb's Stevenson-for-President Committee in the spring of 1960, and Bowles was a fellow alumnus of Choate and an old friend. To newsmen in Chicago that day Stevenson said: "I have satisfactory assurances from the President-elect and the new Secretary that I shall have an adequate voice in the making of foreign policy." He explained that his hesitancy had been only partly due to his desire to know who the Secretary would be; he had wanted also to know that he would have "a degree of autonomy satisfactory" to him and that he would "not be undercut in bureaucratic fighting." As if to underline Stevenson's terms of acceptance, a joint press conference of Stevenson and Rusk was held in Stevenson's New York law office, at 575 Madison Avenue, a couple of days later. Rusk then emphasized that Stevenson was to have a key policy-making role.

Moreover, by that time Stevenson was assured that his long-time Chicago law partners would have adequately prestigious and influential posts in the Kennedy administration. Wirtz would soon be announced as Undersecretary of Labor, Newton Minow as Chairman of the Federal Communications Commission (FCC); and Blair was being given his choice between accompanying Stevenson to the UN or accepting a diplomatic post. He finally decided upon the latter and became U.S. Ambassador to Denmark.*

II

There came now as sharp a break in Stevenson's life—as abrupt a division of "before" and "after"—as had occurred when he first entered elective politics in 1948.

On January 12, 1961, he left the private practice of law, never to return to it again. The day was not for him or his associates a happy one. A photograph taken of him with his Chicago law partners captured the prevailing mood at the ending of what had been, for all of them, a remarkably happy and prosperous relationship. He sat behind a desk which, as usual, was heaped with papers, and he stared straight into the camera lens, his jaw set, his mouth a hard straight line, furrows in his cheeks and sadness in his eyes, while his law partners stood in a semicircle behind hm—Ed McDougal, Blair, Wirtz, Minow, towering John Hunt—with expressions on their faces that were variations on a melancholy theme of farewell. Sad, too, that day, was Carol Evans, who came now to the end of the intimate working relationship with Stevenson that had begun thirteen years before when she became his confidential secretary in the shabby Stevenson-for-Governor headquarters in Chicago's Dearborn Street, in February, 1948. Stevenson had offered her the chance to go to New York. But he had also told her frankly that he would now need an assistant with qualifications different from the exceedingly high ones she possessed—someone who not only knew how to work with him but was also familiar with foreign languages and with the histories and cultures of other countries. Such a person had been on his office staff since shortly before the 1956 campaign and it was she, Roxane Eberline, who would be his top office assistant at the UN Mission. In these circumstances, Carol had decided it would be best for all concerned if she took other employment— employment that "the Gov," deeply appreciative of the immense service she had rendered him, helped her to find. The parting was painful for both of them; because she had joined him at the moment he entered politics, her separation from him now intensified his awareness that his political career was ended, that he was condemned by history to be an also-ran.[8]

Eleven days later, having been sworn in as Ambassador following Senate

---

* Years later, having proved in foreign service the rare diplomatic skill which his long-time intimates had long known he possessed, along with numerous other competencies, Blair was named to the more demanding post of Ambassador to the Philippines. Wirtz became Secretary of Labor when the first appointee, Arthur Goldberg, went to the Supreme Court.

confirmation of his appointment, Stevenson presented his credentials to UN Secretary-General Dag Hammarskjöld and entered upon a new world, a new life. He brought with him as much of the old life and world as he could. He saw to it that his deputy in the U.S. Mission, with the rank of Ambassador, was Francis T. P. Plimpton, who had been a roommate of his at Harvard Law School in 1923–24, a New York law partner of Adlai's Princeton classmate William Stevenson, and hence a good personal friend for some thirty-eight years. To serve as his special assistant handling public relations, subsequently entitled Director of Public Affairs of the U.S. Mission, he brought in Clayton Fritchey. He had Jane Dick appointed a member of the U.S. delegation to the UN General Assembly. He had Marietta Tree appointed to represent the U.S. on the UN's Human Rights Commission. Since this met only one month a year and since she lived in New York, he asked her also to take a full-time job with the U.S. Mission to the UN, which she did, launching a UN career that would include membership (as delegate or alternate) on U.S. delegations to every General Assembly session during Stevenson's period as Mission head as well as service on the Trusteeship Council as American representative. Mrs. Mary Lasker and other of his women friends were also involved from time to time in Mission activities.

In Washington, too, and in several diplomatic posts abroad, he dealt in his work with old friends. He was instrumental in bringing into the State Department as Assistant Secretary for International Organization Affairs (the Washington official with whom he worked most closely) Harlan Cleveland, whom he had known, respected, and liked for more than a dozen years during which Cleveland, a Rhodes Scholar, had been involved in UNRRA, the Marshall Plan, *The Reporter* magazine (as editor), and the Maxwell School at Syracuse University (as dean). Arthur Schlesinger, Jr., was established in the White House as Special Assistant to the President, concerned for the most part with foreign affairs; one of his important functions was that of liaison and occasional ameliorator of personal relations (always somewhat strained) between Kennedy and Stevenson. George Ball was Undersecretary of State for Economic Affairs and later, after Chester Bowles was shifted to another post, became Rusk's second-in-command as Undersecretary. John Kenneth Galbraith was Ambassador to India, Blair, Ambassador to Denmark, John Bartlow Martin, Ambassador to the Dominican Republic, William Attwood, Ambassador to Guinea.

Stevenson's home in New York, the United States Embassy to the UN, on the forty-second floor of the Waldorf Towers, had formerly been the Presidential Suite of the Waldorf-Astoria Hotel. The view from its windows over the city, day or night, was spectacular. His predecessors there, Ambassador and Mrs. Henry Cabot Lodge, had left it beautifully decorated and furnished with eighteenth century French, English, and American pieces.[9] He was well satisfied with it. Nevertheless, inevitably, the suite soon reflected his individual tastes and preferences. The color of his bedroom was changed from pink, which he disliked, to blue, which was his favorite color; the striped curtains in the dining room were replaced with the gold silk curtains that had hung there before the Lodges changed them; and a good deal of his personal memorabilia was soon scattered through the apartment, including framed letters of Washington, Lincoln, and Albert Schweitzer. Within a few months, many of the wall pictures were famous original paintings by American artists on loan from the Metropolitan Art Museum, chosen by Stevenson and Mrs. Mary Lasker (who also loaned him several valuable objects of décor) from among those made available by the Museum director, James Rorimer. In the drawing room a John Singer Sargent portrait was hung over a sofa of oyster-white damask, and a Whistler hung over another sofa; a Goya, loaned by Mrs. Marshall Field, hung over the fireplace mantel. Dominating the décor of the dining room was a magnificent twelve-panel Coromandel screen (also loaned him by Mrs. Field); on the dining room walls were hung, among other paintings, a Monet and a Utrillo. The sitting room had a fireplace with an Adam mantel and was decorated in red and white, both the draperies and the coverings of the upholstered furniture being of these colors. Stevenson loved flowers, and there were always vases of freshly cut flowers in the rooms, most of them from the gardens and greenhouses of Mrs. Field's estate on Long Island.

He also brought with him into the new life his housekeeper and cook, Mrs. Viola Reardy. She had as a young girl worked for his mother for a year or so in Bloomington, and Alverta Duff had got in touch with her on Stevenson's behalf when he was looking for someone to keep the Libertyville house. She became, briefly, something of a celebrity in New York, and subsequently revealed a little of Stevenson's home life when President Kennedy in January, 1962, lunched in the embassy with Stevenson and Acting Secretary-General of the UN, U Thant of Burma. She prepared for the three men a shrimp and artichoke casserole of which the recipe was promptly published in the press. She then, in interviews with metropolitan reporters, unfavorably compared her Waldorf kitchen with that in Libertyville where, she added, "we grow our own lambs . . . and vegetables, and pheasants."

When Stevenson went to Washington overnight, which he did on the average of once a week, he stayed, as he had for many years, in the fine old Georgetown house of Dr. Paul B. Magnuson at 3121 O Street, N.W. (Schlesinger now lived across the street from it.) Magnuson, a surgeon specializing in illnesses of bones and joints, had begun practicing in Chicago in 1908. He and his wife had been of the Lake Forest set of Stevenson's friends for decades. They were happy to have him use their Georgetown house as his own, providing him with a latch key so that, dispensing with all the formalities of a host-guest relationship, he could come and go as he pleased—the same kind of privileged arrangement he had had in earlier years with the John Paul Wellings in Chicago.

But despite all this, the break in his life remained sharp. He had been prepared by earlier experience for the UN world, of course. It remained, nevertheless, a world apart, transitional between a new order struggling to be born and a chaos of sovereignty stubbornly trying to perpetuate itself— a world therefore full of contradictions. Those who lived in it, to the extent of their commitment to its promise, were drawn spiritually taut between hope and despair in an atmosphere of chronic crisis. The novel grated upon the traditional, often in nerve-fraying dissonance. For instance, there had been carried into this new world much the same kind of ritualistic social life—a ceaseless round of cocktail parties, teas, ceremonial calls, formal receptions, formal dinners—that had characterized the polite, leisurely diplomacy of older days. But in those older days an embassy had typically been concerned with relations between two sovereign powers and *only* two—the ambassador's own country and the country to which he was assigned. The social life had been integral, often central, to the embassy's functioning; an ambassador's daily labors, in office or conference room, had not normally been arduous. Far different was the embassy role in the present-day UN! Here each national representative had to concern himself with relations between his own country and a hundred others, doing so through a world organization whose authority, delegated by the member states, was imperfectly defined at best and must, in the most crucial instances, be created by the very act that asserted it. Full and long were the work days of the ambassador. He must operate as a large-scale administrator: the permanent diplomatic and administrative staff of the U.S. Mission totaled 110 and to it, when the General Assembly was in session, were added forty or more Washington specialists in the various subjects indicated by the Assembly agenda. He must also operate as a policy-making member of the cabinet and National Security Council, a negotiator of delicate and dangerous issues, a spokesman of national policy to the world, and a persuasive apologist for the UN to the American people.

Once, at Clayton Fritchey's urging, Stevenson permitted a newspaper reporter to accompany him through a typical day, taking notes and photographs of his activities. It was mid-December, 1961, and the chief crisis was the continuing one of the Congo, where Belgium's sorry colonial policy now bore bitter, blood-soaked fruit. UN military forces, sent in at the urgent request of the legally constituted central government in Leopoldville, were in hostile contact with the forces of rebellious Katanga province, which was backed by European business interests; and the United States, as Stevenson wished, was supporting this UN action despite the opposition to it of Britain and France, both of whom argued that the Secretary-General had exceeded his authority in permitting the UN troops to fight for Congo unification.

He glanced through *The New York Times* as he ate a hearty breakfast, reviewed with Mrs. Reardy plans for a luncheon he was to give at one o'clock (she reminded him he should get a haircut), and at 8:45 left the suite, having stuffed into his briefcase papers he had previously spread out and sorted on the living room sofa. At a little after 9:00 he was in his office in the U.S. Mission building at UN Plaza and East Forty-fifth Street, across the street from the UN headquarters, leaning back in his chair as he was briefed by two aides—brought up to date on overnight cables and messages. His first appointment was at 10:30 when Dr. V. K. Kyaruzi, chief delegate of the new African State of Tanganyika, came to his office. Tanganyika had just been admitted to the UN as its 104th member, and Kyaruzi and Stevenson conferred for some forty minutes on Tanganyika's UN role. Then Stevenson hurriedly crossed the street to the UN building to confer with Mongi Slim of Tunisia, President of the General Assembly then in session, concerning the Assembly agenda on which items were piling up as the delegates drove for adjournment next week. At 1:00 P.M. he was back in his suite hosting a luncheon in honor of Colombian Foreign Minister Jose Joaquin Carcedo. His luncheon was interrupted by an urgent phone call from the State Department. Back in his office he did paper work until a little after 3:00 when he conferred on the Congo problem with Britain's Minister of State for Foreign Affairs, Joseph B. Godben, soon joined by Sir Patrick Dean, Britain's chief UN delegate. It was a lengthy, difficult conference during which Stevenson checked on the cost of the Congo military operation with his delegation's financial expert and at the conclusion of which he used his private phone, marked with a gold and white Federal seal, to put in a call to Secretary of State Rusk, who was attending a conference of foreign ministers of NATO countries in Paris. The time was 3:55 (8:55 in Paris) and Rusk was out to dinner, expected back in forty-five minutes. When the British visitors had left, Stevenson read over the manuscript of the speech on disarmament he was to give that night, penciling changes in the margin, until Rusk in Paris returned his phone call. As he talked, a message was laid on his desk saying the Acting Secretary-General, U Thant, had just turned down Britain's request for an immediate cease-fire in Katanga. Stevenson then put in a call to George Ball in Washington (Ball was Acting Secretary of State in Rusk's absence) and, while he waited for it to be completed, was told that U Thant had called and that Washington had also, the latter to say that Harlan Cleveland would catch the 6:00 shuttle plane in the capital and would be in Stevenson's Waldorf suite by 7:45. Then Ball was on the line; he had been reached at the White House. As soon as the talk with Ball was completed, France's chief UN delegate, Armand Berard, was shown in for conference on the Congo. While the two talked, word came that the forty-nine nations constituting the Afro-Asian bloc of the UN had just adopted a resolution commending the U.S. stand on Katanga and expressing a decided "coolness" toward the British. Berard left. Stevenson returned U Thant's call. At 7:00 he hurriedly left the office and was driven to the Waldorf where, in a rush, he changed to dinner clothes (he had completely forgotten that he was supposed to get a haircut), talked with Cleveland, and then went to the Four Seasons restaurant for a testimonial dinner being given U Thant by Paul G. Hoffman, director of the United Nations Special Fund. He and U Thant managed to get off to one side for a brief conference on the Congo. He left the Four Seasons immediately after dining and was driven to the UN where, to a night meeting of the Assembly's Political Committee, he gave his disarmament speech. (He told his fellow delegates that all of them had been given a "mandate from humanity" and concluded: "We know as all men know that we must not, dare not fail in this historic endeavor to save civilization from the devastation that we ourselves have devised." The tired phrases were given new life by the earnestness with which he spoke them, his voice vibrant with feeling.) It was after 11:00 when at last, his face drawn and his shoulders drooping with fatigue, he stepped out of his limousine at the Waldorf, saying to Danato Tasto, his chauffeur, "Pick me up at 8:45, Danny." And went up to his bed.

Tomorrow would be another such day.

He gave every indication of thoroughly enjoying the UN world, and certainly there were aspects of it that were immensely flattering and richly rewarding. Diplomats from other countries had greeted his appointment with unprecedented enthusiasm. They felt honored by it: he was by far the most eminent statesman ever to be named a permanent delegate. Many of them also knew him personally and honored him, trusted him as they did few others. When he made his first official appearance in his new role at a meeting of the Security Council on February 1, 1961, representatives of the other states seated at the horseshoe-shaped table vied with one another in expressions of praise and welcome of him. Nor did his subsequent performance do anything to detract from his prestige. Honors continued to come to him, too, from outside the UN—and in a steady stream. A signal one, perhaps more pleasing to him than any other, was the establishment, in his name, by the Jewish Theological Seminary in New York of a foundation for which some $1,500,000 was raised to provide scholarships for graduate students of the Seminary's rabbinical school and of the Seminary's Herbert H. Lehman Institute of Ethics to help provide contacts "between the theorist and the statesman, the scholar and the doer." He added to his list of honorary degrees those of Harvard, Brandeis, Boston University, Toronto University, Rutgers, Amherst, Williams, and the New School of Social Research. The Bill of Rights Association and the New York City Professional Council were among the organizations that honored him. He was given the Woodrow Wilson Award at Princeton in 1963, the John Dewey Award by an organization of educators in 1965, and the Eleanor Roosevelt Political and Public

Service Memorial Award in that same year. . . . He could hardly avoid inhaling some of this flattery ("it doesn't hurt you so long as you don't inhale," he often said). Any man would have done so and become happily intoxicated by it on occasion.

But few men would have encouraged, for they could not have borne, the demands made upon him in addition to those of his job or immediately relevant to his public position. He *did* encourage them—invitations to go here and go there, to do this and do that; invitations to private parties, to country houses for weekends of tennis and swimming, to the theater, to concerts, to ceremonies and festivals of all kinds. He escorted Mrs. John F. Kennedy to the New York City Ballet, with a party that included Prince and Princess Stanislas Radziwill, Jacqueline Kennedy's brother-in-law and sister. He escorted her to a Washington Opera Society performance in the following week. He narrated Aaron Copland's "Lincoln Portrait" when this was performed by Eugene Ormandy and the Philadelphia Orchestra at Philharmonic Hall in New York, and again when it was performed out of doors in Washington, reading Lincoln's lines "with precise articulation, simplicity, not unmixed with fervor," as a newspaper critic reported. He attended the opening nights of important plays, the premiere of a motion picture spectacular ("The Greatest Story Ever Told"), the reopening of the remodeled Museum of Modern Art, the opening of the Kirov Ballet. He was the star attraction on Illinois Day at the New York World's Fair. And so on and on.

Simultaneously, he continued to be actively a father to his three grown sons. (He was named National Father of the Year in 1961.) He was mentor to Adlai III as his eldest son entered elective politics and won a seat in the Illinois legislature. He saw Borden frequently in New York, where his second son was still trying to find a job, a profession truly interesting to him. (In the spring of 1966, Borden with others would open a unique night club in New York called Cheetah, catering to teen-agers—a night club in which only beers and wines, no hard liquors, were served. The club prospered.) Stevenson was not only father of the groom but also proud best man, with Borden and Adlai III, as ushers, when his youngest son, John Fell, was married on February 17, 1962, to Miss Natalie Raymond Owings at Big Sur, California. (The bride was the daughter of Mrs. John S. Barnes of Albuquerque and Nathaniel Alexander Owings of New York, co-founder and senior partner of the famous architectural firm of Skidmore, Owings, and Merrill. The newlyweds lived in San Francisco where John Fell was co-founder and partner of the Argo Investment Corporation, a then recently-established real estate and land development concern.) Stevenson gloried in the role of grandfather, too, whenever he visited Nancy and Adlai III, or, soon, Natalie and John Fell—for the latter promptly presented him with another grandson, born February 12, 1963.

When seventy-eight-year-old Mrs. Eleanor Roosevelt fell dangerously ill of anemia and a lung infection in the fall of 1962, the only person permitted to visit her in her New York City home, aside from her family, was Adlai Stevenson. He had long revered that great lady, whose love and admiration of him was known to all, and his visits to her sickbed always greatly cheered her. He thus became the last person, aside from her family, to see her before she died on November 6 that year. Eleven days later, at the Cathedral of St. John the Divine in New York, he delivered the eulogy of her at a memorial service. ("We are lonelier," he said. "Someone has gone from one's own life who was like the certainty of refuge, and someone has gone from the world who was like a certainty of honor.") He accepted chairmanship of a committee to plan a suitable memorial to her, one that would perpetuate the major interests of her life. Out of its deliberations came the Eleanor Roosevelt Foundation, incorporated by act of Congress. President Kennedy ceremoniously signed the bill in the White House's Flower Garden on April 23, 1963, at which time Stevenson accepted chairmanship of the foundation, too. ("I think we are all indebted to Governor Stevenson for his willingness to assume a central responsibility in making this foundation a reality . . . ," said the President.) During the next year he made scores of speeches to raise money for the foundation in cities all over the country.

To most of those who knew him he seemed, on the whole, in this last chapter of his career, a supremely happy human being. He spread gaiety and excitement around him, electrifying all who came in contact with him, as he had done for decades—only more so. He seemed the epitome of buoyant healthiness, his vitality more amazing than ever.

But there were some, a few among his intimates, who wondered if this appearance did not obscure a very different reality. Was there not something driven, feverish, almost hysterical at times in this hyperactivity? Did he not seem, on close inspection, to be operating now sometimes a little out of control, as if his vitality were a kind of fatality?

Always there had been a large measure of compulsiveness in his behavior; but he was now more compulsive than ever before. He couldn't be still for even a brief time, he couldn't even slow down, and whatever he did he did somewhat excessively. He filled his suite with guests, as if he couldn't bear an hour of relaxed solitude. He had completely given up cigarettes years ago on his doctor's advice, but he had begun smoking again, and quite heavily. Despite his love of rich foods he had managed through most of his earlier years to limit his caloric intake, especially when he had too little time for proper physical exercise; but he consistently ate too much, and drank more than before (formerly content with a moderate highball or two before dinner, he now often had three) with the result that his weight, held at a healthful 180 pounds in earlier years, climbed to well over 200. ("I regret I have but one stomach to give to my country!" he said, commenting on the number of food-serving affairs he was required to attend—but the "one stomach" that he did give became enormous.) He began to be pleased whenever he managed to get his weight down to 195 pounds. At the same time he conceded nothing to a need to protect his heart against the extra strain imposed by extra weight. He took no daily systematic exercise, and he was always in a rush, bustling from here to there with bulging briefcase in hand to arrive at the last possible moment (he habitually scrambled into an airplane just an instant before the door was shut). The physical game he played for fun was no such mild form of exercise as golf but, instead, tennis in multiple strenuous sets. He was forever arranging doubles matches with his friends. He played with astonishing agility and skill for so fat a man, scoring points with a forehand of which he was particularly proud.

III

Of all the elements of the break in the continuity of his life when he accepted the UN post, none other was as hard for him to adjust to as the fact of his subordinate position. He had demanded and received assurances that he would be no mere mouthpiece of policy, that he would be consulted on every important matter pertaining to his work before a final decision was made and would function, day by day, as an integral part of the administration's foreign policy-making apparatus. Nevertheless he, who had long been accustomed to running his own show, could now be at best only a major member of the cast in a show largely written and directed by others: he was at the wrong end of the telephone or (when in Washington) on the wrong side of the desk to make any truly final policy decision.[10] And at worst he might find that, promise or no promise, he was *not* consulted nor even adequately informed of important policy developments with whose issue he strongly disagreed personally yet must defend before the UN.

It was the worst that actually happened—and before he had been three months in his new post.

On April 8, 1961, Stevenson was for the first time informed that the United States, having (under the Central Intelligence Agency) trained and armed at a secret base in Guatemala a Cuban exile army of liberation, would facilitate in the near future an invasion by that army of Castro's Cuba. The news was brought to him by Schlesinger from the White House, accompanied by Tracy Barnes of the CIA. The project, he was told, had been inherited from the Eisenhower administration. But it had been carefully reviewed by key people of the new administration, including Secretary of Defense McNamara, Secretary Rusk, and (of course) the President, who now gave it final approval. Its major premise was that the Castro regime had no popular support and was so incompetent, Castro himself being an hysterical fanatic, that it could not effectively react to a well-prepared surprise attack. The attack itself was to be carried out by exiled Cubans and only Cubans; they would fly the air cover, they would comprise the landing parties; and they understood that, once landed, they were on their own, literally and figuratively. There would be no direct U.S. military involvement. Absolutely none. But then none would be necessary: the landing was bound to trigger a popular uprising and an armed force defection whereby the Communist-dominated Castro regime would be swiftly toppled, and at virtually no risk or cost to the U.S. So argued the CIA and the Joint Chiefs of Staff, principal advocates of the project.

Stevenson was dismayed. He was at that time preparing for a General Assembly debate on a resolution introduced long before by the chief UN delegate of Castro's Cuba, charging the United States with planning armed aggression against Cuba. It was now evident to him, and would soon be evident to the world, that the Cuban charge was substantially true; no one could possibly believe that the exiles had trained and armed themselves in Guatemala, sailed the Caribbean, and landed unaided. How, then, was he to answer the Cuban charge? He would be wholly unable to do so if the landing were made before or during the Cuban debate. Would it be? Schlesinger and Barnes were notably vague as to the timing of the operation but their briefing left Stevenson with the impression that the landing would *not* be made until after the resolution had been debated and acted upon.

Later, lunching with Schlesinger, Fritchey, and Harlan Cleveland at the Century Club on 43rd Street, Stevenson gave emphatic expression to his personal disapproval of the project and his regret, not unmingled with resentment, that he had not been permitted to comment on it when the decision was being made. He thought it morally wrong. He believed that even if it succeeded in the purely pragmatic terms in which it had been conceived (and this was by no means certain) it was likely to do immense long-term damage to U.S. prestige, to UN effectiveness, and hence to the cause of peace and freedom in the world. But since the decision had been made he would, as required by his office, defend it as best he could in the UN and do what he could to prevent or mitigate the harm that he foresaw.[11]

Four days later, President Kennedy in his press conference said flatly: "... there will not be, under any conditions, any intervention in Cuba by United States armed forces, and this government will do everything it possibly can ... to make sure that there are no Americans involved in any actions inside Cuba." The quarrel, he insisted, was not between Cuba and the United States but "between the Cubans themselves."

Stevenson took his cue from this, reinforced by information conveyed to him by Harlan Cleveland, when on April 15 he was abruptly required to defend his government against a new charge presented to the General Assembly in passionately embittered tones by Cuba's Foreign Minister Raul Roa. This new charge was that the United States was directly responsible for an attack upon three major Cuban airfields made early that Saturday morning by eight B-26's (World War II planes). These planes had, in fact, been provided by the United States, their Cuban exile pilots had been trained by the CIA, and they had taken off from an airfield in Nicaragua, whence seven of them had returned after the attack. The eighth, having developed engine trouble, had landed in Key West. Meanwhile a ninth plane had acted out a "cover" fiction that had been prepared by the CIA: it was flown directly from Nicaragua to Miami where its pilot announced himself as a defector from Castro's Cuban air force. But none of these facts was known to Stevenson. He had been assured by Cleveland (who was himself misinformed) that the planes that had landed at Key West and Miami were indeed from Castro's own air force and, their pilots defecting, had taken off from Castro's own airfields. He said so to the UN when he answered Roa on Saturday afternoon.

Early in the morning of Monday, April 17, began the tragic fiasco of the Cuban Bay of Pigs. The little army of exiles, numbering some 1400 men, was landed on a beach of the Zapata Swamp and abandoned there, short of ammunition and supplies (a ship in which these were inexplicably concentrated was sunk by the efficient air force Castro was not supposed to have) and with no possibility of further supply or reinforcement unless the U.S. committed armed forces of her own to the battle. This Kennedy had said he would not do and this he steadfastly refused to do, despite intense pressures soon brought to bear upon him by the CIA and the armed services. With his eyes now wide open, he clearly saw the world tragedy that would result from a full-scale U.S. invasion of Cuba. Such an operation, which would brand us as an utterly ruthless aggressor in the eyes of the world, might well require more than half of our conventional armed strength (this had not yet recovered from Eisenhower's reliance on "massive retaliation"), leaving us too weak for effective response to the moves that the Communists would then certainly make elsewhere in the world—in Berlin, in the Middle East, in Southwest Asia. The invading Cubans were perforce classified as expendable; and though they fought bravely, inflicting heavy casualties on Castro forces, which within a few hours outnumbered them twenty to one, they were wiped out, all killed or captured (save a very few rescued by U.S. ships) by Wednesday evening.

But if the Bay of Pigs effort was far too feeble and inept to have a chance of military success, it was more than sufficient to raise a storm of angry protest around the world. Shocked peoples abroad could not but give credence to the Cuban Foreign Minister's words when, on the day of the landing, he charged in the UN that the invasion was "by a force of mercenaries organized, financed, and armed by the government of the United States" and that the CIA was the responsible agency. Nor was Stevenson able specifically to deny the charge. He could only reply in weasel words that "the United States has committed no aggression against Cuba and no offensive has been launched from Florida or any other part of the United States." He "categorically" denied that any United States armed forces were engaged in Cuba.

A short while later, after the UN meeting had adjourned, Stevenson entered a Waldorf Tower elevator just as Jane Dick, bound for a reception, was leaving it. She spoke to him but he walked past her without recognition, as if in a trance, his face drawn, pale, tense. She had never seen him look like that before; she knew something tragic must have happened. She turned back and took the next elevator up to the embassy suite. Stevenson opened the door at her ring. He still looked ghastly. In the suite she watched and listened to his anguished words as he paced the floor. He had told lies to the UN. He had not known they were lies, but he had told them and they had been exposed. On Saturday he had lied about the Florida plans (the CIA cover fiction was torn apart by Sunday afternoon); today he had lied about U.S. involvement, insofar as he denied there had been any. He had lost the respect of his colleagues from other countries. His credibility was destroyed, his effectiveness destroyed. He would have to resign. . . . And yet he couldn't do that either! His resignation now would be a betrayal of the President and the country at a moment of gravest peril, adding to the already terribly high price of folly. What, then, *could* he do? Nothing, it seemed. He could only suffer helplessly in a trap whose iron jaws mangled his spirit.[12]

No small part of his suffering at that moment was the seeming confirmation of his darkest suspicions of Kennedy as man and as President. All men make mistakes, of course. But there was in Stevenson's view a kind of mistake that truly honorable and intelligent men *never* make. Of this kind was the Cuban adventure—or so it seemed at the moment. How could any man of moral sensitivity, with power to control the event, have permitted so criminal a violence to proceed in so soiled and tattered a cloak of lies? How could any man of honor, possessed of normal human sympathies, so ruthlessly use a man of Stevenson's stature, at the expense of Stevenson's honor, merely to lend plausibility to these lies? And how could any mature man possessing common sense have believed that egregious stupidities thus compounded could achieve even a strictly limited, purely pragmatic end?

But Stevenson soon learned, and was vastly relieved to learn, that the young President had *not* truly been in control. Kennedy had been almost as much a dupe of others, almost as much a puppet of events, as Stevenson had been. And while he manfully assumed sole public responsibility for the fiasco, and moved swiftly to mitigate the evil that flowed from it, he blamed himself as bitterly as ever Stevenson could blame him, if on somewhat different grounds. "All my life I've known better than to depend on the experts," he said to Ted Sorensen. "How could I have been so stupid. . . ?"[13] Stevenson also learned from Schlesinger, from Cleveland, from the President himself, that the White House had had no intention of deliberately deceiving its UN representative in order that he might function unwittingly (hence more convincingly) as part of the cover. Kennedy's regret that it had happened was sincere and profound. On the day before sending Schlesinger to New York to give Stevenson the first briefing on the forthcoming operation, he said: "The integrity and credibility of Adlai Stevenson constitute one of our great national assets. I don't want anything to be done which might jeopardize that." [14] The words, reported to Stevenson, were naturally pleasing to him.

Thereafter, with remarkable rapidity, the catastrophe shrank in most minds to the proportions of an episode—an unfortunate episode but one whose effects were by no means all bad. Stevenson's relations with UN delegates from other countries suffered no permanent harm. Indeed, insofar as these were personal they may even have been somewhat improved. His colleagues realized he had been ill-used and publicly humiliated. By enduring the injustice with (in public) dignity and forbearance he gained their sympathy without losing their respect. They continued to believe in his good will; they continued to trust his word. Some of his relations with Kennedy may also have been improved. Certainly the two men felt that they had been in the same boat on stormy seas, and each admired the other's behavior during and after the storm. Moreover, the President and Secretary of State were now resolved, and let Stevenson know they were resolved, never again to permit him to be kept in the dark concerning any development pertinent to the UN operation.

A few weeks later, Kennedy made effective use of Stevenson's immense personal prestige in Latin America to repair some of the damage done U.S.–Latin American relations. In June he sent his UN ambassador on a three-week 18,000-mile tour of South American countries "to consult with officials . . . about what can be done to perfect and accelerate our Inter-American program for social and economic development as well as our cooperation in other respects," to quote the White House statement. Stevenson returned with a generally somber report of conditions in the ten countries he had visited, stressing the "unholy community of interests" between the extreme left and the extreme right in "the overthrow of the working democracy [nine of the ten countries had democratically elected governments] that could frustrate the revolutionary aims of the one and abolish the power of the other to perpetuate social injustices." He opposed "the view that we in the United States have any monopoly on judgment; that we alone know what should be done everywhere; that we are therefore bound to make our aid contingent on acceptance of our conditions as to where, when, and what is to be done." He considered it "both hard and wrong to . . . use economic aid as an ultimatum." The report was accepted with expressions of gratitude; presumably its recommendations became among the guidelines for the Alliance for Progress. . . .

But if the Bay of Pigs aftermath effected an easing of some of the strains between Stevenson and the White House, it heightened others.

The fiasco resulted, understandably, in an abrupt shrinkage in the influence of the CIA and the Joint Chiefs upon administration policy. To protect himself against the kind of single-minded, special-interest views that the men of these agencies had taken, and whose implementation had so dangerously embarrassed him and the country, Kennedy drastically overhauled the Executive's decision-making machinery. He aimed to make sure that never again would his administration be at the mercy of the narrowly expert when important decisions had to be made but that, instead, such decisions would be made in terms of the total picture and the long view. There was an increase in the decisive influence of the White House staff, men whom Kennedy himself had brought into the government. There was a tightening of State Department controls over foreign policy. These changes were, on the whole, greatly advantageous to the country.

They had the effect, however, of emphasizing the subordination of the UN Mission and of "diminishing the value of the Cabinet rank . . . assigned to Mr. Stevenson," as Max Frankel wrote in *The New York Times.* Hence Stevenson continued often to feel that the agreed terms by which he had accepted his post were not being fully honored in Washington; he was not involved in the decision-making process to the extent that he had believed he would be as a ranking member of the Executive. He tried hard (and with success) to avoid developing a prima donna temperament. He tried also to immunize himself against the species of paranoia, highly contagious, to which anyone in his position was dangerously exposed—especially one who had suffered such disappointments as he had suffered. Yet despite the self-deprecation these disappointments had encouraged, he continued to have a shrewd sense of his own worth, and he could not but resent being put in the position (as he felt he was at times) of an errand boy carrying out orders from men less competent, less experienced, than he. It galled him to have his speeches reviewed in advance by State Department underlings who sometimes concerned themselves not only with the policy substance of what he said but also with the language and style in which he said it. It distressed him to define and defend before the eyes of the world positions that he personally thought mistaken, though he loyally did so to the best of his ability whenever this was required.

His resentment was not alleviated, his danger of paranoia was not reduced, by the speed and accuracy with which certain petulancies of his, expressions of personal pique privately made, were reported to the White House. He had always been notably careless of security when conversing with people he regarded as friends—and it was his instinct (he had found it generally sound) to regard almost everyone as a friend. He was naturally guileless and trusting: he loathed the stealth, the secrecy, the calculated deceits that accompany the processes of personal aggrandizement and national sovereignty in an acquisitive, competitive, anarchical world. Wanting a new world, he would help it into being by acting as though it were already here, insofar as he could possibly do so, and if there were obvious risks in this he was prepared to run them. Evidently some of these risks now became actualities. He must assume that there were Kennedy organization people—perhaps bearing grudges from the campaign, perhaps concerned to keep his prestige and authority from encroaching on theirs—who were more than willing to take advantage of what they no doubt deemed his naïveté in order to make trouble between him and the President. Nor were they, it appeared, the sole explanation of Stevenson's occasional embarrassment. They seemed to be only part of Kennedy's private information-gathering system, a system operating outside official channels with a terrifying efficiency.

"It's something like Orwell's *1984*, if you please," Stevenson once complained to Buffie. " 'Big Brother Is Watching You!' Informers seem to be everywhere." [15]

But he refused to be intimidated. He continued to express himself freely and spontaneously in his social relationships. If anything, his sense of eyes that watched, of ears that listened, bred an attitude of defiance that multiplied his indiscretions.

IV

And, despite repeated rebuffs, he continued to press vigorously for new departures in foreign policy.

As regards policy, Kennedy would have said (did in fact say) that the difference between himself and Stevenson, insofar as they differed at all, was one of practical emphasis. Both men knew and practiced the political art as one of compromise between the desirable and the attainable. They were committed to the same goals; they differed only on the best means of reaching them. But this evident difference was rooted in fundamental differences of temperament and philosphy; and these fundamental differences, with the tensions produced by them, were in the classic American pattern of pragmatism versus idealism.

Kennedy's tendency was to measure proposals against the immediate practical context in which they were made, assessing their value or testing their truth in terms of their workability and practical efficacy within this context. Stevenson's tendency was to measure proposals against general (and generally moral) principles, assessing their value or testing their truth by their consistency with these principles and with each other. Kennedy's primary concern was to be realistic (he liked to think of himself as "an idealist without illusions") and he was inclined to regard an insistence upon ideal consistency in policy discussions as evidence of a certain weakness, a certain sentimentality of mind. Stevenson's primary concern was to be right—that is, logically correct and morally sound (there was a basic coincidence of logic and morality, in his belief); he was inclined to regard a willingness to sanction inconsistencies between ideal goals and immediate practices as evidence of a shallow cynicism, bound to be self-defeating in the long run. Kennedy stressed facts, Stevenson ideas. Kennedy emphasized the present, Stevenson the future. For Kennedy a policy idea was true if it worked and because it worked; its truth, indeed, *was* its workability. For Stevenson a policy idea could work only if it were true, and because it was true; its truth was its consistency with all other true ideas and with that ultimate truth of which every particular truth is an aspect.

To some extent these pragmatist-idealist tensions had been revealed by the 1960 preconvention campaign. They had been further revealed by the Bay of Pigs episode, especially by the very different reactions of the two men to that ill-starred proposal when it was first presented to them. The tensions were now nakedly exposed and were emphasized and reemphasized as the administration faced and dealt with the problems of Communist China, disarmament, and relations with the Afro-Asian neutrals.

In the most widely reported of his speeches on Kennedy's behalf during the 1960 campaign, Stevenson had called for a reexamination of our China policy with a view to admitting (and thus committing) Communist China to the UN. It was his opinion that some kind of two-China UN representation—one delegation from Taiwan, another from Peking—could and should be worked out, and that the U.S. ought at the same time to establish direct diplomatic relations with the Red Chinese. The campaign speech in which this was suggested had not been among those most pleasing to the Presidential candidate; it had provided supporting evidence for the President-elect's contention that Stevenson was "too controversial" to work effectively with the Congress as Secretary of State; and its author's efforts to establish its recommendations as new administration policy ran head-on into the President's hard sense of expediency. Kennedy did not deny that Red China *ought* to be admitted. The fiction that Chiang's Taiwan was the real China was, he confessed, utterly absurd. But domestic political opposition to doing the obviously right and reasonable thing remained strong (Eisenhower, for instance, had warned the President-elect that any "threat" of Red Chinese admittance would bring him into open opposition) and Kennedy was determined to postpone facing it at least for a year. The postponement became annual. Stevenson was thus condemned to lead the battle against Communist China's membership every year that he was UN ambassador, an exercise that disgusted him and did nothing to discourage Mao's abhorrent tyranny (indeed it helped persuade the Chinese that the tyranny was necessitated by capitalist hostility) while doing a good deal to encourage Mao's mad-dog rage against nearly all the world beyond China's borders. (Stevenson also failed, and for the same reasons, in his effort to obtain U.S. diplomatic recognition of Communist Outer Mongolia in the summer of 1961, a move that would have given us a much-needed diplomatic outpost in Central Asia; but tactical maneuvering in the battle against Red China's admittance did permit Outer Mongolia to become a UN member in the fall of 1961.)

Concerning disarmament, Stevenson continued to hold the views he had repeatedly defined in public speech during the Eisenhower years. General and complete disarmament was part and parcel of the development of a world community under world law; it was a prerequisite of survival. General and complete disarmament should therefore be not merely a stated goal but also a genuine animating purpose of United States policy. He urged in the summer of 1961 that "the earnest advocacy of disarmament" be presented as "our top priority national interest" in the forthcoming General Assembly. He gave as one reason for so doing the need to "seize the initiative in disarmament which the Russians have held too long," adding that the United States "must appear second to none in its desire for disarmament." [16] He was dismayed to find that only the latter point—the appearance or propaganda point—seemed to interest Kennedy.* (It is possible that Kennedy here was provoked into an exaggerated show of flippancy; he often was in his relations with Stevenson.) Disarmament, said Kennedy, did not seem to concern the American people very much; it was no potent vote-determining political issue; but it certainly concerned peoples abroad and it provided the United States with one great advantage in the propaganda battle with the Russians, namely, that we were willing to permit on-site inspections whereas the Russians were not. Of this "we should take all the advantage . . . we can." Of course we should, said Stevenson, but the really important thing was for us to make serious and substantive proposals for general and complete disarmament. We could do so only if we were genuinely in favor of it. Were we? Was the President? Kennedy, perhaps a little nettled, made no direct reply but merely reiterated his realization of the propaganda values inherent in the disarmament issue. Whereupon Stevenson began so earnestly to lecture the President upon the necessity for good faith in our approaches to disarmament that Harlan Cleveland, who was present at this conversation, hastily intervened with ameliorating statements. The upshot was that disarmament did become a central theme of the U.S. position in that autumn's General Assembly. The President himself, addressing the Assembly, an-

---

* Theodore C. Sorensen, *Kennedy* (New York: 1965), says (p. 518): "His (Kennedy's) initial interest in disarmament was largely for propaganda reasons—a desire to influence neutral and 'world opinion.'" He "underwent a degree of redemption on this subject," Sorensen says, becoming increasingly committed to actual disarmament, but as late as the spring of 1962 the major emphasis in his instructions to the U.S. delegation to the Geneva Disarmament Conference was on the need to counter the sweeping and oversimplified proposals of the Russians with proposals of our own that were not so "complex and cautious" as to have no propaganda effectiveness.

nounced the "intention" of the United States "to challenge the Soviet Union, not to an arms race, but to a peace race: to advance together step by step, stage by stage, until general and complete disarmament has actually been achieved." In the Assembly that followed foundations were laid for the Geneva Disarmament Conference of the spring of 1962.

The problem of U.S. relations with the Afro-Asians was inextricably intertwined with that of relations with Western Europe. The European NATO powers had been, and to a rapidly diminishing degree remained, colonial powers; they were often inclined by special business interests to look with disfavor upon a U.S. policy of encouraging the Afro-Asians to remove the last shackles of colonialism and to develop viable economies and social institutions of their own. This attitude of our NATO allies was very tenderly regarded by those in Washington who continued to look upon world Communism as a unitary force disciplined and spearheaded by an implacably hostile U.S.S.R. Such men continued to regard military force as the chief (if not ultimately the only) effective instrument of U.S. foreign policy; they would subordinate all else in U.S. foreign affairs to the crucial necessity, as they saw it, of maintaining the NATO military alliance at maximum strength. They prided themselves, these men, on their toughness. They were the hard-liners, the men who were not afraid to "face facts" including the possibility or even (as many of them seemed to believe) the probability of thermonuclear war. Their most emphatic spokesman in administration counsels became former Secretary of State Dean Acheson after Kennedy had invited him, in March of 1961, to make special studies of the problems of NATO and Germany.

The polarized, emotionally weighted vocabulary of hard-and-soft was, of course, inimical to clarity of thought. Not even a fully mature mind could enjoy being characterized as soft, whereas adolescent minds were generally eager to prove how hard they were. But Stevenson accepted the stigma of softness as part of the price he must pay for being right concerning our Afro-Asian relations. It was his conviction that the most stupendous historical development of the postwar years was the rise out of colonialism of some forty new African and Asian nations, comprising more than a billion human beings by the end of 1961 (the number increased each year). These new countries constituted a "third world," one belonging neither to that West whose power focus was Washington nor that East whose power focus was Moscow. They were determined to obtain for themselves the instruments of scientific technology and to apply these to their own natural resources in order to close as swiftly as possible "the glaring gap between the material conditions of the rich minority and the poor majority among the world's peoples." [17] Until they did so, or while they were doing so, they presented by far the greatest challenge on earth—fraught with the gravest dangers as well as the largest hopes—for U.S. statesmanship. During the transition period any major element of this third world might become a battleground between Communist and Western power, as the Congo then threatened to become (and would have become if the UN under Dag Hammarskjöld's bold leadership had not intervened militarily), or as Southeast Asia (Laos, Vietnam) threatened to become. Such bloody confrontations in areas geographically remote from the U.S. and historically remote from our national interests could lead to nuclear holocaust for the American people. In view of all this it seemed to Stevenson the very opposite of hard realism —it seemed actually evidence of a soft nostalgic attachment to a vanishing era—to emphasize NATO at the expense of progressive relations with the rising third world. He would not deny that the U.S. must practice power politics vis-à-vis Soviet Russia in the circumstances now prevailing; the balance of power, whereby major war was rendered less likely, must be maintained; but surely realistic power politics must recognize that Western Europe's share of the world's total power was shrinking—it was far less important to America's defense than it had been when NATO was born—while that of the third world (with Red China) was expanding. No longer was it from the capitals of Europe that the destinies of mankind were ordered; and within decades neither Moscow nor Washington would be the world-polarizing power focus that it now was. On these hard grounds alone it behooved the U.S. to do more, rather than less, to help the peoples of the third world to better themselves economically, socially, culturally.

But it was with hopeful possibilities lying beyond power politics that Stevenson in his Afro-Asian views was ultimately most concerned. If any element of the third world might become a battleground, it might alternatively become an area of fruitful collaboration for economic growth and social development—and the proper agency for such collaboration was, obviously, the UN. The UN was already engaged in this effort, of course. "Some 85 percent of the entire staffs of the United Nations system is occupied with the first systematic effort at international cooperation in the field of economic and social affairs," said Stevenson, who saw this as "certainly one of the great phenomena" of our time.[18] It pointed toward an unprecedentedly even distribution of physical economic power over the face of the earth, with a consequent growth of mutual respect and interdependency among the peoples of the earth, under the aegis of an increasingly effective peacemaking and peace-keeping world organization. It pointed toward that world community under world law which, in Stevenson's oft-expressed opinion, should be the major premise and ultimate goal of foreign policy.

With a good deal of this—indeed, with all of it immediately relevant to power politics—Kennedy agreed. In disputes between Stevenson and State Department traditionalists who insisted on dealing with every problem in terms of the Western Alliance, the President generally sided with Stevenson —and with Chester Bowles who, as Undersecretary of State, joined Stevenson in advocacy of new policy attitudes toward the neutral nations. An early instance had to do with Angola where a revolt against Portuguese rule was being bloodily suppressed by Dictator Salazar's soldiers in the spring of 1961. Liberia introduced to the Security Council a resolution requesting Portuguese compliance with a recently adopted UN policy of anti-colonialism and calling for a UN inquiry into the Angolian situation. (The anti-colonial policy had been authored by forty-three Afro-Asian nations; the U.S. delegate, on Eisenhower's orders, had abstained when the vote [89 to 0] was taken during the last month of the Eisenhower administration.) When Stevenson's wish to vote for the Angola resolution was opposed by State Department professionals, Kennedy supported Stevenson, and though the resolution, with U.S. support, failed in the Security Council, it was adopted a few weeks later in the General Assembly. Kennedy and Stevenson also agreed in repudiating that moralistic opposition to neutralism which had been among the determinants of the Dulles-Eisenhower foreign policy. But Kennedy's repudiation was itself less moralistic (in the sense of commitment to principle) and more pragmatic (in the sense of aiming for immediate practical results) than Stevenson's. He repudiated the Dulles-Eisenhower policy because it "didn't work" in a world where most of the people "are not white . . . are not Christians . . . (and) knew nothing about free enterprise or due process of law or the Australian ballot." [19] In Laos, for instance, which the previous administration had tried to make a U.S. ally and where anti-Americanism and communism throve on popular resentment of a corrupt exploitive regime supported by the U.S., Kennedy settled, through negotiation with the Russians and Laotians, for a neutralized state. The Laotian situation remained uneasy but a life- and treasure-consuming battle was avoided. Neutralism worked there better than any other policy.

But by the same token, Kennedy's commitment to the new approach to the neutrals was far less firm, far less visceral, than Stevenson's (or Bowles'). For the view that neutralism *per se* was a moral position superior to that of either protagonist in the Cold War Stevenson seemed at times to have a certain sympathy. Kennedy had none. And there were moments when the President, feeling that the new policy didn't work either, that it failed to produce results, teetered on the verge of repudiating it, with harsh words for Stevenson and Bowles, and shifting to new versions of the hard line.

One such moment, especially bitter, came in early September, 1961, when a summit meeting of twenty-eight nonaligned nations was held in Belgrade. Kennedy at that time was immersed in dangerous problems. Khrushchev had renewed his threat to force the West out of Berlin, having set December 30, 1961, as the deadline for signing a peace treaty with East Germany. In mid-August, driven to desperate and brutal measures by the increasing flow of East Germans into the West, he had thrown up the infamous Berlin Wall. On August 30, the Russians abruptly resumed the atmospheric testing of

H-bombs, Khrushchev having boasted of possessing a 100-megaton bomb—that is, a bomb with explosive force equivalent to 100 million tons of TNT, five thousand times the force of the Hiroshima bomb and hundreds of times greater than the force of all the explosives used in all the wars in history. Had the U.S. initiated these aggressive moves, and especially had the U.S. been the first to resume H-bomb tests, the neutrals, as everyone knew, would have reacted with loud cries of outrage and protest; they would have adopted resolutions condemning the act in the strongest possible language. But no such resolution was adopted at Belgrade. There the heads of the neutral states, including Nehru, Nasser, Tito, and Sukarno of Indonesia, issued pronouncements against Western colonialism but none against the Soviet tests. Kennedy was furious. Nor was his temper improved when the Belgrade conferees, sending Nehru to Moscow, sent only Sukarno (with Keita of Mali) to Washington to convey to the American Executive the sense of the meeting. The order of preference seemed obvious and insulting.

When Kennedy signed the foreign aid bill at that time he said in a public statement that the aid administrators "should give great attention and consideration to those nations who share *our* view of the world crisis." To Schlesinger he said: "Do you know who were the real losers at Belgrade? Stevenson and Bowles." [20] And on September 5, the day he ordered a resumption by the U.S. of underground bomb tests, he openly displayed his irritation with Stevenson when the latter at a White House meeting expressed personal regret that the decision to resume had been made. What else could we do? Kennedy demanded. We might, suggested Stevenson, have exploited the propaganda advantage, the gain in favorable world opinion, that would have resulted from our refusal to follow the Russian lead. Kennedy flatly, profanely disagreed. Look at the so-called "neutrals!" They constituted much if not most of the world opinion we were supposed to court and they employed a double standard for grading the Russians and us, a highly permissive standard for the Russians, a sternly prohibitive one for us. They had behaved abominably. In any case, he concluded, the decision had been made and, right or wrong, could not be unmade.

It was soon made clear to him, however, that the Belgrade conference manifested no such pragmatic failure of U.S. third world policy as he had at first believed. Though no formal protest was made, the conferees in private talk, many of them, expressed angry resentment of Soviet bomb test resumption; there were none of the anti-American speeches that would certainly have been made in such a gathering a year before; and there had been no formal endorsement or much evidence of strong private opinion in favor of the Soviet positions on Berlin, on disarmament (as opposed to the U.S. position), or on the replacement of the office of Secretary-General of the UN with a three-man executive committee (or *troika*), as Moscow had proposed in angry reaction to Hammarskjöld's UN "interference" in

Congolese "internal affairs." According to the U.S. embassy in Belgrade, the conference indicated that recent American attitudes and acts with regard to the neutrals were having a favorable effect. Walt Rostow, then a White House assistant (he soon became an Assistant Secretary of State), revealed through analysis of the issue positions taken by the Belgrade conferees that the six nations whose positions most flatly opposed those of the U.S. had all (excepting Tito's Yugoslavia) received substantially more aid from Russia than from America whereas nearly all the eighteen nations taking moderate (or more truly neutral) positions had received substantially more American than Russian aid. The new approach evidently *was* working after all—and so the President reversed himself as to the proper administration of our aid program. He had never meant to suggest, he now said, "that, in order to be entitled to our assistance" the countries needing our help "must agree with us, because quite obviously these people in the underdeveloped world are newly independent, they want to run their own affairs. . . ." [21]

In the UN General Assembly which Kennedy addressed in late September, 1961—the address wherein he stated the American intention to achieve by practical stages "general and complete disarmament"—Stevenson proved remarkably adroit, persuasive, and resourceful in sustaining his country's positions and at the same time defending the world organization against the gravest threats to its effective existence that it had faced since San Francisco. Kennedy's address followed by a week the martyrdom of Dag Hammarskjöld in the Congo, where the Secretary-General, with five members of the UN Secretariat, died in a plane crash. The Soviets promptly increased their pressure for the *troika,* whereby they would have been enabled to veto the UN Executive's actions, and were defeated in this attempt after seven weeks of negotiations in which Stevenson played a leading part. U Thant of Burma was elected Acting Secretary-General by unanimous vote. (A year later the "acting" was removed from U Thant's title.) The UN's immediate financial crisis, brought on by the extra cost of the Congo operation and the refusal of the Soviets and others to pay their assigned share of it, was alleviated by Assembly authorization of a bond issue of $200 million, the bonds to be purchased by the member states. A resolution calling for a ban on nuclear tests, with effective international inspection and controls, was adopted. And of course Communist China, whose proposed membership became for the first time a subject of full-scale Assembly debate, was excluded by a wide margin of votes; moreover, her chance for future admission was reduced by adoption of a resolution requiring a two-thirds majority for any proposal to change Chinese representation.

Stevenson's China speech measured how far he was willing to go, though always with unhappy aftereffects, toward accommodating principle to practice when the latter was not of his own choosing. He said that the admission of Communist China would place a UN "seal of approval" upon

Peking's aggressive designs on Taiwan, that Peking had "shown nothing but contempt" for the UN, and that it was "wishful" thinking to assume that the admission would bring "this unbridled power" under the influence of the community of nations. The question, he said, was not one of "bringing Communist China into the United Nations" but instead one of finding "a way to bring the United Nations—its law and spirit—back into the whole territory of China." Sophistry could hardly do more.

Yet the pragmatist-idealist tensions remained between Kennedy and Stevenson regarding policy matters, joined and complicated by the unease, the wariness that was constant in their personal relationship. In Jacqueline Kennedy's company, Stevenson was his normally witty, charming self. She liked him immensely and he liked her. (Once, when Buffie commented on the immense favorable publicity that Jacqueline was getting, he replied, "Yes, she has a great flair for this and understands it even better than her husband. I hope she doesn't overdo it." [22]) But in the youthful President's company Stevenson continued to go stiff, to become a bit self-conscious, embarrassed, even pompous-seeming at times, as if his rare spring of laughter had dried up in him. He could not feel *naturally* subordinate to this young man. Nor did Kennedy ease the situation when he subtly (perhaps unconsciously) emphasized, as he generally did with Stevenson, those attitudes of toughness and realism most likely to offend, and in some circumstances even alarm (with their policy implications), the elder man. It was a kind of psychological aggression. The two men had great respect and even admiration for one another—Stevenson's grew as he came to know Kennedy better—but always there was this covert antagonism, a feeling in each that the other was a competitor if not an opponent. And Stevenson remained unsure of his place, his actual status and authority, in the new administration.

v

Indeed, he was given additional reason for such uncertainty in the late fall of 1961. . . .

Of all the Washington press corps, Charles Bartlett of the Chattanooga (Tennessee) *Times* had by far the most intimate relations with Kennedy. The two were of the same college generation (Bartlett, a Yale man, was by four years the younger), both had served in the Navy during World War II, both were wealthy, both were Roman Catholics, and they had been close friends since Kennedy's first days in Washington. It had been at Bartlett's Washington house that freshman Senator Kennedy first met Jacqueline Bouvier in 1953. Rightly or wrongly, Bartlett was believed to have special access to inside information concerning the administration. It was even generally believed among political sophisticates that the White House deliberately leaked news items to Bartlett now and then as a means of applying pressures on individuals or of testing popular reactions.

Hence the furor raised when a Bartlett column in the summer of 1961 indicated that the White House was dissatisfied with Chester Bowles's performance as Undersecretary of State. The dissatisfaction allegedly stemmed from Bowles's soft-line approach to world problems—an allegation that delighted the hard-liners and the political right while causing Stevenson to wonder whether he might not be next on the list of those slated for public humiliation and forced withdrawal from Kennedy's New Frontier.

But if the Bartlett column was in fact a planted story designed to speed Bowles's departure, it wholly failed in its purpose. Bowles's friends, who were many, vociferous, and influential, rallied in his defense. He himself stubbornly refused to oblige by tendering his resignation or asking for reassignment. And the President found it politically inexpedient to take the action he had planned until Thanksgiving weekend when he suddenly announced, among a linked series of personnel changes, the removal of Bowles from his post as Undersecretary. Bowles, it was announced, had accepted a theretofore nonexistent post as Special Adviser for Asian, African and Latin-American Affairs in the White House, a post whose responsibilities and authority were undefined and which the press promptly recognized as a face-saver.

Stevenson was at that moment engaged in the battle to exclude Communist China from the UN and was in consequence far from happy over what his UN job was requiring of him. He moved swiftly, skillfully to protect himself against the kind of humiliation Bowles had been forced to endure. He had at hand a formidable weapon of self-defense. He had begun to shape it several weeks before when Senator Paul Douglas of Illinois had announced that Adlai Stevenson headed his (Douglas's) list of Democratic candidates for the Senate seat now occupied by Republican Everett Dirksen, the Senate Minority Leader, in the coming election of 1962. Stevenson had publicly shrugged off the suggestion with a laugh at the time, but not in such a way as to discourage the flow of letters, wires, and phone calls that followed, urging him to run. He noted with special interest that among those who phoned was Chicago's Mayor Daley. The tough mayor was in a position to dictate the Illinois Democratic nominee for the Senate; he was also a man for whose personal sensitivities and embarrassments Stevenson, after Los Angeles, need feel no deep concern. A few weeks later, at a private luncheon in New York where UN correspondent Milt Freudenheim of the Chicago Daily News was present, Stevenson mentioned that he was seriously considering running for the Senate.[23] Freudenheim promptly informed his paper of this and, within hours, Stevenson received a not-unexpected phone call from Daley, who now offered the Senate nomination outright. Would Stevenson accept it? Daley wanted to know.

Stevenson's response was a typical display of that indecisiveness that was actually a process, a strategy of decision-making. He said he'd "have to think it over" and "talk it over with the President" before he said Yes or No.

He saw the President in Washington two days later. On Saturday morning, December 2, 1961, the day of his UN China speech, he conferred with Kennedy in the White House on general UN problems, with particular reference to Latin American affairs. At the close of the conversation he mentioned that he was being asked to make the Senate race and wondered whether he should consider resigning his UN post in order to do so. The President was unresponsive, saying merely that, while he hoped Stevenson would stay in the UN, the decision must of course be Stevenson's. An unsmiling Stevenson left the office. To the White House reporters who questioned him he replied that he had no plans to run for the Senate but added, in a truly Machiavellian stroke, that Mayor Daley had phoned him last Thursday, urging him to run.

Back in New York, later that same day, he did not hide from his associates his feelings, a hurt feeling, that his continued presence at the UN was not urgently desired by Washington. Nor did he hide it from a highly respected reporter, Max Frankel, whose by-lined story on the front page of *The New York Times* was read by the President at Glen Ora (the Kennedys' weekend retreat in Virginia) on the following morning. Stevenson, wrote Frankel, had told the President that he would decide by January 1 whether or not he would resign his UN post, and though he had declined to say what Kennedy's reaction had been, his report of the conversation suggested that Kennedy "made no strenuous effort to hold Stevenson in his position of cabinet rank." Stevenson's entrance into elective politics would inevitably "engage Kennedy's prestige on his side," Frankel pointed out; it would also increase speculation already rife over the administration's dropping "of prominent members of the liberal wing of the party," though as a matter of fact "Mr. Stevenson's status on the New Frontier has always been somewhat ambiguous and, for him, uncomfortable."

Stevenson had been invited to lunch at Glen Ora that Sunday. He was greeted with rare warmth upon his arrival. By the time he departed he and Kennedy had had a four-hour private talk during which the President was no longer casual in his hope that Stevenson would stay in his present post but, instead, vehemently insisted that he do so. He was, said Kennedy, virtually irreplaceable. And Stevenson promised to review all the factors with great care before making a final decision.[24]

Meanwhile the UN delegates from other countries were publicly reacting with dismay to the possibility of Stevenson's departure. Monday's press reported some of them as offended by what appeared to them to be a threatened "downgrading of the UN" by the United States. (Surely a UN ambassador ought to outrank a mere senator!) Reiterated, and heightened in credibility, were reports that Kennedy hoped to retire Stevenson from the UN.

On the following day, Tuesday, December 5, Stevenson yielded to all this pressure. He phoned a helplessly fuming Daley to say, "I cannot be the Democratic candidate for the Senate" and immediately thereafter released a statement to the press saying that "in recent conference the President has greatly reinforced my view that I can best serve him and the country in the field of foreign policy." Kennedy, in New York that day for a speech, also issued a statement. He was, he said, "delighted" with Stevenson's decision and hoped that Stevenson would "play an expanding role" in foreign policy. . . .

Thereafter for many months relations between Kennedy and Stevenson were more harmonious, and Stevenson seemed somewhat less unhappy and insecure in his UN job.

One pauses here to note a remarkable fact, namely, that a history of Stevenson's UN years need make so little mention of Dean Rusk. The chief UN delegate was in daily communication with the Secretary of State. The two necessarily dealt constantly with one another on matters of routine as on matters of crisis (the latter in the UN were practically routine). But at no time were there significant encounters between the two, friendly or hostile, and in the occasional crises of relations between the UN ambassador and the White House the principal foreign officer of the executive seems to have played no part at all. Why was this?

Part of the answer certainly lies in the manner of Rusk's appointment and in the status pattern that Stevenson tacitly proposed and Rusk tacitly accepted in public, when the two held their joint press conference in Stevenson's office (not Rusk's) immediately after their appointments were announced. Rusk to some indeterminate degree owed his appointment to Stevenson. He had not been appointed until after Stevenson had been; he might not have been appointed at all if Stevenson had not exercised (in effect) a certain veto power over Kennedy's choice of a Secretary. For instance, McGeorge Bundy, then faculty dean at Harvard, had been seriously considered by Kennedy for State. But Stevenson had indicated that he could not accept the proffered UN post if Bundy were named Secretary, for there was a lack of confidence and sympathetic understanding between them. (Bundy, though a Kennedy supporter in 1960, had voted for Eisenhower in 1952 and 1956; appointed a White House assistant on foreign policy by Kennedy, with the National Security Council as his particular concern, he generally favored a hard line in foreign affairs.) Rusk was then named. He was at that time unknown to the public at large.

The manner of his appointment is only part of the answer, however. Not particularly remarkable is the fact that he was plucked from obscurity to fill a high public post (this happens all the time) nor that he should show deference at the outset to Stevenson, a world figure nine years his elder. What *is* remarkable is that, after months and years in this high post of great power, he was still obscure, still to large degree an unknown quantity. Herein lies the basic reason why he figures so meagerly in the Stevenson UN story.

A fierce glare of publicity focused constantly on his office. Yet Rusk himself remained dim and vague to the general public and remained almost equally enigmatic and mysterious to even his close working associates. He may not have had a passion for anonymity (it was hard to believe him passionate about anything), but he managed to retain more of it than one would have believed possible in his circumstances. Soft-spoken, mild-mannered, poker-faced, self-effacing, cautious and precise and industrious, he had at once the qualities of the perfect subordinate and of the efficient administrator, the executive director of a large, long-established, and conservative organization. He seemed in many respects the very type of Organization Man, possessed of a positive (or should one say a negative?) genius for fading into backgrounds while others defined and thereby risked themselves in controversy and decision.

It was as if by conscious choice and effort that he was colorless, carefully avoiding the brilliant word or arresting gesture that might cause people to look closely at him as an individual. In bureaucratic wars—and his had been a bureaucratic career—this amounted to a genius for survival. But it prevented his being a leader of men or effective as an innovator and shaper of policy. Sorensen remarks that Kennedy, who dealt with other cabinet members on a first-name basis, could never bring himself to call Rusk "Dean," and Sorensen and Schlesinger agree that the President and his White House aides could seldom, if ever, discover precisely where the Secretary stood, precisely what the man Rusk truly felt and believed and thought, concerning the critical issues of his time.[25]

The same was true of Stevenson in his relations with the Secretary. He found Rusk easy to work with. Unlike the other key appointees in the administration, Rusk had made his own way from humble beginnings (he was born and raised in an impoverished Georgia rural community), earning his big chance with a Rhodes scholarship awarded while he was a student at Davidson College in North Carolina. Returning from Oxford, he had served in a number of college administrative posts before entering the Army in 1940. He had resigned his colonelcy in 1946 to enter the State Department, where he served for a time, under Truman and Acheson, as Assistant Secretary for United Nations Affairs. Thus he had gained a thorough understanding of how the UN works and of the technical problems, procedural and negotiative, with which Stevenson had constantly to deal. But Stevenson never felt that he knew Rusk personally at all well, and the generally favorable opinion that he had had of him in 1960 was, according to intimates, somewhat reduced in the years that followed. Rusk once told Stevenson—it was the nearest he ever came to an intimate disclosure—that the "hardest decision" he had ever had to make was his decision to leave the Army in 1946. He had actually seriously considered making a career of the Army! Stevenson had found this, as he remarked to one of his sons, rather "damning."

VI

On Tuesday, October 16, 1962, Stevenson flew from New York to Washington to attend a White House luncheon in honor of the Crown Prince of Libya. As the luncheon ended, the President asked him to stay for a talk. The two men went to the study on the White House's second floor, and there Kennedy briefed his UN ambassador fully on a matter of gravest import concerning which he himself had received his first information only a few hours before. . . .[26]

The sad consequences of the Bay of Pigs fiasco had mounted to ominous proportions by the time the UN General Assembly of the autumn of 1962 opened. Ties between Soviet Russia and Castro's Cuba were of course greatly strengthened, the latter becoming virtually a Soviet satellite. Khrushchev, who in the spring of 1961 had threatened war if the U.S. invaded the island, had in the months since made his threat substantial by increasing the flow from his country into Cuba of defensive weapons and specialists to man them. Some 5,000 specialists were believed to be in Cuba by the late summer of 1962, Soviet MIG-21 fighter planes were on Cuban airfields, and (most ominous of all) missile-launching installations of some kind were under construction. It was assumed that the latter were for antiaircraft surface-to-air missiles (SAM's), but John McCone, whom Kennedy had appointed CIA chief after Allen Dulles's resignation following the Bay of Pigs, expressed worry that the SAM's were being placed to protect offensive missile bases, which would be installed later. Why otherwise were they going in? Few took McCone's worry seriously—it seemed incredible that the Soviets could be so foolhardy—but Kennedy had been sufficiently perturbed to issue a warning statement in early September. There was, he said, no evidence as yet of "significant offensive capability" in Cuba but, if there ever were such evidence, "the gravest issues would arise."

Three weeks later, in a policy statement before the General Assembly, Stevenson had described the world as a "powder keg" and protested North Vietnam's "unprovoked aggression" against South Vietnam as well as Cuba's campaign of "subversion and vituperation" against her Western Hemisphere neighbors, a campaign given moral and material support from outside the hemisphere. The Cuban UN delegate immediately replied that

Stevenson's protest was "just a new way of covering up the large-scale aggressions which the government of the United States is preparing against our people." He added angrily: "You tell your aggressive generals, sir, that in our country more than 6,000,000 Cubans will defend the principles of the Charter of the United Nations with something more than sweet words." On the following day, the Soviet Union again warned that an attack on Cuba by the U.S. would mean war, to which Stevenson replied that the "threat to peace in Cuba comes not from the United States but from the Soviet Union."

Meanwhile, the President had ordered an increase in the frequency of U-2 overflights of Cuba—flights whose photographs had provided virtually the sole truly hard intelligence of the Cuban-Soviet arms build-up. On October 14, Sunday, two U-2's had made sweeps of western Cuba, concentrating on the San Cristobal area whence had come reports through intelligence agents of highly suspicious activities. The photographs from these flights were alarming. Expertly analyzed, they showed beyond doubt that the Soviets had begun construction near San Cristobal of a medium-range ballistic missile (MRBM) base, a complex of from sixteen to twenty-four nuclear-tipped rockets whose range of 1100 nautical miles included Washington, St. Louis, Dallas, and of course all the Strategic Air Command bases (and Cape Canaveral) south of that arc. The evident rate of construction, revealed by comparing photographs taken of the area in late August with these latest ones, was such that the entire complex might become operational within two weeks, by which time the protective network of SAM's, plus the MIG's on nearby fields, would render effective U.S. plane attacks on the base difficult and expensive if not impossible.

Kennedy, informed of this and shown the photographs as he arose from bed Tuesday morning, now told Stevenson all he knew of the threat and showed him, too, the photographic evidence. Daily and intensive aerial reconnaissance of all Cuba had been ordered, Kennedy said—the evidence would soon be so overwhelming that no skeptic among our Allies or the neutrals could possibly doubt it—and a carefully selected group of advisers (some fourteen men) was secretly meeting to review possible courses of action. The President would like to have Stevenson join the discussion, postponing his return to New York (where the second annual debate on the admission of Red China to the UN was about to begin) for as long as possible. Time, said Kennedy, was of the essence. Action must be taken quickly. He "supposed" that the action must be an air strike to "wipe them out" before they became fully operational—either that or some other forceful action that would make the weapons inoperable.[27]

Stevenson was almost as greatly perturbed by Kennedy's immediate reaction as he was by the dire development that provoked it. He said quickly that he hoped there would be no air strike until every possibility of a peaceful solution had been fully explored. Sooner or later, he emphasized, the U.S. would have to go before the UN to explain its action and it was "vitally important we go there with a reasonable case."

It was vitally important, too, as both men knew, to probe as deeply and accurately as possible the Soviet intention, in this seemingly mad act, before deciding how to respond to it. Was it a test of American nerve and will when faced with the immediate threat of nuclear war? Was it a diversionary move, designed to lure us into Cuba and leave the Soviets free for forceful action in Berlin? There were other possibilities. And each differed from the others in the amount and kind of threatful danger it presented, hence in the amount and kind of forceful counteraction it suggested. The problem, involving so many unknowns, so many variables, was as full of complexities as it was of fatal danger.

Finally, it was vitally important that the Russians be given no inkling that we knew what they were up to. Only behind a thick wall of secrecy could we, as Secretary of Defense McNamara later put it, "maintain the options" (meaning a free choice among possible initiatives) until we were ready to act. To this end, Stevenson urged Kennedy not to cancel any of his scheduled campaign appearances (the mid-term election campaign then approached its climax) lest it arouse press speculation, spread alarm through the country, and tip off the Russians. Kennedy agreed—he had already reached the same conclusion—and on Wednesday he campaigned in Connecticut, as he had been scheduled to do, for the election of Abraham Ribicoff to the Senate.

Before he left the White House that Wednesday morning, the President received from Stevenson a hand-written note which, according to Sorensen, annoyed him with its "ambivalence." [28] National security must take precedence over all else, wrote Stevenson, and it was impossible for us to "negotiate with a gun at our head." If the Russians refused to "remove the missiles and restore the status quo ante, we will have to do it ourselves— and then we will be ready to discuss bases in the context of a disarmament treaty or anything else. . . ." But Stevenson also stressed the "risk . . . [of] nuclear war" and confessed to "grave misgivings" over the "proposed course of action" (meaning the air strike). He said that "before we start anything" we should make it clear * "that the existence of nuclear missile bases anywhere is negotiable." His own tentative suggestion was that a high-level personal emissary of the President's be sent to Moscow to deliver to Khrushchev himself a message stating our knowledge of the missiles' presence and our insistence that they be removed at once.

(It was soon evident to others, if not to Stevenson himself, that this sug-

---

* Part of Kennedy's annoyance no doubt stemmed from the fact that Stevenson, writing hastily, put this in past tense and gave it thus a chiding tone: "I feel you should *have made* it clear . . ." (Italics mine.)

gestion did not stand up under critical analysis. If the proposed message were a simple statement of our knowledge and a simple request for the missiles' removal, it would hand to Khrushchev the diplomatic initiative we thus far held: he might engage in diplomatic stalling tactics while rushing the missile installations to completion. If the message coupled our insistence with an offer to negotiate the question of bases, Khrushchev might move swiftly to mobilize opinion among our Allies and the neutrals in such a way as to force a summit meeting in which he would hold every advantage. Such a meeting, where the destruction of an effective NATO might become the price of a Soviet withdrawal from Cuba, could prove as disastrous as Munich. If the message coupled our insistence with a threat, warning Khrushchev that his refusal to comply would mean immediate military action on our part against the installations [Soviet personnel would inevitably be killed in an air strike], it would amount to an ultimatum which he might find it impossible to accept and which might even tempt him into a preemptive nuclear strike against us. Sorensen made an attempt to draft a message that combined our request with an air strike threat and found he could not do it save as, in effect, a flat ultimatum. "From that point on, I veered away from the air-strike course," he writes.) [29]

Stevenson remained in Washington through that Wednesday, meeting with others of the select group in George Ball's conference room in the State Department. Among those present at one time or another during the hours of talk were Rusk (who, typically, refused to chair the meeting), McCone, McNamara, Acheson (Elie Abel says that Acheson and Stevenson, who cordially disliked one another, were by accident or design never in the room at the same time), Ball, Bundy, Sorensen, Treasury Secretary Douglas Dillon, and Attorney General Robert Kennedy. It was the last, obviously consciously acting for his brother, who soon emerged as discussion leader, arousing antagonism in many of the older men (including Stevenson) with the sharpness, even the rudeness, with which he questioned those who made suggestions. Yet it was later generally, if somewhat grudgingly, agreed among his detractors that young Kennedy's rough tactics (he was like "a bull in a china shop," Stevenson complained [30]) had been effective in defining and solidifying concrete proposals out of what might otherwise have been an amorphous, wholly inconclusive talkfest. The proposals that emerged as possible responses to the Soviet move ranged from doing nothing at all to launching a full-scale invasion of the island. In between was the air strike proposal, which seemed to command at that time a majority support among the conferees, along with proposals for a total or partial blockade of the island and proposals for diplomatic measures, including the use of the Organization of American States (OAS) and the UN. No firm consensus had been reached when Stevenson flew back to New York.

He returned to Washington on Friday afternoon. Much had happened in the meantime. U-2 reconnaissance, stepped up to six or seven flights a day, had discovered four more MRBM sites, making a total of six at various points on the island. Work on them proceeded apace; they would become operational within a few days. Adding to the alarm was the discovering of excavations for three intermediate-range ballistic missile (IRBM) sites as well. The IRBMs, with a range of 2200 miles, could reach to almost the farthest corner of the continental United States. On Thursday afternoon, Kennedy had had a two-hour conversation with Soviet Foreign Minister Gromyko, who had come to New York to participate in the UN General Assembly and was now returning to Moscow. Gromyko had talked tough indeed about Berlin but had reiterated the Moscow assurance that Soviet military aid to Cuba was solely for the purpose of increasing Cuba's defense capabilities, and that the Soviet specialists were training Cuban nationals to handle defensive weapons only. "If it were otherwise," he concluded, "the Soviet Government would have never become involved in rendering such assistance." Kennedy had then read to Gromyko, without comment, his early September statement warning that we would not tolerate Soviet offensive weapons on the island.[31]

In the continuing strategy discussions that day and Friday, the surprise air strike had, to Stevenson's relief, lost support, thanks in no small part to the vehement and (to Stevenson among others) somewhat surprising opposition to it of Bobby Kennedy. The original belief of some of its proponents had been that the air attack could be a pinpoint or surgical operation in which only military installations were hit and there would be few if any Cuban civilian casualties, but realistic examinaton showed that such an operaton was not possible. A massive surprise attack would be needed to knock out the missile and air bases, and according to one intelligence estimate this might kill as many as 25,000 Cubans, along with many hundreds, perhaps thousands, of Soviet personnel. George Ball, arguing as Stevenson would have done, held such action to be a violation of our own best national traditions which, however successful in purely military terms, must do us irreparable long-term damage. And Bobby Kennedy had emphatically seconded this. He evinced a moral sensitivity few had thought he possessed when he said with passion that a sneak attack at dawn on Sunday, October 21, as had been suggested, would be a "Pearl Harbor in reverse"; it would "blacken the name of the United States in the pages of history." [32] And so the conferees had inclined more and more to the alternative of a naval blockade (it was dubbed a "quarantine" of Cuba in remembrance of Roosevelt's "quarantine the aggressors" speech) to prevent the further shipment of Soviet war matériel into the island. This had its dangers. It could not of itself alone be decisive: it meant an intensification and prolongation of the agonizing tension with which the U.S. awaited the Soviet response, and it was itself an act of war. The U.S. Navy must be prepared to sink any Soviet vessel which, duly warned, attempted to run the blockade. But the blockade dangers were limited while those of the air strike were unlimited. Unlike an air strike, the blockade was a reversible tactic: it could be lifted at any time. It gave Khrushchev a chance to back down without a total loss of face. And it left open a considerable range of choices (it "maintained the options") for the U.S.

With this reasoning Stevenson agreed. He also favored an initial blockade limited to offensive weaponry, retaining the option of extending the contraband list to other items (including petroleum, vital to the Cuban economy) if the initial action failed to work. He recommended, however, that the President's speech to the nation telling of the Soviet missiles and announcing the blockade (or quarantine) be postponed from Sunday night, October 21, to Monday night and that it say not that the quarantine was now in effect, but that it *would be* placed in effect. This would enable the twenty OAS nations to be informed of the action before it was under way and give them an opportunity formally to endorse it. This recommendation was accepted by the President who, on the pretext of a slight respiratory ailment, canceled his remaining campaign appearances and flew back to Washington from Chicago on Saturday morning, the 20th.

The decisive meeting, with the advisory group convened for the first time as a formal convocation of the National Security Council, was held in the Oval Room of the White House on Saturday afternoon. The President presided. He read a two-page summary of the group's conclusions, prepared by Dean Rusk, whereby he was presented with a choice between starting with a blockade and moving from that to an air strike if necessary or starting with an air strike and moving from that to an invasion if necessary. He quickly decided in favor of the blockade, as a majority of the conferees had done. He also agreed with Adlai Stevenson's suggestion that, simultaneously with the President's Monday evening speech, the U.S. should issue a call for an emergency session of the UN Security Council. This would forestall the introduction by the Soviets of a resolution for such a session on the charge that the U.S. naval blockade was an act of aggression against Cuba.

Thus far the meeting was harmonious.

But it ceased to be so. It became, in fact, harshly dissonant when, the immediate decisions having been taken, Stevenson presented to the group his thoughts concerning the diplomatic or political moves we should be prepared to make in addition to the military moves.

Looking at the hazardous confrontation from the UN point of view (it was his duty to represent the UN interest in such councils), yet with due regard for our national interests, he suggested a negotiating program whereby we agreed to a demilitarized, neutralized Cuba whose territorial integrity we joined in guaranteeing through the UN. UN inspection teams would oversee the removal of the Soviet missiles; the introduction of UN influence into Cuban affairs would (hopefully) tend to democratize the Cuban government. This would mean, of course, our withdrawal from the Guantánamo naval base, but Guantánamo was of dubious value to us anyway. Stevenson further suggested that we use our Jupiter missile bases in Turkey and Italy as bargaining counters. To world opinion, Soviet missile bases in Cuba seemed no more reprehensible than American missile bases in Turkey and Italy, and the latter in any case were now obsolescent.*

All this was anathema to the hard-liners in the room and they (chiefly Dillon, Lovett, and McCone, according to several accounts) sprang to the attack. They sprang so swiftly and with such angry scorn that Stevenson failed to make clear just how he intended to time his negotiating proposals in relation to the actions already decided upon.[33]

It was Rusk's impression that Stevenson merely meant to define the position we should take on matters the Soviets would inevitably bring up during the negotiations that must follow their agreement to remove the missiles. Stevenson himself later insisted that this was in fact what he had done. He had, he said emphatically, never suggested that the U.S. "swap bases" with the Russians, offering to remove ours from Turkey and Italy if they removed theirs from Cuba. On the contrary, he had stipulated that the unconditional removal of their missiles was prerequisite to any disarmament discussions whatever and he strongly supported the naval blockade as a first step toward achieving this removal, while opposing with equal strength any suggestion of an air strike or invasion until after the peace-keeping machinery of the UN had been given a chance to work. He had predicted, however, that Khrushchev's political reaction would include a demand that our European bases be removed, and he therefore recommended our saying that the question of foreign bases was on the agenda of disarmament talks— talks that could begin only after the Cuban bases were dismantled.

But when should we have said this, in Stevenson's opinion? The answer remains unclear. He was abruptly obliged to defend his substantive proposals against vehement attacks—attacks that became personally insulting in their implication that he was too soft and timid, too sissified for this tough he-man's world. Amidst this verbal battle, the question of the proper timing of his substantive proposals remained unexplored. He *seemed* to propose including some indication of our negotiation program in the President's Monday evening speech, or in his own speech to the Security Council on (probably) the following day. This suggestion, at any rate, was rejected by the President. Kennedy perhaps found in Stevenson's Saturday statement the same abivalence that had annoyed him in Stevenson's handwritten note of Wednesday morning. He could wholly subscribe at that moment only

* They had been forced upon the reluctant Turks and Italians by the Eisenhower administration. They were removed, without fanfare, in 1963.

to Stevenson's written remark that we "can't negotiate with a gun at our head." There should be no slightest hint that we would consider the Cuban missiles as among the objects of a package negotiation deal; there should be no slightest doubt that those missiles must be *immediately* removed or that, if they were not, we would take whatever steps were needed to render them inoperable. At the same time, according to Sorensen,[34] the President agreed that "we should beef up the political side of the speech."

Sorensen further records that, when the long session at last ended, he went with the President and Bobby Kennedy out onto the second-story back porch of the White House where, as they gazed across the south lawn, bathed in the light of the declining sun, they talked desultorily, wearily, of the afternoon's discussion. "You have to admire Adlai," the President said. "He sticks to his position even when everyone is jumping on him." [35]

But others who had participated in the meeting expressed no such admiration. Some of the hard-liners had a long-standing animus toward Stevenson ("Adlai's not soft on communism," one of them reportedly said; "he's just soft.") and they worried aloud through that weekend lest Stevenson, with his negotiating proposals rejected, make too weak a presentation of the American case before the UN. Bobby Kennedy mentioned this to Schlesinger on Sunday. On Saturday morning, Stevenson, with the President's permission, had told Schlesinger of the missile crisis (Schlesinger had theretofore had no inkling of it, so well had the secret been kept), had said that the blockade approach was certain to be adopted in his (Stevenson's) opinion, and had asked Schlesinger to help him draft the speech he must make to the Security Council early in the following week. He had outlined the argument that he felt should be made, including some of the political program he later presented in the Oval Room. On Sunday, Stevenson wrote out for Schlesinger his revised views of U.S.-UN strategy, eliminating the Turkish and Italian bases as mentionable items but retaining Guantánamo and adding a pledge that there would be no invasion of Cuba. He was not dismayed, however, when the President eliminated these last, too, as mentionable items. He "felt he had done his job as the custodian of our UN interests," writes Schlesinger, "in making the recommendation, and the decision was the President's." [36]

What happened thereafter is history known to all.

At seven o'clock on Monday evening, October 22, 1962, the President, broadcasting from his White House study, told the world of the Soviet missiles; called upon Chairman Khrushchev "to halt and eliminate this clandestine, reckless and provocative threat to world peace;" warned that "any nuclear missile launched from Cuba against any nation in the Western Hemisphere" would be deemed "an attack by the Soviet Union on the United States, requiring a full retaliatory response upon the Soviet Union;" and announced that "all ships of any kind bound for Cuba from whatever nation or port will, if found to contain cargoes of offensive weapons, be turned back."

At 7:30 that same evening, Ambassador Valerian Zorin of the Soviet Union, current President of the Security Council, received from Adlai Stevenson a formal request that the Council be called into emergency session. Attached to the request was a proposed resolution calling for the immediate dismantling and removal of Soviet missiles and bombers from Cuba under UN observation, for an end to the quarantine once the missiles were gone, and for negotiations between the United States and the Soviet Union "on measures to remove the existing threat."

Simultaneously, in Washington, the ambassadors to the U.S. from the OAS countries were briefed by the Assistant Secretary of State for Inter-American Affairs and asked to join the U.S. in the quarantine, while Dean Rusk briefed a meeting of the ambassadors of the neutral countries in an effort to gain, if not their support, at least their sympathetic understanding. The NATO countries had already been informed and asked for formal support, which was soon forthcoming.

In the late afternoon of the following day, Tuesday, October 23, Adlai Stevenson presented the American case to the UN in an eloquent and persuasive address during which he was able to announce (the news was handed him in a note while he was speaking) that the OAS had unanimously adopted a resolution "to take all measures individually and collectively, including the use of armed force, which they may deem necessary" to impose and maintain the quarantine, and demanding immediate removal of the offensive weapons. He also introduced the resolution of which a draft had been handed Zorin the day before. Zorin, having rejected the "false accusation" that his country had established offensive weapons in Cuba, countered with a draft resolution of his own condemning "the actions of the Government of the United States ... aimed at violating the United Nations Charter and at increasing the threat of war."

Next day, Wednesday, October 24, Acting Secretary General U Thant of the UN sent identical letters to Kennedy and Khrushchev suggesting on behalf of the "permanent representatives of a large number of member governments" that there be a "voluntary suspension of all arms shipments to Cuba and also ... of the quarantine measures." On Thursday, Khrushchev made affirmative reply to this letter, saying, "I declare I agree with your proposal, which accords with the interests of peace." Kennedy did not agree. He wrote U Thant that he deeply appreciated "the spirit which prompted your message" but the "threat was created by the secret introduction of offensive weapons into Cuba, and the answer lies in the removal of such weapons." He authorized Stevenson to discuss with U Thant the question of "satisfactory arrangements" for such removal, however—a move responsive to mounting evidence that Khrushchev was trying desperately to find a face-saving way out of his terrifying dilemma. For instance, by Thursday noon it appeared that at least twelve of twenty-five Soviet ships bound for Cuba had halted or turned back to avoid encountering the blockade vessels. And Khrushchev had replied to a world-publicized plea from British philosopher Bertrand Russell with the assurance that the Soviet Union would "take no reckless decisions" in the crisis. There was a slight release of the almost unbearable tension.

But the danger of nuclear war remained acute. The mood at UN head-quarters was one of dark foreboding, when, on Thursday afternoon, the Security Council met again to discuss the American complaint. Stevenson began his restatement of the American position by saying that his government welcomed "the course adopted by the Soviet Union ... to avoid direct confrontations in the zone of quarantine" and also the "assurance by Chairman Khrushchev in his letter to Earl Russell." But he deplored the assertions by Khrushchev and Zorin that the U.S. had provoked the crisis. "This is the first time I have ever heard it said that the crime is not the burglary, but the discovery of the burglar...." He defended his government against the charge that the quarantine was too extreme a response by telling a story, attributed to Abraham Lincoln, "about the passerby out in my part of the country who was charged by a farmer's ferocious boar. He picked up a pitchfork and met the boar head on. The boar died. The irate farmer denounced him and asked him why he didn't use the blunt end of the pitchfork. And the man replied, 'Why didn't the boar attack me with his blunt end?'" His tone throughout was as quietly reasonable, as free from belligerence, as his circumstances permitted.[37]

But the opposite was true of the speech of Zorin, which followed. The Soviet Ambassador, perhaps misled by the relatively mild manner and tone of Stevenson's presentation, spoke harshly, contemptuously as he accused Stevenson of shifting ground since Tuesday, of becoming defensive because the U.S. lacked evidence to prove the assertion that offensive missiles were in Cuba and because world opinion and a majority of the UN were against the U.S. action. Stevenson listened intently, jotting down a note from time to time. He was wearied by the sleep-denying anxiety and activity of the last ten days—goaded, too, by bitter memories of last Saturday's White House meeting—and when he rose to reply he let himself go in a rare display of anger. "I want to say to you, Mr. Zorin, that I do not have your talent for obfuscation, for distortion, for confusing language and double-talk," he began. "And I confess to you that I am glad that I do not!" He addressed himself directly to Zorin's charge that he had lied, that the offensive missiles "do not exist, or that we haven't proved they exist."

"All right, sir," said Stevenson, looking hard at Zorin, "let me ask you a simple question: Do you, Ambassador Zorin, deny that the U.S.S.R. has placed and is placing medium and intermediate-range missiles and sites in Cuba? Yes or no? Don't wait for the translation. Yes or no?"

"I am not in an American courtroom, sir," replied Zorin, "and therefore I do not wish to answer a question that is put to me in the fashion in which a prosecutor puts questions. In due course, sir, you will have your answer."

"You are in the courtroom of world opinion right now and you can answer *yes* or *no*. You have denied that they exist and I want to know whether I have understood you correctly."

"Continue with your statement. You will have your answer in due course."

"I am prepared to wait for my answer until hell freezes over," said Stevenson, "if that's your decision!"

But of course he didn't wait. Having thus proved that he, too, could be tough—and even at that moment he may have felt a twinge of shame at so adolescent an outburst in a situation of such gravity—he put on display before the Council, and before the world that watched TV, enlarged photographs taken by air reconnaissance of the missile sites, explaining in considerable detail what each photograph showed. The evidence was damning.

"As to the authenticity of the photography . . . I wonder if the Soviet Union would ask its Cuban colleague to permit a United Nations team to go to these sites," said Stevenson, turning again to the Soviet Ambassador. "If so, Mr. Zorin, I can assure you that we can direct them to the proper places very quickly."

He paused, then said he hoped that now they could "get down to business" and "stop this sparring."

"We know the facts and so do you, sir, and we are ready to talk about them," he concluded. "Our job here is not to score debaters' points. Our job, Mr. Zorin, is to save the peace. And if you are ready to try, we are."

Shortly thereafter, the Security Council adjourned and Stevenson left the UN building.

He was warmly congratulated by his compatriots on the manner in which he had taken care of the Soviet Ambassador. His mail in the next few days indicated that he had become something of a hero to that vast American audience whose daily TV diet is a compound of crude violence and sex-drenched commercial lying. But he himself was by no means proud of that portion of his performance that most delighted others. What had it contributed to the cause for which he labored? Nothing. If anything it had made more difficult a Soviet compliance with the American demand. He told several people that, in adopting a prosecuting attorney's role, he felt he had "gone too far." [38]

Before the Security Council met again early in the following week, the Russians had pulled back. First through unofficial channels, then through a long letter from Khrushchev to Kennedy, had come in the nick of time a proposal to dismantle the missiles and ship them back to the Soviet Union under UN supervision, provided the United States would pledge itself not to invade Cuba, with Castro in turn pledging that he would not again permit offensive weapons in his country. A second letter from Khrushchev had seemed drastically to revise this: it proposed, as Stevenson had predicted, that we dismantle our Turkish bases in return for their dismantling the Cuban ones: but Kennedy wisely decided to ignore this second letter and reply affirmatively to the first.

By Sunday night, the immediate crisis had ended.

But the hard, tedious work of liquidating the crisis cause had only begun, and the bulk of it fell to Stevenson. He was ably assisted by John J. McCloy who, as a Republican, had been appointed to the UN delegation at the height of the crisis, not only to assure a bipartisan representation and thus reduce Republican criticisms but also because McCloy was an able and experienced negotiator. He and Stevenson had need to be. Many weeks of the most intricate and nerve-fraying negotiations were required before all the missiles had been removed, all the launching sites destroyed, and all the Soviet bombers (these, unlike the missiles, had been outright gifts to Castro) also removed, all under UN inspection. It was not until January 7, 1963, that the Security Council was formally "deseized" of the issue that had been presented to it in Stevenson's resolution of the preceding October 23.

VII

Before that had happened, Stevenson had suffered a public humiliation and gone through a crisis in his relations with Kennedy.

In early December, after much advance publicity, the *Saturday Evening Post* published an article by Stewart Alsop and Charles Bartlett entitled "In Time of Crisis" purporting to give the inside story of the missile crisis. Its most sensational "disclosure" was a deliberate, malicious distortion of the part Stevenson had played and the views he had expressed. It said that, of all those involved in the decision-making process, Stevenson alone dissented from the consensus reached on Saturday afternoon, October 20. It quoted a "non-admiring official" as saying, "Adlai wanted another Munich. He wanted to trade Turkish, Italian, and British missile bases for the Cuban bases." It unmistakably implied that Schlesinger had been assigned to write the "uncompromising speech which Stevenson delivered in the UN on Tuesday" because Stevenson himself was too weak and timorous to do so; and that "tough-minded" John McCloy had been assigned to work with Stevenson in the UN negotiations for the same reason. The piece was illustrated with a full-page photograph of Stevenson looking as though he were about to burst into tears with a caption that identified him with the advocacy of another "Munich." [39]

The article made large front-page headlines even before it was available on the newsstands, and it continued to do so for weeks afterward. Newsmen generally assumed that the White House had collaborated in the article's preparation and that its intention was to force Stevenson's resignation. A Bartlett column, it was pointed out, had presaged Chester Bowles's removal from the State Department. And this view of the matter was encouraged when the White House, as it "limped to Stevenson's defense" (to quote *Time* magazine), issued a statement saying merely that he had "strongly supported the decision taken by the President" and had "brilliantly developed the U.S. position in the United Nations." This left unanswered the question of whether Stevenson had in fact dissented from the consensus on Saturday afternoon and advocated instead "another Munich." Stevenson himself, having at once publicly characterized the article as "inaccurate and grossly misrepresenting my views" and its authors as "irresponsible," was disturbed by the President's failure to back him up. He told Schlesinger, again serving as mediator between the White House and the UN Embassy, that the President need not have been so "circuitous" if his object was Stevenson's resignation. A resignation now, amidst the furor, would cause embarrassment all around. Told of this by Schlesinger, Kennedy profanely denied that he wanted Stevenson to go; he gave Stevenson private assurances of this.[40] He continued suspiciously reticent, however, concerning the part Stevenson had played in the decision-making process. Specifically asked in his press conference whether or not the Alsop-Bartlett story was "authentic," he artfully dodged the question.

But by that time (December 12) it was abundantly clear that the effort to ruin Stevenson had backfired, doing more harm to White House credibility than to the UN ambassador's prestige. Stevenson's version of what had actually happened, of the views he had actually expressed, was fully exposed to the public and proved far more persuasive than the Alsop-Bartlett version. Kennedy had been forced to make repeated public statements of his confidence in Stevenson, including the release of a personal letter to him. "The reaction was so intense and so strongly in Mr. Stevenson's favor," summarized *The New York Times*, "that the President had to keep him on, even if he had wanted otherwise." And Kennedy himself now said, in the aforementioned press conference: "The fact of the matter is that Governor Stevenson renders very distinguished service. . . . I am surprised that anyone would possibly think that it would be in the interest of the country, or the administration, or the White House, that any lessening of his influence would be provided."

In October, 1963, a volume of Stevenson's speeches since becoming UN ambassador was published under the title, *Looking Outward, Years of*

Crisis in the United Nations. It contained a preface by President John F. Kennedy. "Many crises have threatened the peace of the world since Adlai Stevenson became the United States Ambassador to the United Nations," wrote Kennedy. "The force, eloquence and courage with which he has advanced the American viewpoint have played no small part in helping to confine these crises to the council chambers where they belong.... During his presidential campaigns Governor Stevenson raised the level of our national political dialogue. As our representative in the United Nations he has similarly raised the level of the international political dialogue. The proof lies in the pages which follow."

But unhappy personal effects of the missile crisis controversy remained with Stevenson, further inhibiting his communication with Kennedy. He naturally avoided, when he could, words or acts that might encourage Kennedy's doubts of his steadfastness, his decisive courage in dangerous situations. An instance of this occurred during the week *Looking Outward* was published, perhaps contributing in a negative way to a great national tragedy....

On October 24, Stevenson was in Dallas, Texas, to deliver a United Nations Day address. He had anticipated hostile demonstrations by right-wing extremists who were evidently more numerous in Dallas, and less constrained by informed intelligence or decent manners, than they were in any other large American city. Nevertheless he was surprised by the viciousness he encountered. He was booed and heckled by a flag-waving, placard-waving segment of his audience as he rose to speak. Police had to remove one particularly vituperative demonstrator. And when Stevenson left the hall at the close of his speech he was abruptly surrounded by a mob of some eighty angry, shouting pickets who prevented police from breaking through to him and escorting him to his car. Before he could be rescued a woman had struck him on the head with her sign. She was seized by police immediately thereafter, but Stevenson requested that she not be arrested. "It's all right for you to have your own views," he said to her, as if speaking to a child, "but don't hit anyone." She muttered, "All right," and slunk away. When at last he reached his car, two young men rushed up to him and spat in his face.

He knew that the President was scheduled to visit Dallas soon. He knew that handbills had been distributed that day showing front and profile photographs of Kennedy with the caption: WANTED FOR TREASON. And now, shaken by the animal-like ferocity he had just faced, he seriously doubted that it was wise for the President to come here. He said so to Schlesinger next morning when Schlesinger talked to him by phone from Washington; there was, he said, "something very ugly and frightening about the atmosphere." But Schlesinger was, in his own words, "reluctant to pass on Stevenson's message lest it convict him of undue apprehensiveness in the

President's eyes." A day or so later Stevenson phoned Schlesinger to ask if his message had been passed on and was relieved to find that it had not.[41]

On Friday, November 22, 1963, precisely four weeks after Stevenson's visit, the President of the United States went to Dallas and was shot dead on a Dallas street.

Stevenson was in his office in the UN Mission Building when news came that the President had been shot. Immediately after the first news flash several of his closest associates entered. Someone switched on the office television. Stevenson was watching it from his desk, the others standing in stunned silence before the screen, as a newscaster announced that the wound had been fatal, the President was dead. Bill Attwood, then on temporary assignment to the Mission, turned to look at Stevenson. "For a moment he held his head in his hands; then he began quietly giving instructions on what had to be done before finally reaching for a pad and slowly writing the statement that had to be made." [42]

CHAPTER THIRTY-THREE

PRECISELY six hundred days then remained before Adlai Stevenson, too, met death on a city street. . . .

The new President would not hear of his resigning his UN post. He was prepared to do so, of course. An ambassador is a personal representative of the President, and President Lyndon Baines Johnson must appoint his own. Moreover, Stevenson had not found his embassy so great a joy that the thought of leaving it was acutely painful to him; he had, on the contrary, often wished he *could* leave honorably, with no sense of public duty flouted. But this possibility seemed closed to him—he was also personally pleased and flattered—by the vehemence with which Johnson pressed him to stay. In a long conversation in the White House, and in personal correspondence, Johnson made Stevenson feel (the new President actually convincingly said) that his continued service was indispensable to the administration and the country.[1] So Stevenson stayed.

In several respects for several months his personal relations with the White House were easier than they had been before. He felt that he and Johnson understood one another as he and Kennedy had not; he felt that Johnson valued his services as Kennedy had not. The two were of the same generation

(Johnson was by eight years Stevenson's junior) and had stood to some degree in common cause against Kennedy during the nomination campaign of 1960. Afterward they shared to some slight degree a certain wariness, a covert resentment of the relative youngster who had gained the prize they sought and from whom each of them had suffered, on occasion, personal humiliation. All this made a ground of mutual sympathy. And Stevenson admired the political adroitness and commanding will with which Johnson drove the Kennedy legislative program through a theretofore reluctant Congress. He was not at all dismayed when Johnson, in the summer of 1964, paid no heed to voices that urged him to name Stevenson as his running mate in that year's Presidential campaign. He applauded Johnson's choice, instead, of Hubert Humphrey. And he generally approved of the foreign policy statements made by Johnson during the campaign in answer to the Radical Right bellicosities of the Republican candidate, Barry Goldwater. He himself took relatively little part in the campaign that year (the primitive level to which Goldwater's nomination had lowered the national political dialogue appalled him), but he was delighted by the landslide proportions of Johnson's victory in November, accompanied as it was by the election of the most liberal Congress in decades. The very fact that Stevenson and Johnson were so different in character and intellect and natural interests— much more so than Stevenson and Kennedy had been—may have contributed something to the ease of their personal working relationship at the outset. They had wholly different styles of life and politics; they did not grade themselves by the same standards; and so they were not, in this sense, rivals, as Stevenson and Kennedy had been.

But in these differences between them lay also seeds of discord.

Certain of Johnson's personal characteristics—his Southern Baptist preacher's style of oratory; his habit of making flat assertions of sometimes dubious accuracy and then closing his lips in a tight line, as if daring his listeners to challenge him; his increasingly evident more-than-willingness to hide or twist facts in order to achieve his political objectives; his single-minded absorption in politics to the exclusion of every other human interest—were repellent to intellectuals, and particularly academic intellectuals. These had come to admire Kennedy greatly, most of them; they came to loathe Johnson, most of them. They soon saw him as a shoot-from-the-hip Texan whose intelligence was all manipulative shrewdness and whose energy was primarily physical, a man of crude manners, devoid of taste, almost as insensitive to aesthetic and moral values as the oil-and-cattle millionaires whose interests he had represented in the Senate. Those among the academic intellectuals who had accepted posts in the Kennedy administration left (or most did) as quickly as they could after Johnson entered the White House—and if their departure grieved him, he hid it well.

Stevenson was of course very far from sharing *in toto* this hostile view.

He knew it to be unfair. He told Bill Attwood a few weeks after Kennedy's assassination that, having known Johnson for thirty years, he "admired him both as a politician and as a liberal who cared deeply about the basic issues." [2] He had, however, his own doubts and fears concerning the man as President, as he had had concerning Johnson as Senate Majority Leader. And these were not lessened as, the months passing, he watched the development of a new kind of consensus politics. Johnson was an impulsive man, a sentimental man, a passionately proud man. However lacking he might be in the sensitivities admired by academics, he was abnormally sensitive to criticism and was inclined to react to it with a stubbornly defiant insistence upon, or persistence in, whatever trait or deed was criticized. He was also, as everyone knew, an awesomely energetic man who loved the exercise of power, loved to make things happen, and who depended far more upon Will than upon Idea to overcome opposition. The combination could be explosive. And the explosion could be, in a President of the United States, catastrophic for the world. Stevenson had increasing reason to worry about this as Johnson defined in action a foreign policy (or, to put it more accurately, a way of handling foreign affairs) that, despite his continuance in office of Secretary of State Rusk, was different in emphasis if not in defined goals from the one he had inherited from Kennedy. It turned out to be a policy (or way of acting) more exclusive of the UN's peacemaking and peace-keeping machinery than Kennedy's had been. Stevenson soon found that he was having considerably less effective influence on foreign affairs than he had had before, for all Johnson's repeated expressions of admiration and need of him.

II

Of all this, Vietnam, that bitter land, became the prime test and revelation. It was in the lengthening, deepening shadow of events in Vietnam that Stevenson lived out his last six hundred days....

As World War II drew to a close, Franklin Roosevelt, convinced that the age of Western colonialism was coming to an end (and a good thing, too), had strongly opposed the restoration of Indochina to the French, who had held it as a misruled colony for almost a century. He had instead proposed setting up an international trusteeship council, including on it one Russian and one Frenchman along with Chinese and Indochinese and "maybe a Filipino and an American," for the express purpose of guiding the Indochinese into self-government.[3] But this proposal was, unfortunately, the last truly wise one to be seriously made for Southeast Asia by an American President and, having of course outraged the French and been opposed by the British, it had been buried with Franklin Roosevelt in the tragic April of 1945.

The French returned to Indochina. By the fall of 1945 the Vietnamese had declared their independence from Indochina as a Democratic Republic of Vietnam, headed by Ho Chi Minh, a native Communist. Revolutionary war began, transformed into civil war when the French set up a Vietnamese government (the State of Vietnam) as a rival of Ho Chi Minh's Democratic Republic. With that war began what appeared to later critics to be an unbroken series of American blunders, each sinking us deeper into the Vietnamese quagmire.[4]

First, as part of the Truman-Acheson policy of Communist containment, the U.S. supported the French war effort in Indochina, thus tacitly aligning herself on the side of Western colonialism at a time when the tide of history ran overwhelmingly against it. When Eisenhower-Dulles took over it was obvious that the French were in dire straits, though the U.S. believed them when they said they would soon win if only they were given more aid. So the U.S. gave them more aid. Ultimately, the U.S. paid more of the monetary cost of the fighting than the French did—some one billion dollars by the summer of 1954.

Stevenson himself missed an opportunity to serve (as prophet) the cause of peace and freedom when, during his 1953 world tour, he visited strife-torn Vietnam. Here as elsewhere he perforce spent most of his time with the ruling class. He talked with French army commanders, French government officials, French-supported Vietnamese, and American diplomatic representatives. These were agreed in their statements to him that the French war effort was going better than many in the outside world believed and would succeed if a few changes were made and sufficient American aid were given. But some of Stevenson's traveling companions heard a different story from newspaper correspondents and lower-echelon French and Vietnamese. William Attwood, for one, received the general impression that the French were in fact losing the war; he hoped Stevenson would indicate as much in the article on which they worked together for *Look*.[5]

Stevenson didn't. In his hastily written piece published in the June 2, 1953, issue of *Look* under the title "Ballots and Bullets," the portion filed from Saigon opened with what was in effect a statement of the "domino theory" of the Eisenhower administration. "If Viet-Nam falls, all of Indochina is doomed," he wrote; "Thailand and Malaya would be in mortal danger . . . ; Indonesia would be exposed and vulnerable. If this vast area . . . with its 175,000,000 people, its tin, rubber, minerals, and oil, is absorbed into the Moscow-Peking empire . . . [all] Asia would slide behind the Iron Curtain." He then stressed the difficulties the French faced in the fighting war but gave no clear indication of the dire straits to which they had in fact been driven. He closed with "six measures to end the Viet-Nam war" of which the third was to build up "the Viet-Nam army . . . to meet the Communist guerrillas on their own terms and to replace French forces as rapidly as possible"; the fourth was "free elections . . . to give substance to Viet-Nam's democratic intentions and to start the process of developing responsible leaders"; and the fifth was "a land-reform program where needed."

Most of the seven articles that Stevenson contributed to *Look* during his world tour would seem, fourteen years later, to have displayed remarkable prescience. This one would not. Barely a year after it was published, the French suffered their catastrophic defeat at Dien Bien Phu and were forced to quit Indochina after nearly eight years of savage fighting.

The U.S. then actively participated in a Geneva Conference on Far Eastern Affairs (nineteen nations attended, including Russia and Communist China) which negotiated a Vietnamese cease-fire and established independent States in Laos and Cambodia. The U.S. promised to abide by, while declining to sign, the Geneva Agreement whereby: (a) Vietnam was divided along the 17th parallel between Communist North Vietnam, with its capital at Hanoi, and the originally French-sponsored democratic government of South Vietnam, with its capital at Saigon; (b) a ban was placed on any shipment of new troops or weapons and on the establishment of any new bases in the divided land.

The division, insofar as it prevented the free flow of economic goods between North and South, was greatly to the disadvantage of the former, for the feeding of the North Vietnamese required the import of some 250,000 tons of rice annually and most of it had come from the rice bowl of the Mekong Delta in South Vietnam. But by the terms of the agreement, the division was to be temporary. An International Commission of Supervision and Control (composed of Canadians, Indians, and Poles) was established to supervise not only the cease-fire but *also* free general elections by secret ballot in both North and South Vietnam, these to be held in July, 1956, for the purpose of establishing the democratic institutions of a unified Vietnamese State.

The U.S., however, promptly committed herself to the new Prime Minister of South Vietnam, Ngo Dinh Diem, who had no intention of abiding by the Geneva Agreement and indicated as much at the outset of his increasingly authoritarian regime. The commitment to begin with was economic, not military, its purpose "to assist the Government . . . in developing and maintaining a strong, viable state, capable of resisting attempted subversion or aggression through military means," as Eisenhower wrote in a letter to Diem. He added the hope or expectation that, in return, Diem would institute "needed reforms." Diem didn't. Instead he rigged an election whereby (with 98.8 percent of the vote!) he was named Head of State in place of Bao-Dai, the emperor whose prime minister he initially was. He abolished whatever democratic institutions had been established under the French, including elected village government. He suppressed opposition and silenced dissent by brutal force, made little more than token gestures toward reforms that would benefit the peasant majority, and by these means established his family as despotic rulers in the ancient oriental tradition. Simultaneously, he rebuffed every proposal from Hanoi (and they were many between mid-1954 and mid-1956) to plan the promised free elections and meanwhile reestablish normal postal and economic arrangements for the country as a whole.

Yet Washington continued to support him. He was specifically supported in his flouting of that portion of the Geneva Agreement calling for free elections. Eisenhower was convinced, as he writes in his memoirs, that "had elections been held as of the time of the fighting, possibly 80 percent of the population would have voted for Communist Ho Chi Minh . . . rather than Chief of State Bao-Dai." There was no reason to think the outcome would have been markedly different in July, 1956. The possibility (much less the probability) that Communists might win a free election was deemed sufficient justification for a refusal to hold one, though our ostensible reason was that the North Vietnamese had already violated the agreement's cease-fire provisions.*

Not surprisingly, Diem's oppressive rule provoked rebellion among the peasants who were its chief victims and who constituted a majority of the population of South Vietnam. Not surprisingly, Communists who had not gone to the north when the country was divided but had instead remained in their South Vietnamese homes became leaders of the guerrilla warfare that developed, though they seem not to have dominated it at the outset. And not surprisingly, Diem, insisting that what he faced *was* a Communist revolution directed from Hanoi, called for more aid from Washington—and got it. Primarily it was still economic aid, some 1.4 billion dollars of it by 1960, to which was added some 920 millions of military aid. With it went a few hundred military personnel as "advisers." They numbered less than 800 at the end of the Eisenhower administration, by which time the Communists of North Vietnam had formally announced their support of the South Vietnamese guerrillas (now called the Viet Cong) and were giving concrete assistance to them, largely in the form of equipment and strategic advice but also, to some extent (perhaps a few hundred a month), of men.

But this assistance, critics of U.S. policy pointed out, came from Vietnamese *to* Vietnamese and was considerably less, overall, than the U.S., of a different race, across nine thousand miles of ocean, gave a Saigon Government whose concern for human freedom and the economic welfare of the masses was not noticeably greater than Ho Chi Minh's. And the action-reaction pattern was already visible to close critical observers. So was the ultimate catastrophe toward which it pointed. Any increase in U.S. aid to

* The International Commission for Supervision and Control, reporting on its activities in 1956, said that "while the commission has experienced difficulties in North Viet-Nam, the major part of its difficulties has arisen in South Viet-Nam." 6

Saigon would provoke a proportionate increase in aid from the North for the Viet Cong. The process was one of escalating a bloody stalemate until (unless halted) the U.S. invaded North Vietnam with ground forces and there encountered the armed hordes of Red China, after which would come almost inevitably an exchange of thermonuclear bombs.

Soon after Kennedy entered the White House, he was presented with a choice between continuing this fateful pattern or substituting for it a policy and program of neutralizing all Southeast Asia. Vice-President Johnson proposed the former; the Undersecretary of State, Chester Bowles, proposed the latter. Johnson, sent on a tour of Southeast Asia in May, 1961, returned with the recommendation that we enlarge our commitment to the Saigon Government, though not to the extent of sending in American combat forces. "The country can be saved," he said, "—if we move quickly and wisely." The only alternative, in his view, was a cowardly withdrawal in violation of treaties and a return to the Fortress America concept. Bowles proposed instead that we reduce our unilateral commitment by distributing responsibility for a truly neutralized Burma, Thailand, Cambodia, Malaya, and South Vietnam among the member nations of the Southeast Asia Treaty Organization (Great Britain, France, the U.S., the Philippines, Australia, New Zealand, Pakistan, and Thailand), joined by the Soviet Union, Japan, India, and perhaps even China. Bowles felt that Russia might join in guaranteeing this neutrality in order to prevent Red Chinese domination of Southeast Asia. His proposal failed of acceptance. Kennedy chose the course Johnson recommended, a continuation of the pattern already established.[7]

So during his White House years the American commitment in South Vietnam was greatly increased. It also became increasingly military. We sent in more and more military advisers until, when Kennedy died, some 15,500 American military personnel were in the country. By then the Diem regime had been overthrown and Diem himself murdered, after Buddhist priests had begun burning themselves to death on city streets in protest against religious persecutions (Diem was a Roman Catholic)—though their protest was social and political also. A clique of military officers, headed by successive strong men, thereafter ruled in Saigon—men who resisted as strongly as Diem had done every suggestion of negotiation with the Viet Cong—though the crushing of the latter seemed, if anything, farther away than ever. Moreover, the advisory role of our military personnel now increasingly involved participation in active combat. Our men suffered casualties. And thus large portions of the American public became for the first time aware that we were in danger of becoming engaged in a full-scale war against Asians on the Asian mainland.

The American public recoiled. At least it seemed to as the Presidential election campaign of 1964 got under way. Barry Goldwater made Vietnam a campaign issue with his demands that we send American fighting units into the South and bombing planes over the North of that divided land. Johnson, in reply, deplored such calls to "reckless actions which might risk the lives of millions and engulf much of Asia." He refused, he said, to "enlarge" the conflict. "We are not going north and we are not going south," he asserted on September 28, 1964; "we are going to try to get them [the South Vietnamese] to save their own freedom with their own men, with our leadership and our officer direction, and such equipment as we can furnish them." On October 21 he said: "We are not going to send American boys nine or ten thousand miles away from home to do what Asian boys ought to be doing for themselves."

But even before he made these pledges he had in action presaged their violation. On August 2 and again on August 4, according to U.S. Department of Defense announcements, North Vietnamese PT boats made "unprovoked" attacks on U.S. Navy destroyers patrolling the Bay of Tonkin off the shores of North Vietnam. (It seems that South Vietnamese naval craft were attacking a couple of North Vietnamese islands, which two U.S. destroyers were near on August 2.) At least three of the PT boats were destroyed. The ships suffered no damage and there were no American casualties. But Johnson reacted with the wrath of Achilles, terrible in immediate effect and terrifying in its implications for the future. He ordered a series of reprisal air strikes on North Vietnamese shore installations, which left them in smoking ruins. And while the strikes were being made, near midnight EST of August 4, he made a nationwide TV broadcast in which he announced dramatically, ominously that "repeated acts of violence against the armed forces of the United States must be met ... with positive reply" and that "that reply is now in execution. ..."

By Election Day he had nearly decided, if in fact he had not already decided,* to order bombing attacks on North Vietnam as his Republican opponent and his own military advisers were vehemently recommending. Certainly this decision was made within a few weeks after the election, weeks during which (the American people were *later* told) the situation in South Vietnam so far deteriorated that a definite military commitment by the U.S. was required to prevent a total collapse. Bombing of the North was ordered in February, 1965; American combat forces were sent into South Vietnam in March; and by midsummer some 125,000 American troops were there. But still there was no sign of victory, no evidence whatever that the wholesale slaughter of Vietnamese in which the U.S. now engaged (the kill-ratio ran some 20 to 1 in our favor according to official communiqués)

* One journalist, Charles Roberts, White House correspondent of *Newsweek* magazine, says Johnson told him in May, 1965, that he, the President, "had made the momentous *decision* [Roberts' italics] to bomb North Vietnam ... in October, 1964, at the height of the Presidential campaign." See Roberts' *LBJ's Inner Circle* (New York: 1965), p. 20. Schlesinger, Jr., quotes Roberts on p. 30 of his *The Bitter Heritage* (Boston: 1967).

was weakening the enemy's fighting effort or his will to go on fighting. Hanoi reacted to our increasing commitment with an increasing commitment of its own in the South. The bloody stalemate continued, continuously escalating. . . .

III

And in the United States, an outraged intellectual community rose up in protest. Few indeed were the politically-minded writers, artists, scientists, or teachers who did not hate what we were doing in Vietnam. They turned to Adlai Stevenson; they hoped he would be their champion. In private and public communications they called upon him to resign his UN post and speak out against the "lying and brutality" which "defame us and you."

The quotations are of Paul Goodman who was chief spokesman of a small group of writers (Dwight Macdonald, Harvey Swados, two or three others) who visited Stevenson at the UN Mission in June, 1965.[8] They presented their case against our Vietnam involvement with all the force of their deeply-held conscientious convictions. They assumed that Stevenson must feel, deep down, as they did but of course could not say so as long as he remained UN ambassador. He gave them a highly respectful hearing. He was obviously troubled in his own mind. But his response disappointed them. Though he made no great show of it, he resented the implication that, in defending our foreign policies in the UN and in other public speeches, he said things he did not believe true or pretended personal convictions he did not hold—that he was, in brief, an official liar. He also felt that the course that Goodman and the others urged upon him would be, in the circumstances, personally dishonorable. He was, he said (according to Goodman), "on the team" and "it is not the way we play the game, to quit to make a point."

Nevertheless, he had by then virtually decided to quit in a few weeks (before the opening of the next General Assembly in September) or at most in a few months (after the Assembly had adjourned). And a major factor in his decision was his increasing sense of frustration in his job.

He had been angered the previous year when, amidst a European tour, he was abruptly ordered home to make a much-publicized major speech on Southeast Asia in the UN's Security Council.[9] The speech was not of his own composition (its typically flat, limp prose had come out of the State Department and had been approved by Johnson); he had not been consulted during its preparation; and it announced no new departures from a policy concerning which he had some reservations. He was but a mouthpiece (another would have served as well) when, having arrived in New York from London the preceding day, he told the Security Council on May 21, 1964, that the U.S. would back the fight against Communist subversion in Southeast Asia as long as the people there "ask for our help" and that the U.S. was opposed to calling a new fourteen-power Geneva Conference to work out new Southeast Asian agreements. (It was more important, said Stevenson-as-mouthpiece, that the agreements already signed be honored.) Unwelcome, too, had been the necessity, ten weeks later, to defend in the UN the reprisal bombing of North Vietnam—he described it as a necessary "act of defense"—following the Bay of Tonkin incidents.

Frustration had thereafter been compounded.

On August 5, within hours after the reprisal bombing, UN Secretary General U Thant called at the White House to visit the President, a visit that had been scheduled before the Tonkin shooting incidents occurred. Before reporters, Johnson assured Thant that the U.S. was dedicated to world peace. "In all that we do," said he, "America's purpose is to prevent war and to prevent others from provoking war." But of course, he added, this "nation has acted and this nation will always act when necessary in self-defense." The two men then had a lengthy private talk from which Thant emerged without comment to reporters on what had been said. He did say that the UN Security Council, in his opinion, could not be "usefully employed" at that time "in a settlement" of the Southeast Asian crisis because of the "nature of the dispute" and because North Vietnam was not a UN member.

He was determined to do what he could, however, in his UN capacity, to halt the fighting, and later that same month, visiting Rangoon in his native Burma, he had communication with Ho Chi Minh. The President of North Vietnam, it was revealed to the public long afterward, indicated his willingness to engage in private talks with the U.S., through emissaries meeting in Rangoon, in an effort to achieve a Vietnam peace, as Thant had proposed. Thant promptly informed Stevenson of this and Stevenson informed Washington where officials decided that such talks should not be held in the midst of an election campaign in which Vietnam was a principal issue. This reaction was, presumably, passed on by Thant to Hanoi.

Then, in the winter, the election over, U Thant tried again to arrange talks and again obtained acceptance from Hanoi. According to one story,[10] published nearly two years later, Stevenson and U Thant, on their own initiative, set up as far as it was possible for them to do so a meeting to be held in Rangoon on the ambassadorial level. Stevenson informed Washington on January 18, 1965, that all arrangements were completed, awaiting U.S. concurrence and the naming of our emissary. Ten days of silence then passed. Finally, on January 28, Washington replied, negatively, and U Thant "was furious," according to another report by Eric Sevareid, published in late November, 1965. Sevareid, reporting a long private conversation he had with Stevenson on the night of July 12, 1965, in London, goes on to say: "... Secretary of Defense Robert McNamara ... flatly opposed the attempt. He said that the South Vietnamese government would have to be informed and that this would have a demoralizing effect on them; that government is shaky enough, as it is." Even then, U Thant did not cease his peacemaking efforts. He suggested an outright cease-fire proposal by the UN, going so far as to pledge himself to announce the offer in precisely the language dictated by the U.S. if Washington would only "write the terms . . . exactly as they saw fit." Writes Sevareid: "Again, so Stevenson told me, McNamara turned this down, and from Secretary Rusk there was no response, to Stevenson's knowledge." [11]

In the spring had come another frustration, another disappointment.

On a day in early May, Stevenson had been one of a group of high officials meeting with the President in his White House office. Others there included Rusk, McGeorge Bundy (who yet remained as Special Presidential Assistant), and Vice-President Hubert Humphrey. They met to consider the crisis that had arisen in the Dominican Republic, long (under Trujillo) America's bloody doorstep in the Caribbean, where civil strife, a rebellion against the legally-constituted government, was reportedly endangering the lives of American citizens and other foreigners. Johnson read aloud to the group the radio-TV statement he was to make within hours, announcing that a small detachment of U.S. Marines was being dispatched to the Dominican Republic to rescue imperiled foreigners. Stevenson, assuming (as he must) that the reports from the strife-torn island were accurate, had no objection to a rescue mission, but he was disturbed by a sentence in the President's statement to the effect that the U.S. stood ever ready to help the Dominican Republic to preserve its freedom. He asked what that meant. Was this to be a strictly limited rescue operation or was it to be a full-scale armed intervention in Dominican Republic affairs? By his own later account, he received no direct answer to his direct question, and no support from others in the room, who seemed intimidated by Johnson. But the President himself finally said to Stevenson, "I think you're right," and drew a line through the questionable sentence.[12] But a few days later, Stevenson watched and listened with dismay as the President of the United States, on TV, announced that we *were* intervening, and massively (we sent in no fewer than 20,000 marines), to put down a Communist-led rebellion and prevent the Dominican Republic from becoming "another Cuba." He did not believe at the time, he never did believe, that this action was justified. Indeed, two months later, in a private, presumably off-the-record talk with correspondent David Schoenbrun in Paris, he termed it a "massive blunder." * But he nevertheless had to defend the action in public speech at the UN.

---

* Schoenbrun broadcast to the world Stevenson's statement on the evening of July 14, 1965, and called down upon his head the wrath of the White House. Johnson deemed the broadcast a "disservice" to the memory of a man whom death had silenced and who could therefore make no correction of the quotation.

A few days after the visit to him by Paul Goodman and the other writers, he again suffered personal humiliation. At least he felt it so. The President had asked him to draft the speech that he, the President, was to make in San Francisco on the twentieth anniversary of the adoption of the UN Charter, at the close of the 1945 San Francisco Conference. Stevenson worked hard on this assignment, including in his draft several specific proposals that seemed to him indicated by our basic policies. He perhaps leaked these to a newspaper friend inadvertently, hence without proper off-the-record safeguards, when his draft went to the White House, for he remained extremely careless of security in such matters—though one must add that, on occasion, his seeming indiscretions were carefully calculated. At any rate, James Reston's column in *The New York Times* predicted with remarkable accuracy the proposals Johnson would make in San Francisco, whereupon Johnson (presumably for this reason) refused to make them. He ordered the speech rewritten in Washington and gave orders that the final draft be shown no one, *including* (he made a point of it) Adlai Stevenson. And Stevenson was told this by a Presidential assistant when he called the White House to ask that the final draft of the speech be read to him.

He laughed about it, however, and made others laugh with him when, having accompanied the President to San Francisco for the June 26 ceremony, he talked with friends at a party in his honor at the home of his son John Fell. He seemed to them still a supremely happy man, as overflowing with zestful energy and as funny as ever. . . .

IV

The accumulated frustrations of his job, however, were not the sole factor in his decision to resign soon. For all his fervid gaiety, his display of seemingly inexhaustible physical energy, he was now very tired, weary to the point of exhaustion in his deepest self. He spoke with increasing frequency of his weariness—to his sons, to Buffie, to his intimate friends. He said to Sevareid that "for awhile I'd really just like to sit in the shade with a glass of wine in my hand and watch the people dance." To Sevareid and others he spoke of returning to Libertyville and writing his memoirs. Later, some among his intimates wondered if he hadn't known, deep down, that death was near and chosen quite deliberately to defy it—with laughter, with assertive activity.

Certainly he had objective reasons for doubt that his health was fundamentally sound as he entered upon the last months of his life. Marietta Tree knew that for a year or more he had had occasional attacks of what he laughingly called the "flutters"—an erratic throbbing of his heart.[13] But he refused to make the slightest concession to what might be a dangerous condition. He seemed to think that health rules just didn't apply to him: he had been so often warned of dire consequences that did not occur, and he always (almost always) felt so good physically. It was hard for him to believe that he could ever be seriously ill. She later remembered with special vividness a hot steamy September day in 1964 when she and he were among some fifty guests on a country estate near New York. He ate an enormous lunch, including four or five ears of corn dripping in butter, then took papers out in the sun where he worked on them, then played three sets of tennis, went swimming, and had three bourbon highballs before a late dinner. He, who was normally of ruddy complexion, became pasty pale and, immediately after dinner, went upstairs to bed, which was very unlike him.

There were other signs. A cardiograph taken during his last visit to a doctor in New York, late in 1964, was definitely "not good," as Roxane Eberline knew, though he seems never to have mentioned it to anyone else. Appointments were made again and again for his return to the doctor, for further examination, but something always came up to cause, or excuse, his breaking them. In late May of 1965, flying to Canada with his son Borden beside him, he suddenly looked up over his glasses (as usual, he'd been working with papers in his lap) and said: "You know, Borden, I have a heart problem." Borden was shocked; he waited for his father to say more, but his father didn't.[14]

Yet from Toronto (this was when Stevenson received his honorary degree from the university there) he made repeated attempts to reach by phone Arthur Schlesinger, Jr., who was in Washington hard at work on his memoirs of Kennedy in the White House, in order to set up a tennis doubles match to be played when he came down to Washington to narrate, as he had done in New York, Copland's *A Lincoln Portrait*. Schlesinger, when they finally made contact, did as Stevenson wished, and on a Sunday afternoon Schlesinger and his wife played Stevenson and Lani Stern (wife of Phil Stern) on the Stern court. Schlesinger was impressed by how *hard* Stevenson played....[15]

He was scheduled to go to Geneva in the second week of July to speak at a UN Economic and Social Council meeting open to the public. He didn't want to go; he grumbled about it. But of course he went, and on Friday, July 9, he gave an address, originally drafted by Barbara Ward (Lady Jackson), on the problems of urbanization throughout the world, which was enthusiastically received by his immediate audience and, next morning, was fully reported on the front page of the international edition of *The New York Times*. While in Geneva he phoned Buffie Ives who, with Ernest, was in the villa they rented every year outside Florence, Italy. He asked her what they were doing and she said they had just visited some Etruscan excavations. "That sounds great!" he said enviously (he could hardly bear it when others saw sights denied him). "I'm going to try to get down there. I'll fly down from London if I don't have to go home." [16] He was in high spirits when, on the day after his speech, he met Bill Benton in London and went with him to Chequers, the official country residence of the British Prime Minister, Harold Wilson. The two spent all afternoon there. He slept that night in the American Embassy residence in London and tried, Sunday morning, to arrange a tennis match with U.S. Ambassador David Bruce and Benton. ("The Ambassador and I laughed at him," Benton later wrote; "we were too tired. He asked Mrs. Bruce for tennis each day during his five days with the Bruces. . . ." [17] Stevenson and Benton lunched that day with Lady Spears, the former Mary Borden, Ellen's aunt, and then went on to Oxford to dine with Lord Franks, provost of Worcester College, Stevenson being a fellow of that college. On the following day, Monday, July 12, he was again in London where, in the evening, he was interviewed on the BBC concerning American foreign policy, stating as well as he could the basic case for such containment actions as our intervention in Vietnam and the Dominican Republic and answering newspaper reporter's questions afterward (not for direct quotation) with a candor and humility that won them completely.

On that same Monday he asked Marietta Tree to buy a copy of a book by J. C. (Sir John) Masterson entitled *Bits and Pieces*, published by Hodder and Stoughton, and to send it to Sir John for a personal inscription. (The note in which Stevenson wrote down the author, title, and publisher was the last she ever had from him.) Sir John, a don of Worcester College, had been his dinner companion at Lord Frank's, he explained—"a thoroughly delightful man, hale and hearty in his 80's."

Vietnam was very much on his troubled mind during these last days. He had received from Paul Goodman a letter that was a follow-up of the visit Goodman and the other writers had paid him in his New York office. In his letter, Goodman again urged Stevenson to resign his UN Ambassadorship in protest against the "disastrous trend of American foreign policy" and then rally public opinion against it while exposing the "lies" being told the American people. The letter profoundly disturbed its recipient. He had written out in his tight small script an answer to it—a long answer. He had had this typed, and had then gone over the typescript, making longhand corrections, deletions, revisions, before confiding it to his good friend Phil Kaiser, the American Minister in London, whom he asked for comments on it. He was obviously not satisfied with it, and it was destined never to be mailed.[18]

He denied, in this draft, that he shared Goodman's "pre-supposition" concerning foreign policy, and tried to summarize "my reasons for believing that, whatever criticisms may be made over the detail and emphasis of

American foreign policy, its purpose and direction are sound. Our over-riding purpose," he went on, "must be to avoid war. Yet we still live in a state of international anarchy [he drew a line through the last four words when he revised] in which each nation claims absolute sover-eignty...." In such a world, he believed, "the ultimate catastrophe of atomic conflict can be avoided... only by the pursuit of two lines of policy. The *first* is to establish a tacitly agreed frontier between Communist and anti-Communist areas of influence on the understanding that neither power system will use force to change the status quo.... The *second* is to move from this position of precarious stability toward agreed interna-tional procedures for settling differences, toward the building of an inter-national juridical and policing system and toward a whole variety of policies designed to turn our small vulnerable planet into a genuine economic and social community. If you like, the first policy is static and defensive, the second creative and constructive. Both have to be pursued together."

He then described the period from 1947 to 1962 as "largely occupied" with drawing the line between Western and Soviet power. "It is not a very satisfactory one since it divides Germany and Berlin. But the Russians respect it in Europe. So do we." We had, however, no such line with the Communist Chinese, who had proved to be a "very aggressive" expansionist power. Vietnam, like Korea, was an attempt to draw that line and, whether or not the 17th parallel was the best place for it, that was "the line in-herited by the Democratic Administration.... History does not always give us the most convenient choices." It was his "hope in Viet Nam that rela-tively small scale resistance now may establish the fact that changes in Asia are not to be precipitated by outside force. This was the point of the Korean War. This is the point of the conflict in Viet Nam. I believe Asia will be more stable if the outcome is the same in both—a negotiated line and a negotiated peace—a just and honorable peace which leaves the future of the people of South Viet Nam to be decided by them and not by force from North Viet Nam."

This brought him, as he said, to

> my second point—the hope of transcending the static policy of "con-tainment" and moving on to the more creative tasks of building a world security based on law and peaceful settlement. I believe that we must seek a negotiated peace in Viet Nam based upon the internationalization of the whole area's security, on a big effort to develop, under the UN, the resources of the Mekong River and [*sic*] guarantees that Viet Nam, North and South can choose, again under international supervision, the kind of governments, the form of association and, if [they?] so decree, the type of reunification of the two states they genuinely want to estab-lish. If we can achieve this, we begin to offer the small states of the world an alternative to being within spheres of influence. We are more

decisively beyond the age of empires. We would begin to establish procedures by which local revolutionary movements such as the rising in Dominican Republic, and for that matter Zanzibar, are *not* automatically a prey to outside intervention. . . . It is my conviction that American policy is groping its way toward this difficult but essential ideal, and this is the reason both for my support of the policy and for my continuance in a position which gives me some hope of assisting its advance in that direction.

He admitted that "it is possible for honest men to differ on every aspect of this interpretation. . . . I do not impugn the good faith of those who hold different views. I would only ask them, in the name of the courtesies and decencies of a free society, that they should equally refrain from impugning mine."

On Wednesday, July 14, Stevenson and Robert Hutchins, the former president of the University of Chicago, latterly of the Fund for the Republic, both of whom were *Encyclopaedia Britannica* directors, were guests of honor at a luncheon given at Claridge's Hotel, in London, by Benton and Mrs. Benton. Others present were officers of the London *Britannica* office, with their wives. At four in the afternoon, Stevenson met Marietta Tree at the American Embassy in Grosvenor Square.[19] He held a small press conference there, after which he had a couple of hours or so of free time before his evening engagements. He asked Mrs. Tree to come with him for a walk; he had long wanted, he said, to see again the house where he had lived during the UNO Preparatory Commission days in the latter half of 1945. He and Ellen, with Adlai III, and Borden, had been very happy there at No 2 Mount Row, and he would like to show the place to Marietta. After all, a certain amount of early UN history had been made in that house. Alas, he found that it had been torn down; a new building stood on its site.

"It makes me feel old," he said, sadly.

They continued their walk. He talked of what he would do after he had resigned his UN post—he indicated that he had now definitely decided to quit after the next General Assembly adjourned, provided there was no crisis requiring him to stay longer—and mentioned some of the job offers that had come to him. One of the offers was that of czar of the movies, the old Hays Office position, which carried a fantastically high salary and all sorts of perquisites. He asked her advice. But she had learned long ago that advising him on such matters was risky and needless. She *never* gave him advice. Then, suddenly, he made remarks critical of her posture as she walked.

"Keep your head up," he chided her. "Don't slouch!"

They walked along Upper Grosvenor Street where they encountered three teen-agers sauntering along side by side, taking up the whole narrow sidewalk. Both of them went into the gutter to circle the youngsters, Mrs. Tree walking ahead of Stevenson who soon complained, "You're going too fast for me." This was a complaint often voiced by her walking companions; she was one of the fastest walkers in New York, where everyone walks fast. She slowed her pace. But she continued to walk a little way ahead of him. They were walking along an iron picket fence in front of the Sportsman's Club (as she later learned) when, suddenly, Stevenson said in a strange voice, "I feel faint." She turned to look at him. His face was a ghastly gray. She thought she saw, through a gate in the fence, a box, an orange crate, perhaps, and she turned away and was hurrying to get it when she heard behind her the horrible sound of flesh and bone striking concrete, hard. Stevenson had fallen backward. He lay on the sidewalk, his face ashen, his eyes wide open. She ran into the club and asked someone there to call a doctor immediately, and to call Phil Kaiser at the embassy, then came back to find that some man, a passerby, was lifting Stevenson's head to put a coat under it, which frightened her, for she feared he had cracked his skull when he fell and was sure that moving his head in that way was a very bad thing to do.

Then a man came up who said he was a doctor and who, diagnosing a heart attack, began to massage Stevenson's heart, meanwhile asking if there was anyone there who would give the prone man artificial respiration by breathing into his mouth. Marietta Tree said she would, and she did, after the doctor had shown her how (the "kiss of life," London newspapers called it), and in a moment or two Stevenson started to breathe in great long shuddering breaths—a horrible sobbing sound. Very soon thereafter the doctor who had been summoned by phone came. He had his bag with him and immediately gave Stevenson injections. The great shuddering breathing continued—later Mrs. Tree was told that he may actually have been dead then, that the awful breathing was but reflex action—until an ambulance came and, after an oxygen mask had been placed over his face, he was lifted into it.

She was about to climb in to sit beside him when, looking back, she saw scattered over the sidewalk, from the manila folder Stevenson had been carrying, classified ("Secret") documents that, according to regulations, should never have been taken from the embassy. Later, some who heard of this thought it not only typical of the man but also symbolic of the role he had played in history. It was as if he, prophet of world community under world law, thus expressed in the last instant of his life his contempt for the "I-Spy" kind of "security" that accompanies an outmoded, dangerously anachronistic kind of nationalism. But Mrs. Tree, who must go on living in the world as it is and who (like all his close associates) was in the habit of picking up after him, protecting him and the

Mission against such indiscretions, quickly gathered up the papers and took them with her in the ambulance to St. George's Hospital.

Four or five minutes after Stevenson had been carried into the hospital an official there told Mrs. Tree that he was dead. She asked to see him— she was broken, distraught—and was gently dissuaded. "You want to remember him as he was in life, don't you?"

v

And millions all over the world—remembering him as he was in life, shocked by his sudden death at a time when the Vietnamese war was being vastly escalated—mourned his passing as a personal loss. In every quarter of the land there was sudden realization that, in twice (or thrice) rejecting this man's offer to serve as President, the American people may have missed opportunities for greatness that will not come soon again. In every quarter of the globe there was realization that the world's hope of civilized survival was diminished by the silencing of this voice of sweet reasonableness. Who now could speak as he had spoken for man and the human city?

The President of the United States dispatched to London the Presidential plane to bring home Adlai Stevenson's body. Aboard were the three Stevenson sons, and Buffie's son, Timothy Ives, with the wives of Adlai III and John Fell; Secretary of Labor Wirtz; Ralph J. Bunche, UN Undersecretary for Political Affairs; Mayor Daley of Chicago; and an official delegation of Republican and Democratic Senators and Representatives headed by Vice-President Humphrey. Buffie and Ernest Ives, summoned from Florence, boarded the plane in London, returning with the body. So did Marietta Tree, Lady Spears, Mrs. Marshall Field, and William Benton. The plane touched down at Andrews Air Base, fifteen miles from Washington, early in the evening of Thursday, July 15.

Waiting at the airfield were the President, Secretary of the Treasury Henry H. Fowler, Secretary of the Interior Stewart Udall, Attorney General Nicholas deB. Katzenbach, and the British Ambassador to the United States, Sir Patrick Dean. The President stood at the foot of the ramp as the plane emptied, shaking hands with the three sons and their wives, with Buffie and Ernest, and then the others. An honor guard composed of two general officers from each of the armed services lifted the coffin (a plain coffin of white mahogany, an American flag draped over it) from the plane's hold and carried it on their shoulders through a cordon of enlisted men standing at rigid attention. As they slowly marched to the nearby hearse, the Air Force band sounded four ruffles and flourishes and then played, slowly, softly, the trio of "The Stars and Stripes Forever."

The body was taken to the National Cathedral in Washington and placed in the Bethlehem Chapel there. Thousands of mourners filed past the coffin that night and next morning (Friday, July 16) until, at 10 o'clock, two Army noncommissioned officers in dress uniform wheeled the coffin from the Chapel to the Cathedral's Great Crossing. There Adlai Stevenson was given a national funeral.

By 11 o'clock the north and south transepts and the cathedral's unfinished nave were filled with distinguished people: Senators and Representatives, Justices of the Supreme Court, members of the diplomatic corps, the U.S. Joint Chiefs of Staff: and a few minutes after eleven, members of the immediate family entered, taking seats in the first two rows on the right side of the nave looking toward the altar. Then entered President and Mrs. Johnson (she had flown back from Texas for the service) with their daughter, Luci Baines; Vice-President and Mrs. Humphrey; and the cabinet members and their wives. The funeral service was in the tradition of the Stevenson family, conducted according to the Book of Common Worship of the United Presbyterian Church by Stevenson's old friend, Dr. Richard H. Graebel, pastor of the First Presbyterian Church of Springfield, Illinois. The eulogy was given by Carl McGowan, who was now a Judge of the U.S. Circuit Court of Appeals in Washington. His words seemed to some who heard them unnaturally cold, devoid of emotion, but they were such words as would have pleased Stevenson himself, coming from a man he admired as he did few others. For McGowan praised the reasonableness of his departed friend, a "completely civilized man" who had done battle for "the persistence of the very idea of civilization." The "Battle Hymn of the Republic" was sung.

After the service, the body was flown in the Presidential plane to Springfield, Illinois, where the Governor of Illinois, Otto Kerner, headed a waiting delegation of high state officials.

There now began to sound solemn echoes of the death and funeral of Abraham Lincoln, one hundred years before. Under the hot prairie sun, while a nineteen-gun salute was fired by a howitzer of the 33rd Infantry Division, Adlai Stevenson's coffin was carried to a hearse provided by the Smith Funeral Chapel whence, in the lilac spring of 1865, had come the coffin for Abraham Lincoln; and as the eighteen-car funeral procession passed through Springfield's Oak Ridge Cemetery on the way to the state capitol, the hearse and three cars bearing Stevenson's immediate family detoured in order to drive by the Lincoln tomb. The coffin was carried into the rotunda of the Illinois capitol. It was placed there on the catafalque that had borne home from Washington, a century before, the body of Abraham Lincoln. And from mid-afternoon that day until ten o'clock Sunday morning, July 18, save for a brief period on Saturday morning when a memorial service was held for the family and invited guests, the body of Adlai Stevenson lay in state under the 361-foot-high dome of the capitol while people filed by, thousands of them in a steady stream, paying silent tribute.

Sunday was a hot, sunny day, the kind of day when "you can hear the corn grow," as farmers in the Corn Belt say—and since the rains had been good that year, green new-tasseled corn grew more than head-high in endless fields along U.S. Highway 66 as the Stevenson funeral cortege drove northeastward from Springfield to Bloomington. They crossed the Sangamon River on whose banks, at New Salem, young Abe Lincoln had made his start in life. Soon after, they passed out of Sangamon County, which neither Lincoln nor Stevenson had been able to carry in their Presidential election campaigns. They slanted across Logan County through the county seat town, which was named for Lincoln while he was yet alive, along with a college there, to his great pride. Then they were in McLean County, still the second richest agricultural county in the nation, of which Bloomington is county seat. Slowly they drove along Bloomington's streets, lined with thousands of people, to the small Unitarian Church on a rise of ground at the edge of town, and there the body of Adlai Stevenson was carried into the church's Jesse Fell Assembly Room to lie in state until the final funeral services next morning.

The family plans had been to make this last service a small private one, an intimate farewell after the great public ceremonies, but the plans had to be changed when the White House announced that President and Mrs. Johnson would fly out from Washington to be present at the final rites. The Presidential plane arrived at Chanute Field in Rantoul, some fifty miles from Bloomington, shortly before ten o'clock Monday morning, July 19, bearing the President, three of his aides, his wife, Mr. and Mrs. John Steinbeck (who had been weekend guests of the Johnsons), and Chief Justice Earl Warren of the Supreme Court, with Mrs. Warren. Vice-President and Mrs. Humphrey flew in, too, from Minnesota, where they had spent the weekend. All were met by Governor Kerner and Secretary Wirtz at Chanute whence all were taken, in three helicopters, from that field to the small airport at Bloomington. Of course many thousands were gathered to see the President, though he did all he could to remain unobtrusive, to keep this as the family wished it to be, a private service.

It was held in the church sanctuary, which seated only 150 people, with the church's pastor, the Reverend Robert Reed, officiating. The Stevenson family sat on the right side of the aisle in the front row of seats. The President and his wife, the Vice-President and his wife, the Chief Justice and his wife, sat in front at the left side of the aisle. The service itself was starkly simple, yet deeply moving. Twenty-one selected members of the children's choir of Chicago's First Unitarian Church, clothed in red robes, sang without accompaniment, "O God, Our Help in Ages Past." Adlai Stevenson's cousin, the Reverend Martin D. Hardin, associate minister of the Presbyterian Church of Buffalo, read the Biblical verses most often heard at funerals. The Reverend Dr. Reed read selections from Stevenson's writings following which Dr. Dana McLean Greeley, president of the Unitarian Universalist Association, read a beautifully written and profoundly moving tribute. Then the Children's Choir, wherein were represented many races and nationalities, sang "The Parliament of Man."

Came then the last funeral procession, the very last, a three-mile journey through crowd-lined Bloomington streets to the Evergreen Cemetery where an open grave awaited the body, not far from the grave of the first Adlai Ewing Stevenson. Here, too, the service was of the simplest. Doctor Reed read a prayer of St. Francis of Assissi that Stevenson himself had often read, the prayer which begins, "Lord, make me an instrument of your peace." He then led those assembled in the Lord's prayer. Just before the coffin was lowered into the grave, the military pallbearers lifted the flag that had covered it, folded it with ritual precision, and gave it to a Negro captain. The captain gave it to a white lieutenant colonel, who then carried it to Mrs. Ives. Buffie stood to receive it, then sat with it in her lap, weeping quietly before turning to hand it to Borden, who was beside her....[20]

Simultaneously there was held at the United Nations in New York, in the Assembly Hall, a memorial service for Adlai Stevenson, attended by many of the great of New York, of the nation, of the UN. Archibald MacLeish spoke there, saying: "What we have lost, as he said of his friend Mrs. Roosevelt, is not his life. He lived that out, if not to the full, at least more fully than almost any other man. What we have lost is himself. And who can name the warmth and richness of it?" Secretary Dean Rusk spoke, and with an eloquence that surprised. "Three Presidents of the United States sent Adlai Stevenson to the United Nations," he said. "They sent you our best." He also said, as many had said, that Adlai Stevenson was "a universal man.... But not merely because he was informed, well-traveled, urbane, sophisticated, eloquent and gifted; he was all of these. But his universality did not rest upon his being a prince among plain men, but upon his being a plain man among princes. His was the simplicity of fundamental human values—with what is permanent in the midst of change: the love of peace; the instinct of tolerance; the feeling of compassion; the devotion to human rights; the urge to act for human welfare."

When the ceremony ended, the presiding officer's final words were, "The memory and influence of Adlai Stevenson have not ended." Then the hall slowly emptied; the hundreds there who remembered, who were to some degree influenced, went out into New York's crowded roaring streets. And some there were who walked for a time unaware, as if in a silent lonely place, before turning again to the business and the busy-ness of their daily lives....

The memory remains.

NOTES

Chapter One

[1] The portrait of Lewis Green Stevenson and his family, and the story of Adlai Stevenson's maternal and paternal ancestry, derives much from lengthy interviews conducted in 1955 and '56 with Mrs. Ernest Ives, Miss Letitia Stevenson, Mrs. Martin D. (Julia) Hardin, Mr. and Mrs. Carl Vrooman, Mr. Loring Merwin, Dr. E. M. Stevenson, Miss Alverta Duff, and Adlai E. Stevenson. Also used were a Stevenson family album and files of the Bloomington (Ill.) *Pantagraph*.

[2] Adlai Ewing Stevenson, *Something of Men I Have Known* (Chicago, 1909), p. 22.

[3] Allan Nevins, *Grover Cleveland* (New York, 1933), pp. 528-33.

[4] The house is kept much as it was when Adlai Stevenson was a child and the description of it is from direct observation, modified by information from him and Mrs. Ives.

[5] Harriet Fyffe Richardson, *Quaker Pioneers* (privately printed, 1940), gives information on Mrs. Helen Davis Stevenson's maternal ancestry.

Chapter Two

[1] The most useful source of information on the Stevenson ancestry is a "Family History" incorporated in *A History and Genealogical Record of the Stevenson Family, From 1748 to 1926*, by the Rev. Samuel Harris Stevenson, the Rev. J. A. Harris, and the Hon. W. F. Stevenson (privately printed, evidently in 1926), pp. 13-22. The "Introduction" to this work, by the Reverend Stevenson, pp. 3-6, also is valuable as source material. The bulk of the book is a genealogy of the various branches of the Stevenson family.

[2] *Ibid.*, p. 20.

[3] Thomas Marshall Green, *Historic Families of Kentucky, First Series* (Cincinnati, 1889), tells, pp. 155-57, of the Willis Green and Joshua Fry families.

[4] Interview with Mrs. Martin D. [Julia Stevenson] Hardin in 1956.

[5] Francis Milton I. Morehouse, *The Life of Jesse W. Fell* (Urbana, Ill., 1916) is the major printed source of information herein on Fell.

[6] *Ibid.*, p. 71. The story of the Reverend Ellis is on pp. 71-72.

[7] *Ibid.*, pp. 57-62, tells of Fell's promotion of Lincoln's candidacy for the Presidency, including the writing of the famous autobiographical sketch. Harriet Fyffe Richardson, *Quaker Pioneers* (privately printed, 1940) tells the story on pp. 14-15, and her pp. 17-20 consist of a facsimile reproduction of Lincoln's cover letter and of the sketch itself, both in Lincoln's handwriting. Carl Sandburg, *Abraham Lincoln: The Prairie Years* (New York, 1926), pp. 176-77, condenses an account

of the episode written and printed by Jesse W. Fell in 1872. Robert Dale Richardson, *Abraham Lincoln's Autobiography* (Boston, 1947) gives valuable information on Fell's relations with Lincoln.

[8] Richardson's *Quaker Pioneers*, pp. 73-74, tells of the moving of the house and has a photograph of it as it was before the cupola and veranda were destroyed.

[9] Conversation with Adlai E. Stevenson, Christmas Day, 1955.

[10] Morehouse, *op. cit.*, p. 18, quoting a letter from Grace Harwood to Fannie Fell, March 16, 1913.

Chapter Three

[1] Interviews with Adlai E. Stevenson, Mrs. Ernest Ives, Mr. and Mrs. Carl Vrooman, 1956. Mrs. Ives made available to me family papers—letters, etc.—on which much of my account of Adlai Stevenson's boyhood is based.

[2] Interview with Joseph F. Bohrer, 1956. See also Bohrer's "Boys in Bloomington" in *As We Knew Adlai*, Edward P. Doyle, ed. (New York, 1966), pp. 1-4.

[3] Interviews with Adlai Stevenson, Mrs. Ernest Ives, Joseph F. Bohrer, Loring Merwin, 1955.

Chapter Four

[1] Interviews with Adlai Stevenson and Mrs. Ernest Ives, 1955, 1956.

[2] Noel F. Busch, *Adlai E. Stevenson of Illinois* (New York, 1952), p. 47. I heard the story of the accident also from Stevenson himself, from Mrs. Ernest Ives, and from Loring Merwin, in 1956. Mrs. Ives tells of it in her *My Brother Adlai*, written with Hildegarde Dolson (New York, 1956, pp. 72-73).

[3] Interviews with Mr. and Mrs. Carl Vrooman, 1956.

[4] Interviews with Adlai E. Stevenson and Mrs. Ernest Ives, 1956.

[5] Quoted by Ives and Dolson, *op. cit.*, p. 87.

[6] Interviews with Miss Alverta Duff, 1956.

[7] Grade record furnished me by University High School at written request of Adlai E. Stevenson, 1956.

Chapter Five

[1] Interviews with Mrs. Ernest Ives, 1955.

[2] Interviews with Adlai E. Stevenson and Mrs. Ives, 1955 and 1956. Elizabeth Stevenson Ives and Hildegarde Dolson, *My Brother Adlai* (New York, 1956), pp. 106-07, tells of the vacation and quotes in full a lengthy letter from Adlai to his mother.

Chapter Six

[1] Concerning F. Scott Fitzgerald at Princeton, the chief source is Arthur Mizener, *The Far Side of Paradise* (Boston, 1951). The quoted telegram is from p. 29 of that book. Referred to while writing of Stevenson's Princeton years were Ray Stannard Baker, *Woodrow Wilson, Life and Letters, Princeton 1890-1910* (Garden City, 1927); Arthur S. Link, *Wilson, The Road to the White House* (Princeton, 1947); Varnum L. Collins, *Princeton* (New York, 1914); and The Princeton Municipal Improvement, Inc., *Historic Princeton* (Princeton, 1940).

[2] F. Scott Fitzgerald, *This Side of Paradise* (New York, 1920), p. 140.

[3] Mizener, *op. cit.*, pp. 54-55.

[4] *Ibid.*, p. 33.

Chapter Seven

[1] Elizabeth Stevenson Ives and Hildegarde Dolson, *My Brother Adlai* (New York, 1956), p. 151.

[2] Letter in Stevenson family files. Quoted by Ives and Dolson, *op. cit.*, p. 103.

[3] *Ibid.*, pp. 154-55.

[4] Adlai E. Stevenson, *What I Think* (New York, 1956), pp. 180-81.

Chapter Eight

[1] Most of the information presented herein concerning the *Pantagraph* ownership controversy was given me in interviews with Loring Merwin, Mrs. Ernest Ives, and Adlai E. Stevenson in 1955, 1956. Mrs. Ives tells of it briefly in Elizabeth Stevenson Ives and Hildegarde Dolson, *My Brother Adlai* (New York, 1956), pp. 180-81. There is a somewhat more extensive account of it in John Bartlow Martin, *Adlai Stevenson* (New York, 1952), pp. 44-45.

[2] Interview with Adlai E. Stevenson, 1956. Also told by Ives and Dolson, *op. cit.*, p. 179.

[3] Quoted by Martin, *op. cit.*, p. 45.

[4] Adlai Stevenson told me of this project in detail in 1956.

[5] Ives and Dolson, *op. cit.*, pp. 187-91, and Noel F. Busch, *Adlai E. Stevenson of Illinois* (New York, 1952), pp. 53-55, tell of the Russian trip.

[6] Interviews with Mrs. Ernest Ives, 1955-56. She tells of her engagement and marriage in Ives and Dolson, *op. cit.*, pp. 191-94.

Chapter Nine

[1] Interviews with Adlai E. Stevenson, Edward D. McDougal, Jr., and Hermon Dunlap Smith, 1955-56.

[2] Interviews with Mrs. Edison (Jane Warner) Dick, 1955, 1956.

[3] Arthur Meeker, *Chicago, with Love* (New York, 1955), tells of Miss Campbell and, in general, gives some of the flavor of the Chicago society in which Stevenson lived when he first came to the city.

[4] Arthur Mizener, *The Far Side of Paradise* (Boston, 1951), tells of Fitzgerald and Ginevra King, esp. pp. 47-50.

[5] Interview with Mrs. Ernest Ives, 1955.

Chapter Ten

[1] Interview with Dr. E. M. Stevenson, 1956.

[2] Interview with Adlai E. Stevenson, 1956.

[3] Interviews with Mr. and Mrs. Clifton Utley, Mrs. John P. Welling, and Mr. and Mrs. Quincy Wright, 1956.

[4] Adlai E. Stevenson, address to New York *Herald Tribune* Forum, New York, Oct. 24, 1949.

[5] Interview with Adlai E. Stevenson, 1956. The original manuscript of the Lincoln Autobiography is now in the Library of Congress.

[6] Interviews with Adlai E. Stevenson and Mrs. Ernest Ives, 1956.

Chapter Eleven

[1] Interview with Clifton Utley, 1956.
[2] Interview with Ernest Ives, 1956.
[3] Interview with Dr. E. M. Stevenson, 1956.
[4] Interview with Edward D. McDougal, Jr., 1956.
[5] Interview with Adlai E. Stevenson, 1956.
[6] *Ibid.*
[7] The earliest published account of the episode is in Noel F. Busch, *Adlai E. Stevenson of Illinois* (New York, 1952), p. 4.
[8] Interview with Clifton Utley, 1956.
[9] Interviews with Carl McGowan, 1955 and 1956.
[10] Interview with Mrs. Hermon Dunlap Smith, 1956.

Chapter Twelve

[1] Walter Johnson, *William Allen White's America* (New York, 1947), pp. 524-48, tells of White's involvement in this work.
[2] Interview with Walter Johnson, 1956.
[3] All the information concerning Adlai Stevenson's attitudes, thoughts, and feelings during this period derive from interviews with him, 1955-56.
[4] Interview with William McCormick Blair, Jr., 1956.
[5] Walter Johnson, *op. cit.*, pp. 538 *et seq.*
[6] Interview with Adlai E. Stevenson, 1956.

Chapter Thirteen

[1] Interviews with Adlai E. Stevenson, 1955 and 1956.
[2] The story of Stevenson's "Message to Garcia" (as one magazine dubbed it) has been often printed. My account derives from interviews with him (he loved to tell the story) supplemented by his written account. Noel F. Busch tells the story on pp. 64-69 of his *Adlai E. Stevenson of Illinois* (New York, 1952). Elizabeth Stevenson Ives and Hildegarde Dolson tell it on pp. 114-119 of *My Brother Adlai* (New York, 1956).
[3] Interview with Adlai E. Stevenson, 1956.
[4] *Ibid.*
[5] Interview with Hermon Dunlap Smith, 1956. John Bartlow Martin, *Adlai Stevenson* (New York, 1952) tells of the episode on p. 55.
[6] Interviews with Mrs. Ernest Ives, 1956.
[7] Interview with Adlai Stevenson, 1956.
[8] *Ibid.* Also interviews with Carl McGowan, 1955-56.

Chapter Fourteen

[1] Adlai E. Stevenson gave me access to a personal diary he kept during this European mission and to some personal memoirs he wrote of it. These were principal sources of my information concerning this mission.
[2] Interviews with Mrs. Lloyd (Kathryn) Lewis, 1956, and Adlai Stevenson, 1956.
[3] Confirmed in interview with Mrs. Marshall (Ruth) Field III, 1966.

Chapter Fifteen

[1] Interview with Adlai E. Stevenson, 1956.
[2] *Ibid.*
[3] Noel Busch, *Adlai E. Stevenson of Illinois* (New York, 1952), p. 78.
[4] Interview with Mrs. Quincy (Louise) Wright, 1956.

Chapter Sixteen

[1] Interview with Mrs. Quincy (Louise) Wright, 1956.
[2] Interview with J. Edward Day, 1956.
[8] Interview with Mrs. Lloyd (Kathryn) Lewis, 1956.

Chapter Seventeen

[1] Interview with Mr. and Mrs. Louis A. Kohn, 1956.
[2] Interviews with Hermon Dunlap Smith and Adlai E. Stevenson, 1956. John Bartlow Martin tells the story of the candidacy in accurate detail in his *Adlai Stevenson* (New York, 1952), pp. 58-80.
[3] Martin, *op. cit.,* p. 68.
[4] Colonel Jacob M. Arvey in *As We Knew Adlai,* Edward P. Doyle, ed. (New York, 1966), says, p. 52, "When I met with Adlai alone, he insisted that in no circumstances would he be a candidate for any other office than the one of United States Senator. . . ."
[5] Interview with Adlai E. Stevenson, 1956. Martin, *op. cit.,* pp. 69-70.
[6] Interview with Hermon Dunlap Smith, 1956.
[7] Noel F. Busch, *Adlai E. Stevenson of Illinois* (New York, 1952), p. 9.
[8] Interview with Mrs. Lloyd (Kathryn) Lewis, 1956.
[9] Mrs. Edison (Jane) Dick reproduced the letter in a memoir of her campaigning with Stevenson privately printed in the early 1950's. She quotes it in her contribution to *As We Knew Adlai,* p. 276.
[10] Carol Evans and Mrs. Dick gave me circumstantial accounts of this election night, in 1956.

Chapter Eighteen

[1] When I first contemplated writing a biography of Adlai Stevenson in 1955, the problem of handling the divorce with accuracy, yet with a decent respect for the rights and sensitivities of living people, seemed insurmountable. Stevenson himself solved the problem for me. As he and I dined alone one night at Libertyville he told me the story with remarkable fullness and compassionate objectivity, bringing up the subject himself (because he knew I had to know about it). I was thus encouraged to deal with the subject frankly, as I have. What I write here derives not only from him but also from interviews with Carol Evans, Mrs. Edison (Jane) Dick, Mr. and Mrs. Ernest Ives, Mr. and Mrs. Hermon Dunlap Smith, Stanley Pargellis (he came to know Mrs. Ellen Borden Stevenson well when she was a principal sponsor of *Poetry* Magazine, whose office was then in the Newberry Library of which Pargellis was librarian), Mrs. John P. Welling, Mrs. Ellen Borden Stevenson herself, and the three Stevenson sons, Adlai III, Borden, and John Fell.
[2] Interview with Mrs. Ernest Ives, 1956.

Chapter Nineteen

[1] Interviews with Hermon Dunlap Smith, 1956.
[2] Information concerning Stevenson's personnel recruitment and administrative techniques derives from extensive interviews with many of the people here mentioned, including Carol Evans, Louis A. Kohn, and J. Edward Day, 1956.
[3] Interview with Walter T. Fisher, 1956.
[4] Interviews with Fred K. Hoehler, 1956.
[5] Interviews with W. Willard Wirtz, 1956.
[6] Interview with Mrs. Stanley (Betty) Pargellis, 1956.
[7] Interview with Mrs. Edison Dick, 1956.
[8] Interview with William McCormick Blair, Jr., 1956.
[9] Interview with Carl McGowan, 1956.
[10] Interviews with Arthur Schlesinger, Jr., 1956.

Chapter Twenty

[1] Most of the legislative history in this chapter derives (a) from the papers of Governor Stevenson which, in the 1950's, were stored in intimidating volume on on upper floor of the Newberry Library, and (b) from files of *The New York Times*, the Chicago *Tribune*, the Chicago *Daily News*, the Chicago *Sun-Times*, and the Bloomington (Ill.) *Pantagraph*.
[2] The intricate history of Con-Con was explained to me by Carl McGowan, Hermon Dunlap Smith, and William McCormick Blair, Jr., 1956.
[3] Interviews with Blair, J. Edward Day, McGowan, and Carol Evans, 1955-56.
[4] Blair interview, 1956.

Chapter Twenty-One

[1] Interviews with Adlai Stevenson, Carl McGowan, William McCormick Blair, Jr., and Carol Evans, 1956, supplementing press accounts and John Bartlow Martin's *Adlai Stevenson* (New York, 1952), pp. 128-30.
[2] McGowan interview, 1956. Martin, *op. cit.*, pp. 134-37.
[3] Martin, *op. cit.*, pp. 139-40.
[4] Interviews with Mr. and Mrs. Ernest Ives, 1956.
[5] Interviews with the Rev. Dr. Richard Paul Graebel, 1955-56.
[6] Interviews with Harry Edward Pratt, 1956, and Adlai Stevenson, 1956.

Chapter Twenty-Two

[1] Adlai Stevenson, in my talks with him in 1955 and '56, clearly indicated his distaste for certain aspects of the Truman regime while insisting upon his admiration for Truman's courage and judgment in the great decisions of Greece, the Marshall Plan, Berlin, and Korea.
[2] Stevenson interview, 1956.
[3] Harry S. Truman, *Years of Trial and Hope*, Vol. II of his *Memoirs* (New York, 1956), pp. 491-92.
[4] Interview with Newton N. Minow, 1956.
[5] Interview with Walter Johnson, 1956. See also his *How We Drafted Adlai Stevenson* (New York, 1955), which tells the full story of the earliest organized effort to draft Stevenson in 1952.

[6] Adlai Stevenson's Introduction to *Major Campaign Speeches of Adlai E. Stevenson, 1952* (New York, 1953), p. xxii.

[7] Truman, *op. cit.*, p. 492.

[8] Walter Johnson, *op. cit.*, p. 19.

[9] Truman, *op. cit.*, p. 495.

Chapter Twenty-Three

[1] Interviews with William McCormick Blair, Jr., 1956, supplementing press accounts.

[2] Walter Johnson, *How We Drafted Adlai Stevenson* (New York, 1955), pp. 57-59.

[3] Interviews with Kenneth Anderson, John Young, and Milo Sutton, 1956.

[4] Blair interview and interviews with Carl McGowan, 1956.

[5] Adlai Stevenson's Introduction to *Major Campaign Speeches of Adlai E. Stevenson, 1952* (New York, 1952), pp. xxii and xxiii.

[6] Interviews with Edward D. McDougal, Jr., and Mrs. Ernest Ives, 1956.

[7] Elizabeth Stevenson Ives with Hildegarde Dolson, *My Brother Adlai* (New York, 1956), p. 264.

[8] Interview with Newton N. Minow, 1956.

[9] Interviews with Blair, Adlai Stevenson, and Mrs. Ernest Ives, 1956.

[10] Quotations from Adlai Stevenson, *op. cit.*, p. xxvi.

[11] Information on the "Elks Club" derived from conversation with Bernard De Voto, 1955, and interviews with W. Willard Wirtz, McGowan, Arthur Schlesinger, Jr., 1956.

[12] Harry S. Truman, Vol. II of his *Memoirs* (New York, 1956), pp. 491-92.

[13] McGowan interview, 1956.

[14] Truman, *op. cit.*, p. 500.

[15] Stevenson, *op. cit.*, p. xii.

[16] Adlai Stevenson's speech at Cleveland, Ohio, dealing with the Hiss case, on October 23, 1952.

Chapter Twenty-Four

[1] Information concerning Dwight D. Eisenhower and the Eisenhower family and background come in part from direct contact with him, his relatives, his friends and associates, while gathering material for a full-length biography of him, *Soldier of Democracy* (New York, 1945).

[2] The "Grouchy Old Pessimist" phrase was actually coined by Arthur Schlesinger, Jr., who wrote the first draft of this speech.

[3] The photographer was William M. Gallagher of the Flint (Michigan) *Journal* and the hole in the shoe was no more expressive of Stevenson's frugality (or parsimony) than the fact that Stevenson's congratulations went by post card, *not* by cable.

[4] George W. Ball in *As We Knew Adlai*, Edward P. Doyle, ed. (New York, 1966), says, p. 151, that Stevenson reacted with annoyance to his, Ball's, insistence that the candidate "call on a powerful leader of a minority group" in one city—a man Stevenson deemed "a charlatan." "Don't you characters believe," he reportedly asked, "that we are going to win with such a big vote that that kind of noxious business isn't necessary?"

[5] Interviews with Carol Evans, Phyllis Gustafson, Mrs. Ernest Ives, Borden Stevenson, John Fell Stevenson, William McCormick Blair, Jr., Carl McGowan, W. Willard Wirtz, Adlai Stevenson, 1956.

Chapter Twenty-Five

[1] Adlai E. Stevenson's Introduction to his *Major Campaign Speeches, 1952* (New York, 1953), pp. xxvii, xxviii.

[2] Adlai E. Stevenson, *What I Think* (New York, 1956), pp. ix and x.

[3] The Stevenson articles in *Look* provide the best record of the world tour, part of which is described by Barry Bingham's "With Adlai in Asia," in *As We Knew Adlai*, Edward P. Doyle, ed. (New York, 1966), p. 188 *et seq.* The original plan had been to make a book of these plus supplementary material and Walter Johnson worked on a draft of it for several weeks after the party had returned to America. Stevenson found, however, that he simply did not have the time to write the book as contemplated, and so the project was abandoned. Stevenson subsequently used some of the information and ideas his tour had given him in the three Godkin Lectures delivered at Harvard, March, 1954, under the title of "A Troubled World," published in book form as *Call to Greatness* (New York, 1954).

[4] Stevenson interview, 1956.

[5] John Mason Brown, *Through These Men* (New York, 1956).

[6] Interviews with Newton N. Minow and W. Willard Wirtz, 1955-56.

[7] Luncheon conversation with Stevenson and William McCormick Blair, Jr., March, 1955.

Chapter Twenty-Six

[1] Quoted phrases are from W. Willard Wirtz. I was at that time a writer on Adlai Stevenson's staff, resigning later to write, as a free agent, my biography of him.

[2] Adlai Stevenson, *What I Think* (New York, 1956), p. 18 *et seq.*

[3] *Ibid.*, p. 182 *et seq.*

[4] John Mason Brown, "The Road to the White House" in *Through These Men* (New York, 1956), pp. 30-31.

[5] The adviser was myself, 1956.

[6] W. Willard Wirtz and I were then working together on Stevenson's speeches and the quotes are from his remarks to me.

[7] Interview with Newton N. Minow, 1955.

[8] Interview with Adlai E. Stevenson, 1955.

[9] The friend was myself, 1956.

Chapter Twenty-Seven

[1] William McCormick Blair, Jr., made this claim.

[2] For the most part, the description of the convention is from direct observation and conversations at the time with Stevenson staff members.

[3] Interviews with James Finnegan and Wilson Wyatt, 1956.

[4] Adlai E. Stevenson interview, 1956.

Chapter Twenty-Eight

[1] *New York Times*, November 12, 1956, p. 35, column 1. Emmet John Hughes, *The Ordeal of Power* (New York, 1963), pp. 228-29.

[2] J. B. Oakes, *The New York Times Magazine*, November 25, 1956, p. 12.

[3] Interview with Mrs. Marshall Field, Dark Harbor, Maine, August, 1966.

[4] The genesis of the Democratic Advisory Council was described to me in inter-

views with Mrs. Marietta Tree and Robert Benjamin on October 7, 1966, and with Thomas K. Finletter on October 4, 1966.

[5] See James MacGregor Burns, *The Deadlock of Democracy: Four-Party Politics in America* (Boston, 1964). Also his *Presidential Government: The Crucible of Leadership* (Boston, 1966).

[6] Interview with Minow, June 15, 1966, and Wirtz, July 22, 1966.

[7] Undated and unpublished ms. of a talk by Marietta Tree entitled "Memories of Stevenson," given me by her in August, 1966.

[8] According to Arthur M. Schlesinger, Jr., *A Thousand Days* (Boston, 1965), p. 38, the placard-bearing lady was part of the Stevenson demonstration on the convention floor in Los Angeles in 1960, but both Barbara Ward (Lady Jackson) and Marietta Tree remember Stevenson's telling the story as an episode of the 1956 campaign. Barbara Ward speaks of it on p. 213 of her contribution to *As We Knew Adlai*, Edward P. Doyle, ed. (New York, 1966). A recording of Stevenson's speeches issued by the Macmillan Company in 1965, entitled "Adlai E. Stevenson, the Man, the Candidate, the Statesman" has Stevenson himself telling the story during the 1956 campaign.

[9] Kenneth S. Davis, *A Prophet in His Own Country: The Triumphs and Defeats of Adlai E. Stevenson* (New York, 1957).

[10] Information concerning the Council's operation gained from personal interviews was supplemented by a carefully researched account published in Paul T. David, Ralph M. Goldman, Richard B. Bain, *The Politics of National Party Conventions* (Brookings Institute, 1960), pp. 108-110.

[11] Dwight D. Eisenhower, *Waging Peace* (New York, 1965), p. 179.

[12] Transcript of the President's remarks on November 7, 1956, in *Public Papers of the Presidents: Dwight D. Eisenhower, 1956* (Washington, The National Archives, 1958), p. 1090. Quoted by Richard E. Neustadt, *Presidential Power* (New American Library softbound edition, 1964), p. 70.

[13] Quoted by Neustadt, *op. cit.*, p. 72, from *Public Papers of the President, 1957*, pp. 73-74.

[14] Remarks at press conference in New York, August 6, 1957, reported in *The New York Times*, Aug. 7, 1957, 1:5.

[15] Stuart Gerry Brown, *Conscience in Politics: Adlai E. Stevenson in the 1950s*. (Syracuse, 1961), p. 178, quotes the Stevenson memorandum to Dulles. Professor Brown was given access to the Stevenson papers and had numerous talks with Stevenson as he wrote his book and I am particularly indebted to him for his extensive quotations of the papers in his Chapter V, "Stevenson in Washington," pp. 173-188.

[16] Quoted by Brown, *op. cit.*, p. 219.

Chapter Twenty-Nine

[1] Richard E. Neustadt, *Presidential Power* (New American Library softbound edition, 1964), Chapter 4, "Professional Reputation," contains an analytical account of Eisenhower's handling of the budgets of fiscal 1958, fiscal 1959, and fiscal 1960, to which I am indebted.

[2] Dwight D. Eisenhower, *Waging Peace* (New York, 1965), p. 377.

[3] *Ibid.*, p. 378-379.

[4] *Ibid.*, p. 289.

[5] *Ibid.*, p. 304.

[6] Theodore H. White, *The Making of the President, 1960* (New York, 1960), p. 121.

[7] Eisenhower, *op. cit.*, p. 385.

[8] *Ibid.*, p. 381.

[9] *Ibid.*, p. 387.

[10] White, *op. cit.*, tells of the Rockefeller survey on pp. 68-77.

[11] Arthur M. Schlesinger, Jr., *A Thousand Days* (Boston, 1965), p. 16.

[12] My study of Stevenson public statements during this period has been most valuably supplemented and reinforced by Stuart Gerry Brown, *Conscience in Politics: Adlai E. Stevenson in the 1950s* (Syracuse, 1961), wherein Professor Brown makes a succinct, analytical summary of Stevenson's positions vis-à-vis Eisenhower on the H-bomb test ban, the draft, and civil rights. I am much indebted to Professor Brown, whose work was, I happen to know, greatly admired by (and immensely pleasing to) Stevenson. Stevenson spoke often of his regret that Professor Brown's book was not more widely known.

[13] *Ibid.*, pp. 195-96.

[14] *Ibid.*, p. 199.

[15] Transcript of President's remarks, June 5, 1957, *Public Papers of the Presidents: Dwight D. Eisenhower, 1957* (Washington, The National Archives, 1958).

[16] Brown, *op. cit.*, pp. 220-22.

[17] Eisenhower, *op. cit.*, p. 477.

[18] White, *op. cit.*, p. 120.

Chapter Thirty

[1] No one can write of the 1960 campaign without leaning heavily upon Theodore White's brilliant interpretative reporting in *The Making of the President, 1960* (New York, 1962). My debts to it will be obvious to all who have read it.

[2] Stevenson spoke to me of Nixon in approximately those terms in 1955 and '56. I remember being a bit surprised by the vehemence of his hostility.

[3] Interview with Thomas K. Finletter, October 4, 1966.

[4] William Attwood, p. 160 of *As We Knew Adlai*, Edward P. Doyle, ed. (New York, 1966).

[5] William Benton, *As We Knew Adlai*, pp. 200-201. See also William Benton's *The Voice of Latin America*, revised edition, with a Foreword by Adlai E. Stevenson (New York, 1965). It was written as a report and analysis of what Benton and Stevenson saw and heard during their Latin American tour.

[6] White, *op. cit.*, p. 109.

[7] Arthur M. Schesinger, Jr., *A Thousand Days* (Boston, 1965), p. 22.

[8] Donald Murray, a student at Brooklyn College of the City University of New York and at this writing a candidate for a Master's degree in political science, sent me for my review a mimeographed copy of a paper he planned, after revision, to submit as his thesis. Entitled *The Stevenson Campaign at the 1960 Democratic National Convention*, this paper, researched for the most part from primary sources, augmented information I had already obtained and I thank Mr. Murray for his permission of my use of it. Page references to it are useless since the paper, at this writing, is still in ms.

[9] William Attwood, *op. cit.*, p. 161.

[10] Interview with Arthur M. Schlesinger, Jr., Oct. 4, 1966. Interview with Thomas K. Finletter, Oct. 4, 1966. Interview with Mrs. Marietta Tree, Oct. 7, 1966.

[11] Schlesinger, Jr., *op. cit.*, p. 22.

[12] *Ibid.*, p. 22.

[13] Interview with Alden Johnson, Feb. 5, 1967.

[14] Dwight D. Eisenhower, *Waging Peace* (New York, 1965), p. 412.

[15] *Ibid.*, p. 549.

[16] *Ibid.*, p. 550.

[17] Quoted by Stuart Gerry Brown, *Conscience in Politics* (Syracuse, 1961), pp. 280-81.

[18] Eisenhower, *op. cit.*, p. 550.

[19] *Ibid.*, p. 552.

[20] *Ibid.*, p. 555.

[21] Interview with Newton Minow, June 15, 1966. Schlesinger, Jr., tells of the episode in *op. cit.*, pp. 24-26.

[22] Conversation with John Fell Stevenson, June 13, 1966.

[23] Schlesinger, *op. cit.*, p. 24.

[24] Quoted from *This Week* Magazine by A. S. Mike Monroney in *As We Knew Adlai*, p. 248.

[25] Eisenhower, *op. cit.*, p. 557.

[26] Monroney, *op. cit.*, pp. 249-50.

[27] Schlesinger, Jr., *op. cit.*, pp. 27-28.

[28] White, *op. cit.*, p. 126.

Chapter Thirty-One

[1] Interviews with Mrs. Marshall Field, August, 1966, and Thomas K. Finletter, October 4, 1966.

[2] Theodore H. White, *The Making of the President, 1960* (New York, 1962), pp. 119-122.

[3] Arthur M. Schlesinger, Jr., *A Thousand Days* (Boston, 1965), p. 28.

[4] Interview with Walter Johnson, June, 1966.

[5] Schlesinger, Jr., *op. cit.*, p. 28.

[6] *Ibid.*, p. 28.

[7] A. S. Mike Monroney in *As We Knew Adlai*, Edward P. Doyle, ed. (New York, 1966), p. 253.

[8] Schlesinger, Jr., *op. cit.*, p. 26. Kennedy reportedly said to Blair as he, Kennedy, boarded a plane in Chicago en route to Hyannis Port: "Guess who the next person I see will be—the person who will say about Adlai, 'I told you that son-of-a-bitch has been running for President every moment since 1956?'" Blair, says Schlesinger, Jr., answered "correctly. 'Daddy.'"

[9] Donald Murray, "The Stevenson Campaign in the 1960 Democratic Convention." (Mimeographed copy of unpublished ms., written for master's thesis.)

[10] Interview with Newton Minow, June 15, 1966.

[11] White, *op. cit.*, pp. 160-61.

[12] *Ibid.*, p. 161. Murray, *op. cit.*, gives a detailed circumstantial account of this meeting, saying that Lawrence was accompanied by Matthew H. McCloskey, treasurer of the Democratic National Committee and chairman of the Democratic Finance Committee of Pennsylvania. Murray derived much of his information from Mike Monroney, Jr., son of the Senator.

[13] White, *op. cit.*, pp. 159-60.

[14] Schlesinger, Jr., *op. cit.*, p. 37.

[15] Monroney, *op. cit.*, p. 253.

[16] Schlesinger, Jr., *op. cit.*, p. 37. Monroney, *op. cit.*, pp. 252-53. White, *op. cit.*, p. 163.

[17] Donald Murray, *op cit.* Murray obtained his information from an interview with John Sharon, July 12, 1963.

[18] *Ibid.*

[19] William Attwood in *As We Knew Adlai,* p. 163.

[20] White, *op. cit.,* p. 167.

[21] Murray, *op. cit.,* presents detailed account of the genesis and preparation of the Eugene McCarthy speech, Attwood, *op. cit.,* p. 163, says that, in the morning of that day, he "wrote a draft for Senator Eugene McCarthy's nominating speech, some of which he used." Stuart Gerry Brown, *Conscience in Politics* (Syracuse, 1961), pp. 295-97, quotes extensively from a tape-recorded text supplied him by Senator McCarthy.

[22] Mary McGrory in *As We Knew Adlai,* p. 177.

[23] Schlesinger, Jr., *op. cit.,* p. 64.

Chapter Thirty-Two

[1] Arthur M. Schlesinger, Jr., *A Thousand Days* (Boston, 1965), p. 66. William Attwood in *As We Knew Adlai,* Edward P. Doyle, ed. (New York, 1966), p. 164.

[2] Schlesinger, Jr., *op. cit.,* p. 157.

[3] Attwood, *op. cit.,* p. 162.

[4] Mary McGrory in *As We Knew Adlai,* p. 175.

[5] Schlesinger, Jr., *op. cit.,* p. 139.

[6] James MacGregor Burns, *Presidential Government* (Boston, 1965), p. vii.

[7] Interview with Newton Minow, June 15, 1966. Schlesinger, Jr., *op. cit.,* p. 139.

[8] Interview with Carol Evans, June, 1966.

[9] Mrs. Edison Dick has recorded in *As We Knew Adlai,* p. 280, that her "heart sank" as she "looked at those empty, sterile hotel rooms" when Stevenson moved into the embassy, but others remember the suite as I have described it at the time of his moving in.

[10] Interview with Judge Carl McGowan, June 21, 1966.

[11] Schlesinger, Jr., *op. cit.,* p. 271.

[12] *Ibid.,* pp. 271-72. Theodore C. Sorensen, *Kennedy* (New York, 1965), pp. 300-301. Interview with Mrs. Edison Dick, June 16, 1966. Interview with Mrs. Marietta Tree, Oct. 7, 1966.

[13] Sorensen, *op. cit.,* p. 309.

[14] Schlesinger, Jr., *op. cit.,* p. 271.

[15] Interview with Mrs. Ernest Ives, May 3, 1966.

[16] Schlesinger, Jr., *op. cit.,* pp. 468-69. The later quote is from Schlesinger, Jr., also, p. 468.

[17] Adlai E. Stevenson in testimony before the Senate Foreign Relations Committee, March 13, 1963.

[18] *Ibid.*

[19] Sorensen, *op. cit.,* p. 539.

[20] The quotation on foreign aid is from Sorensen, *op. cit.,* p. 538. The quotation on Stevenson-Bowles is from Schlesinger, Jr., *op. cit.,* p. 520.

[21] Quoted by Sorensen, *op. cit.,* p. 538.

[22] Conversation with Mrs. Ernest Ives, May 3, 1966.

[23] "Adlai Decides," *Newsweek* magazine, Dec. 18, 1961, pp. 27-28.

[24] Schlesinger, Jr., *op. cit.,* p. 835.

[25] Sorensen, *op. cit.,* pp. 270-71. Schlesinger, Jr., *op. cit.,* pp. 435-36.

[26] The story of the crisis is told in detail by Schlesinger, Jr., *op. cit.,* pp. 794-841;

by Sorensen, *op. cit.*, pp. 667-718; and by Elie Abel, *The Missile Crisis* (Philadelphia, 1966).

[27] Elie Abel, *The Missile Crisis* (Philadelphia, 1966), quotes both Kennedy and Stevenson directly in p. 49 of his carefully researched (from primary sources) account. Stevenson told Abel in March, 1965: "I was a little alarmed that Kennedy's first consideration should have been an air strike."

[28] Sorensen, *op. cit.*, p. 695. Sorensen does not actually name Stevenson as the author of this note but makes it absolutely clear, in context, that the author could be no other man.

[29] *Ibid.*, p. 685.

[30] Abel, *op. cit.*, p. 58.

[31] Sorensen, *op. cit.*, pp. 690-91.

[32] *Ibid.*, p. 684.

[33] Abel, *op. cit.*, pp. 94-96. Sorensen, *op. cit.*, pp. 695-96.

[34] Sorensen, *op. cit.*, p. 696.

[35] *Ibid.*, p. 2.

[36] Schlesinger, Jr., *op. cit.*, p. 810.

[37] The speech is printed in full in Adlai E. Stevenson, *Looking Outward: Years of Crisis at the United Nations*. Edited by Robert L. and Selma Schiffer (New York, 1963), pp. 100-106. The speech in rebuttal of Zorin is in *Ibid.*, pp. 107-112.

[38] Interview with Mrs. Edison Dick, June 16, 1966, and with Mrs. Marietta Tree, Oct. 7, 1966. Elie Abel, *op. cit.*, p. 169, basing his statement on interviews he had with Stevenson "a few months before his death," says that Stevenson "took no pride in having played 'Mr. District Attorney' at the height of the missiles crisis" and "seemed regretful that," in consequence of his having done so, "the Kremlin leaders no longer considered him 'objective.' "

[39] S. Alsop and C. Bartlett, "In Time of Crisis," *Saturday Evening Post* 235: 15-16 plus, Dec. 8, 1962. S. Alsop, "Footnote for Historians," *Saturday Evening Post*, 236:76, January 26, 1963. Notes and comment concerning the Alsop-Bartlett article, the *New Yorker*, 38:31, Dec. 15, 1962. "Who Done It? Hatchet Job on Stevenson," *Newsweek*, 60:28, Dec. 17, 1962. John L. Steele, "Adlai Stevenson Affair," *Life*, 53:44-46, Dec. 14, 1962. Gilbert A. Harrison, "Why Stevenson?" *New Republic*, 147:7-10, Dec. 15, 1962.

[40] Schlesinger, Jr., *op. cit.*, p. 837.

[41] *Ibid.*, pp. 1020-21.

[42] William Attwood in *As We Knew Adlai*, p. 167.

Chapter Thirty-Three

[1] Interview with Mrs. Ernest Ives, May 3, 1966. Conversations (not formal interviews) with Adlai Stevenson III, June, 1966, and Borden Stevenson, August, 1966.

[2] William Attwood in *As We Knew Adlai*, Edward P. Doyle, ed. (New York, 1966), p. 167.

[3] Quoted by Arthur M. Schlesinger, Jr., *The Bitter Heritage: Vietnam and American Democracy*, 1941-1966 (Boston, 1967), p. 3. See also Robert Scheer, *How the United States Got Involved in Vietnam*, A Report to the Center for the Study of Democratic Institutions (Santa Barbara, Cal., 1965), pp. 3-5.

[4] Of the numerous books referred to, on the Vietnam struggle, those found most useful to me were Bernard B. Fall, *Viet-Nam Witness* (New York, 1966); David Halberstam, *The Making of a Quagmire* (New York, 1965), and the aforementioned Schlesinger, Jr., book, *The Bitter Heritage*.

[5] Interview with William Attwood, June 16, 1967.

[6] Fall, *op. cit.*, p. 78.

[7] Arthur Schlesinger, Jr., *A Thousand Days* (Boston, 1965), pp. 540-45.

[8] Letter from Paul Goodman to Adlai Stevenson III, dated December 12, 1965. Accompanying it was a printed sonnet of Goodman's "Adlai Stevenson," from from which I derive my quotations in the preceding paragraph and at the close of this one.

[9] Interview with Mrs. Ernest Ives, May 3, 1966.

[10] Emmet John Hughes, *Newsweek* Magazine, Dec. 12, 1966, pp. 62-63.

[11] Eric Sevareid, "Adlai Stevenson, His Final Troubled Hours," *Look* Magazine, November 30, 1960.

[12] *Ibid.*

[13] Interview with Mrs. Marietta Tree, Oct. 7, 1966.

[14] Interview with Mrs. Ernest Ives, May 3, 1966.

[15] Interview with Arthur M. Schlesinger, Jr., Oct. 4, 1966.

[16] Interviews with Mrs. Ives, May 3, 1966, and Mrs. Marshall Field III, August, 1966.

[17] William Benton in *As We Knew Adlai*, Edward P. Doyle, ed. (New York, 1966), p. 209.

[18] Mimeographed statement by Illinois State Representative Adlai E. Stevenson III, for release Tuesday, Dec. 14, 1965, to which was attached a photographic copy of the unmailed Stevenson letter, with Stevenson's handwritten notes and revisions.

[19] The circumstantial account of Stevenson's death was given me by Mrs. Marietta Tree in the interview of Oct. 7, 1966.

[20] Interview with Mrs. Ernest Ives, May 3, 1966.

CONCERNING SOURCES AND OBLIGATIONS

Much of the information in this book derives from interviews with the people who are of its subject matter.

My greatest obligation, of course, is to the late Adlai E. Stevenson himself. Without his active support in the early part of this writing I could not have received the cooperation I did from his family and intimate friends. Of these, the most helpful single person was Mr. Stevenson's sister, Mrs. Ernest L. Ives, of Bloomington, Illinois, and Southern Pines, North Carolina, who, in 1955 and 1956, gave me through interviews great masses of otherwise unobtainable information and carefully reviewed, as did her husband, the material.

Mr. Stevenson's aunts, Miss Letitia Stevenson and Mrs. Martin D. (Julia) Hardin of St. Louis, were invaluable sources of information about the family background and about the Adlai Stevenson they knew at various stages of his development. They turned over to me family papers without which it would not have been possible for me to portray, even as well as I have done, their nephews's paternal ancestry, and they checked in manuscript those portions of the book dealing with family history. I am also indebted to the Stevenson sons—Adlai III, Borden, and John Fell—for insights they have given me, sometimes inadvertently perhaps, and to Mrs. Ellen Borden Stevenson.

Many of my other debts, and their nature, are indicated in the book itself and in the chapter notes that precede. Suffice it here to say that I have profited greatly from interviews with, among others: Dr. E. M. Stevenson, Mr. and Mrs. Carl Vrooman, Mr. Joe Bohrer, Mr. Loring Merwin, Mr. Lawrence Rust, and Miss Alverta Duff, all of Bloomington; the Reverend Dr. Richard Graebel and the late Mr. Harry Edward Pratt of Springfield, Illinois; Mr. and Mrs. Quincy Wright, Mr. and Mrs. Clifton Utley, Mr. Edward D. McDougal, Jr., Mr. and Mrs. Hermon Dunlap Smith, Mrs. Edison Dick, Mrs. John P. Welling, Mr. Walter T. Fisher, Mr. Walter Johnson, Mr. Fred K. Hoehler, Mr. and Mrs. Louis A. Kohn, and Mr. and the late Mrs. Stanley Pargellis, all of greater Chicago in the 1950's; Mr. Kenneth Anderson and Mr. Milo Sutton, of Emporia, Kansas; Mr. John Young, of Salina, Kansas; Mr. Richard Stengel, of Rock Island, Illinois; Mr. Wilson Wyatt, of Louisville, Kentucky; and Mrs. Ronald Tree, Mrs. Marshall Field, Mr. Arthur Schlesinger, Jr., Mr. Thomas K. Finletter, Mr. William Attwood, and Mr. Robert Benjamin, of New York.

Of special value to me were interviews with those who were members of Stevenson's immediate staff during all or part (as I was myself, briefly) of the time from 1948 until his death. These include Judge Carl McGowan, who was Governor Stevenson's closest working associate in Springfield; Ambassador William McC. Blair, Jr., who was Stevenson's closest associate through all the 1950's; Secretary of Labor W. Willard Wirtz, who was a law partner of Stevenson's (as was Mr. Blair) in Chicago; and Mr. Newton Minow, also a Chicago law partner, who returned to private law practice in Chicago after serving briefly as Chairman of the Federal Communications Commission. Also extremely valuable to me as sources of information were Miss Carol Evans, personal secretary to Mr. Stevenson from 1948 to 1960; Miss Phyllis Gustafson and Mrs. Juanda Higgens, both of whom worked closely with Mr. Stevenson from the days of his governorship through the 1950's (Miss Gustafson is now personal secretary to Adlai Stevenson III); and Mr. J. Edward Day, a personal aide of Governor Stevenson in Springfield who before that was associated with him in a Chicago law firm and who, in the 1960's, served as Postmaster General of the United States.

For documentary materials I leaned heavily upon personal letters of Adlai Stevenson, as boy and young man, to his mother, father, and sister, and upon letters they wrote to him. I also found invaluable in the portrayal of the early years albums of pictures kept in the Ives home in Bloomington and microfilms of the Bloomington (Illinois) *Pantagraph* kept in the library of the McLean County (Illinois) Historical Society. Voluminous scrapbooks of clippings kept by and for Mr. Stevenson from his first years in Chicago through his two Presidential campaigns were constantly consulted. The war years were illuminated for me by a personal diary kept sporadically by Mr. Stevenson through the early 1940's. The Stevenson papers for the years of the Governorship and for the 1952 campaign were consulted with the cooperation of the Newberry Library of Chicago. I also consulted bound or microfilm copies of the Chicago *Tribune,* the Chicago *Daily News,* and *The New York Times* in the Newberry Library, and of course counted heavily upon these and other current periodicals for information, checking this information when possible against what I could obtain simply by phoning the people directly involved. At several of the events of this period, I was myself present.

My wife, Florence Olenhouse Davis, was of invaluable assistance throughout this labor. She did all the first, basic research on the Stevenson papers in the Newberry Library, made valuable criticisms and suggestions, and typed all the manuscript twice, and some of it a third time, as the work proceeded.

BIBLIOGRAPHY

NOTE: In the chapter source notes I have endeavored to cite the book and periodical sources for specific items of information. Here I simply list, in alphabetical order by author, the books and magazine articles actually used while I wrote, trusting that it will be obvious to the reader how, why, and for what portion of my book each of these was consulted.

Abel, Elie. *The Missile Crisis* (Philadelphia, 1966)

Adler, Bill, ed. and compiler. *The Stevenson Wit* (New York, 1966)

Allen, Frederick Lewis. *Only Yesterday* (New York, 1931)

——. *Since Yesterday* (New York, 1940)

——. *The Big Change* (New York, 1952)

Baker, Ray Stannard. *Woodrow Wilson, Life and Letters* (Garden City, 1927)

Benton, William. *The Voice of Latin America*, with a Foreword by Adlai E. Stevenson, revised edition (New York, 1965)

Billington, Ray A.; Loewenberg, Bert J.; Brockunier, S. H. *The United States, American Democracy in World Perspective* (New York, 1947)

Brogan, D. W. *Politics in America* (New York, 1954)

Brown, Stuart Gerry. *Conscience in Politics: Adlai E. Stevenson in the 1950s* (Syracuse, 1961)

Burns, James MacGregor. *Presidential Government: The Crucible of Leadership* (Boston, 1966)

Busch, Noel F. *Adlai E. Stevenson of Illinois* (New York, 1952)

Collins, Varnum L. *Princeton* (Princeton: Princeton Municipal Improvement, Inc., 1940)

Country Beautiful editors. *Man of Honor, Man of Peace: The Life and Words of Adlai Stevenson* (New York, 1965)

David, Paul T.; Goldman, Ralph M.; Bain, Richard C. *The Politics of National Party Conventions* (Brookings Institute, 1960)

Donovan, Robert J. *Eisenhower, The Inside Story* (New York, 1956)

Doyle, Edward P., ed. *As We Knew Adlai* (New York, 1966)

Eisenhower, Dwight D. *Mandate for Change, 1953-1956* (New York, 1963)

——. *Waging Peace, 1956-1961* (New York, 1965)

Fall, Bernard B. *Viet-Nam Witness* (New York, 1965)

Fuller, Helen. *Year of Trial, Kennedy's Crucial Decisions* (New York, 1962)

Goldman, Eric F. *The Crucial Decade, America, 1945-1955.* (New York, 1956)

Goodwin, Richard N. *The Sower's Seed, A Tribute to Adlai Stevenson*, with a Eulogy by President Lyndon B. Johnson (New York, 1965)

Green, Thomas Marshall. *Historic Families of Kentucky*, First Series (Cincinnati, 1889)

Halberstam, David. *The Making of a Quagmire* (New York, 1965)

Hofstadter, Richard. *The American Political Tradition* (New York, 1948)

Hughes, Emmet John. *The Ordeal of Power, a Political Memoir of the Eisenhower Years* (New York, 1963)

Ives, Elizabeth Stevenson, and Dolson, Hildegarde. *My Brother Adlai* (New York, 1956)

Johnson, Walter. *William Allen White's America* (New York, 1947)

———. *How We Drafted Adlai Stevenson* (New York, 1955)

Link, Arthur S. *Wilson, The Road to the White House* (Princeton, 1947)

Lubell, Samuel. *The Future of American Politics* (New York, Revised Second Edition, softbound, 1956)

Markmann, Charles Lam, and Sherwin, Mark. *John F. Kennedy, A Sense of Purpose* (New York, 1961)

Martin, John Bartlow. *Adlai Stevenson* (New York, 1952)

Meeker, Arthur. *Chicago, With Love* (New York, 1955)

Mitchell, Broadus. *Depression Decade* (New York, 1947)

Mitchell, Stephen A. *Elm Street Politics* (New York, 1959)

Mizener, Arthur. *The Far Side of Paradise, A Biography of F. Scott Fitzgerald* (Boston, 1951)

Morehouse, Frances Milton I. *The Life of Jesse Fell* (Urbana, 1916)

Neustadt, Richard E. *Presidential Power* (New York, 1960)

Richardson, Harriett Fyffe. *Quaker Pioneers,* Privately printed, undated, apparently in 1940 in Milwaukee)

Roberts, Charles. *LBJ's Inner Circle* (New York, 1965)

Ross, Lillian. *Adlai Stevenson* (Philadelphia, 1966)

Rossiter, Clinton. *The American Presidency* (New York, 1956)

Rovere, Richard. *The Eisenhower Years, Affairs of State* (New York, 1956)

Rowse, Arthur Edward. *Slanted News, A Case Study of the Nixon and Stevenson Fund Stories,* With a Foreword by Erwin D. Canham (Boston, 1957)

Scheer, Robert T. *How the United States Got Involved in Vietnam* (A Report [in paperback pamphlet form] to the Center for the Study of Democratic Institutions, Santa Barbara, California, 1965)

Schlesinger, Arthur M., Jr. *A Thousand Days, John F. Kennedy in the White House* (Boston, 1965)

———. *The Bitter Heritage, Vietnam and American Democracy, 1941-1966*

———. *The Crisis of the Old Order,* Vol. I of *The Age of Roosevelt* (Boston, 1957)

———. *The Coming of the New Deal,* Vol. II of *The Age of Roosevelt* (Boston, 1959)

———. *The Politics of Upheaval,* Vol. III of *The Age of Roosevelt* (Boston, 1960)

Sherwood, Robert. *Roosevelt and Hopkins* (New York, Revised and Enlarged Edition, 1950)

Sidey, Hugh. *John F. Kennedy, President* (New York, 1964)

Sorensen, Theodore C. *Kennedy* (New York, 1965)

Stevenson, Adlai Ewing. *Something of Men I Have Known* (Chicago, 1909)

Stevenson, Adlai E. *Speeches of Adlai E. Stevenson,* with a Foreword by John Steinbeck and a brief biography by Debs Myers and Ralph Martin (New York softbound, 1952)

———. *Major Campaign Speeches of 1952* (New York, 1953)

———. *Call to Greatness* (New York, 1954)

———. *What I Think* (New York, 1956)

———. *Friends and Enemies* (New York, 1959)

——. *Putting First Things First* (New York, 1960)

——. *Looking Outward: Years of Crisis at the United Nations,* edited with commentary by Robert L. and Selma Schiffer, with a Preface by President John F. Kennedy (New York, 1963)

Stevenson, Rev. Samuel Harris; Harris, Rev. J. M.; Stevenson, Hon. W. F. *A History and Genealogical Record of the Stevenson Family* (second edition, privately printed, undated, but apparently in 1926)

Sullivan, Mark. *Our Times,* Vol. IV and V (New York, 1932)

Wecter, Dixon. *The Age of the Great Depression, 1929-1941* (New York, 1948)

White, Theodore H. *The Making of the President, 1960* (New York, 1962)

——. *The Making of the President, 1964* (New York, 1965)

Whitman, Alden Rogers. *Portrait—Adlai E. Stevenson, Politician, Diplomat, Friend* (New York, 1965)

Wish, Harvey. *Contemporary America, the National Scene Since 1900.* (New York, Revised Edition, 1955)

Magazine Articles

Alsop, S., and Bartlett, C. "In Time of Crisis," *Saturday Evening Post.* Dec. 8, 1962, pp. 15-16 plus

Alsop, S. "Footnote for Historians," *Saturday Evening Post.* January 26, 1963, p. 76

Anonymous. "Stevenson's Decision," *Newsweek.* December 16, 1957, p. 32

——. "Stevenson's Stature," *New Republic.* March 10, 1958, p. 6

——. "Adlai in '60, The Lively Ghost," *Newsweek.* January 11, 1960, p. 24 plus

——. "Ambassador Stevenson," *New Yorker.* January 28, 1961, pp. 24-26

——. "Bravo, Adlai. You're Needed," *Life,* December 15, 1961, p. 4

——. "Adlai Decides," *Newsweek.* December 18, 1961, pp. 27-28

——. "Who Done It? Hatchet Job on Adlai Stevenson," *Newsweek.* December 17, 1962, p. 28

——. "Bartlett's Quotations," *The Reporter.* December 20, 1962, p. 12

Begeman, J. "Hiss and Stevenson; The Truth," *New Republic.* August 25, 1952, pp. 10-12

Fischer, John. "Footnote on Adlai E. Stevenson," *Harper's.* November, 1965, p. 18 plus

Fisher, Walter T. "Why I Shall Vote for Stevenson," *Christian Century.* October 8, 1952, 1153-55

Harrison, Gilbert A. "Why Stevenson?" *New Republic.* December 15, 1962, pp. 7-10

Lamb, E. "Election Night With Stevenson," *Nation.* November 15, 1952, inside cover

Lindley, E. K. "Impressions of Stevenson," *Newsweek.* April 14, 1952, p. 37

Martin, John Bartlow, and Larrabee, E. "The Drafting of Adlai Stevenson," *Harper's.* October, 1952, pp. 35-43

Morgenthau, Hans. "Stevenson, Tragedy and Greatness," *New Republic.* August 7, 1965

Smith, T. V. "The Serious Problem of Campaign Humor," *New York Times Magazine.* September 28, 1952, p. 11 plus

Stevenson, Adlai E. "Ballots and Bullets," *Look.* June 2, 1953, pp. 35-38

——. "No Peace for Israel," *Look.* August 11, 1953, pp. 38-40

Stevenson, Adlai E. "West Builds a Balkan Barrier," *Look*. August 25, 1953, pp. 54-56 plus

———. "The World I Saw," *Look*. September 22, 1953, pp. 40-46

———. "Must We Have War?" *Look*. November 16, 1954, pp. 47-48

Recordings

Two long-play records were useful to me, chiefly in recapturing the mood, the felt personality, of Adlai Stevenson. One record is "A Recorded Portrait of Adlai Stevenson in Conversation with Arnold Michaelis," produced by Arnold Michaelis, Inc. This was an unrehearsed conversation, which took place in the study of the Libertyville house on June 19, 1956. The other record, produced by Audio Stage, Inc. for The Macmillan Company, consists of excerpts from Stevenson's speeches, connected with narration by Bill Scott. It is entitled, "Adlai E. Stevenson, the Man, the Candidate, the Statesman" and was issued after his death in 1965. It closes with an excerpt from Stevenson's last public speech, at Geneva, Switzerland, July 9, 1965.

INDEX